Courtney D. Fugate
The Teleology of Reason

Kantstudien-Ergänzungshefte

—

im Auftrag der Kant-Gesellschaft
herausgegeben von
Manfred Baum, Bernd Dörflinger
und Heiner F. Klemme

Band 178

Courtney D. Fugate
The Teleology of Reason

A Study of the Structure of Kant's Critical Philosophy

DE GRUYTER

ISBN 978-3-11-048158-7
e-ISBN (PDF) 978-3-11-030648-4
e-ISBN (EPUB) 978-3-11-036791-1
ISSN 0340-6059

Library of Congress Cataloging-in-Publication Data
A CIP catalog record for this book has been applied for at the Library of Congress.

Bibliographic information published by the Deutsche Nationalbibliothek
The Deutsche Nationalbibliothek lists this publication in the Deutsche Nationalbibliografie;
detailed bibliographic data are available in the Internet at http://dnb.dnb.de.

© 2016 Walter de Gruyter GmbH, Berlin/Boston
♾ Gedruckt auf säurefreiem Papier
Printed in Germany

www.degruyter.com

To Maximilian

Preface

This work argues from both historical and systematic grounds that teleological motives lie at the heart of Kant's critical turn, and that a precise analysis of teleological structures can both illuminate the basic strategy of the critical system's founding arguments and provide a key to understanding the unity of Kant's philosophy. In short, it tries to justify Kant's assertion in the *Critique of Pure Reason* that his philosophy, as a philosophy in the genuine sense of a doctrine of wisdom, is ultimately a *"teleologia rationis humanae"* (A839/B867). By comparison with other discussions of teleology in Kant, the present work does not focus on the *Critique of Teleological Judgment* or concern itself with the details of the explicitly teleological elements in Kant's later historical, anthropological or political writings. This is not because I thought these to be unimportant, since quite the contrary is in fact true. The reason is that I desired to go as deeply as possible into the roots of these elements in Kant's thought, and this engaged me in investigations into Kant's pre-critical philosophy and into teleological concepts in general that precluded attention to many other interesting issues.

This work is a revised and greatly shortened version of my doctoral dissertation, delivered at the Higher Institute of Philosophy, Catholic University of Leuven, Belgium, in December 2010. I would like to thank Martin Moors, my advisor, for many years of guidance and support, and the entire faculty of the Institute for all they have taught me. The original dissertation won the Silvestro Marcucci International Dissertation Prize 2009–2010, co-financed by the Accademia Lucchese di Scienze, Lettere de Arti, and judged by Bernd Dörflinger (Trier), Mario Caimi (Buenos Aires), Alfredo Ferrarin (Boston University and Pisa), Luca Fonnesu (Pavia) and Claudio La Rocca (Genova). My thanks to the judges and the staff of the Marcucci Foundation, and in particular to the Marcucci family, Alfredo Ferrarin and Claudio La Rocca for their warm reception of me in Lucca. I also wish to thank the Fox Center for Humanistic Inquiry at Emory University, where I am currently a post-doctoral fellow, along with its director, Martine W. Brownley, and its wonderful staff for all their support while I revised this work. I would like to thank John Hymers for collaborating with me on projects that have certainly influenced important elements of this work and Lucas Thorpe for his unflagging encouragement. Thanks to Tom, Matt, Rob, Nate, Oliver, Brom, Hanno, Jens and Lawrence for enriching my personal and philosophical life over the years. Finally, thanks to my wife Jennifer.

Atlanta
January 6, 2014

Contents

Abbreviations and the Use of Translations —— XV

Part I: **Preliminary Investigations** —— 1

Chapter 1
Motivations —— 3
    Introduction —— 3
§. 1.   Preliminary Sketch of the Telic Structure of Kant's System of Philosophy —— 4
§. 1.1.   The Teleology of Theoretical Reason —— 5
§. 1.2.   The Teleology of Pure Practical Reason —— 9
§. 1.3.   The Doctrine of Wisdom as the End of the System of Philosophy —— 13
§. 1.4.   Teleology and the Transcendental Possibility of the Kantian System of Philosophy —— 15
§. 1.5.   The Unity of Reason —— 20
§. 2.   The Teleological Tradition Before and After Kant —— 24
§. 2.1.   Teleology in the Philosophies of Kant's German Predecessors —— 30
§. 2.2.   The Legacy of Kant's Teleology of Reason in Fichte —— 33
§. 3.   Current Views on the Role of Teleology in Kant's Critical Philosophy —— 42
§. 3.1.   Reactions to the Popular View —— 47
§. 3.2.   Teleology in Special Studies of Kant's Philosophy —— 51
    Conclusion —— 56

Chapter 2
Teleology: Rudiments of a Theory —— 57
    Introduction —— 57
    Teleology: Not Reducible to a Pattern of Behavior —— 60
    Two Examples of this Tendency in Studies of the History of Philosophy: Bennett and Couturat —— 64
§. 1.   Teleological Inferences: From Pattern to Purpose —— 68
§. 1.1.   Teleological and Non-Teleological Inferences —— 72
§. 1.2.   Traditional Teleological Arguments for God's Existence —— 75
§. 1.3.   Concluding Reflections —— 80
§. 2.   Teleological Explanations: From Purpose to Pattern —— 81

§. 2.1.   Maupertuis and the Universal Teleology of Nature —— 88
§. 2.2.   Purposes as Laws of Behavior —— 95
§. 2.3.   Skepticism Regarding Explanation —— 97
§. 2.4.   Teleological Explanations: Concluding Reflections —— 99
§. 3.   The Essential and Inessential Characteristics of Teleological Entities —— 103

Part II:
The Teleology of Human Knowledge —— 109

Introduction to Part II —— 111

Chapter 3
The Historical Roots of Kant's Concept of Experience —— 113
Introduction —— 113
§. 1.   Wolff's Ontological Logic and the "acumen pervidendi universalia in singularibus" —— 117
§. 1.1.   Wolff's Logic of Experience —— 119
§. 1.2.   The Wolffian Roots of Kant's Categories —— 122
§. 1.3.   The Skill of Perceiving the Universal in the Particular —— 126
§. 1.4.   Wolff and Kant on the Possibility of Experience —— 127
§. 2.   Adolph Friedrich Hoffmann and Christian August Crusius —— 130
§. 2.1.   The Logic of Experience According to Hoffmann and Crusius —— 137
§. 2.2.   The Possibility of Experience and the Limits of Human Knowledge —— 141
§. 3.   Anticipating Kant's Account of Experience —— 142
Conclusion: The Nature of Kant's Advance —— 147

Chapter 4
Teleology in the Transcendental Aesthetic and Analytic —— 148
Introduction —— 148
§. 1.   The Problem of the "Critique": How are Synthetic Judgments *a priori* Possible? —— 149
§. 1.1.   The Need for Synthetic Judgments *a priori* and the Structure of Knowledge —— 152
§. 1.2.   Preliminary Outline of the Argument of the Transcendental Aesthetic and Analytic —— 161
§. 2.   Space and Time as Grounds of the Formal Perfection of Sensible Objects —— 167

§. 2.1. The Objective Formal Perfection of Space —— 171
§. 2.2. The Transcendental Aesthetic: Comments on the Text —— 175
§. 3. The Transcendental Analytic —— 177
§. 3.1. The Metaphysical Deduction —— 178
§. 3.2. The Transcendental Deduction —— 181
§. 3.3. The Deduction in the B-edition —— 185
§. 4. Summary —— 196

Chapter 5
Teleology in the Transcendental Dialectic —— 201
Introduction —— 201
§. 1. The Relation of the Analytic to the Dialectic —— 205
§. 2. The Ideas of Pure Reason —— 212
§. 3. The Regulative Principles of Pure Reason —— 224
§. 4. The Transcendental Death of Physico-Theology —— 235
Conclusion —— 238
General Conclusion to Part II —— 239

Part III:
The Teleology of Freedom —— 241
Introduction to Part III —— 243

Chapter 6
The Teleology of Freedom: The Structure of Moral Self-Consciousness in the Analytic —— 248
Introduction —— 248
§. 1. Three Types of Freedom —— 254
§. 2. Our Three Wills —— 261
§. 3. Moral Self-Consciousness —— 276
§. 4. The To-and-Fro Structure of Moral Self-Consciousness in the *GMS* —— 278
§. 5. The To-and-Fro Structure of Moral Self-Consciousness in the *KpV* —— 285
Conclusion —— 290

Chapter 7
Kant on Rational Faith as an Expression of Autonomy —— 292
Introduction —— 292

§. 1.   Problems and Previous Interpretations —— 295
§. 1.1.   Beck's Interpretation —— 296
§. 1.2.   Wood's Interpretation —— 300
§. 1.2.1.   A First Difficulty with Wood's Interpretation —— 301
§. 1.2.2.   A Second Difficulty with Wood's Interpretation —— 302
§. 1.2.3.   A Third Difficulty with Wood's Interpretation —— 304
§. 1.2.4.   A Fourth Difficulty with Wood's Interpretation —— 305
§. 2.   Kant's Argument —— 310
§. 2.1.   Virtue as Moral Strength of Character —— 311
§. 2.2.   How Rational Belief in God's Existence Increases the Moral Incentive —— 315
§. 2.3.   Textual Analysis —— 319
§. 2.3.1.   The Highest Good in *KpV* —— 319
§. 2.3.2.   The Highest Good in the *KrV* —— 327
§. 2.3.3.   The Highest Good in the *KU* —— 328
§. 2.3.4.   The Highest Good in *TP* —— 329
             Summary of the Argument of this Section —— 330
§. 3.   Practical-Dogmatic Metaphysics —— 331
             Conclusion —— 335

Excursus: The Life of Reason —— 337
             Introduction —— 337
§. 1.   From Morality to Life: Three Conditions of the Possibility of the Realization of a Moral World —— 339
§. 2.   Pure Aesthetic Pleasure as a Feeling of Life —— 345
§. 2.1.   Kant's Constitutive Concept of Life —— 347
§. 2.2.   The Historical Roots of Kant's Concept of Life —— 348
§. 2.3.   Pure Aesthetic Pleasure as a Feeling of Life: How the Constitutive Concept of Life is Generalized to Include the Feeling of Beauty —— 353
             Conclusion —— 357

Chapter 8
The Teleological Unity of Reason and Kant's Idea of Philosophy —— 360
             Introduction —— 360
§. 1.   The Unity of Reason —— 362
§. 1.1.   The Unity of Reason: First Reconstruction —— 366
§. 1.2.   Regulative and Constitutive Principles —— 374
§. 1.3.   The Unity of Reason: Second Reconstruction —— 380
§. 2.   Kant's Concept of Philosophy —— 387

§. 2.1. Philosophy "in sensu scholastico" and "in sensu cosmico" —— **390**
§. 2.2. Unity of Reason and the History of Philosophy —— **393**
    Conclusion —— **396**
    Brief Outline of Kant's Conception of Teleology —— **398**

Bibliography —— 404
I.   Translations Consulted —— **404**
II.   Primary Sources —— **404**
III.   Secondary Sources —— **410**

Register —— 425

Abbreviations and the Use of Translations

Aside from the *Kritik der reinen Vernunft* and also the *Reflexionen*, the German text of all writings by Kant are cited according to the volume and page numbers of the Akademie edition of *Kants gesammelte Schriften* (hereafter AA), 29 vols., issued by the Preussischen Akademie der Wissenschaften (vols. 1–22), the Deutschen Akademie der Wissenschaften (vol. 23), and the Akademie der Wissenschaften zu Göttingen (vols. 24–9) (Berlin: Walter de Gruyter, 1902-). References to the *Kritik der reinen Vernunft* use the standard A and B paginations for the first and second editions. Kant's reflections are identified by their numbers as they are listed in AA.

For Kant's main works, I take as my main translation that found in the Cambridge Edition of Kant's Works in Translation. If a translation is not found in that work, then the reader can assume that it is my own. In many cases I have seen fit to emend a translation, or to use an alternative translation, and such is noted. However, in many instances I have found it more expedient either to use an alternative translation or to provide my own. A list of all the other translations I have consulted can be found in the first section of the Bibliography. In all cases my choice was, naturally, based on a desire to render Kant's original German text with as much precision and literalness as possible. It is also worth noting that when quoting Kant's German, particularly in regard to his *Nachlass*, I have taken no pains to make his often fanciful grammar and orthography more regular. I have also chosen not to mark this with the usual "sic" since it would have been needlessly cumbersome considering that such instances are usually of no philosophical significance. The reader will also notice that I have taken no pains to update the spelling used in the titles of some of the older works I will be citing.

AA	Akademie Ausgabe
Anth	Anthropologie in pragmatischer Hinsicht (AA 07)
BDG	Der einzig mögliche Beweisgrund zu einer Demonstration des Daseins Gottes (AA 02)
Br	Briefe (AA 10–13)
DfS	Die falsche Spitzfindigkeit der vier syllogistischen Figuren erwiesen (AA 02)
EEKU	Erste Einleitung in die Kritik der Urteilskraft (AA 20)
FM	Welches sind die wirklichen Fortschritte, die die Metaphysik seit Leibnizens und Wolff's Zeiten in Deutschland gemacht hat? (AA 20)
GMS	Grundlegung zur Metaphysik der Sitten (AA 04)
GUGR	Von dem ersten Grunde des Unterschiedes der Gegenden im Raume (AA 02)
KpV	Kritik der praktishen Vernunft (AA 05)

KrV	Kritik der reinen Vernunft (A/B)
KU	Kritik der Urtheilskraft (AA 05)
Log	Logik (AA 09)
MAN	Metaphysische Anfangsgründe der Naturwissenschaft (AA 04)
MS	Die Metaphysik der Sitten (AA 06)
MSI	De mundi sensibilis atque intelligibilis forma et principiis (AA 02)
NG	Versuch, den Begriff der negativen Grössen in die Weltweisheit einzuführen (AA 02)
NTH	Allgemeine Naturgeschichte und Theorie des Himmels (AA 01)
OP	Opus Postumum (AA 21 and 22)
PhilEnz	Philosophische Enzyklopädie (AA 29)
PND	Principiorum primorum cognitionis metaphysicae nova dilucidatio (AA 01)
Prol	Prolegomena zu einer jeden künftigen Metaphysik (AA 04)
Refl	Reflexion (AA 14–19)
RGV	Die Religion innerhalb der Grenzen der blossen Vernunft (AA 06)
TG	Träume eines Geistersehers, erläutert durch die Träume der Metaphysik (AA 02)
TP	Über den Gemeinspruch: Das mag in der Theorie richtig sein, taugt aber nicht für die Praxis (AA 08)
UD	Untersuchung über die Deutlichkeit der Grundsätze der natürlichen Theologie und der Moral (AA 02)
ÜE	Über eine Entdeckung, nach der alle neue Kritik der reinen Vernunft durch eine ältere entbehrlich gemacht warden soll (AA 08)
ÜGTP	Über den Gebrauch teleologischer Principien in der Philosphie (AA 08)
VNAEF	Verkündigung des nahen Abschlusses eines Tractats zum ewigen Frieden in der Philosophie (AA 08)
V-Lo/Busolt	Logic Busolt (AA 24)
V-Mo/Colins	Moralphilosophie Collins (AA 27)
V-Met/Dohna	Metaphysik Dohna (AA 28)
V-Met-L2/Pölitz	Metaphysik L2 (AA 28)
V-Phil-Th/Pölitz	Philosophische Religionslehre nach Pölitz (AA 28)
VT	Von einem neuerdings erhobenen vornehmen Ton in der Philosophie (AA 08)

Part I: **Preliminary Investigations**

Chapter 1 Motivations

Introduction

Kant's descriptions of reason in the critical writings are replete with teleological formulations. As he explains, reason itself is subject to "needs," "unquenchable desires," "interests," "aims" and "ends" (see, e.g., *KrV* A796/ B824). It is inexorably impelled by a "propensity of its nature" (*KrV* A797/B825), based "on the irresistible law of necessity" (*Prol* 04:368), to seek not only ends, but also an absolute systematic unity of ends under one supreme end, the *final* end of reason, which, most remarkably, pure reason provides for itself through its own practical function. In this respect, claims Kant, something called "metaphysics" – i.e. the implicit project of developing just such a rational and systematic doctrine of ends subservient to one final end – is already a reality contained within "*the natural disposition* of human reason," like a seed that cannot fail to germinate, but which has hitherto failed to throw out a well-constructed and stable root-system.[1]

This chapter presents what I believe to be powerful systematic, historical and scholarly reasons for undertaking a deeper investigation into the telic elements in Kant's philosophy. The first section surveys the textual evidence supporting a teleological reading of the critical philosophy, and does so in a way that aims to make evident the main contours of its purposive structure. In particular, this general structure is treated in three related parts, namely, as it concerns the system of philosophy both theoretical and practical, as it concerns the system of transcendental critique, and finally as it concerns what might be called the systematic epigenesis of philosophical wisdom. Each part of this structure will be further examined in Parts II and III, which form the main body of this study.

The second section of the present chapter draws attention to the significance of Kant's philosophy for the tradition of teleological thought by locating it at the boundary between two radically different manifestations of this tradition. To be specific, the critical turn itself is shown to be located at the dividing line between the telic worldview typical of previous German metaphysics, which locates its ultimate foundation in God's will, and the telic worldview that is typical of the critical Kant and of most post-Kantian German thought, which sees teleology as a product of reason. To anticipate, three points make it evident that teleological motives must lie at the heart of Kant's thought and, consequently, that they de-

---

[1] Kant describes metaphysics in this sense as a "*Keim*" that must be fully formed by transcendental criticism at *Prol* 04:368.

serve to be studied in greater depth. First, Kant himself spent more than the first decade of his philosophical career seeking to better articulate the central teleological framework of traditional German metaphysics. Secondly, since it was Kant who first felt the need to turn away from this worldview to that of the critical philosophy, and since, furthermore, post-Kantian discussions of the telic structure of reason among figures like Fichte, Hegel and Schelling take the critical philosophy as their starting point, it can be said that he almost single-handedly effected this major turn in the tradition. Thirdly, and most obviously, Kant himself explicitly attributes both the possibility and the originality of his critical enterprise to its basis in a radically new formulation of the teleological conception of reason, as we will see further below.

The third and final section of this chapter surveys the secondary literature on Kant's conception of teleology that is most relevant to my project. Specifically, it shows that although a wide variety of views is found in the literature, a few of which see teleology as at best peripheral to Kant's philosophy, the general consensus is nevertheless that it is central to his conception of the structure of reason at the deepest of levels. Yet, despite this consensus, it finds that no sustained investigation has been made into the status or origin of such teleological "talk" in Kant's writings and that there exists no detailed account of how it operates in and unifies the various parts of his philosophy. The present work attempts to fulfill both goals, while showing that Kant works consistently with a single teleology of reason throughout the critical period.

§. 1. Preliminary Sketch of the Telic Structure of Kant's System of Philosophy

In an essay of 1788, entitled "On the Use of Teleological Principles in Philosophy" (hereafter *ÜGTP*), Kant writes,

> *Ends* have a direct relation to *reason*, whether this reason be our own or one foreign to us. [...] Now ends are either ends of *nature* or of *freedom*. That there are ends in nature, no person can see *a priori*; by comparison, one can quite well see *a priori* that there must be a connection of causes and effects in nature. Consequently, the use of the teleological principle in regard to nature is always empirically conditioned. It would be precisely the same story with the ends of freedom, if, prior to these, objects of the will had to be given by nature (in needs and inclinations) as determining grounds, in order for us to determine what to make our ends by the mere comparison of such objects with one another and with their totality. The *Critique of Practical Reason* shows, however, that there exist pure practical principles through which reason is determined *a priori*, and that these hence provide reason with an end *a priori*. If, therefore, the use of the teleological principle for the explanation of nature can never provide the origin of purposive conjunction in a way determined

§. 1. Preliminary Sketch of the Telic Structure of Kant's System of Philosophy — 5

completely and for all ends, due to its being limited to empirical conditions: one must nevertheless expect such from a *pure doctrine of ends* (which can be no other than that of *freedom*), the principle of which contains *a priori* the relation of a reason in general to the whole of all ends and can only be practical. Because, however, a pure practical teleology, i.e. morality, is determined to make its own ends actual in the world: for this reason it may not neglect the possibility of such ends in the world, both as regards what concerns the *final* causes given therein and the suitability of the *highest cause of the world* to the whole of all ends as effect, hence natural teleology as well as the possibility of a nature in general, i.e. transcendental philosophy. For only in this way is it possible to secure the objective reality of practical reason in its exercise in regard to the possibility of the object, that is to say, of the end that it prescribes to be brought about in the world. (*ÜGTP* 08:182–183; my translation)

As this passage clearly attests, Kant's understanding of the telic structure of his philosophy is highly articulated, and comprises at least a theoretical and a practical teleology, which, although initially separate, are finally united within a larger framework of an equally purposive nature.

§. 1.1. The Teleology of Theoretical Reason

Now, that Kant should speak in this passage of a teleology specifically of theoretical reason, i.e. of reason in its role of cognizing physical nature, is not particularly surprising. In the *KrV*, Kant had already traced reason's interest in producing systematic unity in its cognitions, as well as the epistemic limitations that destine it to never fully reach this goal – and thus to remain *perpetually* striving towards it – to the essential conditions or limits of all theoretical knowledge. These were found generally to lie in the understanding's dependency on the giveness of its matter in the form of a sensible manifold, coupled with the requirement that these materials be actively synthesized so that they are capable of being brought under the transcendental unity of apperception. Theoretical reason, it was thus shown, is essentially structured towards the goal of actively producing an absolute unity of experience, a unity that nevertheless can never be completely achieved even in principle.

Indeed, if we look more deeply into the primary texts, as we will in Part II, then it turns out that this teleology of theoretical reason itself has at least three related parts. The first is found in the Analytic of the *KrV* where the very possibility of the understanding and of its application to an object in general are shown to be rooted in several even more basic telic functions. Most of the details of this must be postponed until Part II, but two of these functions can be mentioned here. One consists in the systematic structure of the understanding itself, whose categories, as functions of unity in thought, "must hang together according to a concept or idea" (*KrV* A67/B92), which defines the function or goal (*Zweck*) of all the understanding's activities. According to Kant, this teleology underlies the metaphysical deduction of the categories in which these are derived as the formal means of synthesis necessary and sufficient for the realization of the goal of judgment (i.e. the determination of an object) (*KrV* A67/B92). Another of note comes into view in Kant's attempt to prove specifically that perceptions in spatiotemporal form must be determinable under the synthetic principles *a priori* by means of which alone their objective unity, i.e. relation to an object in general, is rendered possible. The purposiveness here, I will argue, lies in a justified demand for unity in all the understanding's cognition of experience and it characterizes the internal structure making possible the faculty of determinative theoretical judgment. As we will see, so far from meaning that the object of the understanding must be telically structured, this purposiveness, as one for the sake of the employment of judgment itself, in fact has as a necessary consequence that its object be merely mechanical, i.e. not characterized by its own internal end. Still other teleological features that make possible theoretical cognition, such as the unique unity of space and time as forms of intuition, as well as the fitness of this unique unity for the subsuming of objects with spatiotemporal form under the unity of understanding, will be the topic of Part II.

The teleology of this first part thus specifically concerns the inner structure of the understanding in general and its formative synthetic role in bringing perceptions under concepts. It is not directly mentioned in the passage from *ÜGTP* quoted above, but it very much provides the basis for Kant's claim there that "one can quite well see *a priori* that there must be a connection of causes and effects in nature." We can see this *a priori*, precisely because on Kant's view the understanding literally makes or constitutes experience after the form that it requires for its own functioning, and thus telically. Notably, it also provides the basis for the teleology of theoretical reason that *is* specifically mentioned in this passage, i.e. the one that concerns the purposiveness of nature itself. How these two telic structures are related is clarified in Kant's explanation in the *KrV* that the first subjective purpose of theoretical reason, i.e. the unification of experience under concepts, can and must be furthered by the adoption of the transcendental principle that there are objective purposes *in* nature, since the "highest formal unity" or "perfection in the absolute sense" is nothing other than the "purposive unity of things" (*KrV* A686/B714; A694/B722). Kant thus holds, for reasons that at this moment are still unclear, that the ultimate form of the unity within a manifold generally speaking, and thus also in experience, is precisely *teleological* unity, or the unity that makes possible the directedness of objects themselves to ends.

In fact, not only is the subjective purpose of reason itself *benefitted* by the idea of a natural teleology, but indeed Kant goes even further to remark that "the proper vocation of this supreme faculty of cognition is to employ all its methods and principles only in order to penetrate into the deepest inwardness of nature in accordance with all possible principles of unity, *of which the unity of ends is the most prominent*" (*KrV* A702/B730). As Kant explains further in the *KrV*,

> The regulative principle demands that systematic unity as *unity of nature* be absolutely presupposed, which is known not merely empirically, but rather *a priori* (albeit still as indeterminate), and hence as following from the essences of things. [...] The greatest systematic unity, *hence also purposive unity*, is the school and very foundation of the possibility of the greatest use of human reason. *The idea of it is therefore inseparably bound up with the essence of our reason*. This very idea is therefore legislative for us, and thus it is very natural to assume a legislative reason (*intellectus archetypus*) corresponding to it, from which is to be derived all systematic unity of nature as the object of our reason. (*KrV* A693–695/B721–722; emphasis added)

In its highest extension then, reason as a theoretical faculty rests on the indeterminate, but nevertheless legislative, *idea of a transcendental teleology*, i.e. a teleology grounded in the essences of all objects of reason, which comprises both the basic purposive unity constituting nature as mechanical (as a system of perceptions formally constituted by the understanding for the understanding) and the possible purposive unity of the objects of nature themselves (as a systematic unity of mechanisms, i.e. as a teleological system or as an organism).

Nevertheless, as Kant's comments in the quoted passage from *ÜGTP* indicate, this latter teleology of nature only really furthers the subjective teleology of reason, if it is limited to providing a means for furthering the understanding's most essential function, i.e. the bringing of perceptions under laws in an experience. That is to say, its teleology is only purposive for theoretical reason as a whole insofar as it guides us to the further discovery of nature's specifically mechanical/dynamical constitution. Concepts of individual ends, however, have no such immediate function. Indeed, Kant maintains that it is not even possible to *discover* the concept of an end objectively in nature, since such a concept is not only not required for the bare possibility of an experience in general, but is even excluded by the understanding's own most basic need for experience to cohere according to an order of efficient causes and effects. In the case of the further teleological determination of nature, theoretical reason must therefore rely on the faculty of judgment, which Kant says rightfully presupposes concepts of telic objects, but only for the extension of reason's empirical use, and without being able to secure their objective realty.[2] As Kant puts the matter in the *KU*, "the concept of a causality of nature according to the rule of ends ... can indeed be thought without contradiction, but is yet not suited to dogmatic determinations, because, since it cannot be drawn from experience and also is not required for the possibility of experience, there is nothing through which its objective reality can be certified" (*KU* 05:397). Judgment, therefore, presupposes teleological concepts only insofar as they provide reason with additional means for discovering new forms of unity in the appearances. Teleological concepts, in this case, serve reason with what Kant calls "critical principles" (*KU* 05:397), i.e. with principles that allow reason to *immanently* think, and to an extent give content to, the *relation* of the sensible to the supersensible from within, while refraining from positively determining this supersensible and thereby falling into transcendent speculations. The validity of their use therefore stems entirely from the fact that they provide additional means for reason to pursue its own rightful task of systematizing sensible experience through the thought of such a relation of experience to some ultimate unifying ground beyond it. This aspect of the teleology of theoretical reason is directly reflected in the passage quoted from *ÜGTP* where Kant acknowledges that "the use of the teleological principle in regard to nature is always empirically conditioned." Since teleological concepts are not themselves empirical, the empirical condition Kant speaks of here must be that of serving to further systematize the empirical.

Thirdly and finally, Kant argues in the *Critique of Teleological Judgment* that the subjective teleology of theoretical reason, which gives rise to the mechanical constitution of nature, and the objective but merely regulative teleology of nature, are both brought together in the critical and heuristic idea of a universal nature, as object of reason, that would be produced by a supersensible archetypal intellect and in which mechanism and teleology would be united (*KU* 5:405–410). Here, explicitly, it is what Kant calls the characteristic or special constitution (*eigenthümlichen Beschaffenheit*) of our understanding that makes it necessary that we "seek," i.e. adopt as an end of theoretical inquiry, a standpoint in which we are able to unify our reflection in the idea of a nature in which all its products "must [...] be considered by us as intentional and as generated as ends" that themselves are thought of as being conditions of the possibility of those

---

[2] The issue, indeed, is more complicated than expressed here. In the *KU*, Kant both affirms and denies that the concept of a natural end possesses objective reality. At *KU* 05:376 he asserts that "organized beings ... first provide objective realty for the concept of an end that is not a practical end but an end of nature." In §§ 74–75, however, Kant claims that the concept of a natural end cannot be abstracted from experience, and that "the objective reality of the concept of a natural end is not demonstrable by means of reason at all."

very mechanical laws through which nature operates and brings them about (*KU* 05:405).

§. 1.2. The Teleology of Pure Practical Reason

As the quoted passage from *ÜGTP* also clearly indicates, Kant believes the teleology of reason is not restricted merely to these theoretical employments. Indeed, it is evident from many texts that Kant thinks reason is also telic in its pure practical function, and even that in this it is able to provide a constitutive doctrine of ends where theoretical reason could not. He thus describes pure practical reason not only as purposive, but as being the very "faculty of ends in general," i.e. the original source of all true moral objects towards the will is to be determined (*TL* 06:395), and as the basis of a *"pure doctrine of ends"* (see above).

This is puzzling in at least two respects. First, though somewhat superficially, one might be surprised by this claim due to the fact that Kant so often asserts that the moral agent must abstract from all ends (see, e.g., *GMS* 04:400). And some scholars do indeed argue that, despite whatever Kant might say, teleology cannot really be part of the foundation of his practical philosophy. I believe this rests on a relatively simple misreading, as the later chapters of this book will make evident. Kant's actual position is that the moral agent must abstract only from those ends that can possibly be given prior to its consciousness of the law, not those that the thought of the law itself first makes possible.

There is, however, a second respect in which this claim is troubling, and which I think is much harder to successfully work out. The nature of this difficulty runs rather deep and therefore requires some explanation. It begins with the worry that even though Kant employs the language of ends and generally of teleology throughout his practical philosophy, he may not really be justified in doing so. On most interpretations, it is believed that teleology essentially involves the striving to realize a certain state or goal. It was this idea, as we just saw, that made it clear that theoretical reason is an intrinsically teleological power; the realization of a complete cognition of nature serves as the perpetually unachieved measure of theoretical reason's progress. However, in the passage quoted from *ÜGTP*, and in many others we will examine later, Kant asserts that pure practical reason *proves the reality* of its own ends. Hence, these are not ends that pure practical reason first strives to produce; they are much rather ends immediately given in and through its own activity. The rational nature and humanity of the human being, for instance, as ends in themselves, are not something that can either be produced or achieved by anything else, let alone by another's will. These are, to use Kant's own terminology, "*self-subsisting ends*" (*GMS* 04:437). As Kant also notes, pure practical reason is in this respect its own end (Kant 1981, p. 137), because possession of it is precisely what makes one an end in itself for another also possessing pure practical reason. What this indicates, at the very least, is that the unity contained in moral ends, or "ends of freedom" as Kant calls them in the passage above, must have the aspect of an *end*, i.e. something toward which we direct our activities, for radically different reasons than in the theoretical case, and, we should expect, with very different results as well. But there remains the worry that this case is so radically different from the theoretical one, that talk of these things as ends is not really justified.

Another side of the same difficulty can be highlighted by calling to mind Allen Wood's perceptive reconstruction of Kant's compatiblism (Wood 1984). As Wood explains, the moral world, with pure practical reason at its center, is understood by Kant to be something unchanging and established outside of all time, and thus as incapable of being affected in any way by the happenings in the phenomenal world (cf. *KrV* A539/B567-A541/B569). The same conclusion must be drawn from Kant's insistence that the supersensible world must be thought as the ground and never as the effect of the phenomenal world. Thus even if in time there seems to be something called moral striving, which is a purposively structured application of practical reason, it would seem that the inner or supersensible basis of this phenomenon in *pure* practical reason cannot be understood to have a similarly purposive structure or to be realized or otherwise affected by such striving. In other words, even if the appearances grounded in pure practical reason seem to be teleological, pure practical reason itself cannot be, or so it would seem. I believe this conclusion must be drawn by anyone who holds concepts such as striving, achievement, realization, and so on, to be defining characteristics of teleological structure. Such a person must see Kant's use of teleological language to describe the internal structure of pure practical reason as a simple misuse of terms, or else as an illegitimate transferal of the structure of the appearance of moral life to the inner structure of that moral life itself.

In what follows, I will argue that these difficulties can be resolved, though only partially. But to see this we will have to more closely examine the structure of teleological concepts themselves in Chapter 2, and what Kant precisely means when speaking of pure practical reason as a faculty of ends in Chapter 6. Here, let us only note that when Kant says in the passage from *ÜGTP* quoted above that pure practical reason is "determined to make its own ends actual in the world," he most certainly does not mean to indicate by this that such ends are to be first provided with reality through their being actualized in the realm of nature. As I commented above, rational beings as ends in themselves or the moral goodness of a rational being's will are simply not the sorts of things

§. 1. Preliminary Sketch of the Telic Structure of Kant's System of Philosophy — 11

that must first of all be produced by or within nature before they can be ascribed reality; they are rather the sole realities that ground the empirical necessity – and only for this reason, the assumption of the *physical possibility* – of moral progress in the world. Kant's model for moral ends does not appear to be that of a product, as is clearly the model of ends in the theoretical sphere, where the end is in some sense the separate completion of the act and where its achievement, if possible, would mean the cessation of the agent's activity. His model of ends in the moral realm is rather, depending on the point of view one adopts, that of *self-production*, or *reproduction*, or even *preservation*, where the agent and the end are one and the same being considered from two points of view – as that which produces, and thus exists, and as that which is produced, and as such comes to be. The subject of perfect moral activity and the object of the same are formally equivalent, and the act of moral striving towards such activity has the form of attempting to make the object of the will an object that has precisely the same form as that which I discover to be the inner essence of my own rational will. Perhaps a better way to capture this aspect of moral life is to think of its causality not as an unusual form of production, but rather as a kind of self-sustaining activity.

In any case, that the model of ends being employed here is not one of production is further evident from Kant's view that one cannot *determinatively* infer the reality of any such moral entity merely from whatever effects it might appear to have in nature. Such effects only serve as indications, or signs, of a possible supersensible reality underlying it as a cause (KrV A546/B574). It is thus clear that it cannot be through the production of the *appearance* of morality in this world that the kingdom of ends gains moral reality; as the ground of the appearance, the moral world must rather express and strive to re-present itself therein. This is what morality, it would seem, demands of us.

Granting a reading such as Wood's, however, one might validly ask, I believe, why pure practical reason is concerned *at all* with replicating its unity in the empirical world, or how it might feel the need to preserve its unity therein, as if the empirical world could have an effect on the supersensible and somehow corrupt it, or as if some change to our supersensible selves could be effected through our empirical actions, both of which must be considered impossible if we accept Kant's view that the supersensible is the ground of the phenomenal. How, then, can Kant argue that we must also view the moral world as in some sense being produced or realized by our actions or as in some way depending upon them, which is precisely what seems to be required to invest our empirical actions with moral significance? This is a deep question which is not sufficiently answered by noting that the demand to perform certain empirical actions is an obvious feature of moral experience. For, the question is whether the model of moral action and the understanding of the relation of the supersensible and empirical realms that Kant gives us is not only consistent with, but indeed provides grounds for, this feature of moral experience in the basic structure of moral self-consciousness. This must await further treatment in Chapters 6 and 7, but at this point one can nevertheless recognize how damaging to morality it would be to conclude otherwise. For if reason were satisfied with being shut up in its own absolute unity, then moral striving – which is a characteristically temporal process – would lose its entire significance, and the moral law would allow us to contemplate our higher and perfect selves, but would not give rise to any actual motivation. The very same would seem to result from the belief that our empirical selves are merely the phenomenal consequences of a moral destiny already worked out from eternity.

Unlike the previous difficulty, I do not think this one rests on any simple mistake. Rather it points directly to Kant's own difficulty in explaining the binding character of the moral law and, specifically, the imputation of immoral actions. Still, I will argue that despite this unresolved and perhaps irresolvable problem, Kant is nevertheless not guilty of a misuse of teleological concepts. His conception of the activity of pure practical reason, i.e. of freedom in a positive sense, is in fact the culmination of his teleology. In a word, it provides the purest expression of the core teleological concept of an absolutely perfect telic activity such as Aristotle describes as being an activity with its end internal to itself. As such, it also provides the model and measure of perfection for all other examples of teleology in Kant's thought. To put the matter somewhat differently, pure practical reason provides Kant with the only instance of a *constitutive* use of teleological concepts. Thus, far from resting on a mistake, Kant's use of teleological concepts to describe the basic structure of his practical philosophy attests to his extraordinarily nuanced understanding of this tradition.

To briefly summarize the foregoing, we can at last reach a first approximation of Kant's standpoint on moral teleology by stating that the systematic unity immediately given through pure practical reason is also an end for us, i.e. something towards which reason directs its causality in nature, because the moral law, which is authored by pure practical reason and is invested with this unity and reality through itself, is of an intrinsically archetypal nature manifesting itself in moral self-consciousness as a *command requiring unconditionally that the rational human being subject its own empirical will to the consciousness of the reality of its inner freedom*. As a first approximation, this provides us with a description of the larger problem, but it does not yet clarify the rationale according to which Kant can hold the moral unity of reason to be both ground and consequence of the very same set of actions. This deeper rationale, which is the key

§. 1. Preliminary Sketch of the Telic Structure of Kant's System of Philosophy — 13

to the teleological structure of Kant's practical philosophy, will have to be explored in Chapter 6.

§. 1.3. The Doctrine of Wisdom as the End of the System of Philosophy

Finally, not to be overlooked in the passage from *ÜGTP* quoted above is the crucial but tantalizing claim that in order for us to regard moral ends as being really possible in nature (however this is understood), it is requisite to once again *take up transcendental philosophy from a moral point of view*. It is only in this way, Kant claims, i.e. by radically inserting an original purposiveness with regard to the moral in the very *transcendental essences* or natures of things themselves, that objective reality can finally be ascribed to teleological concepts operating in nature, both internally in what is nature within our own faculties of reason and desire, and outside of us in physical nature and in political institutions. Kant's essential claim here is that we must postulate as objectively real a universal purposiveness in the inner natures of all possible things to the very extent that this is required for comprehending the *natural* possibility of realizing the moral world.

Though rarely given weight in the secondary literature, similar claims about the relation of moral teleology, natural teleology and transcendental philosophy are featured in all three *Critiques*.[3] In the Canon of Pure Reason, to take just one signal instance, Kant explains,

> The world must be represented as having arisen *from out of an idea*, if it is to harmonize with that use of reason without which we would hold ourselves as unworthy of reason, namely the moral, as that which depends throughout on the idea of the highest good. Through this all research into nature receives a direction according to the form of a system of ends and is in its highest extension physicotheology. This, however, since it arises from moral order as a unity which is grounded in the essence of freedom and not contingently founded through external commands, *brings the purposiveness of nature down to grounds that must be inseparably connected a priori to the inner possibility of things*, and thereby leads to transcendental theology that takes the ideal of the highest ontological perfection as a principle of systematic unity, which connects all things according to universal and necessary laws of nature, since they all have their origin in the absolute necessity of a single original being. (*KrV* A815–816/B843–844; emphasis added)

---

[3] This, I will argue, is the basic idea underlying the Dialectic of the *KpV*, and the Methodology of the *KU*.

Kant argues here that by virtue of assuming the conditions of the possibility of a harmony between the moral and the theoretical uses of reason, theoretical reason becomes subordinated to practical reason. This is true not only in the sense that practical reason takes precedence, but in the much deeper sense that under such conditions the theoretical use of reason is for the first time brought into unity with reason's practical use through the unification of their respective objects in a single most radical ground. Here the indeterminate but legislative *transcendental teleology of theoretical reason* is united with the determinate and legislative *transcendental teleology of pure practical reason* through the establishment of what Kant sometimes refers to as a *practical-dogmatic metaphysics* of which the "transcendental theology" described here is a basic component. This whole morally purposive unity of nature with the moral agent results from the combination of natural and moral teleology, by means of the postulation of the conditions for their unification, to form a single consistent and complete image of the world that is maximally conducive to the operations of both theoretical and practical reason considered both apart and in unison, and thus as a whole. In this case, both theoretical and practical reason, as we will see in Chapters 7–8, are subordinated to a single end within one encompassing teleology of reason, and without compromising their mutual autonomy, thus as working in a mutually strengthening harmony characteristic of a living organism. At the center, linking together these two faculties by welding together their final and characteristic objects is *transcendental theology,* or the concept of a moral and intellectual God from which derives the ontological and yet also morally purposive perfection of both the essence and existence of the actual world.

It is precisely through the postulation of the existence of such a being that total, indeed *transcendental,* unity is secured both for reason itself and for the system of philosophy. As Kant explains further,

> But this systematic unity of ends in this world of intelligences, which, although as mere nature can only be called the sensible world, but as a system of freedom can be called an intelligible, i.e., moral world (*regnum gratiae*), also leads without exception to the purposive unity of all things that make up this great whole, according to the universal laws of nature, just as the first does according to universal and necessary moral laws, *and unifies practical with speculative reason.* (*KrV* A815/B843; emphasis added)

To be sure, the precise nature and grounds of any such assumption (Kant will call it "postulation") of the unified transcendental and moral purposiveness of things, based upon the postulation of a jointly theoretical and moral God, will have to be investigated before Kant's claims can be rendered fully comprehensible.⁴ However, at the moment I want to underscore the fact that, according to these passages from the *KrV* and *ÜGTP*, it is through the postulation of such a transcendental and at the same time moral purposiveness, that the system of philosophy is forged into a unity, and theoretical and practical reason for the first time prove themselves to be two functions of one and the same faculty of reason.

§. 1.4. Teleology and the Transcendental Possibility of the Kantian System of Philosophy

From the first appearance of the *KrV* in 1781 until his last published writings, Kant maintains that the critical system of philosophy described above is essentially a self-articulating totality the truth and completeness of which can be guaranteed exclusively by the demonstration of its own independent and systematic unity. Yet the very establishment of such a system, according to Kant, presupposes a meta-philosophical, i.e. transcendental, investigation into its possibility, an investigation which, if successful, will be able to outline and verify the overarching idea according to which all the various functions and objects of reason can be put into order in the form of a single system. In analogy with Copernicus, Kant invites us in the *KrV* to think of this idea as a hypothesis or experiment that justifies itself purely through the order and harmony that it introduces into the entire edifice of human reason (*KrV* Bxxiii; see also Blumenberg 1987, p. 595–614). Just as Copernicus believed with regard any hypothesis concerning the wandering stars, it is the "articulation or structure of the system," Kant tells us, that "matters most when it comes to judging [the system's] unity and soundness" (*KrV* Axix).

This view forms the very basis of the way Kant understands his transcendental philosophy and in particular the method by which the *KrV* is itself constructed. Transcendental philosophy, he says, is the science or "system" of "all cognition … that is occupied not so much with objects but rather with our mode of cognition of objects insofar as this is to be possible *a priori*" (*KrV* B25). It thus provides the complete basic structure or idea of the system of philosophy, which is concerned with the special objects grounded in these transcendental concepts. The *KrV*, by comparison, contains "the idea of a special science" (*KrV* B24) whose distinctive aim "is to outline the entire plan [of the idea of a transcendental philosophy] architectonically, i.e., from principles" (*KrV* B27).

---

4 See Chapter 7.

Whether Kant nominally intends this critique of pure reason to be a part of transcendental philosophy or rather as yet a third level of science, a sort of meta-meta-science which establishes transcendental philosophy, is not immediately evident. But what is very clear is that a critique of pure reason for Kant has a quite different purpose than does transcendental philosophy (*KrV* B27); for its defining goal, which provides it with the unity of a science, is to establish "the complete idea of transcendental philosophy" (*KrV* B28), whereas the defining goal of transcendental philosophy itself is "an exhaustive analysis of all human cognition *a priori*" (*KrV* B27). Furthermore, just as is the case with any science according to Kant (*KrV* A832/B860 ff.), the manifold parts contained in a critique of pure reason must be telically organized under its own overarching idea that expresses the science's essential function or end, and from which the proper function of each parts as well as its relation to all others can be discovered.

But how is such a second-order, or perhaps third-order, science itself possible? Does transcendental critique, as some have suggested, require a special organ with which to examine reason's own internal workings? If a critique of pure reason establishes the idea of a transcendental philosophy, then what establishes the idea of such a critique? By such reasoning, are we not led back into an infinite regress of sciences each requiring yet another as its foundation? Kant's answer to this line of thought lies in the unique method of the critique of pure reason itself, which as I mentioned above, draws upon the analogy with Copernicus, although it does so in a very unique way. The full explanation of this point requires a discussion of Kant's theory of transcendental reflection, which must be postponed until later. But the basic idea can easily be gathered from noting that the Copernican analogy provides the basis for Kant's frequent comparison of the unity of the critique to that of an organic body. A characteristic feature of an organic body lies in its having no external model or exemplary idea by which it is to be measured; for even the idea of a biological kind is originally based upon the internal functional unity of its members, not by comparison with an external model. Thus rather than being compared to something else, the fitness of the animal is judged precisely by its own overall health, harmony and the endurance of its parts within a unity, and by the sense that when judged according to its own characteristic form it is in a fully functional state. What is perhaps most unique of the organic being on this account is that the idea of its proper goal or function is inseparably tied to its specific construction and even to the specific character of the parts within it. Put simply, the idea of the whole is inseparable from the whole of which it is the idea, such that when we seek to understand the unity of an organic being we seek to abstract this precisely from an examination of the parts and of the purposive unity evident in the

§. 1. Preliminary Sketch of the Telic Structure of Kant's System of Philosophy — 17

network of their respective functions. Notably, this movement of understanding is circular, and the very possibility of this circle's being virtuous, rather than vicious, is the absence of any external model, or what is the same, the independence and autonomy attributed to the organism as such.

In the *Prol*, Kant points up the similarity between the structure of the critical system and the teleology of an organized being in a way that underscores how essential it is for understanding the nature and, most importantly, the possibility of the critical project itself:

> The sphere of pure reason is so isolated and so thoroughly interconnected within itself that no part of it can be touched without touching all the rest and nothing can be accomplished without the prior determination of the place of each part and its influence on the others. As there is nothing outside pure reason which could correct our judgment within it, the validity and use of every part depends on its relation within reason itself to the other parts, and, as in the structure of an organized body, the purpose (*Zweck*) of every member can only be deduced from the complete concept of the whole. Hence it can be said of such a critique that it is never reliable unless it is whole and completed down to the smallest elements of pure reason, and that in the sphere of this faculty one must determine and settle either everything or nothing. (*Prol* 04:263)

In this passage Kant makes several key claims. One is that pure reason is entirely interconnected, such that each part is uniquely determined in its *function* through its relation to the *total function of parts within the whole*. The complete determination of a part's proper character is therefore only possible on the basis of prior knowledge of the whole. Another is that the total unity and organization of pure reason is a *purposive* unity within which each part becomes a true member only through the incorporation of its corresponding purpose or function under the concept or purpose of the whole. The third and perhaps most important claim made in this passage is that the ground of this unique form of unity, just as in an organism, consists in the characteristic *purity* or *independence* of pure reason from foreign influences or measures. Thus in regard to a critique that would establish the systematic *pure form* of knowledge, pure reason is *all-sufficient (Allgnugsam)*; it neither admits nor requires a further science to guarantee the validity of its own idea. This ability to operate purely, according to Kant, is reason's highest and most characteristic feature, and it explains why reason has no external measure against which to compare itself, no externally given forms to limit or constrain its own form-giving activity. Thus, if there is to be a criticism of pure reason at all, then this can only be carried out by taking up the proper standpoint *within* reason, and from this point outlining its structure as it arises naturally and with complete spontaneity from the isolated nature of reason itself. Consequently, the only justification that can be given for this outline of the critical system is that it agrees with, and thereby furthers the fulfillment of, the intrinsic final end of the whole of reason.

As Kant remarks in the last sentence of the passage immediately above, since this "organic" interconnection implies that the overall truth of the transcendental system cannot be judged in the absence of any one part, the creation of a complete inventory is an indispensable goal. But how do we know that such a complete inventory is possible, and how will we know when our inventory is complete? Kant argues that while completeness is desirable, it is not indispensible for critique, which is concerned only with the idea of the system of the very first sources of knowledge, because a large part of our metaphysical knowledge through pure reason consists actually in the analytical consequences of a small handful of first principles. For this reason, comprehensiveness, which consists only in the complete articulation of these core first principles under an idea, is the true goal of a critique of pure reason. As Kant explains in the A preface:

> I have made comprehensiveness my chief aim in view, and I make bold to say that there cannot be a single metaphysical problem that has not been solved here, or at least to the solution of which the key has not been provided. In fact pure reason is such a perfect unity that if its principle were insufficient for even a single one of the questions that are set for it by its own nature, then this [principle] might as well be discarded, because then it also would not be up to answering any of the other questions with complete reliability. (*KrV* Axiii)

Thus the problem of *completeness of all principles* resolves itself into a problem of *comprehensiveness in regard to first principles* and the former question now becomes: How can we know that a comprehensive science of pure reason is possible, and how will we know when we have comprehended all that is possible through it?

Kant's answer to this question again rests on the characteristic *purity* of pure reason, and its resulting perfect unity. As he writes,

> Now metaphysics, according to the concepts we will give of it here, is the only one of all the sciences that may promise that little but unified effort, and that indeed in a short time, will complete it in such a way that nothing remains to posterity except to adapt it in a didactic manner to its intentions, yet without being able to add to its content in the least. [...] Nothing here can escape us, because what reason brings forth entirely out of itself cannot be hidden, but is brought to light as soon as reason's common principle has been discovered. The perfect unity of this kind of cognition, and the fact that it arises solely out of pure concepts without any influence that would extend or increase it from experience or even particular intuition, which would lead to a determinate experience, make this unconditioned completeness not only feasible but also necessary. (*KrV* Axx)

§. 1. Preliminary Sketch of the Telic Structure of Kant's System of Philosophy — 19

In this passage, Kant bases his claim to completeness, and therefore also to comprehensiveness, on what he refers to as the "perfect unity of this kind of cognition" (*vollkommene Einheit*), which he describes explicitly as being a form of purposive or telic unity. In this specific passage, Kant is not speaking, of course, of the purity of the critique itself, which is what we are concerned with here, but of the purity of the science which it criticizes. However, his key point is that since the unity of this science "arises solely out of pure concepts," and hence independently of the empirical, it is not only possible but even *necessary* that the entire content (*Inhalt*) of metaphysics be exhaustible in a single investigation. That is, if we grasp the kind of knowledge metaphysics is supposed to be, then critique of pure reason, as the investigation of metaphysics' original sources, must be pure as well. Notably, Kant here once again mentions an underlying principle, which is now referred to as "reason's common principle" (*gemeinschaftliche Princip desselben*), and makes the claim that only after the discovery of such a principle will completeness first become possible, indeed inevitable. Kant's idea here appears to be that since the object of critique is itself the idea of something intrinsically pure, namely metaphysical cognition, and hence of something that is to arise from reason independently of any external model, it must either be the idea of an impossible science or else it must be one whose proper governing idea is internal and transparent to reflecting reason itself. This means that the critique of pure reason itself must either be a complete failure, in which case there is no cognition *a priori* of any kind, or else it must be able to discover within itself, through reflection on its own operations, divisions and organization of principles, a transparent measure of its own correctness. Thus the purity of the idea of the kind of cognition being criticized guarantees that the critique must either prove to contain its own measure of success or else be revealed as an utter delusion. By extension, the only measure of incorrectness possible in a critique of this kind will have be one in which reflecting reason detects its own lack of harmony and fulfillment; it can only be incorrect if it remains internally dissatisfied by its results. If reason can be satisfied, however, or can reach a state of perpetual peace with itself (see *VNAEF* in which Kant makes extensive use of this idea), then that very fact will provide a complete, indeed the only possible, guarantee of the correctness of the critique.

If this interpretation is correct, then one would expect Kant to also claim that the critical system, as a self-regulating exercise of pure reason, is self-generating or self-articulating. And indeed, Kant lays great stress on precisely this point in a letter to Christian Garve written in 1783:

> Be so kind as to have another fleeting glance at the whole and to notice that it is not at all metaphysics that the *Critique* is doing but a whole new science, never before attempted,

namely, the critique *of an a priori judging reason.* [...] To no one has it even occurred that this faculty is the object of a formal and necessary, yes, an extremely broad, science, requiring such a manifold of divisions (without deviating from the limitation that it consider solely that uniquely pure faculty of knowing) and at the same time (something marvelous) deducing out of its own nature all the objects within its scope, enumerating them, and providing their completeness by means of their coherence in a single, complete cognitive faculty. Absolutely no other science attempts this, that is, to develop *a priori* out of the mere concept of a cognitive faculty (when that concept is precisely defined) all the objects, everything that can be known of them, yes, even what one is involuntarily but deceptively constrained to believe about them. [...] For I believe I can demonstrate formally that not even a single truly metaphysical proposition, torn out of the whole system, can be proved except by showing its relation to the sources of all our pure rational knowledge and, therefore, that it would have to be derived from the concept of the possible system of such cognitions. (*Br* 10:340 – 341)[5]

This, along with the previous texts, gives powerful indications that Kant seriously considers the teleological structure of human reason to be the key to unlocking the unique methodology of the *KrV* itself. Indeed, in this letter to Garve, Kant concisely reaffirms his position in the *KrV* that it is the inner self-articulating feature of an absolutely pure (i.e. independent) faculty of cognition that makes a critique of pure reason both *possible* and *necessary*. It makes this possible because it means that everything that can ever belong to or derive from pure reason must come from within itself, and must be derivable (because it is so derived!) from the pure idea of such a faculty. It furthermore makes such a critique necessary because at the basis of every cognition of reason, and thus "involuntarily," lies precisely this self-extension of reason to absolute completeness or maximal functionality. It is Kant's view that reason is always already guided in its reflective activities by an at least implicit idea of its own maximal functioning such that any disorder in the system of reason that would hamper this is both detectible by careful self-examination and immediately overridden when properly understood. If this teleological attempt to ground his philosophy truly works, then it would allow Kant to establish a fundamental science without foundationalism and without postulating a special standpoint outside of the system.

§. 1.5. The Unity of Reason

So far in this section I have outlined some elements of the teleology apparent in Kant's system of philosophy as well as in the transcendental system that pro-

---

[5] This is Zweig's very fine translation from Kant 1999, p. 198.

vides it with a foundation. However, in the introduction I indicated, through the analysis of a passage from *ÜGTP*, that Kant understands the complete unity of reason, meaning the unity of its theoretical, speculative and practical functions, as also having a teleological structure. What I wish to do here is to return briefly to that analysis in order to connect it up with my present reflections on the spontaneous and self-formative features of reason discussed above. *ÜGTP* was published in 1788, and from its contents, as well as from the architectonic focus of the *KpV* and the later draft of the *Progress* essay, it would be tempting to conclude that Kant's interest in the overarching teleological unity of his philosophy – the unity of reason as such – is an autumnal bloom, and as such did not figure in the very genesis of the critical system itself. Such is also suggested by the oft-repeated claims in the literature that Kant did not originally intend to write any other work than the *KrV*, and thus that the *KU*, which is concerned chiefly with purposiveness and teleology, sprouted from an unforeseen gap created only by the writing of the *KpV*.

A closer examination of the texts, however, shows that this idea of an overarching teleological system was ripe in Kant's mind even before the writing of the *KrV*. In a reflection penned sometime between 1776 and 1779, for instance, we see Kant sketching the unity of his philosophical system in considerable detail:

> The end (*Zweck*) of metaphysics: 1. To discover the origin of synthetic knowledge *a priori*. 2. To gain insight into the restricting conditions of the empirical use of our reason. 3. To show the independence of our reason from these conditions, and thus also the possibility of its absolute use. 4. Through this, to extend our use of reason beyond the boundaries of the sensible world, though only negatively, i.e. to clear away the hindrances that reason itself creates (from the principles of its empirical use). 5. To show the condition of the absolute unity of reason, so that thereby it can be a complete principle of practical unity, i.e. the harmonization into a sum of all ends. [...]
>
> The dogmatic use of our reason beyond the boundaries of (possible) experiences cannot be objectively determining, and there is no new syntheses here, rather there is only an agreement of theoretical with practical unity, where the practical use is led beyond the boundaries of the pragmatic, and so also beyond the present world, according to the analogy of its empirical use, but in relation to the conditions of a complete unity, and so also that through this the business of our reason is completed *a parte priori* and *posteriori*.
>
> (The freeing of the unity of reason from the limitations of its empirical use makes the transcendental use possible.)
>
> Because the expansion of reason here is purely negative, yet the absolute unity of the knowledge of objects in general and all its ends (free from all restrictions of sensibility) is demanded for the absolute spontaneity of reason, therefore the broadening is practically necessary.
>
> Reason is the faculty of the absolute unity of our knowledge.

> The principles of the completion of our knowledge, i.e. the (the absolute unity of the use of reason) absolute whole of such are syntheses of reason. They contain the conditions of wisdom, i.e. the harmonization with the sum of all our ends. We complete only through what is independent, therefore not through sensibility. The determination of all objects through pure reason is therefore the completion of our understanding's knowledge (*added later:* in the progress of my existence).
>
> 1. In view of the self-knowledge of reason. Completion in progression.
>   a. I belong in a universe (*Weltall*),
>   b. am simple
>   c. free. Intelligence.
>   d. My existence is either externally neither dependent (on body) nor contingent. (*added later:* under empirical principles belong: The manner of existence of all things of the world is contingent, only the original being exits in all regards (or in every sense) in a necessary manner.)
>   Here I consider myself not as soul, but rather as intelligence. The synthesis here is purely negative, namely abstracting from the conditions of sensibility on me as intelligence.
>   And the ground of this synthesis is the freedom of reason from the restricting conditions of sensibility, which is a negative principle of morality, therefore also of wisdom.
> 2. Completion in the regression from conditions to unconditioned.
>   There is an original being,
>   a. which is all-sufficient and unique,
>   b. simple,
>   c. free cause (intelligence)
>   d. necessary according to its nature.
>   These are the conditions of the complete unity of all objects and so also of knowledge. This unity, however, is the condition of the harmony of all that is practical. These cognitions are not dogmatic, but rather only a freeing of the (absolute) unity of the use of reason in theoretical and practical uses from the conditions of its empirical use, in order to secure the principles of the pure practical use. Reason is free from the conditions of sensibility and in practice it must be.
>   The continuation of the function of reason up to the complete unity beyond the limiting conditions of sensibility.
>   (*added later:* The concept of the unity of reason (*Vernunfteinheit*), e.g. the absolute whole – ground, cannot be represented according to the conditions of empirical knowledge *in concreto*. However, it also does not apply to the sensible world, but rather to the world of the understanding, which lies at the ground of the sensible world.) (*Refl* 4849)

The comprehensiveness and depth of detail in this early sketch are truly astounding, and show to what extent Kant's published writings failed, for whatever reason, to communicate to his readers the dynamic teleological interconnection at the heart of the system. Reason is described here as progressively unfolding itself from its first application in theoretical cognition, until the achievement

§. 1. Preliminary Sketch of the Telic Structure of Kant's System of Philosophy — 23

of the complete unity of all its functions under one final practical end. In particular, the five steps outlined in the first paragraph prove that from very early on Kant saw the negative side of his investigation into theoretical and speculative reason as being *at the very same time* reason's realization, first of the possibility, and then of the reality, of its practical vocation as the genuine goal of all its previous, even abortive, efforts. The recognition of the conditions that limit reason in its theoretical employment, i.e. transcendental critique, is thereby identified with the means for releasing pure practical reason from all such conditions, while the dialectic of pure reason is revealed to be reason's own critical response to having mistaken its genuine practical interest in the supersensible for a spurious speculative interest. Thus, when understood from the standpoint of the final end of the system, the disaster of traditional metaphysics turns out to be nothing else than reason's own rejection of an incomplete understanding of its true function, and the critique of pure reason likewise turns out to be the first step of pure reason's reassertion of its practical vocation.

Three further things in particular are important to note about this sketch. The first is that the entire progression is characterized here as the systematic unfolding of the unity of reason from its own inner self-sufficiency, or from an absolutely internal source. It begins with reason as it is submerged in its empirical employment and from reason's recognition of its own spontaneity. Pure reason, then, by means of this recognition sets a standard for the limitation of its own empirical use and in this way opens up the prospect of another fully-unconditioned employment. This other employment is then in turn recognized to be practical in nature. The principles of unity in the theoretical domain are in this regard extended, by abstraction from their sensible conditions, to make possible a pure practical employment for the sake of the complete unity of all the ends of reason. This unity, which Kant identifies in this passage with the unity of philosophical wisdom, is thus not merely practical, but is a unity of theoretical *with* practical reason understood from within the wider scope of the complete unfolding of one and the same reason. Notably, this indicates that the unity of reason for Kant does not lie in their being logically derivable from one original principle, but rather in their purposeful agreement and harmony in regard to the fulfillment of a single end, which is not a *particular* end, but rather the universal final end of reason as an *absolute whole*, the crowning flower of its autonomy. It is this end, viewed however as their origin and inner *conatus*, as a "seed" that cannot fail to germinate, that unifies reason in all its functions under a single idea.

The second is that Kant here again sees the final unity of reason as tied to the representation of a unique object, namely, a divine being that would be the absolute ground of the unity all objects of reason, and thereby also the absolute ground of the unity of the activities of reason in its highest practical function: "There is an original being, a. which is all-sufficient and unique, b. simple, c. free cause (intelligence), d. necessary according to its nature. These are the conditions of the complete unity of all objects and so also of knowledge. This unity, however, is the condition of the harmony of all that is practical." The role Kant ascribes to the idea of God in this passage is further articulated in a reflection penned in the 1780's:

> It is a necessary hypothesis of reason as a principle of the unity of all our knowledge, to assume a single universal primordial being as a principle of everything, to assume this being as intelligent, because only through its being the cause of everything through understanding is the world ordered according to rules, and thereby is an object of our understanding, and finally [it is a necessary hypothesis to assume it] as a cause through rational choice, so that for us it is a principle of a rational will and of the universal unity of all our free actions. Theism is therefore not a dogmatic assertion, but rather a necessary hypothesis of the thoroughly harmonious use of reason, chiefly of its self-sufficiency. (*Refl* 6038)

Thirdly, it is important to note that, as far as content is concerned, such reflections on the teleological unity of reason are neither unique in Kant's *Nachlass*, nor do they express any ideas that cannot equally be found throughout in his authorized writings. The individual parts of this plan, including the view that the *KrV* has as its central goal the rehabilitation of metaphysics for practical purposes, are indeed constant themes in the published writings, while the *FM* essay in particular contains several attempts to sketch out this very same plan with greater depth and scope. Yet the reflections do present the lineaments of Kant's unifying project with a concision and clarity that gives them a particular value. For what we find in these reflections is that Kant understands the structure of the unfolding of his entire philosophy as a progression through distinct steps towards a single final goal in which all ends of reason whatsoever are brought to an absolute unity under the name of "wisdom." Each stage of this progression will be discussed in the chapters to follow, and will finally come together in our discussion of Kant's conception of wisdom in Chapter 8.

§. 2. The Teleological Tradition Before and After Kant

Final causality has been a central motif of western metaphysics since as early as Anaxagoras, or if we follow Aristotle, Hermotimus of Clazomenae (Aristotle 1970, 984b18–22). Nevertheless, the most classic expression of this view – and importantly the one to which subsequent German philosophers repeatedly returned as their point of reference – is to be found in Plato's *Phaedo*, specifically in the passage where Socrates introduces the forms after recounting his disappointment with Anaxagoras' teleology. Interest in this piece of text can be traced back at least to Leibniz's extensive summary, and his many indications of the impact Plato's "very beautiful and very profound thoughts" had on his own conception of teleology (Leibniz 1989, p. 53; Leibniz, 1969, p. 351–354). Moses Mendelssohn, an adherent of the philosophy of Leibniz and Wolff, and a thinker for which Kant had supreme respect, also published a reconstructed translation (using roughly but not exclusively Wolffian ideas) of the entire *Phaedo* in 1767 in which the teleological elements of the dialogue are revised and developed in considerably greater detail than in the original. That Kant was influenced by Leibniz is unquestionable, but the evidence also shows unequivocally that he was deeply affected by this work of Mendelssohn's. Indeed, Mendelssohn's work has rightfully been regarded as a prime source of the distinction Kant makes between phenomena and noumena, and between concept and idea.[6]

Yet this is not the only manner in which the tradition of teleological thought informed Kant's intellectual development. The truth is that all major strands of German philosophy prior to Kant were in some way founded upon a teleological worldview. As a result, the greatest controversies of the time were largely concerned either with the nature of the final end of human reason, for instance whether it is primarily intellectual or practical in character, or with the specific conditions of the possibility of one or another teleological worldview. As the intellectual historian Heinz Heimsoeth once observed regarding the German tradition prior to Kant: "in its center stand the concept and proof of the essence and being of God; a proof without which the whole of philosophy would be useless. The entire totality of things, together with human reason, however, is enclosed by a robust teleology hardly touched by critical doubts" (Heimsoeth 1956, p. 133). Although Heimsoeth is right to say that the systems of Kant's predecessors were not touched by "critical doubts," provided this be taken in its special Kantian sense, it would however be a serious error to suggest such thinkers were not entirely aware of the complexities and controversies surrounding the teleological views on which their philosophies were based. That one must work "dogmatically" within a metaphysically teleological framework was indeed a given, but disagreements regarding the proper articulation of such a framework were precisely what fueled pre-Kantian German philosophy.

---

6 This has been noted primarily in Reich 1939a, but also more recently in Kuehn 1995. Max Wundt also stresses the influence of classical philosophy at this time, tracing it however to Kant's reading of Brucker's *Critical History*. See Wundt 1984, p. 163–167.

Two major features of this tradition directly formed Kant's early approach to metaphysics. The first was the confrontation between the Platonic and especially the Aristotelian aspects of the earlier German philosophy, on the one hand, and the advances made by modern physics, particularly its successful discovery of the universal laws of mechanics, on the other. From as early as the founders of the German Enlightenment, Christian Thomasius and Leibniz, thinkers in this tradition undertook various and radical attempts to reconcile metaphysical teleology with the mechanical view of nature as governed by universal laws. In his *Versuch vom Wesen des Geistes* (1699), Thomasius argued in particular that although mechanism has its truth, it is but the outer appearance of underlying teleological principles, whereas Leibniz argued not only this, but in addition that the mechanical laws themselves should be given a teleological interpretation. Wolff's own *Vernünfftige Gedancken von den Absichten der natürlichen Dinge* (1723), or German Teleology, brought this Leibnizian view to the schools, using it to argue that the unity of nature – even when viewed merely as a mechanical whole – provides direct evidence of the freedom and goodness of the divine will. His very coinage of the term "*teleologia*" in 1728 was intended to bring attention to the moral and religious edification that could be derived in this way from contemplating the purposive structure of physical nature. This and similar lines of thought naturally required German philosophers to penetrate more deeply than ever before into both the inner structure of teleological entities and the meaning of natural law in order to search out a point from which they could be brought within a single consistent picture of the cosmos. As we will see more fully below, this same issue occupied Kant throughout his pre-critical period.

A second feature of this renewed attention to teleological structure that also influenced Kant's approach to metaphysics arose from the related confrontation between these new approaches to teleology and the more practical or humanistic intentions of the philosophical tradition. In particular, attempts to integrate the idea of universal physical law into a teleological framework led almost immediately to the dehumanization of this same teleology. If such physical laws as Snell's law of refraction (Leibniz) or the principle of least action (Maupertuis) – which require the occurrence of physical events so often contrary to human goals – were to become prime models of teleological activity, then the genuine *telos* of nature itself would seem to be indifferent, at best, to human goals as well. If human catastrophes are sometimes the inevitable results of laws instituted by God to bring a greater perfection to the whole, then this clearly places into doubt the very centrality of the human being to the divine plan.

This tension led in two directions, both of which are important to note for their influence on Kant's early development. The first was an attempt to broaden

§. 2. The Teleological Tradition Before and After Kant — 27

and universalize how the very goal of human life was to be understood. To this tendency, which is clearly found in the young Kant, belongs for instance Alexander Pope's chastisement of man's presumption to be the goal of creation and his failure to realize that it is the perfection of the whole that God intends, not the perfection of any one part to the exclusion of another. To this also belongs, of course, Leibniz's *Theodicy*, and his attempt to articulate a purely metaphysical account of goodness in terms of order and harmony amidst the greatest abundance. Many thinkers sought to balance this dehumanization of creation's *telos* by an attempt to see the most significant of human goals, usually by radically reinterpreting their meaning, as in some way continuous with this new teleology of nature. The second direction in which this tension led, most notably in the writings of Leibniz's and Wolff's opponents, was towards even more radical attempts to distinguish the distinctive *telos* of man from that of the rest of the cosmos. This led them in turn to a renewed focus on human freedom, in particular as the condition of the possibility of man's making a truly unique and valuable contribution to the realization of the perfection of the cosmos, and thus also to an emphasis on the priority of man's practical vocation over any other cosmic achievement. This directly led figures like Christian Crusius and later the critical Kant to build their philosophical systems around a teleological principle of the primacy of the practical or moral vocation of man.

It should be no surprise then to find that Kant's pre-critical philosophy shares this very same commitment to a metaphysically teleological worldview, indeed that all of his major writings between 1755 and 1765 seek to articulate a specific version of a telically unified world whose foundation lies entirely in the will of God. It is indeed fair to say that a philosophy of any other kind could hardly be countenanced within the context of German thought in the period. As early as the sketches on optimism (*Refl* 3703–3705, AA 17:229–239), stemming probably from 1753–1754, we see Kant critically engaging with the very foundations of Leibniz's theodicy, indeed forthrightly rejecting it in favor of the one he claims to find in Pope's *Essay on Man*. The chief fault Kant identifies in Leibniz's theory at this time is the view that essences or possibles are absolutely necessary, and consequently that the teleological structure of the created world is restricted to the arrangement of merely its contingent features. As Kant writes, what "precisely constitutes the perfection of his [i.e. Pope's] system," in contrast to Leibniz's, is that it

> even subjects all possibility to the rule of an all-sufficient original Being, under which things can have no other attributes, not even those which are called essentially necessary, that do not harmonize together to give complete expression to his perfection. […] The essential and necessary determinations of things, the universal laws, which are not put in rela-

tion to each other by any forced union into a harmonious scheme, will adapt themselves as if spontaneously [*gleichsam von selber*] to the achievement of perfect purposes. (*Refl* 3704)

By this single stroke, Kant seeks to bring together into a single continuous system his deepest conception of God as all-sufficient (*allgnugsam*), the very first basis of the plan of the created universe (i.e. the realm of possibility itself, which includes the first metaphysical foundations of natural science), and the complete structure of the actual universe. On the basis of such a system, Kant thinks it is possible to assert for the first time that all created things, even those that appear to be pointless or even counter-purpose, such as physical and moral evil, must in fact be good, not only in view of the entire scheme and under the assumption of limitations imposed by the scheme, but even when considered by themselves (*Refl* 3704).

Although the details of Kant's thought evolve considerably from these brief sketches until the middle of the 1760s, the development of this system remains the focus of all his efforts. In the *New Elucidation* of 1755, Kant provides a proof of the existence of just such an all-sufficient God in which all possibility is founded (*PND* 01:395), denies once again the absolute necessity of essences (*PND* 01:395), and claims to prove that all created substance must stand in real interaction (*PND* 01:410–411), which is only possible if God first established each individually through the *idea or schema* of the interaction and harmony of their existences in one whole (*PND* 01:413–415). Kant takes this last point in particular to entail that the essences of all finite substances must conform to this idea so that perfect harmony will result in their actual influence on one another. This is complimented by the *a posteriori* investigations of his *Universal Natural History and Theory of the Heavens*, also of 1755, a work in which Kant diagnoses the failures of the traditional teleological argument for God's existence, argues for the superiority of a proof based upon a teleological interpretation of Newtonian physical law, and then attempts in detail to show how the physical structure of the actual universe, which has developed entirely as the necessary consequence of such laws, nevertheless manifests the greatest perfection of design. And Kant leaves no question that this interpretation of physical law, as the most basic vehicle of design, is made possible precisely by the radically new conception of possibility and of the nature of God that is more closely analyzed in the *New Elucidation* (*NTH* 01:333–334).

Although greatly improved, the same pattern of argument stands at the center of the cluster of works Kant wrote in the first half of the 1760s. In the *Only Possible Argument*, he greatly refines his proof of God's existence, while at the same time better explaining how the inner possibility of all things depends on such a being. He inserts a demonstration that God has a mind and will, which

§. 2. The Teleological Tradition Before and After Kant — 29

must stand in the most perfect harmony with each other (again *contra* Leibniz), and draws this conclusion:

> [...] precisely the same infinite nature has the relation of a ground to all the essences of things, and at the same time it also has the relation of highest desire to the greatest consequences given through this, and the latter can only be fruitful if the former are presupposed. Accordingly, the possibilities of things themselves, which are given through the divine nature, harmonize with his great desire. Goodness and perfection, however, consist in this harmony. And since these harmonize with one [*mit einem*], unity, harmony and order themselves will be found in the possibilities of things. (BDG 02:91–92)

Perhaps the most significant new development in this work is Kant's far more radical attempt to infer the existence of God *a posteriori* from the teleological form of the world. Kant's earlier inference in the *NTH* was merely from the teleological form of the *actual* world. On this basis he had inferred both the teleological character of Newtonian laws and the existence of a ground that would be able to establish these laws in accordance with a most perfect plan. In the *Only Possible Argument*, Kant attempts rather to infer the existence of God directly from the very first laws of nature, and indeed – what is most astonishing and original – from the very first principles of mathematics (*BDG* 02:93–96), which both Leibniz and Wolff had explicitly excluded from being able to play any such role due to their absolute necessity. This extension of his previous theory requires Kant to precisely explain how geometrical forms as well as the first principles of nature are to be understood as being teleological, i.e. as manifesting an essential relation to ends. Kant's answer here lies in a radically new conception of teleology, which as we will see, later plays a central role in his critical conception of teleology. In a word, this new conception is that the most basic and perfect form of teleology is not found in the arrangement of a number of things or conditions as means to the achievement of a single end or set of ends, but rather in the absolute fitness of things to the achievement to an endless number of possible ends, such that every actual thing can be viewed, depending on one's vantage point, as both means and end in relation to every other possible thing, and therefore also every other actual thing. This is what it means for things to be teleological in respect to their very essences or possibility, and hence in the following I will often refer to it as "transcendental teleology."

This transcendental teleology thus consists in this absolute "affinity" of the manifold, where this affinity is conceived of as a universal fitness of the parts to relate to one another reciprocally as means and ends. After recounting the amazing harmony of the manifold of space that makes it such that the construction of a figure for one purpose immediately reveals an infinity of other purposes it could serve, Kant writes:

> Is this harmony any less amazing because it is necessary? I maintain that it is all the more amazing for this very reason. Since a multiplicity, in which each had its own proper and independent necessity, could never have order, harmoniousness [*Wohlgereimtheit*] or unity in their reciprocal relationships to each other, will one not be led through this, just as the harmony in the contingent arrangements of nature leads one, to the supposition that there is a supreme ground of the very essences of things themselves, since unity in the ground also produces unity in the realm of its consequences? (*BDG* 02:95–96)

Teleology, on Kant's new conception, is all the more amazing for being a necessary consequence of the essences of things. And this "all the more" is displayed precisely in that such teleology is not restricted to a single end, but rather gives rise to an inexhaustible fitness to means-ends relationships in the multiplicity. With this Kant extends a thought of Maupertuis, which we will examine in Chapter 2, and gives voice to the radically new form of teleology that guides all of his later investigations into unity, whether it be the unity of the world as here, or the unity of reason, as in the critical period.

Thus Kant's pre-critical philosophy is just as focused on teleology as is his later critical work, although the former locates the deepest ground of this teleology in the nature of God, while the latter locates it in the nature of reason. To further see the great significance of this transformation, and thus also the great importance of studying Kant's teleology for understanding the progress of modern German thought, it will be useful to take a closer look at the teleological elements in the philosophy before and after his epochal turn.

§. 2.1. Teleology in the Philosophies of Kant's German Predecessors

To see this more clearly let us take a closer look at the systems of Kant's German predecessors. The largest division in views during Kant's formative years was that between what are sometimes broadly called the Leibnizian-Wolffian and the Thomasian traditions. While agreeing on little else, both of these traditions share the view that all real determination is at bottom teleological. That is to say, even if they believe there are some merely logical or absolutely necessary truths, which do not attest to the existence of a purposive cause of all things (e.g. those that would be true by virtue of the principle of contradiction alone), they accept that all cases where something is *really* determined by something else to possess a certain predicate, the *ultimate* ground of this determination must lie in a will, i.e. in a causality according to representations. Such real determination is the basis of the truth of all contingent truths. What is more, they agree that this ultimate ground, which is to supply the reason why the creating or directing will operates in the particular way that it does, gives rise to these particular truths, lies purely in the agreement between some formal feature of the representation of that state of affairs as an end and the character of the will that is motivated to adopt this representation as its actual goal.

Let us briefly examine this point in more detail. Firstly, philosophers in the Leibnizian-Wolffian tradition uniformly argue that the ultimate basis determining all contingent properties – and thus of everything actual, including the very laws of nature – lies specifically in the divine will, which chooses these precisely because of their formal agreement into the most perfect possible world, i.e. into the greatest unity in the greatest variety of compossible things. God, being supremely good, primarily wills what is perfect, but due to restrictions imposed by the absolutely necessary essences of finite things, actually wills only the best whole that is possible. Thus Leibniz in his *Theodicy* and Wolff in his German Teleology both argue that all actual determinations of all actual things, all forms of order, all actual laws of nature, all laws of human thought and action, are indeed enclosed in one teleological whole held together by nothing other than their fitness to exit in this very whole, because it possesses the greatest unity amidst the greatest variety possible. And what is God's aim in creating such a world? As Wolff explains in a characteristic passage:

> Since the world is the means through which the purpose is to be achieved, and yet the means is distinct from the purpose, the purpose cannot be found in the world. And accordingly it is to be sought in God, as what is outside of the world and distinct from it. However, because God is independent of all things outside of himself, nothing can be brought into him through the world that he would not already possess. And thus there remains nothing left, except that the world represents God's perfections as in a mirror. This is the purpose that God can achieve through the world, and this is usually called the revelation of the magnificence of God. (Wolff 1983, §. 1045)

All things, including the human being, are but the means to the glorification of God, and thus human freedom, on this view, does not play a particularly central role. It is nothing else than the ability to act from full consciousness of the reasons why one is acting in a particular way, while the highest freedom is the acquired capacity to act in this way for the most or best reasons. What is more, acting freely or morally in this latter case is unavoidably necessary, though only hypothetically so, given that one does indeed represent what is best. In other words, the perfection of action follows necessarily from the perfection of representation of the action *qua* possible. The only determinations that escape this robust metaphysical teleology are thus the purely logical and mathematical truths, as these are absolutely necessary, and thus require no ground of truth outside of their essences.

For present purposes, the most significant result of this metaphysical teleology lies in what it means for how the nature of reason is to be understood. If the very basis of unity or of correspondence between all things rests ultimately on this teleological scheme, then so must that correspondence between nature and our representations that we call "truth." From this point of view, representations and the faculties within the mind that make them possible are treated simply as particular kinds of objects in general. If they possess any particular dignity or significance beyond anything else, this is not because they constitute a unique kind, or require a unique method to approach them, but rather because they provide a particularly excellent means to the realization of the final end of the entire teleological scheme. Indeed, as Kant later observed, on this view the very fact that there even is something called "understanding" or "reason" is merely a corollary of the existence of the same overall scheme (see, e.g., *Refl* 5707); for we represent things at all because there exists a teleological harmony instituted between our representations and the universe, while the fact that we represent things as lawful, and thus possess the faculty of understanding, and as connected, and thus possess the faculty of reason, is owing to the very same scheme.

The Thomasian line, which is most fully developed by Adolph Hoffmann and Christian Crusius, contrasts sharply with the above. Similar to the Leibniz-Wolffians, it defends the view that all real determination is an effect of freedom, which itself consists essentially in an original or first act of a will. It even agrees that all willing, including that through which God creates all things (thereby determining them as regards their real predicates), is founded on a representation or archetype in the intellect. However, thinkers in this school hold that the human being is unique in that it constitutes the genuine end of creation and that it can do so precisely because its willing is not necessarily determined by this overarching teleology, but rather is self-determining, although no less teleological. Only in this way, i.e. if the human being is free in a truly original sense, can it provide a suitable end for the divine will:

> Having considered the matter well, I have previously said that the divine willing of perfection requires that nothing remains in vain not only in regard to the things that exist together and to future consequences, but rather also, that nothing can be in vain in regard to God. This is possible if he 1) so directs the world that through the actions of creatures, insofar as, to the extent they do not depend upon his creation and determination, certain relations to him become possible, which agree with his attributes. This occurs if there are free creatures in the world. For the application and directing of freedom depends not upon God for its actuality, but only for its possibility. And further 2) when the connection of all other unfree creatures are aimed so that they should have an influence on the possibility and result of free actions. If God proceeded otherwise, then in regard to him the entire work of creation

would be in vain. For everything that is not free, or that depends mediately on the free actions of creatures, is adequately ascribed to God as a sufficient and determining cause. Hence, through its actuality there arises no other relation to him than it already would have had before in the state of possibility [...]. (Crusius 1964, p. 506–507)

Thus only a being that is free, i.e. one capable of taking up its own relation to God undetermined by him, can serve as a final end of creation, because it alone is capable of adding something of value beyond what God could do himself. Only a free being can have an act that is its own, and thus is the only kind of being for which genuine obedience to God's law can be comprehensible or indeed of any value. Yet all real determinations are determined, whether by man or by God, through free will after an archetype. In particular, physical things in regard to their real determinations are created by God so as to make the free will possible and to direct it towards perfection, while human beings themselves determine their own moral properties either according to or against this end. As the will is of an essentially teleological nature, all real determination is thus ultimately and *per se* teleological according to this line of thought.

Much more could be said to fully flesh out these teleological views, but it is easy to see that teleology informs the most basic structure of the philosophies of both traditions and that this teleology, even if it leads to a goal located within human reason, is nevertheless first established through a ground external to human reason. Human reason cooperates in and serves this teleological scheme, to be sure, but it is in no sense the complete and original ground of it.

§. 2.2. The Legacy of Kant's Teleology of Reason in Fichte

If the critical philosophy indeed contains a fundamental transformation of traditional teleological structures as I contend, then it should not be surprising that in post-Kantian philosophies the teleological structure of reason is a core concern. And this is precisely what we find. In the early productions of German Idealism, which are contemporaneous with Kant's last writings, the metaphysical teleology found in pre-Kantian philosophers is explicitly reinterpreted as a misunderstood expression of a more fundamental teleology internal to, and originally grounded in, the development of rational self-consciousness. The specific configuration of this teleology of reason differs from thinker to thinker, quickly evolving along lines that would have been unrecognizable to Kant, but are nevertheless undertaken in the basically the same spirit as his own work.

Starting with Fichte, the explicit project of philosophy really becomes the exhibition of the structure of rational self-consciousness as a self-propelling and self-articulating system. Profoundly radicalizing the Cartesian identification of the self with pure thinking activity while at the same time grasping Kant's central methodological insight, Fichte recognizes that whatever is to become of the self, or for the self, must be the result of the self's own free activity. Rationalists from Descartes to Kant had previously realized that one cannot have knowledge accidentally, since to have knowledge means to have taken full possession of truth oneself through a methodical (re)production or (re)construction of the object of knowledge within one's own thinking. Kant himself had expressed the point with unmatched clarity: "reason has insight only into what it produces itself according to its own design" (*KrV* Bxiv). Thus, thinking is knowledge only to the extent that it is constructed from materials already available from within the activity of the "I think" itself. By contrast with pre-Kantian metaphysics, Fichte claims "in all seriousness and not simply as a figure of speech – the object will be posited and determined by our power of cognition, and not vice versa" (Fichte 1994, p. 5).

Fichte followed out the natural logic of this approach by arguing, first, that not only must knowledge be constructed by the self, but indeed anything able to be an object of consciousness *at all* must be the result of such a construction, which means that even the thought of something external to consciousness and effecting it from outside must be in some sense the self's own production. Secondly, Fichte argued that whatever materials there might be within the activity of the self for constructing the objects of knowledge, our possession of these materials must be proven through an act of transcendental reflection in which they are themselves constructed from an assumed original principle of self-consciousness. Thirdly, Fichte recognized that just as the principle of knowledge, and indeed of self-consciousness, cannot lie in a being that is *external* to the self, so also it cannot be a principle strictly speaking *internal* to our empirical consciousness. It must rather be an original act and oneness that for the first time separates and thereby relates some determinate I with a not-I that makes its determinacy possible by providing it with a limit, giving rise to consciousness and its object in one stroke. Self-consciousness, always being the consciousness of some object (and indeed of the self *as limited by an object*), already contains for Fichte the product of an activity that we only first thematize *post hoc* through transcendental reflection. As the active medium fully present in all thought, it can still only grasp itself in particular reflexive acts. And just as for Kant the critical experiment must either be a success or else must lead to the conclusion that knowledge is impossible, so for Fichte one either assumes the original principle and by that fact is in possession of the entire science that follows from it, or one is simply not a philosopher. Intentionally echoing the conclusion Kant himself draws from his teleological statement of method at *Prol* 04:263, Fichte writes:

§. 2. The Teleological Tradition Before and After Kant — 35

"My system can be evaluated only on its own terms and cannot be judged by the principles of any other philosophy. It only has to agree with itself. It can be explained only by itself, and it can be proven – or refuted – only on its own terms. One must accept it completely or reject it in its entirety" (Fichte 1994, p. 5).

Now, because for Fichte this original principle is the original unity of subject and object, it can never fully become an object of consciousness. The original principles, as the absolute self-positing identity of the *I positing I*, the *I positing not-I*, and the *I positing within itself a divisible I opposed to a divisible not-I* are all certainly to be intuited in the sense that in every moment of self-consciousness we are immediately aware of the identity of the subject, the object and the subject-object. Nevertheless, this very awareness of the complex activity of the I must itself be something determinate, and so can only be thematized and pursued in the many guises of subject-object relation through which it manifests itself according to the laws of knowledge. Furthermore, according to Fichte, since the science of knowing must bring itself down to first principles if it is to be genuine knowing, or rather knowing of knowing, the result is that consciousness is compelled from within, thus in its own freedom, to progress from one standpoint to the next in seeking out a fuller consciousness of its basic principle. The self-positing I always by its very nature exceeds any determinate form, and thereby gives rise to contradictions that can only be overcome by freely positing a further object as standing against and limiting it and in which the contradiction is resolved. Fichte describes this as a regression to conditions of possibility, such that each standpoint is found to be possible only on the assumption of yet another, which is at the same time a progression whose "final result" is "the system of all necessary representations," which "must be equivalent to experience as a whole" (Fichte 1994, p. 31), but which can never be other than an idea. The system of knowledge as a whole is therefore nothing other than the articulated presentation of the self-development of absolute principle of the I from which it began, and it possesses among others, the unique feature of teleological structure that its end is at the same time understood to be the full presentation of the condition of the possibility of its beginning.

Although Fichte does often draw attention to the teleological and organic structure of the *Grundlage*, which is to be an expression the system through which self-consciousness articulates itself, and thereby manifests itself as self-determining, this theme is only first explicitly brought to the surface in later writings where Fichte attempts to articulate more radically still the structure of his philosophical system. In the *Darstellung der Wissenschaftslehre* written in 1801, for instance, Fichte explains the difficulty of entering into his system as a result of the fact that although "the *Wissenschaftslehre* is not a system of bits of knowledge, but rather a single intuition," this single intuition is not an "absolute simplicity." Rather it is an essentially "organic unity," which contains "at the same time and in undivided unity both the fusing together of a manifold into a unity, and the radiation of unity into a multiplicity" (Fichte 1845/46, 02:11– 12). As Fichte writes, clearly echoing Kant's similar statements in the *KrV* we examined before:

> This *Wissenschaftslehre* does not conclude forwardly in a simple series, as in a line, according to the law of consequence, which is a kind of method that is only possible within and concerning an organism of knowledge that is already presupposed and reflected. In philosophy this does not lead to anything, and there it is complete shallowness. Rather its conclusions are drawn on all sides and reciprocally, always outwardly from a central point to all points, and from all points back, just as in an organic body. (Fichte 1845/46, 02:12)

Thus any part of the system can only be understood and justified when taken in unity with the whole system, and thus no starting point can be completely justified before the execution of the system itself. Only in its results, namely in the complete self-generating and self-unifying system, is the absolutely first principle self-justifying.

Similar points are made in Fichte's lectures of 1804. In these, Fichte again evidently wishes us to understand the tension between the absolute I, understood as both absolute being and absolute freedom, as only conceivable in the form of an absolutely organic faculty of knowledge, i.e. one that remains at rest in its own being, and preserves itself in this, even while being immersed in the most excessive and infinite going beyond itself. As Fichte writes:

> Since, according to the nature of our science, we must stand neither in oneness nor in multiplicity but instead between the two, it is clear [...] that no oneness at all that appears to us as a simple oneness, or that will appear to us as such in what follows, can be the true oneness. Rather, the true and proper oneness can only be the principle simultaneously of both the apparent oneness and the apparent multiplicity. And it cannot be this as something *external*, such that it merely projects oneness and the principle of multiplicity, throwing off an objective appearance; rather it must be so *inwardly and organically,* so that it cannot be a principle of oneness without the same moment being a principle of disjunction, and vice versa; and it must be comprehended as such. Oneness consists in just this absolute, inwardly living, active and powerful, and utterly irrepressible essence. – To put it simply, oneness cannot in any way consist in what we *see* or *conceive* as the science of knowing, because that would be something objective; rather it consists in what we are, and pursue, and live. (Fichte 2005a, p. 56)

Fichte goes on to remark that, for this reason, it does not matter whether one takes the highest principle of philosophy to be "a principle of oneness or of disjunction," since both would be false or "one-sided" due to the fact that the true principle is neither of these, but rather "is both as an organic oneness and is itself their organic oneness." The goal of all philosophy is therefore to enter into this organic oneness, and to allow it to animate our own thinking, "our own scientific life and activity," with its "self-differentiating" power (Fichte 2005a, p. 56–57).

A second feature of the teleological character of Kant's philosophy that Fichte both absorbs and transforms is its re-conception of the ends of reason as issuing from its practical rather than its merely theoretical capacity. As Fichte famously put it, his "system is from beginning to end but an analysis of the concept of freedom" (Fichte 1993, p.1). In particular, he argues in *The System of Ethics*, that the absolute act "I think" must at the same time be an absolute act "I will," that indeed the entire basis of the possibility of the former can be demonstrated to rest in the latter. And in its final analysis, the end at the basis of all previous developments of the system was but reason itself as freely and absolutely self-determining. By virtue of and for the sake of this sole end, everything, even all traces of individuality are to be thrown off so that one can pursue the infinite project of vanishing into the pure self-positing of the one divine and universal reason: "Our ultimate goal is the self-sufficiency of all reason as such and thus not the self-sufficiency of one rational being [*einer Vernunft*], insofar as the latter is an individual rational being" (Fichte 2005, p. 220). But this gradual elimination of the individual as individual is, according to Fichte, not a mystical leap into the oneness, but rather the development of an organic relation to others; where my freedom is at the same time their willing, where everything purposive for my reason is also purposive for everyone else's: "Accordingly, anything that any one person does would be of use to everyone, and what everyone does would be of use to each individual – and this would be so in actuality, for in actuality they all have only a single end" (Fichte 2005, p. 241). If the center of Fichte's philosophy is truly freedom, then it is the absolutely organic and living character of this freedom that qualifies it as absolute.

The way in which this transcendental teleology of reason relates to the traditional teleology typical of Kant's German predecessors is also central to Fichte's attempts to explain the nature of his system in the first introduction to the *Wissenschaftslehre* and more fully still in the *Vocation of Man*. In the former, Fichte makes the fundamental claim that there are but two possible approaches to philosophy, namely that which seeks to derive the subject from the object, and that which seeks to derive the object from the subject. The former of these contradictorily opposed approaches is embraced by dogmatism, and ends up refuting itself, whereas the latter was first initiated by Kant and proves itself to be the only self-consistent system of philosophy (Fichte 1994, p. 15). Thus in Fichte's view, Kant is responsible for this epochal shift in perspectives.

Later in the *Vocation of Man*, Fichte expands upon and dramatizes this same shift by explicitly narrating the progress of the I as it is driven in search of its own self-sufficiency first to embrace dogmatism, then Kantian criticism, and finally the new teleology of reason characteristic of Fichte's own practical philosophy. Book One in particular describes the manner in which the reflecting I characteristic of pre-Kantian "dogmatic" philosophy begins with the Cartesian decision to take possession of itself, and to become for the first time the genuine owner and author of its own thoughts; how it then passes from this point to a recognition of some of the most basic principles that must be presupposed if it is to ever come to have knowledge of things other than itself, gradually developing the principles of complete determination (i.e. that every actual object insofar as it is such must be determined in every possible respect), of causality, of sufficient reason, and eventually Leibniz's principle of the complete interconnection of all things within nature. From these the I of Fichte's tale comes to take up the standpoint of the complete determinism in regard to nature, and indeed of its own thoughts and actions insofar as these are nothing but natural entities within the great scheme of "sufficiently determined" nature. In light of such reflections, the I comes to recognize itself as a particular product of the great productive force that gives birth to all rational and self-conscious beings, and its own actions and thoughts as but so many variations of this original "anthropogenetic" force (Fichte 1987, p. 13). The I comes thus to see that it possess the specific form that it happens to have, simply because in these particular circumstances the antropogenetic force could express itself in no other way.

Freedom is thus revealed to be an illusion: "In immediate self-consciousness I appear to myself to be free; in reflection on the whole of nature I find that freedom is unfortunately impossible: the former must be subordinated to the latter for it can even be explained by it" (Fichte 1987, p. 15). Still, the I seems to gain satisfaction in this thought, for through the underlying doctrine it becomes clear that the I is connected by necessary laws with the whole expanse of nature. It knows only itself immediately, but can come to know all other things through inference, or by "calculation," using the principles it has so far developed: "The principle of sufficient reason is the point of transition from the particular, which is itself, to the general, which is outside it" (Fichte 1987, p. 16). Moreover, since the I finds these principles within itself, it is clear that the I represents the entire realm of nature through itself, albeit merely from its own perspective. The I is thus elevated above all other things through the fact that it can come to know the whole of nature, and indeed can come to know its own place within nature.

It follows equally from this that all this knowledge is true, since it is nothing but the necessary product of nature within the I. Every thought is thus completely determined and cannot be otherwise than it is. What we call the "clarity and vividness" of knowledge is for this I but the "greater or lesser degree of activity which the force of humanity is capable of expressing" (Fichte 1987, p. 17). The will is likewise nothing but the consciousness of certain productive forces in oneself. When these forces are not in accordance with the general force of mankind, they conflict with the main focus of our drives, inhibit our proper activity, and for this reason are of a lower kind. The higher drives, by contrast, conform to the general goal of our force and thus also to the goal of the force of humanity. The consciousness of the striving of these higher drives is what is called the *moral law*. Remorse is but the feeling produced by the higher drives when these reflect on their failure to overcome the lower ones in the past.

In this way Fichte builds, and none too subtly, the core of the Enlightenment view of man from its first beginnings in Descartes' demand for self-certainty to its full development in what Leibniz called Christian fatalism. And it is indeed remarkable how well Fichte's story coheres with the deepest tendencies of such thought and expresses these tendencies with no attempt to hide their radical nature. But what is the moral of this story? Fichte is here leading the I to develop the teleological view of man that he thinks is distinctive of pre-Kantian thought. The teleology of nature here lies in the view of creation as through and through intellectually determinate, while the specific teleology of man is a teleology of perfectionism in which the essential means and end of such perfection are precisely the cognition of nature as such, but most centrally of man's nature or distinctive goal. Such teleology is a pure intellectualism, and it has the unavoidable result, in Fichte's view, that it leads to a complete determinism in which the I must regard itself as essentially the product of an unknown external force:

> Strict necessity has me in its inexorable power; if it determines me to be a fool and to be given to vice, then without doubt I will become a fool and be given to vice; if it determines me to be wise and good, then without doubt I will be wise and good. It is neither that necessity's fault or merit nor mine. It is subject to its laws and I to its. After realizing this it will be most conducive to peace of mind to give up my wishes to it as well, seeing that my being is wholly given up to it. (Fichte 1987, p. 19)

As I noted, Leibniz called this view Christian fatalism, and held it to be the highest state of mind that one could possibly reach. Nevertheless, the only thing separating it from pernicious and false forms of fatalism is its recognition that everything is determined to be the best because the complete intellectual determinism of creation is grounded in God's good will, and in opposition to these that the things we do and the knowledge we have are integral causes in bringing about our fate.

The I in Fichte's story thus finds after its initial elevation that such a vision of its destiny would be completely crushing, and that what appeared to be its own choice to take responsibility for its knowledge, and to thereby attain its proper dignity, has led it to the ironic conclusion that it has no dignity and that the initial choice was not its choice at all. Fate has itself brought the I to recognize itself as utterly without independence or freedom, indeed to recognize itself as not possessing anything that deserves to be called "self" or its "own" at all. It is at this point that Fichte illustrates how this crushing teleology of dogmatism is transformed by Kantian criticism and thereby opens the path to Fichte's own practical teleology of self-sufficient reason. With this the Kantian I attempts to restore its own proper dignity by retracing the Cartesian path to see where things went wrong. It begins to ponder its knowledge of things and to question how such knowledge is possible, from what inner experiences and ideas in particular it has arisen. Here it discovers an important fact: the I is only immediately aware of itself, of the sensations that are given within it; all else is inferred by principles. Thus everything that can be known by the I must arise from its own construction of an object from these materials, and the I itself, as that which does the constructing, is shown not to be just another object in nature. It is rather more primordial than any object, its essence being the productive ground of the unity of both subject and object in one. Its genuine self is thus this purely productive and free I, which is the very source and author of those principles it previously thought reduced the self to a mere thing.

There is no need to further detail how the *Vocation of Man* proceeds to trace I's development through the all the stages of the *Wissenschaftslehre*, finally achieving the final end at which our earlier discussion of his *System of Ethics* also came to a close. From the above it is abundantly clear that Fichte not only saw Kant's philosophy as effecting a fundamental and irreversible shift in the philosophical tradition, but also that he interpreted this as essentially a radical shift in how the teleology of reason was to be conceived. Similar reflections to these could, I believe, be easily extended to Schelling and Hegel. In particular, it could be noted how Hegel himself carries on this teleological line of thought in his own distinctive way; how he criticizes Kant and Fichte, not for the teleological character of their systems, but for the imperfection and subjectivity in the form of this teleology, which in his view places unjustifiable limits on a productive ground that is in principle supposed to be unlimited; how Hegel repeatedly emphasizes that Kant initiated a recovery of the genuine concept of teleology; and how finally Hegel incorporates Schelling's ideas on natural philosophy into his own explanation of the absolutely and intrinsically teleological process through which the concept manifests itself. But all of this would add nothing essential to my present concerns, but would only further underscore the height to which teleological speculations were raised by the work of Kant.

It is more to the point of this introduction to ask what can be concluded from this about the basic tendency of German Idealism in relation to pre-Kantian philosophy, and what this can tell us about Kant. As to the first question, it is clear that German philosophy both before and after Kant rests on the conviction that the whole of things, including physical nature, is at bottom meaningful and intelligible, and that this truth is grounded in the fact that everything that has being receives its being from the place it occupies in a single unified plan determined by an idea. Prior to Kant, this single unified plan was God's plan, and reason was seen as sharing in this creation, and thus as having reached its highest freedom, only when it came to know this plan and to act from this knowledge. We have also seen that as a post-Kantian, Fichte sought to find an adequate way of relocating the foundation or final *telos* of this teleological scheme in a principle *internal* to reason. The whole of all things, including nature, are intelligible from this point of view simply by virtue of the fact that they are products of absolute intelligence, or are acts of the absolute I.

Regarding Kant, we can therefore conclude that he stands at the turning point between these two teleological schemes. What he brought about, in a first approximation, might be described as an internalization of the teleological structure of creation into the essential ground-structure of rational thought. However, it must be noted that to say this resulted in a "subjectivizing" or "internalizing" of traditional teleology is really to explain nothing at all, since this relocation was not from one place to another place within the traditional metaphysical scheme. In this respect, Fichte was right to argue that Kant's philosophical position has nothing in common with what came before. For the "reason" of Kant's predecessors is simply not the same reason that Kant argues is the genuine source of ends. Indeed, the Kantian subject – which is where things would presumably be relocated when they are "subjectivized" – appears to first come into being in this turning, or is at least strictly delimited for the first time through the activity of self-consciousness that supposedly effects this turn in transcendental reflection. And just as with Kant's "reason," there is simply no such thing as a "transcendental subject" in the writings of Kant's predecessors. Therefore, to say that he relocated the source of teleology from an external source to one within the subject, as if this kind of a subject were already available to him prior to the turn, is really to miss the radical character of the Kantian revolution. Evaluation of the nature of Kant's thought would, of course, be easier if such a path could be taken. As it turns out, however, the subject and the entire conceptual scheme are both transformed at one stroke and in conjunction by the transcendental turn, and Kant himself simply could not have envisaged such a plan of transformation, or its possible consequences, before having enacted it. What this means is that the nature of Kant's turn can best and perhaps only be approached from within the standpoint and exigencies brought to light by the system itself.

§. 3. Current Views on the Role of Teleology in Kant's Critical Philosophy

Outside the narrow confines of Kant scholarship, the prevailing view is that his thoughts on teleology are restricted to the seemingly unimportant *Critique of Teleological Judgment* that takes up a mere fifty-six pages in the Academy Edition. This is a piece of text, as Kant informs us, that discloses no special principle or faculty (*EEKU* 20:243 – 4; *KU* 05:194), and which, if not for its link with aesthetic judgment, could be reduced to a mere appendix to an examination of the theoretical faculty of reason. That teleology is a relatively unimportant notion in Kant's thought, and is indeed restricted to the second half of the *KU*, is further supported by most widely accepted characterizations of his theoretical and practical philosophies: "Nature," for Kant means "the material world of Galileo and Newton" (Collingwood 1960, p. 116). "We must always keep in mind" Gottfried Martin warns, "that when Kant asks about the existence of nature," he is asking about "nature as it is presented in pure mathematical natural science – in mechanics" (Martin 1974, p. 67). Even those who generally seek to emphasize the practical importance of teleology in Kant's philosophy nevertheless regard the aim of the *KrV* to be the defense of a modern view of nature as a mechanical whole devoid of purpose. As Richard Velkley writes, "He [Kant] is the greatest of all philosophic defenders of antiteleological Newtonian science," and for him "the theoretical use of reason is by itself blind to purposes" (Velkley 2001, p. 153).[7] According to most holding such a view, teleology only subsequently enters Kant's theoretical project as a "reflective" and subjective standpoint, required perhaps as a heuristic device for the study of nature in the particular, but ultimately introduced by Kant in order to bridge the immense gulf that his pre-

---

[7] While Velkley expresses this view of the content of Kant's *theoretical* philosophy in a way I disagree with, he nevertheless vigorously defends a robust sense in which teleology is central to Kant's practical philosophy and, indeed, to the architectonic of Kant's philosophy as a whole. He also believes, like I, that teleology motivated the transcendental turn. I will stress, by contrast, that the basic conceptual framework of Kant's thought, which is teleological, penetrates to the deepest level of his transcendental philosophy; it not only motivated it and made it necessary, it also made it possible, since the very transcendental method is internally teleological.

§. 3. Current Views on the Role of Teleology in Kant's Critical Philosophy — 43

vious works had unintentionally introduced between the realm of nature and the realm of freedom. This intuition about the secondary character of teleology is often thought to be corroborated by Kant's severe limitation of its role to that of a merely heuristic standpoint for reflection on nature.[8]

Likewise, on the practical side, the term "deontology," which has come to mean an anti-teleological or duty-centered moral theory, today passes as a synonym for Kantian-style moral theories. In defense of this classification generally and its applicability to Kant in particular, Jerome Schneewind, one of the foremost contemporary historians of ethics, has argued that Kant's moral theory in principle rules out teleology in any usual sense of the term. The idea underlying Schneewind's position is not that Kant's moral theory is without ends and goods – such is easily refuted by even a cursory reading of Kant's texts – but rather that its basic principle for deciding *which* ends and *which* goods are morally acceptable is itself one of "acting for the sake of the law alone," and so of acting independently of any *consideration* of ends whatsoever. Thus if teleology is allowed to enter the moral picture at all for Kant, perhaps under the guise of a theory of value, it is only *after* the notion of freedom and the moral law have been established, and it takes place by means of something added to them from without. Hence Kant's moral theory is not ultimately teleological, since it excludes the conception of an end from playing any role at the most fundamental level. This, it seems, is the most widely held view.[9]

Similarly, Alasdair MacIntyre, one of the most influential writers on ethical theory during the last several decades, has drawn on both of these purported aspects of Kant's philosophy, popularizing a view in which Kant marks the culmination of the anti-Aristotelian, anti-teleological current that, so he claims, characterizes basically all major moral theories of the early modern and modern periods, and which is the result of the "secular rejection of both Protestant and Catholic theology and the scientific and philosophical rejection of Aristotelianism" (MacIntyre 1981, p. 52). After this nearly total "elimination" of "any notion of man-as-he-could-be-if-he-realised-his-*telos*" from both nature and ethics, MacIntyre adds:

---

[8] Bernd Dörflinger observes similarly: "Hence, teleology is apparently not at the centre of Kant's philosophy, but only at its periphery, and although it can indeed serve as a technique for studying nature, its claims are quite restricted" (Dörflinger 1995, p. 813). He however shares my view that this is quite false.

[9] Paulsen held a similar view (Paulsen 1963, p. 326). I don't disagree with the premise of this argument, but with its conclusion, which rests on the assumption that teleological views of the moral principle can only have the form Kant attributes to hypothetical imperatives.

> Reason does not comprehend essences or transitions from potentiality to act; these concepts belong to the despised conceptual scheme of scholasticism. Hence anti-Aristotelian science sets strict boundaries to the powers of reason. Reason is calculative; it can assess truths of fact and mathematical relations but nothing more. In the realm of practice therefore it can speak only of means. About ends it must be silent. [...] Reason for [Kant] as much as for Hume, discerns no essential natures and no teleological features in the objective universe available for study by physics. Thus [Pascal's, Hume's and Kant's] disagreements on human nature coexist with striking and important agreements and what is true of them is also true of Diderot, of Smith and of Kierkegaard. All reject any teleological view of human nature, any view of man as having an essence which defines his true end. (MacIntyre 1981, p. 52)

On MacIntyre's reading, Kant's understanding of human nature, and hence of morals too, is one almost exclusively concerned with rules and formulae of right conduct, and it conceives the good chiefly as does Stoicism, i.e. as the denial of inclination in favor of a fixed law of reason. Thus it is in principle opposed to any Aristotelian or virtue-centered moral theory that seeks to train and incorporate the inclinations so that they contribute to the good life, and which conceives the latter to be a whole of human flourishing with its own internal value. Now because Kant does nevertheless frame his theory in the teleological worldview typical of Christian scholasticism, MacIntyre suggests that this is only because he was insightful enough to realize that without such concessions any moral theory is bound to fail. This framework nevertheless remains something foreign to the essential direction of Kant's thought (MacIntyre 1981, p. 53). Again, the basic view here is that Kant's theory of nature – in this case specifically *human* nature – conflicts fundamentally with his theory of freedom, and that his introduction of teleology is an artificial attempt to cover over this difficulty.

Although of a very different pedigree and tenor of thought, John McDowell built several of his core insights in the 1990s on a similar interpretation. McDowell devotes some of his most interesting work to arguing that the cooperation of passive and active cognitive capacities is necessary for generating both our theoretical experience of the world and our practical conceptions of virtuous conduct. Like MacIntyre, McDowell harkens back to a pre-modern and ultimately Aristotelian view of nature in his attempt to articulate a naturalism that would be robust enough to account for the active and normative capacities of practical reason without overtly or covertly eliminating them. McDowell, however, severely criticizes MacIntryre among others for failing to see that the distinction between Aristotle and Kant is not respectively between a naturalist teleological view and a naturalist anti-teleological view, but rather between a position that sees no difficulty in viewing reason and meaning as developments within a broader conception of "second nature," which is normative and teleological, and a position in which it is thought

§. 3. Current Views on the Role of Teleology in Kant's Critical Philosophy — 45

that if reason and meaning are to be salvaged, then this can only be done by placing them in a "transcendental" realm outside of nature.

According to McDowell, the reason Kant thinks we must place the realm of meaning and norms outside of nature is that his thinking on nature is infected by Protestant individualism and the modern conception of nature as a realm of meaningless natural laws. As McDowell writes in *Mind and World*:

> No doubt the notion of *Bildung* is at Kant's disposal, but not as the background for a serious employment of second nature. For Kant, the idea of nature is the idea of the realm of law, the idea that came into focus with the rise of modern science. [...] Against Hume, Kant aims to regain for nature the intelligibility of law, but not the intelligibility of meaning. For Kant, nature is the realm of law and therefore devoid of meaning. And given such a conception of nature, genuine spontaneity cannot figure in descriptions of actualizations of natural powers as such. (McDowell 1996, p. 96–97)

McDowell explains here that Kant cannot rightfully speak of the pursuit of goals and the observance of norms as taking place as part of the natural world, because the only conception of nature at Kant's disposal is that of "first nature," or nature according to physical laws operating passively and blindly. Now since Kant's theory of knowledge is fundamentally based upon a view of reason as essentially spontaneous or active, and indeed as purposive, this forces him – so McDowell contends – to adopt a special standpoint, called "transcendental reflection," which really should be impossible on the very view of nature that Kant himself attempts to justify. In effect, what McDowell is arguing is that Kant recognizes that a correct understanding of knowing requires that receptivity be fully integrated with spontaneity (intuitions with concepts), but since he lacks a conception of second nature that would make him capable of naturalizing this spontaneity, he is not able to identify the standpoint from which he makes this discovery with the natural or empirical standpoint of the human mind. "And in this predicament," writes McDowell, "he can find no option but to place the connection outside nature, in the transcendental framework" (McDowell 1996, p. 98).

To this McDowell adds the important conclusion – particularly for comparison with the contrary results reached in the Excursus following Chapter 7 – that without a concept of second nature, the "exploitation of the concept of life, which is a quintessentially natural phenomenon, to make sense of a unity in the domain of spontaneity, which by Kant's lights has to be non-natural, is not within Kant's grasp" (McDowell 1996, p. 103–104). McDowell's idea here seems to be that while the concept of life would be the appropriate locus for integrating spontaneity *within* nature, perhaps through the unity of self-organizing and self-actualizing natural powers, Kant's conception of nature as blind physical law precludes him from seriously holding any such view.[10] It is from this standpoint that McDowell suggests in *Mind and World* that what is required is a move beyond Kant to Hegel, who through his view that nothing, not even dead physical nature, lies outside the realm of reason, has provided the key for integrating genuine spontaneity within the natural world. To his credit, McDowell seems recently to have recanted this interpretation, arguing rather that the best way to work out a theory successfully integrating receptivity and spontaneity is by studying what Kant actually wrote.[11] Rather than turning to Hegel, McDowell now suggests, what we need to see is that Kant's theory is not really different from Hegel's. This change in view seems to be tied to a change in the way he understands the transcendental turn.

Another writer that should be mentioned in this connection is Dieter Henrich. Although Henrich recognizes that some deep structural features of Kant's philosophy are teleological, he too presents Kant's moral thought as essentially anti-teleological. In his essay "The Concept of Moral Insight," Henrich argues in particular that Kant's theory could only have arisen after the downfall of the Christian teleological views that dominated German theories of morality practically up to Kant's day (Henrich 1994, p. 55–88). His reason for saying this seems to be that in such theories morality is essentially reduced to an application of metaphysics to the nature of the human being, and from within such a viewpoint there is no room for the idea of a law or *telos* of moral conduct of which we could become immediately and directly conscious. What is good for human beings, in other words, can only be derived within the traditional standpoint through the mediation of certain other metaphysical principles. Henrich argues that through the doctrine of the fact of reason and his rejection of the idea that the notion of what is good must precede the determination of the moral law, Kant essentially asserts that rational human beings have an *immediate* insight into the ultimate criterion of goodness.

In pointing this out, I do not wish to criticize the central idea of Henrich's remarkable essay. He is entirely right to draw this contrast. What I do not

---

10 Is this really Kant's view? Certainly, there is some *prima facie* evidence for such a view in Kant's writings. He does, certainly, place the sharpest possible distinction between the mechanism of nature and the autonomy of freedom, and he certainly also relegates freedom to the supersensible realm. But, on the other hand, Kant speaks both of freedom as "supersensible nature" and as the "supersensible substrate of nature." The other problem with this view is that it blithely claims that natural law is inimical to teleology and normativity. In my section on teleology, and in later chapters, we will see that there is absolutely no antinomy between natural law and teleology.

11 See McDowell 2009, particularly the first three essays, and p. 18n26 where McDowell seems to pin at least some of the blame for this mistake on Rorty.

agree with is the idea that it can be captured in terms of a rejection of teleology. As I will argue, the whole matter should be interpreted with quite a different emphasis. Most earlier theories of morality were, of course, dominated by a *theoretical* or *metaphysical* model of teleology, perhaps with the important exception of the Thomasian line. Just as Kant admits there is a moral fact of reason, i.e., an immediate and self-evident criterion of the good, so Wolff and many others are committed to the existence of a purely theoretical fact of reason, i.e. an immediate and self-evident criterion of truth. This theoretical fact provides the basic principle of a metaphysics that itself serves as the model or archetype of all reality, truth and perfection. The understanding of the perfection of the human being in such a theory is therefore dominated by a theoretical criterion.

Kant, by contrast, argues that the fact of reason is not originally a criterion of truth, but a criterion of the good. His argument for this is complicated, but it begins from the recognition that the supposed theoretical fact of reason relied upon by his predecessors had not been properly examined. If it had, they would have recognized that it is conditioned by certain limitations inherent to human reason, which disqualify it from serving as a criterion of the good. Freedom and the good itself thus lie essentially beyond the territory of theoretical reason, and it is in regard to this open domain that Kant locates his independent moral fact of reason. Still, as the only immediate and truly unconditioned criterion of the good, it too generates an archetype or goal of our practical activity, just as was the case in traditional dogmatic metaphysics. But in this case the archetype is specifically one of all *moral* reality, truth and perfection, and is articulated not in a *metaphysics of nature* but in a *metaphysics of morality*. Kant's moral theory, I will argue, is in fact *even more deeply teleological* than that of his predecessors, because he locates the very source of moral teleology in a criterion (the moral law) and archetype (the pure will) that is *immediately moral* in kind.

§. 3.1. Reactions to the Popular View

According to the interpretations mentioned above, Kant evidently fails to break free of the paradox of modernity that was so well described by Lewis White Beck, when he wrote that:

> It has been one of the paradoxes of science since the time of Descartes that the scientific control of nature for human purposes has been made possible by the denial of the legitimacy of the concept of natural purpose. This denial left man's own purposes unexplained

by nature and jeopardized, at least in theory, by the expansion of natural concepts into the sphere of human conduct. (Beck 1996, p. 234)[12]

Despite its prevalence, however, this view has not gone unchallenged by scholars. Indeed, a whole series of commentators have insisted on the deeply teleological character of various parts of Kant's philosophy and as a consequence believe that to some extent he is able to escape the paradox of modernity.

In regard to his moral theory in particular, some have argued that it is based upon, or at the very least is equivalent to, a theory of value, and that as such it must in some sense be fundamentally teleological. The first in the English scholarship to emphasize teleology in Kant's moral writings was perhaps H. J. Paton, who in the preface to the 1958 edition of his *The Categorical Imperative* admits to having previously failed to recognize the pervasive role of teleology in Kant's "*application* of moral principles." Based upon a recently won insight Paton now believes that "Kant takes into account most fully the desires and purposes and potentialities of men, and indeed that it is on a teleological view of man and of the universe that his application of moral principles is based" (Paton 1970, p. 17). Unfortunately, Paton did not elaborate this thesis in any detail or show how Kant's teleological views might be rooted in the bedrock of his theory of freedom. He only expressed the hope that some future student of Kant would perform what he regarded as an indispensable task.

In "Kant's Teleological Ethics" and *The Development of Kant's View of Ethics*, published in 1971 and 1972 respectively, Keith Ward argues (with considerably more insight than most subsequent commentators) that we must go beyond even Paton and recognize that a teleological worldview forms the underlying context even of Kant's moral formalism. "If Kant's ethics is formalistic," writes Ward, "it is a formalism which means to take full account of all natural and human purposes, and of the essential ends of humanity, perfection and happiness" (Ward 1972, p. 129). While he recognizes that the view of nature required by such a picture might "seem strangely at variance with the concept of nature as a mechanistic and deterministic system of causally interacting substances, outlined in the first *Critique*," in the second and third *Critiques*, he says, Kant developed a teleological view of nature as resting on a supersensible basis that makes it compatible with moral striving (Ward 1972, p. 131).

---

[12] In McDowell's turbid prose: "The upshot is that the philosophy of nature, which aims to deal with how the world comes to expression in *logos*, as it were swallows up the philosophy of practice, which aims to deal with how *logos* comes to expression in the world." See his "Two Sorts of Naturalism," in McDowell 1998b, p. 182.

§. 3. Current Views on the Role of Teleology in Kant's Critical Philosophy — 49

The evidence that Ward brings forward in support of this view is both true and important, but unfortunately it is either ignored by most commentators or at least not given the weight it clearly deserves. The reason for this, I would suggest, is to be found in the very weakness that becomes evident in Ward's own discussion of the topic. The weakness here is that teleology on this view is only introduced in order to bridge the gap between two seemingly anti-teleological realms, namely, that of freedom governed by the categorical imperative and that of the blind mechanism of physical nature. I submit, however, that as long as it has not been shown that the categorical imperative itself, as well as the inner structure of the free will, both require and establish the teleology that would fuse it with nature, and nature with it, then the whole project cannot be taken seriously. The standpoint I will defend holds that Kant in fact *separately* establishes a moral teleology alongside a natural teleology, and that it is only under the requirements placed upon our thinking by the moral teleology itself that natural teleology must be subordinated to it. Rather than being superimposed from outside, teleology arises from the very roots of Kant's system.

In order for such an interpretation to be plausible, of course, one must overcome the notion – seemingly so self-evident to some, but certainly incomprehensible to Leibniz or the Greeks – that "formal" in fact *just means* anti-teleological. Formal is teleological if the matter itself is a product or is essentially and irreducibly infused with the form. As Kant writes in 1796:

> The dismissive habit of crying down the *formal* in our knowledge (which is yet the preeminent business of philosophy) as a pedantry, under the name of "a pattern-factory," confirms this suspicion, namely that there is a secret intention, under the guise of philosophy to actually outlaw all philosophy, and as victor to play the superior over it (*pedibus subjecta vicissim obteritur, nos exaequat victoria coelo* – Lucretius). (*VT* 08:404)

This passage occurs in an essay entitled *On a Recently Prominent Tone*, just after Kant's most extended and precise discussion of the Platonic forms and Aristotelian teleology. As we will see in Chapter 6, far from being anti-teleological, Kant's formalism is tied essentially to the purity and perfection of the telic structure of pure practical reason.

The more recent teleological interpretations by Paul Guyer and Allen Wood are based upon the idea that the categorical imperative is ultimately not the foundation of Kant's moral philosophy (Wood 1999, Ch. 4; Guyer 2000, Ch. 3–7). It is much rather the case, they argue, that Kant arrived at the moral law (perhaps unfortunately) as a way of articulating an insight won regarding the inherent value of human or rational life. The underlying idea would be that since other human beings are inherently valuable, we must relate to them as purposes in themselves, or as purposes that are valuable for no further reason. In attempting to convert this substantive source of value into a workable moral imperative, Kant in their view lost sight of the fact that this material condition of value could not be fully captured in a purely formal law.

There is something to be said for this as a moral theory, and perhaps even as a theory about how Kant arrived at the moral imperative, but it is seems indefensible to me as an interpretation of what Kant thought to be the true subordination of these concepts. In the *Groundwork*, Kant does indeed speak of human beings as ends in themselves as being that alone which could contain "the ground of a possible categorical imperative, that is a practical law" (*GMS* 04:428). But this appears to be only a momentary episode in his conceptual analysis and by no means an announcement that the formal categorical imperative is really grounded for us in the given existence of humanity as a substantive moral value. Contrary to what Wood writes, moral freedom is what first reveals humanity to be intrinsically valuable, and without consciousness of the categorical imperative one could not even become aware of one's own freedom. Clearly, then, the existence of something valuable is only first proven and validated as a consequence of the law, and thus cannot in fact be the original ground of its derivation. In any case, I believe this kind of interpretation has been successfully opposed in the current literature (see, e.g. Sensen 2011).

Although the approaches thus far examined are true to some important features of Kant's texts, I believe they are still too facile to establish the rightful place of teleology in Kant's philosophy. The reason for this is that they fail to recognize where the real challenge lies; for although the anti-teleological readings of Kant may be couched in a dubious historical narrative, this does not necessarily mean that *as interpretations of the foundations of Kantian philosophy* they are entirely incorrect. After all, the fact that Kant introduces teleological notions does not mean that he is justified in doing so. What is missing from the purely expository approach is any deeper historical or systematic account serving to show the possibility and the necessity for Kant to make use of teleological concepts. Thus, I believe that the anti-teleological line of interpretation has one thing right, namely that if neither the theoretical nor the practical dimensions of Kant's philosophy can be shown to be teleological in a genuinely *fundamental* sense, as having *arisen* from teleological speculations, then no matter how important teleological concepts turn out to be for Kant's attempts at formulating a view of reason as a whole, teleology cannot be anything but a derivative notion within his thought. Put more firmly, if it cannot be shown that Kant's founding arguments, i.e., the constructive arguments underlying the analytics and dialectics of the first two *Critiques*, not only permit of a teleological account, but indeed *require* and *establish* one, then teleology – no matter how essential it is to Kant's wider systematic concerns – must be viewed as something foreign

§. 3. Current Views on the Role of Teleology in Kant's Critical Philosophy — 51

and superimposed. It will be precisely the business of the following chapters to show that for Kant the very *essences* (i.e., the most basic normative and constitutive structures) of both human knowledge and human freedom are teleological in a sufficiently well-defined sense.

§. 3.2. Teleology in Special Studies of Kant's Philosophy

Any survey of the place afforded to teleology by the secondary literature on Kant must mention at least a few of the specialized studies that either directly or indirectly broach this topic. In fact, the stimulus for the present study was in part the observation that specialized debates in Kant interpretation seem frequently to resolve themselves into debates over teleological issues, even where one would least expect teleology to arise. In this section, I will only briefly indicate some of the more interesting examples. Others will be discussed throughout the work itself or mentioned in the footnotes.

Several studies of Kant's theoretical philosophy have drawn attention to teleological features implicit in Kant's discussion of the faculty of judgment (Longuenesse), the table of the categories (Brandt and Dörflinger), the complex structure of the rational mind (Henrich and Dörflinger), and even the underlying argument of the transcendental deduction (Rosales, Sellars, Rosenberg). I will speak more directly of these interpretations in the appropriate sections of this work. In particular, Bernd Dörflinger's extended study *Das Leben theoretischer Vernunft: Teleologische und praktische Aspeckte der Erfahrungstheorie Kants* is an important work in this area. After demonstrating the textual foundation for the claim that Kant indeed conceives the understanding, and in particular the system of the categories, as a purposive whole united under a single idea, developing organically from a single root, and so forth, Dörflinger makes several claims with which the present work entirely agrees. Firstly, in regard to the status of the analogy between the structure of theoretical reason and organisms, Dörflinger argues essentially in agreement with Josef Simon, that the analogical relation runs not from given biological entities to reason, "but rather the way can only lead from the immediately known life of consciousness to the mere indirectly comprehensible living character of organisms," and thus "the objects of biology are thought after the analogy with reason" (Dörflinger 2000, p. 31). This is really a fundamental point, because if it turns out rather that teleological concepts have their proper object only in nature, then the analogy must prove to be inadequate for fully understanding the inner structure of reason with any certainty. Pauline Kleingeld has, for instance, argued that the teleological character of reason is based upon an analogy that runs rather from a purposiveness directly perceived in objects of nature to reason, since the latter she says is something supersensible and can thus only be represented on the basis of analogy (Kleingeld 1998). Kant's talk of reason as organic in her view is thus metaphorical or symbolic and is a sign of his critical modesty when approaching the nature of reason itself. While Kleingeld certainly raises some thorny issues, I firmly think the weight of the textual evidence is clearly on Dörflinger's side. Reason may not be a regular sensible object, but its effects and procedures are certainly something of which we can be directly aware. Kleingeld is right, however, that Kant is unwilling to go so far as to say that we are immediately aware of the roots of our own reason in a way that his dogmatic predecessors might have said this. The truth, I will try to show, lies in a synthesis of these two approaches.

In addition to this, Dörflinger argues convincingly, and perhaps most importantly, that from the very beginning Kant understands the internal structure of the entire faculty of knowledge as possessing a sort of intrinsic and self-developing purposive structure and that a knowledge of this structure is key to unlocking a hidden layer of unity and meaning behind such texts as the metaphysical and transcendental deductions in the *KrV*. In a short summary of his main work given at the International Kant Congress in 1995, he claims for instance that: "A project offering a theory of the understanding as teleological must surely lead us to the core of Kant's philosophy, in particular, to the centre of his Deduction" (Dörflinger 1995, p. 813). A close examination shows, for instance, that "the system of the categories" as Kant articulates it in the text of the Metaphysical Deduction, "is not a comparative system, but rather a system of production or a system of descent," for "the 'I think' is not an abstract principle of subsumption, but the principle of the affinity of necessarily combined dissimilar forms of thinking." Kant's account of the transcendental structure of theoretical reason is "part of a theory of rational life" (Dörflinger 1995, p. 823).

Dörflinger raises many interesting problems while articulating this interpretation in his main work. I should, however, mention a few of my misgivings about his more general project so that the difference between his approach and mine is clearer. As it stands, I think the focus on the analogy between an organism and reason is fruitful, but that it tends to steer the investigation away from the true sources of this teleology in Kant's thought and to obscure the unique structure of understanding and reason. Firstly – and this can be seen as operative throughout Dörflinger's book – the comparison of reason specifically with living organisms makes it imperative to stress the presence of an actual complex of causal processes at work in the mind. The understanding thereby tends to be assimilated to the will, and the structure of experience is taken over into a theory of the practical use of the understanding. Such an assimilation would seem to be necessary in order to cash out this analogy fully,

§. 3. Current Views on the Role of Teleology in Kant's Critical Philosophy — 53

because there is no other way to invest the understanding with the causality necessary to think it as an organism. Now, it is perfectly true that the will might take possession of the understanding and direct it in various ways, but I think it is key to properly grasping Kant's theories of both understanding and will to see that they are entirely distinct precisely in the fact that the former is not the source of a genuinely spontaneous *causality*, while the latter in fact is. The teleological character of theoretical reason, I believe, has nothing to do with actual productivity, but rather lies in the sort of intrinsic purposiveness that is presupposed for any actual use of the understanding at all. In other words, focusing on the organic character of theoretical reason draws attention away from the deepest and most original root of its unity and formal perfection, which lies in the inner ground of the *possibility* of its actual use, and confuses this with the specific practical teleology that is presupposed by the purposive directing and determining of theoretical reason by the will to cognize some particular object. The unique purposiveness that lies in the very faculty for representing an object in general has no internal or immediate relation of any kind to a causal activity, except in the sense that it makes the latter possible; it is articulated rather by a pure analysis of the *essence* of the cognitive faculty itself. For a similar reason, I think that speaking of the "life" of theoretical reason, while in a sense justified, threatens to mislead.

The other misgiving I have with Dörflinger's approach also does not really amount to an objection to his actual results, so much as to a sense that its manner of presentation is not precisely right. If we focus on organism and on life, I believe, then the question immediately becomes: From whence does Kant draw this idea? The idea of an organism plays very little part in Kant's pre-critical work, and it hardly plays a greater one in his critical writings. During both periods, living organisms stand as a sort of mystery or symbol of the incomprehensible in nature. Organisms in nature present us with a harmony between mutually independent laws for which we can find absolutely no natural ground. The organism is very nearly a self-contradictory idea, a material being the parts of which operate internally according to the idea of the whole. We can only make sense of the real possibility of such a thing, Kant admits, if we think of an archetypal intellect external to nature, and so also to the organism, as having prearranged the laws of matter to bring it about. The difficulty in both cases is that the real bedrock of human knowledge lies in that which can be known as following with necessity from laws of nature that are universally established. In regard to such laws alone can we have an insight into their necessity and truth. But organisms exhibit a regularity of activity for which no ground can be found within those kinds of laws upon which our objective knowledge of nature depends. In the last analysis, the organism cannot really be understood to posses the purity, self-sufficiency, and true independence that is the unique feature of pure understanding and pure reason. By this I do not mean to deny that the concept of an organism is important for Kant, but only that it is not really a perfectly adequate analogue for articulating the structure of reason. If we add to this the earlier noted fact that Kant always thinks of the structure of organisms on the pattern of the structure of reason, and not the other way around, it seems reasonable to look for a different source of this structural idea.

If not from natural organisms, then from where does Kant derive the purposive conception of reason? To answer this question a natural place to begin would be with any earlier instances in which Kant engages with a similar kind of systematic unity in his writings. What kind of unity is this that is so characteristic of reason for Kant? As we saw in §. 1. above, it was precisely reason's purity, its absolute independence, its self-formative and self-generating character that were essential to its absolute unity. And one notable consequence of this, which Kant underscored precisely by comparing the structure of reason to that of an organism, was that all its functions and parts must cohere together under a single idea or principle, such that each must relate to every other in a perfectly reciprocal means-ends relationship. But as we saw in §. 2., this is essentially the same conception of teleological structure that Kant developed in the pre-critical period in order to articulate the teleological structure of the cosmos, the same which he thought must result precisely from a genuine conception of God as likewise absolutely independent and self-sufficient. Kant, as we saw, believed that just such an absolutely teleological unity was to be found not only in space, but also in the first laws of matter, indeed in the entire structure of the spiritual and physical cosmos, since a proper conception of God's self-sufficiency requires us to think even the essences of things as formed so as to bring about the greatest possible purposiveness in their consequences. This indicates that Kant's teleological conception of reason is modeled directly after his earlier the theory of God as the ground of all real possibility. In a precisely parallel way, the transcendental purposiveness that in the pre-critical period Kant regarded as inhering by virtue of this principle in the necessary essences of things is transformed by him in the critical period such that it is able to guide his formulation of the transcendental affinity and perfection of all cognition within a whole of possible experience. The place previously occupied by God as the unifying ground of the essences of all things in one whole of creation is thereby filled in the critical Kant by the principle of the unity of reason as the synthetically unifying ground of the essences of all objects in one whole of possible experience. This, however, is a topic that must be developed in later chapters.

Studies in regard to the teleology of Kant's moral theory, odd to say, are not nearly as common as one might first expect them to be. The issue has often been

§. 3. Current Views on the Role of Teleology in Kant's Critical Philosophy — 55

debated, as my remarks above indicate, but there are few detailed studies, particularly in the English language, devoted to a thoroughgoing investigation. The work of Peter König, however, deserves special mention. He is the only commentator, as far as I am aware, to undertake a detailed investigation into the inner teleological structure of the Kantian will. His very original analysis in *Autonomie und Autokratie* is based upon the realization that for Kant the very conception of the autonomy of the will is grounded in his understanding of it as rooted in an *idea* of a pure will. As König shows in detail, Kant's notion of an idea as the maximum of reality of a specific kind is a complex notion with its own internal logic and structure. From his exposition of the nature of a Kantian idea in general, König then undertakes a regimented reconstruction of this same idea of a pure will as the idea of a will containing the maximum of reality in its own kind. In order to do this, he begins with an analysis of willing in general that is aimed at determining the essential characteristics of will in general. He then arrives at the idea of a pure will *via negationis*, or by abstracting from all realities associated with willing that conflict with the idea of a will that would be the maximum of its kind. Having arrived at a construction of this idea, which turns out in its fullest expression to include the characteristic of autonomy, König argues that in order to be applied to experience it must be invested with the power of actually opposing those same realties which were abstracted from in the original construction, or in other words, the autonomous will must also be regarded as autocratic.

Illuminating as it is, and admitting that I will draw heavily on it in Chapter 6, I think it must be recognized that König's work does not explain many basic features and problems of Kant's moral theory, some of which directly touch on König's own project. He says, somewhat surprisingly, almost nothing about Kant's conception of freedom, or about the fact of reason, and he fails despite much effort to find a satisfactory answer as to how it is possible for the will to depart from its own law. These limitations, however, stem directly from what is perhaps most insightful in his work, namely his attempt to independently construct the idea of the Kantian will from the very structure of an idea in general. In this regard it succeeds not only in showing that the teleological notion of the Kantian idea is indispensible for understanding the structure of the Kantian will, but that taking this fact seriously opens up the possibility of a very detailed and illuminating analysis of the internal teleological structure of both. Moreover, it also suggests that there may be an internal conflict between this somewhat hidden dimension of Kant's theory and some of the claims Kant makes on its behalf.

The teleology in Kant's moral philosophy has also been commented upon very insightfully by Otfried Höffe, who has written that Kant is essentially an Aristotelian in his moral theory, and to the extent the two differ, Kant's is the more radical (Höffe 2006, Ch. 2). Kant's moral theory, he argues, is itself designed with specifically moral intentions; it is to clarify and fix the precise nature and limits set on our actions by the supreme character of the moral good. It is not anti-teleological, but is rather opposed to a teleology that is naturalistic. Similarly, as in McDowell's criticisms of MacIntyre, Höffe contends that Aristotle's theory is equally universalistic and based upon an original and unsurpassable conception of the good. In this way he suggests that Kant's moral theory is in some sense a radicalized form of ancient teleological theories of ethics.

Finally, there exist several very important studies suggesting that the *unity of reason* for Kant is fundamentally teleological. As I will discuss most of these in Chapter 8, I will mention here in particular the writings of Pauline Kleingeld, Klaus Konhardt, Jürg Freudiger and Paul Guyer, references to which can be found in the Bibliography.

Conclusion

In considering these three sets of motivations I believe to have shown specifically that there exist powerful *systematic*, *historical* and *scholastic* reasons for undertaking a fresh analysis of the role of teleology in the genesis and final structure of Kant's philosophy. Systematically, the teleological character of reason has been shown – according to Kant's own claims and reports – to be required for the very possibility of the critical system. Historically, we have found that Kant's philosophy occupies a moment where traditional teleology undergoes a fundamental transformation such that it can be preserved and indeed further developed in the writings of the German idealists. Finally, examination of current studies of Kant's thought has revealed a radical disagreement over Kant's relation to the teleological tradition in general, and the place of teleology in his own writings in particular. This is strikingly evident in the contrast between the prevailing anti-teleological view of Kant in popular writings and the radically teleological view of Kant found in some of the secondary literature. By examining Kant's philosophy as existing at the intersection of all three sets of motivations, this work attempts to place in the bright light of day the basic reasons for the specific teleological character of Kant's entire way of thought.

Chapter 2 Teleology: Rudiments of a Theory

If one would define what an end is according to transcendental determinations (without presupposing something empirical, such as is the feeling of pleasure), then an end is the object of a concept insofar as the latter is viewed as the cause of the former (the real ground of its possibility); and the causality of a concept in regard to its object is purposiveness (*forma finalis*). (KU 05:219–220)

Yet finalism is not, like mechanism, a doctrine of fixed ridged outlines. It admits of as many inflections as we like. The mechanistic philosophy is to be taken or left: it must be left if the least grain of dust, by straying from the path foreseen by mechanics, should show the slightest trace of spontaneity. The doctrine of final causes, on the contrary, will never be definitely refuted. If one form of it be put aside, it will take another. (Bergson 1911, p. 40)

Efficient causation is that kind of causation whereby the parts compose the whole; final causation is that kind of causation whereby the whole calls out its parts. Final causation without efficient causation is helpless: mere calling out for parts is what a Hotspur, or any man, may do; but they will not come without efficient causation. Efficient causation without final causation, however, is worse than helpless, by far; it is mere chaos; and chaos is not even so much as chaos, without final causation: it is blank nothing. (Peirce 1998, p. 124)

Introduction

All three of the introductory quotes for this chapter express the view that teleology or final causality is a most basic component of just about any conceptual scheme. Kant defines an end *transcendentally*, and thus with no further restrictions, as a thing for which its concept is "the real ground of its possibility." Bergson asserts that teleology and the mechanical theory of nature do not really stand in opposition to one another, as is usually thought to be the case; the latter is a specific theory requiring corroboration, whereas the former is a general framework that can be adapted to almost any specific evidence. Finally, Peirce describes the relation of efficient and final causality in a way that surely harkens back to Kant's statement regarding the relation of intuition to concept: efficient causality without a final cause is "blank nothing," whereas a final causality without efficient causes is "helpless" – he might as well have written "blind" and "empty."

All three see teleology from a standpoint that was first made possible by a transformation that took place in the early modern period, a transformation through which scholastic teleology was expanded and adapted in recognition of the modern conception of universal natural law. This had a complex effect; it both exploded the seemingly essential link between the notion of final cause and that of natural kind, while at the same time reinvigorating teleological speculation and forcing it to reassume the metaphysical depth and breadth it had lost since the Greeks. The full story of this transformation, first in pre-Kantian writers, Newton and Leibniz included, and then in the pre-critical Kant himself, cannot be recounted here, although later in this chapter we will examine one key moment of influence on this aspect of Kant's thought in our look at Maupertuis' interpretation of the principle of least action.

It is my belief that an incisive and clarifying analysis of the role teleology plays in the development of Kant's philosophy requires an equally perspicuous account of teleological structure. There are at least two reasons for this. The first is that a clear account of teleology in general is often thought to be impossible, since goal-directed activity is widely held to be an inherently vague and perhaps contradictory notion, and explanation by appeal to it has long been notorious for its superficiality. In many cases this is surely a fair assessment of how teleology has been employed, although whether it is a fair assessment of its best employment is another matter. More importantly, if a clear account of teleological concepts cannot in fact be achieved, then one certainly has reason to doubt that these could help in clarifying Kant's philosophical intentions. For this reason, while I will draw on traditional formulations and examples in my analysis, I will not assume from the outset that there already exists a well-articulated and generally recognized understanding of teleology. I will not even treat it as settled fact that teleology has anything to do with many of the concepts that are normally associated with it, e.g. biological systems, striving toward a goal or plasticity of operation.

This leads to the second reason why an examination of teleological concepts is necessary here, namely because Kant himself develops a unique and far more fundamental conception of teleological unity than was possessed by any of his immediate predecessors, one based for instance upon the conviction that universal physical laws are one of the highest expressions of the same kind of teleological unity that is only partially, and therefore imperfectly, displayed in teleological arrangements directed to one or a few ends. Since practically all contemporary discussions of teleology simply assume universal physical laws to be the contradictory opposite of teleological laws, and thus see absolutely no commonality between the kinds of unities they express, the basic thought behind Kant's innovation must be more generally explained. By examining teleological concepts in the broadest sense, I hope to avoid many of the objections that would result from the assumption that Kant's teleology is of a more traditional and less refined form.

After some further introductory remarks, I will deploy my argument in three main sections. The overall plan is to begin from the everyday explanatory patterns in which teleological concepts first arise and then to proceed to the more refined philosophical formulations we find in the writings of figures like Maupertuis and the pre-critical as well as critical Kant. In the first section, I will therefore begin by discussing what I call "teleological inferences." These I take very strictly to be arguments that conclude from some existent pattern in nature to the existence of an underlying cause acting on purpose. Here I will argue that teleological inferences of this kind are in fact ordinary inductive inferences, with the exception that they conclude to a unique kind of cause, namely a cause operating through ideas or forms, whatever this may mean. I will argue, moreover, that the fact that they conclude to a cause acting on purpose rather than to a natural law is based upon our prior entrenched beliefs about the way the world naturally operates. In the course of making this argument, I will also seek to highlight the basic features upon which the strength of a teleological inference usually is thought to depend, as well as the weaknesses that make it inevitable that such explanatory practices undergo constant refinement. In the second section, I will turn to what, again in a very strict sense, I call "teleological explanations," which I take to be arguments by which one deduces the existence of a particular range of effects from the previously assumed teleological nature of their cause. Here I will argue two points: 1) that teleological explanations are of the same *form* as any other scientific explanation that proceeds from natural laws, and 2) that the *modern concept of explanation* and, by implication, the modern concept of natural law are teleological under a broadly realist interpretation. The basis of this last point turns out to be rather elementary; philosophers of the modern period take explanation to mean the identification of the reasons that are also the grounds of matters of fact, and as such are the "real ground of their possibility," to recall Kant's insightful formulation at the head of this chapter. Even those, such a Hume, who deny that we can in principle explain matters of fact, do so because they think it is impossible for our reasons ever to be the real ground of their possibility. Thus the broad assumption about what a real explanation would be, and how its metaphysical possibility would have to be grounded, remains an untouched assumption even of those skeptical that such explanation is possible at all.

This analysis will also suggest that the domain of teleological explanations is not only much broader than that of everyday teleological inferences, but indeed that the former are in principle infinitely extensible. That is to say, it shows that any explanatory account can be given a teleological interpretation, as Bergson's remarks indicate. As we will discover, the domain of teleological inferences is usually limited by the fact that these proceed from our unreflective use of a seemingly obvious distinction between intentional agents and the mechanism of nature. And since mechanism is justifiably held in higher esteem from a scientific vantage point, the existence of teleological causes turns out to be defensible in this case only if we can adduce actual things or events whose structure appears to be impossible, or whose existence seems exceedingly less likely than one would expect, if we assume mechanism alone. Thus at the basis of such inferences lies a supposed opposition between teleology and mechanism or physical law. Teleological explanations, on the other hand, proceed rather from our prior assumption – which in principle can only be justified on some other grounds, usually either moral or metaphysical – that a certain cause, perhaps even every cause, is to be characterized by causality with purpose, i.e. by a form of causality for which the real possibility of its operating in a certain lawlike way presupposes a concept of this same lawfulness. Such explanations take the assumption that the causality in question is teleological as a basis for building an account as to how any specific behavior is grounded in the general purposiveness of this causality. Moreover, since any behavior can be an end, at least in principle, causality on purpose can presumably result in any kind of behavior, and this makes it at the very least possible for teleological explanations to be extended not only to beings and events that appear to follow from mechanism alone (since the goal could just be such mechanical regularity of action), but indeed to the natural laws governing such mechanism themselves. This distinction between teleological inference and teleological explanation will be important for sorting out several issues, but mainly for sorting out the distinction between the essential and inessential features of a teleological account. First, however, a few more preparatory remarks are in order.

Teleology: Not Reducible to a Pattern of Behavior

It is not particularly surprising that teleology and mechanism have been seen as contradictory opposites at various times in the history of philosophy and science or that this is the most prominent view held today. It seems apparent that teleology holds the reality of certain wholes existing in nature to be intrinsically irreducible to the simple composition of their component parts, while the principle of mechanism seems to demand – *as the most essential criterion of its manner of explanation* – that every feature of a natural whole result from nothing but such simple composition of preexisting entities, forces and laws. The most original recent work on teleology has accordingly been focused on showing how the existence of causes acting on purpose can be given empirical backing and formulated in way that is as respectable and clear as any mechanistic explanation. Charles Taylor and Jonathan Bennett, for instance, have both done serious work to ward off what they see as the dangers of behaviorism, or the mechanical reduction of specifically human phenomena, by precisely formulating an empirically relevant and testable formulation of the laws by which teleological processes seem to operate. In particular, according to the view developed by Taylor in *The Explanation of Behavior* (1979), a teleological entity is a system governed by laws that account for the order of actions or events in the system in terms of the order that would result from their being governed by exactly these laws. Such systems, he points out, have the special properties of being law-governed (and hence explanatory), holistic, asymmetrical, and irreducible. Bennett's more recent work on language builds upon and refines Taylors's theory by developing the notion of what he calls an "instrumental property" and by highlighting what he takes to be the key condition by which to judge the validity of a teleological law, namely that it should describe an irreducible form of unity in the system for which it is a law, which he terms the "unity condition."

Despite its obvious fruitfulness, I will try to show that the emphasis on empirical backing that is characteristic of this recent work has also furthered a common confusion between the necessary conditions for *empirically justifying* the inference of causes acting on purpose from given evidence and the necessary conditions of something's acting on purpose *in itself*, a confusion, in other words, of what Hegel refers to as the path taken by subjective knowledge with the nature of the thing itself. In Kantian language, it might be described as something like a confusion of the *ratio cognoscendi* with the *ratio essendi*. The manner of thought by which this confusion takes place is rather trivial, and is not remarkably different from the way one ignorant of Spanish might be led to conclude that a necessary part of a Spaniard's being thirsty is that they speak English, since they cannot know that such a person is thirsty unless that person does speak English.

Another source of confusion that I will challenge is the unquestioned assumption that teleology and mechanism are really competing systems of explanation. Both Taylor's and Bennett's analyses take this for granted and for this reason their essential strategy is to formulate a purely syntactical way of distinguishing teleological from non-teleological laws and to show that certain phenomena can only be adequately captured using laws with this teleological form. However, I will adduce arguments and examples to show that no such syntactical *principium divisionis* is possible, and indeed that on the deepest level teleology and mechanism are not mutually exclusive.

The only way to avoid such confusions, I believe, is to strictly separate the characteristics that are essential to *constituting* something as intrinsically teleological, from the structures and concepts without which it *would not be possible to empirically verify and determine* the specific structure of a given telically structured entity or activity. Due to the great importance of this point, it is necessary to spell out the matter in somewhat more detail. In contemporary literature, as I said, discussions of teleology revolve around attempts to characterize the laws governing a certain special class of activities exhibited by human beings, animals, plants, and some complex machines.[1] Now, in these discussions a number of assumptions go nearly without mention, such as:

1) Teleological activities must exhibit the tendency to obtain a certain state under normal conditions (i.e. striving or directedness to a goal).
2) Teleological activities must exhibit a certain freedom in the ways in which they can achieve this state, such that if the circumstances change then the state will be reached by alternative means (i.e. so-called "plasticity of operation").
3) If an activity is teleological, then it must be impossible to explain the same phenomena by any physical or mechanistic law or any set of physical or mechanistic laws (i.e. the irreducibility requirement).[2]
4) The inclusion of a special sort of teleological agent, e.g. a soul, mind, or organism is a necessary, and in some cases a sufficient condition, for an account to be genuinely teleological.

These features will be found on just about any current list of the supposedly essential components of teleological activity. The necessary consequence of assuming them to be essential is that an activity must be regarded as at most teleological only in appearance if the range of activity it covers can also be covered by mechanistic laws, or if it fails to exhibit tendency towards a goal or plasticity of operation, or if it does not include a uniquely teleological agent.

In a later section I will show that these are not essential features of a teleological form of causality, but are rather conditions for being able to verifying the existence of a teleological cause from the pattern of its effects and for determining its specific goal. For now it is important to make clear that while these and similar assumptions might be suitable for this purpose, they are positively disastrous if imported into any interpretation of teleology in the philosophical tradition. In the metaphysics of Aristotle, for instance, it is undoubtedly the case that the unmoved mover is the quintessentially telic entity, because it is fully being,

---

[1] This can be confirmed by a brief glance at just about any entry on teleology that one finds in current dictionaries and encyclopedias of philosophy written in the English language. A case in point is Larry Wright's article in Kim 2009, p. 594–595.

[2] Bennett writes: "The grass bends towards the window so as to get more sunlight; but since this behavior is controlled by one unitary mechanism, it ought not to be explained teleologically, except perhaps in a *faute de mieux* spirit" (Bennett 1976, p. 79).

and because being is good.³ However, if the above conditions were accurate, then such a claim would be nonsensical, since the unmoved mover's own absolute perfection (i.e. its always being one with its end and necessarily so) precludes its exhibiting a tendency or striving towards a state (it is always *in* this state of perfect activity), or having any freedom to depart from the manner of its activity or of achieving its end by a variety of means (*its* freedom consists in its being necessarily in a state of perfection).⁴ However, it is clear that Aristotle regards the unmoved mover as being quintessentially teleological, not despite, but *precisely because* it is not in a state of striving, and because it cannot be in any other state of activity than the one in which it actually is. This is clearly because whatever can be said to *positively and determinately* make certain other things teleological can also be said to apply to the unmoved mover in a yet higher, and indeed highest, sense. For this reason, it is out of love for such a state of absolute teleological perfection that all other *imperfect and less determinate* things exhibit a tendency towards their ends. The same could be argued in regard to the Platonic forms, the Aristotelian soul, the Aquinian creator-God, and – as I will argue in later chapters – the Kantian conceptions of the pure and holy will. All of these must be judged to be non-teleological if the previous criteria were adopted, and yet from the traditional point of view these are precisely the things that are most perfectly teleological, because they are that from which the teleological structure of all other things receives its foundation and purpose. Their activity is the highest precisely because it has its end within itself necessarily, and thus exhibits the characteristics of complete determinacy and self-sufficiency, which have been regarded as essential marks of the good since Aristotle (Mirus 2012). They exhibit in the highest degree that same unity of structure that is manifest in lesser degrees in all other teleological entities, and for this reason alone they constitute the ground by virtue of which all things tend towards an end. Thus the adoption of (1) and (2) would render incomprehensible the sort of teleology that lies at the very heart of most of the great metaphysical systems.

Again, if teleological laws must be irreducible to mechanistic laws as is stated in (3), then this would render incomprehensible those strands in the philosophical tradition that regard physical laws as the means made use of by some teleological agents. A theory such as the critical Kant's that holds the actions of moral agents to be both mechanistically explicable from a theoretical point of view and free and intentional from a practical one, would also be man-

---

3 This has been argued persuasively in Mirus 2004a, 2004b and 2012.
4 Aristotle 1999, 1072b8–9: "But since there is something that causes motion while being motionless, this does not admit of being otherwise than it is in any respect at all."

ifestly contradictory. Contradictory, also, would be the shared view of Leibniz, Maupertuis, and the pre-critical Kant, that the most basic laws of physics manifest the most certain and universal teleological evidence for God's existence.

The list above thus actually turns the traditional conception of teleology on its head, making what in traditional terms would be the least perfectly teleological forms of activity into the most perfectly teleological, and making what would be most perfectly teleological into something that cannot be called teleological at all. This is, however, the necessary outcome of the assumption that the core of teleology really consists, not in a metaphysical account, but in a theory meant to capture a certain class of empirical regularities that is not covered by physical laws.

Two Examples of this Tendency in Studies of the History of Philosophy: Bennett and Couturat

Jonathan Bennett's remarks on Leibniz serve as a powerful example of the errors that can arise from unreflectively importing contemporary accounts of teleology into the interpretation of the philosophical tradition. In his book *Linguistic Behavior* and an article entitled "Folk-psychological explanations," Bennett presents what he deems to be the only "credible" conception of teleology, which is one based upon a description of how teleological entities *behave:* "teleological concepts are nothing if they are not explanatory." As Bennett writes:

> For genuine teleology or intentionality, I contend, the unity condition must be satisfied. That is, a system x's intentionality is genuine only if: Some class of x's inputs/outputs falls under a single intentional account – involving a single goal-kind G such that x behaved on those occasions because in each of them it thought that what it was doing was the way to get G – and does not fall under any one mechanistic generalization. Where that is satisfied, applying intentional concepts to the system brings a conceptual unity to some set of facts about it – a set that is not unifiable under a mechanistic description. (Bennett 1991, p. 177)

In a nutshell, his findings are that a teleological pattern involves four conditions: 1) "For any action-kind A of which Animal is capable, whenever it is so situated that performing A will lead to G, Animal performs A" (Bennett 2005, p. 144). 2) Animal "registers" or "thinks" that the performance of A will lead to G. 3) "[T]hese laws [i.e., those of the form mentioned in (1)] are fully legitimate only if they cannot be systematically replaced by mechanistic ones" (Bennett 1976, p. 81). 4) Animal has the set of mechanisms by which it gets G, *because* having these mechanisms makes it the sort of thing that gets G (Bennett 2005, p. 147).

The correspondence between these and the four conditions mentioned before is obvious.

What interests us presently is how Bennett uses this theory in his article "Leibniz's Two Realms" to strip the latter's philosophy of all its purportedly teleological features. Bennett finds that according to commentators on Leibniz's work, there are essentially four ostensibly teleological moments in Leibniz's metaphysical system: 1) God's creation of the world, 2) the functions performed by the parts of animals, 3) the simplicity of the general laws of nature, but most particularly the fact that Snell's law of the refraction of light can be proven by the assumption that light travels by the easiest path, 4) the appetitive character of monads. The first clearly fails to be teleological, claims Bennett, because there is no reputable theory in Leibniz about how God performs his acts, and so there is no content to the claim that his act of creation is teleological. The second also fails to produce any genuine teleology in Bennett's view, since functional explanations can be captured by a unitary mechanism, and if "behaviour is controlled by one unitary mechanism, it ought not to be explained teleologically, except perhaps in a *faute de mieux* spirit" (Bennett 1976, p. 79). Not surprisingly, Bennett finds the third most perplexing of all:

> Granted that Leibniz's easiest-path formulation accurately expresses Snell's law, why call it teleological? Most writers in this area take Leibniz's word for it, but he and they are wrong. Of course we *can* talk of God's wanting the light to follow the easiest path; but so we can about any physical law. [...] No one who had worked on teleological concepts per se would count Snell's law as teleological. (Bennett 2005, p. 138)

Leibniz certainly should not be treated as a faultless sage, but it is simply irresponsible to suggest, as Bennett clearly does, that Leibniz never gave teleological concepts much thought, or that Leibniz's teleology consists of "concepts from folk psychology with no warrant except their familiarity," which were "taken unanalyzed from armchair psychology" (Bennett 2005, p. 140). By assuming that teleology is in a trivial way opposed to the concept of physical law, Bennett effectively reduces teleology to just another kind physical explanation and thus places it in direct competition with mechanistic explanations. The same can be said for Louis Couturat's equally dismissive claims that Leibniz's notion of purpose and good can strictly speaking have no moral character, since they "consist uniquely in metaphysical 'perfection' – that is, in the degree of essence or of reality – so that the 'principle of perfection' reduces to 'God realizes the maximum of essence or reality,' which is a simple consequence of the principle of reason" (Couturat 1994, p. 8). From this Couturat concludes, quite revealingly, that, "it suffices to say that the *beauty* and *goodness* in question here are entirely rational and metaphysical, having no teleological or moral significance." If Couturat were correct, then one would have to say the same for Aristotle's first mover, which is characterized not only as eternal, unchanging, and necessary, but also as good and beautiful.

What both Bennett and Couturat fail to realize is that teleology constitutes an independent *conceptual scheme* for understanding the very nature of physical reality. That is to say, teleology is not a particular physical theory, but rather a metaphysical one; it is not tied to a particular description of the way physical things behave among themselves, but rather to an essentially irreducible set of categories and structures through which any particular description is interpreted on the metaphysical level. Teleology does not set any limit upon what does or can happen, except in conjunction with some further assumptions about the specific character of the teleology involved. In essence what it really provides is a fundamental orientating context within which what does or can happen takes on a new dimension of directionality and significance. That a bear is in pursuit of food does not tell us anything specifically about what its behavior will be, but it does provide us a guide by which to judge whether a certain behavior is to count as a success or a failure, and whether the animal is healthy or sick, for instance. Again, knowing that the purpose of the heart is to circulate the blood in no way allows us to predict the behavior of any given heart – for a heart can fail to beat at any time for any number of reasons – but knowing this does provide its beating or not beating with a particular significance it would otherwise lack.

A general failure to realize this indifference of teleology to actual behavior is evident from Couturat's expression of puzzlement as to how we should understand rays of light as moving towards a goal and Bennett's reduction of Leibniz's claim to the empty supposition that God simply wants light to follow the easiest path. As Leibniz himself remarked, "all natural phenomena could be explained mechanically if we understood them well enough, but the principles of mechanics themselves cannot be explained geometrically, since they depend on more sublime principles [i.e. *metaphysical and indeed teleological ones*] which show the wisdom of the Author in the order and perfection of his work" (Leibniz 1969, p. 478). Indeed, Leibniz is so far from accepting the opposition – so self-evident to Bennett and Couturat – between natural law and purpose, between the metaphysical and the teleological, or, again, between the rational and the moral, that he says such a distinction is "plausible," only

> to those minds in whom the imaginative faculty predominates, because they believe that they need to use only mathematical principles, without having any need either for metaphysical principles, which they treat as illusory, or for principles of the good, which they

reduce to human morals; as if perfection and good were only a particular result of our thinking and not to be found in universal nature. (Leibniz 1969, p. 478)

In Leibniz's view, human morality and purposiveness are just instances of the moral and purposive structure of God's entire creation, a structure that can be best elucidated and captured using general ontological concepts such as order, contingency, necessity, causality, unity, and so on. His view that Snell's law is teleological rests on his metaphysical interpretation of the principle by virtue of which it comes to be true of the actual world. In other words, the teleology here lies not in the structure of the behavior specifically exhibited by light according to Snell's law, or in God's wanting it to exhibit such behavior, but rather in the very fact that actual nature is governed, firstly, by any recognizable or intelligible laws whatsoever, and, secondly, by such laws as are maximally rational.

Finally, as to the issue raised by Bennett of whether the appetitive nature of Leibnizian monads is an example of teleology, it should now be clear why his and similar contemporary accounts are quick to dismiss the idea. On such accounts, teleological concepts must be descriptive of the activity of a thing's manner of operation, for otherwise it would not be predictive and thus explanatory. The reference to an end must therefore have an irreducible part in the formulation of this description. But Leibniz says little more about the teleology of the monad than that appetition provides the ground and law by which the perceptions within a monad arise and pass away. On Bennett's view there is therefore nothing to warrant a reference to means, ends, purposes or final causes. Indeed, slumbering monads, which Leibniz holds to be just as telically structured as those that are awake, seemingly do not allow, let alone require, the introduction of particular purposes they might have, or for which they might be used, in order to formulate the law governing their appetition. However, Leibniz understands monads to be teleological, and thus to constitute a realm of grace, for a quite different reason than that they have an external use, namely because the laws governing their principles of appetition are constituted in accordance with God's will, the defining end of which is the creation of the most metaphysically perfect world possible, where perfection is understood in terms of determinacy or unity amid variety. The teleology here can therefore only be understood in ontological terms and from a strictly metaphysical point of view, and it has nothing *directly* to do with conscious intentions or manifest behaviors, which Leibniz always regards as physically explicable though mechanical causes. To reject such teleology, as Bennett and Couturat do, is not therefore to correct Leibniz's errors, but to misunderstand the very essence of his approach, and indeed also to fail to recognize its congruence with the earlier metaphysical conceptions of teleology.

In concluding this line of thought, I submit that on Bennett's and Couturat's understanding of teleology – which I take as still expressing the views of most contemporary discussions of the topic – or indeed on any understanding that reduces teleology to its empirical conditions of verifiability, little if anything traditionally called teleological will pass muster. I have taken time to discuss this issue in some detail, because this manner of interpretation also blocks any approach to the kind of teleology that guides Kant in formulating the foundation of his critical philosophy. I take this as sufficient to warrant the alternative approach to which I now turn.

§. 1. Teleological Inferences: From Pattern to Purpose

Much light can be shed on teleology by recognizing that it is not only a core issue in traditional metaphysics, but that it also concerns some of our most common and trusted explanatory practices. Every day we routinely conclude from certain experiences to the existence of causes acting on purpose. Sometimes such inferences are clearly rationally warranted, while other times we seem to make them simply because doing so is deeply embedded in our habits of thought. Consider the following possibilities:

1) John finds nine rocks in the pattern of an arrow in the middle of the Sahara and concludes that someone arranged these rocks to point towards the nearest village.
2) On his laptop John finds the words "Watch Out" typed and concludes that someone is trying to warn him of impending danger.
3) Having just found out that he needs a life-saving operation, which he cannot afford, John buys a lottery ticket out of desperation and wins a million dollars. From this John concludes that "it was meant to happen."
4) John studies the function of the kidneys and other processes in the body and finds that whenever the one organ or system takes water from or adds water to the blood another organ or system does the opposite so that the percentage of water in the blood remains relatively constant. John concludes that one function of the body's organs is to keep the water in the blood at a certain percentage.

Despite the obvious differences in their apparent validity, all of these inferences are based upon three features commonly taken as signs of a cause acting on purpose. First, they each begin from the recognition that a set of things or events fits into a recognizable pattern, and, secondly, that this pattern is valuable or significant in relation to the context. The rocks in the first case resemble an arrow, and

§. 1. Teleological Inferences: From Pattern to Purpose — 69

knowing one's direction in the desert is certainly a matter worth concern. The marks on the laptop are letters, which together form words the meaning of which might turn out to be very significant. In the third case, the winning of the lottery is just what was required for events to fit the pattern of John's needs or hopes, and there is little that would rank as more important to John or his loved ones. In the fourth case, the various and fluctuating processes carried out by the otherwise independent organs of the body all agree in bringing about a constant state without which the body would die.

Thirdly, while in each of the three cases the pattern in question *could* have obtained accidentally, and indeed a rough estimate of their probability is possible on this assumption, such seems to be extremely unlikely. Under normal conditions rocks do not usually end up in arrow-like patterns by accident, although they can; random keystrokes rarely form meaningful patterns, though they may; people rarely win money when they really need it, although it does happen, and independent but accidentally related processes rarely, if ever, perfectly harmonize and cohere to bring about a constant beneficial state for a period of time, although it has been known to occur. Furthermore, it seems evident that none of the three features just mentioned can be omitted without destroying John's tendency to infer a purposive cause. Trivially, if John did not discover a recognizable pattern of things or events, then he clearly would feel no need to introduce a cause to explain its existence. In this regard, it should be noted how much more significant one would find the pattern of coin flips "H, H, H, H, H, H" than that of "T, H, T, T, H, H," although both have a probability of 1 in 64. This can be explained by the fact the former coheres with a recognizable possible intention, while the latter would only do so if one announced beforehand that this pattern would obtain. Again, if the pattern in question were recognizable, but clearly of no importance or value, then, since John would not see *why* an agent acting on purpose would be motivated to have that particular purpose, he would not feel moved to infer such a cause. Finally, if he knew that the existence of a given pattern were very likely to happen by accident, then John would feel little compulsion to infer a cause acting on purpose to explain the pattern's possibility. In fact, it is quite clear that the degree of John's tendency to believe in the existence of a purposive cause is *directly* proportional to the complexity and importance of a given pattern and *inversely* proportional to the probability of the pattern obtaining accidentally through ambient natural causes.

It is also important to recognize that while the discovery of one such simple pattern may leave John, or anyone else, uncertain of the existence of a purposive cause, the repetition of similar patterns to form an overall more complex pattern must quickly lead to an inexorable feeling of certainty. Indeed, if John were to ignore five such patterns, thinking perhaps it could all be a coincidence, we would ourselves feel compelled to call him foolish. To find one pattern of rocks that looks like an arrow might reasonably be judged a coincidence. But it is nearly unimaginable (though, significantly, not *intrinsically impossible*), and certainly unreasonable, to think the same of a series of three, or four, or maybe ten such patterns all pointing in a similar way, unless one is able to identify a clear mechanical cause. This is of course why organisms, which manifest the continuous replication of one enormously complex pattern of behavior, are usually adduced as the primary evidence for the existence of teleological entities.

Now while we certainly try to curb certain extravagant applications of this inferential tendency, as in the case of the lottery where we at least reflectively understand that our need really had nothing whatever to do with our winning, even in these cases the tendency is, I think, based upon very reasonable grounds, and these are worth discussing further. To see this, we must first note that a pattern is nothing but the specific formal unity of a manifold or the ordering of many objects or events according to a general characteristic rule. Now, as was noted above, a key feature that leads us to the inference of a purposive cause is the manifest *improbability* of encountering just such a pattern by way of the accidental results of various independent mechanisms. This means that in a given context the elements that make up the manifold in a pattern must be regarded as *mutually independent* ("orthogonal," as Nagel says) when considered in themselves or apart from the pattern which they happen to form. For if they were not independent, and we were aware of some natural law or unitary mechanism connecting them necessarily so that this pattern could be seen to be the consequence of one single cause, then we would feel no need to look for another source of their fitting into a pattern.

Assuming that the events or elements belonging to a pattern are mutually independent when considered in themselves or apart from the pattern itself, we can thus easily see why the greater complexity or repeatability of a pattern should lead to greater certainty in the existence of an underlying cause acting on purpose. For if there is no such purposive cause, then the likelihood of a given manifold accidentally forming a certain pattern would be just the mathematical product of all the events occurring independently but still in this one particular way. Thus, as it turns out, the likelihood of even a very simple set of events' fitting into a recognizable pattern grows extraordinarily small with even the slightest increase in complexity. As illustration, consider that the probability of randomly spelling the small word "the" on a standard keyboard, taking into account only the letters and numbers, is about one in fifty-one thousand, while the probability of any three letter combination turning out to be an English word is about one in fifty-six. By comparison, the odds of spelling "watch out" is only one in *one-hundred and thirty trillion*, and the odds of nine randomly struck keys meaning something in English is likely no more than *one in several tens or hundreds of billions*. Thus, given that the elements of a manifold are not intrinsically connected by natural rules that would explain the existence of the pattern, it would seem perfectly rational to infer from the occurrence of even seemingly very simple patterns to a cause acting on purpose, i.e., to a cause which was intended or designed to cause just that pattern and no other.

It is also immediately evident from this that the introduction of an underlying intentional activity is intended to explain the fact that the manifold happens to exhibit a specific form of unity. Indeed, the idea of an intentional or purposive activity is nothing but that of a causality that determines each element in the manifold in accordance with the specific unity we see manifested in the resulting pattern. In the cases of inference mentioned above, it seems that what is going on is that the importance of the pattern convinces us first that it is something real and significant, something for which it would be good for there to exist a single explanation. We then intuitively consider the likelihood of its obtaining accidentally,[5] and, if this is excessively small, conclude that the best explanation is that that pattern was somehow integral to the principle governing the causal process from the beginning.

By means of such reflections as these it becomes clear that the tendency to make such inferences is not only very often justified, but in many cases it is actually irresistible *even when* it appears on reflection to be unjustified. Indeed, there are many patterns the existence of which seems intrinsically possible through accident, but which are so unlikely to happen in the peculiar way that they do that we would feel compelled to reject nearly all reputable sources of knowledge if these told us that something of this sort did in fact happen by accident.[6] If John were to toss a coin three times and it came up heads in all three instances, John would not think twice about it, while if it came up heads twenty times, sixty times, or perhaps six-hundred times, John would surely not believe his own eyes; he would be certain for all practical purposes that someone had slipped him a trick coin designed for this result. Yet mathematically it is perfectly possible; indeed, it is just as likely for this to happen as it is for any other result of the same length. As we shall see, this feeling of compulsion is not a feature unique to teleological inferences, and so must not be accounted

---

5 Surely we do not calculate this probability, and in fact it is very unclear in nearly all real cases as to how this is properly to be done. Very much seems to depend on our background knowledge. However, this realization provides a clue as to how we do in a sense calculate it, namely from our entrenched beliefs about the causal structure of the world.
6 It is here that one is particularly impressed with Hume's conception of the Newtonian laws of association in the mind.

to their being rooted in some deeply anthropocentric tendencies of human thought. Indeed, as we shall presently observe, teleological inferences exhibit exactly the same formal structure as any other type of inductive argument and their force stems from the more general tendency to see any form of regularity in nature as the effect of a single underlying cause or unified set of causes.

§. 1.1. Teleological and Non-Teleological Inferences

It is evident that we make teleological inferences continuously and habitually, and often with little or no awareness of the fact we are doing so. Anytime we encounter a piece of language, a tool, or a hand-gesture, we make a move from a visible pattern of events to an underlying cause acting on purpose, and we do so despite the fact that all these things could in principle occur accidentally.[7] The very brief considerations of the previous section have shown that there are at least some rational grounds for thinking this is a defensible though not infallible practice.

Still, it must be admitted that I have not yet even begun to pinpoint what it is specifically that makes an inference teleological. This is evident as soon as we realize that the process of inference described in the previous section is equivalent in form to *any ordinary inductive inference:* Induction, as it is usually described, is the inference of the existence of a cause or law of causality from the repetition of similar events in similar circumstances. So it goes, the larger the number of repetitions that agree in structure, the stronger the inference. This is because the likelihood of these repetitions accidentally occurring in the absence of an underlying law decreases with each repetition. Now, at any moment all the actual repetitions of the same pattern of events can be thought of as just one larger pattern. For instance, if I release my pencil and it moves downward, then this is a single pattern. If I then pick it up and release it again, and again it moves downward, then this and the previous event together constitute a single larger pattern. Clearly with each additional repetition the pattern just increases by one layer complexity. Furthermore, if the movement could in principle have happened by accident the first time, then it surely could have happened the second, and so on, so that after any number of repetitions it still remains intrinsically possible that the entire pattern occurred by accident, though the likelihood

---

[7] Grice's account of non-natural meaning is illuminating on this point. Notably, George Berkeley defends the claim that all meaning is non-natural, or, perhaps more properly expressed, that even natural meaning is reliant upon a reference to God's intentions. This claim is dependent upon his view that nature is itself a language.

of this also becomes vanishingly small very quickly. Thus, after any given number of repetitions, the probability of exactly that *series* of repetitions occurring in the same way is *exactly equivalent* to the probability of the existence of a *single* pattern containing exactly the same number of independent events or elements of a similar type. The logical structure of teleological inference described in the last section is thus equivalent to the logical structure of ordinary induction.

It is clear from this that the inductive inferences of natural science rest on the same foundation as teleological inferences, namely, on the need to introduce a reason that makes necessary the repeated but otherwise apparently contingent patterns we find in the world around us, whether these be of events or of structures. This further indicates that it is not anything about the *form* of the inferential process or what it takes into account that makes a specific argument teleological. Consequently, if there is some reason why in a given case we make inference to a cause acting on purpose rather than to a physical causal law acting blindly, this must have something to do with the *type* of pattern we are trying to explain. In other words, it must be the case that certain types of patterns cry out for a cause acting on purpose, while others do not.

David Hume pointed to analogy as the basis of teleological inferences. If a pattern of events requires an explanation of its uniformity, then all this requires is the introduction of the existence of a single cause, of whatever type, to account for this uniformity. However, if we are attempting to infer something more about the cause than just that it exists, for instance that it has intentions or operates by means of form, then this can only be based upon our entrenched beliefs about the types of causes that usually give rise to the type of uniformity in question. In other words, if we infer from a pattern to the existence of a cause acting on purpose, then this can only be because the type of pattern in question is one that, according to our entrenched beliefs about the world, only arises from things that act on purpose. Now, since we ourselves are the only beings that we know directly as acting on purpose, we can only justifiably infer the existence of a cause acting on purpose when we encounter a pattern in nature that is analogous to human artifacts. If this Humean account of teleological inference were sufficient, then it would clearly account for the difference between teleological and non-teleological inductive inferences in terms of analogy.

Hume's suggestion is certainly illuminating. But it is also quite obviously insufficient to account for the full array of common teleological inferences. For it is a manifest fact that we are compelled to introduce a cause acting on purpose not only where there is a *positive* analogy with our own purposive actions, but also simply where the type of pattern observed conflicts with our entrenched views about the kinds of laws that are possible in nature. When we encounter a pattern in nature it is vacuous to infer the existence of a cause without inferring also something about its character, as Hume rightly notes. The cause, in other words, must be of such a type as will *explain* the existence of the *particular kind* of pattern in question.[8] Now, as it turns out, we have strongly entrenched beliefs not only about how intentional agents behave, but also about the way inanimate or non-purposive nature operates, the types of patterns which it can generate, and when we meet with a pattern that does not positively cohere with these beliefs we are forced to look to the only other kind of cause we are aware of, namely, one acting on purpose. Consequently, a strong *disanalogy* with our well-entrenched beliefs about the character of physical laws is often perfectly sufficient for the inference of a cause acting on purpose.

Historical examples of this type of inference are plentiful and indeed make up the bulk of the more interesting teleological arguments. For instance, when Thales concluded that the magnet possesses a soul in order to explain its actions, this was presumably not because of any striking analogy between the pattern of the magnet's behavior and Thales' own behavior, but rather because the pattern could not be accounted for in the ways that the operations of lifeless things are usually accounted for. Again, when Newton famously inferred from the fact that the planetary orbits are in approximately same plane to God's having arranged them thusly, he did so not because of a striking analogy with how he, Newton, would have arranged the planets, but because this kind of order could not be explained through the laws of nature as he understood them: "though these bodies [the planets] may, indeed, continue in their orbits by the mere laws of gravity, yet they could by no means have at first derived the regular position of the orbits themselves from those laws."[9] Newton says nothing of any purpose that this arrangement might serve, or of any likeness with human purposive activities. If its author is thought by Newton to be "intelligent and powerful" and the system itself "most beautiful," this is not because the order reveals a recognizable purpose, but because order exists at all where nature by itself would seem to be insufficient to produce it. If one presses the issue by claiming that it is precisely in this orderliness that Thales and Newton find analogy with human purposiveness, the obvious response is that clearly the chief reason the phenomena in question are found significant is not that they are ordered (every arrangement would be a kind of order), but that they exhibit a *kind* of order exceedingly unlikely to arise from blind mechanism or chance.

---

8 Quine 1977, p. 170: "To say that one event caused another is to say that two events are of *kinds* between which there is invariable succession."
9 Newton 1974, p. 42.

The basis of this way of arguing lies, it seems, in the fact that we are acquainted with precisely two distinct sources of order in nature, namely natural laws and intentional agents. Thus, in the case that a pattern does not agree with the types of patterns that can be accounted for by natural laws, the only option is to infer a purposive cause or something analogous to one. This explains why much teleological thinking begins with the conviction that a pattern is the effect of some unknown intentional cause and only afterwards seeks to determine the precise nature or goal of this cause. Notably, Aristotle too argues in precisely this way (Aristotle 1968, 199a). Thus, while a positive analogy with human activities certainly strengthens a teleological argument, it is not generally the *nervus probandi* of one.

§. 1.2. Traditional Teleological Arguments for God's Existence

It is precisely these features of everyday teleological inferences that are exploited in the teleological arguments for the existence of God. They proceed from a pattern of effects in nature to a certain kind of underlying cause. As I have also argued, such inferences fall into two distinct parts insofar as they conclude both to the existence of an underlying cause and to the fact that the nature of this cause must be something capable of operating according to forms or purposes. Here are a few versions of the teleological proof for comparison. I have inserted the letters in square brackets in order to facilitate their anatomization below. The letters are inserted in such a way that the basic idea contained in the premise marked for instance "[a]" in the first proof corresponds roughly to the premise marked by the same letter in a later proof. Note that some of the premises are repeated several times.

1) Writes Aquinas:
   [a] We see that things which lack intelligence, such as natural bodies, act for an end, and [a1] this is evident from their acting always, or nearly always, in the same way, so as to obtain the best result. [b] Hence it is plain that not fortuitously, but designedly, do they achieve their end. [c] Now whatever lacks intelligence cannot move towards an end, unless it be directed by some being endowed with knowledge and intelligence; as the arrow is shot to its mark by the archer. [d] Therefore some intelligent being exists by whom all natural things are directed to their end; and this being we call God. (Aquinas 1997, Q. 2 Art. 3, p. 23)
2) Writes Newton:
   [c] Can it be by accident that [a] all birds, beasts, and men have their right side and left side alike shaped (except in their bowels); and just two eyes,

and no more, on either side of the face; and just two ears on either side [of] the head; and a nose with two holes; and either two forelegs or two wings or two arms on the shoulders, and two legs on the hips, and no more? [b] Whence arises this uniformity in all their outward shape but from the counsel and contrivance of an Author? Whence is it that [a] the eyes of all sorts of living creatures are transparent to the very bottom, and the only transparent member in the body, having on the outside a hard transparent skin and within transparent humors, and a crystalline lens in the middle and a pupil before the lens, all of them so finely shaped and fitted for vision that no artist can mend them? [c] Did blind chance know that there was light and what was its refraction, and fit the eyes of all creatures after the most curious manner to make use of it? [d] These and suchlike considerations always have and ever will prevail with mankind to believe that there is a Being who made all things and has all things in his power, and who is therefore to be feared. (Newton 1974, p. 65–66)

3) Writes Crusius:

[a] In the world we meet with an orderly and regular connection and flow of things, which [d] apparently leads us to the conclusion that they are formed according to ideas, and that they have a cause which possesses understanding. It is beyond question that we are not the directing cause of this connection. [c] Matter, as it is not capable of [having] ideas, also cannot have an orderly effect according to ideas without being directed by a cause which possesses understanding. [f] Consequently, this order and regularity shows either that the world was formed through a cause possessing understanding that is separate from it, or one must admit that this order and regularity is only apparent, and is something which arose from chance. [g] Now the latter is an infinitely great improbability: Hence, to nevertheless admit this would be an infinitely great foolishness. Consequently, the former is to be held as demonstratively certain, that, namely, the order and regularity in the world is to be ascribed to a cause possessing understanding and separate from the world, and therefore that there is a God. (Crusius 1964, p. 387–388)

It is important to note from the start that none of these proofs rests on the obviously anthropocentric notion that all things serve human ends or ends that human beings might project into nature. To claim otherwise on the strength of Aquinas' talk of the "best result" or Newton's reference to usefulness is to fail to realize that the metaphysical conceptions of perfection, beauty, and goodness employed in these passages are entirely defined in terms of orderliness and unity, and thus are not characteristics of the form of the whole itself except in the sense that the form is itself the very principle of orderliness and unity.

Thus no form is good except in the sense that, as a ground of order and unity, it is the *measure* or source these features in other things, while all other things are good to the extent that they exhibit the order prescribed by such form itself. Consequently, on this view not even human goods are good because we desire them (some things we desire are not good, after all), but because they possess or result in an internally orderly life. To say, therefore, that the order in nature is best or that it exhibits usefulness is not to find that it fits with a preconceived notion of what is good, defined perhaps by what we human beings presume to be good for us, but only to recognize that it exhibits order and regularity. And whether this is useful to us depends upon whether the regularity of nature provides a ground or means for the regularity in the human being. The key point is that the existence of a purposive cause here is not inferred from actual observed purposes, but rather from the form of purposiveness in general, i.e. the law-like unity of an otherwise contingent natural manifold.

Let us look further at the proofs above. Aquinas' classic formulation begins with [a], an empirical observation that all things are directed to ends. Notably, for this he provides a clarifying statement [a1], which shows that by directedness to ends he chiefly means nothing more exotic than the regularity and repeatability of certain natural motions. Thus the teleological proof begins, as Josef Simon has noted, with an attempt to explain certain empirical regularities (Simon 1983). Premise [b] contains the hidden assumption that regularity is not the effect of chance, and thus asserts that such regularity must be the effect of design. However, as is clear from the following premise, "design" here does not immediately mean something designed, but rather some sort of formal cause of order or arrangement. Premise [c] consequently asserts that unintelligent things cannot be used to account for such order, and thus that since we find unintelligent things in orderly patterns in nature, there must be some *other* being that is responsible for instituting their order. The conclusion, [d], then simply labels this external cause of order with the name "God."

Clearly, there are many gaps in this proof. Nowhere is it proven, for instance, that chance cannot give rise to order or that there must only be a single cause of order in nature. Nevertheless, the basic strategy of the proof is clear enough. If we turn to Newton's version of the teleological argument, we find the same basic strategy with only a slight nuance. Whereas Aquinas' points to the repeatability of natural processes, Newton draws attention specifically to the symmetry in living beings and to the order in the structure of the eye. The evidence here consists not in the eye's being produced in an orderly way, but rather in its internal structure itself; the lens and transparent medium are formed and arranged in a way that is entirely inexplicable if one does not assume the existence of light. But obviously the lens and the medium, and the body in which they grow only become aware of light, are able to detect light, after and by means of these same organs. The structure, as it were, anticipates the existence of light in the way that Newton thinks only an intelligent being could anticipate such a thing. Leaving this slight difference aside, however, it is clear that Newton's proof is essentially the same as that given by Aquinas.

The third proof, which was constructed by one of Kant's important German predecessors, Christian August Crusius, agrees with the proofs of Aquinas and Newton in regard to premises [a] and [c], as well as in the form of the conclusion [d]. Indeed, Crusius cites as examples of natural phenomena needing explanation both the orderly changes in nature and the structure of the human eye. But in Crusius' version premise [b] is replaced by an argument composed of [f] and [g]. Whereas premise [b] asserts that order cannot be the effect of chance, [f] admits that order could arise either from design or from chance. Premise [g] is then introduced to prove that nevertheless, because the probability of such infinitely extensive order as we find in nature obtaining by chance is infinitely small, it is an "infinitely great foolishness" to conclude otherwise than that it is the effect of design. But why should we accept what is least foolish, or in other words, what is most rational? In Crusius' philosophy this principle plays a fundamental role, and is based ultimately on the human being's *moral* duty to trust in the veracity of reason. Thus his version of the teleological argument both accounts for the fact that the empirical evidence for the existence of an intelligent God is never absolutely complete, and provides us with a morally grounded rationale for nevertheless accepting the proof as if it were theoretically sufficient. Thus the teleological proof provides sufficient ground to postulate the existence of God, i.e. to assume it as completely certain even though it cannot be proven with strict necessity.

In line with my previous arguments, all three proofs have the general structure of beginning with a given pattern in nature that requires explanation because it cannot be accounted for by the regular operations of nature alone, and concluding to a cause acting by virtue of ideas or forms as the only kind of cause that is sufficient to produce such an effect. In all three cases, the given pattern is manifestly nothing else than the orderliness of nature that goes beyond what it is reasonable to suppose as possible through chance, and in all three cases the cause concluded to is one that is capable of producing order in a non-accidental way, namely, creative intelligence. Such teleological arguments for God's existence thus appear to draw upon the regular practice of teleological inference. Moreover, they do so in a way that is not susceptible to Hume's objection that the strength of an argument by analogy is directly proportional to the likeness of the initial terms and thus decreases as their likeness also decreases. This is because the argument is not built upon a direct analogy between divine and human causality, as Hume thought, but upon a disanalogy between the production of certain kinds of order and what nature is capable of producing on its own. Of course, these arguments are susceptible to the objection that they have underestimated the kind of order that nature can bring about on its own, although this would have to be shown in each specific case.

Importantly, Kant criticizes this version of the teleological proof throughout his career for quite different reasons. First, he often expresses the view that it is insufficient to prove the existence of a determinate enough concept of such a being to be termed "God." For even if the proof is taken to prove the existence of a creating cause, it proves nothing more than the existence of a finite creator, because the principle of the world need only be as rich in determinations and power as is required to explain the order that we empirically observe. Perhaps its greatest defect in Kant's eyes, however, is that it sees teleological unity only in the contingent order of nature. As he argues already in 1755, the very setup of the proof requires us to assume a distinction between natural and teleological unity, as if the material of nature and the necessary laws of mechanism could exist without the existence of God. This puts the progress of science in direct conflict with the purposes of religion, since the more science is able to explain the apparently contingent order through its necessary laws, the more it ascribes to the operations of nature and the less to God. For this reason, the proof only allows us to reach the concept of an architect of nature, not a genuine creator, admitting only a being that arranges the materials of nature to the extent that science is unable to explain this. And by the same token, it presupposes an original matter existing independently of God's plan. Kant opposed this view from early on by arguing that the genuine concept of a God must be that of an absolutely self-sufficient and original being, an *ens entium*, a being from which absolutely everything else derives without limitaiton. Thus it was one of his central pre-critical projects to reach a new understanding of the character of physical law so that it could be seen not only as consistent with, but indeed as a prime instance of, a broadened conception of teleological causality and unity.

However, Kant also admits that such proofs are only really defective if they are taken to be proofs in the strictest of senses. If, alternatively, we are able to establish the existence of God according to the strictest concept (perhaps on moral grounds), and thus as an original (i.e. independent) being which contains absolutely all reality and from which the reality of all else is borrowed, then such arguments can in fact play the very useful and edifying role of directing us to the empirical traces of God's existence. As Kant is reported to have said in his lectures on philosophical theology from the 1780s:

> Now since the highest being is also the original being from which the essence of all things is derived, it follows that order, beauty, harmony, and unity which are met with in things are not always contingent, but inhere necessarily in their essence. (V-Phil-Th/Pölitz 28:1034)

This is the same as the view underlying his criticism of the traditional teleological proofs and his own original theory of teleological unity as this is expressed in works like *NTH*, *PND*, *BDG* and eventually the *KrV*.

§. 1.3. Concluding Reflections

Having examined the basic elements of teleological inferences, the question arises as to what sort of strict proof they provide. The answer is evidently *none whatsoever*. The tendency to make a teleological inference may be inexorably compelling. Its denial may even require that we compromise our most deeply held beliefs about the nature of the world. But it still can provide no *strict proof* of a teleological cause, since teleological arguments are based upon the improbability of a given occurrence, which implies that no matter how small, there will still be at least *some* probability of an event's happening accidentally. What is more, we have seen that in order to shore up the weakness of a teleological inference, we need to introduce additional premises or rely on entrenched beliefs about what is possible through mere nature, and what is only possible through teleological agents. This of course rests on the dual assumptions that teleological agents exist, and that they operate in a way recognizably distinct from natural mechanisms or things obeying mere physical laws. I think it must be admitted that this shows that any attempt to prove the existence of such teleological agents will not only be lacking in full evidence, but that it will be viciously circular if evaluated by the canons of strict logical proof. But since the very same criticisms can be leveled at ordinary induction, the situation is not all that dire after all. Fortunately, however, we also need not leave the matter as settled at this point. For it remains possible to argue that these additional premises can themselves be justified on the strength of moral considerations, as we saw in Crusius's proof, or rather on *rational* or *metaphysical* considerations, instead of on merely empirical ones. The teleological argument could in this case be interpreted as an empirical *application* of a form of argument that is justified independently of all empirical evidence. Teleology would then turn out to flow from a previously justified *moral* or *ontological framework*, and the teleological inference could then be understood not as trying to justify teleology as a general conceptual scheme, but rather as the specific application of this scheme for the delimitation of particular teleological structures found in nature.

We have also seen that starting from the same foundations an inductive inference can bring us to one of two conclusions, namely, that the pattern is the effect of natural law, or that it is the effect of a cause acting with purpose. The reason for taking one path rather than the other, it became clear, is not based upon logical considerations, but rather turns on whichever explanation would do less violence to our previously entrenched beliefs about the context in which the explanation takes place. This is where the true weakness of teleological inferences take their foothold; to the extent that nature is better explained by regular physical laws, the less justification we have for inferring teleological causes. And if indeed, as is surely the case, all apparently teleological agents and their operations can be explained by physical laws, then the natural consequence is the elimination of teleology based upon inference. Approaches such as those of Taylor and Bennett are thus doomed from the start. However, if there is some other way of justifying the interpretation of nature teleologically, then there remains even the possibility that natural laws themselves will be open to a teleological interpretation. This is the path taken by some in the modern tradition of philosophy.

§. 2. Teleological Explanations: From Purpose to Pattern

> If we recognize the existence of general truths at all, we must also admit the existence of such primitive laws, since from mere individual facts nothing follows, unless it be on the strength of a law. Induction itself depends on the general proposition that the inductive method can establish the truth of a law, or at least some probability for it. If we deny this, induction becomes nothing more than a psychological phenomenon, a procedure which induces men to believe in the truth of a proposition, without affording the slightest justification for so believing. (Frege 1980, p. 4n)

The question has been raised in recent literature as to whether teleological thinking can be avoided by eliminating the locutions "*function, purpose, goal* and *in order to*" from our explanatory practices (Beckner 2006). I will argue that it is doubtful whether the usual language of explanation – which we derive in part from the understanding of explanation generated in the early modern period – can stand at all without at least an implicit assumption of teleology, and I will suggest that we must deny the ability of language to express explanations, at least in the sense of explanation used in modern philosophy, to the very extent that we deny the validity of this teleological foundation. Indeed, I think it can be argued that in this modern sense *all* explanations expressed in common language exhibit teleological features if for no other reason than that such a use of language rests on the assumption that the things being explained fall into distinct and enduring classes, and that the *reason* for their acting the way they do is ultimately *because* of their belonging to such classes. In a word: If we seek to explain particular events or things, we do this by classifying the particulars involved under certain types or kinds. Now we make use of such types because things falling under a type tend to behave in certain typical ways (today such typical tendencies are often called "dispositions"). From this we explain what happens by reference to the fact that, all else being equal, this is precisely how these things typically (i.e. naturally) act in a situation like the one under consideration. Thus the reason we give for things acting as they do is nothing other than the order that they actually exhibit but more broadly conceived as a general tendency to act in just such a way. Stated differently, we explain the actual course of events by means of a more generalized formulation of the very form of order that these events exhibit except as put in the guise of a reason.

Let me make this argument more concrete. I could ask: Why does this thing here in front of me fall as I now let go of it? The answer could be *Because it is a pencil*. In everyday conversation, this is a perfectly fine answer, since we immediately understand that a pencil is composed of matter, and all else being equal, matter behaves in this way. Perhaps after reflection one will prefer the answer *It falls because it has weight*, or *It falls because objects with mass attract one another according to a certain law, and this thing before you as well as the thing at your feet have mass, and there is nothing preventing it like a buoyant force from the surrounding air, etc.* These, however, are simply more complex versions of precisely the same *form* of explanation. In all three explanations a singular event is understood by subsuming it under concepts and categories that have already been accepted as designating things that typically behave in certain determinate and typical ways, all else being equal. Moreover, no matter how far we analyze a singular event that we experience, it seems that we will ultimately end up explaining it – unless we are willing to give up the practice of explanation – by subsuming the objects involved under just such class concepts and laws.

The path taken by this type of explanation, generally referred to as a deductive-nomological explanation ("D-N explanation" for short), can be captured very simply in the following six steps:
1) Why does this singular event e occur?
2) The world leading up to e contained the elements a, b, c, etc.
3) These things are respectively of types A, B, C, etc.
4) Now things of type A, B, C, etc., relate according to laws X, Y, Z, etc., and the necessary outcome of this relation is an event of type E.
5) Hence, we conclude singular event e of type E occurred because its elements a, b, c, etc. were of types A, B, C, etc. that relate to one another according to the laws X, Y, Z, etc., which result in an event of type E.

§. 2. Teleological Explanations: From Purpose to Pattern — 83

6) Hence this singular event *e* occurred because in these circumstances (i.e., elements *a, b, c,* etc.) an event of type *E* naturally occurs under the assumed laws, or just *is* what happens in this case.

Here lower case letters refer to the particular events or elements that make up the initial conditions, while the upper case letters refer to the forms or types of these same elements. For instance, say that *a* is my pen, then *A* refers to my pen *insofar as it is a material type of thing*. This nuance is necessary in order to capture the fact that any particular must first be classified under a certain type before it can be brought under a law, since laws speak only of the relations of types, not of relations of particulars. Thus if I wish to bring my pencil under the law of gravitation, it must be possible to classify this pencil as being a certain quantity of matter, which is a general concept of which the pencil is an instance.

Now if this mode of explanation is supposed to constitute true understanding, then presumably it cannot be the case that despite the entire argument *e* nevertheless occurred entirely accidentally or for some other reason. Rather it *had* to occur, because an event of type *E* had to occur given the circumstances and the laws in place. If it did not occur then we would either have to doubt that we have adequately recognized, i.e. distinguished and classified, the elements of the experience, or else we would have to question the completeness or truth of the relevant laws. There is an important circle to be noted here: A set of concepts and laws that results in an outcome of type *E* explains a system, if and only if the elements of the system and its outcome fall under the types involved in the explanation. Yet the things in question are thought to be of such types only if there proves to be no more adequate explanation that is not of the same basic kind.

It is not important here that D-N explanations have proven insufficient to capture the full character of scientific explanation, indeed to provide either necessary or sufficient conditions for it. What is important is that it captures quite well the way in which modern philosophers understood the explanatory power of fundamental science. Now, teleology enters this picture as the one principal realist way of understanding the objective validity of this form of explanation. For if the given description is straightforwardly true, i.e., if this explanation truly elucidates why event *E* occurred, then it also seems to be true that certain individual things actually possess certain abiding general essences or formal dispositions that relate necessarily according to determinate laws governing the classes to which they belong. To say that they possess such essences need mean nothing more exotic than that they behave as they do *entirely because* they belong to such classes, i.e. they are precisely these types of things or are nothing else than particular instances of these general types. It is thereby assumed that singular experiences can be completely and irreducibly explained in terms of relations among concepts if only we can come to understand the concepts of the things in question and all of the relevant circumstances.

That not only the modern but also the layman's construal of the scientific conception of law implies the existence of dispositions or essences has been recognized for some time.[10] The very concept of a law contains within it the marks of universality and necessity, and for this reason a law always says more than can ever be encountered in any actual experience. The truth of the law of gravitation, for instance, explains not only why my pencil falls when it actually falls, it also implies the *truth* of counterfactual conditionals like *If I had released the pencil a minute ago, it would have fallen*. Such conditionals describe situations that did not, and so cannot ever become a reality, and yet it is commonly agreed that it would be extremely counterintuitive to say they are untrue or meaningless. Indeed, the *normative force* involved in the expression of a law seems to be inextricably linked with the implication of the truth of counterfactual conditionals. This is because the truth of a law *qua* law is understood as independent of actual events, and is thought of as providing the reason for their occurrence. Furthermore, assuming this independence and causal priority, it follows that if particular circumstances were different, then the law would still retain its force although it would have no instance falling under it. In a word, the existence of laws implies the truth of counterfactual conditionals, and counterfactual conditionals in turn lead us, under a realist interpretation of their significance, to the idea that there is an existent condition within things that provides the basis of the real possibility of both the actual states-of-affairs and the counterfactual states-of-affairs. Again put somewhat differently, if the released pencil now falls, then this is understood as necessary because it is the logical consequence of a statement that would remain true, even if counterfactually, the pencil were not at this moment released, namely, *If the pencil is released it will fall*. This real and independent foundation of the necessity of the pen's operations is nothing other than what is referred to as the "disposition" belonging the pencil insofar as it is a material kind of thing. Or, in other words, a disposition is just the law of a given thing's typical activity thought of as belonging to its internal constitution, or to it insofar as it *is* a thing of a certain kind.

The link between these considerations and modal predicates like possibility and necessity is worth dwelling upon further. When we understand laws in this manner we regard actual events explained by a rule as occurring *necessarily*, and

---

[10] The literature on this topic is vast and extremely complex, but the details are not relevant to my basic point. I mention here only Goodman 1983, Chisholm 1946, and Quine 1977.

thereby think the rule as being a law, precisely because we understand events as a consequence of a rule that has a truth and causal priority that extends beyond any actual event or sum of actual events. In other words, any particular event that is explained by reference to a law of nature is thereby understood as an expression of a formal principle that restricts what *can and what cannot* actually occur. If something does not happen, then it may or may not be a real possibility, depending on the existent dispositions of things. However, if something does occur, and it is a proper expression of the extant dispositions in a given set of circumstances, then it is understood as having occurred *necessarily*, because it is an actual instance of a rule governing all possible occurrences. This must not be mistaken to mean that this particular event had to occur absolutely speaking, but only that given the dispositions of things and the circumstances that obtained, nothing else was really possible. Notably, this also implies that if we are presented empirically with a pattern of events which appear to be mutually independent, then in order to regard this pattern as a real one, i.e. one not occurring by accident but rather necessarily, we must think of it as the consequence of some sort of law the reality and truth of which provides the prior ground or reason for the event itself.

But how can a real event in the world be completely explained in terms of non-physical things like concepts and their relations? Does this mean that the latter are in some sense the primary *causes* of events? Before considering possible answers to these questions, we must deal with one obvious but misguided way of attempting to sidestep the issue of teleology from the start. This is to argue that D-N explanations, while they may contain a common mode of understanding, do not reflect our thinking in its best and most consistent moments, because our reliance on them is based on our ignorance of the mechanism underlying the natural laws we make use of in the proof. For example, we might make use of a law such as *Chickens lay eggs* or *Everything else being equal, the pressure of a gas multiplied by the volume it occupies is always a constant*. However, one might say that even if these laws never fail to predict what happens in any given case, it is nevertheless not true to say that these laws *properly explain* such occurrences. The true explanation, it might be argued, lies in the innumerable tiny mechanisms that are commonly found in what we call chickens, and always in gasses, that actually (efficiently) cause them to behave in this way. Furthermore, it might be argued that once the mechanism is recognized, then we will no longer feel a need to make use of class concepts in our explanations, and we will no longer feel a need to introduce mysterious essences like *pullitas* to explain the typical behavior of chickens; we can account this simply to an approximate likeness of constitutive mechanisms. We will then recognize that the introduction of kinds is practically useful, but does not agree with the truth of things themselves. One arguing in this way would likely urge further that ideally we should understand the operations of any given chicken not as operations of the type of thing we call a chicken, but rather as the necessary outcomes of the structures constituting each given individual machine in its own particular circumstances.

It is immediately clear why such a view eliminates traditional physical teleology, which explained the operations of natural substances by reference to specific natures. For according to traditional teleology, classes of natural objects, unless malformed or interrupted by something external, always operate in certain typical ways, and when they do not operate in the natural way this is violent and contrary to their nature, and inevitably the result of outside interference. However, according to the mechanist's view, we tend to believe this only because we do not know precisely enough the mechanical constitution of these objects. All we know is that, on the whole or for the most part, the things we call chickens tend to lay eggs. But this, it would seem, really tells us nothing about what a given chicken will do, and it provides no basis for explanation even if a certain chicken does lay an egg; for what any specific chicken does is a necessary and natural outcome of its particular constitution alone and not of the fact that it possesses something like *pullitas*.

However, such an understanding of nature totally banishes final causes, i.e. most basic and causal forms, from the world only if one thinks that for any given law there must *always* be an underlying mechanism. But even if we are able to multiply the underlying mechanisms indefinitely, we still cannot indefinitely multiply the *laws* according to which these mechanisms operate. And if we cannot do this, then we must admit some first fundamental and irreducible laws, which would then explain the operations of the consequent mechanisms. D-N explanations, along with certain basic classes with specific dispositions, would then once again occupy the ground floor of scientific explanation. Of course, at this point we might no longer make use of *pullitas* in our explanations, or any of the other telic forms previously employed, but we would still have eventually to stop the resolution into mechanisms at a class of most basic things that possess some form of abiding essence to the very extent that their behavior is understood as intrinsically based upon a certain law of activity. We will thus still be left with some most basic but analogous entities in which matter and form are regarded as identical, where it will be true to say that these things behave in a certain way because that is simply the kind of thing that they are.

It is important to note that this way of putting the argument, namely in respect to the most basic and universal laws of nature, avoids the obvious riposte that a mistake is being made here of confusing the cause, which must be an event, with the laws governing the causality of the cause, as would be the case if one were to say, for instance, that the laws of optics are causing me to see the page upon which I am writing. This is because the *most basic and universal laws* are obeyed by everything to which they apply at every moment, and so if the event I am trying to explain by them is simply that something is operating in a way that is a consequence of the law, then there can arise no question as to the event that caused it to do so. The law of gravity provides the reason for the pen's falling, but nothing, so far as we know, "causes" the pen to obey this law. As a result, when described on this level an event itself is nothing else than the manifestation of a law in particular circumstances. Furthermore, it is important to note that if there are such basic and universal laws, and these laws really do give the reasons for the operations of things, then all things that exist or *can* exist must obey them. At this point there is an identity between being a type of thing and acting in a certain typical way, which in metaphysical terms implies a normative conception of being; here being and structure, matter and form, are identical, and it is precisely this fact that makes explanation by reference to this level of things entirely complete in the ideal case. This seems to be what Francis Bacon was indicating when he suggested we call "forms" the laws of motion and the *actus purus* in nature (Bacon 2000, Aphorism 51). To be a piece of matter *is nothing else than* to obey the universal law of gravitation, and to be an electron *is nothing else than* to obey the laws governing subatomic electrical phenomena. When matter and form are identical, there can be no question as to why such a thing follows such a law.

For these reasons, unless we wish to deny that there is any sense in speaking of genuine explanation, or explanation as the moderns understood it, it seems that we must admit some form of teleology. This can either be a real teleology, in the sense of a view that things happen because of certain internal natures, or it can simply be a subjective teleology, such as would argue, for instance, that the human mind is constituted in a way so that it must regard the world as being constituted by such natures. In either case, we will regard the order exhibited in nature as the consequence of the same order, although more generally formulated, as it grounds nature as a whole. And this is just the form of purposiveness, as Kant describes it, namely as the "causality of a concept in regard to its object." This seems to happen also on a higher level of organization in things like living organisms and intentional activities, which we often feel compelled to admit as irreducible unities. But the case of universal laws provides the clearest and simplest instance, because it shows that even mechanistic reduction must rest content with explanation by reference to some most primitive causal unities. The result of this argument is that some form of teleology will always remain possible as a means for explaining the existence of the most basic laws of nature, even if we were willing to accept the reduction of all living and organized beings to machines. Irreducible laws governing a small sphere of nature would be able to form the basis of a new natural kind and a related teleology, while an irreducible and unrestricted law would be able to form the basis of a universal kind such as matter and a related universal teleology.

§. 2.1. Maupertuis and the Universal Teleology of Nature

To this point I have been arguing in the hypothetical that *if* there are fundamental laws in the modern sense and *if* we are committed to what might be called a naïve or realist view of explanation, then some form of teleology seems to be brought along with it. Perhaps this is why the modern conception of explanation is rejected by anyone who believes teleology must go, and has considered their connection in depth, such as Quine. Indeed, the analysis presented here agrees in particular with Quine's assessment of the close connection between the notions of disposition, natural kind and the modern conception of natural laws (Quine 1977). This connection is illustrated nicely by the examples of Descartes and Leibniz, both of whom claim (mistakenly) to be in possession of such fundamental laws of nature, and as a result of precisely the line of thinking I have sketched, do not eliminate but rather transform teleological thinking.[11] However, because of his proximity and influence on Kant, the work of Pierre Louis Maupertuis on the law of least action provides the most appropriate case in point.[12]

In his *Essay on Cosmology*, which appeared in a German translation immediately after its French publication in 1751, Maupertuis examines the whole history of teleological inferences for the existence of God in much the same way as I have in the previous sections of this chapter. His conclusion is that all such arguments suffer from a fundamental and irremediable weakness, namely they fall short of mathematical certainty and draw their persuasive force merely from improbabilities and the limits of our current scientific knowledge. He singles out Newton's argument in the *Optics* for special scrutiny, noting that the probability

---

[11] Descartes admitted a restricted teleology – namely God's aim to preserve the mind-body composite – in order to explain the arrangement instituted between the state of the body and the perceptions of the soul, and he admitted a universal teleology when he sought to deduce basic laws of nature from the perfection of God in his *Principles of Philosophy*. Leibniz, similarly, admitted a limited and explicit teleology to explain the law that light always travels the easiest path, and admitted an unlimited one to explain the interconnection and order among all finite beings.

[12] The translations in this chapter are from the original French, but I have in all cases compared them with the German translation of 1751, which Kant would have read.

that all the planets will be found in approximately the same plane is about 1 in 1,419,856, thus improbable but not impossible (Maupertuis 1751, p. 10–17; see also Newton 1974, p. 138). Moreover, the impossibility of explaining why the planets move in the same direction around the sun is relative to Newton's own physical theory and so might turn out to be explicable from the standpoint of a more comprehensive physics (Maupertuis 1751, p. 18). As for Newton's argument from the construction of animals, which Maupertuis notes is derived from the ancients, it is easily undermined by noting that only animals well-adapted to their environment can survive, and so those now existing may well be a product of chance and "are but the smallest part of what blind destiny has produced" (Maupertuis 1751, p. 26).

More generally speaking, Maupertuis observes that traditional arguments from design always seem to provide fodder for the skeptic (Maupertuis 1751, p. 34–40). If the appearance of order and design is allowed to be evidence for a designer, then those obvious appearances of imperfection found in physical and moral evils must be allowed as evidence against a designer. To avoid this result by limiting God's power by the necessary essences of things in the manner of Leibniz, or limiting his wisdom in the manner of Malebranche, is not a satisfying solution according to Maupertuis (Maupertuis 1751, p. 44–45). Nor does Maupertuis find appealing the conclusion of Alexander Pope, namely that there really is no evil to be found in nature. For in order to believe this, Maupertuis remarks, we must already assume the existence of God, since such a conviction surely does not arise from the simple observation of the world (Maupertuis 1751, p. 47).

In place of such arguments, Maupertuis offers a series of reflections on the laws of nature which he thinks will show that nature considered simply as such is teleically structured on the most basic and most universal level. We should seek God, explains Maupertuis, "in the phenomena which are universal and suffer no exception, and whose simplicity is entirely exposed to our view" (Maupertuis 1751, p. 55). "The supreme being," he writes,

> is everywhere; but it is not everywhere equally visible. We see it better in more simple objects: we search for it in the very first laws that have been imposed upon nature; in the universal rules through which motion is conserved, and distributed, or destroyed; and not in the phenomena that are but the exceedingly complex consequences of these laws. (Maupertuis 1751, p. 61–62)

Maupertuis thus proposes that if we are going to search for proof of God's existence by means of physical science, then we should begin neither with the design of individual objects in nature, nor even with the physical laws that have been reached by induction. The former are too complex for our current understanding and too fine for our scientific instruments, while the latter, although they may be mathematical and precise, are nevertheless never completely certain. Maupertuis proposes instead that we should start from God himself, and attempt to deduce mathematical laws directly from his attributes, in particular from his omnipotence and omniscience (Maupertuis 1751, p. 63–64). If it is then found that these are in fact the laws of nature, then he believes this not only proves the existence of God, but the mathematical form of this proof also promises to offer us the clearest possible insight into the divine perfection at the heart of nature itself.

The core of the *Essay* thus contains an attempt to show how various known laws of nature can be deduced and clarified by reference to a single principle, which itself can be seen as following from the wisdom and simplicity of the creator. Maupertuis first attends to the laws of equilibrium and impact, observing in this regard that the laws of equilibrium, of elastic collisions, and of inelastic collisions have previously been derived from three separate principles, no one of which is able to support the other two. This, as Maupertuis notes, has led to innumerable disputes regarding the first principles of physics, and indeed to disputes regarding the existence of certain phenomena themselves. Worse still, the issue here is not one that can be solved by the empirical-inductive method, since it does not concern the direct explanation of the phenomena (the three laws suffice for this), but rather the systematic unity of the laws governing the phenomena. The only option, Maupertuis proposes, is to search for a single highest mathematical principle from which all three can be formally derived and from which their precise relation can be understood. And if we hypothesize that a single and supremely wise being exists and is the author of these laws, then we should also expect there to be a single principle from which all three can be derived as special cases, or as individual means to a single supreme end.

What then is this highest law? It is what Maupertuis calls the "principle of least action," which states that in all changes in nature the smallest possible quantity of the product of the principal factors is expended. In the case of bodies, he explains that this principle states that in all changes in nature the product of their masses, speeds, and distances travelled is always a minimum. From this single law he proceeds to demonstrate how the laws governing all three sets of phenomena can easily be deduced. In final part of the *Essay*, Maupertuis then turns to the phenomena of light, and shows similarly that from the same principle it is also possible to deduce the principal laws – previously thought to be unrelated – governing direct propagation, reflection, and refraction. In this case, the principle of least action means minimizing the product of time and distance.

While explaining this last discovery, Maupertuis provides us with an interesting insight into his thought process:

§. 2. Teleological Explanations: From Purpose to Pattern — 91

> After meditating deeply on this matter [i.e. refraction], I thought that light, when it passes from one medium to another, soon abandoned the shortest path, which is the path of the straight line, and indeed also could not take the path of least time. In fact, why should it prefer time over space? Now, light cannot at one and the same time go through the shortest path and do so in the shortest time. But why should it go one path rather than another? It takes neither of the two. It takes the route that offers a real advantage: the path it takes is the one for which the quantity of action is the least. (Maupertuis 1751, p. 228–229)

The formulation here is clearly teleological, depicting light as making a selection of its action based upon what it might "prefer" (*préférence*) or foresee as having the greatest "advantage" (*avantage*). Yet it is absolutely central to realize that this formulation rests on a radical re-conception of what these terms might mean, and thus also of the meaning of the most basic of teleological concepts. Firstly, to even understand the kind of goal under consideration here and the "real advantage" it offers, one must understand both the essence of light and its resultant behavior using the tools of a mathematician or a mathematical physicist. One should immediately be reminded here of Copernicus' statement in *De Revolutionibus* that he will only be able to explain the greater perfection of his scheme to one "not ignorant of the art of mathematics" (Copernicus 1995, p. 24), or Galileo's famous assertion that the language in which God composed the universe is that of mathematics. If the essential forms of nature are mathematical, then one would expect, as Maupertuis does in these meditations, that God's intentions can also only be grasped through mathematics, and indeed, that the perfection, harmony, unity, and so on of this design must be similarly interpreted. Secondly, this re-conception of teleology in strictly physical and mathematical terms is not only distinct from any simple anthropocentric view of the universe, it immediately puts all other forms of teleology, including the anthropocentric, into doubt. If the unity of the laws of impact are supreme examples of design, after all, then what is to be said of the natural disasters and human calamities that arise necessarily from these very same laws? To be consistent, Maupertuis and others who follow this path must regard these as merely apparent evils, i.e., as evils only to those who, because they are "ignorant of the art of mathematics," are unable to see their essential perfection.

Maupertuis' proof here thus remains teleological, as he points out, but the formulation in terms of universal mathematical laws fundamentally transforms the structure of the argument in at least two ways. All previous proofs cited by Maupertuis saw God in the realm where physical nature and its laws were seen to be insufficient to account for a certain kind of order, i.e. not in what is necessary in nature but only in that which is contingent. Yet, in all these cases it also had to be admitted that nature could *in principle* account for such order, namely as the result of chance or accident, but that this is really tantamount to denying that this order is a reality, or something more than a mere appearance. Maupertuis' proposal thus departs from previous teleological proofs precisely in the respect that it finds God's intentions most clearly manifest directly in the universal and necessary laws of nature. But is it not nonsensical to suggest that we can see evidence of choice, freedom, providence, and indeed wisdom in that which is absolutely necessary? Maupertuis' reply to this objection is that,

> If it is true that the laws of motion and rest are indispensable consequences of the nature of body, that proves all the more the perfection of the supreme being: It shows that everything is ordered such that blind and necessary mathematics executes what is prescribed by the most enlightened and free intelligence. (Maupertuis 1751, p. 65–66)

In other words, the external character of nature as expressed in these laws (which is necessary given the concept of body) does not conflict with the possibility that the *inner* character of nature (which lies at the foundation of the nature of body itself) might in fact be free and purposive in itself. Indeed, the fact that such a cause is able to act with purpose by originally constituting the very nature of body in accordance with simplicity and perfection indeed shows it to be a freer and more original cause than any that would need to manipulate given physical objects in order to achieve its ends. The first error of other teleological proofs is thus that they look for purposiveness only in that which is not possible through mere nature, and thereby place the perfect causality of God and the blind mechanism of nature in direct opposition to one another.

The second way in which it departs from the previous proofs is by self-avowedly taking up the hypothetical form. Previous proofs, at least on the surface, appear to be straightforwardly inductive; the existence and especially the content of God's intentions were to be drawn from experience, indeed from what I have called teleological inference. Maupertuis' proof begins rather with the *hypothesis* that a God with certain attributes exists, and then makes use of the latter for determining what kind of perfection we should expect to find in the very first law of nature. This move is not inductive, but deductive. It begins from the conviction that the very first laws of nature must fit together with the unity of an intention or as the product of an absolutely perfect intelligence. They will be unified under a single and mathematically most simple law, precisely because the perfection evident in their being unified by this same law must be the reason for its very truth.

One way of understanding this proof is suggested by the fact that all the laws Maupertuis has in mind had at the time been as well established by experimental methods as any laws can be. Thus, it is possible that the real heart of the proof in Maupertuis' mind lies not in the establishment of these laws, or in the confirmation that they individually provide, but rather in the fact that the assumption of God's existence allows us to bring all of these formerly disparate laws under one supreme principle that can be directly deduced from his nature. In this way, the assumption of the existence of God allows us to discover for the first time a non-empirical, or super-empirical harmony not directly between different things, but more significantly between the very laws which govern the necessary behavior of different regions of physical phenomena. If this is the case, then the basis of the proof can be said to lie purely in the theoretical harmony between already established laws of nature, and thus it by itself remains untouched by difficulties arising from the inductive establishment of any one of the laws taken individually.

Beyond these issues, it is important to stress that what really makes Maupertuis' *Essay* most remarkable is that it contains what in Kant's eyes must have appeared to be definitive and undeniable proof of the fruitfulness of a certain species of teleological reflection for the discovery of the most universal physical laws. As Maupertuis himself remarks, Leibniz had made basically the same claim for teleology much earlier. However, aside from his rather obscure references to Snell's law and the law of continuity, he was never able to produce such a convincing example. Maupertuis, by contrast, was able by reference to the minimization of a single metric to unify *for the very first time in the history of science* phenomena as diverse as the behavior of light, of bodies in equilibrium, and the communication of motion for both inelastic and elastic bodies. Moreover, he was able not only to perform such a grand synthesis, but even to show how all three follow from a *newly* discovered and completely universal law, the law of least action. Since Leibniz's attempts to derive physical laws from teleological considerations are in fact faulty, it is fair to say that Maupertuis was the first to give real evidence for the kind of discoveries that might be accomplished in physics by attending to final causes.

The importance of this discovery generally, and on the thought of Kant in particular, must not be underestimated. Today we take it for granted that the laws of nature should fit into a sort of hierarchy, with more general laws at the uppermost peak, and descending from there to particular laws governing different varieties of physical phenomena. Ideally, we believe, science should begin with a single universal principle and all other lower laws should be understandable as nothing other than manifestations of this single law under certain restricting conditions. Biological laws should ideally be reducible to mechanical and chemical laws, and these latter to the fundamental laws of physics. This picture, however, is of much more recent vintage than one might at first suppose. Descartes, for instance, did not envision such a hierarchy, because of the simple fact that he did not believe that there were really any significant lower laws to be concerned with. All physical existence for him was pure geometrical extension, governed by basic rules of push and pull. His system, because of its strict deductive structure, in fact allows for the existence of no specific phenomena such as energy, force, fields, electricity, and attraction, let alone of the special laws that give these concepts meaning. The Aristotelians, on the other hand, did not envision such a hierarchy of physical laws for the very reason that they did not have the abstract conception of law itself, but rather conceived of law as species bounded. Those of Kant's predecessors that attempted to fuse the modern conception of physical law with the species-bound physical theory of the Aristotelians, on the other hand, were forced to admit that the general physical laws were but the external form of things, not the truly fundamental laws governing reality from the bottom up. Kant, importantly, did not envision such a perfectly deductive system either. Throughout his career he expressed the conviction that a perfect hierarchy, though perhaps an ideal of rational inquiry, not only could never be achieved, but that it was perhaps not even a genuine desideratum. His investigations into the basic physical concepts in the pre-critical period seem to have convinced him that an attempt to construct a purely deductive theory of natural science leads to the exclusion of possibilities that are actually found in nature, just as had been the case with Descartes' system. In Kant's understanding, therefore, the universal laws of nature must remain for us something abstract, and do not really delimit the range of unity and interconnection that can actually be found *in rerum natura*. It is for this reason that on Kant's view there can never, for instance, be a Newton to explain the blade of grass.

All of this is just to point out that Maupertuis' discovery must have engendered in Kant, and indeed in many others, the real hope of developing an entirely new kind of fusion between science and natural theology, one in which they complement one another not only as perspectives on one reality, but as dual pillars of a single science. Natural theology could be seen to benefit physical science because a scientifically fruitful way of conceiving final causality, namely as manifest in a mathematically determinate law of simplicity and perfection, had finally been achieved. As Maupertuis observes,

> I know the distaste that many mathematicians have for final causes applied to physics, a distaste that I share up to some point. I admit, it is risky to introduce such elements; their use is dangerous, as shown by the errors made by Fermat and Leibniz in following them. Nevertheless, it is perhaps not the principle that is dangerous, but rather the hastiness in taking as a basic principle that which is merely a consequence of a basic principle. (Maupertuis 1751, p. 234–235)

In exact agreement with the position Kant will later espouse in the *KrV* and *KU*, Maupertuis holds that teleological reflection is indispensable to scientific research, and that it can be kept from causing errors by being properly formulated and restricted from an over hasty use. The proper method is to use teleological reflections in clarifying and expanding the overall structure of our theories, and directing our research into specific laws towards their unification under higher and ultimately supreme laws, but always to precede and limit such reflections by the hard work of experiment and calculation of the phenomena.

As a final note, it is important to recognize that Maupertuis does not base his argument for the teleological character of these laws upon the idea that they show any *striving* towards perfection or any determinate desirable final state, but rather upon the fact that they exhibit the essential unity of a manifold that cannot be comprehended as possible other than through this very same unity, viewed however as a cause or principle. Of course, he does at several points draw attention to the beauty of such unity, and the fact that it makes many desirable things actually obtain. He even highlights at points the peculiarities of this unity that make it appear *as if* the system were striving to achieve the goal of maximal unity by the minimal expense of action, even though this is not strictly speaking accurate since the system is always perfectly obeying these laws in the fullest sense, both in change and in rest (equilibrium). So while these features illuminate and persuade, they add nothing essential to the teleological nature of such entities or to the rational grounds for thinking them to have such a nature.

This excursion through the work of Maupertuis reveals that the very notion of universal law as a teleological entity is not as strange as it might at first appear. Or if it is strange, its strangeness did not deter Kant and his contemporaries from formulating the idea with considerable precision. Perhaps, however, this should not surprise us, for even Aristotle's own teleology was not a separate theory about the purposes of things, but rather the core of a metaphysical account of the ultimate intelligibility of the activity in the cosmos.

§. 2.2. Purposes as Laws of Behavior

To gain the full benefit of this excursion through Maupertuis, it will be helpful to expand upon a common feature of such attempts to interpret the laws of nature as teleological. Though presupposed throughout Maupertuis writings, it is perhaps most fully developed in Leibniz. It is, namely, the idea that what is called a "purpose" in these cases is nothing other than that very unity from which derives the law governing certain activities. Leibniz speaks in this sense of the *en-*

telechie as a purpose which in itself is an *unum per se*. Conceived intensively, it is thus a mere metaphysical point, a genuine unity with no real inner complexity. Yet, considered in terms of its extension or that which it governs, this purpose is also the law governing the manifold of actions performed by the monad which it constitutes. Thought metaphysically it is thus a pure unity, while conceived physically or from the side of the manifold in the behavior of the monad, it is the law according to which these acts flow from one another throughout time. Perhaps the best way to describe this relation in Leibniz, is that the purpose or *entelechie* defining a monad is its unity considered metaphysically or intensively, and thus in abstraction from time, while when taken extensively, physically, or in relation to time, it manifests itself as the law of a series. But why speak of purposes and goals in such an abstract case? The reason is that Leibniz understands what we commonly call purposes in precisely the same general terms, namely as conceptual unities that provide the laws for actions. The concept of a triangle, for instance, serves as the law for the movement of one's hand when one intends to draw a triangle. And indeed, if it were possible to know perfectly the intentions of an agent, then presumably one would be able to use this – just as we would a scientific law – to predict every aspect of that agent's behavior. In either case, if we understand the motion of the hand or the behavior of an agent, or again, if we understand the motion of light through space, in abstraction from the unity that underlies it as a principle, then we have a pure manifold with no unity. If, alternatively, we understand the pure purpose or unity by itself, then we have an indivisible point with no complexity. It seems what must be added to the idea of a manifold to get a whole is the governance by a *unitary law*, and what must be added to the idea of a bare unity or purpose in order to get the notion of a law is precisely the idea of a *possible manifold which it would govern*; the law is as it were the schema that mediates between the unity and the manifold.

I have paused to briefly develop and draw attention to this triad of concepts – namely purpose, law, and manifold – precisely because it forms an important point of contact between this teleological interpretation of the laws of nature and Kant's later arguments in the *Critique of Pure Reason*. Though I cannot develop this point until a later chapter, it is clear that this line of thought – developed first in order to relate teleology to the very foundations of modern science – directly relates to Kant's idea that the most basic principles of natural science are those which make possible cognition itself, which consist for Kant in the bringing of the manifold of intuition under the empty unity of apperception (Kant's *unum per se*), by means of a synthesis carried out in accordance with the transcendental categories. This connection shows itself in Kant's very definition of the understanding:

§. 2. Teleological Explanations: From Purpose to Pattern — 97

> The unity of apperception in relation to the synthesis of the imagination is the understanding, and this very same unity, in relation to the transcendental synthesis of imagination, is the pure understanding. (*KrV* A119)
>
> Rules, so far as they are objective [...] are called laws. (*KrV* A126)
>
> This same unity of apperception with regard to a manifold of representations (that namely of determining it out of a single one) is the rule, and the faculty of these rules is the understanding. (*KrV* A127)

For Kant, the laws of physics and the laws deriving from purposes are manifestations of conceptual unity of a manifold in general. That is to say, they are both expressions of the general lawfulness of experience and as such are understood by him to be vehicles of the unity of apperception; while the manifold of sense is precisely that which must be able to be subsumed under the concepts of the understanding, which provide experience with laws, if it is to be brought under apperception at all. The very structure that makes a purpose a purpose, or an end an end, is therefore manifest all the more properly in the fundamental structural relation of pure intuition and transcendental apperception in Kant's critical philosophy. And to the extent that the defining *telos* of the transcendental faculties of the mind is to synthetically produce a unity of the manifold of sense according to the unity required for transcendental apperception, i.e. to produce experience, this activity and its product will both possess the most general form of purposiveness.

§. 2.3. Skepticism Regarding Explanation

After this brief historical excursion, I return to some concluding reflections regarding my main line of argument. Earlier, I argued that teleology arises in scientific explanation from the claim that such explanation assumes that singular events can be "completely and irreducibly" accounted for in term of concepts and their relations. But why should we seek to explain them completely and irreducibly? Is it not possible to avoid this result by assuming that event *e* occurs because of the confluence of a number of singular and purely efficient causes, and that the explanation in terms of concepts merely functions either accidentally or because we have, for instance, learned to associate mental images in complex ways that happen to provide us with reliable ways to navigate the world around us? Perhaps our concepts do nothing more than allow us to economically track what would otherwise be an incomprehensible welter of sense impressions or efficient causes?

This and other so-called "naturalistic" and "extensionalist" interpretations of understanding and explanation cannot be ignored, but one must not overlook the radical consequences of holding such a view.[13] A simple description of an event like *This rock is falling* is evidently shorthand for a great number of larger and smaller events occurring at the same time, and so would presumably not require an explanation that is irreducible and complete, since one can naturally descend to descriptions in terms of atomic forces and fundamental physical laws (note that the same can be said if we view the experience rather as a complex of sense-data). But in neither case does it vitiate the basic structure of D-N arguments; it just leads to the refinement of one particular explanation. Indeed, as long as we accept that there is *some* true state of affairs that can in principle (though perhaps not in fact) be captured by a description, and can be explained, then this means that there exists a complete and irreducible explanation in terms of concepts, which is just the assumption underlying D-N arguments. This applies just as much to descriptions in terms of efficient causes as to anything else, since in order to understand the efficient causes relevant to a singular event one must be able to describe them and bring them under concepts or classes, which when regarded as adequate or true are in turn assumed to be the reason for the particular efficient causes in question acting in the way they do. Clearly, the only way to sidestep D-N explanations altogether is to completely deny that concepts have any foothold in reality and thus that there is anything like a true explanation or state of affairs, a position actually adopted by some philosophers and scientists. Such thinkers see no absurdity in the claim that even the greatest discoveries of physics provide no truer understanding of reality than do the astrological books of the ancient Mayans, just better methods of calculation.[14]

Nevertheless, even if we no longer think things like rocks are objectively teleological, this is surely not because we no longer describe them in language that implies teleology. The truth is that we have, for one reason or another, come to *assume* despite the possibilities opened by our explanatory practices that such things are not objectively teleological, and we have, as a result, learned to *disregard* the teleological implications of the way we describe these things on a day-to-day basis. If this is true, then the persistence of teleological conceptions

---

13 Quine is, of course, the foremost proponent of this view. One can only admire the ease with which he is willing to see the whole texture of human life and understanding tossed on the trash heap of "scientific progress." The austerity of this vision, and much of its details, brings to mind Spinoza, who also saw the elimination of the teleological world-view as the natural course of human self-understanding.

14 This example was given by Richard Feynman in a public lecture.

in regard to human beings and higher animals is perhaps the result of the fact that we either cannot or will not *accept* that it is right to ignore the teleological implications of these classes of descriptions. Such resistance would certainly not be surprising, considering that the implications in question are precisely what give unity, meaning, and value to our actions, and thus also to our lives.

Of course, all of this is still philosophically fertile ground for further investigation. However, from a historical point of view, it must be admitted that the real opponent of teleology has never really been mechanical or modern science, since the two only disagree about the level at which explanation occurs, i.e. about what the most basic teleological entities in fact are. I think this will be granted readily by even the most skeptical regarding teleology, since they also tend to reject metaphysics in the traditional sense, and so will readily give up on any theory that presumes to inform us about the genuine nature of things, which modern science surely does. The real opponent to teleology, then, is rather the anti-realist view that there is no sense in the notion of an intelligible reality, and consequently that the common understanding of explanation is in error.

§. 2.4. Teleological Explanations: Concluding Reflections

I have argued in this section that, if interpreted in the most natural way, the everyday explanatory practices embraced by most scientists and many modern philosophers imply a conception of things that is essentially teleological. Specifically, in an everyday sense we feel that we have explained events within the world when we can understand them as particular and necessary expressions of universal laws that have a wider ontological status. Furthermore, we have seen that on the most basic level of explanation, and perhaps also at some higher levels, what a thing *is, or the kind of being that it is,* seems to be nothing other than to be a thing that operates according to a certain basic set of laws. Such laws make things possible in the sense that they constitute their natures and in doing so they also provide the causes of the actual world's exhibiting an order that is in accord with these laws and natures. Even if I do not agree with Goodman's and particularly Quine's diagnosis of what this means for scientific explanation, I take it as a sign of their extraordinary insight that they draw the radical conclusion that every human form of explanation and understanding is irreducibly teleological on the most basic structural level. In view of the findings of the previous section, I think it is clear why the deeply teleological character of everyday and scientific explanation – indeed the very concept of understanding – is for the most part overlooked. This stems from a failure to separate the inessential and particular features of certain teleological phenomena from the more general structure that is essential to all teleology. I will try to provide a clear *principium divisionis* later in this chapter.

It should also be clear that, despite my strictures, attempts to formulate teleological concepts in strictly testable terms are still well motivated. The basic idea is that if it cannot be shown that teleological explanations serve some ineliminable function in our knowledge of the empirical world, then they are just so much useless baggage. This conviction, however, is genuinely positivistic and anti-metaphysical in the sense that it manifestly equates meaningful or philosophically respectable discourse with that which is absolutely necessary for describing and projecting (for the sake of predictability) manifest correlations between empirical data. Of course, traditional metaphysics, and indeed teleological thought itself, does not dispense entirely with the concern for empirical relevance. But it does introduce, as we saw in Maupertuis, a large number of further concerns and issues that often override this concern with the empirical, and generates meta-principles and concepts for interpreting empirical descriptions in terms of some specific underlying metaphysical basis. As a product of metaphysics, then, teleological concepts have not generally been introduced as part of the search for an adequate description of a set of physical events, but rather primarily for the sake of developing a way of comprehending how a set of physical events, already describable separately in other terms, can belong to a real whole or unity. The examples I examined in previous sections indicate in fact that teleological thinking is often genuinely motivated by ordinary natural objects and events. But, if I am correct, then these serve it only as a basis for a process of resolving our understanding of such unitary beings back to those principles without which they would not in fact be conceivable as real wholes. Such resolution proceeds towards the causes of teleological phenomena, and in its ideal extension leads to a single highest principle that, by means of its own intrinsic unity, is also the principle of unity in all lower things.

It can be said in favor of the positivistic or anti-metaphysical approach to teleology that it is clearly impossible to *empirically prove* the existence of such internally teleological natures without introducing some, perhaps many, subsidiary metaphysical principles to make up for the lack of strict proof.[15] And unfortunately for traditional metaphysics, these principles often boil down to nothing else than the covert assumption or assertion of the reality of such wholes. In this respect, Plato's introduction of the forms as a *hypothesis* remains perhaps the most honest way of introducing teleology.

---

15 The most common subsidiary principle, of course, is the existence of God, proven in some purely rational way.

Kant provides us with still another kind of motivation, which is neither strictly metaphysical nor moral, for regarding the objects of our cognition as intrinsically teleological on the most fundamental level. His argument, as I will attempt to show, is that the very structure of theoretical and moral reason requires the presupposition that on the most basic and most general levels, the perceptions and objects that are given to us, or the courses of action prescribed for us, must be thought to intrinsically (not accidentally) conform to those concepts without which these uses of reason would not be possible. Furthermore, since the use of reason is in fact at least fourfold – namely, in the theoretical cognition of objects in general by the understanding, in the theoretical cognition of objects as a whole by the higher faculty of reason, in the practical cognition of our moral duties, and finally in our practical cognition of the whole object of pure practical reason – there is at least a fourfold respect in which we must presume the purposiveness of the objects for the sake of the functioning of reason itself.

Granting for the moment that one could perhaps in the ideal case justify the assumption of the internal teleological constitution of things in general and so reach the highest point – either by metaphysical, moral or transcendental arguments – then the bottom-up search for the grounds of the possibility of real unity would give way to a top-down explanation of such unity insofar as it depends upon and is caused by this highest principle. In other words, instead of attempting to infer the effects from the causes, the internal from the external, this top-down form of explanation would allow us to derive the effects from the causes, the external from the internal. This is teleological explanation in its most essential metaphysical form, and it is precisely what we found in the writings of Maupertuis above. Kant's derivation of the laws of nature from the condition of the transcendental unity of apperception, for instance, will provide us with another case in point.

But what does such explanation look like? Its underlying idea is what Aristotle refers to as "hypothetical necessity," and its most basic formulation is found in ordinary practical reasoning:
1) Why does Jane dangle bait in the water?
2) Jane thinks that the world leading up to her doing so contains circumstances such that the most obvious way to catch a fish is to dangle bait in the water.
3) Jane is a rational agent, and thus does what she thinks is obviously required in order to achieve her goals.
4) Hence, Jane would dangle bait in the water if she wanted to catch a fish, and she thought doing so would achieve this aim.
5) Jane wants to catch a fish.
6) It is thus hypothetically necessary for Jane to dangle bait in the water.

The necessity captured in the final line is hypothetical, precisely because it is based upon the assumption that Jane has a particular goal. Moreover, the idea of an agent acting on purpose, which is employed in this proof, clearly is that of a being with broadly dispositional properties. At the head of these properties is the notion of a rational agent, or an agent that will do what it thinks is necessary to achieve its stated goals. (If we wish this account to apply more generally to teleological agency, it could be formulated as saying that an agent acting according to a specific form will cause whatever is required to produce an effect with this form.) Now, in the present case this broad property is made more concrete by reference specifically to Jane's beliefs about what is required to achieve her particular goals. Finally, from this account it is clear that given the circumstances, the nature of a rational agent, and Jane's actual goal – that is, based upon these premises – it is *necessary* that Jane dangle the bait. For if, on the contrary, Jane did not dangle the bait, then one would have to admit either that the explanation does not describe the genuine circumstances or that it does not adequately describe Jane's goal, or that it is incorrect to say that Jane is a rational agent of the usual kind.

It is not difficult to see from this analysis that Hempel and Davidson are correct to conclude that in regard to logical form teleological explanations are identical with D-N explanations.[16] Bennett and Taylor are thus quite wrong to think otherwise.[17] The broadly dispositional property of being a rational agent combined with an individual agent's beliefs and goals together lead to the formulation of a basic law governing Jane's behavior. What Jane actually does is seen to follow necessarily from the truth of the premises and her nature as a rational agent. Of course, no human being is a perfectly rational agent at all times and in all circumstances, but neither will the physicist ever discover any absolutely perfect spheres or ideal gasses with which to demonstrate his or her theories. Nevertheless, we hold ourselves up to the ideal of such an agent, and particularly in the moral sphere we feel compelled to develop such a perfectly rational disposition. For strict adherence to moral laws requires that we clearly formulate

---

[16] See Hempel 1965, esp. p. 469–483 and Davidson's "Hempel on Explaining Action," in Davidson 1980, p. 261–275.
[17] Bennett and Taylor maintain that teleological laws possess a distinctive logical structure. I am convinced, however, that evidently teleological laws can always be reformulated to look like physical laws, and that physical laws can always be reformulated to look like teleological ones. Bennett himself gives a brilliant example of the latter when he unmasks the supposedly fraudulent teleological explanation of Stable Lake. This example, however, proves the exact opposite of what Bennett intends, because the supposed unmasking rests on the assumption that if a teleological law can be reformulated into a physical law, then it is not genuinely teleological.

and evaluate the goals of our actions and perform only those that agree with such laws. Moreover, the more universal our ends, and the more consistently we act according to them, the more our behavior takes on the form of a nature governed by universal laws. The only difference is that while physical laws, under a teleological interpretation, can at most have the systematic unity of nature itself (say, its simplicity, diversity or beauty) as their goal, the laws of human action may have even the systematic unity of such actions as their goal.

§. 3. The Essential and Inessential Characteristics of Teleological Entities

So far in this chapter, I have focused on two different patterns of teleological thought, namely teleological inferences and teleological explanations. I have done this in order to show that certain supposedly central features of teleological entities are actually nothing but conditions without which teleological inferences could not be defended. As we saw, teleological inferences draw their evidence from external behavior, and assume from the outset a distinction between teleological and mechanical behavior. From this it is clear that a given teleological inference would be undermined by the discovery that the piece of behavior it supposedly rests on can be captured by a unitary mechanism. It is equally clear that such an argument would be strengthened by any evidence suggesting that the behavior cannot be captured by one. From this one can see why plasticity of behavior, i.e. the seeming ability to reach the same goal by a variety of different means, which challenges the thought that the behavior is the result of a single mechanism, is usually thought to be essential to teleology. This is reinforced by the fact that plasticity is essential to identifying the specific goal of such behavior once it is assumed to be teleological, and for testing whether an assumed goal is the real goal. For if the goal of a piece of behavior is X, then we can test if the production of X is merely accidental by changing the circumstances. So plasticity is important not because it provides direct evidence of teleology, but rather because it challenges mechanical reduction and helps us to refine our teleological account of a given piece of behavior under the assumption that the goal is relatively constant. By the same token, the very deeply ingrained prejudice that striving towards a goal is an essential feature of a teleological entity can be explained as resulting from the need to adduce some kind of well-defined behavior as evidence. Similar observations can easily be extended to the unity condition and to the requirement that an intentional agent be involved. We also saw that because such inferences are always based upon a certain conception of what kind of unity can be produced purely by the mechanism of nature, it is always limited by the current state of natural science and threatened by its progress.

By contrast with this, we saw that teleological explanations rely directly on what is essential to teleological activity, namely, on the idea that an effect or activity is only possible by virtue of the causality of some kind of concept or representation of this same effect or activity. Teleological explanations have a deductive form and begin with the idea of this type of causality and derive from it a certain range of possible effects or activities. By focusing on this more basic notion of teleology, we have also been able to understand how in the modern period some philosophers, including the pre-critical Kant, came to interpret the most basic and necessary laws of mechanical nature – indeed even the most essential properties of geometrical space – as exhibiting the most basic and universal form of teleological unity. The first step was taken perhaps by Maupertuis, but as we saw in Chapter 1, this thought was soon further articulated by Kant in order to arrive at the conception of a kind of transcendental teleology, i.e. a teleology through which the very essences of things are thought of as constituted such that every possible effect of these same things must give rise to an infinite fitness to ends. This of course profoundly changed the scope and role of teleological structures, and as I have suggested, eventually made possible the kind of arguments through which Kant would later establish the critical philosophy.

Before concluding this chapter, it will be helpful to focus a bit more clearly on this most essential conception of teleology and then to take a brief look at how Kant specifically relates it to that of a natural organism. A key requirement for a genuinely teleological form of causality is that the form of the whole of the effect be characterized essentially by reference to the form that governs the activity through which it is generated as a whole. The circularity of this formulation reflects the essential circularity of teleological causality that was perhaps first noted by Aristotle, but is also central to Kant's own conception. One way this requirement becomes evident is in the thought than in genuine teleology there must be a non-accidental link between a concept and the product of the activity that operates on the basis of this concept.

To illustrate this a bit more fully, consider that a circle can be formed by the joining of the two ends of a line. Such joining evidently does not consist in the placing of the two ends next to one another, because then the beginning and the end would remain two different points, and thus there would have to be at least one point between them, and thus no circle. If we are to transform a line into a true circle, then this can only be by taking the *two most distant points* and identifying them as the *very same point*. It makes sense to say this only because what is now a single point in the circle can also be viewed as the initial point of two contrary movements along the path of the original line. Viewed in the latter way,

§. 3. The Essential and Inessential Characteristics of Teleological Entities — 105

the same point can rightly be regarded as two, namely as that point from which one of these movements begins and as that most extreme point at which it eventually terminates. Now, on the basis of this image we can construct an interpretation of the structure of transparency as like a line that has been transformed in this way into a circle. Something is transparent when the medium that intervenes or stands between the endpoints described by the seer and the seen allows the structure on one side to show through to the other side; the less distorted the image that reaches to the other side of the medium, the greater the transparency. The degree of distortion (and so also of transparency) is in turn judged by reference to the ideal case, namely, when the medium allows the image to pass through unchanged, and thus where the image on both sides of it are indistinguishable. In this case the image can be characterized in the same way as the endpoints that are joined to make a circle, since in the case of perfect transparency the image on one side is in one sense distinct and furthest from the other and in another sense is exactly the same image. It is interesting to note that in regard to images, spatial and even temporal differences are themselves not usually thought to be distinguishing or intrinsically distorting features. This is perhaps because all images must be projected through space and time as through a medium, and if space and time were not intrinsically transparent, there would be no ideal case. However, if there were no ideal case to provide a baseline measure, it would not even make sense to speak of space and time, or anything else for that matter, as transparent to any specific degree.

Now the metaphor of transparency allows us to capture in a single image the two key features of teleological causality, namely the non-accidental link between the concept at the basis of the causality and the form of its product and the normative or measuring relation that stands between the former and the latter. In absolutely perfect teleological activity – i.e. a teleological activity in which the goal is perfectly achieved in every way – the cause and effect are not only non-accidentally identical in regard to their basic form, but rather are non-accidentally identical in regard to every formal determination whatever penetrating down to the matter itself. Since in this case the form is usually the activity through which the goal is brought about, and the matter is the end itself, we can see why for perfectly teleological entities the activity and end are necessarily one and the same. The perfect transparency of the medium lies in its having transmitted the form without having introduced anything accidental into the resulting image. In less than perfect teleology, there must of course also remain at least a degree of formal and non-accidental similarity between cause and effect, even if some accidental features intrude because of the nature of the medium. Now as similarity is nothing but partial identity and partial difference, teleological causality can be said to require at least partial non-accidental identity between the form of the cause and the form of the effect. The degree of perfection is here again measured by the ideal comparison of the form of the cause with the form of the effect in a perfectly transparent medium. Similarly, even if an effect fails to fully manifest the concept that is its ground in a teleological cause, its essential character is nevertheless defined through the degree to which it is faithful, thus to the degree to which the causality can be said to achieve its goal non-accidentally. This requirement for genuine teleological activity, i. e. the requirement of a non-accidental link between the concept as ground and the form of its effect, I will refer to in the following chapters as the "transparency condition."

Finally, it is instructive to notice how Kant specifically understands organic structure as derivative of this more general conception of teleological activity. Organicity is in fact unique in that it is the form of teleology in which the whole is maintained not by the direct causality of the form, but rather by the specific formal interdependence of the causality of the members within the whole. Each member, in other words, is maintained by the whole through its being maintained by another member, and by virtue of this the whole itself holds together in a regular way. The members thus interrelate by mutually producing and strengthening one another, and by this means producing and strengthening the whole of which they are reciprocal parts. This form of teleology has become very prominent, practically to the point of usurping the title of "teleological." However, Kant himself deduces the structure of the organism from the more general conception of teleology in the following passage:

> Now for a thing as a natural end it is requisite, *first*, that its parts (as far as their existence and form are concerned) are possible only through their relation to the whole. For the thing itself is an end, and is thus comprehended under a concept or an idea that must determine *a priori* everything that is to be contained in it. But insofar as a thing is conceived as possible only in this way it is merely a work of art [...]
>
> But if a thing, as a natural product, is nevertheless to contain in itself and in its internal possibility a relation to ends, i.e., is to be possible only as a natural end and without the causality of a rational being outside it, then it is required, *second*, that its parts be combined into a whole by being reciprocally the cause and effect of their form. For in this way alone is it possible in turn for the idea of the whole conversely (reciprocally) to determine the form and combination of all the parts: not as a cause – for then it would be a product of art – but as a ground for the cognition of the systematic unity of the form and the combination of all of the manifold that is contained in the given material for someone who judges it.
>
> For a body, therefore, which is to be judged as a natural end in itself and in accordance with its internal possibility it is required that its parts reciprocally produce each other, as far as both their form and their combination is concerned, and thus produce a whole out of their own causality, the concept of which, conversely, is in turn the cause (in a being that would possess the causality according to concepts appropriate for such a product) of it in

§. 3. The Essential and Inessential Characteristics of Teleological Entities — 107

accordance with a principle; consequently the connection of *efficient causes* could at the same time be judged as an effect through *final causes*. (*KU* 05:373)

After this passage Kant goes on to conclude that such a being is what we call organized or self-organizing. Now what is striking about this derivation is that Kant begins with the completely general form of teleology discussed above, namely with the idea of a thing in which its form is thought to be the real condition or cause of its possibility, which if the form is conceived of as imposed upon the matter from outside results in the concept of a product of art. He then derives the concept of an organism as the single way in which such teleology can be understood as arising from the matter itself. For this to be possible, Kant argues, the whole must arise from the causality of the matter, but in such a way that the product of this causality contains precisely the formal articulation that would have arisen if the form had been imposed upon the matter from outside. The matter must in other words be conceived of as self-organizing. In this passage Kant is addressing himself specifically to the living beings of nature, but if successful this derivation can be generally applied to any kind of matter that would exhibit intrinsic teleological structure, as for instance an ethical community where the place of matter is occupied by the individual who strives for virtue.[18] The important point here is that organic unity is understood by Kant as a particular form of teleology which arises specifically in the case where there is added the condition that the causality of the concept of the whole can only be found in the collective causality of the parts within the whole. In future chapters we will see that this structure is central to Kant's overall conception of the teleology of reason.

---

[18] See *RGV*, esp. 06:93–102; 129–136. I submit that Kant's entire discussion of ethical community is transparently guided by his general understanding of organic structure as the sole conceivable form of a possible intrinsic purposiveness of a manifold.

Part II: **The Teleology of Human Knowledge**

Introduction to Part II

The goal of this part is, first, to sharpen the historical narrative of Chapters 1, §. 2. specifically as it is related to the problem of *knowledge* by showing how Kant's critical investigation into the possibility of experience can be seen as flowing naturally from disagreements that occurred between Christian Wolff and August Christian Crusius on precisely this issue. The second goal is to indicate the nature of Kant's advance in the *Critique of Pure Reason* and to show how his strategy for dealing with the difficulties raised by Wolff and Crusius gives structure to the basic arguments of that work.

It will be useful to state here at the outset what precisely I take my analysis as proving, and how I structure the following investigation. Chapter 3, which is chiefly historical, focuses on the background to Kant's understanding of experience as the ideal and systematically unified totality of all possible perceptions that is the proper goal of theoretical cognition. Here I argue that we can gain insight into Kant's transcendental philosophy, which has for its "supreme problem" the question of the possibility of experience, by viewing it as arising from the tension between Wolff's and Crusius' metaphysical accounts of the possibility of experience. As we will see, whereas Wolff attempts to guarantee the possibility of experience from a metaphysical-teleological principle underlying the operation of reason, and Crusius attempts to guarantee it from a teleological principle in some sense internal to self-consciousness, Kant's strategy is to explain the possibility of experience from the standpoint of a *transcendental teleology*, i.e. a teleological view of cognition justified exclusively on the basis of its status as a condition of the possibility of experience. That is to say, Kant's strategy is not to demonstrate the possibility of experience by exposing the metaphysical conditions that will make knowledge actually develop or that will even assure us that we can or should believe in the reliability of our rational principles, but rather to show that without presupposing these principles are generally valid, no use of reason would be possible at all, not even that by means of which we are able to be aware of ourselves as a single conscious "I." In short, Kant avoids these two dogmatically or metaphysically teleological attempts to explain the possibility of knowledge by developing a transcendentally teleological account. And in doing so, Kant alters the basic question from one about how actual knowledge is possible to how it is possible for our representations to have the form of objectivity, i.e. the form of knowledge, in the first place. The meaning of this will become clearer as we proceed.

In Chapter 4, I will then attempt to show in detail how this teleology underlies the argumentative strategy of the Transcendental Aesthetic and the Transcendental Analytic. The focus of this chapter is on elucidating the precise logic by means of which Kant reinterprets his pre-critical transcendental teleology as the basic ground-structure of the capacity of intuition and the faculty of understanding. I will argue, in particular, that the fact that Kant was able to ask the question of synthetic judgments *a priori* for the very first time, as well as to provide a very subtle framework for answering it, would both be incomprehensible if not for this philosophical background. I also argue, however, that there are certain key alterations that Kant makes to his pre-critical results to allow for their incorporation into a system of self-articulating theoretical consciousness.

Finally, in Chapter 5 I examine the Transcendental Dialectic and in particular Kant's derivation of the ideas of pure reason and his account of the regulative function of the ideal of God. In the former case, we will see how the ideas, as expressions of the purest and most original dimension of human reason, generate an archetype or model which essentially surpasses anything possible through theoretical reason and thus points beyond it to the practical domain, which will be examined in Part III. In the latter case, by contrast, we will see that these same ideas also provide theoretical reason with a sort of archetype of absolutely systematic knowledge, in accordance with which it is able to regulate the purposive use of the understanding. Here, the idea of an absolutely purposive whole, provided by reason itself, transcendentally makes possible the purposive use of the understanding for cognizing the particular in experience.

Chapter 3 The Historical Roots of Kant's Concept of Experience

> Through their conflict, Wolff's ontological logic and Hoffman's psychological logic lead directly to Kant's transcendental logic. The latter must be derived, not from foreign influences, but from this tension within German philosophy. (Wundt 1964, p. 254)

> At the ground of the whole [Kantian philosophy] lies the Baumgarten-Crusiusian system, mingled with Hume's doubts. (Herder, quoted in Erdmann 1888, p.75)

Introduction

At the conceptual heart of Kant's first *Critique* lie the locutions "experience" (*Erfahrung*), "possible experience" (*mögliche Erfahrung*), "possibility of experience" (*möglichkeit der Erfahrung*), and "judgment of experience" (*Erfahrungsurtheil*). Like any good empiricist, Kant tells us that all knowledge begins with experience (*Erfahrung*) (*KrV* B1). Yet, to the extent that the knowledge we gain through experience is *objective*, and thus extends in validity beyond any particular moment of perception, Kant claims further that it must embody rational laws that hold for all *possible experience* (*mögliche Erfahrung*). Finally, according to Kant's view, the objectivity of these laws is underwritten by synthetic *a priori* principles, which are peculiar in that their proofs rest entirely on their relation to the *possibility of experience* (*möglichkeit der Erfahrung*) (*KrV* B294). Thus, as it turns out, the fundamental question of the *Critique*, namely, how synthetic *a priori* judgments are possible, is answered in precisely these terms: "The *possibility of experience* is therefore that which gives all our cognitions *a priori* objective reality" (*KrV* A156/B195). This particular mode of proof by reference to the possibility of experience, Kant tells us more than once, is in fact the key to his critical method and thus contains in crystallized form, as it were, the insight that allowed him to progress beyond traditional metaphysics.[1]

Seen in this light, it is perhaps not surprising that in drafts for an essay on the progress of metaphysics since the time of Leibniz and Wolff, we find Kant claiming that the "supreme problem" of transcendental philosophy is in fact: "How is experience possible?" (*FM* 20:275). Indeed, in the revisions Kant made to the first edition of the *Critique of Pure Reason* between 1781 and 1787, and in still later writings, the question of experience in some respects replaces the earlier and more familiar ques-

---

1 This is particularly clear at *KrV* A216 – 218/B263 – 265.

tion of 1781 – namely, How are synthetic judgments possible *a priori?* – as defining the essential task of transcendental philosophy.

This change in strategy of presentation, if not in actual argumentation, is further underscored by Kant's renewed focus on the concept of judgment, which has been noted by many commentators. In a signal instance, Kant claims in a note to the *Metaphysical Foundations of Natural Science*, published in 1786, that the entire transcendental deduction could nearly be carried out using a single inference from a precise definition of a judgment in general (*MAN* 04:474n2), a suggestion followed out, at least partially, in the B-deduction. The definition given immediately after this bold claim is this: A judgment is "an action through which representations first become cognition of an object." In the B-deduction it reads more fully: "A judgment is nothing other than the way to bring given cognitions to the objective unity of apperception" (*KrV* B141). In both cases, Kant is clearly identifying judgment in general with the idea of a judgment of experience, i.e. with an action of the mind though which perceptions are related to an object by means of their being subsumed under the schemata of the concepts of the understanding. Thus Kant's very definition of judgment, as it stands in heart of the B-deduction, derives ultimately from his definition of experience as "cognition that determines an object through perceptions" (*KrV* B218; see also *Refl* 4679) and this indicates that Kant has reached a very clear and radical position: The essential and real use of judgment in general, thus the guiding idea of judgment for all other uses, is to be found most fully in the kind of judgment which produces experience.

The recognition of these facts brings with it several problems; for the centrality of Kant's concept of experience is matched if not exceeded in degree by its obscurity. Kant himself points to the unorthodoxy of this definition in the *Prolegomena*, where he chides the reader who would imagine that experience is but a heap of sensations with no necessary rational or formal structure.[2] Yet, neither there nor elsewhere does Kant explain the source of this notion, or take any time to tell us why, in clear opposition to the usage of the British empiricists, experience can be *defined* as a product of the understanding, and indeed as *certain* and *objective* cognition. Writes Kant: "What experience teaches me under certain circumstances, experience *must* teach me and everybody always, and its validity is not limited to a particular subject or to its state at a particular time" (*Prol* 04:

---

[2] In the *Prol*, Kant remarks cavalierly that he can do little to help "the reader who retains the long habit of taking experience for a merely empirical synthesis of perceptions" except "recommend him to heed well this difference between experience and a mere aggregate of perceptions" (*Prol* 04:310). Lucas' translation. In the *KpV*, Kant says similarly that such empiricism "can scarcely be taken seriously" (*KpV* 05:14).

299).³ This inherent objectivity of experience is expressed most clearly in what is perhaps one of the most puzzling features of Kant's usage, namely that he takes experience to actually be *composed* of judgments, and takes judgment in turn to be an act of the understanding. This is particularly disturbing since Kant elsewhere in the first *Critique* and even more clearly in later texts claims the very opposite regarding experience, as Kemp Smith has noted (Smith 1984, p. 52). For instance, in the introduction of the first edition of the *Critique of Pure Reason* we read that experience "tells us, to be sure, what is, but not that it must necessarily be thus and not otherwise," and "it gives no true universality" (*KrV* A1).⁴ In the second *Critique*, Kant compares trying to "extract necessity from an empirical proposition" to trying to extract water from a stone (*KpV* 05:12).

To this we must add the suddenness with which Kant introduces his more refined notion of experience in the first *Critique* and the ease with which it allows him to resolve some of the most serious problems in that text, which together lend it an artificial, even *ad hoc* appearance. This was first highlighted almost simultaneously by Salomon Maimon and Karl Leonhard Reinhold, who raised the question as to whether by basing his analysis on such a definition, Kant has not begged the entire question of objectivity.⁵ Notably, Nietzsche later lampoons Kant in *Beyond Good and Evil* for similar reasons.⁶ As a final indication of the peculiarity of Kant's concept of experience, we should note that the key modal concepts of "possible experience" and "possibility of experience," of which Kant makes such an important use, have no equivalents in those texts from the British tradition with which he was familiar.

Setting aside Kemp Smith's implausible suggestion that Kant has no consistent concept of experience, I take the aforementioned evidence as indicating one of two things: either the complex Kantian conception of experience is a discovery of the critical philosophy itself, or else it stems from sources that commentators have yet to fully explore, or in some sense both. The former can, however, be dismissed since the *Nachlass* shows that Kant employed the concept in similar ways perhaps as early as 1763–4, a full decade and a half prior to the appearance of

---

3 Lucas' translation. Emphasis mine.
4 It should be noted that Kant corrected this slip in the second edition.
5 See Reinhold 2003, p. 195 and Maimon 2004, p. 104–106. I thank Richard Fincham for providing me with these references.
6 See especially Nietzsche 1980, §. 11. Here Nietzsche focuses on Kant's idea of a faculty of judgment. However since, as we will see below, Kant's idea of experience is made concrete in certain mental actions called judgments of experience, and since he furthermore identifies the essence of judgment in general with the faculty of judgments regarding experience, it follows that Nietzsche's criticisms amount to the same thing as Maimon's and Reinhold's.

the first *Critique* (see, e. g. *Refl* 3716). I will argue in this chapter that Kant's concept of experience is in fact informed by, but not entirely derivable from, two traditions other than British empiricism, both of which treat of the concept of experience explicitly and at length, and both of which have important things to say about the related modal locutions. I will first discuss the tradition initiated by Gottfried Wilhelm Leibniz and carried through by Christian Wolff, a tradition that dominated German school philosophy throughout most of Kant's life, formed the basis of the books from which he lectured,[7] and holds the distinction of having created the terminological framework or matrix for nearly all philosophical discussion in the German language from the 1730s until at least the eclipse of German Idealism. Here I am interested in answering two questions: 1) To what extent is Kant's view of experience as composed of judgments that apply categories already present or at least implied by Wolff's philosophy? 2) How specifically does Wolff account for the objective laws of all possible experience in terms of the conditions that make such experience possible?

In a second part I will examine two works stemming from what has been referred to in the literature as the Thomasian tradition, namely, Adolph Friedrich Hoffmann's *Vernunftlehre*, and the logic textbook written by his student, Christian August Crusius.[8] It has been shown elsewhere that this tradition exerted a decisive influence on Kant during the years just prior to the critical turn, and that it also enjoys the distinction of having been the only major alternative to, and critic of, the Leibniz-Wolffian tradition prior to Kant. In the course of my discussion of these works I will argue that: 1) Kant's distinction between judgments of perception and judgments of experience, 2) the link he posits between "objective reality" and the modal concept of the possibility of experience, and 3) his claim that the formation of "experience" requires subsuming perceptions under "material" rational principles, are each anticipated by this tradition.

In a third and final part, I will explain how the contrast between these traditions sheds new light on the strategy underlying Kant's critical philosophy, one that has the added significance of clarifying how Kant would respond to recent debates regarding the relation of sensory experience to concepts and the possibility of non-conceptual content. I will suggest that many of the issues around which contemporary debate regarding the naturalization of epistemology centers

---

7 Particularly notable are Baumgarten's *Metaphysica* and Meier's *Auszug zur Vernunftlehre*.
8 As textual evidence shows, Kant studied the works of Crusius for nearly a decade during his pre-critical period (these were still in Kant's personal library when he died), and, despite what some scholars have claimed, I think there is evidence that the impact of Crusius lasted well into the critical period and is as detectible in Kant's moral philosophy as it is in his theoretical philosophy.

were already current in the pre-Kantian tradition, and thus that the critical philosophy should be read as an explicit response to these.

As will become clear as we proceed, I believe this will directly shed light on the specific character of the transcendental teleology that informs the core of Kant's own account of the possibility of experience in the *KrV*.

§. 1. Wolff's Ontological Logic and the "acumen pervidendi universalia in singularibus"

In the preface to his 1783 reissue of the German translation of Alexander Baumgarten's *Metaphysica,* and later in his famous attack on Kant, Johann August Eberhard claimed that the metaphysical tradition stemming from Leibniz and Wolff had already dealt with the problems raised in the *Critique of Pure Reason* (Baumgarten 2004, "Preface to the New Edition"). A similar claim was repeated and extended by Herder[9], Lovejoy (Gram 1967, p. 284–308), and Pichler (Pichler 1910, p. 73–91). Lovejoy's criticism is instructive for being the most trenchant of these views. As he writes, "the substance of the argument upon which Kant relied to refute Hume's skepticism about causality, had already been advanced by the most notorious of the so-called 'dogmatists' [namely, Wolff] over sixty years before the *Kritik* was published – and some twenty years before the appearance of Hume's *Treatise*" (Gram 1967, p. 292). Few, I believe, would defend such a view today, but not because any refutation of it has been produced; rather, until very recently, there has been little interest in early German modern philosophy aside from Leibniz. However, the fact that careful historians of ideas, as I believe Lovejoy and Pichler generally are, could come to such a radical conclusion indicates that this question deserves to be looked at more seriously. Specifically, it indicates that any attempt to come to grips with Kant's account of the possibility of experience, its relation to the work of his predecessors and perhaps eventually its true originality, must look back to the account of experience found in Wolff's writings.

A second and far stronger reason for looking back to Wolff stems from the unique role he played in establishing modern German philosophy. Firstly, it is really from Wolff's work that the Cartesian concern for the deductive form of philosophical knowledge, the very systematic spirit typical of modern rationalism, flows into and takes up permanent residence in German thought. For the most part, German philosophy in the schools had eschewed Cartesianism and

---

9 For Herder, see note 1.

so had the central founders of the German enlightenment such as Christian Thomasius, despite hints from figures like Clauberg and Leibniz. Indeed, Wolff was really the first to succeed in popularizing this view and in producing the textbooks required for infusing the rational method into all areas of academic research. The aim of Wolff's famous "mathematical method" was precisely to introduce the *philosophical* method into all fields of academic research. According to this method, knowing a proposition with certainty *just means* being able to demonstrate it from known premises according to strict logical rules. Thus the certainty of a piece of knowledge is drawn entirely from the certainty of the principles upon which it rests. As a consequence, in constructing a science or a system of sciences, "the supreme law of philosophical method," writes Wolff, "is that those things must come first through which later things are understood and established" (Wolff 1963, §. 133). Obviously, the success of a method of this kind requires that there be a first stage of science and one or more absolutely first principles. In Wolff's system, this initial stage is occupied by first philosophy, or ontology, which treats the universal principles common to all things, being *qua* being, and it rests on a single absolutely first principle, the principle of contradiction. Because of its unique position in the system, Wolff therefore holds the principle of contradiction to be the necessary and the sufficient condition – the "font" – of absolutely all certainty in human knowledge.[10]

On the surface, this looks like the most severe and empty rationalism one could dream up, and it is hard to imagine how for Wolff experience can play any role whatsoever in philosophy. After all, if experiential knowledge is genuinely *derived* from experience (and experience is not simply taken as a confirmation of previously derived *a priori* truths), then it clearly has not been logically demonstrated from the principle of contradiction. Presumably, experience by its very nature would therefore lack the sort of certainty that would make it admissible in philosophy. It would seem to be in this vein that Wolff writes: "Examples merely illustrate propositions suggested by experience, but in no way establish the universality that first comes to light when it becomes evident that, from the determinations in the subject, the predicate can be inferred through a legitimate argument" (Wolff 2005, p. 12). Elsewhere, Wolff states that experience is "the lowest grade of human knowledge" (Wolff 1963, §. 22), the "bare knowledge of fact," and that with such "vulgar knowledge we go no further than those things which we first notice by means of the senses" (Wolff 1963, §. 23).

---

10 Wolff 2005, Part 1, Sect. 1, Ch. 1, §. 55: "*Patet adeo principium contradictionis esse fontem omnis certitudinis, quo posito, ponitur certitudo in cognitione humana; quo sublato, tollitur omnis certitudo.*"

The historical facts, however, indicate that this must not be the whole story. For the views expressed in Wolff's own writings provided key support within Germany for the view that experience was essential *for the foundations of philosophy*, and led many to regard "experience" (*Erfahrung*), its possibility and its principles, as central topics of logic and ontology. Not only was he to devote sizable textbooks in German to "experimental philosophy" and "empirical psychology," he went further and asserted in the *Preliminary Discourse* to the cycle of his Latin writings that in order to have complete certitude "the principles of philosophy must be derived from experience" (Wolff 2005, §. 33). In agreement with this claim, in his German logic (the fifth chapter of which forms the basis for all later discussions of the possibility of experience as we will see) Wolff actually christens judgments of experience "fundamental judgments" (*Grund-Urtheile*), precisely to highlight the fact that they form the basis of all our demonstrative knowledge.[11] And as for first philosophy, the supposed first source of the principles of all other sciences, Wolff states openly that here too "the fundamental notions must be derived from experience" (Wolff 1963, §. 12).

As we shall see below, Hoffmann and Crusius ridiculed this aspect of Wolff's position as so obviously contradictory that the only way he could have expected to avoid criticism is if his readers had fallen asleep. Whether Wolff's position here is truly incoherent is something we will have to consider below. For now, I want simply to note this apparent paradox in Wolff's view of experience – that he apparently holds experience to be both inferior to demonstrated knowledge and the foundation of demonstrated knowledge – and turn to a more detailed discussion of Wolff's views on what precisely constitutes an experience.[12]

§. 1.1. Wolff's Logic of Experience

Given Wolff's influence, it should not be surprising that when we turn to his German logic we find ourselves in territory which on the surface looks not so very different from what we later find in Kant. "Experience," Wolff tells us, is "everything we know (*erkennen*) when we attend to our perceptions" (Wolff 1749, Ch. 5, §. 1). In another of his German works, Wolff explains experience similarly to be "the knowledge (*die Erkenntniss*) we reach through attending to sensations and the alterations of the soul," i.e. to inner and outer sense (Wolff 1983, Ch. 3, §.

---

[11] Wolff 1963, §. 34: "the principles derived from experience provide the foundation of demonstrated truth."
[12] The comparison with Kant's conflicting claims on the status of experience suggests itself.

125). It is important to note here from the outset that Wolff, just like Kant, actually begins by *defining* experience as a particular species of objective knowledge regarding things. This is significant, because it means that unlike Locke or Hume, Wolff does not regard experience as some sort of evidence that precedes and grounds our knowledge, or at least our assumptive knowledge, of objects and their connections. Rather, for reasons not yet apparent, Wolff takes experience as such to be *already constituted* by a type of objective cognition or knowledge intrinsically *about* objects prior to any act of inference. In this respect, Wolff differs even from Descartes, who holds knowledge to originate in the intellect, and not in the senses. What is more, by defining experience in this way, Wolff is essentially distinguishing it from metaphysical cognition, not by its degree of certainty or objectivity – as we will see, he thinks experience can be perfectly certain – but rather exclusively by means of the *occasion* of its acquisition, i.e. the fact that it originates from perception rather than from inference.

Indeed, Wolff is not in the least hesitant to say that by means of experience we know with *strict or metaphysical certainty*[13] such mundane things as that: "A lighted candle makes everything around us visible; spilled water wets the table; the flame of a candle burns paper" (Wolff 1749, Ch. 5, §. 1). Wolff readily classes truths acquired through complex scientific procedures as of the same basic sort as these ordinary deliverances of experience. In fact, the German Logic's chapter on experience is almost entirely devoted to experimental procedure, and to a description of the specific *ontological* principles that make the acquisition of such experiences possible. Let us consider just one example to get a sense of what Wolff has in mind. Writes Wolff: "I may convey a stone wherever I want, and it still remains hard, as long as it remains a stone, or retains its essence. Now as it constantly retains its hardness, and I at the same time remember that what constantly agrees to a thing is an attribute of that thing; I conclude that hardness is an attribute of stone" (Wolff 1749, Ch. 5, §. 6). One's initial inclination, I think, is to interpret this as a mixed procedure, i.e. as a rational argument based upon both certain perceptual experiences of stones being hard, and on an ontological principle defining the relation of essence and attribute. Thus we might interpret it as a syllogism having for its major the ontological proposition, namely, *Whatever constantly accompanies something is an attribute of it*, fol-

---

[13] "Concepts are certain if we know their possibility. Now, since experience shows us that those things exist, of which it equips (*gewehret*) us with a concept, we also know from this that they are possible. Judgments are certain if what we attribute to a thing befits it or can befit it. Now if we have reached a concept by means of experience, then we have come to know, from this, that this or that befits a thing, and it is accordingly clear that this *can* befit the thing" (Wolff 1749, Ch. 5, §. 1.).

lowed by the minor drawn from experience, *I perceive that stone is always accompanied by hardness*, followed by the conclusion, *Therefore, hardness is an attribute of stone.*

This, however, cannot be what Wolff means, since he would be the first to point out that no one can constantly perceive every stone, and that even granting hypothetically that this were possible, it would still not prove that hardness belongs to the essence of stone and thus to any given stone necessarily.[14] Like Leibniz before him, and Hume and Kant after, Wolff fully realizes that induction provides no ground for necessary or universal truths, the conclusion from any number of particular truths to a universal truth being a simple logical fallacy.[15] This explains the striking omission of any reference to induction in his discussion of experimental and scientific procedure.[16] Rather, for Wolff, the experience in this case is actually expressed in the conclusion *Stone is hard*, or more fully *Hardness is an attribute of stone.*[17] This is because the experience is itself an objective thing. Of course, the proposition is not strictly speaking the experience; it *expresses* the experience, and Wolff himself warns against confusing the proposition drawn from experience with the particular experience it is based upon. We can, naturally, fail to correctly express our experiences in propositional form. Nevertheless, the relation between the experience and the proposition that express it remains a matter of immediate *recognition*, not one of inference from pre-

---

14 For to be an attribute is to belong to something necessarily, or as a consequence of its definition, and hence whatever grounds such a connection must also ground counterfactuals like *If a stone that does not now exist, and so has never been perceived, were to be created, then it would be hard.*

15 See the Leibniz 1996, p. 49: "Although the senses are necessary for all our knowledge, they are not sufficient to provide it all, since they never give us anything but instances, that is particular or singular truths. But however many instances confirm a general truth, they do not suffice to establish its universal necessity; for it does not follow that what has happened will always happen in the same way."

16 This, I presume, is the reason Kant never regarded Hume's problem as an issue of induction. For, to the extent that Leibniz and Wolff laid the foundation for explaining the origins of empirical knowledge, induction was never the central problem. Knowledge of fact, if it is to be regarded as knowledge or even the first material for knowledge, must have a certainty that precedes any instance or series of instances.

17 Perhaps we should rather conclude that Wolff's experimental procedures provide only evidence allowing us to make a sort of educated judgment that stone is hard? Such a *juridical* understanding of the relation between experience and judgment is found in Locke, and even more clearly in someone like Reid, but it does not fit Wolff's picture because judgments drawn from experience under this interpretation would not be completely certain, and thus would not be able to serve as fundamental judgments, judgments that form the basis of demonstrated truth.

ceding data. Thus if we have *correctly* recognized and expressed our experience in a judgment, then the judgment actually expresses exactly what was originally contained in that experience or at least in that aspect of the experience; no more, no less (Wolff 1749, Ch. 5, §.3 – 4).[18] Thus in Wolff's view we actually perceive this necessary truth and are aware of its certainty, although properly speaking truth and necessity are not direct objects of perception. They concern the form of the experience, not its content.

What then is the role of the ontological principle if it is not as a premise to an argument such as the one above? Its role is merely to allow us to grasp this experience in a *well-formed* judgment, i.e. in a judgment that combines the right kinds of terms in the right kinds of ways, thereby making it suitable for use as a premise in an argument. Wolff's underlying contention here is that there can be no gap, so to speak, between the content of our perceptions and the judgments that we draw from them, if only we possess sufficient skill in the use of our cognitive faculties and follow the correct method. Now, if absolute certainty regarding the content of experience is to be possible at all, then the addition of ontological terminology or form can be nothing more than the first step of an analysis or resolution of what is already *completely contained* in the perception. If this were not the case, and judgment were to add something that was not somehow already contained in the perceptions, then the judgment would lack complete certainty in regard precisely to this additional element. In other words, the judgment would always rest on an unjustified leap from the experiential evidence for a truth to what is expressed in the truth itself. For Wolff, the immensely complex application of ontological principles to experience in fact adds nothing to the experience itself. This leads to a very unusual notion of containment, according to which a perception can be said to contain implicitly whatever can be extracted by means of rational procedures carried out upon it. In a certain sense, this is just the continuation of Leibniz's own version of an Aristotelian abstractionist view of knowledge acquisition.

§. 1.2. The Wolffian Roots of Kant's Categories

This brings me to a key point in my comparison with Kant, for it shows that well-formed experiences for Wolff are essentially expressed in judgments. The expe-

---

[18] This is supported by Wolff's initially odd sounding claim in §.4 (for those more used to the British tradition) that witnesses can prove that we had other experiences than the ones we think we had.

rience is not some kind of pre-conceptual foundation from which concepts are generated or to which they are added to form knowledge, but are rather the objective foundation of the possibility of the representation of an object, which itself is fully realized and brought to clear consciousness only at the end of the cognitive process called judging. Indeed, like Kant, Wolff actually *defines* experience, when it is correctly expressed, as *consisting* of judgments, and thus as involving the specific mental operation of judging. Following up on this clue we find that Wolff defines a judgment in a more or less traditional manner[19] to be a specific performance of understanding through which two representations or concepts[20] are linked (*verknüpft*) either by combination (*verbindung*) or separation (*trennung*) (Wolff 1749, Ch. 3, §. 2). Presumably, then, a judgment of experience does the same for two sensible representations, expressing how the understanding represents them as connected. Wolff further concludes that since, from a metaphysical point of view, we know that only individual things exist, our perceptions always only regard individuals (*einzenle Dinge, individuum*), which he nominally defines to be whatever we perceive in inner or outer sense (Wolff 1735, §.43). It follows that judgments of experience are *singular* judgments (i.e. judgments the subject of which is an individual (Wolff 1735, §.241)) and not particular or universal ones, which are rather about abstract or general concepts.[21] This argument is particularly revealing because it again confirms that Wolff understands the content of judgments of experience, i.e. what they are *about*, not in terms of their psychological content (the image present immediately to one's mind in perception) but rather in terms of their *objective ontological* content, i.e. their real causes as these might be known by an angel, as Leibniz liked to say.

The metaphysical underpinnings of Wolff's concept of experience are underscored and made more precise by another feature Wolff attributes to judgments of experience. In addition to being fundamental and singular, they are intuitive

---

19 Similar definitions were commonplace in the seventeenth century. Arnauld 1996, p. 23: "*Judging* is the action in which the mind, bringing together different ideas, affirms of one that it is the other, or denies of one that it is the other."
20 Unlike Kant, Wolff makes no sharp distinction between representation (*Vorstellung, repraesentatio*) and concept (*Begriff, notio*). This is in fact symptomatic of his Leibnizian view that sensible ideas are confused representations. In his lectures, Kant restricted the use of the Latin term *notio* to purely intellectual concepts such as the categories and predicables. See, for instance, *V-Lo/Busolt* 24:653.
21 From this we can see that the perceptual character of judgments of experience leads Wolff, by virtue of a *metaphysical* (indeed nominalistic) proposition regarding what exists or is available for being perceived, to the conclusion that all judgments of experience are singular judgments, i.e., judgments directly about individual beings and their states. See Wolff 1749, Ch. 5, §. 2.

(*judicia intuitiva*), which Wolff explains in his Latin logic as meaning that they are attributed to a being or thing "viewing it in its complete [or comprehended] concept" (Wolff 1735, §.51). This is somewhat cryptic, but can be illuminated by noting that Wolff contrasts intuitive judgments with discursive judgments, the latter being a judgment established through inference. A discursive judgment – even if it is about an individual – is thus reached only by the mediation of a universal proposition that precedes it, whereas an intuitive judgment is *immediately* determined in our perception by the very same individual being that is named in the subject term. Now, whatever we perceive is an individual (Wolff 1735, §.42), and an individual, now taken according to its real definition, is on Wolff's view an *"ens omnimode determinatum"* (Wolff 1735, §.74) – a being whose essence is determined in every manner or with regard to every possible predicate.[22] Therefore, in a judgment of experience, as Wolff says, we attribute something to an individual "viewing it in its complete concept," insofar as it is a thing consisting of a manifold of properties. The underlying idea here is one we are familiar with from Leibniz, namely, that perceptions are fundamentally nothing other than confused, though complete, representations of their causes. Only here, Wolff is silently making use of this idea to specifically articulate the content of our judgments of experience, by drawing the conclusion that, since such judgments are based on perceptions, but are also *about* the underlying cause of these perceptions, these judgments express an immediate and intrinsic relation between a being and our knowledge of the same being.[23]

Clearly, for Wolff judgments of experience express objective and intersubjective states of affairs, as I have previously noted.[24] From this fact it follows that the possible types of judgments of experience should be exactly parallel to the different concepts according to which objects themselves may possibly be combined. This, indeed, is nothing more than a special case of the general relationship Wolff claims holds between logic and ontology: "Logic treats of the rules which direct the intellect in the knowledge of all being, for the definition

---

[22] Complete determination is in fact the principle of individuation and the definition of existence according to Wolff. See Wolff 1983, §. 14.

[23] A similar explanation is given in Gottsched 1756, §. 131: "If we consider something as separate in itself which we perceive in regard to a thing in sensation; but nevertheless view it as something that belongs to or is found in a sensible thing: then we decree an intuitive judgment regarding it. E.g. I see the sun go down, and remark its figure, which I represent to myself in my thoughts as something abstract, but yet perceived as belonging to the sun: then I judge according to this experience: The sun is round."

[24] Indeed, as I have noted, they are often the results of complex scientific experiments and procedures involving ontological principles that are used to frame or express these judgments precisely.

of logic does not restrict it to any species of being; therefore it ought to teach us what to look for in order to know things. Now that which pertains to the general knowledge of being is derived from ontology" (Wolff 1963, §. 89). To be sure, Wolff does not, like Kant, use the Aristotelian term "category" to describe these modes of combination, though he does grant them the honorific title of "ontological terms." Nor does he attempt to draw up a table precisely summarizing this parallel between forms of judgment and ontological categories. But that he *could* do this is certainly implicit in his idea that we bring experiences into well-formed judgments by recalling the way beings can be related in ontology.[25] However, since these concepts are all defined and demonstrated in ontology, which encloses the beings we perceive merely as a special case of concepts and principles extending over all beings in general, an additional table would serve no obvious purpose. The truth, then, is not that Wolff, to a great extent himself an Aristotelian, failed to recognize the special function of categories in generating our judgments of experience; he simply had no reason to think that anything could be gained by trying to derive them systematically from the faculty of judgment. On his view, putting logic before ontology in this way would be an inversion of the proper order of the sciences.[26] In truth, we are capable of cognizing these forms, because we are capable of representing the ob-

---

[25] In regard to this basic point, it makes little difference, I think, that Kant regards this as a *subsumption* through which objectivity is brought into our perceptions by the understanding. Subjectively regarded, it is very much a subsumption performed by the understanding. It's only when Wolff's incorrigible ontologism is taken into account, that it becomes clear that objectively this subsumption is analytic, not synthetic.

[26] So did Wolff actually serve as a source for Kant's categories? Kant actually provides an abundance of clues that Wolff and his school were his chief sources. In his lectures on metaphysics, and in the *Critique* itself, Kant several times indicates that his "system of all concepts and principles" serves the same role for objects of experience in general, as ontology was supposed to serve for beings in general. See, for instance, *KrV* A845/B873. Also in the *KrV*, he says that a system of all concepts derivable from the categories, the so-called predicables, could be extracted from any good ontology, particularly Baumgarten's. From the logical side, we need only remember Kant's remark in the *Prolegomena* where he tells us that when he discovered the forms of judgment were the key to systematically deriving the categories, he found everything "finished but not free from defects" in the work of the logicians, the best of which to Kant's mind, as noted above, was Wolff's. Heimsoeth has looked for sources of the categories in Wolff's ontology, and Lovejoy and P. Hauck have discussed the Wolffian sources of Kant's table of judgments. If my interpretation is correct, then neither of these is the most appropriate way of evaluating the relation between Kant and Wolff. The best method would be to focus, not on the forms of judgment in general, but on these insofar as they can be used to express judgments of experience, and to trace the link between these and the related ontological principles of connection. For in Kant's view, the origin of the system of concepts and principles lies precisely in their being the common root of both general logic on the one side, and ontology on the other.

jects themselves, which happen to be structured in a way expressed by the same forms.

§. 1.3. The Skill of Perceiving the Universal in the Particular

Initially, one might think that the singular and intuitive nature of judgments of experience would make it impossible to extract universal and certain truths from them. For even granting that they are true and certain, still they are only judgments about the actual object perceived, and moreover, of the specific determinations an individual happens to have at the moment it is perceived. Yet Wolff patently regards the move from judgments of experience to universal judgments as entirely unproblematic, arguing indeed that all human beings have, and realize to a greater or lesser extent depending on their training, a *natural capacity* for seeing the universal in the particular.

He explains this as follows: Firstly, since individual judgments regard the changes of things, and these are causally determined by the circumstances in which they occur, such judgments can be made universal by adding to them the conditions under which they do occur: "if I have *once* experienced that the assurance of a present good produces joy, I need not doubt in the least that the same assurance will produce joy in other cases" (Wolff 1749, Ch. 5, §. 15; emphasis mine). Secondly, since the individuals perceived by us contain their own essence, which is something universal,[27] and are merely individuated by their contingent determinations, it is possible by comparison and abstraction from these determinations to elicit the universal from the particular (Wolff 1735, §. 57). In fact, this is precisely how, according to Wolff, the basic concepts of ontology arise originally in the mind. Our everyday experiences and locutions contain what he calls a "natural ontology," i.e. a confused apprehension of the true fundamental concepts and principles of all beings. Through use these gain a degree of clarity, and if the correct demonstrative method and order of thinking is achieved, then they become fully distinct and compose an "artificial ontology" (*Ontologia artificialis, künstliche Ontologie*), i.e. a science by which we can reflectively regulate and formulate all our future judgments of experience. Combining this with what was learned earlier, we can say that experience for Wolff is possible because it is, so to speak, *autochthonic*; the certainty that for us constitutes the objectivity of our thoughts arises naturally in the progress of the working up of experiences themselves. As stated in his *Preliminary Discourse*, the existence

---

[27] Wolff 2005, §. 19: "*Universalia autem singularibus, quae perceptimus, insunt.*"

of philosophical knowledge drawn from fundamental judgments proves that it is possible, and thus that it is certain (Wolff 2005, §. 38). Of course, *we* will not know this with certainty along the way, but Wolff is confident that when we do reach knowledge, we cannot help but know that we know it, that knowing it is possible, and that this awareness alone constitutes certainty. Wolff's position here is both fundamental and self-aware: If scientific knowledge is to be possible, then there must exist fundamental judgments that provide the content of knowledge and there must exist in the human mind a natural capacity for extracting the universal principles from these; we have certain and demonstrated knowledge; thus there must exist within us a capacity for seeing the universal in the particular. Ontology is but the artificial cultivation of our intellect and reason, which are those natural optical devices, as it were, by which we resolve sense experience into judgments of experience, and extract from these latter the first metaphysical principles.

§. 1.4. Wolff and Kant on the Possibility of Experience

All of this explains why Wolff takes experience to be objective cognition, and, given that Wolff's view of experience is repeated in the popular textbooks of Baumgarten, Reimarus, Gottsched, Meier and others, it also explains why Kant expected his more informed readers to have no problem with his own definition. But it also makes one suspect that Kant is right in claiming that Wolff and his followers naïvely glossed over the entire problem of the possibility of experience. After all, if Kant is right, and perceptions only first *become* experiences through their being subsumed (or rather being subsumable[28]) under categories in a judgment, then clearly Wolff has failed to explain, in a way that would satisfy Kant, how this is rendered possible. As Kant asks at one point: "How does this representation [i.e. perception] in turn go beyond itself and acquire objective significance in addition to the subjective significance that is proper to it as a determination of the state of mind" (*KrV* A197/B242)?[29]

---

[28] As will become clear, I do not think this is really an accurate statement of Kant's position. His view is not that applying the categories transforms sensations into experiences, as if magically, but rather that we must assume their applicability, in order to regard sensations as related to an object in general.
[29] When Wolff describes the process through which perceptions are analyzed, he already takes them to be representations of objective items, albeit confused ones, and his chief concern is not whether perceptions can be subsumed under concepts of objects, or how they can be so sub-

Wolff, it seems, presupposes the objectivity of perceptions *in general* in order to explain how it is that we can resolve them into distinct or determinate knowledge of objects *in specific*. And this, I think, is how we must distinguish his conception of transcendental truth from that of Kant. Doing so is particularly important because previous comparisons by Lovejoy and others have claimed to find no difference between Wolff and Kant on precisely this point. Briefly stated, Wolff recognized that for any cognition of objects to be possible in general, we must presuppose that objects are themselves thoroughly ordered or connected according to general laws. Wolff terms this complete ordering "transcendental truth" because it is a condition of the possibility belonging to beings in general and in themselves. Now the principle of sufficient reason, which states that everything must have a ground, requires as one of its consequences that all beings be completely ordered both in regard to their own properties and in relation to one another. Thus this principle is the source of transcendental truth, and it follows that unless we presuppose the principle of sufficient reason, no truth of beings will be possible, and thus no knowledge of the truth of beings either.[30] As Wolff puts it, without the principle of sufficient reason there would be no distinction between truth and dreams. As we saw before, Lovejoy considered this to be a Wolffian proof of the second analogy, which was essentially the same as Kant's, except for being superior, since it did not get mixed up in confused talk about subjective perceptual states. Hans Pichler reached much the same conclusion, saying that Kant's theory of the possibility of experience is just a special case of Wolff's superior and more universal proof carried out in regard to beings in general.[31]

However, assuming my interpretation of Wolff's concept of experience is correct, then despite the obvious similarities, Wolff and Kant have in mind two radically distinct problems, requiring equally distinct solutions. Wolff's transcendental truth is nothing other than a general *metaphysical* condition of the empirical cognition of specific objects. It describes an order of objects and their states *in themselves* without which *we* (i.e. finite knowers dependent upon sense experience for the content of our cognitions) could reach no *deter-*

---

sumed – questions that Kant is interested in – but only with whether they are subsumed correctly and judged correctly as standing in their true relations to one another.

30 Wolff 1983, §. 43: "While here truth is explained through the order in the alterations of things, one understands that truth which the philosophers have named *veritatem transcendentalem*, and have given to be an attribute of a thing in general: Thus this kind of truth is opposed to dream. The ground of truth is the principle of sufficient reason, ..." See also Wolff 2005, §. 77.

31 See Pichler 1910, p. 73–91.

minate idea of their relations by means of experience. Kant's, on the other hand, describes an order of *perceptions* – understood not as confused concepts but as subjective states of the mind – that must obtain if they are to be able to be *represented as related to* an external object in general at all. Thus, for Wolff, the denial of the principle of sufficient reason would leave us with a realm of *representations of objects* with no uniform order or real content, a mere dream; whereas for Kant, denial of the second analogy would mean being unable to subsume perceptions under concepts in the first place, and thus would render impossible any real thoughts, even imaginings, that would be capable of having an intentional object, let alone an actual or determinate one. In Kant's own words: "The concept of cause is nothing other than a synthesis" without which "thoroughgoing and universal, hence necessary unity of consciousness would not be encountered in the manifold of perceptions. But these would then belong to no experience, and would consequently be without object, and would be nothing but a blind play of representations, i.e., *less than a dream*." This last phrase is no mistake; it is a clear signal from Kant to his more informed readers of his differences with Wolff, whose understanding of the opposition between truth and dreams was well-known at the time.[32] For this same reason, I cannot agree with Pichler that Kant's distinction between judgments of perception and judgments of experience is already present in this tradition of thought.

In summary, I maintain that Wolff's account of the possibility of experience is not naïve, but rather rests on his steadfastly ontological standpoint. His adherence to this standpoint is made possible only because he thinks that perceptions are indeed nothing but confused concepts that potentially, and thus *essentially*, represent the beings that cause them in a completely adequate way. This belief, in turn, is thought by him to be a necessary condition of the possibility of obtaining knowledge of beings by means of experience, a knowledge that we evidently do possess. Because of this, the logical process through which perceptions are resolved into adequate concepts must be nothing more, in Wolff's view, than a removal of the inessential, the actualization of what is potential, the resolution of the confused into the distinct, a change in form but not in content. It is just a necessary presupposition for the possibility of scientific knowledge, that we pos-

---

32 A 112. Emphasis mine. I think Kant most certainly had Wolff's comments in mind when writing this passage. See *Prol* 04:376n.: "When I oppose the truth to dreams, he [the reviewer] never thinks that it is only a question here of the well-known *somnium objective sumtum* of the Wolffian philosophy ..." Lucas' translation. Wolff's view of dreams was, as Kant mentions here, a very famous doctrine at the time. Though I have no space to argue the point here, I think this is exactly the point Kant is trying to make in §. 12 of the *KrV* where he compares his own transcendental philosophy to that of the "ancients."

sess the cognitive capacities that would allow us to produce within ourselves genuine representations of the objects we thereby represent. Thus the activity of judging, which for Kant is in some way essential to synthetically *making* distinct concepts, and introducing a transcendental *content* into our thinking, is restricted in Wolff's thought exclusively to the analytical role of making *given* concepts distinct.[33] This explains why for Wolff the primary mental operation (*operatio mentis prima*) is the simple apprehension of concepts, which he believes provides judgment and reasoning, the two other mental operations, with their entire content.[34] This contrasts sharply with Kant, for whom the formal content of knowledge, as the relation of perceptions to an object in general, is first generated transcendentally in the activities that make judgment itself possible.

§. 2. Adolph Friedrich Hoffmann and Christian August Crusius[35]

Hoffmann and Crusius – I will be treating their doctrines as essentially equivalent[36] – are remembered mainly for being the most successful opponents of Wolff, and more specifically for their attack on his attempt to derive the principle of sufficient reason, and all its consequences, purely from the principle of contradiction.[37] Their importance for Kant, however, extends beyond this point to in-

---

33 See Kant's *Log* 09:63.
34 Oddly, despite the glaring differences in the underlying presuppositions, this leads Wolff to a position that sounds very much like Locke and Hume. For Wolff and Hume, and to a lesser extent Locke, tend to view simple apprehension as the source of all cognition, and thus regard the clarification effected by judgment as adding no new content. See Hume 1896, p. 97n.
35 For a general historical overview of these thinkers see Beck 1996.
36 Aside from the occasional change in the order of presentation and in emphasis, Hoffmann and Crusius agree completely in regard to the points relevant to this chapter. When Hoffmann died in his prime, Crusius, his student and close friend, seems to have taken it upon himself to revise and publish a complete system based upon what he had heard in Hoffmann's lectures.
37 The following passage is typical of Crusius: "For the principle of contradiction is a totally identical proposition, and thus where it can be applied, it is necessary that one is speaking of totally the same thing, from totally the same point of view, and at exactly the same time. Therefore, no single question, which is brought forward, whether of cause and effect, or of ground and that which it grounds, can be decided from this principle if one does not receive help from another principle that is distinct and independent from it. One represents a thing A, and calls its cause B: Then one would at once see that he who says that A arises, and indeed without any cause at all, certainly says something absurd and unbelievable, but nothing contradictory, and that one must therefore refute him from another ground, a ground which at once would bring forth and furnish the correct limitation of the rule treating of causes and effects. For he says, A arose, B is not, and also has not happened. To arise means to begin to be, or to exist

clude many positive issues regarding both the method and content of philosophy. While the precise nature of the influence of Crusius on Kant during the pre-critical period is still a matter of debate, it is relevant to note that the term "experience" in the sense under discussion here, as well as the phrase "synthetic judgment" first occurs in notes from Kant's *Nachlass* that date from around 1763, a time when Kant described his own method as not essentially different from that of Crusius.[38] This can be explained by the fact that Kant saw Crusius' work as the single most successful attempt to articulate the kind of new synthesis of rationalism with empiricism (i.e. of the commitment to the idea of philosophy as science with the recognition of the radical dependency of reason on experience, not only as regards content but also as regards basic principles) towards which Kant was then moving.

Like most philosophers of the period, Hoffmann and Crusius adopt the greater part of their terminology from Wolff and share his broadly rationalist assumptions about the structure of science and the order of demonstration. In particular, they agree that certainty and necessity are the essence of knowledge, and that certainty, including that of experience, must be derived from just a few basic rational principles that are certain in and through themselves. What they fundamentally reject, however, is Wolff's claim that the method of philosophy is essentially the same as that of all other sciences, including mathematics, and thus that the most basic principles grounding philosophical knowledge consist exclusively of definitions and the principle of contradiction. At the root of this difference is their rejection of what I have referred to as Wolff's steadfastly ontological standpoint, which rests on the conviction that the content of our experiences is essentially identical with whatever can be extracted from them through

---

in a moment of time, but not to have existed in the preceding moment of time. Where indeed is the contradiction? For then he says, A is in another moment of time, it was not in the first; here I see no contradiction. B, however, is not. Also here, I find nothing contradictory. Incidentally, I can scarcely presume that someone would take refuge in the idea that the concept of an effect is already contained in the concept of a cause, and therefore inversely, that one must represent A as an effect which presupposes its cause. For the question here is not about how our thoughts are arranged, but about the thing itself. I will say so much: There is no controversy over whether an effect presupposes a cause (which I concede), if it is accepted that it is an effect. However, what I would very much like to know is if A is an effect, and from where I can find this out" (Crusius 1766, §. 11). Notably, like much else, Crusius' treatment of this issue in his texts is almost identical, sometimes down to the very word and sentence, with previous treatments given by Hoffmann.

38 See, in particular, *Refl* 3716. Kant says that his methodology is very close to that of Crusius in *UD* 02:294. The relevance of Crusius to Kant's discovery of synthetic *a priori* judgments has been treated most fully in Henrich 1967, p. 9–38.

the application of our cognitive capacities. Hoffmann and Crusius, by contrast, argue that reflection on the nature of human experience, and in particular on the axiom of causality (i.e. their version of the principle of sufficient reason) give every indication by their universality that they are not contained within the immediate deliverances of sensation, as Wolff had argued, but rather are *added to* the experience by the mind itself. This leads Hoffmann and Crusius, as I will show, to focus more on the subjective side of the cognitive process and to regard the principles by virtue of which perceptions are first formed into judgments capable of being *about* objects as requiring explicit justification of their objective reality.

This turn is reflected in their view of the principle of contradiction, which rather than being the source of all certainty, is held by them to actually be an identical and indeed empty proposition (*ein leerer Satz*) (Crusius 1965, §. 260). Wolff also maintains, in his way, that it is an empty proposition, but he does so to emphasize that it adds nothing to our original concepts or perceptions, and thus that these latter already contain all the content we might extract from them by analysis. Wolff still holds, nevertheless, that all other fundamental metaphysical principles are true simply because their opposites can be shown to contain a contradiction. For Hoffmann and Crusius, by contrast, the principle of contradiction is empty precisely in the sense that it allows us merely to draw out what we already think in a concept, and since nothing conceptual is contained in a representation that is not placed there in some way by the mind itself, this principle does not allow us to extract any *real* content from our sense experience or our concepts. It therefore says nothing about objects, but only about the *form* in which we must represent objects to ourselves. It remains nevertheless the absolutely highest of all principles, because no thought contravening it is positively thinkable. Yet from it alone it is impossible to extract rules that would capture the real content of objects which might be represented in our thoughts. Thus, unless supplemented by other principles, it provides no ground in their view for adding to any of the determinations merely thought in a given concept or for guaranteeing the concept's objective reality.[39]

From this Hoffmann and Crusius conclude that, if there is to be any knowledge at all, i.e. certain judgments regarding some real object, then there must be one or more fundamental "material principles" of philosophical cognition, i.e. axioms that first provide reason with some objective content or reality. Further-

---

[39] Consequently, in their view, since Wolff had sought to base all cognition on this sole principle, his system was really nothing more than an arbitrary heap of general concepts, and lacked all guarantee of objective reality. In their view, his continuous emphasis on experience was easily explained: It was required to hide the emptiness of his basic principle.

more, they argue that since all human thought begins with perception, and since knowledge consists both in perception and in our conscious relation of this perception to its object, this act of relating must consist in the subsuming of our perceptions under such material principles, or under one of their consequences. It is thus by means of the active addition of these principles from the side of the mind to what is encountered in perception that these perceptions for the first time take on an objective significance. However, in their view it is clear that we are aware of the object only by means of those same perceptions that are supposed to become objective by our addition of such a relation. Consequently, the relation to an object that the mind adds can consist in nothing other than the assertion of a *necessary* connection among the perceptions or representations themselves. Thus the fundamental material principles, by virtue of which thought is related to an external object, are nothing but principles of necessary connection among our thoughts and perceptions.[40] In contrast with Wolff, then, logic or the investigation into the laws of thinking and perceiving must precede ontology or the inventory of the most basic concepts of objects in general.

Given these assumptions, it is clear that at least two things must be explained before one can found a system of philosophy after this model. Firstly, one must be able to outline a clear method for discovering all such material principles, and, secondly, one must prove the truth of these principles, if not absolutely, then at least sufficiently to explain why they are necessary presuppositions of human knowledge. In their textbooks on logic, Hoffmann and Crusius in fact present a multitude of different material principles, for instance: everything that exists does so at some place and at some time; everything that is not a first cause has a determining cause; similar causes produce similar effects, and so forth. These, of course, sound like typical ontological principles of the kind adduced in Wolff's logic and ontology. However, the key point here is that they derive not from the principle of contradiction but from two other supreme principles internal to self-consciousness, which provide it with a lawlike relation to external objects, namely, the principle that two representations that cannot be represented as separate cannot be separate in reality, and that two representations that cannot be represented as combined cannot be combined in reality. These two principles are in their view the original sources of all other material principles, and thus of the objective reality of all cognition.

---

40 As a result of this change in the method of questioning, logic – which outlines and proves these principles – should be understood as a discipline in which we clarify the laws and limits of human thinking, while ontology and special metaphysics should be understood as the system of all that we must think necessarily, and not an unlimited knowledge of being *qua* being.

Hoffmann and Crusius both also expend considerable effort in proving these two supreme principles from several points of view. Yet it seems that the chief series of proofs exhibits one basic strategic idea: If something cannot be *genuinely* represented in a certain way, then whoever claims that it can nevertheless exist in that way is saying something inherently without meaning. Put more precisely, since these material principles govern the connection and separation of our fundamental concepts of things and thereby provide the very ground of the possibility of distinguishing the subjective play of sensations from objective representations, if we say that we can represent an object to ourselves, even if only in imagination, as actually contravening these principles, then we are not in reality *asserting* anything at all; we are uttering word-sounds without any content. For this reason, if we then go on to say that something can exist in this way, we are saying something without any specifiable content. Consequently, if it is correct that these are the very principles through which our representations are able to take on objective significance, then they simply cannot be denied without at the same time denying the very grounds by which such a denial would have any meaning. This basic method of proof, reminiscent in many ways of Aristotle's attempt to prove the principle of contradiction in his *Metaphysics*, is remarkable for the fact that it aims to show from principles *internal* to theoretical self-consciousness, indeed lying at the basis of the possibility of representing an object of cognition at all, that these principles lie necessarily at the foundation of every act of representing an object in general.[41] Hoffmann in this way does not ask whether we *genuinely* have true thoughts about objects; we have all had thoughts that we at one time *regarded* as such, and this surely is possible. What he asks, rather, is *how* it is possible for us to consciously regard our own inner thoughts in this way (i.e. to internally relate our thoughts to ourselves as something objective and set apart), or what must be presupposed for this to be possible. His answer is that if it is possible for us to have true thoughts about objective states of affairs, then this can only be because we consciously presuppose that the necessary connection of our ideas expresses the necessary connection in objects (Hoffmann 2010, Vol. 1, §. 551). There exist necessary laws of the mind of which we become conscious in the course of reflecting upon experience, and unless we take this as expressing the inner connection of objects, we could not presume to even think about objective reality. Kant

---

41 See Aristotle's *1970*, Bk. 4, Ch. 4–5. Aristotle's proof is, however, metaphysical, his point being that if we deny the principle of contradiction, then we destroy the notion of essence, which is the foundation of linguistic meaning. Consequently, denial of the principle of contradiction is at the same time a denial that the utterance through which we deny it is meaningful.

will later refer to such principles as constituting the "real possibility" of an object.

The method both of discovering and of proving all further material principles derives, as it clearly must, from the two highest material principles. The method, in essence, is to reflect on what we think in an experience and to try to abstract from its content until we reach basic combinations of representations that we can no longer separate/unite without destroying the representation as a representation of something objective. The idea is that although it may seem at first blush that two concepts are separable, as soon as we try to separate/unite them in an actual representation, we will find that our representation of one or both of them becomes empty, or, in other words, that the separating/uniting cancels the very objective content of one or more of the representations we are attempting to separate/unite. This impossibility of a certain determinate representation thus signals that the analysis of our ideas has come to an end, i.e. that we can no longer separate any of the remaining representations without destroying the representation as one of an object, and that we have now arrived at the first moment of a necessary synthesis that must occur for the sake of representing objects in general. It marks a transition from pure analysis of experience to what Hoffmann and Crusius call the "synthetic-analytic" or the "analytic-determining method," the necessity of which lies in that in attempting to analyze what is in a given representation we are forced – for the sake of the representation of something at all – to synthetically *add* to a representation determinations that cannot be extracted from it simply by means of the principle of contradiction (Hoffmann 2010, Vol. 1, §. 551). At this turning point from analysis to the discovery of a necessary synthesis, Crusius argues, we can be assured that "these [representations] are combined with one another," not merely in the imagination, but "through the essence of the understanding" (Crusius 1964, §. 50). At such a point we are justified in subsuming the proposition expressing such a relation under either of the two highest material principles, and to conclude from the necessary synthetic connection of these representations in our minds, to the concept's objective reality.

In one key example of the method at work (Crusius 1964, §. 48–50), Crusius asks us to represent an existing being, and then to gradually think away all that we represent in it. Once we remove color, figure, and everything that is peculiar to the thing, he thinks that we will be left with nothing but the space in which it exists, and here, he contends, we will find that if we try to remove this space, then the very possibility of representing an existing object, not only in the imagination but indeed in the intellect, is altogether canceled, and necessarily so. From this Crusius concludes that the representation of any existing object must necessarily be accompanied by that of the space in which it exists. The representation of space, and indeed of something as in space, is thus a condition of the possibility of the representation of an object in general. Put differently, the real definition of existence is that of a substance that is somewhere in space. Our first fundamental concept of space is therefore nothing but that in which it is possible for substances to exist, and which remains in our thoughts when we abstract from everything particular to the substances that are actually represented as occupying it. By comparison, Kant writes in the *KrV*:

> Not merely in judgments, however, but even in concepts is an origin of some of them revealed *a priori*. Gradually remove from your experiential concept of a body everything that is empirical in it – the color, the hardness or softness, the weight, even the impenetrability – there still remains the space that was occupied by the body (which has now entirely disappeared), and you cannot leave that out. [...] Thus, convinced by the necessity with which this concept presses itself upon you, you must concede that it has its seat in your faculty of cognition *a priori*. (*KrV* B5)

This, of course, is exactly the same argument that Kant presents in even shorter form in the Transcendental Aesthetic to establish that space is a necessary representation (*KrV* A24/ B38–39) and a condition of the possibility of representing an object of experience in general.

It is important to note that the two highest material propositions adduced by Hoffmann and Crusius do not directly inform us as to which specific representations either must or cannot be combined in our representations; they are rather general meta-principles of philosophical method. Specific ontological principles and real definitions can only be discovered piecemeal through the carefully conducted analysis directed at specific representations. What the highest principles do ultimately is to guarantee and to give form to the method itself by validating the objective reality of the resultant concepts. One of the key differences between this method and that of Wolff thus lies in the fact that here the consciousness of the necessity of the ontological principles can only be grasped in the very moment of representing the actual content they are thought to govern. It is this emphasis on the absolute impossibility of actually separating or uniting in thought what nevertheless is not necessarily distinct or identical according to the principle of contradiction, that makes the difference between this and the method of Wolff. It is also important to notice that this same emphasis on the connection between the consciousness of necessity and the actual moment of representing is a chief feature of the method of metaphysics that Kant argues for in his *UD* of 1763, the same work in which he claims to share Crusius' general method.

With this basic outline of Hoffmann's and Crusius' philosophical method, let us turn specifically to their discussion of experience and the principles of its possibility.

§. 2.1. The Logic of Experience According to Hoffmann and Crusius

"Experience," writes Crusius, "is used in part to name a particular species of propositions, and in part to name the act or the drawing out of experience by means of which such [propositions] are reached" (Crusius 1965, §. 461). Experience in the former sense consists of propositions in which one *immediately* senses the connection between what are represented by the subject and the predicate, and depending upon whether the connection is sensed in inner or outer sense, these can be further divided into inner and outer experiences. To this extent, there does not seem to be a principled difference with Wolff. For, although Hoffmann and Crusius speak primarily of propositions and not judgments, a proposition is nothing other than the verbal expression of a judgment, which is itself a kind of mental act. And Hoffmann and Crusius also agree with Wolff that the entire stock of these immediate experiential propositions forms the foundation of all other knowledge.

The first real divergence comes when we ask about the content of these propositions or judgments. Hoffmann and Crusius argue that it is absolutely essential that we recognize a distinction between what they call "pure" or "mere experiences" and "mixed" experiences. Just like Wolff, they describe both as being immediate and intuitive, but also add that our immediate perceptual knowledge of things in *pure* experience is actually extremely restricted, indeed that it does not extend beyond what Hoffman calls knowledge according to or after existence (*der Existenz nach*), or what can be grasped in a proposition of external abstraction (*Satz der äusserlichen Abstraction*). What this essentially means is that all that is known immediately in the experience is that we are presented with objects (i.e. mere existences), and that these objects are related to one another according to the laws of spatial and temporal relation (i.e. externally). Crusius expresses this same idea by saying that when we form an immediate judgment of experience, all we are doing is taking the subject and predicate to be signs (*Zeichen*) of one another, or marking that in "certain circumstances certain representations arise in us" (Crusius 1965, §. 465). Because immediate propositions of experience relate two things externally, and not in virtue of their essences, Crusius draws from this the following conclusions: The subject and the predicate can be exchanged in such propositions without changing their content. Such propositions do not state anything regarding the objective reality of what we seem to perceive (Crusius 1965, §. 465). We cannot express a thing's non-existence through such a proposition. Such propositions concern individuals, and thus cannot be universal propositions and so also cannot express causal connections. Finally, if we observe these limitations, claims Crusius, then these immediate experiences possess their own kind of certainty, not a certainty immediately contained within them, but rather one which can be proven by reference to higher-order material principles in application to immediate experience.

In contrast to pure experiences, so-called "mixed experiences" consist of immediate propositions that are based upon pure experiences in combination with other higher and more general material principles. Such experiences not only mark the relation of two things in subjective perception, but also combine them in an essential and necessary way, i.e. objectively, and include claims regarding real existence (i.e. that our perceptions, even if only captured in pure experiences, are of real things), causal connections, powers, substance-attribute relations, and all similar coordinating and subordinating concepts found in traditional metaphysics and empirical science.

As I explained earlier, Hoffmann and Crusius propose to prove the specific material principles that underpin the possibility of mixed experience, and thus guarantee the certainty that the knowledge we draw from our perceptions has objective reality, by means of experiments carried out upon our representations themselves. Just as in Kant, experience consists for Hoffmann and Crusius in the complex unity of all the coordinating and subordinating principles mentioned above, and so the proof of the possibility of experience as a whole has several stages moving from the proof of the fact that our perceptions have a corresponding reality, to such facts as that the things we represent must be causally connected. A full elucidation of this series of proofs would require more space than I have here, so I will simply illustrate the basic strategy of the proofs through the following two condensed arguments:[42]

1) "When we sense something external to us, then such sensory ideas have an actually existing external object" (Hoffmann 2010, Vol. 1, §. 689): Sensations (*Empfindungen*), in their absolute immediacy, are nothing but inner states of the mind of which we are conscious. To think of them as representing an object, is firstly to think of them as signs or marks of an object's *existence*. This, however, means going beyond what is perceived, and thinking the sensations as necessarily related to something outside of themselves. This thought is a *judgment* in which sensations are connected with one another necessarily through their mutual relation to this outer object. However, consciousness of the necessity of a judgment requires consciousness of the real impossibility of thinking its opposite. Now, if we abstract from the existence of objects in themselves and the question as to how it is possible for them to affect us (neither of which are relevant to the problem as to how we can be aware of the necessary relation of the

---

[42] Proof of the causal principle, because of its complexity, requires separate treatment.

concepts through which we represent them), we are left only with the concept of *actual* sensations, which we essentially distinguish from those of memory or imagination through our connecting them with the idea that they do not arise from within us arbitrarily. Thus it becomes clear that it is impossible to think there is a *genuine* distinction between actual and imaginary sensations, if we do not also think of actual sensations as determined by an existing outer object. For to say that we merely *imagine* there to be such an object outside us, would be to say that there *really* is no distinction between thinking an object as truly outside our thoughts and our merely imagining that there is one. "In short, we could not have any concept at all of what one calls an *outer sense*, if objects did not affect the soul from outside" (Hoffmann 2010, Vol. 1, §. 689). Now since we do have such an idea, it is thus necessary to think that objects corresponding to our sensations really exist.

Put concisely, this argument states that if we deny that objects of some sort affect us from outside, then we cancel the real possibility of representing a sensation to ourselves as one that is *actual*. Thus it rests not on a necessity of non-contradiction as Wolff would like, but rather on a necessity grounded in the impossibility of our representing the real possibility of the opposite. To say that there is no real object underlying the sensations that we represent as actual, is not to state a contradiction, since there is no purely logical contradiction between representing sensations as actual and representing that there is no object underlying them. Yet we cannot *really* represent both to ourselves at the same time. Thus the concepts of actual sensation and an object outside of ourselves are linked together in the human mind, not by logical identity, but by a law such that the cancellation of the one entails necessarily the cancellation of the other.

2) "That and to what extent what we sense of objects agrees with the actual constitution of the object" (Hoffmann 2010, Vol. 1, §.690): Truth consists in the *agreement* of a thought with the object outside of the thought. But the object of perception is not itself another perception, and so the truth of the senses can only consist in their agreement with themselves, "that the same things are represented in the same way in unchanged circumstances." "Now, since similar causes bring about similar effects [...] in the same circumstances," which is a material principle that can be proven separately, "therefore the same objects, whenever they affect our senses in the same circumstances, must also bring forth the same perceptions. Accordingly, all our senses must agree with themselves; and therefore are not capable of being deceived" (Hoffmann 2010, Vol. 1, §. 690). Hoffmann thinks that when we say, for instance, that the grass is green, what this really means is that if we were at another time to look at the grass in the

same circumstances that we are in at that moment, then we would have the same perception of green. "Agreement with the object in general (*überhaupt*)" is thus nothing for us except the agreement of our perceptions among themselves (Hoffmann 2010, Vol. 1, §. 690). It is important to note that this proof rests on two separable parts, namely, on the observation that agreement with an object can only manifest itself in the necessary order of our perceptions, and on a higher-order material principle stating that perceptions must be regular, which rests on another series of proofs.

This pair of examples suffices, I think, to illustrate the significance and nature of the distinction between pure and mixed experiences. In view of my previous discussion, the point of this distinction is clear and although Hoffmann and Crusius avoid mentioning Wolff by name, the second of the two leaves no doubt about whom he takes to be his chief opponent. As he writes:

> The system of [some people] does not agree with itself, namely, that which speaks contemptuously of experience in theory, and which calls the unresolved concepts that the senses provide us confused concepts, and nevertheless in application holds clear experiences to be no less certain than the demonstrated abstract propositions; which they must also do in order to avoid being ridiculous. (Crusius 1965, §. 468)

The absurdity of Wolff's entire philosophical system, in Crusius' view, results from the fact that he has no clear concept of experience, particularly of the distinction between pure and mixed experiences. This stems from his failure to distinguish between the immediate content of experience, which is next to nothing, and what we must add to experience, or presuppose, for the sake of representing the objective reality in such immediate experiences. For Crusius, as for Kant, all certainty of experience, including the certainty that experience has an object or, what is the same, that our thoughts can have the intentional property of "aboutness," rests on principles that are not immediately given in the perceptions themselves but rather are added by the mind for the sake of immediate experience.

The entire contrast between the Wolffian and the Hoffmann-Crusius view of experience can therefore be summed up in this one point: For Wolff, judgments of experience are immediate and certain because they and the connections they describe are both directly caused by that same connection as it exists in the object itself. Furthermore, they are possible, because we possess the right cognitive capacities. For Hoffmann and Crusius, however, propositions of experience are immediate and certain because they describe relations of representations that cannot be further analyzed, and which are subsumed under principles without which any thought about an object would be impossible.

§. 2.2. The Possibility of Experience and the Limits of Human Knowledge

The differences between the Hoffmann-Crusius account of experience and Wolff's are subtle but decisive for assessing Kant's relation to the tradition. In both accounts there is discernable a circular and teleological relationship between experiences and the first abstract principles of human knowledge. Namely, both schools of thought construe the basic ontological principles as being the fundamental laws of the human mind of which we only gradually become aware through the reflective act of forming experiences. They thus both provide an explanation of the fact that our cognitive faculties possess an internal teleological structure that makes them reliable instruments of knowledge acquisition. And both accounts argue that, from another point of view, these same laws underwrite the objective reality and certainty of the experiences in which they are first developed and from which they are later abstracted through reflection. Unlike Wolff, however, Hoffmann and Crusius do not make use of the ontologically defined terms "beings" or "things" in their accounts, but rather speak merely of an "object," which is defined by them *relationally*, not absolutely, as "what is represented in a representation, and is distinct from the representation through which one thinks it" (Crusius 1965, §. 117). Underlying this relativized concept of an object are arguments purporting to show that the subjective possibility of the cognition of objects in general must be settled *prior to* ontology and special metaphysics, and that this requires us to recognize certain limits to what can be known by the human mind. Because of this profound change in outlook, Hoffmann and Crusius cannot rest their explanation of the possibility of experience on an ontological identity between perceptions and concepts of real beings as Wolff did. Rather, they must first explain how it is that perceptions, which they recognizes as initially being just subjective states of the mind, can come to represent something distinct from themselves in the first place, i.e. to represent an object, and furthermore what it is that guarantees this object's reality.

The fundamental propositions of human knowledge, as Hoffmann says, therefore "have only a *certitudinem* kat andropon, *seu relativam, non absolutam*," i.e. "a certainty of the human being, or relative, not absolute" (Hoffmann 2010, p. 609). All proofs of the objective reality of certain concepts are thus relative to the conditions of human representation, and may or may not be limited to this. Hence, while we cannot deny with unlimited certainty that what we regard as reality might not be different for another form of intellect, it is true to say that the necessity or objectivity of the objects of our experience flows naturally from the very essence of our kind of intellect. Or as Crusius writes: "The truth is the agreement of thoughts with the thing itself. There can be determined, however, no other natural characteristic mark of the truth than the essence of the understanding itself, or the possibility of thinking" (Crusius 1766, p. 80). From this limitation issues a fundamental principle of philosophical method, one which had already been essential to Christian Thomasius' criticisms of the Cartesian limitation of being to what can be clearly and distinctly conceived, namely, that we must always recognize the laws and limitations of our own thinking as among the essential premises of our knowledge, and thus admit that the limits of what we can rationally conceive are not necessarily the limits of what can be: "We must every one of us be mindful of our finitude (*Endlichkeit*), and thus not permit ourselves in our efforts at judging the truth to pass beyond the nature of finitude" (Crusius 1766, p. 81). As a positive rule of method, this means taking extreme care to frame our propositions precisely in accord with the specific context and limits with which the original analysis of it takes place. This is exactly the principle of method which Kant thought, circa 1763, as providing the solution to all the errors of traditional metaphysics, and which would later be transformed by him into transcendental idealism.

In concluding this section on Hoffmann and Crusius, I want to draw attention to three points. Firstly, it is clear that they, rather than Wolff, are the nearest source for Kant's judgments of perception, since they recognize that prior to subsuming perceptions under material principles and concepts, the objective order of our perceptions remains undetermined. Secondly, Hoffmann and Crusius were demonstratively the chief inspiration for Kant's theory of the categories, even if he departs in large measure from their precise results. This might seem to contradict what I said earlier about the importance of Wolff's logic for Kant's theory. However, although it was most likely the Wolffian textbooks, particularly that of Baumgarten, that Kant most deeply mined for specific concepts, it was certainly Crusius that first impressed upon him the importance of seeking out the source and unity of all ontological concepts in the first fundamental judgments made by the mind, and thus in the logical activities, i.e. acts of judgment, underlying the possibility of ontology in general. Thirdly, even if Hoffmann and Crusius do not reach the sophistication and precision that Kant believes is necessary in this regard, they clearly agree with him that the possibility of experience requires not only logical principles of empirical truth, but also principles underwriting the very possibility of relating perceptions to objects in general, and that this should lead us to a critical limitation of our knowledge claims.

§. 3. Anticipating Kant's Account of Experience

Earlier I observed that in the second half of the 1780s Kant turned increasingly to the question of experience to articulate his critical position, a time when he was being constantly assailed by requests for him to clarify how, if at all, he had taken an essential step beyond his predecessors. I believe that at this time Kant found focusing more directly on the question of experience provided him with three things he dearly needed at this time, namely: 1) a quick and powerful diagnosis of the errors made by his German predecessors, 2) a more natural way to introduce the problem of synthetic *a priori* judgments that would also make the immediate relevance of the critical enterprise to the practice of science more readily apparent, and 3) a way to show that cognition is limited to experience without invoking the complications of the transcendental deduction.

If my investigations have been on the mark, then we can see why these issues are connected. Kant's conception of experience is in fact built upon that of his so-called "dogmatic" predecessors and, because of this, it provides him with a direct point of contact and comparison. This allows Kant to argue that the origin of metaphysics in these thinkers actually arises naturally from a misunderstanding of the sort of principles that are genuinely required for certainty in experience. By this Kant is also able to claim continuity between his own concerns and those of Wolff and Crusius, for whom systematizing the practice of empirical science was a central motivation. As we will see more fully in the next chapter, from Kant's standpoint Wolff and Crusius also correctly observed that experience requires *a priori* principles to ground its certainty, but they both committed errors of subreption, i.e. they conflated the principles of experience with the principles of the things themselves. Wolff did so insofar as he took the certainty of experience to be an unlimited certainty and failed to recognize that space and time, as forms of sensibility, make a material contribution to cognition that is subjective and non-conceptual. Hoffmann's and Crusius' more careful analysis recognized that since the mind contributes something material to the content of knowledge, we cannot rest assured that the principles we make use of in experience are unlimited in applicability. However, in Kant's view they nevertheless failed to precisely determine the source of the necessity of these principles, because they did not recognize that this rests essentially on their relation to the conditions that make experience possible. As a result, they also failed to determine the exact limits of the use of these principles and so could not avoid falling into their own errors of subreption. This is not to say that they took human reason to have an unlimited certainty, as did Wolff, but rather that they failed to precisely locate the genuine boundary of knowledge, and, as a result, took some principles as applying too generally (i.e. in their argument that all objects whatsoever must be in some place and some time) and others as not applying generally enough.

This historical background sheds considerable light on Kant's own solution, which will be to argue that the necessity of the *a priori* principles can only be proven on the condition that all our experience requires the agreement of *both* sensibility *and* understanding in one cognition; and, thus, that the true source of the necessity of such principles is that they are required merely for the possibility of the kind of experience in which these conditions must be combined, and, as a result, are limited to it. For Kant, the question is no longer whether the perceptions do or do not already contain conceptual content suitable to being known. Both options have been fully explored by his predecessors and since found untenable, because they cannot provide a consistent account of both the necessary and the synthetic features of the basic principles of empirical knowledge. Instead, Kant will initiate an entirely new approach by focusing on the modal structure of judgments of experience, particularly on the teleological conception of hypothetical necessity.[43] Reduced to essentials, his master argument as I see it runs as follows[44]:

1) The *telos* of the cognitive faculty is knowledge. Knowledge consists of judgments of experience, i.e. judgments through which perceptions (which are given) are subsumed under concepts and thereby related to an object. The *telos* or intentional point of unity of any cognitive judgment (which is a type of *action*) is the object itself.

2) In order for such judgments about the relations of our perceptions to be justified or objective (i.e. to be knowledge), it must be presupposed that the objects underlying the perceptions contain objectively the connections described by our judgments.

3) However, not all judgments are true; some are false. But in order for knowledge to even be possible, judgments must at least be susceptible of being either true or false, and for this we must at the very least presuppose that the most basic forms of conceptual unity that human beings make use of adequately capture the types of connections that may be found in the objects underlying our perceptions. Consequently, if there are some most basic forms of which we make use in forming *any judgment about objects whatever*, then it must be presupposed that these concepts capture connections that are present in *absolutely all objects with which we may be presented* (cf. KrV A221–222/ B269).

---

[43] The teleological concept of hypothetical necessity, or necessity for the sake of an end, is laid out in Aristotle 1970, Bk. 5, Ch. 5, 1015a20–1015b15 and Aristotle 1968, Bk. 2, Ch. 9, 199b33–200b10.

[44] I have been developing this teleological interpretation of the transcendental deduction independently for several years. I have found similar ideas in the following works: Dörflinger 2000, Rosales 1989, and Rosenberg 2005.

4) Whether this is *truly, really,* or *absolutely* the case is an otiose question; it would require us to step outside of the conscious process of judging and to take a sideways view of the cognitive process, something we clearly cannot do.
5) Judgments, however, are *acts* of a self-conscious "I." Thus, for a self-consciousness involved in such an act, it is necessary *specifically for the sake of* the possibility of knowledge – that is, *hypothetically* necessary – to *consciously presuppose* that whatever presents itself to us can be captured by our most basic forms of conceptual unity.
6) Things are not just given absolutely; they are given through perceptions, which have as their condition two basic forms, space and time. Consequently, because whatever presents itself must be susceptible to such basic forms, and things are hence only given as clothed in those forms, it follows that for the sake of knowledge such a self-consciousness must again presuppose that space and time and whatever is presented by means of them can in principle be captured by these basic forms of conceptual unity.
7) This analysis is capable of claiming not just subjective, but also objective validity, for two reasons:
   a) because of the unique fact that these forms have a pure origin in reason alone, and thus neither correspond to anything in objects themselves, nor does the critical position claim that they do so;
   b) because from the standpoint of any human "I," the unity provided by these forms is really the only thing that can be meant by "relating to an object in general" within a theoretical context.

Do the perceptions already contain all the conceptual content we derive from them as Wolff would maintain? For the sake of knowledge in experience, we must presuppose this absolutely to be the case, for the very assertion of this fact is already contained within any judgment that (whether rightly or wrongly) makes a claim to objectivity. We are furthermore justified in making this assertion because it has only to do with the relation, not to objects absolutely, but to those that may be presented to us in our own finite form of consciousness. Nevertheless, it remains true that without reference to the possibility of knowledge, which as Hoffmann and Crusius held is based specifically in the nature of *human* reason, there is no ground for the necessity of any claim whatever regarding this.

It is a further sign of the fruitfulness of this approach, that interpreting Kant against this historical background also sheds light on what his answer would be to the question of non-conceptual content, which has generated much interest in recent literature.⁴⁵ According to Kant, any content of intuitions that would be non-conceptual would still have to be somehow expressible in concepts, because having such content is tantamount from a critical vantage point to our being able to make judgments about the contents of our intuitions, namely, that they contain some specifiable non-conceptual content. Therefore, that intuitions should contain some non-conceptual content is tantamount to our being justified – *for the sake of knowledge, i.e. for making judgments that would be about objects* – in presupposing either that some content is present in intuition prior to the introduction of concepts, which yet can be captured subsequently by concepts, or that there is some content present that can be captured *only in part* or perhaps indicated (otherwise it would be nothing to us, as Kant would say), but *not fully* captured by the subsequent application of concepts. These two possibilities, however, amount to the same thing, because the latter can only be indicated by the judgment that there is possible an indeterminately infinite series of related judgments regarding the contents of intuition, which is just to say that the content of each further judgment precedes, though in another way (i.e. serially), but still can be captured by, the concepts of which such judgments subsequently makes use. But that there is a content present *before* (logically, not necessarily temporally) the actual application of our concepts, which can also in principle be captured by our concepts, is exactly what is necessarily presupposed for the sake of experience, i.e. for our being able to regard our judgments as objective. However, to question further whether intuition *transcendentally considered* includes some non-conceptual content independently of any connection to the understanding, perhaps by reference to some supposed "objective facts" about the structure of self-consciousness or to an object in itself underlying them, and thus also independently of any reference to the possibility of knowledge, is therefore to slip into a confused and pre-critical frame of mind.⁴⁶

---

45 The literature on non-conceptual content is massive, as is the literature on Kant's understanding of the issue. For further references, see Hanna 2006, esp. Ch. 2. For insightful discussions of what Kant would say regarding this issue, see also McDowell 2009 and Longuenesse 1998.

46 I agree that the experience of the excessive and serial character of judgments regarding intuition (that they never seem to exhaust it) indicates something essentially different is present there, as does the differing structure of intuitional and conceptual forms. But Kant himself explains that this is an illusion created by the intentional structure of the understanding in its determination of sensibility (*KU* 05:362–366).

Conclusion: The Nature of Kant's Advance

I have argued that Kant's critical turn did not come about through a single sudden insight, but rather emerged over time as the only possible synthesis of a number of related philosophical considerations, all of which were tied directly or indirectly to fundamentally teleological issues. Thus at the heart of my thesis in this work lies an account of Kant's motivations for transmuting the teleological dimension of previous dogmatic systems, and indeed, the teleological dimension of his own pre-critical system, into a critical and transcendental theory of the purposive ground-structure of human reason. Furthermore, in the present chapter in particular, I have fleshed out and sharpened this picture by showing how the tension between the metaphysical teleology underpinning Wolff's account of experience and the subjective-practical teleology underpinning Hoffmann's and Crusius' set the stage for Kant's critical reinterpretation of a dogmatically teleological conception of knowledge as being in fact the dynamic and normative *transcendental* structure of human rationality. Rather than being based upon a metaphysical teleology according to which objects and the mind are in some manner structured so as to make the actual development of knowledge possible, Kant argues that reason both must presuppose and has the right to presuppose such fitness for the sake of its own employment. The details of this turn from a metaphysical or psychological guarantee for our cognitive faculties to a transcendental guarantee will be the topic of the next two chapters.

Chapter 4 Teleology in the Transcendental Aesthetic and Analytic

> A project offering a theory of the understanding as teleological must surely lead us to the core of Kant's philosophy, in particular, to the centre of his [transcendental] Deduction. (Dörflinger 1995, p. 813)

> That I am conscious of myself is a thought that already contains a twofold self, the self as subject and the self as object. How it should be possible that I, who think, can be an object (of intuition) to myself, and thus distinguish myself from myself, is absolutely impossible to explain, although it is an undoubted fact; it demonstrates, however, a power far superior to all sensory intuition, that as ground of the possibility of the understanding it has as its consequence a total separation from the beasts, to whom we have no reason to attribute the power to say "I" to oneself, and looks out upon an infinity of self-made representations and concepts. (*FM* 20:270)

> Plato, no less a mathematician than he was a philosopher, admired among the properties of certain geometrical figures, e.g., the circle, all sorts of purposiveness, i.e., fitness to resolve a multiplicity of problems, or multiplicity in resolving one and the same problem [...], from a principle, just as if the requirements for constructing certain quantitative concepts were laid down in them on purpose, although they can be grasped and demonstrated as necessary *a priori*. But purposiveness is thinkable only through relation of the object to an understanding, as its cause. [...] In all of these inferences, Plato at least proceeds consistently. Before him there undoubtedly hovered, albeit obscurely, the question that has only lately achieved clear expression: "How are synthetic propositions possible *a priori*?" (*VAVT* 08:391 and note)

Introduction

In the previous chapters, I have outlined the roots of Kant's teleology of reason, its general structural features, and indicated some of the motivations for its adoption as a way of articulating the unity of the his pre-critical and critical philosophies. In the Chapter 3 in particular, I explained further how Kant's conception of experience emerges from the rich soil of the debate between Wolff and Crusius on the nature and justification of the metaphysical principles of empirical experience, and I proleptically indicated how Kant's critical solution to the same problem rests on a reinterpretation of traditional teleological structures.

In this and the next chapter, I will attempt to describe the underlying teleological structure of the *KrV*. My chief goal is to indicate in the clearest and broadest way possible where the teleological structures I've pointed to in earlier chapters can be located in its basic argument. It is not my intention to provide a complete commentary on the body of this work. Since my investigations in the previous chapter provide a general outline of the sort of interpretation I will be giving, this goal should be possible to achieve without considering all the complications that necessarily arise from a detailed investigation into this most difficult of texts. Some attention to detail, however, will prove indispensable as we proceed.

§. 1. The Problem of the "Critique": How are Synthetic Judgments *a priori* Possible?

As I noted in the last chapter, Kant increasingly turned from the question of the possibility of synthetic *a priori* judgments to the problem of experience in framing the project of transcendental philosophy. Still, it would seem that taking either path will lead in the same general direction. If we begin with experience, we will find first that it requires transcendental principles for its possibility, and secondly that the principles of judgment contained in this transcendental doctrine themselves gain their entire universality and necessity because they answer to this need. Beginning with synthetic judgments *a priori*, by contrast, requires a more circuitous path, since traditional metaphysics presumes to make such judgments about objects that by their very nature lead us beyond the boundaries of possible experience. Here, therefore, it is necessary first for Kant to enumerate all the possible objects that reason might be concerned with, to show what sort of knowledge previous metaphysical judgments regarding them were intended to deliver, and then to undertake an investigation of the actual elements of our knowledge, resulting finally in a decision as to whether or not these elements are of such a kind as allow of being combined to form various kinds of synthetic knowledge *a priori*. If Kant is correct, then we should find the answer to be that a certain class of synthetic judgments *a priori*, namely those that are employed exclusively for the sake of experience, are indeed possible, while another class, namely those presumably enabling us to make judgments about objects in abstraction from sensible experience, turn out to be nugatory. In short, taking up the question of experience allows Kant to avoid entering into the extreme detail of the sort of exhaustive investigation into the structure of reason that would be required for answering the question of synthetic judgments *a priori*, but only the latter kind of investigation can totally fulfill the critical and positive function essential to critique. This is partly because, as we will see, transcendental critique has not only the function of limiting reason's theoretical pretensions, but also of providing a preliminary transcendental sketch of all possible supersensible objects, i.e. ideas, so that these can later be employed by pure reason in its practical function.

These two paths also lead into an analysis of the same inner teleological structure of theoretical reason itself, but from different points of view. The regression from actual knowledge, i.e. from experience, to its grounds, proceeds from consequences to causes, and as such does not necessitate a preliminary analysis of the faculty of knowledge or of the necessity and possibility of just such cognitions arising from it. It moves from the necessity found in certain *actual* judgments that we accept to be statements of knowledge, and the unity of thought contained in these, to the grounds which first make such a necessary unity possible. If, as it turns out, this necessary unity is that of a transcendental perfection and affinity of the matter of sensation that grounds the complete systematic unity of these sensations in relation to an object in general, then the grounds discovered by such an analytical regression will naturally have to explain this possibility. Yet we will not by this be able to show the elements from which it first arises. Such an analysis will also have nothing to say to the objection that the regression presupposes that we in fact possess such knowledge.

By comparison, the question of synthetic judgments *a priori* must begin with an entirely different kind of analysis, namely an analysis of the very essence of the faculty of cognition insofar as it is the *ground from which arises all possible cognition*. It will thus proceed not in a single regressive move from actual knowledge to its grounds, but rather through two stages which move progressively from causes to effects: First, it will have to isolate and establish the most basic elements that belong to the human faculty for knowledge. The drawing of divisions between basic faculties and capacities will be carried out with an eye to the manner in which knowledge has actually been produced, but only insofar as it is possible to determine from this the *universal*, *original* and *pure idea* of the faculty or capacity of which any particular judgment is but an individual act. Each isolated faculty or capacity must for this purpose be examined analytically, thus regressively, in order to isolate the basic and characteristic laws according to which they first produce representations, but then also synthetically or architectonically to see how the products first arise from these grounds. The goal here is to explain why in respect to such faculties and capacities the laws governing their production of representations are necessary and universal. As we will see in what follows, Kant argues that such necessity and universality can only be possible if the concepts and laws governing a certain capacity or faculty of reason provides the conscious or potentially conscious condition of possibility for having a certain kind of representation at all, and if in this respect the mind is also completely undetermined by external limitations and thus stands only under its own laws.

This first stage must then be complimented by a second stage in which it is shown that these initially isolated faculties and capacities belong to a more original whole defined by a more encompassing *telos*. Intuition, for instance, might be isolated in the Transcendental Aesthetic, but this very isolation is shown in later parts of the work to in fact rest on an even deeper unity and harmony among the other faculties of cognition with which it must cooperate in order to bring about the whole edifice of possible knowledge. Not only is it the case that intuitive judgments in fact require the logical use of the understanding, but indeed the Deduction reveals that in their own independent character, the forms of intuition stand in an essential harmony and unity with the understanding itself, and that this harmony alone is the ground of their being objectively united in one function, namely, the purposive generation of experience.

As we will find in what follows, Kant argues that there is in fact a necessary and universal unity of *intuitions*, of *thoughts* and of *experiences*. Such unity as we will also see is not in these cases a general or abstract unity, but rather an absolute and genuinely universal unity, i.e. a unity in which the manifold embraced by such a representation can only be captured *teleologically* by Kant's unique theory of the *idea*, a key feature of which is that the whole must always be thought as a condition of the possibility of the part. Such unity is found, again, in two areas: The unity expressed in individual judgments taken *distributively* (treated in the Analytic), and the unity expressed in the systematic unity of all judgments regarding such objects taken *collectively* (treated in the Dialectic). The correctness of such an analysis, as I pointed out in Chapter 1 and will more fully spell out in Chapter 8, must be judged in the manner of an experiment. That is to say, the initial division will only be confirmed by the fact that by consciously following it up and adopting it in our own minds as the guide to the use of our own reason, the manifold capacities and faculties composing sensibility, understanding and reason, and of which we are all the while making use, all come to cohere into a maximally unified and purposive whole. Likewise, the incorrectness of a certain division or principle will have to be judged from the fact that it conflicts with the perfect harmony of reason with itself and hinders it from extending its powers to the greatest possible sphere.

In view of what was shown in Chapters 1 and 2, it is also important to note that Kant's focus on the possibility of synthetic judgments *a priori* can now be seen more clearly to be a natural consequence of his pre-critical metaphysics. For it is evident that the very possibility of asking the question *How are synthetic judgments a priori possible?* first requires the insight that there even exit necessary and universal truths which are not purely analytic (or which can be captured analytically, but only on the presupposition of a given synthetic ground). In the pre-critical period, as we saw, it was what Kant called the "real contingency" of precisely these same necessary truths that was both grounded in, and required by, his desire to develop an image of all things as absolutely dependent, thus *even in regard to their possibility*, on the nature and will of God. Neither Hume nor Wolff, for instance, could have arrived at this question, because they both take such necessary truths as Kant has in mind either to be not objectively necessary, or else to be reducible to analytic truths requiring no further ground. If we set Crusius aside, then Kant alone is in a position to ask for an *explanation* or *ground* as to why necessary truths are necessary, and why the real essences of things are constituted in such a way that harmony and unity abounds in the whole of nature. This is precisely the point later made by Kant in his comments on Plato's theory of ideas, which I quoted at the head of this chapter. In a related way, in the pre-critical period Kant sees these same necessary but also non-analytic truths as the foundation for the fact that nature necessarily gives rise to unity in all its operations, and of our certainty that all things must necessarily combine into a systematic whole of the greatest teleological unity and perfection. The real contingency of essences, in other words, makes it such that the necessary unity and perfection (which for Kant are the most original forms of purposiveness) found in things must have their source in the very same ground from which things first originate in regard to *both existence and essence*. In the critical period, as we will see, the rules according to which even nature itself – as an object of experience – is seen as necessarily combining into just such a unity in regard to the object of experience in general, is traceable back to the same ground as that from which synthetic *a priori* truths derive (here, however, it is original-synthetic apperception).

In view of this, I submit that if Kant had never sought to develop such a teleological interpretation of the relation between God and creation, then he could never have reached the fundamental view that even mathematical truths require an original and absolute synthetic ground of unity. And without this, he could never have arrived at the question underlying the first *Critique*, nor could he have envisioned the precise path to its solution that he in fact offers.

§. 1.1. The Need for Synthetic Judgments *a priori* and the Structure of Knowledge

Many of the most serious misinterpretations of Kant's *KrV* can be avoided if we have before us from the beginning a clear outline, as far as this is possible, of the processes and structures that he regards as operative in knowledge of an everyday sort. The power of such an approach to illuminate some of the darkest regions of Kant's text has been demonstrated forcefully by Béatrice Longuenesse. In her important book, *Kant and the Capacity to Judge*, she focuses on the teleological concept of a *faculty* of judgment to show the unity of Kant's approach to the foundations of knowledge. One of her chief claims is that the guide to understanding this faculty lies in what Kant refers to as the "logical use of the understanding." In particular, she writes that the argument of the first *Critique* in this regard can be summarized as follows:

> Consider the forms of the analysis of what is given in sensibility (the forms of "comparison, abstraction, reflection" – the logical forms of judgment) and you will have the key to the forms of the *synthesis that must occur prior to analysis*, namely the synthesis required for the sensible representation of the x's that can be reflected under concepts according to the logical forms of our judgments. Consequently, you will also have the key to the meaning and role of the categories, concepts that "universally represent" the different forms of this synthesis. (Longuenesse 1998, p. 11)

It is clear that Kant already had arrived at this theory of the relation of the logical use of the understanding to the formal principles of the matter of cognition in *DfS* and the *MSI*. In those texts it was clear that Kant regarded the logical use of reason – which operates using merely the logical rules of judgment and syllogism – as universally applicable in all science, but most particularly as that use of the understanding through which *appearance* is converted into *experience*. Indeed, several reflections from Kant's *Nachlass* show that when he first began to construct a catalogue of the categories, he referred to them as the basic *concepts of all analysis*. What he clearly meant by this is that analysis determines the objects of thought precisely through the application of these categories in its judgments reached by analysis. The process of analysis, in other words, is that general activity through which we first generate for ourselves a unified and interconnected whole of cognition.

This explains why throughout the *KrV* Kant takes the logical use of the understanding as the "guiding clue" to the pure concepts of understanding and reason. Kant clearly directs the search for formal principles of the matter of cognition precisely to those principles which in his pre-critical metaphysical system were seen as governing the order and connection of all things in the whole of creation. Thus, as Lambert had suggested in his important letter of February 3, 1766, Kant undertakes the discovery and collection of all the basic concepts and principles that would be required to come to a completely connected knowledge of just such a world-whole. Recognizing that such concepts and principles as govern the entirety of material knowledge are the same concepts and principles that must be presupposed and applied by the logical use of the understanding in order to produce knowledge of such material through analysis, Kant came to see the parallel between the most basic concepts and principles of analysis and the first concepts and principles of synthesis. In this way, I believe, Kant came to reorganize and extend the functions to be included in the logical use of the understanding (and reason) such that they would together be *sufficient* to account for the production of the knowledge of a completely determined world-whole. At the same time, he realized that because the entire *purpose* of reason in its theoretical employment is the generation of such a whole of experience by means of analysis, this same reorganized and extended picture of the logical use of the understanding provides the proper point of purposive unity (i.e. viewed as a whole through relation to its function in bringing about a product of a certain unitary form) from which the concepts and principles of synthesis could be completely derived in their systematic relation.

This picture further suggests that a proper understanding of the teleological structure of reason cannot be reached if one does not have a clear understanding of the procedures according to which Kant thinks scientific cognition is actually produced. For the transcendental "fitness" of our cognitive capacities for making possible theoretical reason's essential end, namely the production of a complete system of knowledge, or "experience," is precisely the basis for the deduction of the categories and ideas as conditions of the possibility of reaching this specific *telos*. However, producing such a general picture of the process for acquiring empirical knowledge is not an easy task, since Kant scatters his views on the actual mechanics of scientific method throughout his chief works (perhaps because he takes them to be self-evident, or as easily culled from the logic textbooks), and it is also not a trivial matter to collect this from his writings on logic. Still, the importance of this point requires at least a general attempt.

It seems evident that on Kant's view everyday knowledge in its ideal extension would constitute a system of concepts completely adequate to capturing the structure of the empirical world. Moreover, as concepts are nothing for Kant but rules or functions of unity in our experience, i.e. general and unchanging representations that express the abiding formal unity governing the ceaseless flow of physical processes (or, better, perceptions), this system of concepts would be at the same time a complete system of the laws governing nature as a whole. By reference to such a system, therefore, everything that happens in the world would be seen as happening necessarily from previously cognized grounds, because, assuming the system were completely adequate and thus completely explanatory, then the particular empirical event would have to be nothing but the required exponent of this complete system of rules at a given moment.

The completeness of such a system would have three main aspects. First, it would require a complete stock of all possible concepts of objects that might be given. Secondly, it would require the hierarchical combination of these concepts, through coordination and subordination, into an absolute unity resting on absolutely first principles. In our actual research into nature this ideal of a complete system of knowledge would serve as our essential and guiding end; we would begin by sketching out possible sensed objects in their spatial and temporal relations, and continue by drawing out as many of the virtually infinite number of necessary consequences of these relations as is possible; we would next compare, reflect and abstract our perceptions with the aim of forming judgments, bringing the perceptions under concepts of objects and discovering empirical rules relating them; finally, we would continuously pour over these same objects and rules with the aim of combining them into an indeterminately large, but systematically unified, whole.

If we look at this single purposive activity from the standpoint of the mind from which it arises, we can see that it presupposes the existence and coordination of several component knowledge-seeking activities. First, a capacity (*Fähigkeit*) for sensible intuition is required by the fact that a real object can only be given to the mind from outside, and thus through receptivity (*KrV* A19/ B33). Secondly, a faculty of judging (*Vermögen zu Urtheilen*) the objects and their relations as these are presented in sensation is presupposed for the possibility of bringing the perceptions under concepts, and concepts under each other. This faculty of judging in particular performs at least two functions. First, since all knowledge begins with the senses, this faculty must be able to form what Kant refers to as "judgments of perception" (*Wahrnehmungsurtheile*), or judgments that express merely the subjective appearance of what is presented in perception. Secondly, this same faculty must be capable of forming from judgments of perception, other judgments that make a claim to being about an objective state of affairs, which judgments Kant calls "judgments of experience" (*Erfahrungsurtheile*). As Kant explains, the key to the "aboutness" of these judgments, i.e. their very ability to at least intend to capture more than the merely subjective appearance in our inner consciousness of sensibility, lies in the fact that they connect the subject and the predicate in the judgment by virtue of a special set of concepts which makes the order of the combination necessary, namely, the categories. Obviously more must be said about these categories and their ability to convert a subjective judgment into an objective one, but at the moment I only want to point out that it is the presence of these special concepts in a judgment that makes it possible for a judgment to even *intend* to express an objective state of affairs. Their presence, therefore, makes a judgment for the first time *susceptible* to having a truth value at all, i.e. to being susceptible to either truth or falsity.

Now, it seems clear that empirical judgments that make use of categories are not for that reason necessarily true. They merely intend to express objective states of affairs, and if it turns out that they do not cohere with our further experience of an object they can be rejected as false. Nevertheless, all knowledge must be based upon a stock of judgments of experience, what Wolff referred to as *Grund-urtheile*, or fundamental judgments of experience; for these provide the understanding with all its basic materials for working up a cognition of things.

Thus the first such judgments of experience will be what Kant refers to in his logic lectures as "provisional judgments," i.e. judgments that intend something true but yet are not determined in regard to their actual truth or falsity. If I understand Kant correctly, then these first judgments will fall into two distinct types, namely: 1) intuitive judgments that we recognize to be universal and necessary, and thus certain, 2) and empirical judgments whose truth remains uncertain. The former comprise all judgments regarding the necessary relations of things insofar as they are spatiotemporal entities of a certain shape or form. These provisional judgments by their nature already are judgments of experience, because they are in fact generated in accordance with the category. Notably, although the objective certainty of these intuitive judgments is immediately recognized in intuition itself, their specific applicability to any given object of experience is a judgment of the second type. E.g. it is intuitively certain that if the tower is circular, then there will be a central axis from which the distance to all the sides will be more or less equal, but that the tower is circular in the first place is something that is not intuitively certain.

If we further reflect on these other non-mathematical provisional judgments we will in Kant's view notice something very peculiar. Although they are not immediately certain when considered individually, whether true or false they each still presuppose a certain set of principles by the very fact that they *intend truth*, or insofar as they are purportedly about objects. To see this we must look more closely at the structure of a judgment of experience. Every judgment in Kant's view expresses a connection between concepts. For instance, in the categorical judgment "S is P," S is said to be connected to P by virtue of identity. Now, judgments in Kant's view are of two basic types, namely analytic and synthetic. In an analytic judgment the connection expressed in the judgment is true by virtue of the fact that P is part of the concept of S, and can be extracted from it by the law of identity. In a synthetic judgment, by contrast, P is not a part of the concept S, nor is S a full-blown concept by itself. Rather, S is itself a "partial concept" used to refer to some otherwise unknown object X. The ground of the truth of the judgment "S is P" in this case lies in the fact that the object signified by the partial concept S can also be signified by the partial concept P. If "S is P" is true, then it is not because S is part of P or because we have perceived S to be P, but rather because *S is P*, i.e. S and P are thought as combined in the object itself, *and this is the reason for our experiencing them as connected*. This connection is, naturally, a teleological one; for the ground of the judgment itself is, at least in intention, that which the judgment itself first allows us to explicitly recognize and represent. It is this inner teleological character that makes it suitable to think of such judgments as either succeeding or failing to fulfil their proper goal, thus being either true or false. The teleological relation is thus one of the fitness of our representations to representing the object that is thought to be their cause. To draw again on Taylor's formula, in theoretical cognition the order thought as belonging to the object is at the same time thought of as being the cause of the order through which it is represented to us.

Now all judgments of experience are synthetic judgments, because the concepts connected therein are connected by reference to something given aside from the concepts themselves, namely the experience of their combination. The truth or falsity of such judgments will therefore have to be shown by reference precisely to this experience. But what else is there to validate a judgment than the original experience from which it arose? If I form the provisional judgment *The sun is warming the rock*, because of certain appearances that flit before my consciousness, what could possibly serve for proving this to be more than a subjective connection within my consciousness? Kant's answer is that there can be no other criteria of truth or falsity than the coherence of this judgment with all other judgments generated through experience (cf. *KrV* A57–59/B82–84, A651/B679). Thus, in order to determine the truth or falsity of a given provisional judgment we must be able to compare it with other similar judgments. But in order to do this, it seems that we must already be in possession of higher-order principles of reflection through which provisional judgments can be tested by comparison with other provisional judgments and indeed with the whole scope of a possible cognition in general. As these principles will be called upon as a standard for testing absolutely all provisional judgments regarding objects of experience, it is clear that to be of any use these higher-order principles, as standards for the comparison by which experience is first generated, must be true *a priori*. What is more, leaving aside for the moment the specific truth or falsity of a particular provisional judgment, it should be clear that a judgment must also at the very least – so that it can be subsumed under such higher-order principles and thus be susceptible to being tested at all – possess the specific *form* required for it to possibly fit into any whole of experience of whatever kind. Having such a form can be understood as the bare minimum required for a provisional judgment to be *susceptible* to being tested for truth or falsity by reference to the remainder of experience, and by means of some set of higher-order principles of comparison.

With this we have reached the conclusion that the objective reality (this is Kant's term for "susceptibility to truth or falsity") in empirical cognition requires two things: 1) that there be a form the possession of which makes a provisional judgment a possible term for comparison, and 2) that there must be higher-order principles governing the manner of comparison, and that both must be available *a priori* if they are to make all other *a posteriori* cognition possible. These forms, as one should expect, are nothing other than the categories of understanding, the application of which allows us to form provisional judgments of experience from purely subjective judgments of perception. The principles, however, are of two distinct kinds. The first kind consist of nothing other than those principles of pure understanding, which provide the laws to which *perceptions* must cohere in order to fit into a whole of possible experience. The second kind consist of those principles according to which the manifold of *empirical laws arrived at by the understanding* can be composed into a complete systematic whole of all cognition.

On the basis of these reflections, it is now possible to see that Kant conceives the order through which knowledge is generated to be the following: Firstly, we form judgments of perception, which are merely subjective descriptions of the order of perceptions as these are marked in consciousness. Secondly, by means of judgment we apply the categories to such perceptions in order to formulate provisional judgments. Such judgments, Kant says, have the form of assertions, but they are in fact merely problematic. They are "only thought of as an arbitrary judgment that is possible that someone might assume" (*KrV* A75/B100). "Thus such judgments," Kant explains, "can be obviously false and yet, if taken problematically, conditions of the cognition of truth" (*KrV* A75/B101). They can serve this function precisely because they make a beginning of cognition, and even if they turn out to be incompatible with experience, they still help to mark out the true path. For instance, if we form the judgment *The sun is warming the stone*, and subsequent empirical investigation turns out to prove this false, then we have arrived at the truth of its opposite, namely *The sun is not warming the stone*.

Thirdly, then, after having formed an initial stock of preliminary judgments it is required that we now proceed to reflect upon their relations. Thus begins the logical employment of the understanding which Kant describes in his lectures on logic as consisting of reflection, comparison and abstraction. Guiding this process are several rules, which can be reflectively abstracted from our own process of reasoning. For instance, if we have previously formulated the provisional judgment *The sun is warming the stone* by the application of the category of causality, then this can only be tested if we keep in mind the *a priori* principle that everything that happens must be connected to something preceding it in time by means of a law (the principle of causality). For if we had no *a priori* knowledge of such a general rule, then clearly there would be no rational ground for thinking that another experience of a stone in the presence of the sun should be followed by the observation of the stone's warming. Similarly, without this principle we could not rationally make use of even the simplest experimental reasoning to reach other truths. For instance, say that we form the same provisional judgment, but then find that even with the removal of the sun the rock continues to warm, and then at another moment when the sun is shining on it the rock begins to cool. By means of the principle of causality, the provisional judgment *The sun is warming the rock* came to have the objective meaning that the shining of the sun on the rock must be followed in a law-like fashion with the warming of the rock. But this does not agree with our subsequent provisional judgments. The only judgment that agrees with all these judgments is *The sun is not warming the stone, but something else is warming it.* This judgment is thus more justified than the first. Yet, as natural as this conclusion is, it only flows from the previous ones, and bears some relation of justification to them, because of the *a priori* rule of causality. For since we know by means of the latter that something called "cause" must precede the warming of the stone in a regular fashion, and the sun does not, it follows that something other than the sun must be the cause of the stone's warming.[1]

Again, consider the case where we form a series of provisional judgments all agreeing in that the sun is the cause of the rock's warming. This naturally agrees with the truth of the judgment that the sun is indeed warming the rock, but it does not render this judgment necessary. In order to do this, it must be possible to eliminate all other possible causes of the rock's warming. This is done, as far as is possible, by observing that the rock warms if and only if the sun is shining on it. To do this we must form provisional judgments in cases where the sun is not shining, and where everything else is removed but the sun. If, in this way, it can be shown that nothing aside from the sun stands in a regular relation with the warming of the rock, then *because something must precede the rock's warming in a regular relation*, it can be concluded that the shining of the sun is that event which must precede the stone's warming in a regular fashion. This, of course, amounts to *It is necessary that the shining of the sun be followed by the warming of the rock,* i.e. it is true that *The sun is the cause of the stone's warming.*

Experimentation, which is nothing but a skillful and purposive form of experience in the search for truth, thus rests for its possibility on principles which in turn make possible the interconnection of provisional judgments in such a way that they can be seen as standing in relations of conflict and agreement, and can thus form webs of justification. By their means the understanding is able to reflect upon, compare and abstract, thereby forming general empirical rules and so also experiences.

---

[1] The pattern of reasoning is this: *A priori* rule: Something must cause the rock's warming, i.e. something preceding the warming must stand to it in a regular relation. Provisional judgment: The sun is causing the rock's warming. Provisional Judgment: The sun is not the cause of the rock's warming. First conclusion: The rock is warmed, but it cannot be caused by the sun. Second conclusion: Something other than the sun is warming the rock.

Integral to this process, of course, is the function of comparing and relating the empirical rules discovered in such experiments in order to determine both their truth and their interconnection. For this to be possible, however, there is required what Kant refers to in the Dialectic as the "hypothetical use of reason" (*KrV* A647/B675). In this function, judgment, guided by principles of reason, searches inductively and by analogy for the higher grounds from which the empirical rules might derive, and from which they would in principle draw their status of being not only general rules, but also necessary ones, i.e. laws. The composition of this web of justification through comparison and subordination is a third function served by judgment in addition to the two mentioned earlier. It also, as we will see further below, requires its own underlying principles deriving from pure reason, principles which describe the essential and singular form of any possible totality of human cognition.

In describing these empirical structures of the knowing mind, I have referred to them throughout as purposive because they are actions of the mind that converge in and have their point of unity in an intentional object. However, while it is true that Kant thought of them as purposive in their actual use, this is not what constitutes the teleological structure of knowledge on the most fundamental level. The actual use of intuition, understanding and reason in regard to experience can be purposive in the first place, as we will see, because these faculties find themselves operating within a field of experience that is already *transcendentally* prepared for their purposive application. The transcendental principles, therefore, which account for and constitute this preparation, are teleological in a fundamentally deeper sense; their essential purposiveness consists in their *originally* making possible and necessary any and all purposive use of these capacities and faculties. They constitute, in other words, the transcendental intentionality that makes possible all objectivity whatever, or, what is the same, that makes possible the internal and justified normative structure of these faculties and capacities. Kant famously remarks that we cannot find anything in experience that we have not already placed there; the finding, which is clearly a purposive activity, is thus in turn grounded upon a radically more perfect *teleological activity* that consists in an absolutely original and universal *placing-of-objects-before-us-in-general*. The mind does not produce the objects of experience, but it does produce the field of possible objectivity in all its pregnant determinacy, which makes it possible for the mind to be certain of the "fitness" between its faculties and their objects as if it were in some sense the creator of them. This very placing-of-things-before-us-in-general is teleological in a well-defined and easily understood sense: Experience is the actual product of our cognitive capacities, but the transcendental preparation of the field of this objectivity is achieved by an anticipation, i.e. a preliminary forming of all objects in general in accordance with an original *a priori* representation of a possible experience as an absolutely complete and interconnected whole of perceptions. Thus the cognition that arises in the mind is, on the *transcendental* level, and thus in regard to its very essence as an object of experience, something created after an archetype.

§. 1.2. Preliminary Outline of the Argument of the Transcendental Aesthetic and Analytic

A proper understanding of Kant's argument in these parts of the *Critique* will be greatly facilitated, I believe, by a brief reflection on the position expressed in his *MSI*. In that work Kant clearly already regarded space and time as the essential and necessary forms of the sensible world. Moreover, although it is very tempting to think these forms as mere forms or containers for objects, or as something externally applied to the things within the sensible world, Kant explained that this tendency must be resisted. He thought himself able to prove that these provide the *essential form* of any possible object in the sensible world. Thus the material of the sensible world itself would be internally determined, and thereby also distinguished, essentially through spatial and temporal determinations and relations. To be a thing in the sensible world is therefore to necessarily stand in a determinate place and position within a whole of space and time that embraces all possible sensible objects.

Furthermore, Kant also argued in that work that the determination of sensible objects, in order to become experience, i.e. compared and connected representations, required ontological concepts that spring originally from the pure understanding and are applied to appearances by means of the logical use of the understanding in analysis. This raised a problem, however, because while it was clear to him why space and time must be true features of appearances (namely, because they make them possible), it is not clear why the ontological concepts, which Kant now calls the categories, should also be applicable to objects of experience. The truth of space and time rests on the fact that appearance *qua* appearance is essentially spatial and temporal through and through, and on this *hypothesis* the connection between subject and predicate in certain immediate judgments of space and time are *analytically* valid. The understanding however is free from any dependency on sensibility in its real use (aside from its needing intuition as the occasion of its giving of pure concepts, that is), and sensibility at least appears to be free of any relation of dependency on the understanding. This is precisely the reason, Kant later explains, why the categories require a deduction of their validity. The goal of their deduction is therefore to show that the forms of pure thinking are nevertheless necessary conditions of the objects of the sensible world just as much as are space and time.

On the one hand, such a deduction might seem like a simple matter. Experiences are the product of the logical use of the understanding, and as such they require the application of concepts. From this it is not difficult to show that the very generation of any concept whatsoever takes place by means of the categories; for concepts are the products of judgments, and the table of the categories has been drawn up precisely to contain those most basic concepts required for the universal logical forms of judgment to be thought as determining an object in general. Put differently, the categories are meant to describe the universal forms of any object to which the logical forms of judgment could be applied. The categories are thus simply the most basic concepts without which experience – as a determinate whole of knowledge through concepts – would be impossible. This, I believe, is the basic form of what Kant calls the "objective deduction" of the categories.

On the other hand, a simple deduction of this kind proves to be insufficient because it does not establish the validity of the concepts specifically in their application to *appearances*. If no deduction of this were possible, then the categories would surely be necessary for experience as so defined, but experience itself could nevertheless be something false or merely subjective. One might, of course, wonder if this would really matter. After all, if we cannot but use the categories in all our thinking, then it would remain true that every human being, insofar as we each possess the higher faculty of thought, would necessarily make use of these categories and in this way intersubjective agreement would be possible. What more could Kant's argument offer or require? The problem with such a situation is that the mere fact that we have to make use of the categories is insufficient for explaining the *necessity* we *consciously* attribute to the principles which flow from their use. As Kant wrote in the margins of his copy of the A-edition of the *Critique*:

> If I were simply to say that without the connection of causes and effects I would not grasp the sequence of alterations, it would not at all follow from this that this must be precisely as an understanding needs it to be to grasp it, but I would not be able to explain whence they continuously follow one another. Only I would not raise this question if I did not already have the concept of cause and of the necessity of such persistence. A subjective necessity, habit, would make it worse. An implanted necessity would not prove necessity. (AA 23:26)

Thus the truth of these synthetic judgments *a priori*, just as that of intuitive judgments *a priori*, rests on our consciousness (or at least possible consciousness) of the essentiality of the forms to the objects represented. Intuitive judgments regarding space and time rest, as we have seen, not on the fact that *for us* appearances have to have these forms, but because the appearances *themselves* are nothing but *specifications of these, our forms*. Such judgments are true exclusively because they attach to the representation a predicate that belongs to its very essence, thus merely through *identity*. All truth for Kant must, I believe, be understood in precisely this way. Thus, for synthetic judgments *a priori* in which the conditions of the application of a category to appearances are expressed, it is not enough to show that we have to think experiences in accordance with them. Rather, it must be shown that the objects of experience are precisely *specifications* of categorial unity; that the transcendental form is essential to the transcendental matter itself. Because of this, and because we human beings only have objects given to us through intuition, the mere fact that we can only conceptualize these appearances through the categories (creating thereby experience), is again not enough to show their truth in this regard. What would need to be shown is that we possess consciousness (or possible consciousness) that the objects presented *particularly in the intuitive forms of space and time are also specifications of categorial unity*.

How can such a thing be done? I believe Kant's deduction in the B-edition (which is what I will be focusing on) rests ultimately on the following type of argument:

1) Space and time are *singular* representations, which means that they must be thought of as given all at once as *absolute wholes*, and thus intuitively, but they are *at the same time* the forms of the objects intuited. Now, it may be tempting to think space and time, insofar as they are singular representations given all at once, as being merely applied to a certain matter that is perceived (sensations), and thus to think space and time as intuitions as a sort of preceding indeterminate form which is only later determined through being applied to determinate objects. In this way pure space would be something that precedes empirical space, which latter alone is to be regarded as a determinate representation. But this is entirely wrong. Space and time as pure intuitions, as given singular representations, are the essential forms of the world of appearance. The relation of these forms to the appearances, which is expressed in the phrase "condition of possibility," is such that any possible empirical space is thought as a part of or as a specification (limitation) of original and pure space.

2) In other words, in space and time as pure intuitions, impure and specifically determined intuitions are already thought as *given* in thoroughgoing determinacy and unity. This may seem not only remarkable, but also incredible, yet it is not so very strange considering that space and time are transcendentally *subjective* forms of appearance. This also makes it very clear why Kant

is so certain of their being transcendentally ideal; for to think that the whole containing all that exits would be given to us in a singular representation even prior to our ever thinking any real object as in them would be more than just peculiar, it would be tantamount to attributing to human beings an intuitive understanding.

3) If we grant Kant this much, then it follows that in the singular representations of space and time, there is already thought as *given* an absolute totality of all that can ever be specifically intuited, and thus that the determination of any object in space and time is already thought as determined through the sum-total of all its relations to the whole of universal space and time. Furthermore, even though we do not directly *perceive* space and time except insofar as we perceive spatiotemporal objects, the spatiotemporal unity found in these objects and their relations are likewise thought as *given* already in original space and time. Consequently, the determinate unity thought in original space and time is only *actually represented determinately by us* (although these are given as entirely determinate in themselves, because they are that by relation to which all determination in appearances is possible) insofar as we represent it in *determinate objects*.

4) This requires us, however, to synthetically put together our perceptions in an explicit act of consciousness, which in turn – because it is an act of self-consciousness – must stand under original apperception. Finally, since the categories are nothing but functions through which objects are determined such that pure or original apperception is maintained in the act of representing such objects, it follows that the thoroughgoing determinate unity already *given* in original space and original time as singular representations must be regarded as the *very same unity* expressed in the categories through which it is thereby thought. Put differently, in the singular representations of space and time there is given intuitively, and as it were as an infinite intensive quantity, the whole of actual space and time, but due to the discursive nature of our minds, which expresses itself in the fact that space and time are not given to us intellectually (rather the transcendental unity of apperception is "empty"), these only become thoughts insofar as the manifold given in space and time is successively taken up and unified into a whole. This synthesis, for purely intellectual reasons, is achieved only through the employment of the categories.

5) Consequently: The unity that is already represented as belonging to all things insofar as they are spatiotemporal unities is already presupposed by space and time. This same unity, however, requires a synthesis by which the sensible manifold can be taken up and represented conceptually, and thereby become part of one objective unity of consciousness. The cate-

gories are the most basic forms of conceptual unity through which any object can be represented in thought, and thus the applicability of the categories to the sensible manifold is proven necessary for the possibility of experience and therefore valid. For the appearances as objects of sensible intuition are such that they presuppose such unity, and the categories are just the concepts by which the unity of thought is applied to sensibility in order to reflect its unity in a determinate way. The result is that the unity represented in thought, and specifically by means of the categories, is not to be understood as imposed upon appearances. Much rather, the appearances *qua* appearance, by virtue of the singularity and givenness of space and time, are such that they must exhibit an *internal and essential* thoroughgoing unity, and what is given in the appearance to the understanding for thought, is shown to be necessarily such that the unity of the sensible manifold *reflected in thought* is applicable to it.

This interpretation can be further elucidated by looking at the object from two different points of view. As essentially a spatiotemporal object, it must be thought as determined by its relation to the sum-total of all spatiotemporal positions and times. This sum-total is *given* at once in the singular representations of space and time, for if it were not then any spatiotemporal thing would itself remain indeterminate in an infinitely many respects. And in this case, we could not be said to be intuiting a particular. Consequently, any particular intuition presupposes – as the condition of its possibility – the representation of the completely determined given whole of real empirical space and time. Yet, it does not give these wholes to us as empirical, but rather *a priori*.

Looked at from the side of thought, space and time are not themselves given as actually determined by the categories. Rather, the manifold contained within them must be run through and unified so that it belongs to a whole of self-consciousness. This is an act of synthesis, or, in other words, a self-conscious act of successive combination of this manifold. What this combination does, precisely, is to make it possible for the intuition to be brought under the unity of a concept, thereby allowing us to *think* determinately the relations of spatiotemporal objects. To say, for instance, that X is the cause of Y is nothing but to determinately relate these two things in an objective time-sequence. Thus, as this synthesis according to the categories takes place, we increasingly determine for *thought*, and thus for self-consciousness, the sum-total of all real space and all real time.

This can only be seen if we again resist the temptation to think of space and time as containers for existing objects, and keep in mind the fact that spatiotemporal objects are nothing but determinate regions of space and time represented as objects for thought. Take the example of a red ball rolling across my desk. The ball is a certain region of space that is occupied by the quality of redness. This space itself is regarded here as moving. Now, its shape, size and velocity (which are but certain regions of space thought determinately) are only determined by me through the relation of its parts to one another and to the objects in its immediate vicinity. But the shape and size of these too are indeterminate, unless the parts of this larger space can be related to one another and to a still larger space. The ball may either be moving, or it may be at rest; for if the room is moving, and with a certain velocity in the direction opposite to that the ball seems to be moving, then with respect to an even larger space (namely, that in respect to which the room is moving), the ball is at rest. But surely it must either be moving or not, and with some determinate velocity and it must be so represented for its velocity to be represented determinately. Obviously, the motion of the ball would only be truly thought as determined in this absolute sense when it is held to be moving in relation to the whole of all else in space and time. But in this absolute whole, not only is the motion of the ball thought as determined, but indeed so also is its spatiotemporal relation to absolutely all else. The ball and its motion in this case is just a region of space thought as possessing the same qualities throughout a certain time, and as changing its spatial relations to other regions of space.

This must be qualified in two ways. First, it must be stressed that this does not collapse the distinction between space and time and the objects represented as within it. The pure intuitions of space and time, to be sure, do not contain specific representations and unities of objects represented as in space and time by the understanding. Rather, they present us only with the thoroughgoing unity and determinacy of these objects insofar as they are specifications of a whole of space and time that is itself *singular*. The understanding alone, by means of the categories, is able to represent determinate objects in accordance with these grounds. But this, it must be stressed, does not mean that the unity of objects that would exist in space and time is not for this reason presupposed by the singularity of space and time themselves; much the contrary is true. Secondly, the unity of experience, in the respect that it is thought to contain a systematic unity of empirical laws, extends *in principle* beyond the unity presupposed by space and time. Yet the unity of all things is in essence a spatiotemporal unity, a unity of things that are essentially characterized by determinations of time and position.

With this preliminary sketch in place, let us proceed to the first part, namely, to Kant's account of the purposive unity of space and time as singular intuitions.

§. 2. Space and Time as Grounds of the Formal Perfection of Sensible Objects

It is clear that in Kant's earliest writings space and time played the role of being the forms in which the transcendental teleological unity of God's creation made its first appearance. In working out the position described in *GUGR* and more fully in the *MSI*, however, Kant came to interpret space and time to be the subjective forms of sensible experience, and thus as being nothing but the forms or laws in accordance with which it is possible for us to intuit a sensible object. As such, space and time do not allow us to grasp the transcendental features of objects themselves, but rather only the subjectively necessary condition of our being able to grasp a sensible manifold within a single unity. The unity manifest in space and time is therefore necessary because in no other way is it possible to represent the manifold within one consciousness, and it is essentially subjective, meaning it is a requirement only of human sensibility, not an absolute requirement of the thing itself. For this reason, Kant argues in the *MSI* that when we attempt to represent space and time as independent objects, as for instance we do in the notions of absolute space and absolute time, then all we end up producing are inconsistent and imaginary entities.

In my brief discussion of Kant's pre-critical philosophy in Chapter 1, I also stressed that Kant's transcendental teleology at that time rested on his conception of God as the source of all reality. In particular, we saw that Kant believed the being of all finite things to be inwardly and teleologically constituted because of their common ground in the supreme reality of God. Finite things were indeed thought by him to be differentiated and specified in their being as particular limited expressions of the sum-total of the reality contained in God. In several passages throughout the late sixties and seventies, Kant draws a direct parallel between this relation of God to created beings and the relation of space and time to their own parts. To cite a few cases in point:

> The reason why we find it more conceivable to represent the necessary existence of a most real Being than the necessary existence of a limited one, comes from the fact that we can only think limited things and their negative determinations through the limitation of the more real concept. Accordingly, a greater possibility cannot be put together from lesser ones. And universal possibility is not an aggregate of all particular possibilities, but rather the latter are consequences of the former. The limited thing is that which has some of all possible realities and through this is distinguished from others. Some as distinguished from all possible is only thinkable through all. Duration and external relation (of figure and quantity) can only be known through the limitation of the infinite time and the infinite space, for example, the triangle. (*Refl* 4262)

Of infinite space and time. Time contains the ground of the limitations of the existence of things, space of the limitations of their presence, the highest Being of the limitations of their reality. Therefore, all of these are infinite. Because of this the highest being as the material to all things is thought only sensibly.

Time is that which concerns all things and in which all things exist, through which therefore the existence of each is determined relative to others, when and how long. (*Refl* 4312)

The infinite and single space, which is the condition of the possibility of all external presence of things as well as of their appearing, is to be sure not a proof of the existence of a ground and original being that is connected with everything (*alles befasst*) and in which everything is sustained, from which also comes all unity and relation, because it [i.e. all unity and relation] is as it were possible through its place in the All; but it is nevertheless a proof that the human mind can think of no combination (*Verbindung*) without a common ground and no determination otherwise than in one which contains everything. It is the same with time, in which lies all existence. This serves for the acceptance of such a Being as subjectively necessary, and so also as sufficiently acceptable for what is practical. (Refl 4733)

In the mid to late 1780s, thus well into the critical period, Kant writes with even greater precision:

It does not follow that something is actual because it is possible according to a general concept. However, that something is actual because it is, among all that is possible, completely determined through its concept and is distinguished as one from all that is [merely] possible, means so much as: it is not purely a general concept, but rather the representation of a singular thing completely determined through concepts in relation to everything possible. This relation to everything possible according to the principle of complete determination is just the same in regard to concepts of reason, as the somewhere or somewhen is in regard to the conditions of sensible intuition.* For space and time determine not merely the intuition of a thing, but rather at the same time its individuality through relations of place and moments in time, because in regard to space and time possibility cannot be distinguished from actuality, because both together contain in themselves, as substrate, all possibility in the appearance, which must be given beforehand.

From this it follows only that the most real being in regard to the real concepts of all possibility must be given beforehand, just as equally space cannot be thought beforehand [merely] as possible, but rather [it must be thought] as given; but not as an in itself actual object, but rather a mere sensible form in which alone objects can be intuited; consequently, also the most real being not as object, but rather as the pure form of reason so that it can think the distinction of everything possible in its complete determination, consequently as idea, which is actual [*Wirklich*] (subjectively), yet prior to something being thought as possible; from which it however does not follow that the object of this idea is in itself actual.

Nevertheless, one sees that in relation to the nature of the human understanding and its concepts a highest being is just as necessary as space and time are in relation to the nature of our sensibility and its intuition.

§. 2. Space and Time as Grounds of the Formal Perfection of Sensible Objects — 169

*(Something, the relation of which to everything possible is determined in absolute space and time, is actual. Exactly also that the relation of which to everything possible is determined in the absolute representation of a thing in general, is actual. Both belong to the complete external determination in view of possibility in general and make through this also the complete inner determination of an individual.) (*Relf* 6290)

I know of no passage in Kant's writings in which this relation between space and time and the idea of God is better expressed than in this last one. Others make clearer the fact that in both cases the limited is thought as possible only through the limitation of a maximum, thus the limited part through the unlimited whole, but in this passage in particular Kant most clearly expresses the full sense and significance of this claim for the principles of the critical system itself. Space and time and the highest being, Kant here explains, are not to be thought as forms in the sense of something merely possible (not *mere* forms), but as complete and determinate actualities. In regard to these alone, possibility and actuality cannot be distinguished, meaning that in regard to these everything that belongs to them does so with absolute necessity. In these therefore is thought as *given all at once*, the sum-total of all that is possible, and it is precisely in relation to these that any individual thing can be understood as individual, for this requires for its individuality the complete determination of its properties, which in turn is only thinkable through a relation to the given sum-total of possibility. Just as the idea of God provides the idea of a being in relation to which all determination of existing individuals can be determined, space and time are that through relation to which alone the complete determination of objects in the appearance can be represented with regard to their places and times. The latter is the case precisely because objects in the appearance are through and through appearance, and as such their determinations are all essentially spatiotemporal. For X to be the cause of Y, is thus just for X to precede Y in time according to a determinate rule of time relation.

Yet, unlike the pre-critical versions of these same ideas, Kant warns in this last relfection that what is given here must not be mistaken for something given as actual and also as a thing in itself. Space and time, and God as well, are thought as *given* and thus as actual only in the respect that they are required *subjectively* or strictly in relation to the possibility of sensibility and understanding. When we determine actual things as moments and positions in absolute space and time, we always think these determinations as objectively valid, thus as really essential and applicable to objects, because only in this way are we able to regard them as already belonging to the things *prior to those specific acts of judgment by which we determine them*. This is just what is required to distinguish and explain what it means to have a representation of a real or objective whole, rather than an arbitrarily constructed one. Space and time are thus specifically the real or actual forms by virtue of which it is possible to consciously regard the determinations we make in thought (i.e. by means of the understanding in judgments) as potentially reflecting the true inner or essential unity of the objects of appearances. This is possible only if we have ground to regard the *appearances* as unified and determined *in themselves as appearances* in precisely this way. Space and time are nothing but the representations by relation to which this is made possible.

But space and time share the phenomenological features: 1) that any determinate region presupposes the existence of an infinite region surrounding it; 2) we can conceive but one space and one time, of which all spaces and times are but determinate regions. In the *Nachlass*, Kant often suggests that both of these features have a common explanation in the fact that space and time are nothing but the forms required for the possibility that the sensible manifold be brought under the, as it were, point-like unity of transcendental apperception. For it to be possible for the self-conscious mind not only to contain a manifold of perception, but to be able to represent a manifold of perception to itself, it must be able to *anticipate* the form of such a manifold. In other words, the form of the manifold, as the form of the possible coordination of its parts, must lie already within consciousness *a priori*. Now, if these forms lie within the mind *a priori* as the form of a possible sensible manifold, and are to make it such that whatever is represented belongs to one whole of consciousness, then it follows that every actual region of the sensible manifold must be represented as part of a potentially infinite or inexhaustible field of possible perceptions. In other words, since the *a priori* forms of sensibility are the abiding and necessary conditions of representing a sensible manifold as within one consciousness, it is the case that no actual determination of space or time can exhaust it. Such forms serve as the pre-objective grounds of all possible sensible objects. Furthermore, it is clear that every actualization of these forms will stand in relation to every other by means of their shared relation to this common pre-objective ground, for it is only by relation to this that they can belong in turn to one consciousness. The ideas of absolute space and absolute time would then be nothing but the complete actualization, if such were possible, of these pre-objective grounds. But since such a complete actualization is impossible, these ideas are but imaginary objects. Kant can thus explain his own pre-critical ideas of space and time, as well as the Newtonian idea of absolute space, as having arisen from a confusion of these features of the subjective grounds of intuition with the objective features of some true independent thing.

For all their subjectivity, however, space and time are for Kant nevertheless something empirically real. They may not be the transcendent and archetypal re-

§. 2. Space and Time as Grounds of the Formal Perfection of Sensible Objects — 171

alities that they once were thought to be, but they are nevertheless the real conditions of human sensibility. It is this fact that underlies what Kant refers to as the "empirical reality" of space and time. As real conditions of human sensibility, space and time are essential to the form of every possible sensible object, and for this reason all the features and laws of space and time are necessary features and laws of every object that may in principle be given to the human mind.

§. 2.1. The Objective Formal Perfection of Space

A further and very significant illustration of Kant's continued adherence to his pre-critical views on the teleological structure of space (and time) even after the critical turn, is to be found in §. 62 of the *KU*. Some thirty years earlier in *BDG*, Kant took the formal perfection of space, the essential fitness of its complete unity for the solution of an infinity of problems, as evidence for the existence of a higher being which is the ground of the essential perfections of geometrical forms, and indeed of the essences of all things more generally (*BDG* 02:93–95). In Chapter 1, this provided us with a first precise expression of Kant's transcendental conception of teleology, because in this the absolute perfection of space was clearly exhibited not as an artificial construct for the sake of particular ends, but rather as an infinite fitness of essences to particular ends of all kinds. This illustrated, in particular, that Kant's deepest understanding of teleological structure is that of universal and necessary purposiveness based upon a common ground of possibility.

If in the critical period space is revealed to be nothing but the ground of the possibility of appearances, then it would seem that Kant must argue that this infinite purposiveness found in the necessary properties of space is in fact derivable from the human mind. This is indeed just what we find §. 62 of the *KU*, elucidated under the title "objective formal purposiveness." Drawing attention to precisely the same harmonies and unities in geometrical figures as he did in the *BDG*, Kant writes:

> The purposiveness here is evidently objective and intellectual, not, however, merely subjective and aesthetic. For it expresses the suitability of the figure for the generation of many shapes aimed at purposes, and is cognized through reason. But the purposiveness still does not make the concept of the object itself possible, i.e., it is not regarded as possible merely with respect to this use.

Seen in light of the earlier work, it is clear that Kant is here trying to express the peculiar fact of a purposiveness not based upon an arrangement, which is something with a *particular* end. Geometrical figures, in other words, are useful for an infinity of solutions (i.e. an infinity of particular ends), but without their being intentionally constructed for any of these purposes. The fact that they are not thought of as arranged, is here expressed by the idea that their possibility is not thought as determined by this end or use, which is always the case with arrangements directed to particular ends. "In such a simple figure as the circle," Kant observes, "there lies the basis for the solution of a host of problems, for each of which by itself much preparation would be required, and which as it were arises from this figure itself as one of its many splendid properties" (*KU* 05:362).

Just as in the pre-critical period, Kant also speaks of this purposiveness as belonging to the "essences of things" (by which he now clearly means essences of objects in the appearance):

> For in the necessity of that which is purposive and so constituted as if it were intentionally arranged for our use, but which nevertheless seems to pertain originally to the essence of things, without any regard to our use, lies the ground for the great admiration of nature, not outside us so much as in our own reason; in which case it is surely excusable that through misunderstanding this admiration gradually rose to enthusiasm [in the speculations of Plato]. (*KU* 05:363–364)

The misunderstanding here is not that there is nothing truly remarkable or admirable in such purposive properties, but rather that they are not grounded in anything aside from our own reason. The critical Kant, however, claims to be able to explain quite easily the source of this purposiveness as well as of our (i.e. *the young Kant's*) tendency to mistake it for an indication of an external unifying ground. "The many rules," he explains,

> the unity of which (from a principle) arouses this admiration, are one and all synthetic, and do not follow from a concept of the object, e.g., from that of a circle, but need this object to be given in intuition. But it thereby comes to seem as if this unity empirically possesses an external ground, distinct from our power of representation, for its rules, and thus as if the correspondence of the object with the need for rules, which is characteristic of the understanding, is in itself contingent, hence possible only by means of an end expressly aimed at it. Now of course this very harmony, since it is, in spite of all this purposiveness, cognized not empirically but *a priori*, should bring it home to us that space, by the determination of which (by means of the imagination, in accordance with a concept) the object alone is possible, is not a property of the object outside of me, but merely a kind of representation in me, and thus that I introduce the purposiveness into the figure that I draw in accordance with a concept, i.e., into my own way of representing that which is given to me externally […]. (*KU* 05:364–365)

It is clear from this passage that Kant now regards this purposiveness as a product of the mind, and furthermore that since space is something empirically real

§. 2. Space and Time as Grounds of the Formal Perfection of Sensible Objects — 173

we have a tendency to regard its purposiveness as real as well. What is required to see its transcendental ideality is precisely the "critical use of reason" by means of which we are first able to recognize that what is known *a priori* must always belong merely to appearances. In this case, Kant thus explains that while on the empirical level it is genuinely true that space exhibits a teleological relation to our understanding whereby its properties seem to be suitable not only to the fulfillment of a single set of possible cognitive ends, but indeed an infinite variety of them, this same teleology must somehow be understood to be a product of the mind's own transcendental activity. The mind is thus itself somehow responsible for bringing such infinite teleological unity into its cognitions.

Still, how precisely does this purposiveness come to be in space? Kant first says that it does not belong to the concept of a circle, and indeed this is an important fact; for the illusion of its real and transcendental independence from the mind rests on the fact that it lies in space and not in our arbitrarily assumed concept. But is this unity to be thought as introduced into space by means of its being determined by the concept, and thus somehow as still derivative of the conceptual unity, or rather as truly lying in space even prior to its determination by any concept? If the reader will recall the results of the last chapter, I think it has been shown that Kant cannot and need not answer this question, because it rests on a fundamental misunderstanding of the critical standpoint. The purposiveness of space, to be sure, simply cannot be encountered without determination by the concept, for it is only in such cases that it is ever determinately thought. But for the sake of the objectivity of this very determination by the understanding, the determinations, and so also the purposive unity, must be represented *as if* arising originally from an intuition of space in which they already exist beforehand. But this feature is not something objective and real, but rather is a transcendental presupposition for the sake of the possibility of cognition, and thus outside of this relation there is absolutely nothing further to be said about it. Space is not itself an object, but a form of intuition. To say that apart from its relation to understanding it does or does not already contain this determinacy would be to mistake the very sense in which it figures in the structure of knowledge. This is because the former would turn it into an independent object, and the latter would directly deny that space can play the role required by the understanding for the sake of knowledge. Space must rather be represented *as if* it were something objective and independent, and transcendental reflection must always be called in to make sure that this representation is not mistakenly separated from its limited function, and hypostatized.

That also in the present context, Kant does not think the unity should be regarded as derived from the concept in its determination of space, is evident from the fact that he really believes there is something genuinely remarkable in such purposiveness, even when seen from a critical standpoint. He says indeed, that such a view "cannot be criticized insofar as the compatibility of that form of sensible intuition (which is called space) with the faculty of concepts (understanding) is not only inexplicable for us insofar as it is precisely thus and not otherwise, but also enlarges the mind, allowing it, as it were, to suspect something lying beyond those sensible representations, in which, although unknown to us, the ultimate ground of that accord could be found" (KU 05:365). The purposive unity that is expressed in synthetic judgments *a priori* regarding space is thus nevertheless an indication of the truly remarkable purposive relation between the forms of sensibility and the forms of understanding. It is as if sensibility, by virtue of the form of intuition called space, is infinitely rich in precisely the kind of unity the understanding requires in order to reflect on the sensible manifold and collect it under concepts. The real contingency underlying the pre-critical purposiveness of space is now shown to be located in the real contingency stemming from the fact that sensibility and understanding are heterogeneous sources of representations, which nevertheless must perfectly harmonize to make possible the necessary properties found in all things that fill space.

Here it should be noted that we have discovered a remarkable and, indeed, quite beautiful illustration of the manner in which the notion of real contingency Kant developed in the pre-critical period actually makes possible and shapes his discovery of synthetic *a priori* judgments. The real contingency of space was just what enabled Kant in the pre-critical period to argue that it attests to the existence of a most universal ground of purposiveness in the necessary essences of things. We are now told by Kant that this mistake was made possible by the fact that, in his new terminology of the critical period, such truths are not analytic but synthetic. This indicates most clearly that the real contingency of space in the pre-critical period sets up in Kant's mind the need for explaining our *a priori* certainty of such contingency and the purposive unity that arises in it from a single ground; this is just what the synthetic judgments *a priori* regarding space express. In a word, real contingency in the pre-critical period is the metaphysical problem without which the need for synthetic *a prior* principles would not arise. And now that we know their true source, namely in the inexplicable and admirable harmony of sensibility and understanding which must be presupposed for the sake of cognition, we can at least see that they do not prove the existence of a divine ground at all, although they may lead us to look in that direction.

Still, there is one outstanding question. Although the real contingency of essences has a clear relation to the discovery of synthetic judgments *a priori*, this does not yet explain how the absolute purposiveness that arose in regard to the

§. 2. Space and Time as Grounds of the Formal Perfection of Sensible Objects — 175

former, because of its intrinsic relation to the divine intellect and will, can be taken over and explained by the same grounds that make possible the latter. How, in other words, can we understand that the unity required by reason and presupposed by it in all of its objects is precisely the same kind of teleological unity that in the pre-critical period was seen as arising from God as from a self-sufficient and all perfect ground? This question will be address further below in our treatment of the Transcendental Deduction and further in later chapters. However, at this point it can be noted that Kant himself saw just such an absolute teleology as this to be a necessary presupposition of reason for the sake of experience, and indeed also for the possibility of morality. In *ÜE*, which was published in 1790, Kant admits that the *KrV* itself rests on the presupposition of a Leibnizian pre-established harmony, however not outside us and between the body and the soul, but rather within us in the relations between both sensibility and understanding, and theoretical and practical reason. Such a harmony, which in its ultimate expression requires the idea of a divine coordinator of nature with moral purposiveness, Kant remarks, is not objectively proven by the critical philosophy, but rather proven to be a necessary presupposition for the sake of the employment of reason as a unified theoretical and a practical faculty (*ÜE* 08:249–251).

§. 2.2. The Transcendental Aesthetic: Comments on the Text

Although space and time share many features of the ideas, they are yet not ideas because they belong to sensibility and are intuited. They might in fact be called sensible analogues of the ideas, for they are, as Kant shows, necessary, pure, singular (or unique), infinite given magnitudes which provide the conditions of the possibility of all appearances. They are thus universal representations which contain all particular representations of space and time, and indeed by reference to which the complete determinacy of these particular representations and their reciprocal relations with all other things within the whole are made possible. In accordance with this analogy, and based upon the fact that Kant defines a science as nothing other than a purposive or systematic whole of cognitions unified under an idea, he is able to define the Transcendental Aesthetic as "a science of all principles of *a priori* sensibility" (*KrV* A21/B35).

The text of this section is exceedingly short, and it seems that Kant must have expected his readers to be familiar with the *MSI*, or else he must have mistaken how much would need to be explained. Given what has already been said above, little can be added to my thesis by a more detailed analysis of the Transcendental Analytic itself. Still at least one point is worth further comment. This is that Kant's comment on the Aesthetic in the B-edition helps us to better understand the teleological structure of space in its relation to synthetic *a priori* judgments. Earlier I noted that all judgments are purposive in the sense that they connect two concepts, and thus express a unity, by their relating these concepts to some third thing, and indeed doing so through the representation of this third thing as the ground of this connection. In this respect, in fact, all judgments are purposive activities of the mind insofar as they represent as necessary an otherwise continent unity of these two concepts by relating them to a third thing (the object) in which they are thought as already united. The mind judges in this case in order to fit its own contingently related representations to the model or exemplar that is thought in the object, and it does so on the basis of its own inner representation of this same object. In synthetic judgments *a priori*, this relation is furthermore consciously thought as being universal and necessary, and thus as valid prior to any particular object that might be given. Thus it expresses a universal and necessary, and indeed purposive, relation of our concepts among themselves that is not to be derived from any given object, but rather can only be understood as valid if it somehow provides a rule of the unity of our concepts alone by means of which they can be related to an object in general. At present, however, we are only interested in a particular class of synthetic *a priori* judgments, namely those that are intuitive and are expressed in mathematical propositions. As Kant clearly indicates, these judgments consist in the necessary unity of two concepts that is immediately established in intuition. Consequently, although generally the X that forms the purposive point of unity underlying any judgment is something empirically given, in the case of synthetic *a priori* judgments regarding space and time this X is pure intuition itself. The upshot is that the purposive unity of concepts expressed in *particular* intuitive judgments is in fact the direct outcome of the *universal harmony and purposive relation* of pure intuition for the representation of sensible objects by the understanding. Put differently, particular intuitive judgments regarding what Kant calls "concepts of space" (i.e. concepts of figures and shapes, which are rules of the understanding for determining space as object), which express as necessary the relations of concepts of things in space and time, are in fact made possible by the transcendental teleological relation of pure intuition to the understanding in general for the sake of making just such judgments possible.

In the Aesthetic, therefore, Kant is able to explain both the empirical reality of the forms of intuition as well as their transcendental ideality, and in such a way that this does not compromise either their *a priori* or synthetic character. Their empirical reality rests on the fact that when dealing with objects of appearance, it is identically true that they are in space and time, and are subject to their necessary properties. This is a perfectly analytic truth equivalent to: If something is in space, then it is in space (*KrV* A27/B43). Yet the intuitive judgments of space are themselves synthetic, not because it is synthetically true that spatial things are spatial, but because of the universal and necessary relation these judgments express *between* concepts of the understanding through their mutual relation to the common form of intuition that they are made to determine (in mathematical constructions). The synthesis here is not between the object and the form of intuition, but between two concepts that are not conceptually related (i.e not analytically), and this by means of their mutual relation to the unity of pure intuition: "If we want to go beyond the given concept in an *a priori* judgment, we encounter that which is to be discovered *a priori* and synthetically connected with it, not in the concept but in the intuition connected with it" (*KrV* B73). Still, it is important to note that for Kant even these judgments derive their validity from their teleological relation to the possibility of experience. That Kant would recognize this so clearly is indeed very remarkable. As he writes,

> Even space and time, as pure as these concepts are from everything empirical and as certain as it is that they are represented in the mind completely *a priori*, would still be without objective validity and without sense and significance if their necessary use on the objects of experience were not shown. (*KrV* A156/B195)

A less principled thinker might well accept the validity of mathematical constructions, i.e. the application of certain categories to the synthesis of the manifold of space and time, based upon their internal necessity and possibility alone. Yet Kant recognizes that the deduction must not only establish the possibility and necessity of such an application, but must do so precisely by relating this unity to the ultimate *telos* that defines the theoretical faculty of understanding. That is to say, Kant thereby recognizes that the objective validity of even mathematical constructions can only be guaranteed by proving that they can and must play an indispensable role also in the generation of experience. In a word, according to Kant even mathematical constructions derive their validity from the role they play as means to the fulfillment of the ultimate *telos* of theoretical reason, i.e. the generation of experience.

§. 3. The Transcendental Analytic

To many the Transcendental Analytic is the core of Kant's entire philosophy. Generally speaking, this is certainly not true, because Kant's philosophy is ultimately directed to the practical, and in regard to this the *KrV* is but a necessary preparation. Yet, from a systematic point of view, the Transcendental Analytic certainly is a core piece of the larger puzzle. The reason for this is that the Analytic provides the key to the discovery of the table of the categories, which in Kant's view provides the specific pattern for all scientific thought. This is because all science consists in the systematic unity of judgments, which are reached by means of analysis, or what Kant calls the logical use of the understanding. From early in the pre-critical period, as we saw, the logical use of the understanding was for Kant the tool through which all science is constructed. The categories are, however, "concepts of an object in general, by means of which its intuition is regarded as *determined* with regard to one of the *logical functions* of judgment" (A95/B128). Thus if the logical use of the understanding is to be applied to anything in order to determine an object, then the structure of this object in general must be determinable by the categories. The categories, therefore, as the first absolutely pure product of reason in the wider sense, articulate the inner purposive structure that must be thought as the determinate structure of any object in general, if it is to be able to be brought under the logical use of the understanding, and thereby known. This purity and universality of the categories is thus reflected in the fact that all knowledge of any kind is expressed in judgments, and it makes necessary the employment of the categories for articulating every possible science. "The categories," Kant explains, "of course must lie at the foundation of every division of principles of a scientific knowledge from concepts" (*Br* 23:494). The deduction of these categories from the logical functions of judgment is the goal of the metaphysical deduction, to which I now turn.

§. 3.1. The Metaphysical Deduction

Several commentators have drawn attention to the teleological themes that permeate the Metaphysical Deduction. Kant, for instance, describes the process of the analytic as the tracing of the categories to "their first seeds and predispositions in human understanding" (*KrV* A66/B91). More importantly still, he asserts that as a science, and indeed as the scientific outline of all possible science, the table of the categories must form an absolute whole unified under a single idea, a system of which "the completeness and articulation [...] can at the same time yield a touchstone of the correctness and genuineness of all the pieces of cognition fitting into it" (*KrV* A65/B90). Kant reinforces this vision of systematic, indeed purposive, unity by stressing the purity and self-sufficiency with which the understanding produces these concepts: The understanding, he says, "separates itself completely" and "is therefore a unity that subsists on its own, which is sufficient by itself, and which is not to be supplemented by any external additions" (*KrV* A65/B90).

It is impossible not to hear in this again an echo of Kant's pre-critical cosmology, and in particular of his concept of God as the all-sufficient being. Indeed, it was precisely the all-sufficiency of the original being that guaranteed that all of its products necessarily cohere into an absolute unity, which entirely depends upon the fact that this unity is made possible by a single common ground. Certainly, the understanding is in many ways quite distinct from this idea of God, and I do not think that Kant in fact ever thought of his procedure as one in which certain features of God were directly transposed into the structure of the understanding, i.e. as a sort of deification of the understanding, as one might find in Fichte. The manner in which Kant arrives at this likeness is rather this: The logical use of the understanding is aimed essentially at an absolute whole of cognitions, and in this way it moves from experience towards the first principle of all things. Such an employment presupposes for its objectivity that experience itself is internally unified in accordance with the kind of ground that would make it suitable for such cognition. The model for just such a world-whole and the principle alone which would be sufficient to think it as a real or objective whole, furthermore, is precisely that of a community of substances interrelated by means of their common derivation from a single common ground. Thus the pure ontological concepts gain their validity and employment entirely from the fact that through these concepts alone is it possible to determine distributively the objects that would exist within such a whole. But such concepts and principles are presupposed by any experience, and thus are *a priori*, which is only possible if they arise originally from within the mind. Thus the understanding must make possible just such a unity of cognitions as is thought in such a whole of experience. But it must do so from its own absolute purity and spontaneity, and with at least implicit consciousness of this, for otherwise it would not represent to itself such concepts and principles as both necessary and universal.

Kant's argument here could almost be read as a radicalized version of the Cartesian position: Descartes takes it as the highest principle for determining what is within the I in the proper sense, that it must be a product of the activity of this I. Yet he also admits that the objective reality contained in the concept of God found within the I proves that a being with greater formal reality than the I must exist, and be the cause of this very concept. Descartes even argues that I can only have the concept of myself as limited, if it is presupposed that I have the concept of the unlimited, or infinite against which to cognize it. By contrast, Kant might be thought as arguing thusly: If the idea of God could not be produced by the I, then it could not be said to be possessed by the I either; for the act of consciously producing a concept or idea is the only genuine ground of possession. Consequently, if we have a true cognition of limited things, and indeed of ourselves *as limited* (the empirical self), then we must indeed have a representation of God, but this representation must also be the *product of the activity of our own thinking*. The fact that we are conscious to ourselves of our own limitedness, indicates that there is a more fundamental transcendental level to consciousness by which it creates for itself an archetype of the unlimited. As we will see later on, it is precisely the shared purity, independence and complete originality of the sources of transcendental cognition (intuition and concept), that secures and justifies the fact that nature, as the whole of possible experience, must also be understood as a singular entity completely unified by transcendental laws.

The Metaphysical Deduction thus exploits this unique character of the understanding as a basis for arguing that, although the manifold of concepts and rules associated with judging throughout the history of logic have been discovered piecemeal, all of these must nevertheless fit into one complete systematic whole unified under an idea, namely the idea of a pure and *a priori* faculty for judging. Judgments, Kant explains, are "functions of unity among our representations, since instead of an immediate representation a higher one, which comprehends this and other representations under itself, is used for the cognition of the object, and many possible cognitions are thereby drawn into one" (*KrV* A69/B94). This can be explained as follows: Judgments determine objects by connecting concepts under which objects fall. For instance, "rose" and "red" are both concepts, and thus general representations. As such, both have the truly astounding ability to apply to a veritable infinity of things. For instance, "red" applies as much to all actual red roses at any moment as to all possible ones, and perhaps even to some that never will exist, but perhaps could. In this respect, concepts as it were cut out and bring under one whole swaths of our possible experience. Thus when we judge, for instance, *All roses are red*, what we are in fact doing is determining experience more thoroughly by connecting up in a determinate way all those possibly infinite things that fall under the concept "rose" with all those other things that fall under or are associated logically with the concept "red." Judging is thus the means, and a very powerful one at that, through which unity is brought into our cognitions. Indeed, Kant claims, although he does not prove the fact, that the functions of the understanding are exhausted precisely by the manifold ways in which it can form judgments.

It is at this point that Kant introduces the table of the logical functions in judgments, which is supposed contain a complete systematic enumeration of the basic forms of judging. I will not dwell on this table, except to point out that it is clearly formed, not with a view to traditional logic, but rather with a view to the manifold forms of judgment that are required by the logical use of the understanding which aims essentially at cognition of a whole *logical world of cognition*, as it were, just as in the pre-critical period this use of the understanding was cut to produce a cognition of a world-whole. The various adjustments Kant makes throughout, and explains in notes to this section all indicate that he is evaluating the validity of the different divisions in terms of what they add to *cognition as a whole*. Thus, in order to see the completeness and necessity of the divisions we have to place before ourselves the idea, or perfect whole, consisting of all possible concepts required to achieve the goal of determining an object; for it is precisely in being able to completely capture the content of such a whole in judgments that lies the perfection and purity of the understanding. The modal forms of judgment, however, clearly do not relate to this whole of possible logical forms in the manner of the others. They do not belong to this table because they are necessary for capturing the content of this whole of logical forms in judgments, but because they are necessary for capturing the manifold ways in which judgments relate to the idea of such a whole.

The key point here, however, is that Kant's basic idea is to derive the table of judgments from the very idea of a pure faculty for judging, and his claim is that if we attend to the action of judgment in its purity, thus to what it is supposed to be, it is possible to see how the manifold forms of judgment arise systematically from this single idea. Once this self-articulating unity has been developed, it is then possible according to Kant to discover with the same systematic unity the categories of the understanding; for these are nothing but the complete system of all possible concepts through which the forms of judgment are thought as determining an object in general.

§. 3.2. The Transcendental Deduction

In "Kant's Notion of a Deduction," Dieter Henrich writes, "the process through which a possession or a usage is accounted for by explaining its origin, such that the rightfulness of the possession or the usage becomes apparent, defines the deduction" (Henrich 1989a, p.35). Henrich here is speaking more generally about the kind of legal deduction that was common in pre-Napoleonic Germany, but his description is intended to clarify the way in which Kant understood his own method of philosophical deduction. In the Transcendental Analytic of the first *Critique*, he therefore argues that, "the purpose of the deduction is to determine, with regard to origin, the domain and the limits of the categories' legitimate usage" (Henrich 1989a, p. 39). In the same essay, Henrich puts forward three criteria of a "successful interpretation" of Kant's deductions. One must, he says, be "capable of comprehensively explaining the vocabulary," the manner of composition, and the similarities between the transcendental deduction of the categories and the transcendental deduction of the *KpV* (Henrich 1989a, p. 42).

I think this is a fitting introduction to a teleological interpretation of the argumentative structure of the transcendental deduction for two reasons. First, I think that in addition to Henrich's own results, it is only a teleological interpretation that can explain the remainder of the terminology Kant employs in this section of the *KrV*. For Kant not only situates his deduction in legal terms, but also in explicitly teleological ones. Aside from the comparisons Kant makes between the understanding as a faculty of judgment and an absolutely perfect systematic whole, i.e. an organism, there is also the fact that the precise use Kant makes here of traditional ontological concepts cannot be understood apart from the role they were shown to play in his pre-critical teleology. I submit, in fact, that there is simply no way to explain how Kant came to form the argument as he did without bringing it into direct contact with this pre-critical result.

The second reason this is a fitting introduction is that the distinction Kant draws between the order of justification and the order through which representations are produced, which is highlighted by Henrich's focus on the legal nature of the proof, is key to separating out the different levels of teleology implicit in the Deduction itself. Let me illustrate this by further elaborating the parallel between legal claims and Kant's transcendental investigation. Possession, in the legal sense of the term, is in fact a teleological relation between an agent and an object. To physically possess something is to make use of it, or to hold something particular before oneself with the awareness that it is at one's disposal, and thus can be made use of at any time. An act of possession is thus always something particular, and although it does not mean that we are actually making use of something, it provides an essential guarantee of the *rightfulness of any possible use* we might make of the thing. But a right of possession can only be proven by the agreement of this particular act with a universal condition: "Any action is right," Kant explains in the *MS*, "if it can coexist with everyone's freedom in accordance with a universal law, or if on its maxim the freedom of choice can coexist with everyone's freedom in accordance with a universal law" (*MS* 06:230). Proof of the right of possession thus is based upon a universal law, and by means of it *all possible particular uses and acts of possession* in accordance with it are guaranteed to be justified. The law of right does not justify teleological acts of possession or use, however, by immediately containing them within itself, but rather by putting forward a universal condition by means of which all possible acts of possession can be fit into an absolute systematic whole. It thus presents us with a universal condition of the purposive relation of all purposes, and as we read above it is precisely the reciprocal unity and harmony of these purposes that is the highest condition of right itself.

To extend this comparison to the claims made in synthetic judgments *a priori*, we must see that the specific preliminary judgments that form the basis of a transcendental investigation are not like other judgments about objects. Transcendental reflection considers these judgments, not in regard to their object, but in regard to their very nature as preliminary *judgings*. It is not the product that is reflectively thematized, i.e. the judgment as an object, but rather the *act* of forming this product, the judging. What is in question in the investigation are precisely the activities and commitments presupposed by the very conscious operation by means of which we first form any preliminary judgments regarding objects in general. Just as in acts of physical possession, an act of knowing an object might well be teleologically structured in the sense that the modes of mental activity must all be employed in relation to a single object of consciousness and guided by it *qua* consciousness. But this is merely a teleological relation of *empirical* intentionality. However, through its focus on the *quid iuris*, Kant's transcendental investigation is concerned with a far deeper level of teleological structure, namely, with the very source and possibility of such a purposive relation of consciousness considered universally. Like acts of possession that are deemed rightful, acts of knowledge make a universal claim upon others; indeed such acts demand that others agree in their own purposive use of the understanding with one's own results. But at the basis of any such claim, *if it is to be justified*, there must lie a set of structures and laws by which the possibility of such universal agreement is first guaranteed.

If I make a knowledge claim, then there must therefore be a universal standard or basis by means of which the rightfulness of this claim can be adjudicated. Clearly, if this is to be possible, then the standard of adjudication must be justified in itself; it must be such that no action in agreement with it could possibly contradict the rights of others. Similarly, the deduction of the categories, as the deduction of the concepts without which any intentional relation to a particular object would not be possible at all, is at the same time the justification of those standards without which no claim to knowledge would be possible (the principles), and thus these standards are at once guaranteed as universally valid.

The case of legal acts of possession can be brought even closer to Kant's transcendental investigation if we recognize that in any system of justice there must be certain *original actions,* which require no further defense than that without one's right to them no system of justice would be possible at all. Cases in point might be the right to make a claim, the right to present one's evidence in a court of law, the right to appeal to a judge, the right to draw up a contract of sale – such are indeed rights to particular actions, but they are *essentially different* from any specific act of justified possession. The difference lies in the fact that without such original actions there could be no general practice of rightful possession at all, and thus no individual acts of justified possession would be possible either. Put differently, one could say that if we do not admit that these original acts are justified, then there can be no justified acts whatsoever.[2] In the cognitive realm, by comparison, Kant speaks of certain original actions of the mind (he in fact calls them "original acquisitions," which he points out is a term used in the field of natural right (*ÜE* 08:221)), which are indeed always particular actions, but which at the same time require no other justification than that without them no cognition of any object would be possible at all. *They are particular acts, which are also universally justified.* Although we are always aware of them, they are not empirical but *transcendental*, because they are those original actions by means of which alone an object can first be represented. These are what Kant refers to under the name "transcendental synthesis." It is important to stress that they are transcendental not because they *temporally* precede all empirical acts, or because they take place on some mysterious non-empirical plane of mental reality, but simply because of the fact that they are in themselves absolutely justified in regard to objects in general. The transcendental acts of synthesis therefore precede absolutely all empirical acts of knowing *in the order of justification,* and this is what makes them transcendental. That the categories are justified in regard to objects in general, therefore just means that the synthetic action by which the manifold of sensibility is collected and brought under categorical unity is universally valid as well.

With this in place, we can now draw out in a preliminary way the following three elements of Kant's investigation: 1) Particular teleological or intentional relations between knower and object (and between perceptions and objects). 2) The universal and transcendental horizon of all possible such justified relations, constituted by a universal rule of harmony. 3) The original acts, which, like the former, are always manifest in particular relations, but which are also connected with the latter such that no particular and justified relation would be possible without them.

This analogy serves well for pointing out these two levels of teleological relation, and the place of certain original acts in respect to them. Yet it also has its limits. The rightfulness of our knowledge claims in regard to others is in fact a mere *consequence* of the rightfulness of knowledge claims in regard to objects in general. This, as we will presently see, can only be guaranteed by their agreement with the unity and harmoniousness of reason with itself in the representation of such objects. For this, however, I turn to the Transcendental Deduction itself.

---

[2] This is perhaps the weakness of the comparison: Something can be justified even if there is no practice of justification in the legal realm, but in the cognitive realm it is by means of these original acts that ownership is first made possible.

§. 3.3. The Deduction in the B-edition

In both editions Kant announces that the principle towards which the transcendental deduction must work is that the categories "must be recognized as *a priori* conditions of the possibility of experiences (whether of the intuition that is encountered in them, or of the thinking)" (*KrV* A94/B126). The deduction, as many have pointed out, therefore consists of two steps. In the first step (§§. 15–21), Kant aims to show that with respect to the understanding, the categories are conditions of the possibility of any knowledge that rests on intuition, and in the second step (§§. 25) he aims to show that these are also conditions of the possibility of objects presented to us in the specific forms of space and time. I have already indicated above in my preliminary outline that I understand the relation of these parts as consisting in the agreement of two distinct teleological structures within a teleological structure which embraces both. In speaking of space and time, we already saw that they possess their own teleological structure, which is manifest in the fact that they are singular intuitions, and as such are given as absolute wholes, which are presupposed by the possibility of their parts. Space and time are thus the sensible equivalents to ideas, and the consequence is that what is given as within them (particular spaces and times) are thought as completely determined by relation to them. In the first part of the Deduction, Kant argues that there is also a structurally parallel transcendental teleology which issues from the synthetic unity of apperception. Just as space and time provide the universal and necessary form of intuitions, so the synthetic unity of apperception in the guise of the categories (which are functions of its unity) provides the universal and necessary form of all thought of an object that might be given to it. Then, in the second part, Kant argues that the very same singularity of space and time *presupposes exactly the same kind of synthesis*, however such that it might be reflected in determinate acts of thought. Consequently, the two teleological structures harmonize such that the categories can be held to be conditions of the possibility of *experience*, which lies in the objective unification of perceptions under concepts. And by means of this result, it is shown that every particular act of knowledge presupposes – indeed holds before itself as a guide to the conscious formation of its judgments – an absolute whole of possible perceptual experience determined in itself. Like space and time and pure apperception, this image of a whole of nature is singular, or is such that each experience is only thought as thoroughly determined by reference to the whole of possible experience.

With this outline, let us begin with the first part of the Deduction. Kant begins this part in §. 15 with a general explanation of the concept of combination and its possibility. His first point is that although all cognition consists in a combination of the manifold given to us in intuition, the combination itself of this manifold cannot be given in the intuition. The reason for this is that sensibility is something passive, whereas combination is something that consists in an active awareness of the unity of what is given. Such an active awareness cannot therefore be given, but must be produced by the mind. Furthermore, combination contains two things, namely the manifold that is combined and a unity in accordance with which it is combined. The unity does not result from the combination, Kant explains, but rather the combination is first produced by the application of the unity to the manifold. The act of combining Kant calls "synthesis" and the unity by the application of which the combination of the manifold is made possible he calls the "synthetic unity." It is important to note regarding the latter, that although this unity is called "synthetic" by Kant, it is not the result of a synthesis, but it is much rather the case that the manifold must be synthetically combined so that it can first be brought under this unity.

After laying out these concepts, Kant makes the pivotal claim that the category "already presupposes combination." This might be somewhat surprising, since the categories are most often understood to be forms of synthesis, and thus as preceding it. In what sense, then, can the categories be said to "presuppose" a synthesis? Kant is very clear: "all categories are grounded on the logical functions in judgments, but in these combination, thus the unity of given concepts, is already thought" (*KrV* B131). The categories are the most basic concepts of *analysis*, and only for this reason are they also the guiding concepts of any synthesis. In the analysis, which applies the categories in judgments, the synthesis of the manifold is already presupposed. Thus as *actual concepts applied in judgments* the categories presuppose a synthesis of the manifold a priori, just like any other concept. This, it must be noted, does not preclude the possibility that the categories might also precede synthesis in the order of justification, namely, in the sense that only the synthesis carried out such that the categories can be applied is to be called justified transcendental synthesis. In other words, even if the concepts are only applied later in judgments after synthesis has taken place, the same categories may still be able to be said to be prior to the synthesis through the fact that only the acts of synthesis that are consciously guided by the categories are justified. In any case, Kant claims in §. 15, that since the unity which makes combination possible precedes the categories, it must be "someplace higher, namely in that which itself contains the ground of the unity of different concepts in judgments, and hence of the possibility of the understanding, even in its logical use" (*KrV* B131).

In §. 16, Kant investigates this qualitatively higher unity under the name of the "original-synthetic unity of apperception." Kant's strategy here is to show, firstly, that this unity is the absolutely first and active ground of the possibility

§. 3. The Transcendental Analytic — 187

of any representation whatsoever. Secondly, he derives from this fact several transcendental properties of this apperception. Thirdly, he attempts to argue from the nature of this apperception to the essential structure of any representation that might be possible through it (this begins in §. 16, but is only worked out in §§. 17–18). In this way, his argument parallels the pre-critical argument of the first part of the *BDG*. The reader will recall that in that text Kant first proves the existence of an absolute unity that is the ground of the possibility of all things, and proceeds in his second and third steps respectively to establish the transcendental properties of this being, showing only after this that these properties are the ground of the essential form of the object of God's will which is at the same time the ultimate object of human knowledge, namely, the whole of all creation.

Here, Kant argues firstly that this unity of apperception is absolutely necessary in regard to cognition as follows: 1) "The *I think* must *be able* to accompany all my representations" absolutely speaking for otherwise they "would either be impossible or else at least would be nothing for me." This is an *analytical truth*. 2) Intuition is found in us even before thinking. 3) Therefore, the intuition must have "a necessary relation to the *I think*." 4) But this requires an *activity of synthesis* by means of which the manifold of intuition is capable of being related to the analytic unity of the I think. This establishes the necessity of this unity in regard to cognition, and it shows furthermore that the unity itself *presupposes* a synthesis without which no representation would be possible as mine. It also, however, establishes in Kant's view the spontaneous, pure, original, singular and transcendental character of this apperception. Its spontaneity, as we just saw, stems from the fact that the synthesis presupposed by this unity cannot be given by the senses, as we earlier saw was the case in regard to all combination. For similar reasons, this unity is *original*, meaning it is the *absolutely first condition of all representations*, and as such has no representation prior to it; as regards unity, it is absolutely *unconditioned*. By contrast with empirical apperception, which is conditioned by it, this apperception can be called *pure* for the reason that, because it is first and active it cannot be mixed with what is given from without (passively). Kant does not explicitly refer to this apperception as singular, but nevertheless draws attention to the role it plays in producing the I think, which itself "in all consciousness is one and the same." This is confirmed in the paralogisms chapter of the B-edition: "That the I of apperception, consequently in every thought, is a *single thing* that cannot be resolved into a plurality of subjects, and hence a logically simple subject, lies already in the concept of thinking, and is consequently an analytic proposition" (*KrV* B407–408).

To this list Kant adds *transcendental*, he says, in order to note that it is a ground of the possibility of cognition *a priori*. In making this claim he shifts the focus of §. 16 from original-synthetic apperception itself, to the necessary connection between this unity and the unity of the representations brought under it. The major claim Kant makes in this regard is that the production of the "I think" in connection with the manifold of intuition requires a synthesis that is indeed of a very unique kind:

> The latter relation [i.e. between representations and the unity of the subject] therefore does not yet come about by my accompanying each representation with consciousness, but rather by my *adding* one representation to the other and being conscious of their synthesis. (*KrV* B133)

Synthesis, as Kant has stressed several times, is an act of the spontaneity of thought. The analytical unity of apperception, as we have also seen, presupposes such a synthesis for its possibility. But now we learn that this synthesis must consist specifically in an act by which one *consciously adds* each representation to the others and *retains this act of synthesis within consciousness*. This is a fundamental claim regarding what it means for consciousness to *act*, and it amounts to the contention that acts of consciousness are by their nature *intentional* or *teleological*; for it declares that an action can only properly be an action of consciousness if the *form of this act of consciousness* is identical with the *form of which we are conscious in the product of this act*. The two must be convertible. This is just the teleological condition of transparency, which must be presupposed for any operation of consciousness as something which acts essentially in a formal way or in accordance with the kind of unity found in concepts. Here, however, Kant supports this identity more explicitly by arguing that without consciousness of the unity of the synthesis produced, there could be no synthesis as an act of consciousness at all: "Namely, this thoroughgoing identity of the apperception of a manifold given in intuition contains a synthesis of the representations, and is possible only through the consciousness of this synthesis" (*KrV* B133).

From this Kant draws the important conclusion that it is the synthetic combining in one consciousness (i. e. a synthesis that takes place "before the eyes" of a singular self) that is presupposed for the possibility of an identity of the same self throughout all one's own representations. "The analytic unity of apperception," Kant explains, "is only possible under the presupposition of a synthetic one." It is important to note that this is not just a repetition of the claim of the last paragraph, but indeed includes the further inference above. For in this sentence, Kant is not saying that analytic unity of apperception presupposes synthesis simply, but that indeed it presupposes a synthetic *apperception*. This is key because it incorporates into the former claim the insight about the fact that this synthesis cannot be a sort of dead or mechanical activity, but rather must be an intentional act in which apperception is aware of its own progressive synthesis of the manifold.

Kant is very careful in the last paragraph of §. 16 to make this structure clear. The unity of apperception he stresses is merely an analytical unity, which belongs to all actual thinking merely through identity. But this analytical unity, because it does not produce the representations that are to be included under it, presupposes a synthesis by which the manifold is combined such that the manifold *can* be brought under it. In characterizing apperception in this way, Kant is able to make use of his pre-critical reflections on the relation of God to the world, but at the same time make a principled distinction between the two. Both God and apperception are thought as absolutely original, singular, unchanging conditions of the possibility of the unity in what they produce. And this is what makes it possible in both cases to think their objects as necessarily and essentially formed in accordance with these principles of unity. Unlike God, however, apperception is not an unconditioned ground, but rather merely an unconditioned *condition of unity*. Apperception does not produce its matter, but yet is the source of an absolutely original condition which requires for the possibility of any cognitions arising in accordance with it, that the matter given from without be thought as formed *as if* it had been produced by the understanding itself. Unlike God, apperception is an *empty* condition, but it is this very emptiness combined with the authorization that comes from being absolutely original, that makes such a projection of its own unity into experience both possible and necessary. Thus the transcendentally purposive structure in both cases is almost exactly parallel; that alone which is different lies in ground of the necessity of the laws grounded in it. In the case of God, they were thought to follow from the *originality* of his fullness and all-sufficiency, whereas from the standpoint of apperception they follow from the *originality* of its emptiness and finitude (dependence on sensibility).

Yet despite this difference, Kant does not entirely leave apperception high and dry. Although it is empty and conditioned by sensibility, it is still absolutely original and thus unconditioned in respect to form and thus also to unity. It is also active, and has before it an *a priori* manifold of pure sensibility with which to work. For this reason, pure apperception not only makes necessary, but indeed is able *to produce with absolute spontaneity*, the unity of thinking in its own representations, and thereby a unity of thought within one consciousness. It thus makes this unity possible originally, which means that the same unity belongs to its representations essentially and thus internally. The spontaneity of the mind in this respect is genuinely free, at least in regard to the unity of thinking, and it forms a world of thought for itself. Whether this extends to intuition and thus also to experience, however, is yet to be decided.

In §. 17, Kant begins by noting that we have arrived at a parallel between the supreme principles of intuition and the principle of understanding. Namely, just as space and time are the first formal principles of all intuition in regard to sensibility, so similarly the "supreme principle of all intuition in regard to the understanding is that all the manifold of intuition stand under the conditions of the original synthetic unity of apperception." The difference is only that the former relates to what is given, while the latter to what is thought in one consciousness (*KrV* B137). The overall aim of this section is clearly to connect up the original-synthetic unity of apperception with the understanding, and thereby also with the concept of an object in general. The basic claim for such a connection rests on an identity Kant points to between the unity of the manifold of intuition, which is thought as necessary through the conscious relating of it to an object, X, in which it is already objectively combined, and the unity of consciousness in the synthesis of such a manifold. This might be put simply as: The original-synthetic unity of apperception has been shown to be an absolutely necessary principle of all representation whatsoever insofar as this can only come about through the consciousness of the synthesis of the intuitive manifold. Now, when the understanding thinks an object, all it really does is to represent to itself the synthesis of a manifold of intuition as necessarily united. The concept of an object is not originally that of a thing, but rather is the consciousness of the necessity of just such a synthesis. That we constantly relate our perceptions to objects in general, and indeed think of them as necessarily relating to some object, is just our consciousness of the necessity of a synthesis of these perceptions. Thus, the same synthetic unity of apperception is presupposed by and manifest in the action of the understanding when it determinately represents any actual object. But more generally, the possibility of representing something as objective at all rests on the necessity of this original apperception. For, aside from this singular unity, there is no other that could render the action of the understanding necessary, and thus valid without restriction. For this reason Kant also refers to original apperception as the "objective unity of self-consciousness" later in §. 18.

In §. 17, however, Kant concludes from this reflection that:

> The synthetic unity of consciousness is therefore an objective condition of all cognition, not merely something I myself need in order to cognize an object but rather something under which every intuition must stand *in order to become an object for me*, since in any other way, and without this synthesis, the manifold would *not* be united in one consciousness. (*KrV* B138)

Objects in general, which are represented by the action of the understanding, are thus nothing but particular consequences of this synthetic unity of apperception. The unity it brings into the manifold is entirely free and unlimited by anything outside of itself, but it is not for this reason to be regarded as a mere invention or something falsely imposed upon our intuitions. It is rather true of them simply because it is the first absolutely necessary condition which makes possible all representations of objects in general. This unity is not true because it agrees with the constitution of some transcendent object, but because it is that unity with which all further unity of thought must agree if it is to be possible at all. The transcendental condition of the truth of cognition is therefore nothing but its agreement with the original-synthetic unity of apperception.

With this basic structure in place, Kant now turns in §§. 19–20 to unite with this the logical form of judgments, and thus also the categories. In principle, however, the main argument of this first half of the deduction is complete. We have just seen that the action of the understanding whereby it represents an object presupposes an original-synthetic apperception whereby the manifold is synthetically combined such that it can be brought under this same unity of an object. In §. 19, Kant makes an essential move by defining judgment to be "nothing other than the way to bring given cognitions to the objective unity of apperception" (*KrV* B141). Kant's idea here is that judgment is precisely that action of the understanding whereby an object is represented. It is thus also that whereby analytic unity is extended throughout our cognitions. The analytic unity presupposes, however, the original-synthetic one, and so the basic concepts employed in judging also presuppose one (this, notably, agrees with Kant's claim in §. 15 that the categories presuppose a synthesis). The original-synthetic unity, however, consists in the singular consciousness of a synthesis by means of which the manifold of intuition is gathered into and reflected under a concept. Consequently, when I judge that, for instance, "X is the cause of Y," the *aim* of this judgment is to indicate that the synthesis by which the manifold relating to X and Y is gathered into a unity that is itself necessary. The contention, thus, is that a synthesis in accordance with precisely this category and no other is generally valid. All the deduction aims to establish in this first part, however, is that the absolute necessity of the original-synthetic apperception makes it equally necessary that some synthesis is possible of such a manifold whereby it can be reflected under the categories.

This can be seen further by noting that nothing can become an object of thought except through analysis, and the basic system of concepts employed in this analysis is precisely that through which alone given things are represented objectively. Now, this unity is and can only be objectively valid because it is the consequence of the original-synthetic unity of apperception. The categories are therefore nothing other than the reflected concepts through which consciousness of the original-synthetic unity of apperception is expressed, and thus in accordance with which any valid act of synthesis must take place. The categories are only actually applied in judgment that already presupposes a synthesis, but because the synthesis must be one of which we are conscious, and the categories are just the basic forms of such consciousness, the synthesis must be one in accordance with these forms. This is just to say that the categories are not simply valid because we synthesize in accordance with them as our rules, but rather because if it were not the case that synthesis in accordance with the categories were regarded as valid, then the intuitive manifold in this case would be nothing to us. The conclusion is that it is true for any possible object in general, that the intuitive manifold for which it provides the unity must necessarily be able to be synthesized in accordance with the categories.

With this the first part of the deduction arrives at its conclusion: The synthesis of the intuition, which takes place before the eyes of original apperception, is that alone by which the representation of an object is possible. It is thus absolutely necessary and unconditioned. Moreover, the analytic unity that this synthesis makes both possible and necessary is the same unity that is articulated in accordance with the logical functions of judgment. The categories, however, were shown in the Metaphysical Deduction to be nothing other than the basic concepts by means of which such logical functions are thought as determining the object. The synthesis overseen by original apperception must therefore be in accordance with the categories. This explains why Kant can claim that: "The same understanding, therefore, and indeed by means of the very same actions through which it brings the logical form of a judgment into concepts by means of the analytical unity, also brings a transcendental content into its representations by means of the synthetic unity of the manifold in intuition in general" (*KrV* A79/B105).

Skipping over the explanatory §§. 21–26, we arrive finally at the second step of the deduction, which aims to show that these forms of thought are not only necessary in regard to thinking, and in regard to an intuition in general, but even in regard to our specific forms of intuition, space and time. Kant's essential goal here is thus to show that space and time as they are established in the Transcendental Aesthetic presuppose (just as the analytic unity of consciousness does) the original-synthetic unity of apperception. In order to do this, Kant refers us back to the *singularity* of these forms. Earlier, in a footnote to §. 17, Kant had already brought attention to the fact that space and time are not mere forms of intuition, but are also intuitions, and thus are singular, and that this means space and time are "many representations that are contained in one and in the consciousness of it; they are thus found to be composite, and consequently the unity of consciousness, as synthetic and yet as original, is to be found in them." In §. 26, Kant explains this more fully by introducing a distinction between space and time as forms of intuition and as formal intuitions. As formal intuitions space and time are represented as singular unities, but as forms of intuition they are thought to contain a manifold within them that is united into this one. From this he draws the conclusion that space and time as formal intuitions presuppose a synthesis "through which all concepts of space and time first become possible."

This requires some explanation. Firstly, by "concepts of space and time" I understand Kant to mean determinate and actual representations (for instance, of a square), and not space and time themselves as forms of intuition. Such a usage is attested in Kant's discussion of mathematics in the Doctrine of Method (*KrV* A720/B748). In the Aesthetic it was shown that determinate concepts of space and time presuppose for their possibility a relation to space and time as formal intuitions. This is because the complete determination of any part of space or time presupposes its relations to the actual whole of which it is a part. However, Kant here notes that the singularity of such formal intuitions already presents us with a representation in which the manifold is essentially seen as belonging within a fully determinate unity. The *pure* intuitions of space and time, therefore, contain within themselves the unity of the synthesis (though not the synthesis itself) of what lies within them. Now, if something is given empirically it must be given in accordance with this form, and thus also in accordance with this complete unity. But nothing can be *thought determinately* as combined that is not combined by the original synthesis, which itself is governed by the categories. Thus not even determinate concepts of space and time can be given without the action of such a synthesis in accordance with the categories. This, importantly, does not mean that the singular unities of space and time are generated or infused into the manifold of intuition by the categories. Categorial and intuitive unities are essentially heterogeneous, as the schematism chapter makes clear. But space and time as well as all of their parts are perfectly determinate unities, as the Aesthetic shows, and this means that in order to represent these the mind must run through, collect and synthesize the intuitive manifold in accordance with its own unity of thought, which latter is possible only in accordance with the categories. One might put the matter thusly: The categories are conditions of any synthesis that can result in an object of thought. Space and time are conditions that prescribe the necessary unity of the manifold of what can be sensed. So when we encounter something given in space or time we represent this sensibly and necessarily as a manifold contained in one. But to *think* this for ourselves determinately, and to thus bring this sensible unity *within thought* in a determinate way, we must actively synthesize it, and for the sake of this the original-synthetic apperception must follow a concept by which its action is grasped as one by consciousness itself. Of course, the concepts that can play this role are nothing but the categories.

Kant explains this point with great clarity in the body of §. 26:

> We have *forms* of outer as well as inner sensible intuition *a priori* in the representations of space and time, and the synthesis of the apprehension of the manifold of appearances must always be in agreement with the latter, since it can only occur in accordance with this form. But space and time are represented *a priori* not merely as *forms* of sensible intuition, but also as *intuitions* themselves (which contain a manifold), and thus with the determination of the *unity* of this manifold in them (see the Transcendental Aesthetic).* Thus even *unity of the synthesis* of the manifold, outside or within us, hence also a *combination* with which everything that is to be represented as determined in space or time must agree, is already given *a priori*, along with (not in) these intuitions, as condition of the synthesis of all *apprehension*. But this synthetic unity can be none other than that of the combination of the manifold of a given *intuition in general* in an original consciousness, in agreement with the categories, only applied to our *sensible intuition*. Consequently all synthesis, through which even perception itself becomes possible, stands under the categories, and since experience is cognition through connected perceptions, the categories are conditions of the possibility of experience, and thus are also valid *a priori* of all objects of experience.
>
> *Space, represented as *object* (as is really required for geometry), contains more than the mere form of intuition, namely the *comprehension* of the manifold in accordance with the form of sensibility in an intuitive representation, so that the *form of intuition* merely gives the manifold, but the *formal intuition* gives unity of the representation. In the Aesthetic I ascribed this unity merely to sensibility, only in order to note that it precedes all concepts, though to be sure it presupposes a synthesis, which does not belong to the senses but through which all concepts of space and time first become possible. For since through it (as the understanding determines the sensibility) space or time are first *given* as intuitions, the unity of this *a priori* intuition belongs to space and time, and not to the concepts of the understanding.

Kant does not spell out in detail the reasons for his conviction that sensibility and understanding rest on heterogeneous kinds of unity here, but this is no doubt related to their differing relations to synthesis, which I think Kant clearly stresses in the passage above. The analytic unity of thought, as we have seen, presupposes a synthesis which in fact precedes it, and which actively brings the manifold under the otherwise empty unity of apperception. Concepts of any kind, therefore, "presuppose" a synthesis by means of which they are possible as concepts, i.e. general representations. The unity of intuition, however, as it is described in the passage above, itself presupposes a synthesis in quite a different sense. The unity of sensibility must be regarded as itself preceding any synthesis, because the very *singularity* of space and time as pure intuitions, which is essential to their concepts, rests on the idea of an absolute totality that is *given all at once*. No synthesis, therefore, could possibly produce them fully or in a manner congruent with these original intuitions. Yet they presuppose a synthesis, because they contain a manifold, and only through synthesis

§. 3. The Transcendental Analytic — 195

is it possible for *thought* to represent anything to itself at all. Thus, in order to be grasped in thought, and thus also in order to belong to the whole of determined self-consciousness, spatial and temporal concepts must be constructed through an act of synthesis on the part of original-synthetic apperception. Space and time therefore are absolute unities, and they presuppose a synthesis not like concepts, because they first become possible through it, but rather because, as passive forms, they would not be able to be taken up into thought itself (which is active) unless we were able to form concepts of them, and this latter requires a synthesis. Expressed in one formula, space and time as pure sensitive intuitions do not require a synthesis as such, or include a synthesis (they are, after all, not activities); rather such a synthesis is required for us to gain knowledge though them, only because we must be able to have *concepts* of space and time (i.e. representations of them produced by the activity of thought) if anything represented by means of them is ever to belong to one whole of objective consciousness.

The unity of thought is in this case *merely a means* to the partial determination, in respect to thought itself, of the unity already contained in the pure intuitions of space and time *a priori*, which as singular representations are in themselves completely determined. The fact that we can only represent these as mediated by the unity of thought (in concepts of space and time) makes this unity no less originally sensible. It is indeed a unity that we represent *as given* independently of thinking, although it is only first presented to us in relation to concepts in accordance with which the manifold is actively synthesized for the sake of thinking it.

This, to be sure, is a difficult point. But it can be illuminated by recalling our earlier discussion of the sort of deception that Kant saw as arising from the perfection of mathematical figures constructed in space. In that case, Kant noted how one almost inevitably becomes convinced that there is required an external ground of space that is the source of its formal perfection, because the purposive unity found in the constructed figure always contains infinitely more formal perfection than resides in the concept of this figure. The concept of a circle, for instance, which is merely a rule for its construction, contains nothing of the infinity of different solutions that it can provide to mathematical problems. It is for this reason that we seem to genuinely discover something more in space than we place in it through this act of construction. Now, when we looked more closely at that example before, we found that Kant does not in fact deny that there is a far richer kind of unity in the figure than is to be found in its concept. What he claims rather, is that this unity is entirely produced by us *in the activity of constructing a figure in space according to this concept.* The key here is that the unity in question lies not in the concept, nor in some absolute space considered as transcendentally given apart from our determination of it through this concept, but rather *in the very unity of this act of construction* in which the concept is used to synthetically combine the pure manifold in accordance with the form of space. It is thus just as incorrect to say that this unity genuinely belongs in some objective manner to a thing called "space," as it would be to say that it is first infused into the intuitive manifold by the understanding. For the same reason, it would be wrong to interpret the pure intuitions of space and time as being some kind of indeterminate forms, which only gain determination from the understanding. There is simply no sense to any talk of space and time in a real sense prior to their determination through the understanding in the act of construction. Yet, and this is most important, relative to these same acts of construction, the richer unity that comes about through it, in order to be represented as objective (and as empirically real), must also be represented as being there prior to the act of construction, like the statue already there in the marble.

The conclusion of this second part of the deduction, then, is that the forms of sensibility are subject to the categories for no other reason than that they too (like the analytical unity of thinking) presuppose by their own singularity in regard to sense a synthetic act in regard to thought whereby *concepts* of them become possible. The categories, therefore, are not only the concepts in accordance with which the thought of objects becomes possible, but indeed in accordance with which all representations become possible in general.

§. 4. Summary

The teleology underlying the Transcendental Deduction is not one of art, but of creation. The understanding itself creates "nature" as the lawful connection of the appearances, through its transcendental synthesis, and yet this nature is but the form of a whole of possible cognition (i.e. nature taken formally, not materially), and thus not the whole of anything transcendentally real. Such a creation of nature in a formal sense is made possible, as we have seen, by the *purposive harmony in relation to a single common goal, i.e. the production of experience,* that Kant has discovered between the transcendental teleological structures underlying sensibility and understanding. Both have been shown to be the sources of a manifold that is internally unified and governed by absolutely original and determinate principles of possibility. And in both cases, it has also been shown that the complete determinacy of the unity arising from them rests on the singularity and originality of these grounds in their respective domains. There is but one space and one time; there is but one original-synthetic apperception; and, finally, there is but one whole of experience in which the two

§. 4. Summary — 197

are combined to form the field of all possible human cognition. Each of these original wholes are presupposed as given in order to allow us to represent as necessary the complete determinacy of the manifold in which the respective cognitive functions are thought to agree. As Kant explains in the Deduction of the A-edition:

> There is only one experience, in which all perceptions are represented as in thoroughgoing and law-like connection, just as there is only one space and time, in which all forms of appearance and all relation of being or non-being take place. If one speaks of experiences, they are only so many perceptions insofar as they belong to one and the same universal experience. The thoroughgoing [i.e. complete] and synthetic unity of perceptions is precisely what constitutes the form of experience, and it is nothing other than the synthetic unity of the appearance in accordance with concepts. (*KrV* A110)

The transcendental purposiveness of experience explains, for this reason, how it is possible for an individual's sensations to be self-consciously related to an object, and how this object, as a ground that does not itself appear, but which is rather the point outside, or on the boundary of our appearances, is also able to provide a ground of their universal significance. In this way, in an *actual* judgment of cognition, the otherwise *contingent* order of an individual's perceptions is *purposively determined in one way* that is regarded as *hypothetically necessary* in relation to the assumption of an object upon which this order is represented as depending.

Now, Kant has further demonstrated that since it is impossible for the object to appear in its inner constitution (since no determinate combination can be given), and since an implanted "necessary" rule for ordering perceptions would not be experienced by the thinking subject *as* necessary, this rule must have its source in the understanding. Thus, according to Kant, it is only by being subordinated to an *intellectual unity* that gives a rule to the series that the perceptions within it can relate *purposively* to an object in the first place. In other words, the self-conscious activity of forming judgments depends upon an ability to bring the otherwise independent faculties of sensibility and understanding to an intentional or teleological unity, and the logical functions of judgment, as well as the categories that underlie them, describe principles of the possibility of precisely this.

This does not, however, explain how such intentionality is possible, or give any clue as to why a rule that is *hypothetically* necessary in regard to particular perceptions, might have objective validity, i.e. be a *law*, and thus why we should have any right to claim this subordination is necessary *in itself* and *universally* for all human experience such as is required to relate the subject, at least in intention, to an object apart from how the subject might happen to accidentally represent this object. Consequently, the possibility of an intentional relation (of specific perceptions to a specific object) that would be objectively valid has required a transcendental proof that: a) certain rules governing this teleological relation are in fact *laws* required for the possibility of any intentional act whatsoever, and b) that this act of legislation regarding the subordination of given material to necessary laws is in fact rightful, i.e. that it occurs within a domain over which the legislating body, in this case understanding, has absolutely free and uncontested domain.

To establish the first of these points, Kant calls on the principle that the unity of a self-consciousness containing a manifold of perceptions, without which there would be no subject and hence no thought of an object either, is only possible through the consciousness of the (synthetic) unity of its perceptions. Now since the first unity is necessary, so is the latter, and since the unity of the object is only possible through the determination of perceptions under the categories, the first point is established. With this in place, it is now possible to see that since perceptions are related purposively to an object only by virtue of being brought under a rule, but this rule, if it is to be objectively valid, must in turn be subsumed under a unity that is necessary for the possibility of having knowledge of an object at all, it must be the case that "empirical laws are only particular determinations of the pure laws of the understanding, under which and in accordance with whose norm they are first possible" *(KrV A128).*

Thus because any judgment that intends an object is *only possible* if it is based upon a self-conscious act of subordinating one's sensations to a rule through which they are determined in view of the understanding's form of a *thoroughly determined* unity of appearances (experience), the transcendental structures that make experience possible are necessarily valid laws with regard to any possible object of experience. The rules of experience, then, do not relate to the whole of experience as individual to general, or even as means to end, but rather as *particular to universal*, and the synthetic *a priori* principles that hold for the former are nothing other than the manifold ways in which objects can be determined in view of belonging to, or being contained within, a completely determined whole of human experience. Nature in a transcendental sense, then, is nothing less than a universal horizon of within which the purposive relation between the thinking subject and an object first becomes possible, and it can in a certain sense be called a *system of systems of cognition*, or the science of sciences, or, again, a principle of teleological unity with regard to objects universally speaking. For it is, in intention at least, an absolute unity grounding the possibility of experience as a completely determined system of connected cognitions, and determinative judgment, which is based upon the idea of this unity, is from its very foundation directed in a purposive way towards a universal and infinite field of cognitive "ends," i.e. possible objects of knowledge.

Point b mentioned above is equally essential, and really underlies Kant's entire argument, but has received less attention in the literature. It is established by recognizing, first, that we are always dealing with mere appearances that exist only in relation to our sensibility, and second, that what is given in such sensibility contains no laws.[3] The first establishes the freedom of the understanding in its legislation from any dependence upon, or claim with regard to, the objects as they are constituted in themselves, while the second does the same for the understanding in its relation to sensibility. The upshot is that, as the only source of *a priori* laws in regard to objects, the understanding is absolutely free to extend the conditions that are necessary for it, over all possible objects of cognition; it is thus autonomous and self-sufficient within the bounds of possible experience. The price of this autonomy, of course, is the doctrine of transcendental idealism.

It is thus on the transcendental level that the most basic place and function of teleology in the Analytic becomes evident, and all similarities with organisms or with a form of life are merely ways of partially describing the Analytic's far richer and more perfect teleological structure. Kant's transcendental deduction thus aims to establish in an *essential* and *intensive* manner the unity or necessity of the connection between the pure analytic unity of apperception (without which there would be no *thought* of an object), and the absolute synthetic unity of a possible empirical experience (without which this thought would lack relation to a real object, i.e. objective reality), and it does this by reference to *idea of a whole of possible human experience* in which sensibility and understanding are to be combined and in relation to which the understanding enjoys absolute freedom and independence. The idea or form of a *unique whole of all possible empirical experience*, then, is an *end that is also a whole or totality*, which founds not only the possibility of a total system of the human cognitive powers (transcendental psychology), but also the possibility of a total system of objects of human cognition (ontology), and thereby establishes a two-sided teleological structure. The teleological unity manifest in empirical cognitions relates to the transcendental unity of the mind in the same way as actuality relates to the real ground of possibility, or as the extension of a concept relates to its intension. That is to say, the teleological unity of actual cognition displays in an *extensive* way (with regard to the subject in its manifold operations) the

---

[3] This point is somewhat more complicated, since the aesthetic seems to argue that space and time as pure intuitions are sources of laws for the appearances. I submit that this is, at least in part, the reason for Kant's attempts in the B-Deduction to show that "this synthetic unity can be none other than that of the combination of the manifold of a given intuition in general in an original consciousness, in agreement with the categories, only applied to our sensible intuition" (*KrV* B 161).

very same unity that transcendental philosophy establishes *intensively* as belonging originally and autonomously to the essence of human cognition. Teleology, then, describes the idea and schema that lies at the basis of self-consciousness and through which it relates the actual in human cognition to the grounds that make it possible, and thereby explains why certain features of the actual are not only subjectively necessary, but are also *recognized as objectively necessary* by theoretical self-consciousness. The interrelation of these two teleological structures (i.e. the transcendental and the empirical) is the structure of self-consciousness in the *activity* of particularizing itself in its objects. In the case of human cognition, transcendental teleology thus turns out to be nothing other than the inner ground of cognitive normativity.

Finally, we have seen that at the teleological core of determinative judgment lies the transcendental synthesis of the imagination. As a *synthesis* it is an act of the mind which produces a unified representation from a previously given manifold. And as *transcendental* synthesis, it is one that produces with absolute spontaneity and originality an absolute whole of all intellectual representations, the singular whole of all possible experience insofar as it is thought. However, as itself "empty" or as dependent upon the receptivity of sensation, this same transcendental synthesis presupposes or requires a pure manifold of intuition given to it from outside, and if this, again, is not to compromise the absoluteness of such synthesis there must exist a perfect harmony between the unity required for thought and the unity of this pure sensible manifold in itself. Thus, it cannot be proven or derived, but it can be shown to be a presupposition of all knowledge, that the absolute purposive unity (i.e. complete determinacy of the interconnection of the parts within the whole) produced by transcendental synthesis is in agreement with the absolute purposive unity contained within space and time as pure intuitions (as shown in the Aesthetic). Consequently, the transcendental synthesis through which the form of all knowledge is produced, and indeed produced in accordance with or as guided by the unity found in the categories (as vehicles of the unity of apperception) is an absolutely purposive or teleological action of the mind. Furthermore, since every action of the mind through which an object of cognition is determined in regard to a real predicate (found only in experience) is a *specification* of this original action, and for this reason the pure transcendental action can be regarded as the *proper essence* of determinative judgment, it can be concluded that all real determination is *per se* teleological, or is teleological when viewed in terms of its transcendental possibility. And this is nothing but the Kantian apology for Leibniz's claim that the principle of sufficient reason is at the same time the principle of final causes.

Chapter 5 Teleology in the Transcendental Dialectic

Introduction

The Transcendental Dialectic has three functions, the most famous of which is to show that all purported knowledge of the noumenal realm is based upon a natural and unavoidable illusion. Such illusions are natural, Kant explains, because reason in all cases demands the absolute, or assumes that when the conditioned is given, so also are all the conditions (*KrV* A307–308/B364). Since the conditioned in this case is an object or law of experience, and reason in fact only introduces the unconditioned in order to support and explain the existence and truth of such an object or law, it naturally leads us to think of the unconditioned as itself objective and secure. Indeed, it would seem that the very objective validity of the conditioned rests on the unconditioned, and thus that the denial of the validity of the idea of the unconditioned would lead to the denial of the validity of the conditioned as well. The illusions, Kant thus argues in the Dialectic, arise from a natural and avoidable teleology of reason (*KrV* A298/B354–355), which compels it to assume the infinite in order to provide a ground for the finite.

For Kant, however, the criticism of reason, in which consists this first function of the Dialectic, requires more than just the proof that no such knowledge is possible. Because of the inevitability of such illusions, they can only be genuinely defused if transcendental philosophy manages to explain their source and necessity from the structure of reason itself. Only in this way – by means of an active and reflective self-regulation of reason – is it possible to avoid the negative consequences of this subreption. Indeed, as we saw in Chapter 1, due to the very isolation and purity of the higher faculty of reason, Kant is in fact certain that even such a necessary tendency to error must rest on positive and useful grounds. This is because the very possibility of this error must lie entirely within reason itself, and thus the key to correcting it must lie in making use of transcendental reflection to bring these grounds of error into harmony with the whole of reason's activities. In another respect, however, these errors are not genuine errors at all, but rather part of the very self-regulation that constitutes the intrinsic structure of pure reason as an essentially *self-conscious* faculty. In other words, the chaos and disharmony that results when the conditions of sensible experience are conflated with reason's transcendental ideas are in fact the positive grounds that provide, and have historically provided, the incentive for reason to undertake its own self-examination. The conflicts arising within reason are therefore no mere contradictions, but rather reason actively developing itself from its character as a mere disposition into a secure critical science. As Kant explains, "the conflict between these propositions is not a logical conflict of analytical opposition [...], i.e., a mere contradiction," but rather "a transcendental conflict of synthetic opposition" (*FM* 20:291). For this reason a resolution is possible in which one, neither or both propositions are shown to be true, if only their synthetic roles are critically set apart. One might put the matter this way: The apparent disharmony and contradictoriness that arises in an uncritical use of reason, first make possible and necessary a more original harmony of reason that can only be reached through an essentially self-reflective examination. The role of self-reflection is thus shown to be essential to the activity of reason, and thus in such transcendental reflection reason does not abolish or cancel the lower-order illusions, for these are in their own way inevitable and beneficial for the empirical use of reason; it rather limits and relativizes their significance to the conditions in accordance with which they serve a healthy function. In fact, I believe that if properly understood, the link between transcendental illusions and reason's self-reflective character could not be more essential. For if the illusions were to be totally removed, then there would be no ground for thinking of reason as an *essentially* self-reflective and self-regulating or autonomous activity. Moreover, if reason is indeed essentially such a kind of activity, then there must be some most basic imperfection and disharmony in its functioning when this self-regulatory component is left out of view. In this way, the critical philosophy is genuinely the spur to an active use of reason, and not a pillow to fall asleep on (*VNAEF* 08:415).

For Kant, reason is an essentially self-reflective activity, and it never fails to function in accordance with its proper nature (*KrV* A294/B350). At the basis of this reciprocal relation, in Kant's mind, lies the fundamental fact that pure reason – reason considered in its very essence – is a *transcendentally purposive* form of self-consciousness. In other words, its deepest roots lie in an absolutely pure and original principle of unity in self-consciousness, and all else that arises from it naturally and necessarily has its purposive function in articulating and maintaining the whole of reason in its own perfect harmony. This idea of a self-articulating and self-formative faculty is just what we saw in Chapter 1 provides for Kant the guarantee of the possibility of an exhaustive and systematic critical examination of pure reason. This same purity and originality is thus what also guarantees that the transcendental illusions must belong to a wider economy of pure reason's own purposive activity.

Drawing on our examination in Chapters 1 and 2, we can see that this same unity is modeled by Kant on the dynamic teleology he developed in the pre-critical period, particularly as this is evident in the *NTH* and *PND*. Kant's goal at the time was in part to discover a teleological structure that could, in the way described by Pope's *Essay*, do justice to the relation between the world and its all-sufficient and most perfect cause, but which at the same time would not lead to the denial of the reality of certain things like evil. The problem was one of maintaining at the same time that something like evil is a reality and that everything considered in itself is good, as is required by the fact of God's all-sufficiency. The solution for Pope, and even more clearly for Kant, was located in the essential *dynamism* of creation. An evil is really opposed to some *particular* good, and relative to *this* good it certainly should be overcome; but this overcoming lies precisely in the taking up of the spur to activity that lies at the basis of this evil itself. Like attraction and repulsion, which are both real forces, the conflict between evil and good on the level of the particular results, they argued, is a dynamic activity that operates according to a law by which an infinity of unities and purposive relations, i.e. goods, necessarily and naturally arise on a more universal level. The opposition of forces, in other words, leads naturally and inevitably to the development of an even more perfect system of activity, just as in the *NTH* this conflict of forces and activities is seen as leading to the development of an infinity of cosmic systems unfolding within cosmic systems. That the ultimate cosmos is, however, the most perfect and most dynamically articulated was thought by Kant to be already guaranteed by the basis from which these original forces and the laws of their interaction first arose, namely God's perfect and all-sufficient being.

A precisely parallel problem faces the critical system in its discovery of the antinomies: Reason, which is a pure, original and thus self-sufficient principle, discovers within itself what appear to be counter-purposive operations, secondary principles that are each directed to knowledge but which in particular combinations actually lead to a nest of contradictions and opposed maxims of judgment under the assumption that they are constitutive. Kant's solution here, as before, is to relativize these principles to the *dynamic unfolding of reason from its original principle*. The seemingly contradictory principles are thus revealed by Kant to be just so many different and *complimentary* principles, which through both their unity in one system of reason *and* their heterogeneity as constituting separate sub-systems regulating reason's differing forces and tendencies, serve to produce a self-image of reason as a dynamic and self-articulating whole of rational self-consciousness.

This tracing of transcendental illusions to their roots thus leads to a second and third positive function of the Dialectic of the *KrV*. The first of these is to systematically outline all the distinct ideas of the absolute insofar as they spring originally from pure reason's essential function. This serves to systematize the criticism of our supposed knowledge of the objects of these ideas, but also has the much more important function of providing a scientific cognition, indeed a complete structural outline based upon a principle, of all the principles of completeness, which reason always strives in its cognition to equal. These are thus seen to be the archetypes or models which contain, as it were, the transcendent focal point and norm of all reason's activities.

Of course, the unveiling of the dialectical inferences of pure reason proves that such concepts cannot be objective, and this puts reason in a peculiar situation. Reason demands the absolute, as Kant remarks, and thinks as in the absolute the highest ground without which no employment of reason would be possible. But at the same time, it is able to recognize with equal certainty that this ground cannot be objective. Reason needs and even demands the absolute, but it can never truly represent it. How is reason to escape from this difficulty? In accordance with what I claimed above, Kant's solution is to trace the problem to its root source in reason, and to show that although the idea of the unconditioned arises purely and spontaneously from reason itself, the assumption of the objectivity of this concept in a theoretical respect is in every case only required for the sake of the use of the understanding in its greatest possible extension, and thus exclusively as limited to an empirical employment. In other words, the unconditioned must be assumed as objective, but only for the sake of the employment of reason insofar as it gives unity and direction to the understanding in its research into experience. In this employment, furthermore, the unconditioned is represented *as if* objective, and indeed *as if* it were the ultimate real ground of all objects represented by the understanding. Transcendental reflection, however, is that alone which allows us to restrict this assumption of the unconditioned *as if* objective to the function it plays in regard to the understanding, and prevents us from thinking that this necessary assumption is itself absolutely valid, or constitutive of the unconditioned, which in fact would undermine reason's own activity. The explanation of the possibility and nature of such a "regulative" employment of the ideas, which is nothing but the positive function of these illusions themselves for the sake of empirical knowledge, constitutes the third and final function of the Dialectic.

In the following, I will attend chiefly to the second and third functions of the Dialectic in order to examine how Kant here takes over the core of his pre-critical teleology, namely the idea of God as the self-sufficient ground of the *omnitudo realitatis*, and transforms it into the highest focal point of reason. In particular, it will become clear through this analysis that the two positive functions of the ideas are precisely what make it possible for Kant to wed theoretical and practical reason into a single whole. The ideas, as we will see, extend essentially beyond anything theoretical reason can represent (they are transcendent) and in this respect they point beyond theoretical reason to its possible practical employment. In this function, the ideal of pure reason in particular constitutes an absolute and "faultless" pure image untainted by any relation to the sensible. In this respect, however, it is destined to remain merely a *critical principle* for theoretical reason. But as we will see in Chapters 6 and 7, it is precisely this purity that allows the same ideal to be given an immanent and constitutive moral function.

This same purity, however, also makes it necessary to explain how it can be *possible* for something that is *heterogeneous* in respect to absolutely everything derived from the senses to be employed for the regulation of our empirical use of the understanding. The answer, as we will see, is that to fulfill such a function, the absolute must be provided with something like a *schema*, or an mediating image that is cut to fit this function in regard to the understanding. The idea of God, in particular, is in this regard constructed by Kant on *analogy* with human reason itself, such that the assumption of the existence of such a being is at once the assumption that the world is constituted in accordance with a *transcendental teleology of which particular ends are mere consequences*, i.e. it is constituted in regard to its essential, universal and necessary laws in a way that is maximally fit for comprehension by human reason (i.e. as made possible by concepts, which is the transcendental definition of purposiveness). We must think the world as if really designed purposively by an archetypal intellect, because only in this way can we maximally subject the empirical world to our methods of research. In this function, the ideal serves to articulate the normative teleological structure of reason in its regulation of the empirical employment of the understanding. As we will see, however, the function of mediation that is played by the analogy in the Transcendental Analytic is cashed out in terms of specific methodological principles through Kant's little noted concept of a maxim of reason.

§. 1. The Relation of the Analytic to the Dialectic

Before looking more closely at the Dialectic itself, it is important to see how Kant distinguishes it from what was treated in the Analytic. As we saw in the last chapter, the Analytic explains the possibility of particular teleological or intentional relations of the mind to empirical objects by exhibiting precisely how the mind itself, from its own spontaneous resources, constitutes a transcendental horizon of objectivity, i.e. a field within which perceptions can be regarded universally and necessarily as belonging to just such a complete unity as is required in order to think them as related to an object. In other words, in order to show how such an empirical relation to an object is possible, Kant adduces arguments by means of which he is able to prove that the field of perceptions can and must be thought of as *already constituted* with precisely the unity which would be captured in any such empirical relation generally speaking. It is this same transcendentally purposive unity of perceptions that both makes the application of the categories objectively valid, and allows us to regard as necessary and objective the rules of unity (the principles of understanding) that can be derived from their validity.

The laws governing the transcendentally teleological relation to any possible object in general, however, do not yet in Kant's view exhaust the field of cognitive normativity. Thus the Transcendental Analytic is described by Kant as providing merely the principles of a possible *distributive* unity among the objects of experience, by contrast with which, the Dialectic is said to treat the ideas of pure reason, which are concerned rather with the *collective* unity of objects (*KrV* A670/B697). In order to understand what Kant means by this distinction, it is first necessary to recognize that the results of the Analytic must be limited in at least two important and related ways. The deduction of the categories and the proofs of the principles that arise from them are necessary for the determination of any given object based upon their essential relation to the form of a possible experience. However, such experience must first be given empirically, and cannot be given with the unity that can only be produced by the activity of thinking. Hence, actual experience is a *synthetic* totality, which must rather be progressively constructed from the objects that are offered in perception. Now, as this progressive act of construction is also an act of determining what is given in intuition (in regard to thought), the specific manner of this determination is entirely *contingent in relation to our minds*. In other words, although the Analytic proves that all perceptions that might be given must fit into a possible whole of experience, and a whole of experience is indeed, at least in intention, a whole that is thoroughly determined, nevertheless, *the specific manner of this determination* is only revealed in the process by which experience is generated. Thus while it is indeed true that the categories and principles relate universally to individual intentional relations or judgments as universal to the particular instance, they have only a *general* significance with regard to the empirical objects of such judgments. Thus every judgment determines an object in relation to a whole of possible cognitions with a completely determinate form, but whether any real objects are in fact given to fill out and realize that form in a specific manner or in sufficient quantity to allow us to analyze them so as to determine the particular for ourselves in thought is something that only actual experience itself can decide. Put most precisely, the Analytic justifies the expectation or anticipation that perceptions are completely determinate through their relation to an object, but how this or that perception will be connected up

§. 1. The Relation of the Analytic to the Dialectic — 207

when this actually takes place cannot be derived from the transcendental grounds of experience, although it is certainly required by this.

For this reason, Kant explains that the synthetic truths demonstrated in the analytic apply to *each and every* empirical object of which we have perception and about which we make judgments, and they bring such objects necessarily into one formal whole of empirical nature. However, since this judgment always determines the given perceptions through relation to an object, and merely in view of the form of a whole, and so constructs an empirical whole of experience synthetically by the progressive composition of its parts, it can lead to absolutely no assertions regarding the whole *as a given totality, or as one complete object*. The Analytic then is doubly limited: It provides no principle for completely determining the empirical particular *a priori*, or for grasping the whole of nature as one determined object. The unity its principles do provide, then, is merely "distributive," i.e. it applies to each and every object that can be given, but is not "collective," i.e. it does not apply to each and every object *and to the one in which they are all contained.*

In the Dialectic, Kant clarifies the difference between the roles of pure understanding and pure reason through a number of comparisons, the upshot of which is that just as understanding as a faculty of rules determines the otherwise contingently related *manifold of perceptions* by relating them purposively to concepts of an object in general in which their combination is represented as necessary, reason for its part as a faculty of principles serves to determine the otherwise contingent *manifold of the rules of the understanding* by relating them to the ideal of an object in which they are combined into one absolute systematic unity. Kant puts this nicely by saying that "The understanding constitutes an object for reason, just as sensibility does for the understanding" (*KrV* A664/B692; see also *KU* 05:183). Correlatively, just as there are *a priori categories* and *synthetic principles* grounded in the necessary unity of the pure understanding that govern the former teleological relation, so, as we will see further below, there must be *a priori ideas* and *maxims* grounded in the necessary unity of pure reason that govern the latter. In exact parallel with our previous analysis, then, theoretical self-consciousness, here however on the level of reason in the narrow sense, necessarily projects for itself a universal field within which any purposive use of the understanding first becomes possible, i.e. a universal system of possible subjectively teleological unity.

Kant employs other, more concise, ways of characterizing this distinction, but none of these are sufficient to explain Kant's true point. For instance, Kant clearly thinks of distributive unity as the unity expressed in judgments, and collective unity as the unity that is expressed in the major term of a syllogism. Again, he explains that distributive unity applies to perceptions in relation to an object in general, whereas collective unity applies, or is supposed to apply, to the relation of all objects to one world-whole. In other places, Kant also characterizes the principles of the understanding as principles (first grounds of cognition) exclusively in relation to the unity of intuitions, whereas the principles of reason are to be principles in an absolute sense. Another way of characterizing this same distinction is by making the comparison of the division Analytic/Dialectic with the traditional division between ontology and special metaphysics.

What is missing in all of these ways of describing the difference is an explanation as to why this division belongs essentially to the transcendental structure of reason, and how we are to understand not only the division, but also the relation between these two kinds of unity. This deeper reason for the division, I believe, can only be fully articulated through an analysis of Kant's own manner of constructing the idea of a pure faculty of reason which we will turn to below in considering his derivation of the ideas. In a sense, then, like all other divisions within the critical system, the division between principles of understanding and principles of reason must be seen to arise from the very *idea* of a certain kind of pure cognitive faculty. Thus, if the demonstration of the principles of understanding rest on the idea of a pure faculty of judging, then it will make sense that the demonstration of the principles of reason will rest on the idea of a pure faculty of reasoning, i.e. of the faculty for the determination of propositions through the syllogism.

As for the relation of these two kinds of unity, I think the best way of clarifying this matter (which has caused much difficulty for commentators) is by looking to Kant's pre-critical theory of the world-whole, and by relating this to his understanding of the process through which knowledge about this whole is acquired, which we described earlier in Chapter 4. In the pre-critical period, Kant had in fact to deal with a similar sort of division. The divine intellect, as the ground of possibility, according to his view at the time, certainly contained a schema of a world-whole in which was grounded the complete determination of creation in the particular and as a whole. Kant thought of such a schema as grounding not only the minimal principles of the possibility of a world-whole in general, but indeed every possible particular relation that might ever obtain in the actual world. For this reason, he regarded God's will as not adding any predicate to the real essence of a created thing, not even its predicates of place and time, but rather as merely positing it along with all its predicates. Of course, in doing so, God also created at the same time the entire world with which such a thing would be essentially connected, by means of this same schema, into a community of real interaction and influence. Now, although Kant saw this original schema as leaving nothing to be determined or filled in, aside from the existence of what it described, it remained his view that human reason would be able to determine *a priori* almost nothing of the infinite wealth of purposive unities that would arise from such a schema. This was a direct corollary of the all-sufficiency of the divine nature; not even the essences themselves could be comprehended apart from the plan of creation, which was only really known in its full extent by God. Yet Kant thought himself able at the time to adduce several examples of such purposive unity in experience, for instance in the purposive structure of space and in the basic teleological tendencies found even in the universal laws governing matter. On this basis, Kant clearly held it to be the ideal of philosophical research, whether achievable or not, that we should attempt to trace all particular unities and determinations back to these most universal and necessary laws. However, he was forced to admit that until we are able to do this, the universal laws of nature will perforce remain merely general laws of nature, i.e. laws which surely apply to all things, but which have at least not yet been shown to be the absolutely first principles from which derive all possible determinations of things within the world-whole. That is to say, it had not been shown, and Kant was rather certain that it never could be shown, that all particular teleological relations in nature are nothing but specifications of the transcendental teleology of creation, although this is the ideal of our empirical research.

If such were achieved, however, then the law that all material things operate according to mechanical laws (distributively), for instance, would be understood as being a mere consequence of the genuinely universal principle that the world-whole is a whole essentially unified by these mechanical laws (collectively). But to show the latter, we would have to also show that the world is essentially constituted through one being, and that the mechanical structure found within it is a direct effect of its derivation from this single common ground. To show, in other words, that the universal laws of matter alone are responsible for the unity and reciprocal purposiveness of things in the world-whole, one would have to be able to show how this fact is a direct effect of the nature of the divine being. Kant, however, was convinced that such a derivation would be impossible, not only because each extant thing we find in experience is in fact the result of an infinitely expansive, complex and dynamic process, and as such could never be traced back by us to its first grounds, but also because there exist certain kinds of fundamental irresolvable connections (like causality), which are such that the human mind can have no insight into them *a priori*. Thus, even if the genuine laws that bind together the world-whole in every possible way would be open to our view, there would remain an insuperable barrier in the nature of things themselves to our ever being able to understand creation in its complete determinacy *a priori*.

From this arose, indeed, a certain tension. While the transcendental concept of the divine schema was seen to be the principle of the complete determination of things in one whole and as one whole (collective), the content of this schema, insofar as we would be able to determine it for ourselves, would at most place general (distributive) conditions on the objects we study in nature. Notably, when Kant makes the critical turn, this tension is by no means relieved, for although Kant is able to explain in the Aesthetic and Analytic how it is possible for the human mind to know these universal and necessary laws with perfect certainty without at the same time having direct cognition of the principles of all things in themselves, there remains the difficulty that determination of particulars for thought only takes place in the act of empirically determining them in accordance with transcendental conditions of unity, and hence cannot be arrived at completely or even in part *a priori*. Yet, in the critical position, it still remains the case – because this is the only way in which cognition can be consciously regarded as experience, i.e. as objective cognition – that Kant understands the particular as being an instance or as a subordinate case of the determination through the universal. The understanding judges, in other words, in accordance with the guiding idea that the determinations it expresses belong to a whole of completely determinate and purposively unified experience. But such unity, Kant now explains in the critical system, is only justified *relative to this very act of progressive determination*. Thus, if we attend only to the determination by judgment, then it is clear that something must always remain undetermined in the object, and this, even though the guiding idea of such determination is indeed an absolute whole of experience completely determined in itself. Consequently, if our research is to ever go beyond the mere connecting of perceptions, there must exist another activity of judgment or reason by means of which we are able to move from these basic connections to more general ones. This is what Kant calls the "hypothetical" use of reason, and its essential function is to inductively search for the universal under which stands a certain series of particulars. By means of it, particular connections are seen as consequences of more general ones, and the perceptions that are collected under concepts by the understanding, are brought under more extensive and differentiated ones, thereby further determining experience itself. Thus although understanding already has before it a whole of completely determinate experience, at least as its guiding idea, it is not by itself able to reach such determination without the help of principles borrowed from reason.

Importantly, this supposition of a system of experience, which is transcendentally purposive for cognition, cannot be immediately identified with that underlying the merely reflective notion of teleology that Kant takes up in the *KU*. It differs from the teleology of natural ends in that it does not initially consider particular ends or individual systems that are teleological in themselves (organisms), but rather serves to "make the systematic unity of nature entirely universal in relation to the idea of a highest intelligence" and gives a "regulative principle of the systematic unity of a teleological connection, which, however, we do not determine beforehand, but may only expect while pursuing the physical-mechanical connection according to universal laws" (*KrV* A691–692/B719–720). The purposiveness here is entirely transcendental; for in it the unity of nature is regarded not as determined and made possible by any particular purpose, but rather as determined by the idea of the complete use of our reason in regard to the whole realm of possible nature. Thus, since the mechanical connection of things is what is first discovered in the *a priori* laws of the understanding, this purposiveness in the first instance grounds the unity and specification of the system of nature according to physical causality, i.e. it provides the foundation for the maxims for investigating nature as a universal system under empirical laws (*KU* 05:376–377). The teleological causality of a natural end is in this respect to be regarded as just one more form of unity in experience that is purposive for our cognitive faculty, and which is in a real sense made possible entirely by the necessary unity of experience itself, which is the transcendental basis of such purposiveness.

If this analysis is correct, then it is clear that the seemingly obvious differences between the results and arguments of the Analytic and Dialectic are actually quite superficial. For, as it turns out, the determinative/regulative distinction has nothing directly to do with the strength, depth, or validity of the principles of the use of reason so described, but rather stems entirely from the different domains in which the two faculties are intended to function. The understanding just happens to be the name for the faculty the unity of which is required for thinking objects in the first place, while reason is that the unity of which is required for any purposive use of the understanding in respect of experience as a whole; and when each is limited to its proper domain and function, it is fully secure and autonomous.[1]

This is absolutely crucial for my broader thesis, because it shows that both of the major constructive arguments of Kant's *KrV* establish the autonomy and purposive use of our cognitive faculties in a way that at the same time proves them to involve essentially a reference to the concept (or idea) of a realm of experience that is purposive *for the use* of our cognitive faculties, i.e. that contains the necessary unity required for their use. Thus, so far from being "blind to purposes," nature as an object of knowledge, and even if limited to purely physical laws,

---

1 See my discussion of the constitutive/regulative distinction in Chapter 8.

culminates problematically in an absolute system that is conceived as uniquely purposive for human reason, as indeed constituting a system in which each part is itself a cognitive end completely determined in regard to the whole of which it is a part. Furthermore, as Kant argues in the *KU*, mechanical connection is not the only sort of connection that is possible for us. Our own faculty of acting according to concepts, as well as examples of organisms in nature, proves that it is possible to regard some objects of nature as possible only according to analogy with a *specific* intention, i.e. a causality based upon a particular concept of the product of the same causality. Thus nature, as Kant understands it, is not only teleological in a transcendental sense, but this same transcendental purposiveness allows Kant to regard particular teleological relations as arising from nature's own resources. Contrary to McDowell's view, Kant's nature is already through and through a second nature, because it is the product of an original and spontaneous faculty of reason.

I turn now to the second function of the Dialectic, namely, the derivation of the transcendental ideas.

§. 2. The Ideas of Pure Reason

> The idea is singular (*individuum*), independent and eternal. It is the divinity in our souls that we are capable of [having] ideas. The senses provide only ectypes or mere appearances. (*Refl* 5247, late 1770s)

The second function of the Dialectic, as I noted above, is to outline the transcendental ideas in their purity and to show that in this form they can never be theoretically determined. This means that when considered in themselves, these ideas are pure transcendental thought-entities whose theoretical existence is neither provable nor disprovable. Thus, in a theoretical respect, as we will see, both the assertion and the denial of the existence of anything corresponding to these ideas would be pointless, simply because there is simply no means by which they can be given sense or meaning. They are, as it were, pure logical transcendental concepts, which, like the pure categories, have a sort of independence and validity as thoughts, but which in their purity lack any meaningful employment for cognition. Unlike the pure categories, however, the pure ideas cannot even be provided with a schema. They are what Kant calls "transcendent" concepts, by which he means not that their objects lie somehow beyond the boundaries of reason – since through them we are not able to represent any real object at all – but rather that they always drive reason itself in this direction. By "*transcendent* principles [...] I mean principles that actually incite us to tear down all those boundary posts and to lay claim to a wholly new territory that recognizes no demarcations anywhere" and not "the *transcendental* use or misuse of categories, which is a mere mistake of the faculty of judgment when it is not properly checked by criticism" (*KrV* A296/B352). Transcendent principles or concepts are thus not those of a certain kind of object unknown to us, or even the mistaken thought about an object supposedly beyond the boundaries of experience; they are rather those principles or concepts that lead reason necessarily to overstep its own boundaries, thereby giving rise to transcendental illusions.

This theoretical nullity of the ideas, of course, is perfectly consonant with Kant's intentions, because their true vocation will later be loacted in the moral realm, where they provide the principles of that "exemplar" of moral perfection, namely the intelligible world, which Kant first announced back in the *MSI*. And in this function, the fact that no sensible object would be congruent to them, and thus that they cannot be schematized, is interpreted as an essential positive feature of moral concepts, one which serves to keep them free from all admixture with sensible representations. This purity, indeed, will be interpreted by Kant in the *KpV* as essential to the protection of moral philosophy from empiricism, "which destroys at its roots the morality of dispositions" (*KpV* 05:71). Yet the ideas will be provided nevertheless with sense and meaning *indirectly* through what Kant later calls a "typic," which rather than being a rule for sensibility, serves as a ground for higher-order *maxims* of the application of the understanding in experience. In this function, the pure ideas for the first time gain a meaning and a specifically defined content through the moral law. Kant's goal here in the Dialectic of the *KrV* is thus in part to secure the originality and independence of the ideas from their service to theoretical knowledge, so that they can later be given a pure practical employment.

Kant's original derivation of the ideas, however, is not practical, but rather transcendental. Parallel to the way he derives the categories, Kant looks to the logical use of the understanding, or in this case the logical use of reason, and asks what synthetic principles must be presupposed so that the logical procedure can be thought as determining something objective. In the Analytic this logical procedure was described by functions of judgment, whereas in the Dialectic it is now seen to be described by the functions of the syllogism. This, of course, reflects a continuation of Kant's pre-critical division between judgment and reason respectively as between the function of the understanding whereby concepts are made clear and that whereby they are rendered complete.

In order to provide a point of unity for this derivation, indeed a *telos*, Kant seeks to discover a basic *idea of pure reason as a whole*, one which shows the absolute origin of both reason's logical and its pure use. This "universal concept of the faculty of reason," he claims, is nothing but that of a faculty of principles, or of a faculty which cognizes its objects from principles (*KrV* A302/B359). A principle, Kant further explains, only genuinely deserves the title if it is an *absolutely original* source of cognitions. Such a principle would be a first universal concept, suitable for providing the major term of a syllogism for which there could in principle be no higher syllogistic demonstration. Evidently, since all concepts drawn from experience, or indeed even those derived from the pure understanding, only serve to cognize objects under certain conditions of sensibility (or intuition), a principle of pure reason in the absolute sense can only be understood as cognition from pure concepts alone, thus without any other source or condition. Consequently, a "cognition from principles" must be understood as one in which we would "cognize the particular in the universal through concepts" (*KrV* A300/B357). Of course, how or even if such a pure concept is able to gain relation to a real object is an open question. But at the moment this is not a relevant concern, since Kant is attempting merely to develop the basic idea of such a faculty as pure reason.

Now the logical use of reason consists in the procedure of attempting to bring empirical cognitions, by means of prosyllogisms, to just such a first principle. Reason, as it were, teaches that the ground for the particular laws must always be sought in a more universal one, because only in this way is the manifold of its cognitions reduced to a unity. Cognition thus becomes increasingly perfect to the extent that we can find a higher and more universal concept from which the lower ones can be derived, and so shown to follow with necessity. In this way, Kant directly models the logical use of reason, which seeks a higher condition for every cognition, on the three kinds of syllogism: categorical, hypothetical and disjunctive. The difference between these kinds of syllogism lies in the different relations that the higher condition (i.e. the major term) has to the lower one (i.e. the conclusion) (*KrV* A304/B361).

But for this principle of economy, or of reducing laws to as systematic a unity as possible, to be considered something objective and grounded in pure reason itself, it must be shown to rest on some fundamental *material* principles by means of which the cognitions themselves are represented as *already existing* in such a thoroughgoing systematic unity. In other words, if this logical procedure is to be anything more than an artful, but arbitrary collecting together of pieces of cognition under fabricated general representations, or, expressed differently, if the universal conditions under which this logical procedure collects certain particular conclusions are to be regarded as in fact the grounds for the *truth* of such particulars – then there must be some principles that ground the objective significance of this very procedure. Therefore, if prosyllogisms are to be useful for generating and extending knowledge, then there must be some ground for regarding reality apart from these considerations as structured in a precisely parallel manner. If we then take into account the fact that the logical use of reason aims essentially at cognizing the logical particular under a logical universal, it would seem to follow that such material principles must allow us to cognize the *real* particular as deriving from the *synthetic* universal. As Kant explains:

> But this logical maxim cannot be a principle of *pure reason* unless we assume that when the conditioned is given, then so is the whole series of conditions subordinated one to the other, which is itself unconditioned, also given (i.e. contained in the object and its connection). (*KrV* A307–308/B364)

And again,

> This complete magnitude of the domain, in relation to such a condition [as is expressed in the major of the syllogism], is called *universality* (*universalitas*). In the synthesis of intuition this corresponds to *allness* (*universitas*), or the totality of conditions. So the transcendental concept of reason is none other than that of the *totality of conditions* to a given conditioned thing. Now since the *unconditioned* alone makes possible the totality of conditions, and conversely the totality of conditions is always itself unconditioned, a pure concept of reason in general can be explained through the concept of the unconditioned, insofar as it contains a ground of synthesis for what is conditioned. (*KrV* A322/B379)

A principle in the genuine sense should therefore be a source of "synthetic cognitions from concepts," and as it is to rest on no further conditions, and thus provide the condition of all the rest, then it must be an absolute principle of synthesis. Thus, in accordance with such a principle, whatever whole is grasped through it is thought to be absolutely unified through the fact that everything within this whole derives from a single ultimate common and real ground. The logical use of reason therefore rests, if it is to have any kind of objective significance at all, on the idea of the givenness or reality of an absolutely first condition, with which is also already thought to be given the entire totality of conditions down to any particular conditioned thing.

The principles of reason, Kant thereby explains, will be that of the highest synthetic concepts required by the logical use of reason. From the fact that there are three distinct kinds of syllogisms, it is clear that there must therefore also be three fundamentally different principles of reason. The question of what precisely these principles are, however, is not such a straightforward matter. For what is the idea which corresponds to the unconditioned universal in the categorical, hypothetical and disjunctive syllogisms? Kant argues that these are precisely the ideas which provide the absolute unity of the thinking subject (I), of the appearances (world) and of all things whatsoever (God) (*KrV* A334/B391). I would like to skip the general details of this argument, and focus only on the way Kant attempts to deduce the last of these ideas from the faculty of pure reason in order to better grasp the unique nature and status of these concepts of reason. As described above, the basic strategy Kant employs is to deduce the ideas as transcendental or material principles grounding the applicability of the logical forms of syllogism to the determination of real objects. The key presupposition of this derivation is itself the *idea* of pure reason as a faculty of knowledge, which, like the idea of the pure understanding Kant drew on in the Analytic, is that of an absolutely unconditioned, thus original and pure source of cognitions.

Now, Kant connects the idea of God specifically with what he refers to as the "logical principle of determinability," which states for every concept "that of every two contradictorily opposed predicates only one can apply to it." This, he further explains, is nothing but the principle of contradiction, which is a mere logical principle, applied however to the determination of a concept with regard to its predicates. This is obviously a general and distributive principle which applies to each and every given determination of a concept. However, if this logical principle is to be seen as applicable to objects, and thus as not only taking into account the form of determination but also the material content of such determinations, then it requires a further principle, namely, that in regard to every *possible* pair of contradictorily opposed predicates, the object is determined as possessing one of them. This principle is distinct from its logical counterpart precisely through its reference to the *collective* idea of a totality of all possible pairs of such predicates. It is therefore not just a principle of determination, but indeed of the *totality* of all determinations of a thing.

Having outlined this principle, Kant further examines the grounds of negation. His claim is that a negation is not, properly speaking, a feature of a concept or of its content, but rather expresses a relation to another concept. Presumably, Kant means that when I, for instance, deny the faculty of locomotion to rocks, I am not by means of this attributing something positive to rocks, but rather only denying of rocks a certain positive content originally expressed in the concept of locomotion. This basic idea, of course, is nothing new for Kant, as he defended basically the same view in the pre-critical period, along with its consequence, namely, that every real determination of a thing relies for its objective significance on a relation to some reality. According to this, purely positive predicates directly express a reality, while negative ones express the denial of a certain reality. Consequently, things only differ in regard to their limits, not in regard to their realities as such. In view of this fact, the collective idea of the totality of all possible pairs of contradictorily opposed predicates itself contains an inner relation – as the ground of the reality of what is positive in each and every concept – to the equally collective idea of a whole of reality. "All true negations,"

Kant writes echoing his own similar thoughts developed in notes from the late 1760s, "are nothing but limits, which they could not be called unless they were grounded in the unlimited (the All)" (*KrV* A575–576/B603–604).

Kant also explains the dependence of the applicability of the logical principle of determinability to objects on the transcendental idea of an *omnitudo realitatis* by reference to the disjunctive syllogism (KrV A576–579/B604–607). As I stated earlier, Kant's original claim was that the ideas can be derived from the logical forms of syllogisms in a way parallel to the derivation of the categories from the logical forms of judgments. Now a disjunctive syllogism, as Kant describes it in his *Log*, has the following forms:[2]

Major: X is A or not-A.
Minor: X is A.
Conclusion: X is not not-A.

Major: X is A or not-A.
Minor: X is not-A.
Conclusion: X is not A.

In both cases, the major consists of the division of a general concept, X, into two smaller spheres, namely A and not-A. The minor restricts the same concept to one sphere, and the conclusion determines the concept by this part. From this it is clear that the disjunctive syllogism depends both upon the principle of determination and upon the givenness of some original material, A, to provide the content for the disjunction *A or not-A*. For instance, drawing an example from Meier, we can form the disjunctive syllogism as follows: "Matter can either think or not, now the latter is false, so the former is true."[3] For such a syllogism to provide knowledge, it must not only be logically valid, but indeed it must be the case that the predicate "thought" corresponds to some reality, i.e. to some positive thinkable content, so that the disjunction "can think or not" can be understood as expressing an objective inherence/non-inherence of a reality in the subject "matter." Consequently, if we now ask what is required for the completeness in the determination of an individual it would clearly be a major premise in which is contained the disjunctions of all possible real predicates. This, however, again presupposes the givenness of a sum-total of all possible reality which is to serve as the content of these predicates so that by comparison with this the object is determined in regard to every real predicate as either possessing it or lacking it.

---

[2] The sections in Kant's *Log* which treat the disjunctive syllogism are literally identical with those in Meier's *Auszug*, and thus I feel confident in generalizing Meier's examples, which Kant omits.
[3] See his *Auszug*, AA 16:749.

But this raises a problem, because, as Kant points out, the major premise, if understood in this way, would consist of a disjunction in which the concept of reality is itself divided into smaller spheres. The concept of reality, however, cannot be so divided, "because apart from experience one is acquainted with no determinate species of reality that would be contained under that genus" (*KrV* A577/B605). What precisely is meant by this? In Kant's pre-critical philosophy we find him claiming as early as the late 1750s that two realities cannot be distinguished qualitatively *qua* reality, because reality is nothing but the positive content of a thing as such (see *VKK*). His conclusion was that two realities can only be distinguished by means of their external limits, and thus purely quantitatively. Quantitative distinction, however, as depending upon external limits, rests again on the relation both to other things and to a maximum, which provides the positive content contained within the limits. Here, I believe, Kant is making a similar claim, based however upon the fact that "reality" in the critical philosophy is nothing but the givenness as such of some sensation. If we turn to the Anticipations of Perception earlier in the *KrV*, Kant explains that all differences in regard to reality (i. e. the quality of what is given in experience) are discovered only empirically, and thus that in regard to the transcendental concept of reality, which is in fact the higher concept of which empirical realities are specifications, "we can cognize *a priori* nothing more than their intensive quantity, namely that they have a degree" (*KrV* A176/B218). Thus on the transcendental level, realities can be distinguished only as regards their magnitude, and indeed, just as in the pre-critical period, this magnitude is intensive.

From this we can conclude that the transcendental concept of an all of reality that is required by the principle of complete determination is not a general concept, since a general concept is always one that can be treated as a predicate, and thus under which other concepts are classified and thereby unified into one. For instance, that "black" is a general concept means it can function as a representation, and indeed as a rule, under which various other concepts are brought. So in a judgment like *The cats in my house are black*, the predicate is understood by Kant as something under which I bring the cats in my house, and thereby relate the cats to other things that also fall under the concept of black. The general concept is thus a rule for the unification of our cognitions, and as such it rests ultimately on a transcendental synthesis. But the transcendental concept of reality is not a predicate such as could be used to restrict, and thereby unify, other concepts. Rather concepts themselves only serve a function, and thus are genuine concepts, insofar as they signify some reality. Again, all realities are understood to be parts of one whole of reality, and as such are contained within it, not under it, as is the case with general concepts:

> Thus the transcendental major premise for the thoroughgoing determination of all things is none other than the representation of the sum total of all reality, a concept that comprehends all predicates as regards their transcendental content not merely under itself, but within itself; and the thoroughgoing determination of every thing rests on the limitation of this All of reality, in that some of it is ascribed to the thing and the rest excluded from it, which agrees with the "either/or" of the disjunctive major premise and the determination of the object through one of the members of this division in the minor premise. (*KrV* A577/B605)

Kant here clearly understands the all of reality in terms of a maximum which contains within itself all other realities, which latter thus consist essentially in a limited portion of this sum-total. Consequently, the individual realities, viewed as parts of this greater whole, do not make this whole possible by being synthetically brought together into one, but rather by being *given*, or at least being *thought as given*, all at the same time in this sum-total. In other words, in the idea of an all of reality, we have the concept of an analytic totality in which the parts are only possible through, and as analyzed out of, an original whole, just as if it were not a concept but rather a genuine intuition.

This all of reality is thus no ordinary concept. It is rather, as Kant explains, "the one single genuine ideal of which human reason is capable, because only in this one single case is an – in itself universal – concept of one thing thoroughly determined through itself, and cognized as the representation of an individual" (*KrV* A576/B604). The exact grounds for this claim are difficult to discern, and Kant makes use of language that indicates this passage contains only a sketch of the genuine argument. Uniqueness or singularity, of course, is precisely what distinguishes the all of reality as an ideal from the remaining concepts of reason, which are but ideas, and makes it into the supreme principle of reason itself. All the ideas are principles of totality, so the property of uniqueness cannot rest on this alone, or all the ideas would really be ideals. Kant would seem to be suggesting that singularity can be derived from this concept's being a principle of totality only in combination with its complete determinacy, as this is done, for instance, in the Pölitz lecture notes on religion (*V-Phil-Th/Pölitz* 28:1037–1038). The argument would then be: There can be but one all of reality, because, firstly, this idea is a principle of totality. Thus in the idea itself is included the notion of completeness. Secondly, this idea is also completely determined, because the very idea of it is arrived at in order to provide a principle for the complete determination of other things. That is, since it contains – in the *idea* at least – the reality in each and every real positive predicate, it must not only possess one from every set of contradictorily opposed predicates, but moreover its very concept determines which one of the two (i.e. the positive one) must belong to it. However, if we assume there to be two such beings, then these could only be distinguished by a difference among their realities, and so we would have to deny of one of them something that is contained in the other. But this can only be the denial of a reality, which contradicts the assumption that they both contain all reality.

However, the principle of totality is not by itself sufficient to establish this conclusion, since it is perfectly possible to have two principles of totality of the same kind, just as we can have two instances of freedom, as principles of totality in a causal series. Similarly, we could have two different instances of "all the apples in the orchard," if there are two orchards. Kant's contention is that this is only possible because these principles of totality are in fact conditioned universals, i.e. their universality is based not upon what they contain, but upon what they lack. The phrase essentially leaves out an infinite wealth of determinations that can be distinguishing features of the individuals that are such wholes, thereby allowing them to fall under the same general concept. However, a contradiction arises when we recognize that in order for there to be two sum-totals of reality, there must be a distinguishing feature among them, but in regard to the all of reality it is the case that every feature is determined through the concept itself. Thus, the very principle of totality as a totality of reality means that this concept in principle leaves no further determinations by which it might be distinguished from another of the same kind.

The idea of an all of reality is, like that of space, the idea of a singular and of a maximum that makes possible its parts as limited portions of itself. It is not just a ground, but also a model, or, as Kant describes it, an "original image (*prototypon*) of all things, which all together, as defective copies (*ectypa*), take from it the matter of their possibility, and yet although they approach more or less nearly to it, they always fall short of reaching it" (*KrV* A578/B606). Consequently, it can be said that all determinations of things take their very "being" from an original maximum containing all being originally (as an *ens entium*). The being of finite things is clearly thought of here as being *per se* normative, because all being of this kind is seen as originating in a maximum such that the very identity of the finite individual is determined by this relation.

However, as in Kant's pre-critical analysis of this ideal, he finds that the description of it as a sum-total, which is the first "silhouette" (*Schattenriss*) we arrive at through the derivation from the principle of complete determination, is not actually proper to the inner nature of its concept (*KrV* A579/B607; cf. *BDG* 02:86). Kant's move here, I believe, can be understood as follows: The derivation from the principle of complete determination, as a regressive derivation from consequences, allows us to arrive at the idea of the original being only as a sum-total. However, once we begin to analyze this concept on its own, it becomes clear that it must possess many other properties including singularity, originality, supremacy, originality, infinity (i.e. unlimitedness) and so forth. This, however, means in turn that the ideal cannot be an aggregate of any kind, or a composite of realities as would be a sum-total. Hence, if the many realities found in things spring from it, and indeed so does every real difference encountered in the world, then this difference, not found in the original being itself, must be among its consequences. With this Kant again defends the thesis that only a dynamic evolution of realities from the original being can suffice to explain creation. There are, in Kant's view, a multitude of realities, evil and deprivation being among them, that cannot be found in the original being, but are nevertheless both real and are the consequences of God. The sum-total of realities, therefore, that Kant sees as presupposed (only by reason, of course) by the principle of complete determination should, I think, be regarded as the sum-total of the realities that actually occur, and many of which are first *produced*, in the actual world. This is a difficult point, but I think in a fuller discussion Kant would have to argue that such realities are contained in God, but only as a ground, and indeed also in God's intellect insofar as they are first actualized according to his plan, but yet that they are not to be ascribed to God either as parts or as properties. God's creative activity is seen as taking place through the creative activity of nature itself.

In any case, Kant clearly views the ultimate ground of the possibility of things, just as he did in the *BDG*, as "a ground and not as a sum-total." For this reason, it is not the highest being that is in fact to be viewed as the sum-total and thus as limited in each thing, but rather the highest being's "complete consequences." The world, therefore, as all that is the real consequence of God, is that by the limitation of which we alone are able to cognized any object as completely determined. Kant is here drawing on traditional conceptions, but also combining them in a unique fashion. The idea that all things are first fashioned, in regard to their reality, by a kind of mixing of being and non-being, and thus that they all attest in their own determinations to a common well-spring of all reality, is an ancient theory that Moses Mendelssohn approvingly mentioned in his *Phädon*. And Kant too uses this idea to support the claim, also expressed in Mendelssohn's work, that it is a direct result of this single common source of the being of all things that they exhibit the most precise similarities and continuities (cf. Kant's discussion of the regulative principles). But whereas Mendelssohn speaks simply of a mixing of being and non-being, Kant goes further to argue that the being here mixed is not that of the original being, but rather the whole of being that is its consequence. This similarity and continuity, then, is not one of the individual with God himself and only thereby with all other things, but rather among all things as his consequences. For this reason, Kant is able to fuse with this conception one that is remarkably Leibnizian, although transformed by Kant's own original understanding of the kind of principle required for real community, namely, that each individual even in regard to its most inward real determinations stands in a relation and thus reflects the entire world of which it is a part. The world is thus not only a whole viewed in terms of similarity and continuity, but also in terms of causality, and for this reason it is an absolutely or universally organic whole. Put differently, the unity of the world Kant has constructed here by following out the consequences of the principle of complete determination is one in which the very real possibility of the individual essentially presupposes the entire reality in the whole of which it is a member, "just as all figures are possible only as different ways of limiting infinite space" (*KrV* A578/B606).

From this we can conclude that the ideal of pure reason, as regards its content as a singular concept, is for Kant the highest teleological principle of his entire philosophy. As a result of it, all real determinations of reason's objects, if they are to be cognized at all, must be viewed *as if* intrinsically teleological, i.e. as if caused by an intellect through the idea of a whole of all being. The moments of this teleology are worth dwelling upon. First, the ideal of pure reason, as a ground, provides a model or image of which all other things must be cognized as but limited copies. It is able to play this role universally because the ideal is being itself, and the source of all being (i.e. reality or thinkable content) of anything whatsoever. Secondly, this determination is represented as belonging to the inner essences of things, and thus as regarding what is necessary in them. Thirdly, although this determination is absolutely internal, it is nevertheless founded – by virtue of the inner reference to the divine ground at the basis of each thing's essence – on a real relation to absolutely all other beings in the world-whole. Fourthly, because of this fact, the real determinations of all things, as regards their internal possibility, thus *transcendentally*, already stand in a relation to all other things according to principles of harmony and unity. Fifthly, because the actual determinations of things, viewed metaphysically or as a consequence of the essences of things taken both individually and in community, are the specifications of the same structures discovered from the transcendental standpoint, all real determinations of things must also be objectively viewed by reason, to the extent that the ideal is necessary for its operations, as specifications of this absolute teleology. For reason this means that insofar as it operates under the ideal of pure reason, it must regard the acts whereby it determines objects, in an anticipatory manner, as necessarily fitting in an essential way into a possible absolutely unified teleological whole. Sixthly, this purposive relation of reason to all things, supported however by reason's viewing all things in turn as purposive for it, provides the source of those regulatory principles or maxims of the theoretical use of reason that will be discussed below. The upshot of all these

§. 2. The Ideas of Pure Reason — 223

points is that all specific real determinations, hence also those that are necessary, must be viewed as *per se* teleological from the perspective of reason. This teleology is a universal and not a particular teleology, permeating even the necessary laws of physical matter, and in relation to it all particular purposive relations between beings are to be seen as its concrete specifications.

These are the essentials of Kant's derivation of the idea of the transcendental ideal and the foundation for what he refers to as "transcendental theology." This same ideal will later be given determination and objective reality through the act of moral postulation in the practical sphere. Here, however, although it is a transcendentally justified and "faultless" ideal, Kant assures us that it expresses only a concept that reason must assume in relation to its own use of concepts in order to think them as objectively determining. Nevertheless, for the most basic use of reason in regard to experience, we neither need it as a principle of determination, nor are we able to provide it with any determinate content. Indeed Kant claims to show that all reason's concepts, and so also the ideal, actually cancel in their very concepts the conditions under which alone they could be employed theoretically: "None of the concepts through which I can think any object determinately will attain to it, and the conditions for the objective validity of my concepts are excluded by the idea itself" (*KrV* A676–677/B704–705). Thus the ideas are in this sense self-purifying, and it is this intrinsic feature that makes them unsuitable for any constitutive theoretical use. According to their concepts as unconditioned "firsts," the ideas thus separate themselves off from everything sensible, and since human reason can have an object given to it only under the conditions of sensibility, they can never have a use in regard to objects of knowledge. For example, Kant argues that the I, as the ultimate ground of all thought, must be represented as pure spontaneity. But determination of the self, even in regard merely to its existence, can only occur through the application of the category of existence to the form of inner sense, and thus in accordance with the condition of receptivity (*KrV* B429–430). The existence of the self is thus only given in receptivity and can in no way be cognized in accordance with pure spontaneity, which is required by the idea of an absolutely first subject. The world, similarly, cannot be cognized as such because in every case the determination of the unconditioned totality of conditions cancels the conditions within which such determinations can possibly have objective significance. And in regard to God, understood as ground of all possibility, Kant notes in his lectures on natural theology that reality must be provided to our concepts empirically, thus only within the forms of space and time. As a consequence, this reality can only be that of the appearance or that given under certain limitations that cannot be removed without at once removing also the grounds that make our cognition of it possible. In other words, a being that is of infinite reality cannot be given specific content because all concepts possible for us are made possible by certain limitations intrinsic to the finite human mind, which if they are removed, entail the removal of the grounds whereby we can cognize anything at all (*V-Phil-Th/Pölitz* 28:1021–1023). Again, in regard to God understood as the absolutely necessary being, Kant argues both in the Dialectic of the *KrV* and more fully in the *KU*, that since absolute necessity in fact cancels the difference between possibility and actuality, but this distinction itself rests on the distinction between what is thought in concepts and what is given in intuitions (which distinction is the basic condition of objectivity itself), the idea of God is precisely the idea of something that cancels the most fundamental conditions of human thinking: "The unconditioned necessity," Kant concludes, "which we need so indispensably as the ultimate sustainer of all things, is for human reason the true abyss" (*KrV* A613/ 641).

§. 3. The Regulative Principles of Pure Reason

> The pure concepts of reason have no exemplars, but rather are themselves the archetypes; however, the concepts of our pure reason have this reason itself as their archetype, and therefore are subjective and not objective. (*Refl* 3981, circa 1769)

In this section, I wish to more fully clarify my earlier comments on the regulative function of the ideas and to examine in particular the single most central case of such a principle, namely, the use of the concept of God. I think consideration of this, the most important of the regulative concepts, will again provide a sufficient understanding of Kant's general theory of the regulative employment of the ideas. First, however, I will describe more fully Kant's general conception of a regulative principle.

As I noted in the introduction, Kant seeks to combine the demand for the unconditioned with the finitude of human reason through the restriction of the idea of the unconditioned to a transcendentally *subjective* validity. His essential strategy is to argue that the ideas in this employment actually arise from the fact that reason requires principles in order to support its ascent from the rules cognized by the understanding in its application in experience to a unified system of cognitions. The understanding itself, Kant argues, requires for its own use in regard to experience the assumption that experience is intrinsically constituted not only such that the understanding can cognize objects in general, but indeed even in the particular, and this is only possible through the idea of a sum-total of reality that would be cognizable only in an absolutely complete system of knowledge. Thus, although the concepts of the understanding have been proven

§. 3. The Regulative Principles of Pure Reason — 225

to be generally valid in the Analytic, still their application in experience is always to the determination of the particular, and for this to be possible further principles of specification are required. Now as is clear from the description of the process through which knowledge is acquired, which was laid out at the beginning of Chapter 4, we must begin with provisional judgments, and attempt to arrive at particular laws through analysis, i.e. through the comparison, reflection and abstraction of the manifold given empirically. In this way we seek, by keeping the transcendental laws in front of us as guiding principles, to determine for a given event the previous event with which it is connected according to a rule. But for this to even be possible, we must assume that the provisional judgments will deliver us a manifold of preliminary cognitions that is more or less systematically constituted. If, for instance, there was at one moment a bright ball in the sky, which was now hot, and now cold, and now no longer a ball, its changes following no determinable rule, then it would be impossible to ever arrive at the concept of "sun." But with no concept of "sun," it would not only be impossible to see that some such object caused the rock at one moment to warm, it would really make no sense to say this at all, since there would be no general rule connecting them. In other words, the possibility of the application of the transcendental laws to the particular rests in part on the possibility of bringing the particular under concepts through the analysis of the sensible manifold. Consequently, the use of the transcendental principles in part presupposes that the empirical manifold given in experience is systematically organized such that it will be possible to arrive at general concepts of things. For only if we are able to subsume sensible particulars under general concepts of kind, will it be possible to formulate particular empirical laws governing their relations. It is with such considerations in mind that Kant claims that without the *assumption* that experience presents us with a systematic connection in accordance with empirical laws, we would not even have a criterion of empirical truth.

There remains, to be sure, quite a bit of obscurity in Kant's meaning here. For one might (justifiably) object that if the transcendental deduction guarantees the applicability of the categories, and so also of the transcendental laws, to experience in general, then it must have already guaranteed the application of these concepts and principles to the particular as well; for systematic knowledge of the particular is exactly what experience is. Two replies can be made to this objection. Firstly, Kant does not claim to have demonstrated the applicability of the categories and principles in the Analytic so much as the *validity* of such an application. It remains sensible to say that the possibility of actually applying these concepts and principles might require the satisfaction of some further conditions, even though we know such an application, if it were possible, would in fact be justified. This seems to be Kant's chief explanation. Secondly, one might grant the point entirely, admitting that the transcendental deduction guarantees this applicability, and yet still reply that some additional principles of judgment are required for this application. In this case, one would argue that these additional principles are themselves implicitly already justified in the transcendental deduction, and that the Dialectic only completes or makes explicit this fact by showing that they are indeed required for the application of the categories and principles to experience, which contains the particular. This line of reasoning too, I believe, agrees with much of what Kant says.

A third and better reply, in my view, would focus on the connection between the complete determination of the particular and the concept of an absolute totality of experience. If the validity of the categories and principles rests upon the fact that in the determination of experience we always necessarily have before the "eyes" of consciousness a singular whole of possible experience to which every perception (which is particular) must belong, and the determination of every perception as particular requires in principle the given totality of all possible experience in one determinate whole, then it would follow that the determination of the particular by the categories and principles in fact requires a principle of totality. However, since the categories and principles are always and only directed to the progressive determination of experience (which can never be completed), and we thus can never arrive at cognition of the particular in its complete determination, they can in fact be employed without presupposing any principle of totality. Perhaps we can even form concepts of specific objects in accordance the understanding and its rules. Yet, and this I think is Kant's central point, without a principle of totality we would lack any objective, or at least non-arbitrary, ground or norm against which to compare these concepts in order to distinguish the lower from the higher in respect to truth. We could, in other words, determine experience in all kinds of ways without the idea that we are actually proceeding in this way towards some ultimate or complete truth. In scientific practice it is often the case that a rule in agreement with experience is rejected in favor of another simply because it does not fit, or fit as well, into a possible system with other pieces of established knowledge. A principle of judgment, like that of Ockham's Razor, places a systematic criterion of truth on laws, which itself goes essentially beyond what can verified in experience. In this way the principle of totality will provide us with such general criteria for judging systematic unity and generating higher-order laws even when these are not strictly speaking required to account for the empirical evidence.

In such a case the "subjectivity" of the assumption of the unconditioned is not the subjectivity of something *arbitrarily* assumed. The unconditioned is something without the assumption of which even the understanding would not be able to be reliably applied to the appearances. For without it we could

§. 3. The Regulative Principles of Pure Reason — 227

well arrive at several competing sets of laws covering exactly the same empirical evidence, and lack ground for selecting any of these as more suitable than the rest. Furthermore, the idea of the unconditioned is not that of a general principle of unity or of something purely assumed for the economy of the understanding. As Kant explains, the goal of all understanding is truth, and it would therefore conflict with the very nature of understanding and reason to assume something arbitrarily only for the sake of its own economy (*KrV* A651/B679). Indeed, if reason thought the unconditioned as providing a unity that is *imposed upon* the matter of its systematic knowledge (i. e. the cognitions given through the understanding), then it would in fact be representing something to itself *as* unjustified and false. To think the unconditioned as is required by its very idea, it must rather be thought of as providing the inner and essential form of the knowledge first generated by the understanding. In other words, the unconditioned must be thought as the genuine and completely determinate ground through which all conditioned and determinate cognitions of things are first made possible and from which they are derived in their complete determinacy. The transcendental purposiveness of the whole of experience for the sake of the understanding, but provided by a principle of reason, must therefore be "that systematic unity [...] presupposed absolutely as a *unity of nature* that is recognized not only empirically but also *a priori*, though still indeterminately, and hence as following from the essences of things" (*KrV* A693/B721). We must, in other words, represent the unconditioned just as Kant originally thought it in the *BDG*; for only if we represent all the objects of cognition as resting on just such a ground, can we regard the unity and perfection we discover in the world, which extends over and above that required by the simple unity of experience, as genuinely objective.

Kant indeed argues that reason has every right to assume such a ground, precisely because this assumption takes place only for the sake of directing the understanding and so only for the sake of cognition. Reason's assumption of the ideas is valid, therefore, and is a justified transcendental assumption, because reason is in this respect entirely autonomous or free and thus concerned only with the unity of its own cognitions. Kant summarizes these points in a single key passage:

> Pure reason is in fact concerned with nothing but itself, and it can have no other concern, because what is given to it is not objects to be unified for the concept of reason, i.e., to be connected in one principle. The unity of reason is the unity of a system, and this systematic unity does not serve reason objectively as a principle, extending it over objects, but subjectively as a maxim, in order to extend it over all possible empirical cognition of objects. Nevertheless, the systematic use of the understanding furthers not only its extension but also

> guarantees its correctness, and the principle of such a systematic unity is also objective but in an indeterminate way (*principium vagum*). (*KrV* A680/B708)

Kant here claims explicitly that the regulative principle is one that reason gives to itself, and in its own freedom, in order to guide the use of the understanding. The unity of a system, like the unity of an experience, is itself a pure product of the mind in its transcendental function. Yet the unity of reason provides a principle of judgment that is not related directly to the object, but rather to the understanding and its own unity. Thus rather than being the source of a genuine principle of cognition, the regulative principles provide judgment with *maxims of reason*, i.e. "subjective principles that are taken not from the constitution of the object but from the interest of reason in regard to a certain possible perfection of the cognition of this object" (*KrV* A666/B694).

Kant wavers in his characterization of these maxims as objective, sometimes stating outright that they are merely subjective, but also, as in the quote above, that they are "objective but in an indeterminate way." His meaning seems to be that they are objective in the sense that they cannot be understood as mere principles of economy, which would be something arbitrary, because in order to perform their chief function of supporting and guiding the understanding, they must be represented as providing the principle of the inner possibility and form of all objects of knowledge. In this respect, the ideas of pure reason play a function that is perfectly analogous to those of the forms of intuition and the categories previously discussed. The ideas, however, are entirely distinct in one key respect, namely, in that they are conditions of the possibility only of the systematic unity of objects of experience, while the supposed objects of the ideas lie in principle beyond any possible experience. In this respect, it is important to recall that the truth of space and time rests on the fact that the appearances are mere specifications of them. Similarly we saw that the categories are true of experience because experiences are just specifications of categorial unity and this categorial unity is only the reflection in thought of the unity already presupposed in the singular intuitions of space and time themselves. In these cases the object of knowledge is only possible on the basis of this subjective condition, and so on this transcendental level the subjective and the objective are convertible. Space and time are formal intuitions, but they are also the forms of intuition. The categorical unity is the unity presupposed by all experience, but it is also the unity of actual experience. This identity is thus the basis of their truth. The ideas, by contrast, may be thought as the condition of the possibility of a real systematic unity of things, but this systematic unity definitely cannot be regarded as the object of the ideas. The reason for this disanalogy is that the unconditioned by its very concept can never become an object for us, and so its employment in relation to experience can never be of the same status as that of the categories or of space and time, and this in two respects. Firstly, since there can never be an identity, or indeed any determinate connection whatever, between the object represented in the idea of the unconditioned and the experience that the idea supposedly grounds, the form that we think in experience by relation to such an idea can never be objective or true. Secondly, because the unconditioned not only presents us in the idea with a form of unity that can be applied to the understanding, but also presents us with a supposedly new object, the same lack of identity assures us that this idea determines no object that can be given sense and meaning according to what it would be in itself.

The upshot is that in the Dialectic, Kant is able to secure a place for the ideas only under what he calls their "regulative use" or only insofar as they guide the understanding and provide it with a systematic unity of its cognitions. And he claims that in this respect – i.e. exclusively in their relation to sensible experience – the ideas must be represented *as if* objective. From the point of view of transcendental reflection, the dialectical syllogisms can be kept at bay, not to be sure by removing their grounds or even by forcing us to no longer assume the ideas as if they were objective (for this we cannot do without damage to empirical knowledge itself), but rather by allowing us to *reflectively recognize* these dialectical syllogisms for what they are, namely, logically valid forms of reasoning that do not however possess any real content (or at least move logically from arguments with content to conclusions without content, etc.). It is thus the act of transcendental reflection which allows Kant to integrate reason's demand for the unconditioned with its finitude.

Still one key question remains: How is it possible for the ideas, which are absolutely pure, and which separate themselves from everything empirical, to guide the understanding in its empirical use at all? Not only is it the case that the ideas cannot be brought into contact with the sensible in this way, or determined theoretically, but Kant argues in addition that the unrestricted assumption of the ideas as constitutive would even be detrimental to the use of the understanding. Kant claims, for instance, that if we assume a God as the all-sufficient ground of nature, then we by this fact represent everything that is in the world as absolutely contingent. One reason for this is that we would thereby think of things as really determined by an understanding that in principle exceeds human understanding. But the understanding can operate only on the assumption that there is recognizable necessity in nature, and indeed that the rules by which the mind must consciously think its object are also the laws of things.

The problem is this: How can the unconditioned be brought into relation to human reason in a theoretical respect, which is essentially conditioned, and thereby provide it with a guide? This general problem contains three particular ones, namely: 1) How is it possible to make use of the idea of the unconditioned in regard to the understanding, if it in fact excludes any homogeneity with the empirical? 2) How is it possible to determinately think the idea for such a use, and indeed *as if* objective, when the assumption of the idea as objective in fact cancels the conditions in accordance with which it could be thought? Or if, as Kant puts the matter in §. 76 of the *KU*, "the very thing that reason regards as constitutive of the object and adopts as principle is for understanding, in its human form, transcendent, that is, impossible under the subjective conditions of human thought" (*KU* 05:402–403)? 3) How can the ideas be assumed *as if* objective, and indeed in order to further the purposive use of the understanding, when Kant at other times admits that the assumption of them as objective destroys all purposive use of the understanding? I will restrict my description of Kant's answers to the case of God, as was noted earlier.

Generally expressed, the problem is one of mediation between the finite and the infinite. If the ideas are to be employed in respect to the understanding, then Kant must be able to provide a middle term between the understanding and the ideas, which will allow these two heterogeneous unities to be brought into relation without detriment to either side. Kant provides just such a mediation on three separate but equally essential levels, namely on the level of form, on the level of judgment, and on the level of critical self-consciousness. In regard to form, Kant states that for a regulative use of the ideas to be made possible, it must also be possible to construct a sort of image of them on *analogy* with what is required by the understanding in its specifically empirical use:

> Yet although no schema can be found in *intuition* for the thoroughgoing systematic unity of all concepts of the understanding, an *analogue* of such a schema can and must be given, which is the idea of the *maximum* of division and unification of the understanding's cognition in one principle. For that which is greatest and most complete may be kept determinately in mind, because all restricting conditions, which give indeterminate manifolds, are omitted. (*KrV* A665/B693)

Thus, in order for the ideas, or the unity of reason, to be applied to the determination of the understanding, there must be some form common to both. We thus think the idea, not in itself or in accordance with its supposed internal determinations, but rather in such a way that it can provide determination to the understanding. Now since the table of the categories contains a complete enumeration of the basic forms of understanding, it follows that the ideas will have to be formed in agreement with these. This will be a most basic case of analogy, because the rule of the understanding in accordance with it will be transferred to the determination of the idea, which is something essentially different. We will thus form the idea by attending to the category while at the same time re-

§. 3. The Regulative Principles of Pure Reason — 231

moving from it all restricting conditions. If, for instance, we think of the idea corresponding to the concept of cause, this will be that of an uncaused cause, or a cause without further condition.

Kant makes this analogical procedure most clear in its application to the determination of the concept of God for regulative use. In the *KrV*, he writes:

> Thus according to the analogy of realities in the world, of substances, causality, and necessity, I will think of a being that possesses all of these in their highest perfection, and since this idea rests merely on my reason, I am able to think this being as *self-sufficient reason*, which is the cause of the world-whole through ideas of the greatest harmony and unity; thus I leave out all conditions limiting the idea, so as – under the auspices of such an original ground – to make possible the systematic unity of the manifold in the world-whole and, by means of this unity, the greatest possible use of reason, by seeing all combinations *as if* they were ordained by a highest reason of which our reason is only a weak copy. (*KrV* A678/B706)

Thus while the ideas in their regulative use must obviously each be thought according to such an analogy, in the case of God, this analogy is most determined. In the quote above, indeed, Kant says it is based upon the analogy with four concepts, namely, "of realities in the world, of substances, causality, and necessity." In the *FM*, Kant expands even more fully on the analogical construction of the idea, which in this text he calls its symbol:

> The symbol of an Idea (or a concept of reason) is a representation of the object by analogy, i.e., by the relationship to certain consequences as that which is attributed to the object in respect of its own consequences, even though the objects themselves are of entirely different kinds; for example, if I conceive of certain products of Nature, such as organized beings, animals or plants, in relation to their causes like a clock to man, as its maker, viz., in a relationship of causality as such, qua category, which is the same in both cases, albeit that the subject of this relation remains unknown to me in its inner nature, so that only the one can be presented and the other not at all.
>
> In this way I can indeed have no theoretical knowledge of the super-sensible, e.g., of God, but can yet have a knowledge by analogy, and such as it is necessary for reason to think; it is founded upon the categories, because they necessarily pertain to the form of thinking, whether it be directed to the sensible or the super-sensible, even though these categories constitute no knowledge, and this is precisely because they do not by themselves yet determine any object. (*FM* 20:280)

Kant thus constructs the idea of God for regulative use by beginning with "our reason," and particularly with the concepts most basic to it, and then by separating off from these all limitations. In this way he arrives, by analogy and abstraction, at the image of a self-sufficient reason, a reason that creates its objects in the very thinking of them. But this does little more than allow us to think of an intellect that possesses categorial determination abstracted from any dependency on sensibility.

Although it is no surprise, it is important to note that the symbol of the Idea of God that Kant constructs in this way is identical with his pre-critical concept of God, which also grounded his previous transcendental teleology. Above we saw that Kant describes this being as possessing reality, causality, substantiality, and necessity in the highest degree and also as "*self-sufficient reason*, which is the cause of the world-whole through ideas of the greatest harmony and unity." Kant's specific arguments for these properties are in fact drawn directly from his pre-critical justification of them in *BDG*. The complete determination of the individual in regard to all its properties, requires the foundation of an *omnitudo realtitatis*, Kant argues, because all properties consist of a certain limited magnitude of positive thinkable content, i.e. reality, and the representation of the limited is only possible by reference to the unlimited. Such a being thus is represented as containing the sum-total of the material of all possibility, and because without this there would be nothing at all available for thought, it is also represented as absolutely necessary. Kant argues furthermore that the being possessing this reality must also be represented as a singular being, the ground (cause) of all other things (*ens entium*), the first of all things (*ens originarium*), and the highest of all things (*ens summum*). In other words, now in an employment explicitly restricted to the determination of the systematic form of empirical knowledge, it is to be regarded as "the original image (*prototypon*) of all things, which all together, as defective copies (*ectypa*), take from it the matter of their possibility" (*KrV* A578/B606).

However, Kant argues that if viewed from the standpoint of the thing in itself, these properties cannot at all be proven to belong to one and the same being. The idea itself of an absolutely necessary being, for instance, has nothing in it from which we can analytically derive its status as an *omnitudo realitatis* or as the ground of such a sum-total, nor is there anything in the latter concept to guarantee its absolute necessity. Yet by analogy with our empirical cognition, and in accord with the categories as they are employed by the understanding, we can form the idea of an *omnitudo realitatis* and also see that it is absolutely necessary from a subjective point of view to *assume* such a being for the sake of the use of reason in regard to experience. Thus as the *sum-total of the highest conditions required for our particularly human kind of cognition*, but only as this, can these properties be seen as belonging necessarily to *one ideal*, namely the single focal point in which the activities of the whole of reason are combined into one supreme principle, which is thus the ideal analogue of human reason itself (*KrV* A581–582/B609–610). Just as we have but one faculty of thought which is an absolute unity, so also must all the necessary conditions of such a faculty belong to a single highest condition. The key difference with Kant's precritical position, however, is that he now formulates these arguments as expressing the requirements of a finite faculty of reason – based in how it is internally compelled to think the ground of the world-whole – so that it can regard its own cognition as objectively valid. God, under the title of the "ideal of pure reason," is thus now seen to express not only an abyss for thinking, but indeed on the basis of an analogy, also the focal point and normative principle of all theoretical use of our cognitive activities as a whole. In his lectures on the philosophical doctrine of religion, Kant is recorded as saying:

> The absolute necessity which we indispensably need as the final ground of all things is the true abyss for human reason. Even eternity, as described in its dreadful sublimity by a Haller, does not make as dizzying an impression on the mind; for it only does away with the duration of things, *but it doesn't sustain them*. [...] In short, an absolutely necessary thing will remain to all eternity an insoluble problem for the human understanding. (*V-Phil-Th/Pölitz* 28:1032–1033; emphasis added)

We absolutely need the representation of this being, as the sustainer of all things, *for the sake of the use of our reason* and indeed "it is unavoidable, by means of a transcendental subreption, to represent this formal principle to oneself as constitutive, and to think of this unity hypostatically" (*KrV* A619/B647). But we are also conscious of the basis of this very condition and thus also that its absolute necessity is not one *of the thing*, but of the *relation of the thing to our thinking*.

Now, specifically on the level of judgment, Kant locates a second point of mediation between the finitude of the understanding and the infinity of reason through his use of the related terms "goal" and "maxim" (*KrV* A666–668/B694–696). These terms mediate this relation by restricting the infinity of reason's ideas to the notion of a goal to be achieved through the progressive and systematic unification of the operations of the understanding, which is performed by the faculty of judgment. So the infinity of reason is thought specifically in terms of a goal, because only in that form can it provide a basis for maxims, i.e. subjective guiding principles, suitable for a properly immanent employment. This moment might be termed that of teleological mediation. Its highest maxim is to proceed as if all that might ever enter into a possible experience as its actual material condition were already formed and structured in agreement with the ideal image of reason. Or in other words, proceed as if every object of experience were actually contained in a real and objective systematic whole determined in every respect according to the nature of God, as this idea has been determined above. Since this maxim deals merely with a modal goal for cognition, namely, a goal according to which reason projects an unlimited image of its own structure into the ground of the real as the source of its necessity, and thereby presents its own cognitive needs as necessarily fulfilled by experience, it can be called a maxim of the self-determination of reason in its immanent or theoretical employment. As Kant explains,

> The ideal of the highest being is, according to these considerations, nothing other than a regulative principle of reason, to regard all combination in the world as if it arose from an all-sufficient necessary cause, so as to ground on that cause the rule of a unity that is systematic and necessary according to universal laws; but it is not an assertion of an existence that is necessary in itself. But at the same time it is unavoidable, by means of a transcendental subreption, to represent this formal principle to oneself as constitutive, and to think of this unity hypostatically. For, just as with space, since it originally makes possible all forms which are merely limitations of it, even though it is only a principle of sensibility, it is necessarily held to be a Something subsisting in itself with absolute necessity and an *a priori* object given in itself, so it also comes about entirely naturally that since the systematic unity of nature cannot be set up as a principle of the empirical use of reason except on the basis of the idea of a most real being as the supreme cause, the idea is thereby represented as an actual object, and this object again, because it is the supreme condition, is represented as necessary [...]. (*KrV* A619/B647)

This chief maxim is based upon reason's "single unified interest," namely its end of making the most extensive and systematically unified employment of the understanding in respect to experience. But, according to Kant, this is the basis of a number of seemingly competing maxims whose "conflict [...] is only a variation and limitation of the methods of satisfying this interest" (*KrV* A666/B694). If these are taken as constitutive they seem to contradiction one another, e.g. the maxim of interest in cognizing the manifoldness of experience and the maxim of reducing experience to a unity, but when understood merely as maxims, i.e. subjective principles for how to proceed in the application of the understanding towards a certain end, then they are not only consistent, but converge in one and the same final end.

Finally, on the level of self-consciousness or of transcendental reflection, Kant provides a further critical term to mediate between the finitude of the understanding and the infinity of reason. This consists in the act of transcendental reflection in restricting the infinity of reason to the governance of the conditions under which its demand can be realized in a finite subject. In regard to God, we saw earlier that this concept is essentially that of an absolutely necessary being and that this concept cancels the very conditions of our possibly cognizing it. Kant is careful, however, to show that this is not contradictory as long as we recognize the proper limiting task of transcendental reflection itself, which allows us to see that the idea of the absolutely necessary being is required only as an idea to which we relate our use of the understanding, and thus *subjectively*. It is absolutely necessary to think such a being, and indeed to represent it as if it were objective; but, at the same time, we must recognize that this idea has been derived from the concept of a sensibly conditioned, and hence finite, faculty of human thought. To think God as the absolutely necessary being is absolutely necessary, in other words, only for a mind which possesses the distinction between possibility/concept and actuality/intuition, and thus needs such an idea to ground the systematic form of its cognition. Outside of this relation to our own kind of understanding, however, there is simply no place for the notion of absolute necessity. For this reason its absolute necessity is merely subjectively valid. As Kant sometimes says, it is treated as an object only in the idea, whereas the idea itself is restricted to a subjective employment. That is, the apparent contradiction between the fact that we must assume the absolutely necessary being, but cannot cognize it in itself, actually vanishes if we recognize that the ideal of pure reason is merely subjectively necessary as a goal, and not as an object that is to become actual for reason itself. The critical restriction of the ideal to such a *subjective necessity* constitutes the final, transcendental moment of mediation between the understanding and reason.

Transcendental reflection thus reveals the ideal of pure reason in its regulative function to be the ideal analogue of finite reason itself and it restricts the assumption of this ideal, under the term "subjective necessity," entirely to the effect it has in supporting and providing a most ultimate norm for the dynamic activity of reason in the theoretical cognition of all its objects.

§. 4. The Transcendental Death of Physico-Theology

If we compare Kant's position in the Dialectic with his position in the pre-critical period, then we find that the conceptual core of the former rests essentially on the latter, and would not have been possible without it. Kant's very understanding of the function and structure of the ideas is manifestly derived from the teleological image of God and his relation to the world which was the core achievement of the pre-critical period. This is so much the case that Kant's description of the transcendental ideal in the Dialectic could function well as a precise summary of his pre-critical findings almost down to the last detail. Similarly, his treatment of the "maxims of judgment" in regard to the purposive unity and perfection of the world, which he elucidates in connection with the regulative use of the ideas, is in most respects little more than an expansion of his treatment of the same principles in the *BDG*.

Yet in examining the Dialectic, it will be noted that there is one crucial difference between the critical and the pre-critical discussions of these and similar topics. In fact, it becomes evident that Kant's attempt to smoothly transform these pre-critical structures into their critical garb to a certain extent conflicts with some of the key doctrines of the *KrV*. For instance, we saw earlier when looking at space and time that in the critical period Kant argues that the same unity and perfection which he located in the essences of things in the *BDG*, is in fact only the unity and perfection in the essences of phenomenal objects and is actually introduced into the appearances by the mind itself. Furthermore, the universal laws of nature and the ground of all necessity even in empirical laws, which again in the pre-critical period were seen as necessary consequences of God's nature, are revealed in the critical period to be necessary consequences of the unity of the forms of sensibility and apperception working in unison.

For these reasons, when Kant arrives in the Dialectic at the teleological relation of God to the world, the discussion must be entirely altered. The revised method of physico-theology is the clearest fatality of this transformation. Kant cannot now argue that the universal laws of nature must be seen as if issuing from God, because the whole effort of the Transcendental Aesthetic and Analytic went into showing how they are grounded in the limits and needs of the human mind. But on the other hand, the discussion of the regulative use of the ideas does indeed show that it is necessary and valid to think the most universal laws of nature, as well as all the more derivative empirical ones, *as if* they "shot out" from the intellect of a creator-God. But because this is proven to be a valid assumption only in a certain respect or relative to the conditions of human thought, and to be meaningless aside from this relation (for theoretical reason), the assumption of such a God no longer really belongs within physico-theology, which is the attempt to determine the existence and nature of God *in himself* from the structure of the physical world.

For this reason, Kant's discussions of the regulative maxims of judgment and of physico-theology turn out to be more complex than one would first expect. For through the restriction of these issues to subjective principles of reason, the original intention behind them as well as their place in the structure of philosophy has fundamentally changed. The pre-critical relation of tension and support that existed between the *a priori* proof of God's existence and the teleological character of his creative activity, taken on the one hand, and the teleological inference from creation to creator, taken on the other hand, is in the critical period entirely dissolved in respect to theoretical and speculative reason. Not only is the *a priori* proof no longer objective, but in its subjective form it does not even prove that we must assume the existence of a God determined by pure or transcendental predicates. The image of God that is assumed *as if* objective is rather one entirely cut to fit the employment of the understanding for the sake of empirical knowledge. The image of God himself as a pure and "faultless

§. 4. The Transcendental Death of Physico-Theology — 237

ideal" is thus off limits in a theoretical respect, and has nothing to do with the analogical image of God required to ground the maxims of reason. A consequence of this alteration is that physico-theology in the *KrV* is stripped of precisely those elements that belonged to Kant's favorite revised method. On this new story, we must presuppose the existence of a creative intellect in order to think experience as internally structured in a way required for the possibility of maximal unity in our knowledge, but this is presupposed only relative to reason for the sake of its own employment. In other words, the transcendental teleology is a presupposition made by reason itself, and thus provides no evidence whatsoever for the real existence of God apart from this. If there is anything left, then, for a genuine physico-teleological proof to consider, it is only those entirely contingent arrangements that appear to be found in nature, such as natural ends. However, even in regard to these it is by no means perfectly clear that they retain their original function in Kant's critical thought. Indeed, just as Kant holds in the pre-critical period that we should seek to extend the transcendental teleology as far as possible in our research into nature, and that we also must do this if we are ever to know these things in an adequate way, so here in the *KrV* Kant strongly suggests that as respectable as the physico-teleological proof might be, it is not proof of anything. I think one might wonder, particularly given the treatment of teleology in the *KU*, whether there is room left in the critical system for any kind of physico-theology.

This effect of the turn in Kant's thought on the physico-theological proof can be seen clearly in one of his most damaging criticisms of it:

> According to this inference, the purposiveness and well-adaptedness of so many natural arrangements would have to prove merely the contingency of the form, but not of the matter, i.e., of substance, in the world; for the latter would further require that it be able to be proved that the things in the world would in themselves be unsuited for such an order and harmony according to universal laws if they were not in their substance the product of the highest wisdom; but entirely different grounds of proof from those provided by the analogy with human art would be required for this. Thus the proof could at most establish a highest architect of the world, who would always be limited by the suitability of the material on which he works, but not a creator of the world, to whose idea everything is subject, which is far from sufficient for the great aim that one has in view, namely that of proving an all-sufficient original being. If we wanted to prove the contingency of matter itself, then we would have to take refuge in a transcendental argument, which, however, is exactly what was supposed to be avoided here. (*KrV* A626–627/B654–655)

In view of the findings of the previous chapters, Kant's point in this paragraph is immediately comprehensible. He is not arguing that teleology in general is no ground for a proof of a highest all-sufficient being, but only that a proof attempting to base itself upon a teleology regarding the contingent and particular arrangements in nature at best allows us to infer a finite God, a God which like an artist is himself limited by the material upon which he operates. If a teleological proof is to be sufficient to the genuine concept of God, then it must rather base itself on the transcendental teleology found in the essences of things, which requires the idea of a God that establishes the reciprocal unity and harmony of substances in his creation of them. Such a transcendental argument alone is sufficient to provide a basis for inferring an all-sufficient and original being in a theoretical respect. However, the very necessity of these laws rests on our ability to cognize them *a priori*, or at least as based upon ones cognized in this way, which however proves in Kant's view that the idea of God as an all-sufficient being is purely a product of our reason, and must be entirely restricted to a regulative theoretical function.

Conclusion

The Dialectic, like the other parts of Kant's critical philosophy, exposes a teleological structure internal to human reason, and indeed one that is established originally and purely by reason in accordance with the conditions of its own self-reflection. Those same grounds that constituted the basis of traditional teleology, and also of the revised teleological method of Kant's pre-critical period, are revealed by transcendental reflection to be objects assumed by reason and for the sake of reason, in order to provide itself with a system of cognitions congruent with its own internal structure. As Kant explains, "here the questions are not laid before us by the nature of things but only through the nature of reason, and they are solely about its internal arrangement" (*KrV* A695/B726). Philosophy is, and always will be, nothing more than "a study of our inner nature" (*KrV* A703/B731). It is able to be this, and yet to also claim to provide a complete treatment of the foundations of knowledge, because of its isolation from any concern with things in themselves. This isolation is precisely what allows it to regard its own form-giving faculties as unconditioned.

Kant thus offers an account of finite human cognition in which the very activity of transcendental reflection plays an essential role in generating reason's own unity, and it does so by relating the unconditional demand of reason in the narrow sense to the specific conditions under which it can be realized in agreement with reason as a whole. It emerges from this self-conscious restriction that the real (not merely logical) unity of subjectivity is essentially practical in the wide sense and consists in the self-conscious – though by no means arbitrary – legislation of maxims for cognitive activity that formally ground the possibility of the use of the understanding. Yet, as we have also seen, when the finitude of the subject is fully taken into account, this absolute self-legislation with regard to the form of maxims structurally entails the projection of a material condition, namely, an object that reason sets before itself as a goal, which by its very essence cannot be achieved under the conditions attaching to a finite reason.

In this respect, transcendental philosophy in general is nothing but absolute autonomy. Here, reason out of its own original essence legislates its laws and sets its own goal as the formal condition of the possibility of the complete *realization* of its own unity. Yet under the conditions of the finite subject, this self-legislation entails the *self-conscious* subordination of the judging subject to the pursuit of a goal in its cognitive activities that can only be fulfilled by something outside of itself. So while the Kantian "I think" is the absolute transcendental and formal ground in the theoretical realm, the actualization of this formal unity is seen as dependent upon the *ideal* of the causality of a material ground *from within the autonomy of the transcendental perspective itself.*

General Conclusion to Part II

We have seen that the possibility of objective representations rests in all cases on a bounded, but spontaneous and legislative, act of the conscious mind. The laws of sensibility rest on the formal analytic unity of space and time; the principles of understanding rest on the formal analytic unity of apperception; and the maxims of reason rest on the formal analytic unity of the higher faculty of reason. Each of these unities is "analytic" in the sense that it is absolutely necessary for the mind in its respective function, and so must be presupposed in relation to it. Thus, given a perception, it is analytically true that it has temporal and spatial unity; given an object, it is analytically true that it has unity of thought; and given a system of cognitions it is analytically true that it has unity of reason.

But that an object in itself must have temporal and spatial unity, that it must contain in its concept the unity required for thought, and that it must fit into a system of cognitions – these are neither analytically, nor synthetically true. What is synthetically true is rather that any object: *if* it is to be an *object* of our intuition, it must have temporal and spatial unity; *if* it is to be an *object* of our experience, it must have the unity required by thought; and, finally, if it is to be empirically determinable as fitting into a complete whole of cognition, it must contain the unity of reason. The synthesis in these cases is that between the concept of an object of our minds *in general*, and the specific laws that such objects must necessarily obey in order to be given to us in experience, and in such a way that we can form such a concept of them. The basis of the validity of this synthesis lies in the fact that there exist within the finite mind certain conditions in accordance with which alone the representation of an object *qua* object, i.e. in regard to its necessary and essential determinations, is first made possible. The ground of synthesis, in other words, lies not in any of the particular conditions in relation to what they specifically make possible, but rather in that *all the conditions* (or faculties of mind) *must be able to be combined into one whole of conscious representation* for any one condition to be capable of having an object. In particular, the synthesis in intuitive judgments is required for us to represent intuited objects because this also involves the understanding in its logical or judgmental use. The understanding, on the other hand, requires a synthesis because it must collect together the manifold offered to it by sensibility, if it is to represent an object in accordance with its own conditions. The unity of a system of cognitions through the logical use of pure reason, again, requires a synthetic ground in the ideas in order to think the unity of understanding (which is nevertheless a manifold seen from the standpoint of reason) such that it is objectively determinable by the unity of reason.

In all three cases, Kant ultimately rests the validity of such synthesis on the originality and purity of the principles of unity involved. Such originality and purity, along with the fact that these principles of unity can be shown to make their corresponding objects possible, allows Kant to argue that the whole can and must be represented as in some sense preceding the parts and as making them possible; for only in this way can their application be represented as objectively valid in even a limited sense. In its structural outlines this is just Kant's most lasting and richest conception of teleological unity in its theoretical function.

Part III: **The Teleology of Freedom**

Introduction to Part III

Serving as both the centerpiece and foundation of Kant's moral philosophy, the *KpV* has the chief task of limiting the pretensions not of pure reason, but of practical reason insofar as it is conditioned by empirical principles (*KpV* 05:139). As Kant himself points out, this may seem like a strange change of fortune for pure reason after its treatment in the *KrV*. In the analyses that occupied us in Part II we saw that pure reason has a twofold function within the theoretical domain. In its first function, it is subordinated to and limited by the goal of knowledge and in this capacity it serves the understanding in order to further the latter's purposive use for the comprehension of experience as a system. While in its second function, pure reason also serves the purpose of theoretical cognition, but this time by setting a limit to theoretical knowledge itself, thereby extricating it from the contradictions it necessarily falls into when it takes its knowledge to extend to the absolute. It is important to note that pure reason is able to serve this function precisely because it is only through a direct contrast with the model of an absolute or pure, but unreachable, divine intellect that reason is able to become reflectively aware of its own finitude. As Kant writes, "it is pure reason that itself contains the standard for the critical examination of every use of it" (*KpV* 05:15). In this respect pure reason's self-reflection is in fact the organ of transcendental critique and, as we saw, at the core of this critique stands transcendental theology. As we also noted there, through transcendental criticism reason becomes reflectively self-limiting and self-regulating, a sort of autonomous and organically structured system of self-consciousness.

The one key feature of reason insofar as it is directed to the *telos* of cognition is that its entire use is subordinated to the systematization of what is given to it empirically. As a result of this, the use of pure reason, and so also of its ideal, is restricted to the regulative and critical functions just outlined. This means that as far as cognition is concerned, reason is *required* to regard the empirical realm as the complete field of its valid use, and must act on the maxim that the path of empirical research is the only valid way of investigating any object with which it may be presented.

Transposing then to the moral sphere, it seems that consistency would require Kant to say that questions about the nature and laws of the human will can only be validly approached by the methods of empirical psychology. Indeed, as long as we have no justification for thinking that morality can be anything more than an empirical study of laws that govern the faculty of desire, *reason itself* seems to be impelled by the results of the *KrV* to work on the maxim that the empirical path exhausts the field of meaningful questions that can be asked about the human will. Furthermore, if every valid question about the will allows of an empirical explanation, then this means that every act of practical reason must be explicable from, and so also conditioned by, a prior cause extant within the empirical world.

It is precisely this state of affairs, as Kant explains, that makes it necessary to criticize practical reason when it is conditioned by sensibility. Since the will is nothing but the reflective application of reason to the faculty of desire for the sake of determining the best course of action, conditioned-practical reason for its own part and *by its very nature* is led to presume as part of its own decision-making process that "it, alone and exclusively, furnishes the determining ground of the will" (*KpV* 05:16). Thus an entirely healthy and necessary principle of theoretical reason, when it becomes practical, is the reason why

> we find our nature as sensible beings so constituted that the matter of the faculty of desire [...] first forces itself upon us, and we find our pathologically determinable self [...] striving to give its pretensions priority and to make them valid as first and original claims, just as if it constituted our entire self. (*KpV* 05:74)

Thus the very striving for happiness that Kant calls "self-love" is not in the first instance a blind urge, but rather a reflective disposition to determine our actions exclusively according to cognitions constituted by the transcendental principles of theoretical reason in so far as these are applied to empirically given impulses. Now, since Kant thinks it fully possible to show not only "that pure reason can be practical but that it alone, and not reason empirically limited, is unconditionally practical," and thus that there is more to the self than its empirical appearance, it follows that in the moral realm it is theoretical reason, in the guise of conditioned practical reason, that threatens to overstep its boundaries and therefore requires criticism (*KpV* 05:15).

It is also important to note that this way of framing the project of the *KpV*, namely as a defense of moral cognition against the encroachment of theoretical cognition, has a deep historical basis in the fact that the moral theories of both Leibniz and Wolff rest essentially on a naturalistic view of morality and freedom, one in which the *telos* of the will is a mere consequence of our achievement of the *telos* of knowledge. The dogmatic and unfettered use of theoretical reason typical of such thinkers has as its necessary corollary, in Kant's view, a moral theory based upon the concept of rational self-love, which is subordinated to end of theoretical cognition, and both ultimately spring from the misuse of the otherwise valid and healthy maxims of theoretical reason. However, since Kant regards genuine morality as consisting in the disposition for determining one's actions through the moral law immediately ("for the sake of the law"), and hence not with a view to the principle of self-love or to any end or set of ends that would be given by nature prior to this law, we can draw the highly significant conclusion that the project of the *KpV*, as the full and systematic limitation of theoretical reason's pretensions to legislate within the practical domain, is itself essentially a *moral* project, i.e. a project aimed at directly increasing the morality in our actions, and not merely a dry architectonic exercise. "*Common human reason*," Kant thus states,

> is impelled not by some need of speculation [...], but on practical grounds themselves, to go out of its sphere and to take a step into the field of practical philosophy, in order to obtain there information and distinct instruction regarding the source of its principle and the correct determination of this principle in comparison with maxims based on need and inclination, so it may escape from its predicament about claims from both sides [i.e. the sides of conditioned-practical and pure practical reason] and not run the risk of being deprived of all genuine moral principles through the ambiguity into which it easily falls. (*GMS* 04:405)

The reclamation of the will from this service to the end set for it by theoretical reason, through the limitation of the latter's claims, and the placement of theoretical reason in a proper balance with pure practical reason, is a reflective procedure through which we *as self-conscious beings* construct a mode of thought about our actions that is essentially moral. To fail to perform this act of criticism leads naturally and thus necessarily to an immoral theory of morals (i.e. one based upon self-love), or, if one still admits the true moral principle in some form, to a natural dialectic in which the effects of this principle are eroded through competition with the rational principle of self-love.

From this we can also see that the apparent reversal of fortunes for pure reason in the practical domain is really just a shift in perspective. In both *Critiques* it is pure reason that has the function of preventing the norms of theoretical knowledge from extending themselves into the absolute. Since theoretical knowledge, as Kant shows, is *essentially* a purposive activity aimed at systematizing the deliverances of empirical intuition, and is therefore also conditioned by the latter, the very locution "pure theoretical knowledge" is literally shown to be a mongrel concept akin to "absolute conditioned knowledge." Now outside of the proper domain of theoretical knowledge, in a practical field where pure reason in the guise of the will is able to produce its own objects, and thus where it does not depend upon anything given from outside, a locution like "theoretically-conditioned pure willing" is shown by the *KpV* likewise to be a kind of mongrel. However, in this case – since the field in question properly belongs to an absolutely unconditioned or pure faculty reason in its determination of the will – it is the not the word "pure" but rather "theoretically-conditioned" that is misplaced. So in both cases, transcendental criticism is not aimed at *extin-*

guishing either the limited or the unlimited exercise of reason, but rather in limiting each to their proper domains. It is only fitting then, that in its own domain, where reason itself enjoys an unlimited employment, the pure use of reason would be the one requiring protection.

In the moral realm we are therefore dealing with a structure of self-consciousness that is organized under principles quite different from those of theoretical reason, where everything was subordinated to the *telos* of the knowledge of what is given. I will argue in this and the next chapter that the structure of moral self-consciousness is actually organized according to its own complex teleology, one that constitutes its inner normative structure and content. Now, since conditioned-practical reason, according to my interpretation, is nothing but theoretical reason reflectively applied to the causality of the will for its determination, and its tendency to overtake the domain of morality is a corollary of the teleological or purposive character of theoretical reason, it is only to be expected that the criticism of conditioned-practical reason will have to be divided in a way parallel to the critique of pure reason. Accordingly, we will discover in the present chapter that the function of judging, particularly in respect of the categories by which it determines its objects, and the grounds it holds as valid for determining practical judgment, occupy Kant in the Analytic of Pure Practical Reason. In my discussion of the Dialectic in the next chapter, we will also find that the idea of God, which guides the complete determination of the object of pure reason, and so here also of pure reason in its practical employment, is provided by Kant in this respect with an entirely new set of determining concepts.

In both respects, we will thus find in the course of these chapters that the natural teleology of practical reason is limited by the supremacy and legislation of the pure will, which lies at its foundation, and reveals itself to be the pure root of practical reason. This pure will as an *idea*, in Kant's view, provides reason in its pure practical employment with the archetype of all moral reality in the idea of God, both in regard to the basic character of possible objects of willing in general, and in regard to the total object of pure practical reason, i.e. the highest good as the *bonum consummatum*. So here, just as in the *KrV*, we will see that it is pure reason – through its ideas – that again serves as the organ of criticism, or in other words, as that by comparison with which the empirical employment of practical reason is both limited, and set in the right balance for its purposive use. Additionally, since practical reason as such is conditioned, *pure* practical reason, guided by this idea, must be understood as one and the same function of reason insofar as it is *by itself*, and thus in its own *purity*, the source of its own actions both in regard to their causality as well as their content. Thus pure practical reason is itself nothing other than that idea – in the strict Kantian sense – of a free faculty for practical reasoning that would be self-legislating or autonomous. As in the theoretical case, here also in the practical one, the reflective act of criticism consists in pure reason's employment of its own ideas upon itself.

Chapter 6 The Teleology of Freedom: The Structure of Moral Self-Consciousness in the Analytic

> Here, then, we see philosophy put in fact in a precarious position, which is to be firm even though there is nothing in heaven or on earth from which it depends or on which it is based. Here philosophy is to manifest its purity as sustainer of its own laws, not as a herald of laws that an implanted sense or who knows what tutelary nature whispers to it. (*GMS* 04:425)

> That I want to be free [...] means: I myself want to make myself whatever I will be. I would, therefore – and this is what is most puzzling and apparently totally incoherent in this conception – I would already have to be, in a certain sense, what I am to become, so that I could make myself be it; I would have to have a double kind of being, of which the first would contain the basis of a determination of the second. [...] Here, to be sure, it is merely in thinking of my purpose that I *already am* what I will thereafter and as a consequence of this thinking *really* be through willing and acting; I am first a thinker what in virtue of this thinking I subsequently am as an agent. I make myself: my being through my thinking; my thinking simply through thinking. (Fichte 1987, p. 22)

Introduction

> Plato was right, however, to see clear proofs of an origin in ideas ... where human reason shows true causality, and where *ideas become efficient causes* (of actions and their objects), namely in morality. (*KrV* A317/B374)

> There are cognitions *a priori* through which the objects are possible. It is strange that an object should be possible purely through a cognition; however, all instances of order, all purposive relations are possible through a cognition, e.g. a truth is not possible without a cognition that precedes it. The cognition *a priori* through which the object is possible is the Idea. Plato said: one must study the ideas. (*Vor-Met-L2/Pölitz* 28.2:577)

The place of teleology in Kant's moral philosophy has long been a matter of dispute. Outside the narrow confines of Kant scholarship the prevailing view has nearly always been that Kant's philosophy marks the culmination of the modern rejection of Aristotelian teleology. As this particular story goes, the early moderns eliminated the explanatory function of purposes in the realm of physics, but, with perhaps the exception of Spinoza and Hobbes, they left teleology unchallenged in the spiritual realm. This led immediately to the question as to how human beings could pursue their moral and religious destiny when nature, of which the human body is itself a part, is not intrinsically purposive. The pineal gland, pre-established harmony, occasionalism, and all similar metaphysical monstrosities, can on this view be understood as just so many attempts to heal the rift, felt most acutely within the human being's own complex nature, between the cold mechanical universe and the teleologically rich realm of the soul.

Depending upon whether one favors a continuation of modernity or a return to Aristotle, Kant enters this story either as its imperfect but clear-headed hero, or else as its most sinister and deceptive character. In either case, Kant is seen as carrying modernity to its logical conclusion by showing the transcendental necessity of the mechanical worldview, while at the same time extending the modern anti-teleological conception of natural law, in the form of the categorical imperative, into the inner sanctuary of the soul. Deontology, according to this interpretation, should be understood as the natural extension of modern science into the field of morality.

But if this is how the matter truly stands, then what are we to say of all that is so evidently teleological in Kant's moral writings, such as his conception of the highest good, of moral striving, of virtue, of reason as an absolute purposive unity, and of the inevitability of moral progress in history? If Kant is as sinister as some champions of Aristotle claim, then one might view this as nothing but clever deception; just enough "merely regulative" teleology and religion to satisfy the unstudied eye and the censors, but not enough to compromise the deeply anti-teleological foundations of his thought. If, on the other hand, Kant is our sober hero of modernity, then his overtly teleological views can be excused as simple human weakness, a tribute to the metaphysics of his predecessors and the morally sound Pietism of his parents.

Finally, there is a third possibility, one that is firmly grounded in Kant's own writings. This possibility is that, because of the subjective constitution and limitations of human reason, we can only fully commit ourselves to acting according to the moral law if we can *conceive* how this is possible and what it will mean. Thus on several occasions Kant explicitly claims that thinking in terms of ends, which includes viewing our own actions as directed to specific purposes, is not objective, but rather is based upon the particular or subjective character of human thought (*RGV* 06:8n). The key here is that teleology is seen not as the foundation of the moral law, or even as on the same objective level as the law, but is rather introduced solely on what Kant calls the "subjectively logical" level. The teleological world-view would then be a mere *as if* reality, to be used as a regulative but never as a constitutive concept.[1]

Admittedly, this latter story is not without support in Kant's texts. Yet over the last few decades, commentators have put together a picture of Kant's

---

[1] I will interpret these passages differently below.

moral philosophy in which teleology plays an indisputable role both in the application of the moral principle and in securing the overall unity of Kant's moral philosophy. As a result of this, I think it has become clear that we cannot have a moral theory that looks anything remotely like Kant's if we try to entirely excise teleology from the picture. Although I do not want to generalize too much about recent scholarship, it seems to me, however, that on the whole the pendulum is beginning to swing perhaps too quickly in the opposite direction, making Kant look like just another modern theorist of the value of humanity as the end of creation. I am hesitant about these developments, because I do not think we have quite yet begun to understand how such teleology actually flows from the basic principles of Kant's moral philosophy. Surely, there must be a constitutive place for teleology in Kant's philosophy, particularly his moral philosophy. For, barring this, we will have to accept the suggestions made by Allen Wood and more recently and radically by Patrick Frierson, that according to Kant – because our character is timelessly constituted through our absolute or transcendental freedom – our earnest moral striving, our attempts to morally educate our children, and our attempts to develop ethical communities, all of which consist in the achievement of specific purposes, are of no intrinsic moral significance.[2] Being "not literally true," to use Wood's expression, we will have to view them as the mere appearances or expressions of a moral character that was mysteriously decided by us in a timeless way, though we never had any conscious awareness of making any such decision.

Nevertheless, for those who seek to retain Kant's stress on the deep moral significance of striving towards and to some extent achieving a moral world, it has become common to sweep aside the problem of providing an internal justification of the reality of this teleology, and to start from the assumption that our

---

[2] Writes Wood: "Since the noumenal world for Kant is a timeless realm, his solution requires us to regard even such basic features of the moral life as moral striving and moral progress as having only figurative or allegorical and not literal truth" (Wood 1999, p. 179). Patrick Frierson, however, accepts and even extends this basic idea, while trying to deny that it affects the moral importance of our striving and progress in the empirical world. As Frierson writes, "As the expression of one's noumenal will, one's appearance in the world is morally relevant in the strongest possible sense. It is by being a certain sort of appearance that one shows oneself to be a certain sort of free agent" (Frierson 2003, p. 99). In my opinion, Frierson fails to make this idea plausible, because the whole issue of moral striving turns on the idea that *through it* we think that we can *become* better people. But if this is nothing more than the expression of a moral character that is constituted prior to, and thus apart from this moral striving, like my taste for music is expressed in what I choose to listen to, and which this striving only expresses but does not bring about, then moral striving is not *literally* true. This is not to say that a solution to this problem is easy or that Kant in fact possessed a workable solution.

progress in time for Kant is simply reality itself, and therefore that concepts of a timeless realm of transcendental freedom, of God, of the moral law, and even of the unity of reason itself (which is practical), are nothing more than mere *regulative* ideas, the sole function of which is to provide us with an indeterminate focal point for the complete systematization of our actions in the empirical world. I do not, however, see how this or any similar attempt at a solution can be thought to work. If all that is actual or real is our progress in the empirical world, then this means that the concepts Kant sets up to guide this progress, *which all either belong to the noumenal realm or gain their moral significance by relation to it*, are themselves nothing but necessary and universal fictions just like the regulative ideas of *KrV*. Worst of all, it seems we can and must, from a transcendental perspective, become perfectly aware of their fictional status. Now, if the idea by which we measure our progress is purely a fiction, then I do not see how Kant can count the progress we make towards realizing it to be anything but fictive as well. For, in this case, our supposed progress in time, when viewed objectively, will not be a real progress, and our very attempt to save the reality of teleology in the moral realm will collapse by itself.[3]

What Kant's theory requires, I believe, is a way of retaining two seemingly incompatible views at one time, namely, a point of view from which the empirical dimension of moral action is viewed as the core of reality and the supersensible objects as mere ideas, and another point of view from which these objects are viewed as the supreme realities and the empirically observed moral action as the mere appearance or expression of this noumenal reality. One thing to notice is that a simple division of theoretical and practical standpoints will not suffice for this task, since both of the points of view I have just described involve different views on the relation *between* theoretical and practical reason within a broadly practical perspective. Kant's own attempt to settle this tension through the reality/appearance distinction in the *GMS*, I would suggest, is by itself just too simple to account for the richness and complexity of his own view of the moral self.

The question at issue when we ask about the place of teleology in Kant's philosophy, then, is not whether he draws on teleological formulae throughout his moral writings or whether these can be fruitful for the sake of interpretation. The question is rather one as to how deeply this teleology runs and whether it can ultimately be made consistent with what Kant says regarding the reality and ab-

---

[3] To be sure, these arguments are not sufficient to defeat constructivism. They do, however, tell against any constructivism that claims to be an interpretation of either the letter or the spirit of Kant's moral philosophy.

solute spontaneity of freedom and the emphasis he places on the purity of moral motivation from all consideration of ends. For if teleology is deeply ingrained in Kant's moral thought, then it must be possible to show how it follows naturally and necessarily from his most basic principles as they are expounded not only in the *GMS* but also in the *KpV*. Given what I said before, this means that we must be able to trace the basic arguments through which Kant constructs his theory of freedom, and from this show how the reality of the timeless supersensible realm, as well as the reality of our moral striving in the empirical world, fit into a complex but consistent unity immanent to moral self-consciousness.

In the following sections I will outline a way this can be achieved by attending to the distinctive teleology that I believe lies at the very heart of Kant's concept of freedom.[4] To be precise, I will defend the thesis that Kant's account of human freedom, the very principle of unity underlying the human will, is *constitutively* teleological. In essence, the problems I just sketched, as well as the problems I will sketch in the next several sections, cannot be resolved in my view if we jettison Kant's moral ontology, as Korsgaard and other constructivists would have us do (e.g. Korsgaard 1996, p. 183), or if we undertake "staggering revisions in our commonsense conception of our agency" as Allen Wood thinks we must (Wood 1984, p.99). Kant's distinctive moral theory, I contend, can be saved only if we recognize that from within the first-person experience of moral self-consciousness both views are generated in a single complex movement of thought. I will further argue that the unity of this movement – through the contrast and tension generated by our awareness of the competing reality of both the supersensible and empirical perspectives on the self – is what *constitutes* freedom as itself a teleological concept. If my argument succeeds, it will show that from *within* moral self-consciousness, and thus immanent to the practical perspective, Kant would have us view freedom as teleological in a twofold way, namely, as the *causality of an idea* through which we are constituted as absolutely self-determinative or as self-formative beings, and from another perspective as the causality of a being that must be viewed essentially as involved in an infinite striving towards an unrealizable goal of moral perfection.[5]

---

[4] Stephen Engstrom perhaps comes closest to what I have in mind. See Engstrom 2002b. Although he does not use the term, Engstrom clearly recognizes the teleological structure of freedom in Kant. He does not, however, investigate the origin of this teleology in the basic structures of Kant's moral theory, which is what I propose to do here.

[5] In demonstrating this, I aim to support the wider thesis also held by Dieter Henrich that the unity of subjectivity in Kant, in this case of moral subjectivity, is essentially teleological. See his "On the Unity of Subjectivity" in Henrich 1994, p. 17–54.

My reasons for desiring to develop such an interpretation of Kant's moral theory stem from two sources. First, there are the internal sources which I will examine in the next few sections. My suggestion here will be that the explicit claims Kant makes about morality cannot be made sense of apart from an *intrinsically* teleological, indeed quasi-Platonic account of moral agency. Secondly, the historical backdrop to Kant's moral theory, and the way in which he situates his theory in relation to this backdrop, leave little room for doubt that Kant's moral thought is directly motivated by a felt need for a reformulation of the very foundations of the teleological structure of moral agency. Cognizance of this fact, I believe, shows particularly how wrong-headed the anti-teleological interpretation of the categorical imperative in fact is. In particular, it shows how this interpretation fundamentally misconceives Kant's very motivations for seeking to clarify the grounds of morality, which are in fact aimed at a reformation and a deepening of the teleological structure of our practical nature. In particular, the categorical imperative, through its absolute immediacy and purity, allows Kant to break through the metaphysics of an endless mechanism of theoretical nature, and simultaneously allows him to lift the rational agent into a realm in which conscious purposes can for the first time genuinely become *our* purposes, and not just purposes that nature, as it were, works through us.

Just as in our examination of Kant's pre-critical teleology, this gives rise to the idea of a pure willing whose goal is the complete systematic unity of the absolute whole of all willing, and it relates to the particular will as the source of absolutely all practical objective reality (as it were, an *omnitudo realitatis moralis*), the principle of complete moral determination, and as the model or archetype of complete moral perfection. Morevoer, just as in Kant's pre-critical view of teleology, the determination to specific ends is here a mere consequence, and not the prior determining ground, of a will constituted by this intrinsic teleology. The teleology here is not the finite production of moral ends, but the unlimited, reciprocal and harmonious relation to every other moral being as to a final end. Partial or particular instances of moral harmoniousness and agreement are but instantiations of the infinitely rich teleological structure that the pure will is determined to sustain through its activity.

As we will also find, the Kantian moral intellectualism evident here relates to that of Leibniz and Wolff in much the same way that Socrates relates to that of the *physikoi:* For the speculations of the *physikoi*, the practices of man constituted but a limited and derivative portion of the cosmos, and so the question as to what man should do was subordinated to the natural law of the cosmos of which he was seen to be but a part. In the thought of Socrates, by contrast, the practices of man gained for the first time their own distinctive *arché*; the good, along with justice, piety, virtue and so forth, in his view proved the existence of laws that are immediately internal to *nomos* itself. Neither Socrates nor Kant, to be sure, were the first in their respective traditions to engage in moral speculations, but they share the uncommon distinction of having raised moral speculations to a new height by granting to the human will its own distinctive principle in relation to nature. As we saw in Chapter 1, Kant emerges from a tradition in which the operative contrast was one between a cosmic teleology governed by the principle of sufficient reason, and an inner teleology of self-consciousness that rebelled against this cosmic law, and thus sought by means of a conception of an absolute uncaused causality of freedom to reinvest the realm of moral purposes with an independent significance and normativity. The influence of this latter tradition of thought on Kant, particularly through the work of Crusius, indicates how deeply any view that would reduce moral choice and striving to a mere consequence would go in the teeth of one of the central motivations behind Kant's moral theory.

I will now turn to the part of my argument that is based upon internal textual evidence. In its first half, I distinguish three seemingly incompatible concepts of freedom in Kant, namely, *freedom of responsibility*, *freedom as idea*, and *freedom as self-mastery*, and afterwards three corresponding concepts of will, namely, the *empirical will*, the *noumenal will*, and the *phenomenal will*. These will serve as the moments of the teleological structure I will articulate in subsequent sections. In its second half, I try to show how these seemingly incompatible concepts are generated by Kant in one continuous and consistent movement of moral self-consciousness. I will conclude with some comments on what I see as serious deficiencies in Kant's account.

§. 1. Three Types of Freedom

The practice of keeping track of the different types of freedom in Kant's works can become something of a pastime for the careful reader. If allowed to leave aside technicalities, however, I think that there are basically three distinct manners in which Kant tends to speak specifically about the inner freedom of the human being. I will now sketch these three manners in the broadest of strokes. Those familiar with the debate surrounding Henry Sidgwick's claim to have found two incompatible notions of freedom in Kant will notice that my tripartite division has similarities to his, but that it also differs in crucial respects (Sidgwick 1888).

Freedom in a first sense – and this I will call the *freedom required for responsibility* – is a universal property belonging to every single act of the will, and not admitting of greater or lesser degrees. The universality of this type of freedom in respect to choice stems from the fact that every action is first made possible according to Kant, *as an action belonging to or as imputable to a person*, precisely through the freedom with which the action is chosen. So while a person *can* be more or less responsible for a movement of their body viewed as an *empirical event*, a person *cannot* be more or less responsible for their actions *qua* action.[6] It is precisely to clarify this point that Kant introduces the term "deed," which describes an action that springs originally from freedom, and as such is unconditionally imputed to a person (*MS* 06:223).

Kant often speaks of freedom in this sense, particularly in his discussions of imputation. The following is a most clear case:

> So considered, a rational being can now rightly say of every unlawful action he performed that he could have omitted it even though as appearance it is sufficiently determined in the past and, so far, is inevitably necessary; for this action, with all the past which determines it, belongs to the single phenomenon of his character, which he gives to himself, as a cause independent of sensibility, the causality of those appearances. (*KpV* 5:98)

Kant would seem to suggest that practical freedom of this kind plays a very similar role in relation to the manifold of actions as transcendental apperception plays in relation to the manifold of intuition in general. That is, just as representations do not belong to me simply in virtue of the fact that I can be conscious of them as analytically united representations, but require a further *synthetic* ground, namely transcendental apperception, to make this analytic unity possible as belonging originally – *collectively* – to one consciousness; so, similarly, in order to be imputed to me, actions and choices require not only an analytical relation to the causality of my will, but additionally also a relation to the *synthetic ground* in virtue of which my will itself forms an original and distinctively *practical* unity. This latter ground is freedom itself, and is what distinguishes the causality of a rational will and its capacity for taking possession and being responsible, in a word, of performing deeds, from the causality of a non-rational agent that lacks all such capacities. In short, Kant suggests that both apperception and freedom function as the ground of the *synthetic* unity of a manifold. The difference is that the manifold in the practical case is composed of our empirical actions. From this we can see that freedom of responsibility provides a synthetic unity of the empirical will under the determination of the noumenal. It is also clear from this that the empirical will plays the role of a determinable matter

---

6 Kant does often speak as if there are degrees of responsibility, for example, Immanuel Kant, *Lectures on Ethics*, trans. Louis Infield (Gloucester, Mass.: Peter Smith, 1978), p. 62–70. Clearly he means by this, however, not that there are degrees of responsibility, but rather that there are degrees to which one is responsible.

that can be made determinate under a higher formal principle stemming, as we will see, from the noumenal dimension of the will.

A first point that must be stressed here is that according to this concept freedom must not be understood as something merely ideal, but something real and present within us, a genuine causality; for it is precisely what constitutes the particular human being both as a particular morally responsible agent and as an individual moral substance or person (*MS* 6:223). Just as the spontaneity of the synthesis belonging to apperception provides a ground through the association with which a manifold of intuitions can first become "mine," or be seen as belonging to one whole of consciousness, so freedom seems to be something like that character of my causality that must obtain if its effects are to be seen as "mine" and so as being a manifold of *actions* belonging to one will. Thus freedom with regard to the choice of my actions can be described as the condition of the possibility of an action's being a deed, and being counted as "mine" at all. Whether this concept can be put to a constitutive use for cognizing one's character is something that must be decided later on.

A second point requiring emphasis is that on this concept absolutely all actions of whatever moral quality must be accounted as free in this sense, for otherwise they could not be imputed. Indeed, since according to this idea of freedom all acts are entirely free to the extent that they are acts at all, such freedom is not open to quantitative determination. For this reason, even apparently the most evil of acts must be entirely free in this sense; for to the extent that it was judged to not be free, it could not be imputed, it would be without moral quality, and thus could not rightfully be called evil at all. Sidgwick calls this kind of freedom, "neutral freedom" precisely to highlight the fact that we must be free in this sense whenever we perform both good and evil acts. I think one might be tempted to equate freedom in this sense with what Kant calls the negative definition or concept of freedom (*GMS* 04:446, *KpV* 05:29), but it seems to me that the freedom required for responsibility requires something more than mere freedom from external determination, namely, it requires an inward and *positive* faculty for self-determination which is yet not equivalent to positive freedom either, since it may go against the law.

A second type of freedom featured in Kant's writings is what I will call *freedom as idea* (cf. *GMS* 04:448–453). Kant also refers to this as the causality by virtue of which pure reason is practically or morally determining. Freedom as idea, according to Kant, can only be conceived as an intelligible causality operating in accordance with the moral law (*GMS* 04:452–453), and is also supposed to provide an actual moving force in relation to actions. This is because it is the single causal ground in relation to which one can *consciously* view the whole of one's actions as either belonging or failing to belong to an ideal system of pure and autonomous willing (e.g. *MS* 06:379–82). In other words, this sort of freedom is present to consciousness in the form of a *real* motivational force, a principle of discriminating actions into good or bad, and as a universal ideal or goal placed upon it as a duty by the moral law. Hence it is something we are morally required to take as our archetype in particular empirical actions, and to the extent that this idea can or at least ought to also be the complete efficient cause of actions – the immediate incentive of the will, as Kant says – it is also the real causality alone through which it is possible to carry out genuinely moral actions.

This notion of freedom will become clearer when I explain Kant's conception of the pure will in the next section. But it will be helpful at this point to note two of its key structural features. Firstly, in one respect this notion of freedom has the character of a mere idea that has not yet been achieved (cf. *GMS* 04:455), and which always remains the outstanding and unreachable model of moral determination. Secondly, and in another respect, this idea of freedom, for all its seeming ideality, must also be thought of here as having real causal efficacy, as providing a genuine and potentially effective motivation for determining the actions that a moral agent performs in the sensible world. For only if we grant such an idea genuine causality can it be possible for an action in the world to occur through it and for the sake of it. The form of the act must, in other words, not only resemble but indeed internally *be* the form that is to govern its production, for otherwise we would at most have a case of legality, not morality, in respect to action. Now, Kant argues throughout his moral writings that this causal agency, by virtue of which it is possible for an action not only to outwardly and accidentally agree with the model of moral perfection, but also to be internally and essentially determined by it, is nothing but the transcendental idea of freedom (e.g. *KpV* 05:29) once this has been fully filled out, as it were, with a determinate content, i.e. the moral law. The action of an agent can be essentially and immediately determined by the thought of the law, Kant thereby claims, only if the action is itself produced by a causality that is the absolutely first link in a causal chain. To make use of the terminology developed in Chapter 2, transcendental freedom as the immediate production of an action through consciousness of the law, thus by means of an uncaused causality operating according to a presentation, is the condition of teleological *transparency* that is essential to the moral determination of an action; for only on this condition can the action be an *immediate* consequence of our consciousness of the moral law.

Some textual evidence for this concept of freedom is in order:

> The lawgiving form, insofar as this is contained in the maxim, is therefore the only thing that can constitute a determining ground of the [free] will. (*KpV* 05:29)

> That *independence*, however, is freedom in the negative sense, whereas this *lawgiving of its own* on the part of pure and, as such, practical reason is freedom in the *positive* sense. Thus the moral law expresses nothing other than the *autonomy* of pure practical reason, that is, freedom. (*KpV* 05:33)
>
> First, the moral law determines the will objectively and immediately in the judgment of reason; but freedom, the causality of which is determinable only through the law, consists just in this: that it restricts all inclinations, and consequently the esteem of the person himself, to the condition of compliance with its pure law. (*KpV* 05:78)
>
> [T]he two concepts [i.e., freedom and the moral law] are so inseparably connected that one could even define practical freedom through independence of the will from anything other than the moral law alone. (*KpV* 05:94)

Kant first arrives at this idea of freedom, as Peter König has noted, by means of a reflective procedure whereby he separates out from the very idea of willing all that could be regarded as a limitation (König 1994). This occurs both at *GMS* 04:446–7 and in the sixth section of the first chapter of the *KpV*. In both texts Kant argues very succinctly that: 1) An absolutely free will, which can only be a will from which all limiting conditions have been removed, must be a will that is determining independent of all conditions of sensibility. 2) Because the essential notion of willing lies in the determination of its actions through representations of possible actions, i.e. maxims, the free will can only be a determination according to that aspect of maxims which is independent of sensible conditions. 3) This feature of the maxim is not the matter, but the lawgiving form. 4) Therefore, this form alone, which itself is captured only in the categorical imperative as in the only representation of the determination of actions that is absolutely unlimited, is the only law that a free will can possibly have. In this argument, Kant very carefully constructs the positive concept of freedom as idea by removing from the essential core of the concept of the will all possible limiting conditions, conditions that would restrict the validity of this freedom to any particular object. In reading these passages, I think it is crucial to notice that Kant begins with an idea of a causality that already presupposes a form or concept at the basis of its determination, namely with the idea of the causality of a will, which as a form of causality, must obey a law of some kind. This is the reason why freedom as idea is essentially tied to a particular form or content, why indeed it is an *idea*. For Kant arrives at the idea of the categorical imperative here, which is the form of positive freedom, by precisely the same kind of deduction he uses in the *KrV* to arrive at the ideas of reason, namely by the move from a conditioned to an unconditioned causality. The only difference is that here he deduces specifically the idea of the unconditioned causality of a will, i.e. something determined originally and teleologically by a representation of its own possible activity. Furthermore, as the causality through a representation is, as we saw, Kant's own transcendental definition of teleological causality, it is clear that *this same construction of the idea of freedom is at once the construction of the most absolutely unlimited form of teleological activity.* I will return to this point when I speak of the pure will in my next section.

Turning then to a third type of freedom in Kant's writings – which I will call *freedom as self-mastery* – we discover this kind of freedom in places where Kant speaks in a way that suggests that the closer an action comes to fulfilling the moral law, its letter and its spirit, the freer it is. It is with this conception of freedom in mind that Kant says, for example: "To be able to compel oneself is the highest degree of freedom" (*V-Met/Dohna* 28:679). "The more a man can be morally compelled, the freer he is . . ." (*V-Mo/Collins* 27:268–9). And again: "His freedom increases with the degree of morality . . . the more he accedes to the moral ground of motivation, the more free he is," and hence "he [i.e. the moral agent] proves his freedom in the highest degree by being unable to resist the call of duty" (*MS* 06:382n).[7] This concept of freedom is clearly linked with, but not identical to freedom as idea. For in freedom as idea, while it was clear that freedom and causality according to the moral law are the same thing, we are still talking about freedom as such. Freedom of self-mastery is, and is for the first time, clearly possible of quantitative determinations such as increase and decrease, greater and lesser, and is attributable to a deed only to the extent that the latter is *purposively* ordered to the fulfillment of the moral law. Kant here speaks of the "magnitude of freedom" which can be estimated from the degree of the sensible impelling causes that must be overcome in the performance of a moral act (*V-Met/Dohna* 28:256). Just as in freedom as idea, freedom as self-mastery presupposes that freedom and action determined by the moral law are one and the same. It is, however, ascribed to a will – which in any case is to be considered a will – only to the extent that it is determined in its actions by freedom as idea. Again, as I have described it, freedom as idea is a causality *determining through the idea*, whereas freedom as self-mastery is more properly expressed as a causality *determined by the idea*. Freedom as idea is always in itself already a causality in accordance with the idea, whereas freedom of self-mastery is a freedom that arises through the determination of causality by the idea.

In freedom as self-mastery it would seem that freedom arises only *in and through* the performance of specific actions appearing in the empirical world, be-

---

[7] The most remarkable expression of this struggle for freedom is perhaps found in Kant's *RGV* where he states: "That [the human being] be free, [...] this is the highest price that he can win. [...] and, to assert his freedom, which is constantly under attack, he must henceforth remain forever armed for battle" (*RGV* 06:93).

cause only in these acts do we actually practice and develop our moral strength. Freedom in this sense thus appears to be equivalent to what Kant calls "virtue," i.e. "the moral strength of a *human being's* will in fulfilling his duty, a moral *constraint* through his own lawgiving reason," which "we can assess only by the magnitude of the obstacles that the human being himself furnishes through his inclinations" (*MS* 06:405). Notably, from this point of view, freedom as idea is viewed as merely an *ideal state of activity* that is only first realized when, in accordance with this idea, we actually succeed in constraining our actions to the norm set out by the categorical imperative. Correlatively, since morally bad actions are counter-purposive, these are not to be regarded as free in this sense, but rather as evincing a sort of heteronomy or slavishness in relation to external causes. This conception of freedom is clearly of Stoic provenance. As Epictetus says: "No one is free who doth not command himself" (Epictetus 1807, p. 371).

What is distinctive about this way of talking about freedom, then, is that it requires us to regard freedom as idea as being merely an *ideal* ground of actions – i.e. something we envision in our minds and strive to achieve but which first *becomes actual or real* only in the self-determination of our actions themselves, insofar as through these actions we cultivate a state of self-mastery. This state is then one of being free in the sense of possessing a faculty for carrying out the command of the law in opposition to our inclinations. Evidently, the emphasis in this case is placed upon the reality of the human being as an empirically given being, and not on the reality of its noumenal freedom, which latter for this reason looks more like an aspirational model. It would seem that if we reduce Kant's theory to this kind of freedom, then Christine Korsgaard would be correct when she writes:

> Nothing in this development requires any ontological claims, or requires that we be radically different sorts of creatures than the mundane rational animals we suppose ourselves to be. All that Kant needs is the conclusion that the moral law does indeed represent the positive conception of freedom. The idea of freedom motivates us to cultivate the virtues, and, in turn, virtue makes us free. (Korsgaard 1986, p. 183)

§. 2. Our Three Wills[8]

Just as Kant has three concepts of freedom, so he also has three concepts of will. These triplets are not perfectly parallel, but they are closely related. That Kant holds at least a two-will theory is plain enough from the texts. In the *KU*, we read that: "The will, as the faculty of desire, is one of the many natural causes in the world, namely that which operates in accordance with concepts" (*KU* 05:172). Here, unequivocally, the human will is asserted by Kant to be an object of experience, and so to this extent it must be regarded as falling under the universal determinism of nature. However, in the *GMS* Kant speaks very differently about the will: "A rational being counts himself, as intelligence, as belonging to the world of understanding, and only as an efficient cause belonging to this does he call his causality a *will*" (*GMS* 04:453). This passage indicates that the very notion of will is possible only as belonging to a noumenal world. Finally, in another important passage we find Kant combining these two concepts of will, stating: "To my will affected by sensible desires there is added the idea of the same will but belonging to the world of understanding – a will pure and practical of itself, which contains the supreme condition, in accordance with reason, of the former will" (GMS 04:454).

The bridge between these two conceptions of will is in fact articulated by Kant in the section of the *KpV* entitled "On the concept of an object of pure practical reason," which culminates in what he calls the table of the categories of freedom:

> However, since actions *on the one side* indeed belong under a law which is no law of nature but a law of freedom, and consequently belong to the conduct of intelligible beings, but *on the other side* also as events in the sensible world yet belong to appearances, the determinations of a practical reason can take place only with reference to the latter and therefore, indeed, conformably with the categories of the understanding, but not with a view to a theoretical use of the understanding, in order to bring *a priori* the manifold of (sensible) *intuition* under one consciousness, but only in order to subject *a priori* the manifold of *desires* to the unity of consciousness of a practical reason commanding in the moral law, or of a pure will. (*KpV* 5:65)

Kant here argues that the will, as a kind of causality in the sensible world, must be subordinated to the categories of the understanding. It thus, insofar as it is *already* determined, must become an object of consciousness under the limitations of theoretical consciousness. But insofar as freedom is *to determine* this

---

[8] Some of the material in this and the next section has previously appeared, although in a slightly different form, in Fugate 2012.

same will, the theoretical categories by which such a causality of the will is cognized must be reformulated such that their basis can be thought to lie in a noumenal principle of determination. This limitation, to be sure, is not one that affects the essential content of the law or would compromise its purity as a law commanding absolutely, but rather is a limitation on us or in our thinking due to the fact that this law must be carried out and used to determine a will that is itself sensible in its appearance. The limitation is thus nothing more than that the determination be thought as a determination of a sensible world in general, or of a will belonging to such a world. Another way of expressing the same idea, is that the limitation consists in that the moral law must be the source of a law according to which we *reflect*, and in reflecting *determine*, the maxims of our otherwise sensible will. If it is to be a rule or law of reflection, it must obviously be in accordance with the forms of reflective determination in judgments, and these are nothing but the categories. In this way, the transcendental categories are transformed into the categories of freedom, or the categories that take into account the fact that this causality can be determined by the moral law, and thus as having its origin in freedom. Furthermore, since the natural categories do not yet include the fact of such determination, but only its possibility, these categories regard the determination of the will's causality to *both* good and evil. In other words – and this will be important to recall when I speak afterward of the specific structure of moral self-consciousness in the *KpV* – the very concepts through which it is possible to cognize the will as determined by freedom, since they are firstly of theoretical provenance, *include the possibility of its not being determined by freedom*. Finally, when Kant speaks of freedom, he is most clearly thinking of a *causality in the world of sense* which is noumenal only in regard to the "basis" of its determination.

Later in the *KU*, Kant makes use of this same division between the empirical and the noumenal sides of the will in order to precisely articulate the boundaries of what should go by the name of practical philosophy. He does this by noting that just because a form of cognition addresses itself to the will and its capacity, this does not entitle said cognition straightaway to be called "practical" in the most proper or moral sense. This use of the term should rather be limited to the cognition of that which is possible through freedom alone, and while the will is certainly free, still it is not always cognized in accordance with its freedom:

> All technically-practical rules [...] must, so far as their principles rest upon concepts, be reckoned only as corollaries to theoretical philosophy. For they only touch the possibility of things according to the concepts of nature, and this embraces, not alone the means discoverable in nature for the purpose, but even the will itself (as a faculty of desire, and con-

sequently a natural faculty), so far as it is determinable on these rules by natural motives. (*KU* 05:172–173)[9]

Here the will is considered as "just one of the many natural causes in the world" (*KU* 05:172), and the cognition of it in this regard is a mere corollary of theoretical philosophy. On the other hand, the moral law reveals that the same will stands under the noumenal concept of freedom, and that what is possible through the will considered in this respect is what belongs properly to practical philosophy. It is interesting to note here, that Kant is unwilling to regard the inclusion of a rational agent, and even the inclusion of an agent acting according to concepts, as sufficient for regarding a theory as in principle more than mechanical or technical. What is required is rather the inclusion of the *right kind* of agent acting in the *right kind of way*, namely an agent whose causality according to concepts is such that it cannot in principle have arisen from mechanical causes of whatever kind, be they physical or psychological. A dolphin, for instance, is a type of agent that we cannot really comprehend without the thought that it operates according to concepts, but since all of its actions can be understood as arising from a configuration of matter that has been designed by an external being, who perhaps also created the matter from which it is composed precisely for this purpose, it remains merely a unique kind of mechanical object. It is precisely for this reason that it is incapable of the kind of teleological self-determination required for morality, i.e. the determination of our actions for the sake of the law. This is just to say that while such a thing might be the object of teleological reflections, it does not in principle require anything other than mechanical principles to understand its real possibility. The moral or free will, as we will see more clearly below, has the special character that it is a causality according to concepts which is unique in the fact that it cannot *in principle* be comprehended as arising from external design, or indeed from anything at all prior to its own internal act of determination.

From these observations it is evident that the causality of the will itself has both an empirical and a noumenal dimension in Kant's writings. The empirical operation of the will, on the one hand, is something that I can observe within myself, and as such is nothing other than the capacity to use reason in order to make choices that are directed to an end. In this function, reason simply represents a concept as an end, and hence also as a logical principle from which hypothetical imperatives governing the necessary means to that end can be derived. This is what Kant refers to as empirically-conditioned practical reason in

---

[9] I have preferred Meredith's translation here.

contrast to *pure* practical reason, and it at first appears to be teleologically structured in the sense that the representation of an end is also the ground of the action whereby the end is to be brought into existence. In a deeper respect, however, the empirical will is not an intrinsically teleological unity at all. For, although it is, to be sure, a causality operating by means of concepts and thus for ends, still the presence of these concepts and the motives that lead to the willing of them can all be seen as belonging to the order of nature, and so as generated from an unlimited series of prior efficient causes. In this respect, the teleological unity of the will could at most be that of a living organism as this is discussed in the *KU*. It thus does not require us, as the ground of its real possibility, to attribute to it any intrinsic purposiveness. In close parallel to Socrates' objection to Anaxagoras in the *Phaedo*, Kant claims that this notion of freedom, even though it grants the mind a role in the causal process, is still the freedom of a turnspit; for in it mind is not a cause in the way mind should be a cause. Thus, if the empirical will appears to be spontaneous, then this is only a *relative* spontaneity, and the conditions that make it spontaneous in regard to a particular set of outer impressions or ideas, ultimately serve to enslave it further to other internal but nevertheless natural ones. Conditioned-practical reason's adoption of an end is therefore not self-determined, but pre-determined in time and in concept through a combination of perceptual and psychological conditions (*GMS* 04:447–51).[10]

The noumenal will or the noumenal dimension of the will, on the other hand, which Kant also calls the "pure will," is however teleological in the most supreme and perfect sense, in accordance with the conception of teleology I developed earlier. "If pure reason has causality," Kant writes in a note penned in his copy of the *KrV*, "then the will is a pure will, and its causality is called freedom" (AA 23:41). Such a will is teleological precisely because, if pure reason is practical, then reason "is *by means of ideas* itself an efficient cause in the field of experience" (*KpV* 05:48). As Kant explains in the comment to the deduction in the *KpV*, the idea of freedom as a type of causality has been introduced by him solely to help us conceptualize the fact that "the *idea* of the law of a causality (of the will) *itself has causality* or is its determining ground" (*KpV* 05:50). Freedom here is nothing but the causality of an idea, namely, the idea of the law insofar as it can be the determining ground of actions taking place in the empirical world.

---

10 In this case the manifold choices of the will form a mere aggregate of empirical events governed only by the natural laws of human desire and the objects that are available to it. If this were all there is to the human being, then in Kant's view it would lack both personality and a moral character. See *Anth* 07:285.

Compare this formulation with Kant's transcendental definition of purposiveness in the *KU*:

> If one would define what an end is in accordance with its transcendental determinations [...], then an end is the object of a concept insofar as the latter is regarded as the cause of the former (real ground of its possibility); and the causality of a *concept* with regard to its *object* is purposiveness (*forma finalis*). (*KU* 05:219–220)

Clearly, Kant's understanding of the determination of the will by the categorical imperative contains in its essential structure the definition of an end, and so also of purposiveness. The object or end of freedom, or causality according to the moral law, is not a particular good object, but rather is the good as such and universally, which as an *ideal and fully determinate end* becomes precisely that of the highest good (*KpV* 05:109). For Kant, the universal character of the end of the free will, and thus the fact that it is determined to specific ends by first being immediately determined to a universal end, is in fact a necessary and essential consequence of the absoluteness, or non-relative and non-contingent character, of this end with respect to it. Thus every other end that might be proposed for the will, unless it is *incorporated* as an instantiation under the universal end of the free will under the name "good," will lack that essential characteristic by which it is able to be a genuine end of the free will. Correlatively, according to the definition above the absolute moral purposiveness that will attend such willing consists in nothing else than that the good moral act be determined (i.e. caused) by the thought of the law *alone* (i.e. solely by a concept). For in this act of self-determination, the individual act is literally first caused, and thus first made possible, by the concept of the perfect whole of all possible ends of willing of which it is therefore also a part:

> But now since the whole would in that case be an effect (*product*) the *representation* of which would be regarded as the *cause* of its possibility, but the product of a cause whose determining ground is merely the representation of its effect is called an end [...]. (*KU* 05:408)

There is thus no denying that determination of choice by the moral law provides us with a most precise formulation of a kind of end.

Thus, the condition that Kant places on genuinely moral actions, namely, that they must be motivated by the mere thought of the law alone, is in fact the direct outcome of his teleological notion of the causality of an idea. For, if an action is to be seen as issuing from an idea as from its necessary and sufficient cause, then the action must have an *intrinsic* and *non-accidental* link to the idea itself (the transparency condition). But to think that an action is only possible through the idea is to say that our entire motive for bringing an action into existence must lie in the fact that the concept of this act is itself derived from or contained within the idea alone. Thus an act is an act of pure practical reason, and is internally moral, only if it finds its complete sufficient cause in the thought of the law. Pure practical reason, as Kant notes, is itself the supreme faculty of ends, and thus everything that can be an end for it actually is an end for it (*MS* 06:395).

This can be illustrated through an act of drawing a triangle. I may for instance have a concept of a triangle in my mind, and also proceed to draw a triangle, but the act of drawing is not intrinsically purposive unless the most basic cause of the resulting sensible figure's *being* a triangle is in fact the concept I had in my mind. For indeed, it is completely possible for me to have the idea, and to draw a triangle merely by accident, perhaps by following a connect-the-dots puzzle while simultaneously thinking about the shape of the great pyramid of Giza, in which case no one would say that the picture I drew was a triangle *because* of the concept in my mind, except perhaps accidentally. Thus, as an act of drawing a triangle, the action I performed should not be regarded as intrinsically purposive. What is missing here? Aristotle very precisely located the key omission, namely, that the idea of a triangle in this case is not a cause in the way it is of the nature of an idea to be a cause, that is, *qua* idea. For this to be the case it must be something intrinsic to the idea that determines the causal act to occur; it must not only explain the form of the act, but also its actuality. Whatever intrinsic purposiveness is at bottom, it is nothing if the idea *as* idea does not somehow govern the entire chain leading to the action or product in which it becomes visibly manifest.

To further illuminate the teleological structure of the pure will under discussion here, it will be helpful to compare it with two of its teleological analogues. The first is what Kant calls a natural end, and which he describes in the *KU* as being conceivable as an organized whole, only if we presuppose that it is made possible by an idea had by a creative intellect standing outside but at the foundation of its natural mechanism. The reason for this condition is that, because a natural end itself is first and foremost *natural*, meaning a product of the mechanism of nature, if we choose to think it as teleological in an objective sense we must place the underlying idea or purpose that makes it possible in the causality of a being extrinsic to nature. To theoretically determine such a ground, however, transcends all our conceptual capacities, and this makes it impossible to prove the objective reality of natural ends. The pure will as Kant describes it, however, is provided with objective reality *immediately* through the law itself, and according to its concept it is not only the efficient causality of the idea, but is the efficient causality of the idea of that very same being which it produces, or perhaps better, *reproduces* through its own activities. Thus in another note, Kant remarks that "the pure will is its own end."[11]

Another analogue to the teleological structure of the pure will is what Kant refers to in the *KU* as objective formal purposiveness. As Kant explains,

> [W]e also find in ourselves, and even more in the concept of a rational being endowed with freedom (of its causality) in general, a *moral teleology*, which, however, since the relation to an end together with its law is determined in us *a priori*, and thus can be cognized as necessary, needs no intelligent cause outside of us for this internal lawfulness, any more than we need to look beyond what we find purposive in the geometrical properties of figures (for all sorts of artistic exercises) to a highest cause which has imparted this to those figures. (*KU* 5:447)

Here Kant is asserting that moral teleology is comparable to that found in the essences of mathematical objects, and thus in space, for in both we are dealing with the intrinsic and self-subsistent unity which is characterized essentially by its being an inexhaustible source for the finality in everything that is a consequence of it. In such cases we find, as Kant says, "a purposiveness perceived in the essences of things" (*KU* 05:364). Regarding the formal purposiveness of geometrical figures, Kant writes in particular:

> All geometrical figures that are drawn in accordance with a principle display a manifold and often admired objective purposiveness, namely that of serviceability for the solution of many problems in accordance with a single principle, and indeed of each of them in infinitely many different ways. This purposiveness here is evidently objective and intellectual, not, however, merely subjective and aesthetic. For it expresses the suitability of the figure for the generation of many shapes aimed at purposes, and is cognized by reason. But the purposiveness still does not make the concept of the object possible, i.e., it is not regarded as possible merely in respect to this use. (*KU* 05:362)

This purposiveness, which is not immediately aimed at purposes at all, but rather freely gives rise to an infinitude of them from the inner bountifulness of its underlying principle of unity is what Kant says led Plato to his theory of ideas, and indeed is characteristic, as we have seen, of the unity that ideas in general are thought to be the source of in Kant's view.

This occurred when "Plato," as Kant writes,

> himself a great master of this science, was led by such an original constitution of things, in the discovery of which we can dispense with all experience, and by the mental capacity for

---

11 This is from a note Kant penned in his copy of the *KpV*. It can be found in *Kant Studien*, 72 (1981), p. 137.

> drawing the harmony of things out of their supersensible basis (to which pertain the properties of numbers, with which the mind plays in music), to the enthusiasm that elevated him beyond the concepts of experience to ideas, which seemed to him explicable only by means of an intellectual communion with the origin of all things. No wonder he banned from his school those who were ignorant of geometry, for he thought he could derive that which Anaxagoras inferred from objects of experience from the pure intuition internal to the human mind. (KU 05:363)

First, the reader will no doubt recall how this very same teleological idea played a central role in Kant's pre-critical thought, and that at that time he actually adduced this same objective purposiveness as genuine evidence that space is grounded in an absolutely original and divine being. It is also deeply revealing, that here, some three decades later, Kant is placing his own pre-critical views in the mouth of Plato, and attempting to explain how that great sage might have fallen into such a serious error. Secondly, this passage also makes clear that, in Kant's mind at least, this universal formal objective purposiveness, which is not aimed at a purpose nor defined by one, would in fact provide a ground for explaining the abundance of particular purposes in nature, if only it were really grounded in a source external to our minds as Plato had thought. This is precisely what Kant indicates when he says that through this idea Plato thought he had found the internal intellectual source of the particular purposive arrangements Anaxagoras noted in given nature.

The continuation of this passage is also worth reproducing here:

> For in the necessity of that which is purposive and so constituted as if it were intentionally arranged for our use, but which nevertheless seems to pertain originally to the essence of things, without any regard to our use, lies the ground for the great admiration of nature, not outside of us so much as in our own reason; in which case it is surely excusable that through misunderstanding this admiration gradually arose to enthusiasm. (KU 05:363–364)

While again stressing in this passage that the purposiveness of space that gives rise to particular purposes without, however, being aimed at them (i.e. not by being determined by any particular end beforehand), Kant proceeds to excuse Plato (and so also his younger self), because he finds that there is something genuinely marvelous and deserving of respect in this idea. Of course, Kant will later argue in this paragraph that transcendental reflection reveals that this purposiveness is not to be discovered in things themselves, but rather is inserted by the human mind through the *act* of mathematical construction. Nevertheless, after recognizing this fact, Kant adds that the source of this harmony in the mind should still be regarded as something wonderful and as suggesting a supersensible basis.

§. 2. Our Three Wills —— 269

Now, the passage cited above indicates clearly that Kant sees that there is a similar kind of purposiveness to be found in the essence of the pure will as well. One might of course wonder how strictly Kant is willing to take such a parallel between the structure of the purposiveness exhibited by geometrical figures and that contained in the causality of the pure will. In Chapter 1, however, we noted Kant's claim that:

> The *Critique of Practical Reason* shows, however, that there exist pure practical principles through which reason is determined *a priori*, and that these hence provide reason with ends *a priori*. If therefore the use of teleological principles for the explanation of nature can never provide the origin of purposive conjunction in a way determined completely and for all ends, due to its being limited to empirical conditions: one must nevertheless expect such from a pure doctrine of ends (which can be no other than that of freedom), the principle of which contains *a priori* the relation of a reason in general to the whole of all ends and can only be practical. (*ÜGTP* 08:159)[12]

"The principle of which contains *a priori* the relation of a reason in general to the whole of all ends and can only be practical" – this genuine doctrine of ends, which in direct contrast to natural teleology's indeterminate rise from the individual to the universal, genuinely proceeds from the universal to the particular, is to be found, Kant is telling us here, in morality alone. Of course, this highest principle of morality is nothing but the pure will and the causality that can be determined by it. It is furthermore clear that in the passage above Kant is not employing the concept of extrinsic purposiveness discussed by his predecessors in order to explain his moral teleology. He is rather drawing on the idea of a purposiveness, or a source of relation to ends, that is not determined by limited ends, but rather provides a principle for the complete determination of all ends in a single unified system or whole and in every possible relation to reason. It is precisely this that allows it to form the basis of a *pure doctrine of ends*.

Taking this in conjunction with what was said above, it seems that an understanding of the pure will can be approached by triangulation. Like a natural end, the pure will rests on the idea of a *causality* according to a concept, or a causality the product of which presupposes its own concept as the only sufficient real ground of the activity by which it is produced. However, unlike the natural end, the objective reality of the pure will, along with its intrinsic unity, can be understood in complete independence from any external or material conditions. Due to our immediate consciousness of the moral law, the objective reality of the pure will does not require validation through sense experience, as does the concept of a natural end. The causality of the pure will is not just purposive in the

---

12 My translation.

sense that in order to comprehend the possibility of its products they must be *represented as if* based upon the causality of a concept, but rather they *must be* caused by such. In view of the comparison with mathematical figures, we can add to this a more refined characterization of the sort of internal or formal purposiveness that Kant has in mind here. The pure will, it seems, is not just purposive in the sense that its particular products presuppose the causality of a particular concept, but rather it is such that everything that flows from it will necessarily manifest the highest possible degree of purposiveness and harmony in such a way that any of its particular products will presuppose causality according to a concept of the whole of all possible ends, according to an idea. If the pure will were to become fully manifest in nature, then, things would be good not only in relation to one end, but unlimitedly in relation to everything else reciprocally. Nevertheless, the pure will remains different from objective formal purposiveness because of the feature it shares with a natural end, namely, its inclusion of the idea of a real *causality*.

In a reflection probably penned in the mid-1780s, Kant clarifies how it is possible for such a thing as the idea of a pure will to provide an actual measure for determining moral actions:

> How can the maximum be a guiding measure of our judgment, where the idea of such surpasses all our given concepts? Because the limitations are positive, all of which I leave out in the maximum. Therefore, [this is possible] because it is a pure idea, just as the concept of totality arises from multiplicity without limitation.
>
> Thus the divine understanding is a pure understanding, the divine will is a pure will, the divine presence is pure, the eternal, etc. etc.
>
> The idea of the maximum is that which is most determined and therefore also determining.
>
> The idea of the maximum alone is precise, e.g. perfect righteousness and morality.
> (*Refl* 6211)

What Kant says here not only agrees with my previous claim that the notion of the pure will arises by the setting aside of limitations, but it indicates a few other important points. Firstly, it shows that Kant thinks of the divine will as a *pure* will, precisely because it is an unconditional or unlimited will. It also shows that Kant regards the pure will as providing a model or measure, because to think it one must remove the limitations which we actually think in something of a specific kind. In other words, such an idea can provide a measure for our judgment if we recognize how it first arises in the mind, namely by the lifting of limitations. Thus, what is thought with fewer limitations will be more in accord with the unlimited.

This might make it seem that the unlimited is therefore empty or without any content. But Kant here claims the exact opposite: The maximum is both the most determinate and the most precise. This has to be understood through the fact that our very ability to think limitations rests on there being some positive thought-content, which these limitations exclude. As we saw in earlier chapters, a limitation is only possible because of an underlying whole of reality that provides a ground of determination, a backdrop, as it were, against which such a limitation takes place. Now in the case of the will, the limitations are nothing other than the specific manners in which it may be particularized in relation to some given end, and the underlying principle of determination is the positive content or essence of willing as such that is found in all these different determinations. The unlimited will is not an empty will, but is rather the self-subsistent and independent essence of willing that provides the inner reality that encompasses what is positive in absolutely every possible particularization of willing. Again, if particular willing always rests on a limited relation to ends, and gives rise in its products to a limited unity due to its determination by a limited concept, then absolute willing, if it is to contain within itself whatever is positive in all such willing, must have an unlimited but still positive relation to all ends, and it must give rise in its products to an unlimited but still positive unity in its consequences. Such a pure will is certainly not to be understood as an empty one; its purity is a consequence of its supreme inner determinacy, independence and perfection. So much at least is contained in our *idea* of such a will. Yet Kant clearly also thinks that we have no determinate knowledge of this or any other such idea except through the process of continually removing limitations and expanding our own determinate concept of it thereby (*GMS* 4:462).

After this clarification, the next question is obviously: Do we limited human beings have such a seemingly divine thing as a pure will? This, actually, is just what the analytic of the *KpV* sets out to prove, namely, that pure reason can be practical or have efficient causality, and thus that we are free. As Kant writes, "but in reason's practical use the concept of freedom proves its reality by practical principles, which are laws of a causality of pure reason for determining choice independently of any empirical conditions [...] *and prove a pure will in us*, in which moral concepts and laws have their source" (*MS* 06:221; emphasis added). This is perfectly consistent with Kant's earlier explanation that "this 'ought' is strictly speaking a 'will' that holds for every rational being under the condition that reason in him is practical without hindrance" (*GMS* 04:449). Thus, from a practical standpoint, the pure will is a reality within us, not a mere ideal, and the causality through which it determines our choice is what Kant takes to be the most definitive statement of what freedom is essentially or is according to its positive concept.

The pure will, as we have seen, only ever relates to particular purposes in the case that they are *particularizations* of its universal purposiveness and unity. This is what genuine and absolute teleological unity in Kant's more general view means. It thus moves from the universal to the particular and at the same time from the whole to the part. But does Kant not characterize human reason as essentially discursive, and thus as having always to conclude from the particular to the universal, from the part to the whole? It is only in regard to its moral consciousness, i.e. in regard to what is commanded as duty, that human reason is exempt from such discursively, and here alone the human mind must essentially be able to determine the particular through the universal. This is evident at many places in Kant's moral writings, and is indeed the consequence of his view of the absolute originality and independence of the moral command. However, his clearest explanation of this point is found in his lectures on the philosophical doctrine of religion, delivered in 1783–1784:

> Insofar as our cognition of human actions is derived from the principle of a possible system of all ends, it can be called human wisdom. *Hence we are even able to give an example in concreto of a highest understanding which infers from the whole to the particular, namely in our moral conduct, for here we determine the worth of each end by means of an idea of the whole composed of all ends.* In the idea of happiness, on the contrary, we have no concept of the whole, but rather we only compose it out of parts. And just for this reason, we cannot arrange actions according to the idea of happiness, because such a whole cannot be thought by us. (*V-Phil-Th/Pölitz* 28:1057; emphasis added)

Precisely in the respect that we can determine our causality in accordance with the pure will our action is perfectly analogous to creation by a being in possession of an intuitive intellect. Such an intellect, as Kant describes it, "goes from the synthetically universal (of the intuition of a whole as such) to the particular, i.e., from the whole to the parts, in which, therefore, and in those representations of the whole, there is no contingency in the combination of the parts" (*KU* 05:407). Notably, just as Kant draws a parallel between moral teleology and the purposiveness of geometrical objects, Kant also compares the structure of such an *intellectus archetypus* to the structure of space, which "has some similarity to the real ground which we seek in that in it no part can be determined except in relation to the whole (the representation of which is thus the basis of the possibility of the parts)" (*KU* 05:409).

In another passage, Kant compares the good moral agent to God in quite some detail:

> The need for a final end assigned by pure reason and comprehending the whole of all ends under one principle (a world as the highest good and possible through our cooperation) is a need of an unselfish will extending itself beyond observance of the formal law to production of an object (the highest good). This is a special kind of determination of the will, namely through the idea of the whole of all ends [...]. In this the human being thinks of himself by analogy with the Deity who, although subjectively in need of no external thing, still cannot be thought to shut himself up within himself but rather to be determined to produce the highest good beyond himself just by his consciousness of this complete self-sufficiency. (*TP* 08:280n)

We are not God, of course, because our cognition of the synthetic universal extends only to the moral, thus only to what ought to be, and so does not even embrace the whole of all possible ends, natural or otherwise, but only those that are moral and any that might follow from our moral determination. Nevertheless, the pure will within us still has the one key advantage over even that of the divine will, namely, that the objective reality of the former is given immediately to us in the moral law, while that of the latter can only be thought negatively and postulated insofar as this is required for our moral purposes, i.e. so that we can best strive to see our actions determined by the pure will within us.

I have thus far claimed that there is evidence to think that the teleological unity of pure practical reason, in Kant's mind, shares certain key features with both his concept of the divine will and his concept of the unity of space. Now another key feature, which pure practical reason shares with these other two, is to be found in the *necessity* of the purposive determinations arising from it. This requires some explanation. Throughout the pre-critical and critical periods, Kant repeatedly draws attention to the fact that in regard to God and in regard to space, there is no distinction between possibility and actuality, and what is possible in them is by that very fact actual, or at least this is what is contained in the idea of them even on the interpretation given by the critical philosophy. But what is actual simply by virtue of its possibility, is the very definition of the necessary. Here, I will cite only three of these passages as illustration of this feature of Kant's thought:

> The effects are symbols of the cause, therefore space (through which indeed actual things are in fact represented as necessarily connected by means of a common ground) [is] a symbol of divine presence or the phenomenon of the divine causality. In space possibility is not distinct from actuality. (Refl 4208; circa 1770)

> Everything that belongs to his [i.e. God's] determinations, belongs to his essence, for this is thoroughly determined through his own concept.
> His possibility is not distinct from his actuality, and therefore also his essence is not distinct from his nature.

> Indeed here it is not a question of the existence, but rather of the concept of the most real being. (*Refl* 6271; circa 1783–1784)
>
> It does not follow that something is actual, for the reason that it is possible according to a universal concept. That something is actual, however, because it is completely determined in regard to all possibility through its concept and is distinguished from all possible as one, means precisely that: It is no longer merely a general concept, but rather the concept of a unique being that is completely determined by concepts in relation to all that is possible. This relation to everything possible according to the principle of complete determination is just exactly the same according to concepts of reason, that the somewhere and somewhen are according to the determinations of sensible intuition. For space and time determine not merely the intuition of a thing, but rather also its individuality through the relation of place and the moment in time, because with respect to space and time possibility cannot be distinguished from actuality. This is because both together contain within themselves, as in a substrate, all possibility in the appearance, which must be given beforehand.
>
> From this it follows only that the most real being must be given prior to the real concepts of all possibility, and so just as with space cannot be beforehand as [merely] possible, but rather as given [...] (*Refl* 6290, circa 1783–1784)

Now compare this with Kant's explanation in the *MS* that pure practical reason is the basis of a duty to ends, because:

> What, in the relation of a human being to himself and others, *can* be an end *is* an end for pure practical reason; for, pure practical reason is a faculty of ends generally, and for it to be indifferent to ends, that is, to take no interest in them, would therefore be a contradiction, since then it would not determine maxims for actions either (because every maxim of action contains an end) and so would not be practical reason. But pure reason can prescribe no ends *a priori* without setting them forth also as duties, and such duties are then called duties of virtue. (*MS* 06:395)

This compressed passage is said by Kant to contain the very deduction of the necessity of certain ends from the nature of pure practical reason itself. In other words, it is supposed to lay bare the precise manner in which pure practical reason relates to ends in general. Now, without our previous analysis I think this argument would have to be regarded as terribly obscure. But on the basis of it we can almost immediately see that the crux of this deduction goes something like this: 1) Pure practical reason is just the pure and unlimited (thus universal) faculty of ends, meaning it is that alone in relation to which an absolutely complete system of all possible ends is first made both possible and necessary. 2) Determination of the will to any ends at all requires the *specific* representation of *particular* ends to provide a basis for determination. 3) Thus, pure practical reason according to its own nature must set particular ends before the will, for otherwise it would not be a faculty of ends at all. 4) As pure practical reason is the ground of the possibility of any particular willing at all, however, all those ends that it sets before the will are necessary, or are *duties*, if for no other reason than that the ends it sets arise from it purely and without limitation. In sum, whatever is a *possible* end for *pure* practical reason is by this very fact an *actual* end for the human being to the extent that it possesses pure practical reason, or what is the same, a pure will.

To summarize, we have seen in this section that Kant ascribes to the pure will an absolutely unique teleological character. It is absolutely unique, namely, in combining the following features: 1) Of all teleological objects, it alone can be provided with objective, though practical, reality. 2) It possesses the kind of unlimitedly teleological purposiveness we represent as being present in the divine will and the essence of space. 3) Even granting that Kant thinks the empirical will offers an example of causality according to representations, only determination by the pure will provides us with an example of an absolutely original, uncaused causality according to representations. Combining this with 1, we can conclude 4) that such determination also provides us with the only constitutive use of teleological concepts, i.e. the only case where we can actually determine both the positive character of a noumenal object (i.e. the pure will), and derive from it, as from the universal, the entire system of particular consequences (actions) it is to have in the empirical world.

This finally brings me to yet a third notion of will in Kant's writings, namely the phenomenal will, which is distinct from both our inner pure will, and our empirical will. I call it the "phenomenal will" because this is what Kant generally calls it, and because it relates to the empirical will in the same way as phenomenon relates to appearance, namely as the conceptually determined to the empirically determinable. The phenomenal will is, in other words, just the empirical will to which the idea of an underlying free self has been added as a principle of unity and from the standpoint of which one can reflectively assess the character of this individual's will. It is not necessary to develop the matter here, but I would suggest that this assessment has two parts, namely, the assessment of the general character of oneself as a moral agent in general, and the assessment of the moral quality of this character from the specific actions one finds oneself performing in the world. Having an empirical component, the phenomenal will is clearly distinct from the pure will. But it is also distinct from the empirical will because, rather than being an empirical manifold of motives and possible actions that are to be determined by the pure will, the phenomenal will is precisely the empirical will insofar as it has already been determined to actions, and has thus displayed to a certain extent indications of its underlying character. The phenomenal will, in other words, is the determined appearance of our moral character, and from it we can with caution make a teleological inference to the kind of will that we possess overall.

On the basis of this notion of the phenomenal will, it is now possible to say something more about the notion of a holy will, which is the model towards which the pure will bids us to strive. The holy will is the image of a phenomenal will, thus a will that is determined in respect to its causality in the world of sense, but formed or determined in such a way that it is absolutely in accord with the archetype set out in the pure will. The holy will, insofar as it is relevant to human willing, is thus the idea of a particular phenomenal will that has reached absolute self-mastery amidst the conditions of nature, and has thus entirely subordinated its sensible nature to its supersensible nature. Of course, since on Kant's view this is impossible in principle, the holy will for him is the object of an infinite task. It is the fictitious idea of a finite expression of an absolute and infinite teleological model. But at the same time, it must be the object of all human moral striving.

Before concluding this section, it will be helpful to briefly indicate the relation of these notions of will to the notions of freedom examined earlier. Firstly, it is clear that freedom as responsibility is that activity and synthetic ground of determination which makes possible the phenomenal will; for the phenomenal will is a morally determinate empirical will that can be of any moral quality. Furthermore, freedom as idea is quite obviously the causality of the pure will. And finally, freedom as self-mastery is the determination of the empirical will, by which it becomes a phenomenal will, insofar as it agrees with the pure will. The holy will, in turn, is just itself the phenomenal will that would result from the empirical will's complete determination in accordance with the pure will, or, in other words, from absolute freedom as self-mastery.

§. 3. Moral Self-Consciousness[13]

As different and as incompatible as freedom as responsibility, freedom as idea, and freedom as self-mastery may seem, not to mention their attending conceptions of willing, I will argue nevertheless that they are all implied in Kant's description of the movement of moral self-consciousness as we find it in the *GMS* and the *KpV*. However, before entering into an analysis of the structure of this movement, it is important to make sure that we are not importing into Kant a standpoint that he could not himself adopt. The first question to be decided,

---

13 I owe the inclusion of this section to a discussion with Paul Guyer, who expressed doubts about my textual warrant for speaking of moral self-consciousness in Kant.

§. 3. Moral Self-Consciousness — 277

then, is whether Kant himself employs a notion that is anything like what I will describe moral self-consciousness to be.

Let me first list reasons for thinking this to be a genuinely Kantian notion. The first thing to note is that this self-consciousness is essentially nothing but our awareness of ourselves as moral agents, i.e. as beings with intentions we regard as potentially efficacious in the empirical world. To be a moral agent is more than to just be the cause of certain types of events. What is added to this in moral agency is precisely our explicit awareness of a range of possible events, and the consciousness that our evaluation and deliberation, and ultimately our decision, will be the ground for the actuality of one of these states of affairs. Thus to have a will is to engage in self-conscious acts of practical reasoning that one regards as possessing causality. Furthermore, to be a genuine moral agent, i.e. to be a being *responsible* for its causality, it seems we must deliberate under the idea that our thinking is not only efficacious, but that it is even an absolutely first or spontaneous causality. To be unable to will without thinking oneself as free in an absolute sense, is then just, as Kant says, to *actually be free* in a practical respect (*GMS* 04:448). Kant can make this claim because it is just this sort of necessary representation – namely that which is unconditionally necessary for a specific function of self-consciousness – that *constitutes* the objective reality of a concept or idea. We thus cannot say that we necessarily have to think ourselves as being free in the consciousness of our action, and nevertheless at the same time allow that we may not be free, simply because there is no other conceivable standard against which this freedom would turn out to be an illusion. To "really be free" cannot be anything else but this. Thus, it is impossible to actually will anything as one's own without at once regarding oneself as *really* free. For this reason, the concept of freedom is in Kant's view a *constitutive* concept for our moral agency, i.e. it is a concept without which actual moral agency (which is something essentially self-reflective) would be impossible. This is just to say that it is essential to the act of willing that we think ourselves as free.

Of course, this does not provide freedom with theoretical objective reality. But this is of no relevance, because from within the perspective of moral self-consciousness the idea of freedom is absolutely necessary as a condition of the possibility of this very same consciousness, and for this reason it possesses all the *practical* objective reality that is required. It is also important to note in this connection that one essential component of moral self-consciousness is moral feeling, or what Kant also calls the moral incentive. But since the moral incentive is nothing but our consciousness of the law insofar as it determines our will, and thereby indirectly has the effect of frustrating our sensible incentives (*KpV* 05:73), the explanation of the genesis of the moral incentive will have to be based upon the more general explanation of the genesis of moral self-consciousness itself. The moral incentive, in other words, must be seen as but an effect of the very structure of this consciousness.

Now the importance of the concept of moral self-consciousness is that it allows us to delimit this most basic conceptual core of Kant's moral philosophy. With a clear view of its structure in place, everything else that may be seen as belonging to the theory of morals or to moral religion, will have to be traceable back to this basic core, and grounded in it, if we are to ascribe to Kant a consistent philosophical view. Now, since the entire inner structure of morality will presumably be exhausted by this basic conceptual core, it follows that whatever else belongs to moral philosophy or to religion can at most have the function of explicating this core or of facilitating the realization in our moral practice of the demands it places upon us. Such realization, according to Kant, requires two parts, namely, a metaphysics of morals that will instruct us in the determinate rules of moral conduct, and a theory of religion, whose sole aim will be to develop the moral incentive within us by presenting it in an intuitive form that is appropriate to its majesty.

§. 4. The To-and-Fro Structure of Moral Self-Consciousness in the *GMS*

My aim in tracing this movement is to begin with the first moment that we become aware of ourselves as moral beings, and sketch how from this initial moment the rest of moral consciousness, or at least its basic core, develops through a number of standpoints. I will call this the "to-and-fro structure" of moral self-consciousness to emphasize the fact that it always begins with immediate self-consciousness and passes from this to the noumenal self before finally terminating again with our immediate selves, but as transformed or illuminated by the noumenal perspective.

There is, however, one serious difficulty to telling a general Kantian story here. This is because the version in the *GMS* and that in the *KpV*, as we will see, do not coincide in the most important respects. For this reason, I will discuss only the version of the *GMS* in this section, leaving that of the *KpV* for the next. However, in both works, Kant says that we first enter into something like moral consciousness at the very moment we set about to will anything at all. Although Kant does not provide a very explicit description of this initial moment, it is clear that prior to it we must already possess at least a theoretically constituted understanding of our faculty of desire, or what Kant calls conditioned practical reason. For to even set about willing something, even in a

§. 4. The To-and-Fro Structure of Moral Self-Consciousness in the GMS — 279

non-moral way, I must have the awareness of possible states of affairs and of a natural ability to make at least some of these actual. Now specifically in the *GMS*, Kant argues that if I set out to will something, anything, and thus take the operations of this empirically given will to be my own, then I must think of myself as the absolutely first cause of this same faculty of desire, and thus as a cause by virtue of a transcendentally free causality lying at the foundation of my natural will. This, as he says, is because more generally I cannot conceive of a will that would belong to an agent and yet would be caused by something outside of it. I must therefore think of myself as absolutely the first ground or as free, because otherwise I would not be able to regard the act as being mine at all. From this it is evident that, in the *GMS*, moral consciousness opens or is first generated by the concept of freedom as responsibility, and that the assertion of this freedom is first reached independently of our specific consciousness of the moral law. This is important to note, because it shows that the further development of moral consciousness, no matter where it might lead, presupposes a prior moment in which I recognize an empirical act *as mine*, or potentially mine, and thus as occurring freely or through my own causality alone, regardless of whether it is in agreement with the moral law.

However, as soon as we rise to the idea of freedom, we recognize firstly, that since it constitutes me as a person with a will, it must to this extent be regarded as real. The mere idea that I am free will certainly not make an action mine. But we also recognize that this freedom cannot fall under the laws of experience, and so must be a reality existing in an intelligible world. Thus I now know myself as free, and as belonging to a different order of things. Furthermore, since the rules followed by our empirical wills are all mechanical, it is clear that they can tell us nothing about the nature of this freedom. Here we discover, for the first time, that we have a higher will or self, and this is able to enter into our rational deliberations as an additional non-empirical motive. Clearly, in making a rational decision we cannot be indifferent to any motive that would stem from our higher will, just by the very fact that we view it as higher or as more properly expressing who we actually are. From this we are brought to the question of whether any specific type of action agrees with this higher will. Kant's conclusion, of course, is that yes, indeed, there is but one law conceivable according to which this noumenal freedom could operate, and just as the thought that we are free is practically constitutive for the possibility of willing, so too is this law practically constitutive of our conception of freedom. At this moment we have reached a practically grounded metaphysical standpoint according to which the moral law is thought as the inner law or essence of freedom. From a practical perspective we are really free and, as we now discover, to be free is just to act according to the moral law, and to not act according to it is something that cannot positively be understood. More importantly, it is something we cannot recognize as the outcome of a motive with which we can identify our true selves.

We now find ourselves at the fourth moment in this basic movement of moral thought, which is certainly the most complex. The whole movement of practical consciousness began with our concern to call certain acts our own, or to think ourselves as having a will in regard to actual or possible empirical acts of the will. This immediately set us on a course through which we discovered a higher self within us, and a new source of motives. Now if we return to the original standpoint of our empirical wills, as we must since the whole story began from an actual moment when we set out to will something in the empirical world, it must now appear in an entirely different light. As the phenomenal will it must be viewed from two points of view, namely, as both the effect of a free causality, and as the effect of a being whose most proper freedom is described by the law. Now the empirical will, as always related to empirical causes or motives, is always by its nature in a position where it has to be actively determined to exclude these causes or motives in order for us to act from the idea of the moral law. Since this condition can never be eradicated as long as our will is empirical, and thus is always open to determination by sensible inclinations, the teleological progress in which such determination appears is in principle never ending.

We can now see that from a *theoretical-reflective perspective* within moral consciousness, the concept of a noumenal self is in fact a mere idea, because its reality cannot be given in experience, which is the most basic *criterion* of theoretical reality. It can in this respect at most play a regulative function for judging to what extent our empirical actions reveal a disposition purposively subordinated to the moral law. On the other hand, from a *strictly practical point of view* the same noumenal self, and with it the freedom of pure practical reason, are not mere ideas but are rather *realities*, since they are regarded as real conditions of the possibility of our thinking that we have a will of our own in a practical respect, and thus of our actually having a will of our own. But the theoretical "mere" idea of the pure will, when it is provided practical reality, is not just another noumenal object, it is our own most proper will. The pure will, or pure practical reason operating with freedom, demands of itself that it be regarded not as a mere idea but as an idea with real efficient causal power, in fact as an idea with unconditioned real causality. Thus the same idea that theoretical reason views as being merely regulative turns out not only to be constitutive *for* practical reason, but also constitutive *of* it, because it is a condition of the possibility of consciously and rationally thinking of ourselves as willing anything at all, and thus of really doing so. Thus, practical reason gives rise to a true practical metaphysics of the self as a noumenal being, and from this point of view, Kant thinks, the empirical self must be judged as the mere appearance of our proper or real selves.

The movement I have just described has a fairly clear structure. It begins from the theoretically constituted conception of our own empirical causality. Moral self-consciousness interrupts this by the impulse to take particular actions as one's own, thus from a need to think of ourselves as possessing freedom of responsibility, and moves from this to the inward construction (*via* purification) of the positive *idea* of freedom in our own self-consciousness, only to return to the actions from which it began, but with a transformed vision of itself as acting freely only to the extent that it determines itself by the moral law alone. It is only in this last moment that the moral "ought" is fully present within self-consciousness, because the difference between a mere law, on the one hand, and a merely empirical will on the other, is that in the "ought" the empirical will is held up to the model of the pure will: "If we think of ourselves as put under obligation we regard ourselves as belonging to the world of sense and yet at the same time to the world of understanding" (*GMS* 04:453). "The moral 'ought' is then his own necessary 'will' as a member of the intelligible world, and is thought by him as 'ought' only insofar as he regards himself *at the same time* as a member of the world of sense" (*GMS* 04:455). This conflict between the image of the empirical will, which we *find* as always already empirically given to us, and the pure will, which we actively *discover* at the innermost basis of the possibility of our willing, thus generates this active state of conflict that is yet motivational in respect to our noumenal selves insofar as it in part opposes the empirical self.

The moral "ought" is thus marked by a complex and *purposive* state in which a comparison takes place between the theoretically constituted will and moral archetype of the will, alongside the recognition of the superiority and rightfulness of the latter. This conscious state is purposive, even if our subsequent actions fail to exhibit practical purposiveness, for the very reason that in it we find the natural constitution of our wills motivationally constrained, and thus affected, in accordance precisely with an *idea*, in Kant's technical sense of this. Put differently, the state of mind in which we experience the "ought" is one whose *real condition of possibility* must be regarded as lying in the real effect of the consciousness of such an idea, namely the pure will, on the consciousness of our empirical wills. This is a teleological relation in the strictest transcendental sense. It is also important to point out that this movement suggests a way to explain the imputability of immoral acts, because the very transition to the second moment was occasioned by our actual interest in taking responsibility for acts in general. It was precisely in doing this that we discovered the very essence of willing, and its higher claim upon us. This would also explain the seeming equivalence of freedom and the law, because it would show this to be a discovery that takes place in the second moment, which is in turn applied to the empirical self in the fourth.

The structure uncovered here, however, has very clear difficulties, not the least of which is that Kant repeatedly rests his description of this movement on the second stage, namely on the taking of an action as one's own. This is what made the account robust enough to perhaps account for immoral actions, but it is clearly unacceptable as a proper description of how moral self-consciousness arises. I think this is in fact already clear in the *GMS* itself, for if the genesis of moral self-consciousness rests on my taking actions as my own, the first question that arises is why one should do this, and how one could be motivated to take such responsibility in the first place. It is clear that if one bases this taking-up of responsibility on anything other than the moral law itself, then one will implicitly be grounding our interest in morality on our interest in having a will of our own. However, it clearly violates the unconditional nature of the law to say that the thought of having a will of one's own must precede, and thus condition, the recognition of the claim of the law upon us. Much rather, consciousness of a moral law must itself *immediately command that we take actions as our own*; it must provide the necessity through which actions are ascribed to the moral person in the first place. Otherwise, the law will only really be binding for those actions, which on other grounds, we already have an interest in accounting as our own. The moral law, because of its own inner normativity in regard to our wills, may on this account still have an effect on those actions we in fact take as our own, or plan to take as our own, but it has nothing to say about extending the range of our responsibility, or seeking to increase our moral scrupulousness. Put differently, if we *assume* as Kant constantly does, that we are dealing with human beings that already take themselves to be rational, and thus draw up maxims and reasons about what they should do, then the moral law may hold some normative sway in this reasoning. But it still would have nothing to say about one's debasement or abandonment of one's rational nature altogether, and so could not bid us to more fully examine and rationalize our behavior. This will leave us with a kind of moral subjectivism, or perhaps with something similar to Rawls' theory insofar as the validity of the law will rest on some prior interest in autonomy or rationality itself.

Still another problem arises if we ask about the principle of the *unity* of this movement. First, I think it is clear that the movement which I have described includes all the notions of freedom and willing that I worked out above, and that it combines them into a scheme in which they do not give rise to the contradictions I claimed earlier must arise in any dogmatically metaphysical theory. However, to prove these consistent is different from proving that they must be unified, that

§. 4. The To-and-Fro Structure of Moral Self-Consciousness in the GMS — 283

indeed the moments of moral self-consciousness *must be combined* in the final moment in the feeling of moral obligation. Why, after all, should we ever return to the first empirical will, and compare it with the pure will, after we have discovered that our innermost willing is one with the law? Why should we not take the discovery of the pure will in the second moment to be an *unmasking* of a false empirical image of our wills, and so remain rapt in the blissful idea that we are presently members of a purely spiritual kingdom of ends? Again, why should I take the appearance of my will to be symbolic of, or indeed related in any sense, to my noumenal pure will? In sum, how can we explain that morality is "determined to make its own ends actual in the world" (*ÜGTP* 08:159)?[14] The question here is, as Kant explains, the question of the necessity of a *synthesis:*

> And so categorical imperatives are possible in this way: that the idea of freedom makes me a member of an intelligible world and consequently, if I were only this, all my actions *would* always be in conformity with the autonomy of the will; but since at the same time I intuit myself as a member of the world of sense, they *ought* to be in conformity with it; and this *categorical* ought *represents a synthetic proposition a priori*, since to my will affected by sensible desires there is added the same will but belonging to the world of the understanding – a pure will and practical of itself, which contains the supreme condition, in accordance with reason, *of the former will.* (*GMS* 04:454; last emphasis added)

In the *GMS*, Kant gives a very unsatisfactory answer to the question regarding the necessary principle of such a synthesis. He argues, in particular, that the necessity of relating the empirical to the noumenal, by means of the active subordination of the former to the latter (and not just the rejection of the former by the latter), is required by the manner in which the object of theoretical reason is subordinated to the object of practical reason. As he writes, the moral agent must synthetically combine the two images of the self into one, "since it [the moral law] arose from our will as intelligence and so from our proper self; *but what belongs to mere appearance is necessarily subordinated by reason to the constitution of the thing in itself*" (GMS 04:461; emphasis added). In another instance Kant writes the reason that the moral agent "must represent and think of himself in this twofold way, however, rests as regards the first on consciousness of himself as an object affected through the senses and as regards the second on consciousness of himself as an intelligence, that is, as independent of sensible impressions in the use of reason (hence as belonging to the world of understanding)" (*GMS* 04:457).

Kant's claim here can be understood in a couple of ways, but none of them, I think, will reach a satisfactory result. The first quote suggests that the necessary

---

14 My translation.

unity of the synthesis that gives rise to the moral "ought" is in fact the same principle that makes us subordinate mere appearances to things in themselves. This can be understood in two ways. First, reason here could be taken in its speculative employment. But the subordination of the phenomenal to the noumenal is only required in this respect *for the sake of the systematicity of our knowledge of the phenomenal*. Indeed, outside of the moral domain Kant explicitly argues that the noumenal is introduced solely in order to provide the theoretical employment of reason with boundary concepts, which make possible its maximally purposive use. Now, obviously the introduction of a noumenal self answering to *this* ground of justification could not justify the introduction of a noumenal self the essential nature of which stands in *contradiction* with what one would infer from reflection on the will's empirical side. We can thus conclude that this strategy does not solve the problem precisely because, although it might lead to the subordination of the phenomenal to the noumenal generally speaking, it can do so only for the sake of theoretical (not practical) purposiveness and cannot explain why the phenomenal must be subordinated *specifically* to the noumenal image of a pure will. Secondly, we might instead think that Kant has reason in its pure practical employment in mind here. But this is obviously a non-starter. Pure practical reason is precisely the noumenal side of the will itself, and so it can hardly be used as the principle for explaining the necessary *synthetic* subordination of the phenomenal to the noumenal.

The second quote suggests another line of attack, namely that the movement of moral self-consciousness shows that the agent must consider *itself* (of which there is one) as possessing both selves, or as having both dimensions to itself. Such an interpretation is supported by a passage from the *MS:*

> I, the prosecutor and yet the accused as well, am the same human being (*numero idem*). But the human being as the subject of the moral lawgiving which proceeds from the concept of freedom and in which he is subject to a law that he gives himself (*homo noumenon*) is to be regarded as another (*specie diversus*) from the human being as a sensible being endowed with reason, though only in a practical respect – for there is no theory about the causal relation of the intelligible to the sensible – and this specific difference is that of the faculties (higher and lower) of the human being that characterize him. (*MS* 6:438n)

This suggests that moral self-consciousness, as that unified and morally purposive state of mind, originally arises from 1) theoretical self-consciousness, 2) pure practical self-consciousness, which are synthetically linked by 3) a requirement that there be a total unity of self-consciousness as belonging to a numerically identical being. This is implied by the idea that we must combine them because we find both within our identical selves. Furthermore, this could also perhaps explain not just the linking here but also the subordination; for if the two images must be linked into one, it is very possible that there is a good argument that this can only occur by *subordinating* the empirical self to the pure self.

But what then is the ground of the necessity of that third element, namely the total unity of self-consciousness? If it is traced back to the unity of apperception and the faculty of cognition which rests upon this, then it is nothing but the necessary unity of theoretical self-consciousness, which again cannot be used to justify its own necessary unity with *pure* practical self-consciousness. For the same reason, pure practical self-consciousness cannot serve such a function either. But what is left?

§. 5. The To-and-Fro Structure of Moral Self-Consciousness in the *KpV*

In the *KpV*, Kant provides a more nuanced and careful explanation of this second moment of moral self-consciousness as well as of its relation to the first. Here too, Kant says that the movement of thought begins when we set out to will, but in this case he says more precisely that our goal here is not to have a will of our own, but rather *to determine* our empirical will: "It is therefore the *moral law*," writes Kant, "of which we become immediately conscious (as soon as we draw up maxims of the will for ourselves), that first offers itself to us and, inasmuch as reason presents it as a determining ground not to be outweighed by any sensible conditions and indeed independent of them, leads directly to the concept of freedom" (*KpV* 05:29–30). Clearly this act of drawing up maxims for determination of the will already presupposes a theoretically given manifold of possible empirical actions, and thus an empirical will. So rather than starting from the taking of an action as one's own, Kant starts here with the drawing up of maxims, or what is the same, the formulating of possible ways in which an empirical will could be determined. As we further learn, it is precisely and immediately at this moment that we become conscious of the moral law. Here, the law as it were interrupts conditioned-practical reason mid-act by announcing its own necessity. As Kant says, we thus become conscious of the moral law "by attending to the necessity with which reason prescribes them [the practical laws] to us and to the setting aside of all empirical conditions to which reason directs us," and in this way, he further explains, "the concept of a pure will arises" (*KpV* 05:30). As we saw in the quote above, it is only by reflection upon this unconditionality, and indeed on the fact that it requires absolute independence, that the idea of freedom for the first time enters moral self-consciousness. This freedom, it is important to note, is indeed transcendental freedom, because it is an absolute independence, of which the independence from empirical motives is a mere consequence.

Now looking over these two initial stages in the progress of moral self-consciousness, we should focus more explicitly on the fact that rather than beginning in the taking-up of responsibility it started with the consciousness of a necessity placed upon the maxims we draw up for the will. Thus the moral law actually announces itself, as Kant describes it here, most originally in the form of an "ought." But as Kant explains, the experience of an "ought" already *includes* the consciousness of a *comparison* between our empirical will, as open to determination by sensible motives, and our pure will, as a willing in accordance with the law alone. The second moment of the dynamic movement of moral self-consciousness is thus not properly speaking a *pure* awareness of the moral law or of the pure will, but rather of the *interruption* or *tension* manifest in the experience of the "ought" itself. This interruption or tension thus, for we human beings, constitutes the first *datum* of properly moral self-consciousness.

As a kind of rupture, then, the "ought" can be understood as *bifurcating* our inner consciousness into, on the one hand, the factor that is *interrupted* and, on the other, the factor that *interrupts*. The unity of the "ought" is, according to this interpretation, to be considered more basic than either of these other two factors, and as that which *originally* makes us conscious of their difference and their relation. Now the interrupted factor here is itself conditional-practical reason, which becomes thematized in self-consciousness precisely in the form of that which must be excluded from determination of the will, and as that which for this reason always, as it were, presses back towards determination of the will. The interrupting factor, on the other hand, is pure practical reason itself or the pure will, which we only become distinctly aware of when we abstract from the sensible conditions of the "ought," thus leaving behind the complete unity of our original *datum*, and raising ourselves to the consciousness of a law not only without limits, but without anything material that requires its limitation. Now, if we abstract from the sensible limitations in this way, it is clear that the tension of the "ought" really contains, insofar as it manifests to us a direct motive and a curbing of sensible incentives, the idea of a law that in the image of a noumenal or higher self we at the same time fully and independently will.

If this is correct, then Kant's story in the *KpV*, which rests on the idea of the categorical imperative as a fact of reason, opens up an entirely new way of understanding the unity of moral self-consciousness, and thereby avoids the problems that would arise from accepting Kant's story in *GMS* as his considered account of the genesis of moral self-consciousness. In particular, rather than beginning with the generation of two separate images of the self, and attempting to locate a principle of their necessary synthesis, Kant begins with the original fact in which both sides are already synthetically combined into one.

But in this case the fact that the "ought" and the law of a pure will are actually two quite different things takes on special importance. For while the "ought" is a synthetic unity of the sensible and the intelligible images of ourselves, the law of the pure will is the quite independent and unlimited content of our exclusively intelligible side. This is clear from the fact, as Kant himself claims, that the law of the pure will is the same in all rational creatures, and even in God for whom there are no sensible impulses, and hence also no "ought" (*KpV* 05:32). The law of the pure will is thus not itself necessarily or essentially an imperative, but rather has the form of an imperative only in finite rational beings, which have a sensible side. However, if we are originally given the imperative, then as I claimed above, we must only arrive at the law and the idea of a pure will by abstracting from the original conditions that are essentially contained in the "ought," or as Kant says, "according to certain dynamic laws" (*KpV* 05:42). The image of an unlimited pure will, and indeed of our own intelligible nature, it would seem, is something *inferred from* and *constructed out of* a reality that is only given to us under quite specific limitations.

And on the other side, this would mean that the image of a purely theoretically determined will, or of a will determined by conditioned-practical reason, is itself equally something arrived at by abstracting from the unconditional dimension of the "ought." In other words, the consciousness of ourselves as sensibly determined or as acting according to maxims that are normative but not unconditioned must be first made possible by the demand that the law makes on us to *not be thusly determined*. Just as awareness of the possibility of acting badly presupposes and rests upon the awareness of what we ought to do; perhaps so also the awareness that we can be externally determined to act presupposes and rests upon the awareness that we must not allow this to happen. The idea that I have a will at all, and of any kind, and am not merely another cog in the machine of nature, will thus first arise from the consciousness of something that interrupts and awakens my consciousness through a call to something higher than nature. If this is not Kant's exact meaning – though I think there is much in Kant, and more in German Idealism, that speaks in favor of it – it is certainly an important possibility to consider.

But what about taking responsibility for our immoral acts? In a certain way, it is clear that the *possibility* of freedom as responsibility is given ground in the fact that the moral "ought" manifests the law as originally in tension with one's sensible nature. Yet even granting this possibility, why should we ever actually take ourselves to be responsible for any given action that appears to conflict with the law? This is a complicated issue, but the short answer, I believe, is that Kant is able on this theory to make a move from the possibility of this determination to its actuality, and thus to the requirement that we take responsibility for actions not in accord with the law, based upon an argument to the affect that the practice of doing this is itself required for the sake of increasing the moral incentive within us, which is something in turn required by the very unconditionality of the moral law. We may practically speaking know that we have a pure will, and furthermore that we must fight our sensible nature, but that we have actually determined ourselves for or against the moral law is something of which we can never in principle become conscious. Nevertheless, as Kant argues, the law in its unconditionality enjoins us to do everything in our power to strengthen and to extend both our consciousness of, and our resolution to obey, the moral law (*MS* 06:393). Now, it is on this basis alone, I believe, that Kant can justify the holding of ourselves and others as responsible, and thus also justify the practice of reflectively seeking to determine a person's moral character. The freedom of responsibility, in other words, should be nothing other than a postulate for the sake of fulfilling the command of the law.

This story, I think, is appealing, and it does indeed resolve a number of serious issues. But I am afraid that it conflicts with another key feature of Kant's moral philosophy, namely his notion of autonomy. In a characteristic expression of this autonomy, Kant asserts that the free will "must necessarily be able at the same time *to agree* to that to which it is to *subject* itself" (*KpV* 05:132). But if the above interpretation is correct, then one should more precisely say that, in the moral law we find a case where we must agree to something to which we originally find ourselves to be genuinely subjected, i.e. obligated. In other words, if there exists within us a genuinely *original* consciousness of obligation as such, then it seems that we must, in order to conceive this obligation properly, think of it as expressing who we really are and who we, on another higher level, actually will ourselves to be. In this case, one would be tempted to say that the idea of our own pure will is in fact of the same status as the moral idea of God, about which Kant says we may make use of it only in order to make moral obligation intuitive to ourselves, thus exclusively according to a subjective requirement (*MS* 06:48). If the image of God is required to make the commanding force of the "ought" intuitive, then is the image of our own inner pure will required only to make the "mineness," so to speak, or the rightfulness of the law's obligation intuitive for ourselves? Kant defines autonomy, however, as the giving of the law to oneself, or as the independence of the principle of willing along with the determination of ourselves by this principle (*KpV* 05:33, *GMS* 04:440). And, unlike the case of God, he never suggests that it is anything less than a practically objective concept.

§. 5. The To-and-Fro Structure of Moral Self-Consciousness in the *KpV*

We have arrived finally at the question of the unity of Kant's account of freedom, and so also to the question of the unity of the Kantian analysis of the human will, about which I can say only this in closing. Above I have tried to explain this unity as consisting in a series of standpoints through which the moral agent is dialectically determined to progress in the unfolding of the consciousness of itself as a transcendentally free but also finite and empirical being. This kind of dynamic integration of differing ontological standpoints on the self, even conflicting ones, within a whole of self-consciousness, is in essence I think the kind of solution sought by Fichte and others, and it is perhaps the approach that remains most faithful to the structural priority Kant gives to autonomy, the self-given character of the law. As I have noted, he seems at first to coordinate rather than subordinate the otherness of the law, its legislation by God's will, to the moment of autonomy, but he just as soon explains the former to be an ideal position taken up for the sake of increasing the moral incentive, while leaving the latter, autonomy, in its original place at the foundation. However, if we recognize that autonomy, though essential to moral self-consciousness, is not the foundation, and thereby give up hope of an absolute closure for the dialectical process of our moral being, there remains an open alternative: Namely, to take the actual moral state of mind that consists in consciousness of the moral ought, i.e. of practical normativity, as itself constituting the most basic *datum* which calls for and demands interpretation, and to which differing ontologies relate only as partial interpretations, none of which can be taken as most fundamental without falsifying the original experience. In a word, we could think of these concepts of freedom and will as constituting independent conceptual schemes or ontologies, which in their own terms certainly contradict one another and cannot be brought into a single linear-deductive system that is either complete or closed, but which when viewed as interpretations required by the base *datum* itself, fit into a consistent and complete covering articulation. In this case, we can see them as not really conflicting with one another, because the base *datum* itself is manifold and calls for manifold ontological articulations and various perspectives, and because the unity of its manifold is not a theoretically graspable unity already given. The unity of moral self-consciousness would be understood rather as the unity of a life situation towards which we constantly strive. Seen in this way, theoretical conflicts would really be correctives and impelling causes towards more complex and sustained ways of being moral.

Conclusion

In the *KU*, Kant speaks of the moral human being as the final end of the existence of the world. All other beings in the world, even natural ends, he says, must be thought of as instruments for the production of ends external to themselves. The causality of the human will as a moral will, however, has only itself for its end, be it in one's own person or in that of another. As Kant says in §84, such a will is the single natural being about which we can "cognize, on the basis of its own constitution, a supersensible faculty (freedom) and even the law of the causality together with the object that can be set for itself" (*KU* 05:435; emphasis added). We are in Kant's *own words*, the "*single* sort of beings whose causality is teleological," and as such we are not only the sole beings that can be counted as ends of nature, we are also the only beings that know ourselves to be self-determining *within* nature, but yet also absolutely independently *from* nature, and thus can be called an end *for* ourselves. Of course, when Kant speaks of the human being as the single sort of being whose causality is teleological here, he is not thinking of it as a biological (for then there would be many sorts) or even simply as a rational being, but rather as a being whose pure faculty of reason has causality.[15] Thus, Kant is claiming in effect that our causality, which is nothing but freedom, is the single sort of causality that is *constitutively* teleological.

In this chapter, I have argued that Kant's notion of freedom is not encumbered with the sort of difficulties sometimes attributed to it, though it may still be encumbered by many others.[16] This can be seen by recognizing the

---

[15] "Further, the commonest judgment of healthy human reason is in complete agreement with this, namely, that it is only as a moral being that the human being can be a final end of creation, if we but direct its judging to this question and gave it occasion to investigate it" (*KU* 05:443).
[16] One important result that follows from this interpretation is the following: It is generally admitted that despite his direct assertions to the contrary, Kant must accept a morally neutral conception of freedom, a sort of freedom of indifference. This seems to follow from the fact that freedom of responsibility requires immoral actions to be a product of freedom. Yet in the *Metaphysics of Morals*, Kant says freedom cannot be defined in this way, because "only freedom in relation to the internal lawgiving of reason is really an ability; the possibility of deviating from it is an inability" (*MS* 06:227). Now a teleological account makes this immediately comprehensible since a potency is always defined by its end, that is, essentially by its being a potency *for* something. For example, within a seed lies the potency to be a tree, and it is only for this reason that seed can both grow or fail to grow (note that a rock cannot fail to grow). Yet this cannot be used as the definition of being a seed, because its form is determined not by the accidental, but by its essential end. Similarly, the human being has a potency to be free (signaled by freedom of responsibility), and only for this reason can he become free or not free (freedom of self-constraint). But the possibility of being indifferent to the achievement of its essence cannot be

unique *teleological unity* of the human will as it is constituted in moral self-consciousness. And although we certainly cannot have theoretical insight into the specific operations or even the possibility of the teleological structure of its causality, we do nevertheless have a duty, in Kant's view, to acknowledge at the same time the practical reality of freedom and our obligation to theoretically realize this same freedom in the world. Indeed, it is precisely this tension that constitutes the dynamic and normative structure we call moral self-consciousness.

---

counted as a positive capacity of freedom. Hence, since freedom and the law reciprocally imply one another, and this in relation to the empirical phenomenon of the will is its defining essence as end, there can be no morally neutral concept of freedom. Rather, freedom as a faculty, is *essentially* the faculty to be free.

Chapter 7 Kant on Rational Faith as an Expression of Autonomy

> My son, keep your soul in a condition where it always desires that there be a God, and you shall never doubt it. What is more, whatever decision you make, bear in mind that [...] without faith no true virtue exists. (Rousseau 1979, p. 311–312; emphasis added)

Introduction

According to Kant's own lights, the highest good and the postulates of pure practical reason together form the apex of the entire critical philosophy. From the standpoint of its speculative employment, reason strives unceasingly towards its final aim in the unconditioned, which it at last locates in three highest objects, namely the freedom of the will, the immortality of the soul, and the existence of God (*KrV* A798/B826). The same three, through their regulative employment, necessarily guide the understanding in all its activities, both theoretical and practical, by providing it with maxims pointing in the direction of reason's essential ends (cf. *VNAEF* 08:416). At the same time, Kant also firmly maintains that, despite this natural, even *necessary* drive towards the transcendent, all speculative reason's endeavors would ultimately remain empty, without object – indeed without *value* – if the practical interest of reason were not capable of providing these very same ideas with objective reality and content. The warrant for this in turn, as we will see further below, lies in reason's practical need, arising from the moral law, to postulate objects corresponding to such ideas. This move is made possible in Kant's view because, seen from the practical side, the need of reason, which Kant claims can only be satisfied through the moral postulates, *must* be satisfied, or is a "need having the force of law," since without this the necessary end of all moral action, i.e. the highest good, would have to be regarded as impossible and illusory (*KpV* 05:5).

Thus, on Kant's account, it is in this complex of ideas – the highest good, and the three conditions of its possibility, namely freedom, immortality and the existence of God – that pure reason, both as a faculty of knowledge and as a practical faculty, and thus *as a whole*, for the first time discovers its own destined vocation and the means for attaining it. In a word, without the moral postulates Kant's own notion of philosophy in the sense of *wisdom*, or as he says, as a science of the "essential ends of human reason (*teleologia rationis humanae*)," would be without objective reality (*KrV* A839/B867).[1]

---

[1] See also his late essay VNAEF, especially 08:417–418.

Although this will be dealt with more fully below and also later in Chapter 8, it should already be noted here that the postulates thus not only provide an end to all theoretical disputes regarding the principles of the human being's true destiny, but indeed form the foundation of a practical-dogmatic metaphysics, which is to provide the indispensable doctrine leading to wisdom in its highest, practical sense. Kant's theory of the postulates is thus one of impressive depth and scope, particularly considering its implications for both the history and the future of philosophy. Through it Kant claims not only to have definitively resolved the internal tensions within his own project, and to have completed the system of critical philosophy by disclosing its highest point of unity; he further claims that this doctrine puts an end to the debates that have plagued the doctrine of the highest good since ancient times, and that by revealing the essential goal of all true philosophy, it thereby establishes for all future time a lasting state of peace among genuine philosophers (see *VNAEF* 08:419–421). Thus, Kant's theory of the postulates is meant to give voice to the hitherto obscured, but nevertheless universal eternal source and goal of all human striving, and to uncover its single means of fulfillment.

This means that on Kant's own view, his philosophical enterprise *as a whole* genuinely rests on the strength of his arguments for the moral postulates. Indeed, since Kant's critique is a critique of the thinking and willing subject, and thus consists in the examination of the proper grounds for *asserting* truths and *adopting* maxims, the whole structure would seem to rest not only on the fact *that* the postulates are established, but more importantly on the *way* in which they *must* or *can* be established, i. e., on the *comportment* of the rational agent towards articles of belief that is required for a specifically delimited type of rational faith. As a consequence, the *type* of argument Kant uses to establish the postulates and the unique *modality* (for instance, subjective or objective necessity) that it establishes must harmonize with, and indeed express, the essential way in which the rational subject relates itself both theoretical and practically to their truth, and thereby to its own final end. Kant thus recognizes that belief in freedom, immortality and the existence of God is not sufficient as such, but only if this belief is motivated by the right reasons and circumscribed by the right limitations; "for, this moral law is based upon the autonomy of his will, as a free will which, in accordance with its universal laws, must necessarily be able at the same time *to agree* to that to which it is to *subject* itself" (*KpV* 05:132). This is because the same beliefs, if adopted on improper grounds (i.e. not on grounds to which the subject could agree), could well be a source of heteronomy, and thus lead to the further corruption of the moral disposition. From this immediately follows the crucial point that if Kant's philosophy is ultimately one of autonomy, i.e. of free and absolute self-legislation, then the justification for the moral postulates, as the unifying element of this same philosophy, must not only be compatible with, but indeed directly express this same autonomy.[2] In the best examination of the postulates to date, Allen Wood underscores this point crisply, writing that: "Moral faith, in fact, is the outlook, the *Weltanschauung* of the critical philosophy itself, and in gaining an understanding of it" it is "possible to grasp most clearly the critical conception of man's condition, and the rational response to that condition dictated by the principles of the critical philosophy" (Wood 1970, p. 249). In view of this, it is key to recognize that in regard to the postulates, Kant is not chiefly interested in the discovery of new theoretical or practical knowledge, but rather his interest lies in sketching a picture or an outlook within which the true unity of reason is set in the most proper relationship to the rational agent so as to guide it towards a form of life that is fulfilling and meaningful in an ultimate way.

In this chapter, I will attempt to clarify the natural logic behind the moral postulates and its significance for understanding Kant's conception of the unity of reason by attending to the chief postulate, namely that concerning God's existence. I will argue in particular that the postulation of God's existence, insofar as it is a free act undertaken for the sake of cultivating our moral character and increasing our moral strength (e.g. virtue), is an intrinsically moral activity, one in the absence of which we cannot in principle be *fully* devoted to the development of a virtuous disposition. The necessity of such belief will therefore be seen to rest on the direct and essential impact it has on the believer's entire moral disposition. This interpretation, as will become clear, builds upon previous ones, particularly on those of Lewis White Beck and Allen Wood. But it also goes significantly beyond them not only by seeing the relation of belief to moral striving to be the genuine basis of the proof-strategy of the postulates, but also by showing for the first time why the two stand in such a relation in the first place.

---

[2] Denis 2005 defends only the compatibility of the postulates with Kant's theory of autonomy and on grounds that I cannot fully accept (see below). Packer 1983 goes further by claiming that in some sense "to will one's true happiness is to will one's autonomy" (Packer 1983, p. 118), although he does not provide any strong reasons as to why one must think this is true. See also Mariña 2000 and Caswell 2006. Beiser 2006 gives a good overview of the arguments for and against the postulate, but ends up presenting it in either the teleological form of Beck (Beiser 2006, p. 595) or as an *absurdum practicum* as in Wood (Beiser 2006, p. 604). For this reason, he finds the objections to these views to be strong.

§. 1. Problems and Previous Interpretations

It has been shown elsewhere that the concept of God serves both a synthetic and a symbolic function in Kant's moral philosophy (Moors 2004). The former derives from its familiar role as the *tertium quid* that must be postulated in order to provide a causal connection between the two necessary but heterogeneous elements of the highest good, namely perfect virtue and the happiness proportioned thereto, as this is explained in the Dialectic of *KpV*. While the latter symbolic function, for its part, is introduced briefly already in the same work (*KpV* 05:129), it is only fully articulated in the Doctrine of Virtue of the *MS*. However, in both texts, and in still others, Kant argues that we must regard all duties as divine commands – and hence God as the legislator of the categorical imperative – because it is only through the image of a righteous, all-powerful and all-knowing moral being that inspects us from above and from within that we can make our moral obligation "intuitive for ourselves" (*MS* 06:487). In the Doctrine of Virtue itself, Kant further qualifies the need we have for making obligation intuitive by saying that it is merely "subjectively logical," which he clarifies as meaning that it is not "an obligation to perform certain services for another, but only subjective, for the sake of strengthening the moral incentive in our own lawgiving reason" (*MS* 6:487). It should be noted that Kant not merely suggests in passing that we must regard our duties in this way, but rather asserts it so often that it must be considered as absolutely central to his argument for rational belief.[3]

So belief in God's existence is necessitated, Kant would have us think, in order to 1) explain the possibility of the highest good and 2) in order to provide the moral agent with a symbol through which moral obligation, which is something inherently intellectual and not sensible, is nevertheless represented so as to bring it closer to intuition and to provide it "with access to the human mind and influence on its maxims" (*KpV* 05:151). Yet there also remains quite a bit of obscurity regarding how these dual functions of the concept of God are intended to support the fundamental insight of Kant's moral philosophy, i. e. the essential link he claims to have discovered between freedom and autonomy, genuine spontaneity and self-legislation. Indeed, the Kantian postulation of God's existence, and the subsequent claims that we must regard all duties as divine commands, are often thought to corrupt the moral incentive and to undermine his

---

[3] Although commentators rarely refer to it, this view is asserted by Kant at least eleven times in the course of the *KpV*, the *KU*, the *RGV* and the *MS*. Kant also mentions it over a dozen times in the *OP*.

very conception of freedom as autonomy in several obvious ways.[4] In addition to this, it has yet to become clear how, or even if, these dual functions as ground of synthesis and as symbol for obligation share a common root or serve a common function.

In his respected commentary, Lewis White Beck has managed to provide a valid reconstruction of a Kantian argument for the postulation of God's existence. But the price of accepting his reconstruction is that we must also accept that the argument rests merely on theoretical, aesthetic or teleological grounds, and that it thus lacks any real practical ground or significance, a conclusion that is clearly at odds with Kant's own intent. Allen Wood, by contrast, has provided a valid reconstruction aimed at providing it with a practical core, thus emphasizing its deep moral significance. But in order to do so, Wood is forced to prefer arguments found only in Kant's unpublished notes and lectures to those that Kant specifically authorizes in the *KpV* and elsewhere. Furthermore, Wood's strategy, as I will argue, also fails to provide the act of postulation with any genuine moral significance, although it claims to be able to do just this. Thus neither commentator, in my view, is able to show the deep moral significance of the postulates. Nor are they able to explain the intimate connection between the postulation of God's existence as the ground of synthesis and Kant's insistence that we must think this same God as the legislator of the moral law itself. This idea, indeed, plays no part in either of their reconstructions.[5]

§. 1.1. Beck's Interpretation

Prior to Beck's analysis, commentators generally adopted one of three approaches to the Dialectic of Kant's *KpV*: reject it, ignore it, or exposit it with apologies.[6] All three approaches are motivated by the basic intuition that Kant's introduction of the highest good is not only superfluous, but that it also introduces an ignoble desire for being rewarded with sensual pleasures for our moral con-

---

[4] Hegel 1995, p. 463: "The ground on which God is accepted – that by the conception of a holy law-giver the moral law may acquire additional reverence – contradicts the fact that morality really consists in reverence for the law simply for its own sake." By contrast, Denis 2005 argues that the two views are compatible, although only under a weaker formulation.

[5] Wood attempts to find a home for this idea in another part of Kant's *Religion*, asserting that it "is derived from the *social* character of man's highest end" (Wood 1970, p. 191). Wood is correct at least that one formulation of this idea is connected to this, but as the quotations earlier in this section prove, it is not in the first instance *derived* from this, but rather from the personal need to make the moral obligation in our own reason intuitive for ourselves.

[6] This also applies to most current commentators. An exception is Willaschek 2010, p. 168–196.

duct.[7] Beck himself generally agrees with the usual objections to Kant's introduction of the highest good. As he writes, "the existence or even the possibility of the *summum bonum* [...] cannot be held, in consistency with his settled views, to be logically or ethically necessary as a motive to genuine morality" (Beck 1960, p. 244). But Beck also does not think that Kant is necessitated by *his own* theory to hold that the existence or possibility of the highest good is required for morality. According to Beck, "the concept of the highest good is not a practical concept at all, but a dialectical Ideal of reason" (Beck 1960, p. 245).

Beck reaches this conclusion by the following analysis. In a first step he breaks Kant's argument down into seven parts, which I reproduce here verbatim:
1. Happiness is the condition of a rational being in the world in whose whole existence everything goes according to wish and will.
2. Man's will is not the cause of nature and does not bring nature into complete harmony with the principles of his will.
3. There is, therefore, no ground in the moral law (or in nature) for expecting a necessary connection between the morality and happiness of men.
4. But such a connection, in the concept of the *summum bonum*, is postulated in the command that we ought to seek the *summum bonum*.
5. The highest good must, therefore, be possible.
6. Therefore, a cause adequate to it must be postulated.
7. Such a cause must be the Author of nature, acting through understanding and will. Such a being is God. (Beck 1960, p. 274)

Beck then focuses his criticism of this argument on the fourth premise, which he claims to be almost self-evidently spurious. The problem is that according to Kant himself, the moral law, as the single law of autonomy, must be the source of all duties, because duties from any other source, even from the highest good itself, would violate this autonomy. Thus the concept of the *summum bonum* cannot be the source of any additional duty on pain of introducing a principle of heteronomy, and so the most that Kant can really mean by saying that we are commanded to promote the *summum bonum* is that we are commanded to seek that part of it which is already required by the moral law itself, i.e., perfect virtue, or what Kant calls the "supreme good" so as to distinguish it from the complete good (Beck 1960, p. 274–277). However, the supreme good, which is nothing but virtue, must in Kant's view be thought by us as possible through our power alone. What is not in our power, and what therefore requires the ex-

---

[7] For bibliographical information relating to such claims, see Wood 1970, p. 38–39, as well as the notes to these pages.

istence of God for its possibility, is rather the proportioning of happiness to this virtue, but this is also not our duty on Beck's view for the very reason that it is not within our power.

Beck claims on the basis of this line of thought that the fourth premise is really a cover for Kant's extra-moral commitment to the unity of his system. Such unity, according to Beck, is "important for the architectonic purpose of reason in uniting under one Idea the two legislations of reason, the theoretical and the practical, in a practical dogmatic metaphysics wholly distinct from the metaphysics of morals" (Beck 1960, p. 245). Thus Beck would have us believe that despite the misleading label of being a "moral" argument, Kant's proof is not moral at all, but is rather based upon the "ideal of the rationality of morals" (Beck 1960, p. 275), an ideal which is at best founded, in Becks view, on aesthetic or teleological grounds that are independent from, and perhaps also inconsistent with, Kant's moral theory.

It is notable that the breakdown provided by Beck and quoted above is almost an exact translation of a mere one-half of a paragraph from the second *Critique* (*KpV* 05:124). This indicates that Beck does not take any of Kant's remarks in the introductory or concluding paragraphs of this section of the work as relevant to the central argument, which ignores the fact that Kant informs us several pages after the paragraph in question that he had "deliberately postponed" discussion of the precise ground upon which moral postulation rests until this point (*KpV* 05:145). Beck's analysis also does not consult any of the other six extant versions of the proof, several of which were written after the *KpV* and thus indicate that Kant was perhaps not fully confident in his earlier explanation. It should not be surprising then if it turns out that Beck has missed the deeper point underlying Kant's argument.

Yet there are two aspects of Beck's account that are most certainly correct, and which must be given weight by any attempted interpretation of the proof-strategy behind the postulates. The first is that the duty to seek or promote the *summum bonum*, which underwrites the force of the argument as a whole, cannot consist in an *objective* duty that is distinct from or that goes beyond the duty to be virtuous. Nothing can be a duty that is not required by the moral law, and as Kant never fails to remind us, the moral law commands the conformity of our wills to the law and not the *achievement* of ends. Indeed, it is a cardinal aspect of Kant's moral theory that we must seek to fulfill our duties without any concern whatsoever for their practicality or for the real possibility of achieving such ends (*GMS* 04:417). The deeper moral reason for this is that since the moral law is to command objectively and immediately, any concern for the practicability of achievement can only distract us from the single moral aspect of action, namely choosing to do good and the development of a disposition for making choices out of respect for the moral law alone. As Kant writes with perfect clarity:

> This formal character of our actions – their subordination to the principle of universal validity – which alone constitutes their intrinsic moral worth, lies entirely in our own power; and we can quite easily make abstraction from the possibility or the impracticability of the ends we are obliged to promote in accordance with that law – for they only form the extrinsic worth of our actions. Thus we put them out of consideration, as what does not lie altogether in our own power, in order to concentrate our attention on what rests in our own hands. (*KU* 05:471n)

This, as Beck correctly notes, poses a serious challenge to the consistency of Kant's account of the postulates. For in this account, Kant seems also to maintain that one has a duty to promote the highest good as an end that includes not only virtue but also happiness, and that if one does not regard this end as achievable, then one could not at the same time obey the moral law. And yet it is clearly Kant's general position that the practicability of the achievement of ends must be abstracted from for strictly moral reasons.

The second aspect of Beck's analysis that seems indisputably correct is that for Kant's argument to be moral, the necessity that belongs to the belief in the possibility of the highest good must also be moral in kind. This means not only that it cannot be purely theoretical or aesthetic, as Beck believes it to be, but also that it cannot be merely the kind of necessity that belongs to propositions involved in what Kant calls "technical-practical" rationality. The key point is that while all uses of practical reason are certainly rational, and as such are objectively subject to logical rules of rational consistency, i.e. imperatives in the broad sense, not all imperatives are categorical, and so not all uses of practical reason are genuinely moral or are what Kant calls "morally-practical." As a rational being, it might seem proper to test my course of action for logical consistency, but should I freely decide to forgo this and to risk acting in ways that do not fit into a nice logical system, this does not necessarily make my actions immoral. It just risks seeming foolish or erratic. The logical necessity of consistent action is thus in principle distinct from moral necessity, unless it can be shown that logical inconsistency by itself either directly or indirectly leads to actions contrary to the moral law. And this is obviously untrue. For if the majority of my rational intentions are selfish, then possible moral actions will be inconsistent with the greater part of my willing, and so, as far as consistency goes, should not be pursued. Yet, in Kant's view, I obviously (morally) should adopt these nevertheless. From this it follows that if the necessity supposedly demonstrated by the arguments for the postulates in any way presupposes an antecedent interest in an end or a concern for rational consistency, which cannot be shown to be subordinated to a genuinely moral interest (of which there is only one, namely conformity to the law), then the proof will not be moral in kind.

§. 1.2. Wood's Interpretation

In *Kant's Moral Religion*, Allen Wood puts forward a very subtle attempt to defend the moral significance of the postulates against objections like those voiced by Beck. He locates the core of this defense in an idea expressed in Kant's lectures on the philosophical doctrine of religion that the postulates rest on what is there called an argument "*absurdum practicum.*" Rather than relying on theoretical or aesthetic considerations, or on a *reductio* argument aimed merely at showing that only by belief can we escape falling into theoretical contradictions, the *absurdum practicum* is a *reductio* which purportedly shows that only by such belief can we avoid a practical absurdity, in this case the unacceptable conclusion that we are morally reprehensible human beings. Wood further claims that although this argument can only be found in Kant's lectures and notes, it nevertheless gives us the least distorted picture of the kind of argument Kant intended to articulate in his published works.

As will become clear in the following, I sympathize with much in Wood's approach. But I fundamentally disagree with his understanding of the structure of the *absurdum practicum*, the conclusions he draws from it, and his view as to what this argument is able to achieve. He summarizes the core idea as follows:

> Kant thinks that I can act rationally in pursuit of an end only as long as I believe that the end is possible of attainment through the actions I take toward it. This means that if I do not believe I can achieve an end E by taking action A, then I cannot rationally do A with E as my end; further, it means that if I do not think any course of action on my part has any possibility of reaching E, then it cannot be rational for me to make E my end at all.
>
> Now suppose there is an end that as a rational agent I am morally bound to set myself. In that case, I can neither rationally abandon this end nor rationally pursue it without believing that it is possible of attainment through the actions I take toward it. (Wood 1992, p. 401)

Now, as Wood notes, Kant argues in addition to this that the moral law obliges us to work towards the achievement of the highest good. So, according to the argument summarized in the quotation above, we must also believe the good can be attained. Furthermore, the existence of God is required as a condition of this attainment. The *absurdum practicum* is thus: If I believe that God does not exist, then I cannot rationally regard the highest good as possible, and so by this fact I cannot rationally obey the moral law. I must therefore admit I am a scoundrel. Or more precisely, I cannot deny God's existence and still obey the moral law unless I act irrationally by pursuing an end I also hold to be impossible to achieve. "But in this case," observes Wood, "I will have to admit that I am acting 'irrationally' and that according to my beliefs I should (in a logical, but not in a moral sense of 'should') give up my pursuit of the highest good and my obedience to the moral law, and become a *Bösewicht*" (Wood 1970, p. 30). Now since this is an unacceptable conclusion about myself, I must not believe that God does not exist.

§. 1.2.1. A First Difficulty with Wood's Interpretation
This line of interpretation, however, faces four major difficulties, which I do not believe it will be able to resolve. The first is that if this is actually the entirety of Kant's argument, then it still clearly suffers from the kinds of difficulties raised by Beck when he noted that the arguments for the postulates cannot be termed *moral* or *morally-practical,* in a genuinely Kantian sense, unless they are ultimately shown to rest on an explicitly moral ground of necessity. For if the argument is structured as Wood sees it, then the postulates clearly rest both on moral considerations *and* on one's commitment to the rational integrity of one's beliefs. The true structure of the argument should then be formulated as a practical *dilemma* containing two interrelated *reductio* arguments, namely: If I believe that God does not exist, then either,
1) I will retain the rational integrity of my practical beliefs, and not follow the law, and thereby become a scoundrel in my own eyes, or
2) I will follow the law and choose to be moral, but give up the rational integrity of my beliefs and as a result be a fool in my own eyes.

Wood does not himself mention that in many other places where Kant lays out the *absurdum practicum* more fully, it is formulated precisely as what he calls a "*dilemma practicum.*"[8] And in all of these texts it is clear that an essential component of this argument is the desire to not seem to oneself a moral fool or a "*tugendhafter Phantast.*" The proof of the postulates would therefore require Kant to show the moral unacceptability of *both* horns of this dilemma, but as Wood himself admits, there is seemingly nothing morally wrong with being a

---
[8] Kant discusses this argument at AA 28:385–386, AA 18:20 (*Refl* 4886), AA 18:194 (*Refl* 5477), AA 18:484 (*Refl* 4255), AA 18:485 (*Refl* 4256). Finally, the fullest discussion is in the Pölitz metaphysics lectures 290–294.

moral fool, as unsatisfying as that might be for other reasons. The important point is that this means that if we have already decided to follow the moral law, and Kant clearly thinks the argument for the postulates presupposes that we have (cf. *KU* 05:450–451n), then the real *nervus probandi* of the argument for the necessity of belief can be seen to rest on the commitment to rational integrity *alone*[9], unless, of course, it can be shown that this commitment is also somehow of moral significance, something Wood's argument most certainly does not do. Notice that in the quote above Wood himself writes "in a logical, but not in a moral sense of 'should,'" thereby admitting that logical and moral necessity are distinct in kind. Consequently, if either the argument as Wood presents it or the more fleshed-out version of it in terms of a dilemma, is all Kant has to offer, then we would have to conclude that it does not show belief to be necessary for strictly moral purposes. For it seems clear that as long as we inure ourselves to doubts stemming from the fear that we are acting in a pragmatically foolish way, we can still fully strive to conform our disposition to the law, which is all morality in the strict sense requires of us.

§. 1.2.2. A Second Difficulty with Wood's Interpretation

Another significant difficulty with Wood's analysis is that if it indeed represents Kant's intended argument, then this argument does not really prove that *positive belief* is necessary, but rather only that we cannot positively believe that the highest good is impossible.[10] There is nothing inherently absurd, Wood admits, about simply following the law without thinking about its consequences, or in simply following the law with the opinion that the highest good *might* be possible. We can escape the dilemma, it would then seem, simply by refusing to concern ourselves with anything other than our most immediate moral duties. But if

---

9 To see this more clearly consider the case of one who is devoted to the moral law as a law they find powerfully present in their own conscience, but who does not think that for this purpose they need to believe in God. Clearly such a person is possible, because many such actually exist. But how would one then prove to such a person that they should or need to believe in God as well? According to Wood's argument, the only thing one could say to them is that if they do not believe, then they will be acting irrationally. Not only is this not morally significant, but it could even seem to be an assault on this person's morality itself. For, if they are already committed to morality, then the only new effect engaging in this line of discussion could have is to generate doubts about the validity of this commitment. This problem vanishes, however, if it can be shown that such a person can become *even more fully committed* to morality though striving to believe. If such could be shown, then this morally committed person would seek belief as part of that very same commitment. This is the gist of the interpretation presented in this chapter.
10 Wood 1970, p. 30. Also see Denis 2005, p. 43.

§. 1. Problems and Previous Interpretations — 303

all that is required to avoid absurdity is not positively believing the highest good to be impossible, then all that would be required to fulfill Kant's argument is the idea that there *might* be a God, or that it is not the case that there certainly is not a God. As Wood interprets Kant, then, the explicit argument for the postulates does not prove that positive belief is in any way necessary, but only proves the extremely weak conclusion that one cannot at the same time dogmatically maintain the non-existence of God, follow the moral law and also act in a rationally consistent manner. This amounts only to saying that the rational atheist cannot be committed to morality, and thus, to the extent that we are committed to morality, that we cannot be explicit rational atheists. But this is almost trivially true, since it would mean rationally accepting – contrary to all empirical evidence – that we can be happy and be moral, when we know that being moral will not make us happy and pursuing happiness will not make us moral. "Religious skepticism," on the other hand, "is in Kant's view morally tolerable," according to Wood (Wood 1970, p. 31).[11] As can be seen from the above, the weakness of this conclusion is a necessary consequence of Wood's interpretation of the structure of Kant's argument, since one only finds oneself engaged in a practical absurdity in the case that one *actually* and *explicitly* maintains the non-existence of God, the validity of the moral law, and the rationality of one's moral commitment and all three at the same time. The argument as interpreted by Wood, therefore, proves neither that we must believe that God exists, nor even that we must give a thought to his possible existence, nor that we must be concerned with the rationality of our moral commitment.

Wood himself is not insensitive to the oddness of this conclusion. Although he initially attempts to read it as a positive expression of Kant's enlightened moral tolerance, he also notices that it does not seem to sit well with Kant's stated intentions of providing a "moral proof of the existence of God" (*KU* 5:448). But given his understanding of the argument, the best Wood can do is to say that anything less than actual belief is "not the most appropriate or rational attitude for the moral man to hold" (Wood 1970, p. 32), although this again is not something directly shown by the argument as he construes it.[12]

Wood is right to be uneasy with this conclusion, because there can be no question that Kant regards his argument as proving that "it is morally necessary

---

[11] One must be careful here not to confuse the tolerability of another's lack of faith, i.e. our recognition that it is not our concern, with a supposed moral tolerability *toward oneself* of one's own lack of faith.
[12] The same can be said of Lara Denis's interpretation. She hits on something like the right idea at Denis 2005, p. 53, but does not seem to realize the significance of the point for Kant's general argument.

to assume the existence of God" (*KpV* 05:125). Only this squares with Kant's statements that "the moral law leads through the concept of the highest good, as the object and final end of pure practical reason, *to religion, that is, to the recognition of all duties as divine commands,*" (*KpV* 05:129) and that there therefore exists a "*duty of religion*, the duty of recognizing all our duties *as (instar)* divine commands" and, finally, that "to have religion is a duty of the human being to himself" (*MS* 06:443–444).[13] As we will see more fully below, Kant takes his argument as establishing that devotion to the moral law and positive belief in God stand in a *necessary although synthetic* connection to one other.[14] Thus by interpreting the argument of the postulates as consistent with religious skepticism, Wood directly obscures the unity of Kant's moral and religious thought. In this regard, it should also be noted that Wood's reading of Kant's claim that the possibility of the highest good requires only that God's existence be possible, not necessarily actual, is dubiously consistent with Kant's own conception of possibility, and is certainly insufficient to establish the full possibility of the highest good.[15]

§. 1.2.3. A Third Difficulty with Wood's Interpretation

A third difficulty with Wood's version of the argument, which incidentally also affects Beck's account, concerns the structure of the highest good itself. Namely, Kant is quite clear in the *KpV* that God's existence is required to account for the possibility of "happiness *in exact proportion to* morality" (*KpV* 05:110; emphasis added; see also *KpV* 05:125). Wood's interpretation of the argument as an *absurdum practicum*, however, does not seem to be able to account for the proportioning of dissatisfaction with evil actions, which this "exact proportioning" neces-

---

[13] The connection between the moral proof and these remarks from the *MS* will become clear in the sequel.
[14] "This [rational belief] is, accordingly, *a need from an absolutely necessary point of view* and justifies its proposition not merely as a permitted hypothesis but as a postulate from a practical point of view," and moreover "this is the only case in which my interest, because I *may* not give up anything of it, unavoidably determines my judgment" (*KpV* 05:143).
[15] Wood's argument makes use of a sense of "possibility" that is common today, but to which Kant never ascribed: "What is possible only under conditions that are themselves merely possible is not possible *in all respects*" (*KrV* A232/B284). As for the last point, Kant maintains that we must believe the highest good to be possible. But belief in the mere possibility that God exists is insufficient for this purpose as can be seen from the following: The highest good will only be possible if there is a God. For the possibility of God's existence is consistent with his nonexistence. But if God does not exist, then the highest good will not be possible. Consequently, the mere possibility of God's existence is consistent with the impossibility of the highest good.

sarily entails, since on his reading we strictly only need to believe in the possibility of achieving happiness in order to be able to rationally follow the law. For the same reason, Wood's argument also clearly does not preclude our believing that we could reach happiness by means other than virtue or our hoping to achieve more happiness than we perhaps deserve based upon the particular amount of effort we put forward in this life.

Perhaps this is a problem with Kant's own argument, but an interpretation that is able to account for this exact proportioning is highly desirable, since its omission would have disastrous consequences for Kant's religious thought. The reason for this is that Kant does not simply make use of any given concept of God, but rather believes that the true nature of this concept can only be deduced from the precise role it is required to play in making the highest good possible. Thus, it is entirely in order to make an object of the form that the highest good possesses, with its exact proportioning, that makes it necessary on Kant's view to think of the cause of the world as not only a powerful being, but also as one that is perfectly moral (so that it always distributes happiness based upon a judgment of our virtue) and omniscient (so that it is able to know our innermost disposition throughout our entire existence) (cf., for instance, *KpV* 05:140). Thus if an interpretation like Wood's cannot account for this exact proportioning, then it also cannot explain any such derivation of Kant's specific concept of God. And without this, in Kant's view, the concept necessarily remains without any moral significance.

§. 1.2.4. A Fourth Difficulty with Wood's Interpretation

This final difficulty is a rather deep one because it rests ultimately on what I take to be a flawed understanding of Kant's basic views on moral motivation. Because similar views are found in other important articles on this topic, I feel the need to address it in some detail in this section.[16]

According to Wood's argument, the highest good must contain both virtue and happiness because the end aimed at in virtuous conduct itself (i.e. perfect virtue) turns out to be extensionally equivalent with the achievement of the ends of a finite will in general (i.e., happiness). He tries to justify this equivalence, as far as I understand him, by an appeal to the structure of rational willing as follows:[17] All maxims of a rational will must have an end at which they are

---

[16] See Engstrom 1992, Bowman 2003 and Denis 2005.
[17] This line of thought is most fully articulated in Engstrom 1992. It is also discussed briefly in Denis 2005.

directed, and so every moral maxim just by this fact must also have an end as its matter. Now happiness is just that state in which everything that I will as an end actually comes about, so a directedness to happiness is already contained even in moral maxims. This object, which contains my own happiness as at least a part, is thus the highest good.

As I said above, I believe this argument rests on a fundamental misunderstanding regarding Kant's view of motivation. It presupposes, namely, that the material and the form are in fact independent and separable features of a practical law, and thus, for instance, that the material or object of the maxim can be my own happiness or a happiness in which my own is included, while the form that restricts it is also of a genuinely moral character. As Wood writes: "Every maxim, to be sure, has a matter, and represents an end which the subject actually desires and labors to attain. But this matter need not and *ought* not be the motive for the adoption of the maxim, and hence not the motive for its own attainment" (Wood 1970, p. 47). I agree that every maxim has a matter or end, even moral ones. Kant makes this clear in several places (e.g. *KpV* 05:109). But it is simply not Kant's considered view that the matter of a maxim or law need not be the determining ground of the will that acts on it, and even taken on its own it would be hard to defend philosophically. Wood himself tries to make sense of this claim employing the example of a man whose goal it is to improve the housing situation of the people around himself, and who indirectly improves his own situation thereby. Cleary, this man's intentions are moral if his motivation is to improve the housing situation of others as the result of his consciousness of the moral law, and this obviously remains true although his own happiness constitutes in part the object that will be brought about by following the maxim. So far so good. However, if the man's own situation improves only indirectly as a result of this action, then it quite evidently should not be thought of as included in the material or end of the maxim itself unless we are willing to also say, for instance, that the maxim Einstein followed in theorizing about the matter-energy relationship contained as part of its material or end the development of the atomic bomb. And if we allow this, then there is nothing to prevent us from taking as the object or the material of the maxim every single consequence that should arise from the action in the future. This would make little sense.

Contrary to the way Wood characterizes it, a maxim is not an objective fact in the world that may have some completely unforeseen end, but is rather the self-conscious or potentially self-conscious formulation of a rational intention. The material of a maxim can therefore be nothing other than, and can extend not further than, the end *by the representation of which* we bring about the action, and thus in the case of moral choices it can in no way be separated from the form of the law. As Kant explains, an "end is an object of choice (of a rational being), *through the representation of which* choice is determined to an action to bring this object about" (*MS* 06:381, emphasis added). Also when Kant introduces the highest good as the complete object of the moral law at *KpV* 05:109, he then goes on to say that this object, as end, can genuinely be thought of as the determining ground of a moral will. This is because the law itself introduces this very end, so that aiming at it and willing for the sake of the law are equivalent from the standpoint of the moral agent.

Consider another case: I form the maxim to will my own happiness. Now, as Kant describes this, the application of the moral law requires me to universalize this maxim such that I will the happiness of all other persons as I would my own. Should we say that the material of the first maxim, namely, willing my own happiness, is somehow preserved in the latter as part of its end or material? I cannot see why. Application of the moral law changes nothing regarding the maxim of willing my own happiness, and it certainly does not make the willing of my own happiness any more of an object of pure practical reason. Rather, it seems to drive me to form a quite different maxim, with an entirely different though descriptively related material, namely, the willing of *other peoples' happiness* as if it were my own. This is why Kant can say that

> since the sensible inclinations of human beings tempt them to ends (the matter of choice) that can be contrary to duty, lawgiving reason can in turn check their influence only by a moral end set up against the ends of inclination, an end that must therefore be given *a priori*, independently of inclinations. (*MS* 06:381)

I can thus see no sense in which it would be correct to say that for Kant the willing of other peoples' happiness is the direct generalization of willing my own happiness. These are entirely different ends, which are essentially connected with morally heterogeneous kinds of motives. Moreover, after such restriction, I may just as before will my own happiness, but only under the restriction that I also follow this other quite different law *at the same time*.[18] This is just to say that when the form of morality is made to restrict a materially determined maxim, it does this by limiting it through the introduction of a different law and a different material altogether.

---

[18] This is a tricky point. Kant's view seems to be that we can include happiness among our ends in this case only to the extent that it does not violate the moral law. Here we perform certain actions (*Handlungen*) for the sake of happiness, but we do not perform deeds (*facta*) with moral content. The existence of such permissible actions certainly does not make it the case that "Our own happiness becomes an object of pure practical reason when it is pursued on a maxim that gives priority to virtue, and when we also adopt the end of the happiness of others" (Denis 2005, p. 35), because such actions are precisely morally indifferent.

This can be seen still more clearly by taking a look at how this confusion arises in cases where the material of the maxim before and after restriction by the moral law happen to fall under very similar descriptions. Take, for instance, Kant's favorite example of the shopkeeper who deals honestly with his customers, not because this is the right thing to do, but because he is afraid that if he cheats a customer and someone discovers this, his business and so also his happiness will suffer (*GMS* 04:397). One might formulate his maxim in this case as: Treat others honestly insofar as this is required for the sake of my own happiness. The object of this maxim might appear to be treating others honestly, and to this extent one might think it agrees in its material, though not in its formal aspect, with the maxim to treat others honestly because this is what the moral law commands. However, in this case the object and thus the material is really the shopkeeper's own happiness, as Kant makes clear. Treating others honestly is only the means to this, not the purpose itself. However, when I treat others honestly because this is required by the moral law, I do not do this as a *means* to fulfilling the law, but rather because the law itself – *as the inner law of all that is good* – immediately constitutes being honest with others as an act that is good in itself, and thus is a duty for no other purpose. The matter in this case is again a particularization of the moral law itself under specific conditions, and so *the moral law is already included in the particular practical law as the essential form of the matter within it*. This is just to say that all duties are already contained in the moral law and that specific duties arise as the various ways in which this one law is to be applied in a specific set of circumstances.

Thus if we recognize that maxims concern *representing to ourselves* the object we intend to produce through an action, then it should also be clear that the physical product of an action and its material are not the same, even if they happen to fall under similar or even identical descriptions. It also follows from this that one cannot have something as one's end without at the same time being motivated by it. That Kant thinks this is true for all non-moral choices, is clear from his equation of these with choices motivated by the representation of an empirically given object (*KpV* 05:21–22). But this is no less true of our moral choices, if properly understood. This does not violate Kant's principle that no moral action can be determined by its material or end, as Wood suggests it does, because by this Kant means only to exclude material that would be given to us as a source of motivation *prior to the law*. Indeed, as must be the case given his theory of motivation, as I noted above, Kant admits that moral actions also have their determining ground in an object or end, namely that of the highest good itself (*KpV* 05:110, Passage 7 below). The material of genuinely moral actions is not therefore an external material given from elsewhere that has been incorporated by us under the law, but rather is an end that is *first produced by the law itself* in its restriction of our non-moral maxims (cf. *TP* 08:279). This production, again, must not be thought of as a forming or universalizing of our immoral maxims, but rather as an instance of the law generated by means of its restriction of these. Thus whatever is left of the original material of the immoral maxim, say some aspect of one's own happiness, is thereby restricted so that it can be pursued, but only because it now no longer conflicts with the law, and thus is no longer of any moral significance (i.e. it is adiaphorous). Thus when Kant says we should abstract from the material of a maxim in judging its moral content, he is directing us to check for the presence of the law itself in our maxim by abstracting from the limitations that particularize it to some specific maxim, and prove or disprove it to be a particular application of the moral law. The upshot of this whole discussion is that no attempt to account for the presence of happiness in the highest good can succeed that rests on Kant's understanding of the material element of a maxim; for one's own happiness in any form cannot in principle be the immediate material of a maxim that is both morally significant and good.[19]

Notwithstanding this, it may nevertheless be quite true that happiness, defined most broadly as the achievement of the material or goal contained in our maxims and not simply as the satisfaction of our inclinations, is to be directly included in the highest good for this very reason. Kant in fact often makes use of such a broad or formal concept of happiness in order to articulate the kind of non-selfish happiness that can be an object of the virtuous person. But the guarantee that this will be the kind of state that we are *capable* of enjoying, and thus that can fittingly answer to the *natural* drive for happiness from which Kant's argument in the postulates begins, is not something that we can understand. The decisive point is that Kant thinks we need to believe in God not because our virtuous actions might end up failing to achieve some kind of reformed world,[20] but rather because of the mismatch between the "extreme heterogeneous concepts" involved in "the endeavor to be virtuous and the rational pursuit of happiness" (*KpV* 05:111) and the fact that such happiness is always going to be a possible object of the human will. If, as this interpretation suggests, the happiness Kant has in mind were just whatever we would will when were we to will virtuously, then the achievement of virtue would by itself just mean the pursuit of this

---

19 I say the "immediate" material, because Kant does suggest at some points that our own happiness can be an indirect duty, but only because it may serve the further aim of putting us in the best situation to develop our own virtue. So here, the matter of the maxim is really virtue, or as Kant formulates it, "to seek virtue with all one's might."

20 This suggestion arises repeatedly in the secondary literature, but as far as I am aware is never suggested by Kant.

end, thus virtue and happiness would be thought to fall together in the way suggested by Stoicism, but rejected explicitly by Kant himself (*KpV* 05:111–113).

To conclude, Wood's account is clearly built upon a genuine recognition of the centrality of rational belief to the kind of moral disposition Kant thinks is essentially moral. And much in his treatment is sensitive to the way in which Kant also thinks rational belief helps to stabilize one's moral character, which lends support to the idea that the argument for the postulates has a deeply moral significance. In this respect his account genuinely anticipates the present one. The core problem with Wood's account is that rather than try to show that the moral significance of the postulates is intended by Kant to provide the very basis of the version of the argument found in the published works, he substitutes for it the rational principle of practical consistency quoted above, the necessity of which is not only dubious, but which, even if true, does not provide a morally practical ground for belief. So despite his recognition of the moral significance of the postulates, Wood regards it as lying outside of the argument proper.[21] The other deficiencies I have pointed out in Wood's account, I believe, can all be traced back to his attempt to make sense of the argument while omitting this, its most essential component.

§. 2. Kant's Argument[22]

Having assessed the interpretations of Beck and Wood, I will now turn to what I take to be Kant's own argument. Due to its complexity, I will break down my presentation into three sections. Section one will briefly explain Kant's conception of virtue, what it means for the duty of virtue to be a wide obligation, and how Kant thinks such virtue can be cultivated. In the second section, I will show that rational faith in the existence of God is a central way of attempting to fulfill this wide obligation, and thus is indirectly required by the moral law itself. The key idea here will be that this belief is the core of the single theoretical conception of the world as it might be constituted in itself that, if assumed as true, would lead to or facilitate a *maximal increase* in one's moral strength of character, i.e. in one's virtue. As we will see, this means that the *free and active adoption* of a belief in God's existence is a way of striving for virtue, and thus falls under the duty of virtue and thus has a moral foundation. Finally, in section three I will present

---

[21] Wood 1970, p. 33–34 is indeed the closest he comes to the account I will offer. I do not, however, see how it can be made consistent with his central argument.
[22] I make a similar argument, although drawing on different evidence, in Fugate 2014.

additional textual evidence to corroborate this reconstruction and further specify the nature of the necessity underlying the moral postulates. For ease of reference, I will number the key passages throughout.[23]

§. 2.1. Virtue as Moral Strength of Character

To understand the underlying argument of the postulates, we must first come to a better understanding of what Kant means by virtue as moral strength. This concept plays a central role throughout Kant's moral writings, eventually forming the concept at the very heart of the Doctrine of Virtue. However, already in the *KpV* Kant writes that "the utmost that finite practical reason can effect is to make sure of this unending progress of one's maxims toward this model [i.e. of holiness] and of their constancy in continual progress, that is, virtue," which latter is a "naturally acquired ability" (*KpV* 05:32–33). Later in the *MS*, we read that virtue is "the strength of a human being's maxims in fulfilling his duty" and is "recognized only by the obstacles it can overcome, and in this case [...] natural inclinations, which can come into conflict with the human being's moral resolution" (*MS* 06:394).

But why does Kant think it is necessary to employ such a concept in a moral philosophy that has at its basis the idea of a transcendentally free agent? This is neither immediately obvious nor obviously consistent. Indeed, it would appear that since freedom guarantees our ability to act for the sake of the law whenever necessary, i.e. whenever we are faced by an actual choice, there should really be no need to develop any additional kind of strength. Why may we not simply seek to act according to the law in every individual action, which is something the consciousness of our own freedom assures us we can do? Although Kant does not provide a detailed explanation of this point, and although it is not my concern in this chapter to prove the consistency of this notion with his general theory of freedom, it is still necessary to examine his stated reasons for introducing it. I cite the whole passage because of its significance for what follows:

[Passage 1] The greatest perfection of a human being is to do his duty *from duty* [...]. – At first sight this looks like a *narrow* obligation, and the principle of duty seems to prescribe with precision and strictness of a law not only the *legality* but also the *morality* of every

---

[23] The reader might wonder why I have chosen to present a reconstruction of Kant's argument before looking at the central texts. However, the direct method has so far failed to yield a satisfying account, and as I think this chapter shows, the central texts become much clearer when related to the other texts from which the reconstruction draws its foundation.

> action, that is, the disposition. But in fact the law, here again, prescribes only the *maxim of the action*, that of seeking the basis of obligation solely in the law and not in sensible impulse (advantage or disadvantage), and hence not the *action itself*. – For a human being cannot see in to the depths of his own heart so as to be quite certain, in even a *single* action, of the purity of his moral intention and the sincerity of his disposition, even when he has no doubt about the legality of his action. [...] In the case of any deed it remains hidden from the agent himself how much pure moral content there has been in his disposition.
>
> [...] The law does not prescribe this inner action in the human mind but only the maxim of the action, to strive with all one's might that the thought of duty for its own sake is the sufficient incentive of every action conforming to duty. (*MS* 06: 392–393)

This passage is from the *MS*, but Kant also makes a similar argument, though more briefly, in a key passage of the *KpV* (*KpV* 05:32–33). In both of these passages, Kant argues that since one cannot ever really know that one is acting for the sake of the law alone, and since one nevertheless knows that in doing so lies precisely the goal of all morality, what the moral law really in fact demands is that one follow the maxim to "strive with all one's might" to assure this is true.

So the opacity of one's own true motives in combination with the absolute command of the law makes it the case in Kant's view that the fundamental moral maxim, the central duty of the moral agent, is one of *striving by all means available* to obtain a moral strength of character, i.e. virtue. Or as he also states, referring specifically to virtue itself,

> [Passage 2] It is also correct to say that the human being is under obligation *to virtue* (as moral strength). For while the faculty (*facultas*) to overcome all opposing sensible impulses can and must be simply *presupposed* in man on account of his freedom, yet this faculty as strength (*robur*) is something he must acquire. (*MS* 06:397)

Although Passage 2 clearly indicates that striving is a duty, one must be careful to note that by this Kant does not mean to say we have a duty *to be* virtuous, but rather only that we have a duty *to seek to become* virtuous, to strive with all our might – and thus presumably by all available means – to develop a virtuous disposition. As he explains a few pages later, "virtue itself, or possession of it, is not a duty (for then one would have to be put under obligation to duties" (*MS* 06:405). In other words, there cannot be a separate duty to be virtuous, because this would be redundant, a duty to fulfill duties. Duties rather *just are* the things to which we are obliged, and consequently virtue can be nothing other than the subjective strength of character required in order to counter sensible incentives, thereby allowing the moral law to become an "irresistible" constraint on our actions (*MS* 06:405). As such, a duty to virtue (not a duty to possess it) is already contained in the very concept of a duty for beings subject to sensible incentives.

§. 2. Kant's Argument — 313

This explains Kant's further claim in Passage 1 that since the duty to virtue is properly only a duty to seek virtue, *how* we are to do this is not objectively prescribed by the law. It is for this reason that he classes it among the duties of "wide obligation," the distinctive character of which lies in that they "leave a playroom (*laditudo*) for free choice in following (complying with) the law, that is, that the law cannot specify precisely in what way one is to act" (*MS* 06:390). In the case of such duties, when it comes to how it will be fulfilled, a person can "decide as he chooses" and is able to exercise "free choice" in regard to means (*MS* 06:392). Thus although "it is true that in its idea (objectively) there is only one virtue (as moral strength of one's maxims)" it is also true that "(subjectively) there is a multitude of virtues" and that "our cognition of ourselves can never adequately tell us whether it is complete or deficient" (*MS* 06:447).

So virtue is a strength, which must be "naturally acquired" and which we have a duty to acquire in order to earnestly attempt to counter our natural inclinations. But how is this acquisition to take place? Kant's compressed answer in 1797 is the following: "The way to acquire it [virtue as strength] is to enhance the moral incentive (thought of the law), both by contemplating the dignity of the pure rational law in us (*contemplatione*) and by practicing virtue (*exercitio*)" (*MS* 06:397). On the surface this hardly seems helpful, since it does not tell how specifically this possibility for increase is supposed to be understood philosophically or how one should practically go about such "contemplating" and "exercising." Both, however, can be clarified by attending to two other passages in which Kant discusses how an increase in the moral incentive is to be understood. In the *KpV*, Kant writes:

[Passage 3] There is indeed no feeling for this [moral] law, but inasmuch as it [i.e. moral feeling] moves resistance out of the way, in the judgment of reason this removal of a hindrance is esteemed equivalent to a positive furthering of its causality. (*KpV* 05:76)

[Passage 4] Whatever diminishes the hindrances to an activity is a furthering of that activity itself. Recognition of the moral law is, however, consciousness of an activity of practical reason from objective grounds, which fails to express its effect in actions only because the subjective (pathological) causes hinder it. (*KpV* 05:79)

Thus "in the judgment of reason," whatever that may mean, the curbing of inclinations as such is the same as increase in the strength of the moral incentive itself (cf. *TP* 08:284–285 where Kant explains this more fully).

From Passages 3 and 4 it is clear that Kant understands this connection through analogy with dead and living physical forces, where a dead force is a kind of internal effort (*conatus*) checked by an external obstacle such that upon the removal of this obstacle, the dead force would automatically become living or operative.[24] Accordingly, Kant asserts that, in the absence of opposing sensible incentives, the power of the moral incentive is intrinsically self-manifesting, explaining that:

> [Passage 5] For, the pure thought of duty and in general of the moral law, mixed with no foreign addition of empirical inducements, has by way of reason alone [...] an influence on the heart so much more powerful than all other incentives [...] On the other hand a mixed doctrine of morals, put together from incentives of feeling and inclination and also of rational concepts, must make the mind waver between motives [...]. (*GMS* 04:410–411)

> [Passage 6] It is utterly mistaken to worry that if it [the moral incentive] were deprived of everything that the senses can recommend it would then bring with it nothing but cold, lifeless approval and no moving force or emotion. It is exactly the reverse: for where the senses no longer see anything before them, yet the unmistakable and inextinguishable idea of morality remains, there it would be more necessary to moderate the momentum of an unbounded imagination so as not to let it reach the point of enthusiasm, rather than from fear of the powerlessness of these ideas, to look for them in images and childish devices. (*KU* 05:276)

Consequently, whatever else contemplation and exercise might specifically entail (this will be discussed further below), it is clear that they will consist of practices aimed at combating our sensible incentives and establishing a character in which rational concern for such incentives plays as little part as possible with the expectation that a genuinely moral disposition will thereby automatically develop within us. In other words, because we lack all insight into the true springs of morality, we can do nothing better *practically* than to regard striving to become moral as equivalent to actively striving to combat the power of all non-moral incentives. We must "strive with all our might" to make sure we are motivated by the law, but the only available way to do *that*, it now turns out, is to seek to perform moral acts while at the same time doing all we can to *exclude* the role of non-moral incentives in our decision-making process and more generally to cultivate a character that actively guards against and rejects so far as possible all possible sources of non-moral incentives. "The true strength of virtue," Kant thus writes, "is a *tranquil mind* with a considered and firm resolution to put the law of virtue into practice" (*MS* 06:409). It is the striving to develop just this kind of tranquil character, we can now see, that Kant holds in Passage 2 to be something commanded by the moral law, and as such to be a duty.

---

[24] For the clearest expressions of this distinction see *Refl* 3583 and *Refl* 3585.

§. 2.2. How Rational Belief in God's Existence Increases the Moral Incentive

It should now be clear that if there is to be a genuinely moral ground for postulating the existence of God, which latter is not a duty in the narrow sense, then this is only possible in one way, namely, if the rational integrity of our beliefs, under the condition of the moral law, in some special sense nevertheless *serves and furthers our observance* of the moral law in the narrow sense. That is to say, rational belief can only be necessary if in some sense it can be shown to be an unavoidable means to *fulfilling* the duty to virtue, which, as we saw, is a duty of wide obligation.

Nevertheless, it still remains unclear how asserting that the world is one in which happiness is proportioned to virtue, and thus that there is a God to underpin this relation, can strengthen the moral incentive. However, if we can solve this problem, then we will for the first time have shown that the postulation of God's existence in its synthetic role truly rests on a moral foundation, and has a moral significance insofar as it is necessarily contained within the intention to become virtuous by all available means. I believe the following argument establishes this very point: Ordinary practical reason, or what Kant often calls conditioned-practical reason, is nothing but the conception of practical reason found in Wolff's writings, clad however in slightly new terminology. On both Wolff's and Kant's understanding this practical reason gains the material of its maxims from its reflection upon our empirical state – i.e., on what *actually* pleases us in our *present* state – and gives these a form and coherence by progressively integrating them into a total theory of human perfection which is at the same time a theory of happiness (*GMS* 04:390–391, *GMS* 04:417–419). Such a function of reason is said to be "conditioned," on Kant's view, because it takes the material of its maxims from the empirical, just as Wolff had explained. Now it is also reflective and rational, and this means that through its reflection upon these conditions practical reason is able to abstract empirical laws, which can then be used to construct maxims of action for *increasing* the overall harmony or perfection of our empirical nature, thereby giving rise to greater natural happiness (Wolff 1752, §192; cf. *KpV* 05:41 & *TP* 08:282–283). The production of these maxims is guided not only by the empirical laws, but also by the goal of absolute universality and harmony of willing, i.e. of completely systematic and thus perfect willing. But only reason, not understanding or sensibility, can gain such insight into the systematic character of the laws of nature, and reason is therefore the master who teaches what Wolff calls the moral law (Wolff 1752, §23; cf. *KpV* 05:36), or what Kant identifies with the law of self-conceit (*KpV* 05:74).

For instance, say I find that drinking large quantities of alcohol leads to intense but merely fleeting pleasures and, by harming my health, decreases my capacity for more sustained pleasurable activities. Good health, on the other hand, is both pleasurable in itself and it opens up the possibility of developing capacities, all of which occasion pleasures, that would not otherwise be possible; personal pleasures, social pleasures and even pleasure in others. Proceeding in this way, conditioned practical reason, simply by following its own law of selecting maxims that genuinely lead to the greatest amount of perfection and therefore also pleasure (and not the most at a certain time, or to the detriment of the total pleasure in a life), tends necessarily towards an increasingly rational and systematic theory whose single goal is the achievement of the greatest perfection which is at the same time the greatest possible sum-total of pleasures. Its unifying principle, when understood as Kant understands it, i.e. from the vantage point of *motives*, is precisely the idea of *happiness* as a *systematically maximal sum-total*, and without this guiding idea practical reason would have no rational criteria for either accepting or rejecting practical maxims. This theory, in turn, because it is guided by the normative idea of happiness, serves as a source of maxims for *cultivating* our sensible incentives and inclinations in a way that maximally fulfills this ideal. Thus, to live or will rationally is to actively cultivate by rational means a certain type of character, a character purposively formed for achieving the maximum satisfaction of the totality of our natural inclinations (Wolff 1752, §169 and §188; cf. *KpV* 05:22–25). Indeed, for the sake of this ideal the calculating Wolffian moral agent will freely endure partial or temporary displeasure if this will lead to an increase in the scope or degree of pleasure of a rational variety, meaning a variety that is more universal and more permanent and thus which is more consistent with the perfection of the will. But ultimately Wolffian virtue, or the capacity to readily act (*Fertigkeit*) according to the law of nature, is a means to the highest natural happiness.

The chief point I want to draw from this sketch, is that the true function of conditioned practical reason, if left to itself, is not only to systematize those pleasures we are presently capable of enjoying, but moreover to rationally cultivate and to increase, by means of knowledge and exercise, our *global capacity for enjoying and being motivated by this kind of pleasure* and even to help us discover entirely new types of pleasure that are more rationally consistent and in principle more intense and extensive, which can afterwards provide further incentives for new types of maxims of conduct. In the end, the most perfectly rational agent will enjoy, as Leibniz also claims, the most perfect and everlasting happiness.

Based upon this sketch, I think we can better understand why Kant considers conditioned-practical reason, if left to itself, to be not merely morally neutral, but even to be directly *opposed* to morality.[25] This is because it not only opens us up to the temptation of adopting non-moral incentives as the basis of our maxims, but because it moreover leads naturally and directly to the adoption of maxims aimed at *discovering, cultivating* and *strengthening* these non-moral incentives, i.e. to the establishment of a character or a principled and firm disposition unyielding to Kantian moral sensibility. But to make it one's "maxim to foster the influence of such motives [i.e. those of happiness] [...] is the death of all morality" (*TP* 08:287). Hence, from Kant's point of view, the Wolffian conception of virtue as the acquired habit for rationally pursuing the greatest possible perfection, which is at the same time the greatest possible pleasure, is precisely the opposite of genuine virtue, which consists in willing independently from all such motives. And this remains the case even though both systems will often provide motives to the very same action. It is not the action that matters in respect to virtue, but the motive which generates the action.

But conditioned-practical reason only necessarily leads to this result if it is left to operate on an empirically based conception of the good. If I as a rational agent, however, *actively assert for myself* that this idea of happiness as the guiding idea of conditioned-practical reason can in fact *only* be reached on the condition that I cultivate virtue within myself above all else, then the whole eudemonistic and rationalistic project is not thereby canceled, but is rather *incorporated* under a more embracing maxim of pursuing virtue through increasing the moral incentive. This is true for three reasons. Firstly, the claim that the achievement of happiness is conditioned by virtue *internally* transforms the otherwise natural assumption of theoretical reason that happiness can be reached by cultivating our non-moral incentives, and this in turn halts one from engaging in otherwise rational practices that lead directly to the development of new competitors to the moral incentive. Secondly, based upon the intrinsically self-manifesting character of the moral incentive this *indirectly* leads to its increase simply by clearing a space in which it can assert its own intrinsic power without opposition. Thirdly, just as the project of increasing our non-moral incentives is a rational one in which we empirically seek out improved means for attaining

---

[25] As Kant writes, "if one wanted to give the maxim [i.e., of one's own happiness] the universality of a law, the most extreme opposite of harmony would follow, the worst conflict, and the complete annihilation of the maxim itself and its purpose" (*KpV* 05:28). Again: "The direct opposite of the principle of morality is the principle of one's own happiness made the determining ground of the will [...]. This conflict, however, is not merely logical [...] it is instead practical and would ruin morality altogether [...]" (*KpV* 05:35). In both these passages, Kant is clearly criticizing Wolff's universal practical philosophy, although he does not mention it by name.

higher degrees of pleasure and formulate these into a system of maxims for conduct, the project of decreasing these same kinds of incentives is likewise a rational and indeed empirical one, in which we construct just such a system, however this time in a way that serves to further our pursuit of virtue. This, in essence, is the project of pragmatic anthropology (cf. *MS* 06:217).[26]

The postulation of the existence of a God that distributes happiness only on the condition that one exerts all one's powers to develop a character of choosing the law for its own sake, and thus without regard to happiness, directly undermines the rational project that would otherwise systematize, develop, and strengthen the pathological causes that hinder the determination of the will by the moral law by replacing it with an analogous project, which, however, aims at furthering morality itself. When conditioned-practical reason is itself in turn conditioned by the moral law, this second conditioning is in fact a lifting of the first. Conditioned-practical reason becomes one with the *unconditioned* legislation of the pure practical reason, i.e. the pure will. But for this to happen, the former's conditioned ideal of natural happiness must be limited absolutely by the ideal of the latter, i.e. by the condition of perfect virtue. The act of postulation, therefore, can be understood as a correlate, on the level of reason and its ideas, to the understanding's production of moral feeling on the level of incentives; for just as the moral law stands to sensible incentives, the act of moral postulation stands to self-conceit, i.e. the self-love that "makes itself lawgiving and the unconditioned practical principle" (*KpV* 05:74), and so also just as the ideal of perfect virtue stands to the natural ideal of perfect happiness. To spell this out just a bit further, one could observe that in the first the constraining effect of the law on non-moral feelings produces in turn a moral feeling; while in the second, the constraining effect of moral postulation on self-conceit in turn produces a rational faith in which the rational desire to become happy is replaced by the equally rational desire to become worthy of happiness. And both of these are analogous to the third, in which the condition of perfect virtue places a constraint on the natural conception of our end producing in turn the Kantian concept of the highest good.

From this we can now see that what essentially takes place when the existence of God is postulated is that the space is cleared which was previously occupied by the incentives that were fortified and cultivated by means of practical reason guided by the natural ideal of happiness, and it thereby becomes one in which the pure moral incentive can automatically manifest itself. The ideal of happiness in its most general form cannot, however, be entirely supplanted be-

---

[26] See also Frierson 2003, Ch. 3.

cause it is nothing more than the name for the focal point of all rational human willing. When the capacity for pure willing is set aside, reason indeed justifiably evaluates the maxims of the will according to the empirical connection it discovers between certain types of actions and the satisfaction that it anticipates as resulting from them. However, once the moral law *is* taken into account, and thus also the capacity for pure willing, reason no longer recognizes the empirically observable rules connecting actions with satisfaction as a proper means for evaluating the relation between its maxims and its final natural goal. That the idea that God, or a moral creator, stands as the ultimate root of *nature itself* means therefore essentially that, despite all appearances to the contrary, a will that is motivated according to empirically observable rules of conduct – simply because this is not the right kind of motive – will inevitably be frustrated in its overall project. The postulation of God is in this respect equivalent to the rational assertion that conditioned-practical reason *necessarily* does not lead to happiness as naturally defined. Once such an idea is postulated, then, practical reason continues to function, but it does so according to the maxim that the only way to reach happiness is to actively attempt to totally disregard our natural motivations, and to focus exclusively on the moral quality of any particular action. The resulting conception of our natural end is thus one that is disengaged from our first empirical nature, and consists rather in a second moral nature that can only arise in conjunction with the pursuit of virtue itself.

§. 2.3. Textual Analysis

That this is the core of Kant's actual argument can now be confirmed by attention to what he actually claims in the published writings to be the basis of the postulate of God's existence. As we will see, every extant version of the argument, from the *KpV* until the *TP*, agrees that belief is necessary, not to solve the *purely* architectonic or theoretical issue of the synthesis of virtue and happiness, but in order to develop the kind of character within which the moral incentive can maximally manifest itself. I will begin, however, with the extended account provided by *KpV* itself, since it is clearly the most central.

§. 2.3.1. The Highest Good in *KpV*

The argument of the Dialectic of this work has the following structure. In Chapter I, Kant announces that just like speculative reason, pure practical reason falls into a dialectic when it seeks the highest good as the "unconditioned totality" of its object. He then explains that properly speaking the science which determines this idea practically – "that is, sufficiently for the maxims of our rational conduct" – is what has traditionally been called the "doctrine of wisdom." But before passing on to the analysis of such a doctrine Kant pauses to clarify the relation of the highest good to the determining ground of the will. For although he previously explained that the moral law, which "is the sole determining ground of the pure will," requires us to abstract entirely from ends and thus also from objects of willing, he now notes that the highest good is the only object for which this is not true. It is, he says, both object *and* determining ground of a good will at the same time,

> [Passage 7] because in that case [i.e. the case of the highest good as object] the moral law, already included and thought in this concept, *and no other object*, in fact determines the will in accordance with the principle of autonomy. (*KpV* 05:110; emphasis added)

This point is of the utmost importance. For here Kant is asserting the equivalence, from the point of view of motivation, of being determined by the law alone and being determined by the idea of the highest good alone. This means that whatever might be the content of the highest good, determination though it must be able to generate nothing more or less than a moral disposition conforming to the law itself. And this, clearly, has both an intensive and an extensive aspect; *intensively*, determination by the highest good must yield an absolutely *pure* form of motivation, whereas *extensively* it must yield one that conforms in the absolute *totality* of one's possible actions. Without the first aspect it would not be an object of the *pure* will *at all*, and without the second it would not be the *complete* object of this will. It is essential to note also that in the italicized clause in Passage 7, Kant recognizes that only the highest good of this kind can serve the will as its object, and that it must not be combined with any additional object besides. For to allow the latter would be to introduce non-moral incentives, and hence heteronomy. As Kant emphasizes, "the moral law alone must be viewed as the ground for making the highest good and its realization or promotion the object" (*KpV* 05:109). One can already see from this that to be the object of the pure will, such that it neither introduces nor allows any form of non-moral motivation, the good of the pure will must be both intensively and extensively maximal. As we will see, the rest of the argument for the postulate of God's existence is based precisely on this very condition.

After making these crucial remarks, Kant introduces Chapter II with a closer look at these intensive and extensive aspects of the highest good. "Highest," he says, can be taken to "mean either the supreme (*supremum*) or the complete (*consummatum*)," where supreme means unconditional in regard to the subordination of conditions and complete means unconditional in the sense of a "whole which is not part of a still greater whole of the same kind" (*KpV* 05:110). As we saw above, the purity, thus unconditionality, of the determination that would arise from this object is nothing but the morality of one's disposition or virtue, and this is accordingly the supreme condition of the good. But the moral law, insofar as it is absolute, also requires its object to be extensively maximal, for in regard to such a will motivation by any object other than the highest good cannot be admitted without introducing sensible incentives. Thus, in the highest good itself, all possible objects of willing must be subjected absolutely to the supreme condition. Now, as Kant points out, virtue itself is by no means the only possible object of our faculty of desire. Indeed, the finite will, for which the pure will is a model, is naturally inclined to many kinds of objects, and as we saw in previous sections, when left to itself, it rationally pursues these under the guidance of the idea of perfect happiness. Consequently, if the highest good is going to be the object through which a finite will determines itself in accordance with the pure will, in this concept all these other possible objects, thus happiness itself, must be subordinated absolutely to the supreme condition of the highest good.

Thus in the idea of the highest object of a finite will perfectly conforming to the moral law, virtue and happiness are necessarily combined, because to leave them uncombined would be for there to remain objects of motivation unconditioned by conformity with the moral law. But Kant says more than this, namely, that they must be thought as necessarily combined "in exact proportion." Why in exact proportion? Kant provides no extended explanation in the text itself. But from what has gone before, I think the reason is not difficult to discover. For suppose this were not the case, and I could expect either more or less happiness than I deserve. If the former, then I could expect that some of my desires can and perhaps will ultimately be fulfilled (without being cancelled by a future punishment) even though I do not subject them fully to the limiting condition of virtue. If the latter, then I could expect that in some of the cases in which I do not pursue a desired end in the name of virtue, I could in fact have increased my overall happiness by being less virtuous. In both cases, the complete object of my will would include ends potentially reachable without limitation by virtue, and thus the same object could in principle be a source of non-moral incentives. Only if happiness is thought to be precisely conditioned by virtue will it be *impossible* to conceive of a will motivated by this object alone as having anything but moral incentives. It is thus the optimal object for a will seeking virtue with all its might.

At this point Kant argues that the necessary combinations of two concepts must be either analytic or synthetic. Leaving the possibility of a synthetic necessity for consideration in sections I and II of Chapter II, Kant first turns to showing that the link cannot be analytical. The basic reason for this is that an analytical link would contradict the view of moral motivation explained earlier in the *KpV*. As he notes, if the link were analytical then "the endeavor to be virtuous and the rational pursuit of happiness are not two different actions but quite identical, in which case no maxim need be made the ground of the former other than that which serves for the latter" (*KpV* 05:111). But from the standpoint of motives, the Analytic has shown that the "maxims of virtue and those of one's own happiness are quite heterogeneous with respect to their supreme principle; and [...] they are so far from coinciding that they greatly restrict and infringe on each other in the same subject" (*KpV* 05:112). From this one can already anticipate, that 1) since the maxims of one's own happiness must be prevented from infringing on the moral law, and yet 2) the object of these maxims, i.e. happiness, must somehow be incorporated into the highest good, while 3) the highest good must remain a source of nothing but moral maxims and incentives, happiness must be incorporated precisely in such a way that it gives rise to no other maxims than moral ones. Put differently, the highest good must incorporate happiness in such a way that the latter essentially vanishes as a competing source of motivation.

It should be noted that, unlike its competitors, this line of thought shows why Kant need not be concerned with the objection voiced by Garve, Hegel and others that his argument would turn virtue into a means to happiness. This would be a valid objection only if Kant thought we needed to include happiness in the highest good because it would be intolerably disappointing to think that the object of our striving will never be attained; for this would mean we must include happiness in order somehow to satisfy our natural desire for it. But clearly Kant thinks quite differently that it must be included in the highest good because only in this way can we seek to eliminate it as an actual motive for our actions. This is particularly evident from the way Kant formulates this dependency as one of happiness, not on the performance of certain actions alone, but rather on the development of a pure or virtuous *disposition* itself, i.e. virtue. Thus only to the extent that we are not motivated by happiness, i.e. we are motivated by the moral law, can we ever expect to achieve happiness. We trust in God as the ground of the highest good not so that we can believe happiness is possible by means of virtue, but rather because this is the only way to strive to focus our entire attention on virtue itself.

Kant delineates this point very precisely in another passage of the Dialectic, which has so far gone unnoticed:

> [Passage 8] It can now readily be seen that all worthiness depends upon moral conduct, since in the concept of the highest good this constitutes the condition of the rest (which belongs to one's state), namely, of one's share of happiness. Now, from this it follows

that morals in itself must never be treated as a *doctrine of happiness* [...]; for morals has to do solely with the rational condition (*conditio sine qua non*) of happiness and not with the means of acquiring it. But when morals (which merely imposes duties and does not provide rules for selfish wishes) has been set forth completely, then – after the moral wish, based on the law, to promote the highest good [...] has been awakened, which could not previously have arisen in any selfish soul, and for the sake of this wish the step to religion has been taken – then for the first time can this ethical doctrine be called a doctrine of happiness, because it is only with religion that the hope of happiness first arises. (*KpV* 05:130)

This passage is so clear that it is hard to imagine why Kant has been so deeply misunderstood. As described here, Kant's conception of the highest good, along with the postulation of God's existence, has the function of so conditioning the rational project of happiness by the project of acting for the sake of the law alone that it converts the former into a sublimated hope. And what is distinctive about this hope is that it can provide no motives aside from that provided by the moral law itself, precisely because God will only grant happiness to the extent that we do not act for the sake of it. But once this is fully taken into account, then it is proper to present this same hope as the fulfillment of absolutely all of our ends, because otherwise they would remain sources of temptation.

Let us return to the main line of the argument. Having rejected the possibility of such an analytical necessity for the link between virtue and happiness, Kant moves in section I of Chapter II to a presentation of the Antinomy itself. A synthetic link between happiness and virtue, Kant explains, must consist in a causal relationship, i.e. either in happiness producing virtue or in virtue producing happiness. But the first is "*absolutely* impossible because maxims that put the determining ground of the will in the desire for one's happiness are not moral at all and can be the ground of no virtue" (*KpV* 05:114). Yet, if we look at the world around us, the second also appears to be impossible, again because the maxims of virtue rarely if ever produce happiness and certainly are not related to it *necessarily* as cause and effect. So an antinomy has arisen that threatens to undermine the concept of the highest good and, by extension, the moral law which requires that we make this good the object of all our willing. Thus if the antinomy can somehow be resolved, then it must be resolved, because this is a requirement stemming from the moral law itself. Thus the necessity of resolving this issue is not a merely logical necessity, but rather a pure moral one.

And as it turns out, a solution is possible, because although it is absolutely impossible for maxims of happiness to bring about virtue, the appearance that it was impossible for virtue to produce happiness was based merely upon the laws of natural necessity discovered in the empirical world. Thus, to satisfy what the moral law demands, because we can assume that the empirical world is not the only reality, and that from the point of view of the world in itself virtue might somehow be the causal ground of happiness, we must make this very assumption. This leads directly to the proof of the postulate of God's existence in section V. After running again through what came before, Kant adds that in order to assume that the highest good is possible, i.e. to resolve the antinomy, we must assume the conditions under which alone it can be conceived of as possible. Thus we must assume, or as he now says, we must *postulate* "the existence of a cause of all nature, distinct from nature, which contains the ground of this connection." Moreover, since this cause must be able to proportion happiness to the extent to which rational beings conform their wills to the representation of the law, this cause must possess a power of representation, i.e. an understanding, and a causality based upon this, i.e. a will, and the moral righteousness to proportion happiness to virtue. It must, therefore, be God.

Kant has thus traced a direct line from the command of the moral law, *via* the concept of the highest good which it makes necessary for a finite rational will, to the moral necessity of postulating the existence of a God. Or as Kant himself states:

> [Passage 9] In this way the moral law leads through the concept of the highest good, as the object and final end of pure practical reason, *to religion, that is, to the recognition of all duties as divine commands* [...] as essential laws of every free will in itself, which must nevertheless be regarded as commands of the supreme being because only from a will that is morally perfect (holy and beneficent) and at the same time all-powerful, and so through the harmony with this will, can we hope to attain the highest good, which the moral law makes it our duty to take as the object of our endeavors. (*KpV* 05:129)

Clearly, the central idea throughout this derivation has been that without these further assumptions one would not be able to completely conform their moral disposition to the law itself, because otherwise happiness would remain to some extent a possible source of motivation in competition with the law.

Most importantly, at this moment the essential link between the synthetic and the symbolic functions of the idea of God also becomes clear for the first time. For in order to think of a being that would proportion happiness to virtue we must think of it as a moral being possessing omnipotence (so it has absolute control of this proportioning) and omniscience (so it can know our innermost disposition in all our choices), and thus as a being external to ourselves that in essence demands nothing other than our complete conformity to the moral law itself. And when we think of God in just this way, Kant explains, what we are doing is presenting the moral law itself, now personified, as if it originated in the will of an external being, although it in fact originates in our own. As Kant later clarifies in the *MS*, the reason for this is that because the moral agent gives himself the law and yet must also hold himself accountable to it, the only way to present this obligation to oneself and to do so in a way that is appropriate to the absolute obligation of the moral law, is to think of it as if it were an obligation to another person, but not just to any other person, but only to one that is also an omnipotent and omniscient moral being, i.e. God (cf. *MS* 06:438–439). So what we postulate in order to think of happiness and virtue as appropriately combined is just the existence of the same idea that is thought in the symbol of God.

Consequently, we can understand the relationship between the symbolic and the synthetic functions of the idea of God to be the following: The idea of God functions firstly as a symbol in which the moral law is personified with the appropriate properties such that being obligated to the will of this person just means nothing else than being obligated to the moral law itself in its greatest possible extent. Now, for our wills to be fully submitted to the moral law, i.e. for all other motives to be subordinated to it on the level of reason, we saw above that we had to think of the highest good as including happiness and indeed in such a way that it is absolutely subordinated to the condition of virtue. Thus the synthetic role that the idea of God plays here is to enable us to think or represent happiness as subordinated to that very symbol in which the moral law was originally personified. The same idea of God thus serves two related functions, each of which aims at facilitating our development of a moral disposition in a different respect. The symbolic function provides us with an extended way of "contemplating" the moral law and its absolutely comprehensive validity, and thereby provides us with a direct way of increasing the moral incentive. The synthetic function, however, as we saw earlier, allows us to think the object of all non-moral incentives, i.e. happiness, as subordinated absolutely to the condition of virtue, providing us with an indirect way of increasing the moral incentive by removing obstacles thereto. This difference between these two is in turn reflected in their differing relations to the existence of the object of this idea. For Kant argues that we need merely the *idea* of such a God in order to fulfill the symbolic function, while we need nevertheless to think of the object of this idea as *existing*, and so must postulate its existence, in order to fulfill the synthetic one.[27] The reason for this is that to fulfill its synthetic function, this

---

[27] Kant brings these two functions together in a key passage in the *Critique of the Power of Judgment*, thereby confirming our interpretation to be the view he held as late as 1793: "It is at least possible as well as well-grounded in a moral way of thinking to represent such a purely moral need for the existence of such a being, by means of which our morality acquires either more strength or (at least as we represent it) more scope, namely, by assuming a new object for its exercise, i.e., a morally legislative being outside of the world, without any regard to a theoretical proof, but on a purely moral ground, free from all alien influence (and thus, to be

being must be thought as the real causal ground of happiness and thus also of nature.[28]

If we return to the main argument of the Dialectic, it would now seem as if Kant has established that the necessity of postulating God's existence and thus that it is an objective duty. But as we saw in Passage 1, the moral law does not command that we conform our moral disposition to the law, but rather that we strive by all possible means to do so. Unlike duties of narrow obligation, which always command the performance of specific actions, duties of virtue leave some latitude such that the means by which we can seek to fulfill them are not individually duties in a strict sense. Now, as it turns out, for beings for which happiness produces incentives that necessarily compete for supremacy with the moral law, we find ourselves in a unique case where the rational belief in God's existence is the only way in which this conflict can best be resolved for reason. In section VIII of the Dialectic, Kant therefore qualifies his proof, explaining that such a belief is not itself a duty but a "need connected to a duty," and that it has its basis in the merely *subjective* (i.e. it is based upon the nature of human beings) fact that through it alone is it possible for the highest good to be the complete object of the rational human will, and thus for such a will to become maximally conformed to the moral law. Consequently, although the moral law does not command rational belief as a duty, the adoption of such belief is at the same time the adoption of the optimal worldview for the pursuit of virtue, and so possesses a subjective moral necessity.

Just as we saw earlier regarding a duty of virtue in general, Kant here in the Dialectic points out that although the moral law commands us to pursue the highest good as our object, "*the way* in which *we* are to think such a harmony of the laws of nature with those of freedom has in it something with respect to which we have a *choice*," and again, that "the way in which we would think it [i.e. the highest good] as possible rests with our choice." To make such a free choice, is therefore a way of seeking to promote our own virtue, and thereby the highest good itself, by all possible means. It is "the only way

---

sure, only subjective), on the basis of the mere recommendation of a pure practical reason legislating for itself alone" (*KU* 05:446). God, we read here, is assumed in order to provide morality with strength (intensive magnitude), and scope (extensive magnitude). The former is achieved through the removal of impediments to the self-manifesting power of the moral law, while the latter is achieved by providing the moral law with a kind of symbol for use in conscience.

28 Compare the argument for the postulates with Kant's statement at *MS* 06:439, in the context of the symbolic function, that "this is not to say that a human being is entitled [...] to assume that such a supreme being *actually exists* outside himself."

in which it is theoretically possible for it to think exact harmony in the realm of nature with the realm of morals as the condition of the possibility of the highest good, and at the same time the only way that is conducive to morality"; it is not a command but "a voluntary determination of our judgment, conducive to the moral (commanded) purpose." The argument of the postulates thus provides, as he says, "the ground of a maxim of assent for moral purposes" (*KpV* 05:146). In the *FM* essay, Kant expands on this key feature of moral postulation. "Belief, in a morally-practical context," Kant explains, "also has a moral value on its own account, since it contains a free affirmation." And as he continues,

> [Passage 10] It is necessary only in a moral sense, in order to add a supplement of the theory of possibility of that to which we are already ipso facto constrained, namely to strive for promotion of the highest good in the world [...] since the effect of assuming them [i.e. God, freedom and immortality], upon the subjective principles of morality and their reinforcement, and thus upon action and omission themselves, is again by intention of a moral kind. (*FM* 20:298 – 299)

This, along with the passages from the *KpV*, shows that the necessity of moral postulation is precisely of the same wide obligation as is found in a duty of virtue, with the only caveat being that whereas most courses of action that would satisfy such duties can be equally well replaced by others, there is no replacement for rational faith. This special feature of rational faith allows Kant to regard religion as a freely adopted way of attempting to pursue virtue and at the same time as something very close to a duty of narrow obligation.

§. 2.3.2. The Highest Good in the *KrV*

We are now in a position to understand a passage that has garnered a great deal of criticism from commentators. In the *KrV*, Kant writes,

> [Passage 11] It is necessary that our *entire course of life* be subordinated to moral maxims; but it would at the same time be impossible for this to happen if reason did not connect with the moral law, which is a mere idea, an efficient cause which determines for the conduct in accord with this law an outcome precisely corresponding to our highest ends [i.e. the highest good], whether in this life or in another. Thus without a God and a world that is now not visible to us but is hoped for, the majestic ideas of morality are, to be sure, objects of approbation and admiration but not incentives for resolve and realization, *because they would not fulfill the whole end that is natural for every rational being and determined a priori and necessarily through the very same pure reason*. (*KrV* A813/B841)

This passage is usually taken as direct evidence for the view that Kant, at least in this work, believes that happiness is required as part of the highest good in order to positively supplement the moral incentive. However, Kant actually only says in this passage that without the possibility of the highest good, and thus without the postulation of the existence of God and an invisible world, the moral law would not provide "incentives for resolve and realization." He does *not* say that by assuming their existence the moral law will gain an *additional* incentive from happiness itself, though this is how this passage must be glossed if we are to reach the conclusion that the introduction of happiness spoils the moral incentive. If my interpretation is correct, then what Kant is really saying here is that without postulating God and an invisible world, we will *by that very fact* remain within a rational view of the world where the goal of our practical reasoning is at least in principle the development of natural happiness. By the same fact, we would simply not be fully devoted to the cultivation of our moral dispositions. The whole of our practical reasoning, the maxim of which would consist in the development of a character directed to natural happiness, would thus constitute an insuperable hindrance to the full determination of the will by the moral law.

§. 2.3.3. The Highest Good in the *KU*

Kant is no less clear in his reformulation of the proof in the *KU*, where he says that "without it [i.e. the belief in God's existence] the moral way of thinking has no way to persevere in its collision with theoretical reason's demand for a proof" (*KU* 05:472) and stresses that God "is assumed only for the sake of the *practical use* of reason" (*KU* 05:471). In fact, in this text Kant comes very close to formulating the *dilemma practicum* discussed in §. 1.2.1., when he speaks of the case of someone like Spinoza, who would both be of good moral intentions but convinced that there is no God. But instead of introducing the principle of rational integrity, which I criticized in my discussion of Wood's argument, Kant writes:

> [Passage 12] The end, therefore, which this well-intentioned person had and should have before his eyes in his conformity to the moral law, he would certainly have to give up as impossible; or, if he would remain attached to the appeal of his moral inner vocation and *not weaken the respect* (*Achtung*), by which the moral law immediately influences him to obedience, by the nullity of the only idealistic final end that is adequate to its high demand (*which cannot occur without damage to the moral disposition*), then he must assume the existence of a moral author of the world, i.e., of God, from a practical point of view [...]. (*KU* 05:452–453)

This, I believe, is Kant's revision of the *ad absurdum practicum* described by Wood. As the italicized phrases make evident, in it Kant has manifestly replaced his earlier requirement of rational integrity with an emphasis on the direct impact such rational belief has on the moral incentive and so also on one's moral disposition. It furthermore makes clear that one cannot be genuinely motivated by the law without also believing in God, which is something that did not follow from the earlier formulation of the *absurdum practicum*. For Kant here clearly states that without belief in God the *respect (Achtung)* for the law is necessarily weakened. Kant's use of the technical term *Achtung* here is highly significant, for as we read in the *KpV*, "respect for the law is not the incentive to morality; instead it is morality itself subjectively considered as an incentive inasmuch as pure practical reason, by rejecting all the claims of self-love in opposition to its own, supplies authority to the law, which now alone has influence" (*KpV* 05:76). If consciousness of the moral law is what actually produces the feeling of respect in us, then the only way this can be squared with Kant's present claim that disbelief can weaken this respect, is if such disbelief actually creates obstacles to the moral incentive itself. Of course to do this, a worldview of which God is not a part must necessarily lead to the production of non-moral incentives to action, thereby hindering the development of a moral disposition.

§. 2.3.4. The Highest Good in *TP*

Finally, Kant's brief reformulation of the Dialectic's argument in the *TP* agrees with the present interpretation. In it he writes:

> [Passage 13] For without some end there can be no will, although, if it is a question only of lawful necessitation of actions one must abstract from any end and the law alone constitutes its determining ground. But not every end is moral (e. g. that of one's own happiness is not), but this must rather be an unselfish one; and the need for a final end assigned by pure reason and comprehending the whole of all ends under one principle (a world of the highest good and possible through our cooperation) is a need of an unselfish will *extending itself beyond observance of the formal law to the production of an object (the highest good)*. This is a special kind of determination of the will, namely through the idea of the whole of all ends, the basis of which is that *if* we stand in certain moral relations to things in the world *we must everywhere obey the moral law* [...] (*TP* 08:279)[29]

As the last sentence makes clear, the "basis" of our having to determine our will through the highest good (i.e. "the idea of the whole of all ends") is that *"we must everywhere obey the moral law."* But if we must obey this law everywhere and, of course, unselfishly, then it must in its concept rule over all our possible ends. Yet, as Kant points out here, not all our possible ends are moral. Conse-

---

29 Last emphasis added.

quently, our possibly non-moral ends must be incorporated in such a way that renders them no longer contrary to an unselfish moral disposition. As I argued earlier, this is done precisely by displacing happiness altogether from our immediate practical reflections, whereby it becomes a hope without any motivational role to play. Thus by taking the highest good as our object, which also means assuming its conditions of possibility, we go beyond the law not by adding to it, but rather by taking the additional "God-like" step of unselfishly subordinating the entire object of our conditioned-practical reason to the development of a will in conformity to the law.

Summary of the Argument of this Section

I have argued that: 1) The symbol of God as an omnipotent moral creator of the world and as divine law-giver is specifically constructed to be maximally conducive to the cultivation of virtue if held to be true by the moral agent. 2) Since faith in the existence of such a being helps to increase the moral incentive, and indirectly furthers the cultivation of virtue by removing obstacles to this increase, the act of freely affirming (postulating) God's existence is itself an act with moral significance. 3) Indeed it is one through which reason as a whole freely, that is to say autonomously, asserts the law of its own nature. 4) It is this subjective ground, which lies in the free self-determination to the cultivation of virtue in the single way that is most in accord with reason's own nature, which underpins Kant's argument for the postulates of pure practical reason. 5) Belief in God, according to Kant, is the immediate product or expression of reason's employment of all its own faculties in an optimal way for the active cultivation of virtue, i.e., the strength of one's moral character, and as such belongs under the duty to virtue described in the *MS*.

The present interpretation has four major advantages over its predecessors. Firstly, it is able to provide a consistent interpretation of passages in which Kant speaks of the postulates without hypothesizing a violent change in his central views. Secondly, it is able to account for Kant's description of belief as based upon subjective and moral grounds, in the strict sense of "moral" as concerning one's inner disposition towards the law. Thirdly, it is able to account for Kant's insistence that the argument proves the necessity of positive belief in God's existence. And fourthly, by exploiting the second and third of these points, it is able to show the deep unity of Kant's theoretical, moral and religious philosophy by articulating in detail how the necessity of religion in fact derives from the duty to virtue, when this duty is taken as the basis for adopting a theoretical world-view most conducive to virtue's development.

§. 3. Practical-Dogmatic Metaphysics

In the previous section I have focused on the postulate of God's existence, partly because I take it to be the chief of the postulates and partly because I believe that exhibiting its basic structure provides sufficient insight for my purposes into the general teleological structure by which Kant seeks to unify his theoretical, moral and religious philosophies. In this section, I want to briefly clarify this more general structure by a different line of attack.

It has been noted that in his moral and religious writings, Kant frequently makes use of an argument that can be described as "from ought to can" (in the following I will simply call it the "ought/can" argument). Kant first makes use of this kind of argument in order to draw what is perhaps the most basic connection within his entire moral philosophy, namely, that between consciousness of the moral law and the reality of transcendental freedom. Writes Kant: "He [the moral agent] judges, therefore that he can do something because he is aware that he ought to do it and cognizes freedom within him, which, without the law, would have remained unknown to him" (*KpV* 05:30). This quote reveals that the "ought/can" argument is first introduced simply as a way of expressing Kant's understanding of how the fact of reason leads to the assertion of transcendental freedom. As significant as this particular employment of the "ought/can" argument evidently is, it is also important to note that it nevertheless enjoys a quite limited scope. The argument in this case says only that when I stand in a moral context that requires a choice, the "ought" accompanying it reveals my freedom to choose rightly, and thus that I can choose rightly regardless of whatever degree of resistance I might encounter from my inclinations. Hence the argument here is in fact restricted to the level of individual choices governed by locally determined maxims, saying only that any state of self-consciousness that is accompanied by consciousness of an ought, can in principle be followed by an act that obeys this ought. Another important way in which this version of the argument is restricted is that Kant patently disclaims any attempt to provide a metaphysical theory about precisely how this move from a moral "ought" to a theoretical "can" would actually operate. Indeed, it is an important feature of Kant's moral standpoint that when it comes to individual moments of moral choice, it is necessary for strictly moral reasons that we cast off all such concerns for practicability, since these can only distract us from the moral features of the choice at hand.

In comparison with this, however, other subtler and much broader versions of the same argument play central roles in many of Kant's later works. For instance, on more than one occasion in Part One of the *RGV*, Kant makes recourse to a type of "ought/can" argument that is exemplified in statements such as the following: "If the moral law commands that we ought to be better human beings now, it inescapably follows that we must be capable of being better human beings" (*RGV* 06:51). Similarly, broad examples can be found in the *MS*, the concluding sections of the *KU*, the unpublished essay *FM*, and so forth. Above we saw that the moral proof of God's existence takes the same form: The moral law commands us to pursue the highest good, and so the highest good must be possible. What is distinctive about this and similar uses of the argument is that it is here broadened from its application merely to individual choices such that it applies to the entirety of one's choices as a whole, i.e. to one's entire moral life or to the entire object of one's moral life. For this reason, I will refer to this and similar versions of the argument as "global," as opposed to its "local" application, which latter regards only individual moral choices.

Now, one of the most significant things about these global versions of the argument is that, unlike the local case, Kant is quite willing to busy himself with untangling the metaphysical difficulties that arise when one asks how the move from ought to can may be thought of as a real possibility, i.e. how the supersensible above us (God), within us (the free will), around us (nature and the moral community), and after us (immortality) must be constituted for it to be thinkable that I can achieve that goodness of will that I know I ought to achieve. More than this, Kant actually claims that in the global case it is not only necessary to busy ourselves with working out these conditions of possibility, we must even postulate or judge *assertorically* that they obtain. All three of the postulates in the *KpV* have this form, and argue for the necessity of believing such conditions of possibility obtain, but there are still other examples of this in Kant's writings, as we will see in a moment.

The key question then is on what grounds Kant can say that such a postulation is necessary. Indeed one should wonder if it is even consistent for Kant to make this claim when he draws the exact *opposite* conclusion in regard to the local use of the same argument. Before turning to this thorny question, however, I want to characterize more precisely the conditions of possibility just mentioned in a way that shows their common source and interconnection. This, I hope, will take us part of the way to an answer.

At first blush, the conditions of the possibility Kant introduces to explain the various global versions of the "ought/can" argument seem to compose an unsystematic aggregate: We need immortality, he says, to understand how it is possible for a being that is imperfect at every moment of time to actually become perfect in the end. We need an intelligent and just God to explain how happiness can be exactly proportioned to virtue. We need grace to explain how it is possible for a will that is radically evil to be transformed into one that is entirely good. We need the idea of a universal ethical community, and the idea of God as its inner uniting father, for the possibility of overcoming the source of evil that springs necessarily from the very fact that we are in society with one another. In a similar vein, in *FM*, Kant says that we need the idea of "virtue as strength" for the possibility of overcoming the power of our natural inclinations. In the same text he also claims, quite importantly, that there must exist a metaphysics *covering all these conditions of possibility*, but most particularly the chief condition, namely the existence of God, because otherwise we, as self-reflective rational beings, would not be able to understand how the good, which it is our duty to work towards, can really be possible (*FM* 20:294). To mention just one final, though extremely intriguing example from the *MS*, Kant argues that even the capacity for having certain types of feelings (that is to say empirical states of my own self-consciousness such as respect, conscience, love of others, etc.) must be *presupposed* as existing in any rational agent as a condition of the possibility of its being receptive to the moral law.

Now the reason the list I just gave appears to be a rather loose collection, I think, is because each condition springs individually from a different limitation or imperfection that is accidentally to be found in the human being. But in Kant's mind they do in fact form a tight system, not because of their specific content, but because they collectively serve a single *function* and belong to a single but very important image of the way the world might be constituted. The function, which uniquely defines this group of conditions of possibility, and brings them into a systematic unity, is that they *as a whole* consist of the total theoretical image of a world, modeled at least in its sensible aspect on our own, that is precisely constituted such that the moral agent's holding of it to be the true image of the world would be most conducive to the cultivation of this agent's own virtue. In other words, they are all components of the theoretical world-image that is optimal for increasing the believer's strength in overcoming sensible incentives to transgress the moral law.

What I have here referred to as the "optimal image" is in fact what Kant refers to in the *FM* as "practico-dogmatic metaphysics." Regarding this doctrine, Kant writes:

> This ultimate purpose of pure practical reason is the highest good, so far as it is possible in the world, though it is to be sought not merely in what Nature can furnish, namely happiness (the greatest amount of pleasure); it lies, rather, in what is also the supreme requirement, or condition, under which alone reason can accord happiness to the rational world-being, namely that the latter's behavior should simultaneously conform to the utmost with the moral law. This object of reason [i.e. the highest good] is super-sensible; to progress toward it, as ultimate purpose, is duty; that there has to be a stage of metaphysics for this transition, and for progress therein, is therefore indubitable. Yet without any theory this is still impossible, for the ultimate purpose is not wholly within our power, and hence

> we must frame to ourselves a theoretical concept of the source from which it can spring. Such a theory cannot, however, be framed by what we cognize in objects, but at most by what we impute to them, since the object is super-sensible. Hence this theory will be framed only from a practico-dogmatic viewpoint, and will be able to assure to the idea of the ultimate purpose an objective reality sufficient only from this point of view. (*FM* 20:294)

Thus the optimal image, or the image of the world as framed in a practical-dogmatic metaphysics, is that of a world which, if taken as the image of the real world, would be most conducive to assuring that our conduct will "conform to the utmost with the moral law." The seemingly loose set of "ought/can" arguments is here drawn into a unity in the service of pursuing the highest good, because they all belong to the theoretical conditions of believing in its possibility, and this belief is most conducive to the actual pursuit of virtue. If this is correct, then our previous investigation of the moral proof of God's existence also suggests an answer as to how Kant can be consistent when denying we should explore the theoretical conditions of individual moral actions, while also arguing that we must do this in the global case. This is because both are conducive to the same goal, namely, to the pursuit of virtue; denial in the local case does this by preventing distraction from the moral features of the choice at hand, while postulation of the correct conditions in the global case allows us to bring reason – which is unavoidably concerned with the rationality of action – into line with the same moral vocation. Thus as Kant further describes such a metaphysics in this essay, it must include: 1) Belief in the autocracy of pure practical reason, i.e. "the power, in regard to its formal condition, namely morality, to attain this final purpose here in our earthly life … despite all the hindrances with which the influence of Nature may exert upon us as sensory beings." "This," Kant explains, "is the *belief in virtue*, as the principle *in us*, for attaining the highest good" (*FM* 20:295). In another passage of the essay, Kant describes this same belief as one in the fact that there exists "in the human soul a disposition which renders it capable of a never ending progression towards this" (*FM* 20:300). 2) Belief in God as the original and highest principle of good, and the creator of a world in agreement with this end. Again, later in the essay Kant seems to equate this belief, at least in part, with the belief that "there exists in the nature of the world an original, though incomprehensible, propensity to conform with moral purposiveness" (*FM* 20:300). 3) Belief in immortality, or the conditions required for the possibility of a never ending progress in our morality.

In this way, by means of rational belief, a moral teleology, which is inherently universal, is grafted onto the transcendental teleology underlying the possibility of the systematic unity of our theoretical cognitions. Practico-dogmatic metaphysics thus allows a person, "despite the obstacles placed in the path of such progress by the course of the world-as-appearance – to assume therein, as object-in-itself, a morally teleological connection, such that, by an ordering of Nature beyond his comprehension, it tends to the final purpose, as the super-sensible goal of his practical reason, namely the highest good" (*FM* 20:307).

Conclusion

My strategy in this chapter has been to highlight a side of the Kantian moral disposition that is often overlooked, namely, that it consists not only in the subordination of sensibility and inclination to our rational nature, but, more precisely, in the active subordination of our own nature as thinking beings (in the act of moral postulation) to our nature as moral ones. For a genuinely moral disposition, which consists in relating my *whole* self purposively to the law's command, also contains – *as an essential part* – my own active subordination of all my faculties, including theoretical reason, to the essentially *subjective* project of increasing the moral incentive. Thus in the act of asserting the existence of the objects of these ideas, reason asserts the focal point for all of its manifold activities, and in doing so does nothing else than self-consciously maintain its own lawfulness and unity in its dealings with the world. In a word, "the final end of our true being is delineated to our minds quite freely, and in virtue of the precept of our own reason, by a reverence for the moral law" (*KU* 05:481). The assumption of God's existence is required, from a moral point of view, because "virtue [...] contains a positive command to a human being, namely to bring all his capacities and inclinations under his (reason's) control and so to rule over himself" (*MS* 06:408). It is therefore not only compatible with, but indeed an essential expression of our autonomy.

This shows that the unity of reason is essentially grounded in morality, but it is not an analytical outcome of it. The moral law, through the very absoluteness of its command, and the teleology at the basis of moral self-consciousness, requires that we make every effort to cultivate our moral disposition. However, we are essentially reflective beings containing a complex of cognitive powers, and our knowledge of the world and of ourselves is limited by the specific constitution of our reason. Because of this, the teleological structure of theoretical cognition is not unrelated to the will, but rather expresses itself in the demands of conditioned-practical reason. For this reason, the only way that we can be entirely devoted to the cultivation of our morality is if some agreement can be reached such that the demands of theoretical reason are fully satisfied without, however, this interfering with the moral teleology demanded by pure practical reason. According to Kant, this agreement can only be reached through another reflective act of self-determination, namely the purposive activity through which we freely postulate a single object that simultaneously satisfies and combines the teleologies of theoretical and practical reason. Thus, at the conclusion of Kant's moral philosophy the first two teleologies come to be combined into a final teleology the object of which is the concept of a world maximally conducive to the cultivation of the moral incentive. And just as the purposive use of theoretical reason is furthered by our assumption of the transcendental idea of God in its regulative function, the purposive pursuit of morality is furthered by our assumption of God as the highest moral ground of absolutely all reality. It is through this assumption that all finite things, the inner reality and essence of which is constituted by the same God, can be thought to spontaneously agree with one another and with mankind's final end in a way exactly suited to the fulfillment of what morality demands.

Excursus: The Life of Reason

> If [... we] ask whether it is ever possible to attain such knowledge of the nature of the soul from experience – a knowledge sufficient to inform us of the manner in which the soul is present in the universe, how it is linked both to matter and to beings of its own sort – we shall then see whether *birth* (in the metaphysical sense), *life*, and *death* are matters we can ever hope to understand by means of reason. (*Br* 10:72)

> [T]he moral law reveals to me a life independent of animality and even of the whole sensible world, at least so far as this may be inferred from the purposive determination of my existence by this law, a determination not restricted to the conditions and boundaries of this life but reaching into the infinite. (*KpV* 05:162)

> By means of reason, the soul of man is endowed with a *spirit* (*mens*, *nous*), so that he may lead a life adapted, not merely to the mechanism of *nature* and its technico-practical laws, but also to the spontaneity of *freedom* and its morally-practical laws. This life-principle is not founded on concepts of the *sensible*, which collectively begin by presupposing *science*, i.e., theoretical knowledge (prior to any practical use of reason); it proceeds initially and at once from an Idea of the *super-sensible*, namely *freedom*, and from the morally categorical imperative of which the latter first informs us; and thereby forms the basis of a philosophy whose teaching is not, say (like mathematics), a good instrument (or tool for arbitrary purposes), and thus a mere means, but a doctrine which it *is in itself a duty* to make into a principle. (*VNAEF* 08:817)

Introduction

From his discussion of the paralogisms, it is clear that Kant thinks questions regarding the nature of the soul, the possibility of its possessing immanent and transeunt causality (i.e. inner activity and causality with regard to what is external to it), and of the possibility of the soul's living independently of the body, all naturally arise for human reason and constitute, as he says, the "proper goal of rational psychology" (*KrV* A384). Yet Kant also recognizes explicitly that, along with this science, the answers to any questions regarding the metaphysical concept of life surely surpass the essential limits of theoretical reason. Thus if we do not look beyond the first *Critique*, we might be justified in concluding, I think, that the metaphysical concept of life has no proper place in Kant's philosophy.

As it turns out, however, this concept, as well as other cognate concepts such as the "feeling of life" (*Lebensgefühl*), "enlivening" (*beleben*), "liveliness" (*lebendigkeit*), "vital force" (*Lebenskraft*), "health" (*Gesundheit*), and "strength" (*Stärke*) – all of these begin to play an increasingly significant role in the development of Kant's philosophy in works written after 1781. One need only think of the third *Critique's* characterization of the pleasure underlying aesthetic judgments regarding beauty as "a feeling of the promotion of life" (*Gefühl der Beför-*

derung des Lebens) (*KU* 05:244) or of the activity of the mental powers involved as an enlivening (*belebenden*), strengthening free play; of the sublime as that which "calls fourth our power" (*KU* 05:262), "reveals the consciousness of an unlimited faculty" (*KU* 05:259) in us, and gives rise to pleasure through the "momentary inhibition of the vital powers and the immediately following and all the more powerful outpouring of them" (*KU* 05:245). Alternatively, one can recall Kant's description of virtue in the *MS* as a vital power, and his reference to freedom as the life-principle in the human being (*MS* 08:417). As evidence for this development, one could equally adduce Kant's little essay *VNAEF*, where he claims not only that his critical philosophy alone is able to promote "nature's intention of continuously revitalizing [*Belebung*] him [man], and preventing the sleep of death," but also that the concept of freedom secured in his moral philosophy first reveals to us the hyperphysical basis of human life, literally its "life-principle" (*Lebensprincip*) (*VNAEF* 08:417).

These pieces of evidence are explicitly found in Kant's published critical writings. However, examination of Kant's *Nachlass* and the lecture notes taken by Kant's students, further deepens the impression that the concept of life played some sort of essential function in his thought, and indeed that it did so well before this became manifest in his published works. In fact, it is evident from these texts that Kant not only uses the concept of life in full consciousness, and seemingly with full confidence, but also that he exerted considerable effort in analyzing this concept and in trying to articulate its specific relationship to other parts of his philosophy, most particularly his moral and aesthetic doctrines.

Still, despite all these indications, it must surely be admitted that the interpreter of Kant's thought is still faced with the difficulty that in his published works Kant neither explains the interconnection of these various usages of the concept of life in terms of a single core concept, nor does he clearly indicate how his concept of life differs from those of his dogmatic predecessors in such a way as would make such a clearly *metaphysical* concept suitable for incorporation into his critical philosophy. We must also keep in mind that, as we will see more fully below, the concept of life as Kant understood it, and indeed as the entire tradition of which he is a part understood it, is that of a genuinely spontaneous *spiritual* activity, an activity of which bodily motion and organic structure are at best an *external* signs.

In this excursus I will argue that Kant's mature understanding of life is the fruit of the very same shift in method that led him from doubts regarding the possibility of metaphysics in his late pre-critical period, to his critical avowal that metaphysics can in fact attain its goal of being a perfect and dogmatic science if it is reconstructed on a practical foundation. Kant, I will argue, sees moral freedom, i.e. the absolute and perfect spontaneity belonging to the autonomous causality of the rational will, as the very *idea* of life itself. The objective reality of this idea, just as that of the idea of freedom, therefore has a strictly *practical* foundation. Its objective reality thus derives exclusively from its demonstrated ability in practice to facilitate the grip of morality upon us. Every other valid use Kant makes of the concept of life, therefore, must have at least two features if this interpretation is correct: 1) It must contain a specific limitation of the supreme reality contained in the specifically *moral* idea of life. In other words, the degree of life found in all other things must always be quantified as a limitation of the supreme degree of life found in the perfect spontaneity of the rational will. 2) The reality of any instance of life must be established by showing how it is grounded in the specifically *moral* idea of life. As will become clear in what follows, Kant extends the notion of life beyond the moral idea by means of analogy and postulation. But as I will also argue, the central and indeed constitutive use of this concept nevertheless applies exclusively to the freedom within the rational human being.

This topic is in itself extensive, and although a full and careful discussion of it belongs to any complete treatment of teleology in Kant's thought, it is beyond the scope of this work to do more than indicate the broad outlines of such a Kantian theory. I will thus explain what I take to be the key structures and considerations that would have to inform such a discussion, and instead of attempting to give a general overview of Kant's texts, I will attempt to treat in detail one particular instance, namely the pure aesthetic pleasure which Kant characterizes as a feeling of the furtherance of life.

§. 1. From Morality to Life: Three Conditions of the Possibility of the Realization of a Moral World

In Chapters 6 and 7 we saw two things. Firstly, we saw that from within the practical standpoint, the concept of freedom, as absolute spontaneity in the determination of our actions, is provided with objective reality. This means that within the practical standpoint there is warrant to regard our own nature, particularly insofar as this is expressed in choices and actions we see ourselves making in the empirical world, as the effect and expression of ourselves as absolutely self-determining beings. This, however, did not as yet allow us to extend such a supersensible principle to the *explanation* of nature in general; indeed freedom itself provided no ground for explaining even our own actions. Now, secondly, I also observed that in order to strengthen the moral incentive within us we were authorized, on Kant's view, to postulate the conditions both within us and outside us that are required to theoretically conceive (though not know!) the highest good as possible within the natural world. For if we do not do so, then by that very fact we will not have purposively related our *whole selves* to the service of the moral law.

I now would like to suggest more specifically that in regard to such conditions as must be found directly *in* nature there are basically three distinct kinds. The first kind consists of those conditions or predispositions *within our very nature as human beings* that are required for us to be susceptible to determination by the moral law. These consist firstly of "moral feeling, conscience, love of one's neighbor, and respect for oneself" (*MS* 06:399). These, as Kant says, "are natural predispositions of the mind for being affected by the concepts of duty, antecedent predispositions on the side of *feeling*." Such dispositions, Kant further informs us, are such that "anyone lacking them could have no duty to acquire them," since "it is by virtue of them that he can be put under obligation." Feeling is of course something empirical, but since these feelings in particular are supposed to consist really in the effect of the moral law on feeling itself, their source is nevertheless purely intelligible. It is important not to overlook the significance of this claim, for here Kant is manifestly asserting that we must presuppose on the side of our empirical nature this susceptibility to being affected by ourselves as something purely intelligible, and indeed we must do this precisely in order to make comprehensible our determinability by the law. These feelings thus manifest the effect of the intelligible upon our inner empirical nature. But not only this; since determinability by the law is at bottom autonomy, and thus consists fundamentally in the *self-determination* through the thought of the law, moral feeling must be understood as a species of *self-affection*, i.e. a causality in which the intelligible consciousness of the law affects the empirical consciousness within us. Moral feeling is thus at heart a *self-formative* causality, a causality in which the form of its product, though not the matter, is the unique effect of a cause acting purely by means of concepts. This single supreme act of pure self-determination by means of self-affection is thus an archetypal instance of living activity at work in the human breast.

Or put more precisely, even in a sense the matter here is to be made possible by the intelligible. This takes some explanation; for at first blush it seems evident that feelings are something empirical, since they appear in inner sense, and they would for this reason seem to be the material which is brought under the form required by moral feeling, and in this restrictive act it would seem that we produce within ourselves an empirical matter with a purposive form, a form that shows its own origin in something supersensible. However, if we focus more explicitly on what should most properly be called the matter of moral feeling, i.e. its object or what it is about, it seems that this characterization is not accurate. For moral feeling in general is not merely empirical feeling that is restricted by a principle of form. If it were this, after all, then moral feeling would not be something intrinsically different from pathological feeling, for it would be at most a limited or restricted example of pathological feeling itself. Rather, moral feeling, if it is to be genuinely moral, must be something intrinsically different from pathological feelings of any kind. In the *MS* Kant explains, however, that "feeling, whatever may arouse it, always belongs to the *order of nature*" (*MS* 06:377). Nevertheless, "pleasure that must precede one's observance of the law in conduct follows the *order of nature*; but pleasure that must be preceded by the law in order to be felt is in the *moral order*" (*MS* 06:378). Thus, while it is true that feeling of whatever kind appears empirically within us, this does not mean that all feeling has only the necessity and origin from natural causes. This means that the material of moral feeling, though given empirically, does not first appear as pathological feeling that is then subsequently restricted by consciousness of the law, but rather first originates and appears in a way that is inwardly and essentially dependent upon consciousness of the law for its very possibility. It is thus something given empirically, but its empirical manifestation is itself thought to be conditioned by an even higher non-empirical ground lying at its foundation. Thus the moral or purposive form of moral feeling is not imposed upon the matter, but rather the matter is essentially and intrinsically determined even in regard to its first possibility by the intellectual moral form. If there is thus to be genuine moral feeling, then pure moral consciousness does not operate upon feelings and arrange and limit them like an artisan, but rather gives rise to an empirical matter (feeling) that is inwardly infused with morally directed force. Pure moral consciousness expresses its *living activity* in moral feeling.

Also belonging to this first kind is what Kant calls virtue regarded as strength. If moral feeling and other similar susceptibilities are required on the part of our sensible nature for the *possibility* of our determining ourselves in accord with the law, then *actual* success and firmness in obeying the law presupposes, according to Kant, the possibility of cultivating an *actual state of strength* in opposition to our inclinations. The concept of virtue is precisely that of a strength of soul in the performance of our duties. However, although it is an internal principle of the soul, it still can only be measured by the strength of the obstacles it is able to overcome, and thus only through the *purposive form of its effects*. Now, surely, such a purposive form could be the result of our acting artificially in a way that outwardly looks moral, but which is based entirely on considerations of prudence, for instance. But in Kant's view this would be merely a case of legality, and not one of morality. For genuine moral virtue can only be displayed in acts which are first inwardly and essentially determined or made possible by the intention of obeying the moral law. By comparison one seeking merely to perform legal acts would resemble an artisan, or one who is attempting to restrict or limit his acts in external agreement with the law without fundamentally changing the mode of thought underlying them. Therefore, although all evidence of virtue is empirical, genuine evidence for morality is to be found only in those acts that are first animated and inwardly informed again by the consciousness of the law.

Such strength, of course, insofar as it is to be the effect of the exercise of our freedom and the strengthening of the moral incentive, is again a *power of life*; for it consists precisely in the determination of our sensible natures in accordance with the spontaneity of the free soul itself. In the following passage, Kant makes particularly clear how the *measure* of the strength of soul in general is to be understood:

> It is not only unnecessary but even improper to ask whether great *crimes* might not require more strength of soul than do great *virtues*. For by strength of soul we mean strength of resolution in a human being as a being endowed with freedom, hence his strength insofar as he is in control of himself (in his senses) and so in as state of *health* proper to a human being. But great crimes are paroxysms, the sight of which makes one whose soul is healthy shudder. The question would therefore come to something like this: whether a human being in a fit of madness could have more physical strength than when he is sane. This one can admit without attributing more strength of soul to him, if by soul is meant the vital principle of man in the free use of his powers; for, since the basis of great crimes is merely the force of inclinations that *weaken* reason, which proves no strength of soul, the above question would be tantamount to whether someone could show more strength during an attack of sickness than when he is healthy This can be straightaway denied, since health consist in the balance of all his bodily forces; and it is only by reference to this system that absolute health can be appraised. (*MS* 06:384)

This, as we will see further below, is a very important passage. For in it Kant is not only making a statement about virtue, but indeed about the most general principle of life in the human being. "The state of health proper to a human being," Kant here claims, must be determined by the balance of forces which is required for the *purposive function that is distinctive to the human being as a free being*. Furthermore, genuine strength of soul it seems must be measured not by the external violence or apparent liveliness of the act itself, but rather by its agreement with the system that defines the distinctive and maximal exercise of the vital principle within the human being. In this respect, vices may appear to consist often in great feats of strength, but as Kant explains here, if we take into account that the true strength of the human being lies essentially in its ability to control its sensible nature in accordance with its inner freedom, it turns out that only actions carried out for the sake of the moral law can really be regarded as expressions of strength. As violent and powerful as a crime may be, it is nevertheless a sign of weakness and of failure to assert one's own free self-determination. So while moral strength can only be measured by the strength of the obstacles it can overcome, it is not simply the overpowering of these obstacles that must be taken into consideration. The obstacles overcome must be ones *opposed* to the proper freedom of the human being and its inner law, and indeed to the *complete* vocation or destiny distinctive to this *form of life*.

For this same reason, Kant argues that violent acts in accordance with virtue are not genuinely acts of moral strength, because since they have the tendency often to exhaust and weaken our moral resolve in general, they are not truly purposive in view of our moral vocation *as a whole*. Virtue, therefore, as the acquired and cultivated capacity to act from the law in opposition to all forces is the general state of a genuinely *healthy* human being, or as Kant writes:

> The strength of virtue is a *tranquil mind* with a considered and firm resolution to put the law of virtue into practice. That is the state of *health* in the moral life, whereas an affect, even one aroused by the thought of *what is good*, is a momentary, sparkling phenomenon that leaves one exhausted. (*RGV* 06:409)

In the *Religion*, Kant mentions yet another extension of this first kind of life, namely that which consists in an ethical community unified under the laws of virtue. In such a community alone, Kant argues, is it possible to achieve such a state of health in the moral life. And, not surprisingly, the possibility of just such an ethical community rests on the possibility of an inward and living unity of the hearts of all members into a genuine whole, where the parts are for the sake of the whole and the whole for the sake of each part, and in which the moral life of each individual is supported and strengthened by such unity. Similarly in *Refl* 567, Kant writes:

> Everything increases or furthers the feeling of life that favors the activity of its powers; and this goes for the knowing as for the performative powers. The sufficiency of free choice is the complete life. The more it is in agreement with itself, the more is its choice, according to its nature, in agreement with the wills of others, and the more is it a ground of the unification of other's choice with our own: the more it agrees with the universal principle of life, the less its obstacles also, and the greater the influence on the relations and free choice of others. The free will, that at the same time unifies others with itself, possesses the greatest life.

The second kind of condition consists, unlike the former, in that which must be presupposed on the side of *external nature*, so that it is conceivable that the moral law can eventually come to have an effect in the empirical world. This external nature is not indeed that of physical matter, but rather that of the human being regarded externally, i. e. in regard to its actions and associations in the empirical world. It regards the dispositions of human beings in regard to civil society and international law. I will say no more of it here.

The conditions that belong to the third kind are of an entirely different nature than the former two, and will be the focus of the remainder of this excursus. These do not consist in what must be presupposed in order for the determination of nature through the moral law to be possible. They are postulated rather for the sake of our susceptibility to aesthetic feelings for the beautiful and the sublime in nature. These, as I will show below, are of a more complex nature than the aforementioned conditions because they cannot be directly derived from our moral determination itself. Both kinds of feeling indicate, but do not provide proof of, a moral disposition in the person experiencing them. As I will show in the case of the pure aesthetic feeling for the beautiful in particular, the formal structure according to which alone a genuine case of such feeling is possible is precisely analogous to moral feeling in several respects. This analogical structure in fact lies precisely in that such a feeling must be thought as inwardly conditioned by a universal form which alone can make it possible. Nevertheless, morality does not place on us any duty whatsoever to take pleasure in beautiful objects, and so also taking such pleasure is in no way a proof of our virtue. But like morality, there is a sense, as we will discover, in which others rightfully *demand* of us that we judge in accordance with the universal sense for beauty. For our very engagement in the culture of aesthetic judgment involves a commitment, and the very presumption to judge aesthetically rests its possibility on the idea of just such a common sense.

All of this is very interesting, but the key issue that connects the feeling for beauty with the feeling of life, as we will discover, is that the culture of beauty forms as it were a bridge from the pure requirements of the culture of knowledge (the principle of communicability) to the pure requirements of the culture of morality. The practice of judging beautiful objects is in a sense analogous to the practice in both of these domains. But crucially it is not strictly speaking required by either. It rather furthers and eases their development within us, although it arises from a basis that is all its own. In this respect it is just like those principles of teleological judgment which Kant says serve both theoretical and practical purposes, but are assumed by judgment for its own sake and thus independently of *determination* by either theoretical or practical reason. The concept of life made use of in this case, I will argue, is borrowed from the concept of moral life. Thus to the extent the powers furthered by the experience of beautiful objects create within us a purposive activity that by this analogy furthers the cultivation of our moral freedom, it can rightfully be called an instance of living activity.

I have run through all of these conditions only for the sake of completeness. What is really important is the red thread that runs through them all, that each presents us with a clear instance of life or vitality in Kant's philosophy and each contains an essential reference to the moral concept of life. Indeed, the degree of life found in each, as my discussion of pure aesthetic pleasure will suggest, is seen by Kant to increase to the very extent that the law manifest in them more fully approximates to the law of freedom itself, i.e. the moral law. In properly Kantian terminology, this means that the degree of life manifest here is dependent upon the extent or degree to which they *analogically* conform to the idea of moral life. For instance, since the standpoint of morality requires an autonomous and self-critical use of reason, and is based upon a universal and holistic point of view, these instances of life – Kant explicitly states – are more intense, more active, and more powerful to the very extent that they are more self-determining, autonomous, universal and holistic.

Let us turn now to the case of beauty.

§. 2. Pure Aesthetic Pleasure as a Feeling of Life

In the first section of the Analytic of the Aesthetic Power of Judgment Kant connects aesthetic judgment with the concept of life. He says, namely, that in an aesthetic judgment "the representation is related entirely to the subject, indeed to its feeling of life, under the name of the feeling of pleasure or displeasure, which grounds an entirely special faculty for discriminating and judging" (*KU* 05:204).

In the recent secondary literature this cryptic remark has aroused some degree of interest. John Zammito, for one, sees the feeling of life in this context as nothing less than an "awareness of our empirical freedom, our status as practically purposive in the world of sense" (Zammito 1992, p. 295). This conclusion is a natural outcome of his two central interpretive claims, namely: first, that life for Kant is "freedom of the will in its actuality," – and I should here note that Kant does indeed define life in the moral works in this way – and secondly, Zammito argues that the aesthetic feeling of life must therefore be a feeling or affective awareness of the furtherance or hindrance of our freedom in the empirical world.

Similarly, Rudolf Makkreel attributes a great deal of importance to Kant's references to life and liveliness in relation to aesthetic judgment, and to this passage in particular. His explanation of its significance, however, unfolds in an entirely different way than does Zammito's. The central difference lies in Makkreel's contention that the passage I have quoted signals the initial stage of an attempt on Kant's part to develop an entirely original concept of life, one that is essentially *aesthetic* and *constitutive*, and in relation to which Kant's definition of life in the moral works, namely, as the actuality of the faculty of desire, must be seen as a merely limited psychological definition (Makkreel 1990, p. 90). In fact, Makkreel makes the very bold claim that this aesthetic usage is the sole constitutive use of the concept of life, and furthermore that it is therefore "the basis for attributing organic life to nature" (Makkreel 1990, p. 93).

Now I have briefly introduced these two interpretations because they correspond to two very natural but opposed ways of interpreting Kant's notion of life in the context of aesthetic judgments regarding beauty. The first possibility, Zammito's, is to take as fundamental Kant's definition of life in terms of desire and to attempt to move almost immediately from this to pure aesthetic pleasure understood as a feeling of this very same life. However, in my view, this leaves two insoluble problems. The first arises when we recognize that freedom of the will – and indeed actual desire – cannot be involved in *disinterested* judgments on beauty, judgments that by their very nature abstract from all possible forms of willing. How then can pure aesthetic pleasure be a feeling of agreement with life, if life is identical with desiring? The second problem is more general. If life indeed consists in desire, how is the aesthetic feeling of life related to or distinguished from the feeling of respect, which is a feeling determined not by our actual desires but rather by what the moral law commands us *to* desire? Zammito's solution is to place these in opposition to one another by arguing that the feeling of life is based on actual desiring, while moral feeling or the feeling of spirit is a feeling of the authority of the law within the will. The difficulty with this solution is that Kant often explicitly refers to freedom as the principle of life, and speaks in numerous places of moral *Geistesgefühl* as a type of *Lebensgefühl*, namely as that of spiritual life.

The second route, Makkreel's, is to abandon such a strict interpretive scheme, and to search for a foundation of the relation between feeling and life within aesthetic judgment itself by locating there a constitutive use of this concept. However, in this case we immediately run into the problem that aesthetic judgments are not cognitive, and so cannot provide a foundation for a constitutive use of any concept, even if they are based upon a constitutive principle of judgment, as Kant admits. Since Kant precisely means by the constitutive use of a concept that use through which our cognition of an object is determined through said concept, I can see no foundation for such a claim. Rather, if there is indeed a ground within the analytic of the beautiful for using the concept of life constitutively, it seems evident that the principles of this application cannot be the same as those which make pure aesthetic judgments possible *a priori*. Consequently, these principles must be drawn either from those of theoretical or practical cognition, and only *subsequently applied* to the case of pure aesthetic judgment.

I will argue that these interpretations fail because they do justice neither to the historical richness and complexity of Kant's notion of life, nor to the critical dimension of the problem that underlies it. My central aim in the following is to gain, through a brief historical excursion, the conceptual core of an interpretation that can make sense of Kant's remarks on the concept of life, and yet can be understood according to authentically Kantian principles.

§. 2.1. Kant's Constitutive Concept of Life

To understand Kant's mature concept of life we must recall that despite all appearances, it is the outcome of a long evolution of ideas reaching back to the Ancients and that this hidden genealogy leads Kant to often employ the term in a very strict and idiosyncratic sense. Evidence of this idiosyncrasy can be found in Kant's considerable reservations about applying the concept even to such indisputably living beings as natural ends, or organisms. This occurs in an oft-cited passage where Kant claims that the causality involved in a natural end is indeed closer to an analogue of life than to one of art (*KU* 05:374). What is not usually mentioned, however, is that Kant denies that even this analogy is sufficient, concluding rather that: "Strictly speaking, the organization of nature is not analogous to any causality that we know" (*KU* 05:375). This is not because life can be used only as a regulative concept, as one commentator has suggested, but because life in its true sense, as self-determination through a faculty of desire, cannot be attributed to material nature at all without violating the basic metaphysical principles of natural science. Finally, conclusive evidence for this view is provided by the second fascicle of the *Opus postumum*. Here Kant explains,

> Because man is conscious of himself as a self-moving machine, without being able to further understand such a possibility, he can [...] introduce *a priori* organic-moving forces of bodies into the classification of moving bodies in general – although only indirectly, according to the analogy [...]. He [must], however, generalize the concept of vital force (*Lebenskraft*) and of the excitability of matter in his own self by the faculty of desire. (*OP* 21:213)

Notably, in the continuation of this passage Kant goes on to state that, nevertheless, only desires are *Lebenskräfte* in the true sense. From this it is clear that Kant's definition of life in terms of the faculty of desire is indeed really the central one, and not merely a narrow psychological definition.

I have said that this concept of life has Ancient sources. In fact, the idea that life consists most essentially in the absolute inner activity of an uncaused causality, that indeed this is the source and measure of all life itself, is found already in Plato, who divided all things into the self-moving and the moved, equating the former with soul and the latter with physical matter. It is a key feature of this Platonic tradition, even as it is found in Mendelssohn's philosophy, that not only is the body not essential to life, but that it is even a *hindrance* to it. Life is pure activity, and its engagement with body can at most interfere with such activity and bring it into a state of lethargy. Aristotle too, who otherwise gives a more positive function to matter (but understood only as potency for a *specific* activity) nevertheless holds that the activity of the unmoved mover is pure life.

In this tradition, and generally in the tradition of which Kant is a part, organic or purposive structures found within nature can never be direct proof of the presence of a living activity, but only external signs of it. This is why in Kant's pre-critical essay *TG*, he was fully willing to admit that we perceive organic beings within nature, but that nevertheless this is no proof of the presence of life in nature. Life, in that essay, met the same fate as the concept of a spirit precisely because life is the activity distinctive to an *immaterial* being. Thus if there are no immaterial beings, or if we have no grounds for assuming them to exist, then there is no foundation for thinking that anything found in nature might be alive, i.e. regulated or governed by the activity of an immaterial principle. Under the following heading I will look more specifically at the historical sources of Kant's own view of life.

§. 2.2. The Historical Roots of Kant's Concept of Life

To clarify the source of Kant's usage here, let us briefly sketch the historical background that leads him to this conception of life. In the following I will focus on the work of Christian August Crusius, because I believe that Crusius is the single most important influence on this aspect of Kant's work. As regards the proof of such influence, I restrict myself to the following observations. Firstly, in opposition to Leibniz and the Wolffians, Kant agrees broadly with Crusius' analysis of the ontological issues most relevant to the concept of life. Two such issues in particular are worth noting here. Firstly and most fundamentally, like Crusius, Kant disclaims Leibniz's (supposed) identification of substance with a living force of perception. The concept of substance, they both contend, is simply that of an absolute subject of all changes and accidents. As such, substance is neither a force, nor does it need possess only a single force; it is rather the substrate of a possible plurality of forces, while forces themselves are in fact merely relations between an underlying substance and its accidents. In a word, forces provide the sufficient reason or ground for changes in the states of substances, while substance provides the ground for the unity of many forces in one subject.

Secondly, this particular innovation issues immediately in an important criticism of Leibniz's understanding of the soul as a *substantial force* of representation, and of his contention that the other faculties of the human mind, namely, sensibility and desire, are derivative modifications of this single fundamental power. In Kant's view, again following the analysis of Crusius, this purely conceptual mistake leads Leibniz to his two most fundamental errors, namely, to the identification of the power of sensibility with that of confused concepts, and to his identification of desire with the faculty to change states of representation. In contrast, Kant's critical position is that since substance is never to be met with directly in experience, the heterogeneity of the effects of the mental powers requires that we consider them as basic and distinct to the extent that their effects cannot be comprehended empirically as the effects of a single principle. Indeed, Kant claims that if we consider the mind merely from its empirical side it forms a mere aggregate of powers, and not a true system of such (*EEKU* 20:206). This is clearly an anti-Wolffian idea that Kant shares with Crusius. In the following I will refer to it as the "plurality thesis" since it claims that a single and truly unitary being, for instance the human mind, may contain a plurality of distinct fundamental powers. The impact of this thesis on how life is to be understood will be addressed below.

For now let me just mention the second observation that suggests an influence by Crusius on Kant's conception of life. First of all, the majority of Kant's *Nachlass* that deals specifically with the concept of life stems from the late 1760s, around the same time that Kant composed *TG*, the very text in which he first expresses the concept of life that he will later employ in the critical period.[1] Now in this text Kant not only explicitly refers to Crusius, but he also employs the term *pneumatisch* to describe the laws that govern the beings of the spirit world, and this is most likely, although of course not necessarily, a reference to the chapter of Crusius' *Entwurf der notwendigen Vernunft-Wahrheiten* that deals with the attributes of spiritual beings. Thirdly, and most significantly, the very concept of life used throughout *TG* and later in the *MAN* is essentially the same as that expounded by Crusius in opposition to the similar Wolffian concept.

---

[1] *Refl* 3855 is the single significant note on life predating *TG*, but it contains a nearly perfect articulation of the position I am here claiming Kant still employed in the critical period. Unfortunately the translation of it in the Cambridge Edition contains several errors that obscure Kant's argument.

Let me develop this last point by briefly outlining Crusius' concept of life. In the sections of the *Entwurf* devoted to this, Crusius begins with a characterization of a non-living natural substance as one possessing a power that acts only with a determinate degree and according to a single direction (Crusius 1964, §. 458). By contrast, a living being is a substance that can be "active in many ways from an inner ground," and consequently it must be immaterial. Now Crusius argues further that in order for such a being to be possible it must first of all have an internal representation of the possible ways in which it might act, and so it must possess a power of representation. Moreover, it must also have power for determining itself to one particular course of action among the many that it represents to itself, and consequently, it must also have a will (Crusius 1964, §. 445). Notably, according to this argument the will is the ruling power (*herrschende Kraft*) that internally directs the other powers within a substance and is for this reason the seat of life within it (Crusius 1964, §. 454). Kant's complete agreement with this idea is recorded in his lectures on metaphysics, where he claims that the possession a faculty of desire, that is, the faculty to be a cause by means of representations, can be made into a definition of a living being (V-Met-L2/Pölitz 28:587).

From this point Crusius proceeds to outline the different types of living beings that are possible on this model (Crusius 1964, §. 468–470).[2] What interests us here is that Crusius' hierarchy depends on the grade of spontaneity belonging to the internal principle of life involved in each case. The first form of life is spontaneous merely in relation to the *external* form of nature, but is neither spontaneous with respect to the form of its own nature nor to the causal power that it must always borrow from external sources. This would be a sort of spiritual machine constructed according to the idea of a master craftsman. The second form is spontaneous both in relation to the outer form of nature, and, in certain circumstances, to the power of nature as well. This would be something like a spiritual machine with the addition of a limited capacity for self-motion. Thirdly, a being may possess perfect spontaneity, meaning that it is both the author of its own nature and is in possession of the causality to act through itself alone. Very importantly, this last capacity, according to Crusius, is precisely what we mean by the concept of freedom, which ought to be the ruling power within the will (Crusius 1964, §. 450–454). Clearly then, these correspond to three grades of liv-

---

[2] My account here is admittedly greatly simplified with a view to the following comparison with Kant. However, it is important to realize that a real gradation of living powers, even if it is not identical to Kant's, is simply not to be found in Wolff or Baumgarten, and presupposes intersubstantial causality.

ing activity, with freedom as the principle of the greatest and most perfect form of such activity.

Now compare these two reflections Kant penned respectively in the mid-1760s and the mid-1780s:

> Life is the faculty to begin a state (one's own or another) from an inner principle. The first is not a complete life, because that the alteration of which is possible, requires something external as cause. Bodies have indeed an inner principle to affect another (e.g. cohesion) and also to preserve an externally received state, but not to initiate one from themselves. Therefore, all change proves origination from a first beginning and thus also freedom. Because, however, the beginning can be comparatively the first, namely according to mechanical laws. E.g. if a dog smells a carcass, there begins in it a motion that was caused through the activation of desire, and not because it is generated according to mechanical laws by the smell. In animals, however, this is just as much an external necessitation as in a machine, and for this reason they are called spiritual automata. But in human beings the chain of determining causes is in every case cut, and because of this one distinguishes the immaterial as a principle of life from the material. In regard to human beings the spirit is free and wills the good; the animal is automaton. [...] (*Refl* 3855)

> If I think of a life in nature beyond material [...] mechanism, i.e., an activity of natural things in accordance with laws of the faculty of desire, there arises the concept of needs and of an organism. [...] The causality of this living being, i.e., the determination of its faculty of desire, is either autonomy or heteronomy; in the latter case there is always only a formal mechanism of nature in accordance with physical laws, [while] in the former there is a spontaneity in accordance with practical laws, and its nature is not determinable merely organically and physically, but also morally. To this extent these beings do not direct themselves merely [...] in accordance with a foreign and imprinted idea, but in accordance with their own idea, which can originate from themselves *a priori*, and their causality is freedom. Consequently the causality of nature is either natural mechanism or instinct or freedom. (*Refl* 5995)

In another note, Kant articulates a hierarchy of liveliness similar to the one found in Crusius, expressed however this time in terms of feeling: "The feeling of life in perception is great, but I feel an even greater life in an enlivening that is voluntary (*willkürlich*), and I feel the greatest *principle* of life in morality" (*Refl* 824; emphasis mine). Another note states simply: "The self-sufficiency belonging to free choice is the complete life (*das vollständige Leben*)" (*Refl* 567).

Finally, the essential connection between freedom, the moral law and deepest root of life in the human being is nowhere more clearly articulated by Kant than in the following passage from the second *Critique*. Kant begins the passage I am about to quote with a hypothetical. Suppose, he says, that human nature as well as the moral law remained essentially as they are now, but that we also had insight into the supersensible, and consequently that "*God and eternity with their awful majesty* would stand unceasingly *before our eyes*." At this point Kant continues:

> The spur to activity [...] would be promptly at hand and *external*, reason would have no need to work itself up so as to gather strength to resist the inclinations by a lively representation of the dignity of the law [...] human conduct would thus be changed into a mere mechanism in which, as in a puppet show, everything would *gesticulate* well but there would be *no life* in the figures. (*KpV* 05:147)

This shows quite beautifully, I think, that the constitutive use of life with regard to the human being is not only tied to and revealed to us through morality, but that it is also bound up with the specific way in which the moral law is a spur of our own internal and active pursuit of virtue in the natural world. Of course, we know such pure life is possible, only because the exercise of such life is an actual duty placed upon us by the moral idea itself.

Let us now return to Crusius one last time. In conjunction with the plurality thesis, the analysis given above leads Crusius to make a distinction that, as I will illustrate at the conclusion of this excursus, is absolutely indispensable for understanding Kant's use of the concepts of life and liveliness, which will be central to the interpretation that follows. This distinction is that between life (*das Leben*) in the substantive sense, and which can only be applied to substances with a faculty of desire, and the adjectival form "liveliness" (*Lebendigkeit*), which can also be attributed to individual powers in order to designate their heightened activity (Crusius 1964, §. 458). Notably, for Crusius a power can be designated as enlivened or lively even if its activity *conflicts* with the life of the substance to which it belongs, or even if it is a power belonging to a non-living substance. In this case, however, the apparent liveliness is not at bottom an expression of life, because it is not grounded in a living being or substance. The point here is that the plurality thesis makes it such that there is no immediate connection between a living power or a lively power and life in the substantive sense of the term. Importantly, this opens up a possibility that did not exist for Leibniz and Wolff, namely, that the liveliness of an individual power within a living being may be inconsistent with the substance's ability to determine itself according to will, and so may even be the cause of a decrease of life in the being as a whole. In terms of pleasure and pain, this means that there is no immediate connection between these and the furtherance or hindrance of life in the whole, although these may be associated directly with the increase or decrease of liveliness in the part.

Unsurprisingly, Kant himself expresses this very opinion in a series of notes, the most clear of which is the following: "All enlivening through spirit is deeply internal and increases life as a whole; all enlivening through the body enlivens only a part. [...] The furthered feeling of life in a part can perhaps subsequently be connected with a decrease of life in the whole. Although immediate feeling does indeed signal increased life" (*Refl* 570).[3] In *Refl* 943, Kant makes a similar observation regarding genius. He says, namely (my translation): "Because enlivening is sensible, genius always relates to the perfection of sensibility. But in this case genius is dependent on an idea. Yet something can also be merely the occasion of liveliness, without being a living principle, for example, mere images that bring the imagination into activity. The perception of genius alone enlivens us deeply and internally through sympathy."

So the question arises: when *is* liveliness in the part or of a single power also an expression of the life of the whole being to which it belongs? In the human being, as we have seen, the principle and measure of all life is to be found in freedom and morality respectively, the latter of which is the ultimate arbiter in deciding whether the enlivening in the part is indeed agreeable to, and hence an expression of, the spiritual life of the whole. From this it follows that the liveliness of the part is only an actual expression of life in a substantive sense, when it furthers the end in the world that morality sets for humanity in view of its ultimate spiritual vocation. Or to put it another way, the moral form that belongs essentially to the life of the human in a substantive sense, that is, to the normative structure of its faculty of desire, gives a rule in relation to which the actuality of any occurrence of liveliness in the parts can take place.

§. 2.3. Pure Aesthetic Pleasure as a Feeling of Life: How the Constitutive Concept of Life is Generalized to Include the Feeling of Beauty

With this set of questions in place, let us return to the passage in which Kant equates the pleasure in judgments of taste with a feeling of life. On the face of it, at least, this remark does not appear to call for extended interpretation since Kant routinely defines pleasure and displeasure respectively as feelings of the agreement or disagreement of an object with our life-force. In the *KpV*, for example, Kant just flatly states that "pleasure is the *representation of the agreement of an object or an action with the subjective conditions of life*" (*KpV* 05:8n). Put simply, then, pure aesthetic judgment involves feelings of pleasure and displeasure, and so it relates to life. That Kant accepts this connection with-

---

[3] Kant explicitly calls attention to this fact in his discussion of the strength of virtue. See the Remark, *MS* 06:384.

out argument is further supported by his claims in the *KpV* that this definition is simply borrowed from psychology.

But perhaps it will be fruitful to press Kant a bit on this point by following up on this reference to psychology. Now what sort of psychology does Kant have in mind here? This begins to puzzle as soon as one realizes that the relation of life to pleasure is not something that can be drawn from either empirical or rational psychology when these are isolated from one another. For as for the first, on Kant's own admission we are only aware of life *through* the feelings that come to us in interior sense, and this only insofar as our life-force is furthered or hindered by an external object. Clearly a single act of introspection cannot secure a connection between an empirical representation of interior sense, namely pleasure, and the pure rational concept of life. On the other hand, rational psychology also cannot be the source of our knowledge of this connection. For to use Kant's own description, the pure concept or judgment 'I think' is the "sole text of rational psychology," and so on principle this science excludes everything empirical including feeling.[4]

Obviously the difficulty in connecting feeling with life lies in this: that the former is an empirical and indeed a non-cognitive representation, the possibility of which we know only from experience, while the latter is a metaphysical concept, namely, that of the "faculty of a *substance* to determine itself to act from an *internal principle*" (*MAN* 04:544) and as such it falls essentially outside of the bounds of possible experience. To add to the difficulties surrounding this question, Kant demonstrates in the paralogisms chapter, that although the question "about the possibility of the community of the soul with an organic body, i.e., the animality and the state of the soul in the life of the human being" constitutes in part the "proper goal of rational psychology," this science is unable to validate this possibility, let alone prove the existence of such a causality (*KrV* A384). Life is then not only a metaphysical concept, but also a transcendent one for theoretical reason. What we are left with, then, are two interconnected puzzles: 1) On what basis can Kant assert that pure aesthetic feeling is a feeling of life in the rigorous metaphysical sense of the term? 2) Granting for the moment the truth of Kant's claim that we feel life only indirectly through its increase or decrease, on what basis can we discriminate between the two? Pain it seems, just as much as pleasure, can signal an increase in vitality and living activity. Pulling an infected tooth, for instance, certainly causes great pain, but it also evidently in-

---

[4] *KrV* A343/B401: "The least object of perception (e.g., pleasure or displeasure), which might be added to the general representation of self-consciousness, would at once transform rational psychology into an empirical psychology."

creases the vital power of the whole organism. Likewise, practicing virtue certainly checks our self-love and thereby causes palpable anguish, but on the other side it also builds within us the spiritual strength to persevere in our future moral conduct and opens us to an intellectual pleasure in the good.

How then is it possible to throw a bridge across these two heterogeneous domains, and to establish a *critically* acceptable connection between pure aesthetic feeling and life? If my analysis in previous sections has been accurate, then Kant can determine a systematic relation between sensibility and constitutive concept of life only through a psychology that presents the structure and unity of the mental powers based upon the order that they must be able to take up if self-determination through pure practical reason is to be possible. Hence the moral law and the actuality of freedom that it reveals would found an endpoint or goal toward which the powers of the mind, namely, cognition, feeling, and desire, must be able to orient themselves and in relation to which they must take up a systematic unity. Notably, this method is in agreement with Kant's notion of system, which is that of the ordering of parts according to and under an idea as end. And it is also confirmed by Kant's deduction of the moral incentive in the second *Critique*, where, I would like to remind the reader, he claims "here we have the first and perhaps the only case in which we can determine *a priori* from concepts [namely, the moral law] the relation of a cognition [...] to the feeling of pleasure and displeasure" (*KpV* 05:73). In this specific case alone, it seems, the dynamic unity of all the mental powers can be determined from the idea of a rationally self-determining faculty of desire.[5] Moreover, with this system in place, one could proceed regressively to an analysis, and perhaps even a postulation (though not a *derivation*) of the conditions of the actuality of such life in a natural being with our particular characteristics and capacities.

Let me now take a moment to briefly summarize the main points of my interpretation. Firstly, I have stressed that a constitutive concept of life is inherently metaphysical and transcendent for theoretical reason. Nevertheless, in Kant's work this metaphysical conception is instantiated and provided with reality from a practical point of view through his proof that pure reason is indeed practical.

---

5 According to the lecture notes, Kant had this to say about the connection between freedom and pleasure in the mid-1770s: "*Freedom* is the greatest degree of activity and of life. Animal life has no spontaneity. Now if I feel that something agrees with the highest degree of freedom, thus with the spiritual life, then that pleases me. This pleasure is intellectual pleasure. One has a satisfaction with it, without its gratifying one. Such intellectual pleasure is *only in morality*. But from where does morality get such a pleasure? All morality is the harmony of freedom with itself. [...] *Whatever harmonizes with freedom agrees with the whole of life. Whatever agrees with the whole of life, pleases*" (*V-Met/Pölitz* 28:251).

Defined as the spiritual life of freedom, then, this concept becomes the fixed point without which all talk about life would lack foundation and reality. Additionally, I have also argued that life *appears* always in the guise of liveliness (internally in inner sense, and externally in the formative powers of organisms), and that since this spontaneity is something inherently *partial* and *relative* to the whole, the recognition of it as a true expression of life requires that it be measured as such through its relation to freedom's fixed point. Still, despite this division of life into an absolute and a relative conception, the relationship between the latter and the former can be described as non-reductively teleological. That is, regardless of its material source, we recognize the appearance of liveliness as rooted in life itself through the way in which it contributes to the universal and harmonious functioning of the whole by virtue of its *form*, but not through any direct conceptual derivation of it from the moral law. On the other side, the moral law determines the whole of life as a singular and determinate unity through the form it requires of the empirically given and hence contingent set of capacities and faculties that belong to the human being. What stands in the middle of this non-reductive teleology is precisely the finite *given* human being as a *whole* with its infinite and essential potency for formal perfection (culture). As a consequence of this, the relative expression of life really has freedom as its principle as far as form is concerned, but with purposiveness as universal harmony providing the middle term between them. Furthermore, it remains consistent to say both, that the specific character of these expressions of life is not conceptually determinable *from* the moral law, or by the free will, and that these expressions, to the extent that they are *true*, must be fit to the furtherance of the freedom and the moral life of beings like ourselves.

Before concluding this excursus, I wish to venture a brief but precise statement of how life is involved in the Analytic of the Beautiful, and thereby provide an application of the conceptual framework I have been developing. Firstly, Kant's statement that pure aesthetic pleasure is a feeling of life can initially be only an empirically grounded and hence *hypothetical* generalization of the way in which interior sense usually relates to the activity of the mind and body. Notably, this leaves entirely undetermined what type of relationship, causal or otherwise, holds between pleasure and the liveliness in question, or whether this particular appearance of liveliness in the natural mechanism of the mind is actually an expression of life in the substantive sense, or rather an expression of momentary agitation or even a decrease in overall vitality.

Now in the case of beauty something more is possible because the pure aesthetic judgment "postulates," as Kant says, the universal communicability of such pleasure (*KU* 05:216–219). On this basis, Kant argues that such pleasure is only possible if it is grounded not only on the stimulation of the cognitive powers, but precisely on the stimulation of the mental powers to the free and subjective harmony that is required for cognition in general. Consequently, taste is the capacity to judge whether and to what extent the mental liveliness afforded by a particular sensible representation is in agreement with a universally valid cast of mind. This means that the liveliness associated with pure aesthetic pleasure is inherently consistent with the life of the whole, and thereby can be seen as inherently suited to the furtherance of life in the substantive sense.

If we apply this to the case of art we can see that genius truly is a principle of life, for Kant, and not only of liveliness (agitation), only because the material aspect of liveliness that it provides through the stimulation of our mental powers also has a form in agreement with and purposively related to a universal life of the mind understood in a substantive sense. What is particularly interesting about this special form of life, then, is that it consists in the formal and purposive subordination of a *natural activity* resting on *material* conditions to a *form* of life that is pleasurable and natural but yet is structurally the same as that which would result if morality were to determine its form from the top down, as it were. And this shows that the liveliness involved in pure aesthetic judgment is an external mark of a specific form of natural life (Kant calls it "humanity") that is structured according to a universal purposiveness just *as if* it were determined by morality, without however being so determined with regard to either form or content. Consequently, despite being actually grounded and structured in quite different ways, the life of taste and the life of morality *insofar as they relate sensibility purposively to a universal substrate of humanity as end* may mutually strengthen and play off of one another. And this, I believe, is the idea that underpins Kant's long series of apparent *non sequiturs* at the end of the Critique of Aesthetic Judgment, to wit, that taste is the faculty for judging the "sensible rendering of moral ideas," that genius is the natural capacity to render moral ideas sensible, and that "genuine taste" can "assume a determinate form" only through the "development of moral ideas and the cultivation of moral feeling" (*KU* 05:356).

Conclusion

In *Refl* 6862, penned probably between 1778 and 1789, Kant remarked that:

> Everything finally comes down to life; that which enlivens, or the feeling of the promotion of life, is agreeable. Life is unity; hence all taste has as its principle the unity of enlivening sensation. Freedom is the original life (*das ursprüngliche Leben*), and its coherence is the

condition of the reciprocal agreement of all life; hence that which promotes the feeling of universal life, or the feeling of the promotion of universal life, produces a satisfaction. Do we, however, take pleasure in the universal life? Universality makes all our feelings agree, although there is no special type of sensation of this universality. It is the form of *consensus*.[6]

Drawing upon the general structure of Kant's teleology, which we have uncovered in previous chapters, it is clear that this *consensus* of life consists not in a sort of a general collective agreement in the sense of a simple lack of conflict or an external arrangement, but rather in the sort of rich and universal harmony from an inner ground. The activity of freedom in accordance with the moral law is the archetype or idea of life itself; it is the only manner in which we can conceive an absolute spontaneity from concepts, which is just what life in the highest degree means. In regard to such an idea Kant notes,

> The idea is (exemplar, to which a cognition is related, unity of genesis) the unity of the concept as a principle of the determination of the manifold* in the intuition that corresponds to it. All parts are there for the sake of the others and all are there for the sake of each one, just as in an animal.
>
> * (They are not associated and collected together, but rather are generated through it. The spirit is wholly in the whole and wholly in every part.) (Refl 945)

"Just as in an animal," Kant says. The key difference is that an animal cannot be understood as genuinely alive in the supreme sense required by the idea, as the quotes above clearly indicate. For the animal has its pattern or idea given from without, while it is only in a free being that the spontaneity is one in which even the law has its source in the subject's *own* activity.

This idea of life, as we have furthermore seen, can be employed firstly in deriving certain dispositions within our own nature as this is required by morality itself and secondly can be extended by use of analogy. I did not say anything specific here about Kant's treatment of organisms, or natural ends, but these are in many ways parallel with the teleological structure we found in the case of pure aesthetic judgments. In both cases, the teleological character cannot be derived from the idea, but rather the idea provides a regulative pattern in analogy with which certain things in nature are cognized. Unlike the cases of moral feeling and virtue, the reflection guided by these general patterns must base itself on an actual experience of the structures found in nature. Reflection guided by such patterns then allows us to relate specific patterns in nature

---

6 Translation emended.

(found in pure aesthetic judgments and in organisms) with their basis in the supersensible. They can never be grafted onto the intelligible world, and seen in a determinate relation to it, but they indicate by their analogical structure the dependence on such a supersensible ground. Unlike the case of organisms, however, pure aesthetic judgments regarding beauty, because they purely concern the free use of our faculty of judgment and thus have not even the slightest pretense to objectivity, are able to rest on their own principle and found an independent and self-formative activity distinctive to the *human being* as such.

Chapter 8 The Teleological Unity of Reason and Kant's Idea of Philosophy

Nothing is more rarely the subject of philosophy than philosophy itself. (Schlegel 1971, p. 161)

What is Philosophy, as the Doctrine which, of all Sciences, Constitutes Man's Greatest Need? It is that which its name already indicates: the *Pursuit of Wisdom*. But wisdom is the concordance of the will to the *ultimate purpose* (the highest good); and since this, so far as it is attainable, is also a duty, and conversely, if it is a duty, must also be attainable, and since such a law of actions is called moral, it follows that wisdom for man will be nothing else but the inner principle of *willing* to obey moral laws, of whatever kind the *object* of this willing may be. (*VNAEF* 08:417–418)

According to this moral strength, as courage (*fortitudo moralis*), also constitutes the greatest and the only true honor that man can win in war and is, moreover, called wisdom in the strict sense, namely practical wisdom, since it makes the final end of his existence on earth its own end. (*MS* 06:405)

Introduction

In his criticisms of the Kantian philosophy, Hegel argued that the basis of its whole way of thought lies in an inconsistent teleology of human reason. To be sure, Hegel recognized that Kant had made great strides by showing that the system of reason is intrinsically teleological, and thus self-articulating and self-limiting, but he had also gone astray, in Hegel's view, through his restriction of this teleology to a merely subjective validity. For in addition to its intrinsic purposive unity, Kant had also interpreted the teleology of reason to be essentially involved in a *perpetual striving* toward a completion which could never in principle be realized within the limits set by the critical system. This, in Hegel's view, contradicted Kant's initial insight that metaphysics must be everything or nothing (see, e. g. *FM* 20:259), which genuinely underlies the speculative standpoint of the transcendental deduction, because it placed the ground and limit of reason, the very measure of its truth, in a transcendent realm. Thus the entire Kantian concept of philosophy, according to Hegel, proves its own falsity by holding up to itself a measure of truth and unity that, on its own principles, it can never equal.

Since Hegel's initial assessment, the issue has received attention in the writings of many scholars, the most notable being Klaus Düsing, Dieter Henrich, Klaus Konhardt, Bernd Dörflinger, Richard Velkley, Paul Guyer and Pauline Kleingeld. Richard Velkley in particular has noted that "the very heart of

Kant's philosophy is a new way of seeing reason as purposive or teleological, that is to say, as a source of an architectonic order of ends" (Velkley 2001, p. 155). All agree that the *unity of reason*, as Kant describes it, has something to do with its possessing a genuinely and intrinsically purposive structure, i.e. with its constituting a self-formative system the parts of which each have their own distinctive parts, functions and goals, and yet each of which nevertheless coalesces into a purposive whole under the legislation of pure reason. These writers also agree in sharing the somewhat unpopular view that, far from being an artificial imposition, Kant's teleological-systematic idea of reason is in fact the key to understanding the deep structure and purpose of the entire critical philosophy.

Hegel's criticisms, however, prove to be in a certain sense prescient in regard to these later investigations. For, although perhaps unwitting of their agreement with Hegel, many recent commentators have located in Kant just such a tension between two distinct teleological schemes, namely, between the intrinsic (teleological) unity required for the completeness – and therefore also the closure – of the critical system, and the never-to-be-completed ("zetetic") view of the activity of philosophizing that is one of its defining features. Just such a tension has been seen as infecting and threatening with internal inconsistency both Kant's understanding of the unity of reason and his general concept of philosophy.

The previous chapters of this work have sufficiently proven, I believe, that teleological issues do in fact inform the most basic structure of Kant's critical philosophy, and that they do so on an even deeper level than is usually supposed even by those who defend the central role of teleology in Kant's thought. In line with this deeper understanding, I want to achieve two goals in this final chapter. Firstly, I want bring more closely into focus the general character of the unity of reason as it has been articulated at least implicitly in previous chapters. In the first section of this chapter, I will therefore set about reconstructing Kant's broader views on the unity of reason, and I will defend the thesis that it does not suffer from the tension between a closed and an open structure as some commentators have suggested. Kant is not forced into making a choice between a constitutive (i.e. closed) or regulative (i.e. open) conception of this unity for the very reason that the system itself both requires and makes possible a double-standpoint on the unity of the system. Depending upon the vantage point one adopts, namely as either theoretical or practical, the unity of reason must respectively be regarded as either merely regulative or as actually constitutive. Having defended this result, I will pursue my second goal, which is to show that Kant presents us with a very powerful and well-articulated concept of philosophy, one that in fact incorporates within itself the dual nature of the unity of reason elucidated in section one.

§. 1. The Unity of Reason

My claim at the conclusion of Chapter 7 was that the unity of reason is secured in the act of moral postulation. Reason's unity is thus an activity of this very same reason in its free assumption of a theoretical world-view that is cut to fit its most essential moral vocation. Indeed, the very validity of this way of unifying reason rests on the fact, as we saw there, that only by means of it do the manifold faculties and functions within reason cohere and harmonize into an *absolutely purposive whole under its final practical end*. The question remains, however, as to what the precise status of this unity might be. Is it to be regarded as regulative or as constitutive? Is the unity of reason an open and progressive unity, which allows for innovation and possibly for a radical shift one day in our understanding of this unity, or is it rather a closed systematic whole finished for all times?

Before approaching such questions, it is important to say something about the locution "unity of reason" itself, since it has been used with varying meanings in the secondary literature, and since I will be using it in still another meaning in the pages that follow. In the main, it is used as a translation of the single word "*Vernunfteinheit*," which for Kant has at least three meanings, two of which stand parallel to the wider and narrower meaning he gives to the term "*Vernunft*." In the narrower meaning, the "unity of reason" refers strictly to the unity conferred upon representations by the higher faculty of reason through its employment of the transcendental ideas. In this sense, it is to be sharply distinguished from the unity of the understanding, which confers unity merely upon the manifold of *perceptions* by means of a concept: "The unity of reason is therefore not the unity of a possible experience, but is essentially different from that, which is the unity of understanding" (*KrV* A307/B363). Such unity, Kant explains, is "of an altogether different kind" from that of the understanding, which only unifies perceptions by bringing them under concepts, thereby generating rules (*KrV* A302/B359). Characterized positively, the unity of reason is said by Kant to consist in the systematic unity of all our cognitions (*KrV* B365 and A680/B708). The very narrowness of this definition is, however, a source of surprising breadth; for, since the unity of reason in this sense proves to have an entirely different source from that of the understanding, it need not, like the latter, be restricted to an empirical or theoretical employment alone. Or better, because of its own higher spontaneity, the unity of reason need not be restricted to serving the understanding, and indeed in the practical domain it actually turns out to command the use of the understanding. As we have seen, this separation from the understanding is precisely what allows Kant to reinterpret the unity of reason, and with it the transcendental ideas, as ultimately stemming from pure practical reason.

The second sense in which Kant speaks of the unity of reason is the same as the narrow sense above, except that it is explicitly restricted to the service of the understanding. Kant often refers to this as the unity of reason in its empirical use. In this sense, the unity of reason serves only to bring unity into and extend the use of the understanding, which is itself restricted to the conditions of sensibility. It is this unity of reason that underwrites the regulative use of the ideas, and the introduction of a teleological view of nature. In reference to this sense of the term, Kant claims:

> This unity of reason (*Vernunfteinheit*) always presupposes an idea, namely that of the form of a whole of cognition, which precedes the determinate cognitions of the parts and contains the conditions for determining *a priori* the place of each part and its relation to the others. Accordingly, this idea postulates (*postulirt*) *complete unity of the understanding's cognitions*, through which this cognition comes to be not merely a contingent aggregate but a system interconnected in accordance with necessary laws. One cannot properly say that this idea is the concept of an object, but only that of the thoroughgoing unity of these concepts, insofar as the idea *serves the understanding as a rule*. (*KrV* A645/B673; emphasis added)

In examining the Dialectic of the first *Critique*, I noted that one of its chief functions, in respect to the wider system of philosophy, is precisely to show that the unity of reason is not restricted to the material conditions implied by its service to the understanding, and thus to open up the distinction between the first sense of *"Vernunfteinheit"* and the present one.

In any case, it is clear that Kant's claim in this passage that "the unity of reason always presupposes an idea" holds for both of these senses of the term, and is by itself of considerable importance. Kant often speaks of the unity of reason as the unity of our cognitions insofar as this is achieved by the logical use of reason, that is to say, through the systematic integration of cognitions into one complete whole through the employment of syllogisms and prosyllogisms. But this unity itself, Kant remarks here, requires a principle of unity, called an "idea," which he literally says "postulates" the complete unity of this process. It postulates in other words the existence of some highest principles or laws from which the particular laws, which reason first encounters, can in principle be derived by means of a series of deductive arguments. The logical procedure of reason in other words, presupposes for the sake of its own justified use, a transcendental principle through which the manifold that it is to unify is thought as unified in itself through its being *internally derivative* from an underlying and absolute principle of unity, an idea. Now, in the practical domain, the unity of reason is not the indeterminate thought of a highest principle of this kind, but is rather an idea *given* in the moral law and the actual maxims of our conduct can in fact be *derived* with strict necessity from this highest principle through practical syllogisms. This we saw in Chapter 7.

The third way Kant uses the term "*Vernunfteinheit*," which accords with the wider sense of "*Vernunft*," is to describe the absolute or complete unity of reason as a whole, thus as comprising all our cognitive faculties under one end. Drawing attention to the fact that this unity is a kind of activity, Kant sometimes also refers to it as the "absolute unity of the use of reason" (*absoluten Einheit des Vernunftgebrauchs*) or, literally as "the unity of reason" (*die Einheit der Vernunft*), presumably because it has the primary function of unifying the theoretical and the practical employments of reason under a single principle (see *AA* 23:471–472; *KrV* B868 and *Refl* 5119). The chief text in which Kant speaks of this unity is in the famous final section of the analytic of the second *Critique*, where he suggests that "at some point" we might be able "to attain insight into the unity of the whole pure rational faculty (theoretical as well as practical) and to derive everything from one principle – the underlying need of human reason, which finds complete satisfaction only in a complete systematic unity of its cognitions" (*KpV* 05:91). Presumably, in view of what we saw with the previous two meanings, this unity of reason would presuppose an idea by means of which the unity of reason in the service of the understanding (theoretical) and the unity of reason commanding in the moral law (practical) are somehow brought into an overarching systematic unity of all possible cognitions of whatever kind (wisdom). As we saw in Chapter 7, this idea is precisely that of the highest good as the *bonum consummatum*.

It must be noted, furthermore, that all three of these senses of the unity of reason contain an interesting and notable ambiguity, since they can be taken to mean either reason's own unity, or, alternatively, the specific type of unity that reason confers upon cognitions given from another quarter. Kant actually uses all three senses of the term in both ways, although he never expressly states the difference. The reason for this ambiguity stems, it would seem, from Kant's conception of the structure of reason as an autonomous or self-legislating faculty. This makes it possible to view reason from two points of view, namely, as the *source* of its own unity, i.e., as legislator, and as a whole *governed by* the laws in which this same unity is expressed, i.e., as the subject of legislation. "Reason," in other words, "is the faculty of absolute unity in our cognitions" (*Refl* 4849), but it is also a faculty of principles – *in the plural* – each of which can be employed in several distinct areas and accordingly must obey a rule in order to harmonize with the others. So, not surprisingly, reason itself has the unity of reason, i.e., it is a system that is unified through its own underlying idea or law. Its autonomy is here expressed through its unique status of being essentially a self-unifying or self-formative and original faculty.

Finally, there is a fourth sense in which the phrase "unity of reason" may be employed, and this is the sense in which I will mainly be employing it. If the entire faculty of cognition, i.e., the whole complex of theoretical, practical and judgmental powers forms a unity of reason, and this unity, as Kant suggests, is *absolutely organic or purposive*, then it seems that there is a most basic sense in which the unity of *each individual faculty* can be described as containing within itself the unity of reason. For at least in the idea of an organism each part is to contain the form of the whole within itself, as the condition of its own possibility, and so as grounding its own essential unity: "An organic body is such that each of its individual parts contains the absolute unity of the principle of the existence and motion of all others in the whole" (*OP* 21:210). Indeed, it is precisely because all the parts exhibit such a common inner form that they are able to mutually strengthen and harmonize with one another, and also objectively with the form of the whole, thereby forming an inwardly or architectonically, rather than a merely technically, unified whole. The unity of reason, in other words, is just a transcendentally generalized version of the Principle of Coexistence, which Kant developed in the pre-critical period.

This fact is directly manifest in Kant's very definition of *science:*

> What we call science, whose schema contains the outline (*monogramma*) and the division of the whole into members [*Glieder*] in conformity with the idea, i.e., a priori, cannot arise technically, from the similarity of the manifold or the contingent use of cognition *in concreto* for all sorts of arbitrary external ends, but arises architectonically, for the sake of its affinity and its derivation from a single supreme inner end, which first makes possible the whole; such a science must be distinguished from all others with certainty and in accordance with principles. (*KrV* A833–834/B861–862)

Science, according to Kant, is thus nothing other than a system of cognitions into which has been brought the unity of reason. The cognitions within such a system are therefore related, as Kant claims here, not because they have been brought together for the sake of "arbitrary external ends" which one might achieve by means of them, but rather through their "derivation from a single supreme inner end, which first makes possible the whole." Cognition no doubt relates to certain particular cognitive ends (i.e. for the sake of knowing this or that object), but the kind of cognition that is called "science" is only that which is intrinsically purposive as an *absolute whole*. It is the idea of a whole of cognitions whose purposive form is both essential to the manifold of cognitions within it (by virtue of the fact that it is thought as the principle of their possibility), and which is manifest in a fitness of the manifold to the production of all possible particular cognitive ends. Kant originally arrived at this conception of system, as we saw in Chapter 1, through his investigations into the transcendental teleological structure of the cosmos, which he theorized to be the direct effect of the all-sufficiency of the divine nature. Here Kant has reinterpreted this same structure as the fundamental normative horizon which reason projects into any and all of the cognitions which arise originally and purely from within it. For this reason, Kant is able to recognize as "science," and presumably then also as containing the "unity of reason," those investigations contained in the subdivisions of his writings, e.g. the Transcendental Aesthetic and Analytic of the *KrV*, the Analytic of the Beautiful of the *KU*, and so on. And it is indeed true that Kant claims each of these constitutes a specific science to the extent that it rests on an inner supreme principle (end) which makes possible *as a real whole* a certain kind of cognition.

This fourth use of the locution "unity of reason" is thus already detectible in the common thread running throughout the three previous senses in which Kant speaks of the unity of reason. For complete systematic unity or the unity constitutive of *any science whatever* is nothing but the unity of reason through an idea, and each faculty composing reason, insofar as it is the object of a specific science (e.g. the "science of all principles of *a priori* sensibility") must as such exhibit the unity of reason. The unity of reason, then, should not on this reading be understood as a separate sort of unity belonging to a special compartmentalized faculty, but rather as the specific form of unity that belongs to the transcendental structure of the thinking subject as such. It should thus be understood as consisting in the form of the whole system of reason only because this whole itself develops or arises independently and autonomously from its own parts through the fact that its form is *iterated* in the composition and hierarchy of the parts themselves (Zöller 2001, p. 66). Here, it seems, the autonomy or self-formative structure of reason is actively displayed in transcendental reflection through the very analysis and synthesis through which reason (re)produces its very own structure from the smallest seeds of self-consciousness up to pure reason's highest practical goal. The unity of reason is thus contained in every sub-faculty of reason, and they are each thereby constituted in conformity with the essential *telos* of pure reason itself.

§. 1.1. The Unity of Reason: First Reconstruction

With these complexities in mind, I will now turn to the first stage of my reconstruction. As noted in Chapter 1, Kant's favorite image for describing the unity of reason is that of an organized body. Two passages in particular are worth recalling here. The first occurs in the introduction to the B-edition of the first *Critique*, and is clearly a reworking of a similar but less precise passage from the *Prolegomena*:

> [P]ure reason, so far as the principles of its knowledge are concerned, is a quite separate self-subsistent unity, in which, as in an organized body, every member exists for every other, and all for the sake of each, so that no principle can safely be taken in *any one* relation, unless it has been investigated in the *entirety* of its relations to the whole employment of pure reason. (*KrV* Bxxiii)[1]

This point is considerably amplified in the Architectonic of Pure Reason, where Kant speaks more generally about his conception of system. A system, he explains, is precisely an articulated (*gegliedert*) self-subsistent unity of the sort mentioned in the passage just quoted. It consists first of all in an *idea* of the whole, or, in other words, in an *a priori* concept which completely determines its internal structure, "not only the scope of its manifold content, but also the positions which the parts occupy relatively to one another" (*KrV* A832/B861).[2] This can be clarified by returning to a note I quoted back in the Excursus on life:

> The idea is (exemplar, to which a cognition is related, unity of genesis) the unity of the concept as a principle of the determination of the manifold* in the intuition that corresponds to it. All parts are there for the sake of the others and all are there for the sake of each one, just as in an animal.
>
> * (They are not associated and collected together, but rather are generated through it. The spirit is wholly in the whole and wholly in every part.) (*Relf* 945)

Just as I argued above, Kant sees the idea as a principle that brings a manifold into a whole precisely by being internally present to each part, which for him just means to be a real presupposition of their possibility. The parts are generated by and in accordance with its form, and in this way they, as it were, grow and fuse together into a genuine unity. Such a common origin is then manifest in that the parts reciprocally support and depend upon one another in their actual activities.

Yet the idea, by itself, is not yet the system of which it is the idea. The system is a whole of *actual content*, whereas the idea is merely the *a priori* form of such a *possible* system. Now, to construct an actual system there is further required a *schema*, or a mediating representation containing an "essential manifold and an order of its parts" (*KrV* A833/B861). But, again, this schema iteslf is still only the outline of a *possible system* or, better, of *the possibility of a system*, albeit one having the same unity represented in the idea. An actual system still requires an actual manifold of particular cognitions, and *the unity of such a mani-*

---

[1] I have chosen to follow Kemp Smith's translation here.
[2] Again, Kemp Smith's translation.

fold, insofar as its complete internal structure is determined *a priori* though an idea, is called an "end" (*Zweck*).³ The equivalence Kant posits here between an actual system determined by the idea and the concept of an end is, I believe, of fundamental importance for understanding the inner structure of his teleological conception of system. First, it reveals that idea and end in Kant's philosophy relate universally and precisely as do the *a priori* representation of an archetype, and the *a posteriori* reproduction of this same archetype in the medium of actual cognitions, i.e. the ectype in perfect agreement with it. In other words, the idea is the *a priori* representation of a possible perfect system, while the end is the concept of the very same system *embodied* in a whole consisting of an actual manifold of cognitions. Thus, the end is precisely that which, because of the legislative force of the idea, either *needs* to be (in the theoretical sense) or *ought* to be (in the practical sense) effected through the cooperation of the parts, while the idea is precisely the *representation of the form of this end* prior to and independent from its actual existence. Now as both idea and end are representations of absolute perfection (namely, as possible and actual respectively), they can never be fully *given*, but can only be objects we strive to realize.

Again, in view of the differing structures of theoretical and practical reason, one must more carefully distinguish between the relation of idea to end in these domains. In the theoretical respect, the idea can never be instantiated in our thinking, and thus can never be fully represented, because it prescribes an absolute unity of intuitions, while intuitions for us are always determined progressively in actual acts of judgment. In the practical respect, however, the idea is afforded objective and determinate practical reality, and serves as a principle from which unity is deductively specified (as discussed in Chapters 6 and 7 above). Yet, although this reality of a moral world is given by pure practical reason, it remains an object valid merely for practical employment, and so is not afforded theoretically determined content. The latter always requires among other things, the existence of corresponding intuitions, to guarantee the objective reality of its cognition. Thus, the moral idea is constitutive for moral *practice*, but the same idea can at most be regulative for speculative purposes.

The second passage, this time from the *KpV*, clearly shows that there exists an *essential* relationship, in Kant's mind, between the purposive structure of reason and the method of transcendental criticism:

> When it is a matter of determining a particular faculty of the human soul as to its sources (*Quellen*), its contents (*Inhalte*), and its limits (*Grenzen*), then, from the nature of human

---

3 See also *KU* 05:373: "For the thing is an end, and is thus comprehended under a concept or an idea that must determine *a priori* everything that is to be contained in it."

cognition, one can begin only with the parts, with an accurate and complete presentation of them (complete as far as is possible in the present situation of such elements as we have already acquired). But there is a second thing to be attended to, which is more philosophic and *architectonic:* namely, to grasp correctly the idea of the whole and from this idea to see all those parts in their mutual relation by means of their derivation from the concept of that whole in a pure rational faculty. This examination and guarantee (*Gewährleistung*) is possible only through the most intimate acquaintance with the system; and those who find the first inquiry too irksome and hence do not think it worth their trouble to attain such an acquaintance cannot reach the second stage, namely the overview, which is a synthetic return to what had previously been given analytically; and it is no wonder that they find inconsistencies everywhere, although the gaps they suppose they find are not in the system itself but only in their own incoherent train of thought. (*KpV* 05:10)

It is very easy to mistake the sense of this passage, I believe, and to think that it in fact speaks against, rather than for, a close connection between system and method. For is Kant not claiming here that the collection and analysis of the parts, "complete as far as is possible in the present situation," is merely preparation for the later and genuinely philosophical task of deriving the parts in their relation from the concept of a pure rational faculty? If so, then a significant part of the critical method, namely that having to do with the analysis and enumeration of the parts of a faculty, would be a quite *external* and *accidental* means to the discovery of a system that exits independently of it. In other words, the analytical part of the method would necessarily precede the synthetic return only because of an accident of our nature, namely the imperfection or finitude (i.e. receptivity) of our knowledge, and thus would in no way figure in determining the actual content and structure of the system which we discover by means of it.

This interpretation, however, can be set aside definitively by attending to Kant's actual wording of the passage and by attending to what he says elsewhere concerning the relation between method and system. Method, Kant explains in the *Logic*, is a rule the observance of which converts a mere aggregate of cognitions into a system (*Log* 09:139). But when we are dealing with a pure rational science, as in the critique of an *a priori* faculty of thought, then the individual cognitions contain no character or content aside from their determinate location within the system. System or science, in this case, is then nothing but cognition *first generated* through the observance of a method, and thus the connections within the system are in fact nothing but the rules of method that have been reflected upon and represented objectively to oneself. The critical method, in other words, is the self-constitution or self-justification of reason's own *original* procedure, and its immanent and consistent self-development and self-limitation is the only measure of its truth. This can be seen simply from a comparison of Kant's definition of method with the function of an idea: Method is a rule which when observed converts an aggregate into a system. An Idea, however, is the rational principle by means of which alone an aggregate can be conceived of as internally unified in the way required for a system. *Method, which is the practice of science, will only be true or genuine when it is guided by the idea underlying the unity of the object it allows us to cognize.*

With this conception of method in mind, it is now possible to detect the nuances of the view Kant expresses in the passage above. The analytic procedure as Kant describes it must not be conceived as accidental or as external to the synthetic return, since its indispensability stems "from the nature of human cognition" itself, and as such it must form a part or moment of any system that articulates the essential structure of *human* reason. That is to say, the need for an analytical point of departure must become comprehensible as necessary through the architectonic grasping of the sources, contents and limits of the cognitive faculty as a whole. It is only with this in mind that one can explain the circular claim that the architectonic must be able "to grasp correctly the idea of the whole" and "from this idea to see all those parts in their mutual relation by means of their derivation from the concept of that whole in a pure rational faculty." Indeed, if the analysis is not carried out in accordance with the idea, then how can it be anything but a merely arbitrary division? And if this analysis is guided by the idea of the whole, then what need is there to derive the relations of the parts from such an idea? The circularity here, we can now clearly see, is not vicious but virtuous. The analytical division gains its guarantee (*Gewährleistung*) from the fact that it leads to a complete and determinate idea of a whole which *proves itself to be complete through the very harmony, purposive unity, and perfection that follows from making just such a division*, and in which all parts are seen as maximally cooperating for the sake of the pure cognitive faculty in question. Moreover, the test of this guarantee lies precisely in that:

> the unity of the end, to which all the parts are related and in the idea of which they are also related to each other, allows the absence of any part to be noticed in our knowledge of the rest, and there can be no contingent addition or undetermined magnitude of perfection that does not have its boundaries determined *a priori*. (*KrV* A832/B860)

In a word, this guarantee is provided by our ability to derive any one of the parts discovered in the analysis from the idea of the whole when this is compared to all the other parts discovered in analysis. This is why such a guarantee "is possible only through the most intimate acquaintance with the system."

But still, admitting that the internal circle is virtuous in the sense that the method of analysis must be guided by the idea, and the idea must become manifest and active in the process of analysis, one might still wonder how it is possible to break into this circle in the first place. How, in other words, can the correct method be first discovered if the guiding idea only becomes manifest once we have already found the proper method? Kant is entirely aware of this issue, but rather than seeing it as a serious problem, he interprets it as evidence for the self-sufficient character of human reason. The system in question is the essential system of our very own reason, after all, and so it is always operative even if not always properly employed or understood. Moreover, the absence of a proper employment will automatically make itself known from the overall weakening and disharmony that will result within reason. Kant takes the closed circle of method and idea to be an unavoidable and appropriate feature of all scientific thought. No one can, as he admits, arbitrarily create a science; its basic idea must rather be hit upon "as if" by accident. The systematic or purposive structure of science is that of a self-sufficient whole; it cannot be justified or arrived at from anything external to the system itself. But once the basic idea has been recognized, then the method and along with it the entire science develops and articulates itself necessarily as if from a seed. This is presumably what Kant means when he says that in reason "nothing here can escape us, because what reason brings forth entirely out of itself cannot be hidden, but is brought to light as soon as reason's common principle has been discovered" (*KrV* Axx). "Reason's common principle," which Kant mentions here, is in fact nothing but the idea of the unity of reason itself.

It is now evident why the guarantee that a correct analysis of reason has taken place is not a mathematical deduction, but rather consists in the ability to deductively return from the idea to that very same whole that was first arrived at by means of analysis. For the manifold reached through analysis has an essential *cognitive priority* over the idea that it leads us to discover because only in this *activity of analysis* does the legislative power of the idea make itself manifest or operative; it is not available to us apart from the activity of analysis it inwardly governs. Yet, nevertheless, it is equally true to say that this same *idea* possesses its own unique kind of priority, a priority through its justification of the analysis, in that it allows us to grasp the inner unity of all the parts through a form that precedes each taken individually as that through which alone they constitute members of a perfect or complete whole. The virtuous circle here is exactly the same as the one contained in that concept of an intrinsically teleological being; it is what God's creation would be if the pre-critical position were not ultimately faulty, and what a natural end would be if it were not intrinsically limited by the mechanism that makes it possible.

To use Kant's own term, the natural end might well be called a *monogram* of the unity of reason; for in a natural end the characteristic marks of such unity are combined and thought as existing in a natural object external to reason.[4] This, of course, leads to the incomprehensibility of a natural end, since only reason in its complete autonomy, as both speculatively architectonic and morally archityponic (if I may coin the word), is known to be both cause and effect of itself. For unlike the natural end, which has to do with the concept of a being possible only through the idea, but also actualized in the medium of mechanical causality, reason has to do only with itself, and here its own concept of freedom, revealed through the moral law, guarantees that the mechanical conditions of its activity are mere appearances, that indeed they all belong to a character which reason gives entirely to itself as absolute spontaneity.[5] We can certainly think the possibility of a natural end, but we can have no guarantee of its objective reality. Pure reason as an end in itself, by contrast, is not only conceived by us as possible, but *is given in its actuality* to us. For, as Kant explains,

> There is even one idea of reason (which is in itself incapable of any presentation in intuition, thus incapable of theoretical proof of its possibility) among the facts, and that is the idea of *freedom* the reality of which, as a particular kind of causality (the concept of which would be excessive from a theoretical point of view) can be established through practical laws of pure reason, and, in accordance with these, in actual actions, and thus in experience. – It is the only one among all the ideas of pure reason whose object is a fact and which must be counted among the *scibilia*. (*KU* 05:468)[6]

In view of the forgoing analysis, we are now in a position to see precisely how the practical knowledge of the reality of freedom provides, according to Kant, the keystone to the teleological-systematic unity of reason. For if the prac-

---

[4] For Kant's use of the term "monogram," which admittedly is not very consistent, see *KrV* B181, A570/B598, and A833–834/B861–862. Schelling also refers to the natural end as a monogram of the original identity of reason. See F. W. J. Schelling, *System of Transcendental Idealism* (1800), p. 218. Notice, however, that this unity for Kant, contrary to Schelling, is *not* the expression of the original identity of the conscious and the unconscious activity of the self. Nevertheless, for both Kant and Schelling the natural end is not properly speaking a schema or presentation of the unity of reason itself, but only a symbol of it, which is clear from the fact that strictly speaking a natural end is incomprehensible.

[5] See *KpV* 05:98: "So considered, a rational being can now rightly say of every unlawful action he performed that he could have omitted it even though as appearance it is sufficiently determined in the past and, so far, is inevitably necessary; for this action, with all the past which determines it, belongs to a single phenomenon of his character which he gives to himself and in accordance with which he imputes to himself, as a cause independent of all sensibility, the causality of those appearances."

[6] I have changed "in real actions" to read "in actual actions" to keep the distinction, which I think is important, between *Realität* and *Wirklichkeit*.

tical idea is revealed as something actual, and thus as a cause through itself alone, then in this case and this case alone the distinction I previously noted between *idea* and *end* entirely falls away. Freedom as idea is, for practical self-consciousness, a reality that is concrete and actual in itself, and as such is to be regarded as the preceding real ground of any possible act of the self. If there is something self-sufficient, and quasi-divine within the human being, then it is not the theoretical idea, but rather the practical idea of freedom as absolutely unconditioned causality. The theoretical self, by contrast, always requires some material given from without in order to stimulate it to activity, whereas pure practical reason is an activity that manifests itself absolutely and in its purity from all external stimuli. In the practical field, the whole issue of the circularity in the relation between method and idea thus becomes almost trivial, since the power and activity of the idea in this case requires no previous and dependent act of analysis in order to become manifest in consciousness. When we engage in theoretical or speculative enterprises we can, for this reason, long remain in error, and the guiding principle of reason in this employment is easily mistaken; but when it comes to the moral employment, Kant claims that the correct moral principles separate themselves out as if spontaneously and without any lack of clarity or need for effort on our part, just as "when an analyst adds alkali to a solution of calcareous earth in hydrochloric acid, the acid at once releases the lime and unites with the alkali, and the lime is precipitated" (*KpV* 05:92).

To take stock of what we have seen to this point, Kant's work contains three distinct but closely related teleological systems. The teleological system underlying what Kant calls transcendental philosophy consists in the grasping of the entire structure of the faculty of pure reason through the *idea* of just such a pure rational faculty. Moreover, this idea is essentially that of a faculty which actualizes the idea itself, and thus constitutes itself as an end in this respect, through the very *activity* of self-reflective analysis. Such an analysis is the genesis of the transcendental science, and just like the individual members themselves, this act of analysis proves itself to belong to the system through the very fact of its success. In the process of this, pure reason unfolds the entire necessary structure of all possible knowledge, including the structure of the transcendental ideas themselves.

The second teleological system is that of pure practical reason, and it distinguishes itself precisely through the fact that it does not require such a preliminary analysis. It is in fact *self-analyzing or self-purifying*. The moral law manifests itself here immediately within consciousness by the force of its absolute demand, and requires no long period of development throughout history, or any collection of its specific acts which is always required by the analytical procedure. Pure practical reason rather is self-activating, self-articulating and genuinely self-producing in the highest sense. By virtue of this fact, pure practical reason is able to authenticate and justify the use of all the higher ideas of pure reason, and to employ them for the sake of fulfilling its own teleological determination.

The third teleological system is that by means of which the ideas are to be brought into connection with the *particular* in experience. This is the proper focus of the *KU*, which I in part analyzed back in the Excursus. What is unique about this teleological structure is that it consists in the combination of an *a priori* determination of the supersensible with certain phenomena discovered within nature *a posteriori*. This combination is carried out by means of an analogy between the form of these natural phenomena, which indicates a supersensible ground, and the actual determination of this supersensible ground through pure practical reason. What is key here is that this consists in a teleological mediation between the transcendental teleology of theoretical reason and the moral teleology of pure practical reason. And thus in regard to this third teleological structure, there must be something answering to the demands of both. The demands of theoretical reason are satisfied by the *a posteriori* component, which requires that for natural teleology we must be able to find actual physical objects possessing such a uniquely purposive structure. And the demands of pure practical reason are satisfied by the fact that the form of this physical structure must be purposive for pure practical reason itself. Indeed, this purposiveness is the basis of the analogy between the two. In the previous chapters, I have said less about this structure only because it is in a certain sense merely a special case of theoretical teleology, and because it remains limited by the fact there is no way to genuinely unite, according to transcendental principles, the theoretical and the practical directly in the empirical. The true unity of these two realms, I have argued, is secured *transcendentally* through the act of moral postulation.

§. 1.2. Regulative and Constitutive Principles

But is it not still the case that the end of pure practical reason is something we are eternally destined to strive after, but never to fully achieve? Is it not the case that freedom, as Kant repeatedly describes it, is in exactly the same position as theoretical reason, and of the latter's concept of a natural end, i.e. that it has to reproduce itself in the external medium of empirically given actions, and thus first and foremost submit to the conditions of nature? Because of this, must we not restrict the idea of freedom to a merely *regulative* use?

§. 1. The Unity of Reason — 375

Given that Kant understands reason as a whole to be nothing but pure practical reason in its fullest application, his answer to these questions must be negative. For this view of a freedom as that which is never actually given in experience attaches not to pure practical reason, but only to reason insofar as it seeks to *theoretically conceive the possibility of such freedom from the evidence of the senses*. By virtue of the fact of freedom, then, the concept of intrinsic teleological perfection *serves indeed as both a regulative and a constitutive concept of the unity of reason*. The importance of this point cannot be overestimated. The idea of freedom and the postulates that follow from it are *constitutive* of and for the unity of reason as a practical faculty, and for this reason, they are *also necessary regulative concepts* for our cognition of a nature in which freedom is supposed to operate. Kant expresses precisely this point in a number of key passages:

> In [the practical capacity the ideas of pure reason] become *immanent* and *constitutive* inasmuch as they are grounds of the possibility of making real the necessary object of pure practical reason (the highest good), whereas apart from this they are transcendent and merely regulative principles of speculative reason, which do not require it to assume a new object beyond experience but only to bring its use in experience nearer to completeness. (*KpV* 05:135)

> Thus it was strictly speaking the *understanding*, which has its proper domain indeed in the *faculty of cognition*, insofar as it contains constitutive principles of cognition *a priori* [...] In just the same way reason, which contains constitutive principles *a priori* nowhere except strictly with regard to the *faculty of desire* ... (*KU* 05:168)

> Hence the moral judgment is not only capable of determinate constitutive principles, but is also possible *only* by means of the grounding of its maxims on these principles and their universality. (*KU* 05:354)

> Pure reason, as a practical faculty, i.e., as a faculty for determining the free use of our causality by means of ideas (pure concepts of reason), not only contains a regulative principle for our actions in the moral law, but at the same time also thereby provides a subjectively constitutive one, in the concept of an object that only reason can think and which is to be made actual by means of our actions in the world in accordance with that concept. The idea of a final end in the use of freedom in accordance with moral laws thus has subjectively *practical* reality. (*KU* 05:453)

> But when it comes to the practical sphere, such a regulative principle [...] namely, to act in conformity with something, as an end, which given the constitution of our cognitive faculties can only be conceived by us as possible in a certain way – is at the same time *constitutive*, i.e., practically determining; whereas the very same thing which is by no means theoretically determining as a principle for judging the objective possibility of things [...] is rather a merely *regulative* principle for the reflecting power of judgment. (*KU* 05:457–458)

In view of these passages, it is clearly impossible to agree with Susan Neiman that what unifies Kant's notion of philosophy is precisely the fact that reason in all its domains, and thus as a whole, is *merely* regulative. Kant denies this not once, but on many occasions, and in at least three different areas, namely, in regard to understanding and reason, as is clear from above, as well as in regard to reflective judgment, which he says is constitutive for the feeling of pleasure and displeasure. Neiman is certainly correct to say that reason, in the sense of the higher faculty of cognition, is never *theoretically* constitutive, and thus that the theoretical essence of freedom remains forever beyond the bounds of knowledge. But this is the least interesting half of the story, and certainly provides no foundation for characterizing the *entire* structure of reason, the true vocation of which is in fact practical.

One might still wonder, of course, how precisely one is to understand the notion of a principle's being *subjectively* or *practically* constitutive. Perhaps, after all, Kant is saying nothing else than that freedom and the moral law are practically constitutive in the sense that actual maxims, which are to determine our actions, can be directly derived from them, and thus does not mean by this that it opens up an additional field of positive cognitions. Two things must be said in response to this. Firstly, even from a cursory glance at the texts above, it is clear that Kant thinks the constitutive principles in the practical sphere include the *entire* field of reason's ideas (i.e., all the moral postulates) insofar as these belong within the image of a world maximally conducive to the performance of moral actions. Secondly, the underestimation of the importance of constitutive principles in Kant's philosophy derives, it seems to me, from a failure to understand the deeper structure of the unity of reason. The distinction between constitutive and regulative principles is not between two inherently different kinds of principles with differing claims to validity, but rather between a principle *applied within the domain it first constitutes* on the one hand, and this same principle taken in relation to *a field it helps to unify* but does not originally constitute, on the other. Every transcendental principle, as a principle of autonomy within a certain sphere of activity, is necessarily constitutive within that sphere. This follows from the fact that transcendental deduction, which every such principle requires, rests on a relation to the conditions of the possibility of the use of reason in the sphere in question – the deduction proves that certain concepts are constitutive for a certain use of reason. Put in other terms, it is a general feature of Kantian self-consciousness that cognitive activity of any kind requires the representation of an objective (i.e. non-arbitrary and law-like) principle which allows it to consciously grasp the unity of all its possible cognitions in original-synthetic apperception. Such an object is, as it were, the necessary counter-image by means of which the activity of consciousness is reflected and grasped in *self-consciousness properly understood*. Such an object is thus always necessarily thoroughly determined in accordance with the requirements of such self-consciousness. In this respect our cognition of it can rightfully be called constitutive.

Still, this might appear to be an abuse of Kant's terminology. Yet Kant himself is far from consistent. In accordance with Kant's way of speaking in the Dialectic of the *KrV*, a principle is constitutive if we regard it as determined in itself through reason. Clearly, the terminology comes from the Latin *constitutiva*, which Kant applies in his *Logic* to describe the true essential or primitive marks which compose the concept of a thing (see, e.g. *Log* 09:61). Thus a principle is constitutive if it allows us to actually determine the essential marks of an object. God is not a constitutive concept from the vantage point of knowledge, as Kant says, because speculative reason is able to determine absolutely nothing about what such an object would be in itself. It is rather *regulative*, meaning it is the source of a rule or maxim for extending the use of the understanding. But this does not seem to me to be a very clear way of expressing the essential idea. More importantly, Kant's other uses of the terms "constitutive" and "regulative" are quite different. For instance, Kant often also speaks of a principle as "constitutive" if it allows us to determine the necessary or essential features of the objects it makes possible as objects of reason. What I think Kant should have said is that the pure idea of God is not constitutive *or* regulative, because in its pure form it cannot be made use of theoretically at all. However, in the regulative employment he speaks of in the Dialectic, it is not the pure idea that serves to guide the understanding, but rather a certain idea of God constructed by analogy with human reason. Of course, this idea does not constitute or determine God in himself, but this is entirely clear from its origin; it arises entirely for the sake of reason's empirical employment. But in this respect, the idea of such a being is entirely determined, because it is determined through the specific need of reason, in regard to which there is nothing hidden. The upshot is that if we properly understand the regulative idea of God, then it is not in any sense really an idea of God, or of a transcendent being, at all. It is rather the specifically determined idea of an intellectual ground for a whole of experience created such that it would completely satisfy the very needs of finite human reason. Thus, it makes no sense to deny that it is constitutive, if only because it bears no relation to any concept of an object thought of as independent of the conditions of human reason, let alone of God in himself.

The only other reason we should wish to call it regulative and not constitutive, is because it does not allow us to determine the objects of experience, but provides rather merely rules (*regulae*) for research into them. But this too is not a consequent way of getting at what Kant intends, because the regulative ideas simply do not have the function of theoretically determining objects, which belongs rather to the understanding. It is only the understanding as a faculty, as Kant notes, that is an object for reason in its theoretical or regulative employment, and in this respect reason does indeed provide an "objective" and justified principle for its systematic use. Indeed, it does this by presenting determinate objects "as if" they were the underlying grounds of the validity of its activity. Thus ideas are said by Kant to be regulative and not constitutive with regard to objects precisely because they are not *required* for the possibility of the unity of objects of experience. Still, this does not make them in any sense dispensable or open-ended, because in their proper field, i.e. in regard to the use of pure reason for the guidance of the understanding, they are in another sense *constitutive* and well-defined – not in regard to specific objects, of course, but with resect to the use of the understanding – and indeed allow us to derive necessary and completely determinate maxims for its use. Thus, such principles are regulative when viewed in relation to the cognition of objects of experience, but they should be characterized as constitutive when viewed within that specific sphere of reason's activity for which they are a condition of possibility. For, if qualified in this way, such principles do allow us to determine the essential marks of the objects thus qualified, just as the axioms of space and time are constitutive and true of objects if only we add to the latter the condition of being spatiotemporal. The ideas of reason justify not the universality of rules governing the connection of objects, but rather the universality of the rules governing the connection of our reasoning about objects (*KrV* B675). An experience not in accordance with these could possibly present objects, but not a possible systematic whole of cognition. It is true that Kant did not, as I have argued, express this as clearly as he might have while he was composing the *KrV*, perhaps because he was still wedded to a pre-critical way of speaking about reason's relation to its objects. But I think it elucidates many of Kant's apparent fluctuations on the status of the regulative principles in the Dialectic of the *KrV*. Moreover, it also provides a genuine insight into the necessity of transcendental illusions, since these can be explained on this view by the fact that the regulative principles are indeed constitutive of the *use* of reason (thus, in a sense, practically), which means they also possess the necessity that is generally the mark of objectivity, but that only through transcendental reflection on the specific sets of conditions of the possibility of different uses of reason is it possible to discover that this necessity is only required by, and so limited to, the guidance of the understanding.

When seen from this point of view, it is immediately clear that the categories and principles of possible experience possess no deeper foundation and certainly no absolute privilege over any of the other transcendental principles. They simply govern their own autonomous domain, which happens to be that of the unity of objects in general. As Kant explains,

> An analogy of experience will therefore be only a rule in accordance with which unity of experience is to arise from perceptions [...], and as a principle it will not be valid of the objects (of appearances) *constitutively* but merely *regulatively*. The very same thing will also hold for the postulates of empirical thinking in general [...], namely that they are only regulative principles, and that they differ from the mathematical principles, which are constitutive, not, to be sure, in their certainty, which is established *a priori* in both cases, but yet in the manner of their evidence, i.e., with regard to their intuitiveness (thus also their demonstration). (*KrV* A180/B222–223)
>
> In the Transcendental Analytic we have distinguished among the principles of understanding the *dynamical* ones, as merely regulative principles of *intuition*, from the *mathematical* ones, which are constitutive in regard to intuition. Despite this, the dynamical laws we are thinking of are still constitutive in regard to *experience*, since they make possible *a priori* the *concepts* without which there is no experience. (*KrV* A664/B692)

Note Kant's formulation: The dynamic principles are regulative *in respect to intuition*, but constitutive *in respect to experience*, because they are not required for the possibility of intuition, but they are indeed required for the possibility of experience. The mathematical are constitutive with respect to intuition, because without them there would be no intuition at all. The only reason the mathematical principles have no regulative use is because they are the very first conditions of the possibility of cognition of any object at all. Does this, then, give them a greater objectivity or a deeper foundation? Not at all: In fact, it is precisely the fact that they are absolutely constitutive of all objects of knowledge, that proves them to be transcendentally ideal, i.e., merely *subjective* conditions of the possibility of empirical intuition. For, since they first constitute the appearances themselves, they can have no possible use beyond the appearances. About the categories in general, then, Kant says, "their objective reality is founded solely on the fact that because they *constitute the intellectual form of all experience*, it must always be possible to show their application in experience" (A310/B367). This underscores the important fact that the terms "subjective" and "objective" in Kant's philosophy gain their entire content and meaning from the specific domain within which they are being employed; for what is objective in one domain, i.e. what constitutes the object of reason within it, may well be subjective from the vantage point of another, and *vice versa*. The matter turns simply on whether the concepts in question belong to that most basic set of concepts without which no object at all of a specific kind (theoretical, speculative, moral or aesthetic) could be represented, or alternatively to those concepts that allow us to think these objects as possessing a richer mode of unity.

This brings me back to the point that when Kant emphasizes that the ideas of pure practical reason are only *subjectively* or *practically* constitutive, I think he means by this simply that they are not *theoretically* constitutive. Furthermore, since, as I have argued, *every* function of reason consists of a specific field of the *active use* of reason constituted by unique conditions of possibility, which are also to provide it with a law or norm, it is fair to expect that pure reason as a whole will form a unity under the guidance of one supreme constitutive practical principle, which when seen from a merely theoretical point of view will nevertheless be theoretically regulative in regard to objects of cognition, but at the same time constitutive for the *use* of theoretical/speculative reason in accordance with its practical vocation.

§. 1.3. The Unity of Reason: Second Reconstruction

I have claimed in the first stage of my reconstruction that in regard to the transcendental system the necessity of an analytical point of departure would have to be a proven to be an essential part of the system itself. I did not, however, explain how this is accomplished by Kant, except to indicate that it has something to do with the fact that the system only becomes operative in specific acts of cognizing. I will now attempt to repair this omission.

Kant's basic insight in this regard, I believe, is that much of the structure of rational cognition can be discovered by analyzing the very notion of the *consciousness of necessity* in order to elucidate how such a thing can be possible at all. Kant famously says that there is nothing in the object that we have not placed there ourselves. He is also typically presented as claiming that we impose our thought-forms upon the objects given to us from outside. Any reader, I think, should immediately wonder: Why then is this truth and not illusion? Is not the idea of a reason that freely and originally constructs its objects that of a reason rapt in its own dreams? Moreover, how can reason's own impositions be experienced by reason itself as necessary and universal laws when it is all the while at least implicitly aware that it has constructed them itself? The appeal to the idea that every person has precisely the same faculty of reason, and so poeticizes in exactly the same way, is of course no answer, because this itself would have to be a cognition. Thus at most we could be dreaming that others dream like us. Likewise, an appeal to the idea that the principles according to which this poeticizing occurs are just the basic facts of human consciousness, provides no genuine answer, because the fact that we have to think according to them is entirely distinct from our *consciously recognizing them as necessary*, not to mention that it would subject reason to heteronomous principles. The problem underlying the *consciousness of necessity* is that in order to be *conscious* it must in some sense be a product of our active thinking, but in order to be *objective* or *necessary*, it must be present within consciousness also as something imposed upon it from another quarter. This is the basic problem of autonomy, and it is just as much an issue for Kant's theoretical as for his practical philosophy.

This conundrum is directly reflected in the question of the purposive unity of the mind that the transcendental system sets out to discover. Kant is quite clear, as I noted before, that the mind first becomes aware of itself exclusively in determinate acts of representating. These might be called "parts" of the mind in the sense that we find them as actively occurring within ourselves without immediately seeing how they fit into a larger whole. There are, however, three ways in which a given multiplicity can be a unity. The first possibility, which Kant famously rejects, is that they all be derived from a first fundamental power, as in Leibniz and Wolff. In this case, all the faculties of reason would stand unified through their being nothing more than distinct specifications of one and the same fundamental activity of the mind, and all representations would likewise be unified by being nothing more than distinct specifications of an originally unitary representation (perhaps the self's consciousness of its own substantial unity). In Kant's view, the conscious mind *qua* consciousness would not, however, in this case be a truly purposive unity, since the contingency of the unity of the mental faculties, by virtue of their common root, would be denied, and thus there would be no need to introduce the notion of a *conscious goal or end* in order to ground this unity. To be perfectly precise, the unity of the something called "mind" *could* in fact turn out in this case to be purposive, but the *self-conscious* use of reason, which is what Kant really means by "reason," still would not be intrinsically purposive. That is to say, if it were revealed that the unity of the mind were the effect of a previously hidden root, then this fundamental power could admittedly be directed to a goal, and thus require a teleological explanation, but this teleological unity would be inevitable, and would not rest in an essential way on the *reflective self-consciousness* of the human being. It would flow with necessity from a root that precedes the individual faculties, and indeed precedes the very activity of self-consciousness which judges by means of these faculties. The latter would then be teleological, not in the sense that it has an end exclusively *because it recognizes an end for itself and strives towards it*, but rather in the sense that its actions are necessary as a means to the achievement of an end already constituted prior to and outside of the operations of this same self-consciousness. The unity of mind would be a metaphysical necessity for the mind, viewed perhaps as a substance first constituted in accordance with a divine intention, but without its also being shown to be an end the possibility of which is grounded in the self-activity of consciousness. But not even this would be true, at least strictly speaking. For if self-consciousness or reflection were still involved at all, it would not be able to *recognize* this "necessity" as a necessity (objective), but rather as something *subjective* in the sense of arbitrary or contingent, because it would be aware of no *cognitively transparent (i.e. justifiable to itself)* connection between such a condition and the essence of its objects (cf. *KrV* B168).

What is more, even if the common root of the faculties of the mind supported a teleological reading of the unity of the mind from a metaphysical standpoint, this unity would not be purposive in the precise sense of the term as it is used by Kant; for purposive unity requires that the whole, and thus the end, consist not in something distinct from the parts, but rather in their mutual interdependence and harmony as a whole. If the parts could all be derived from a common root, however, the functions of reason would each exist exclusively for the sake of the common root, as so many means to the end it essentially prescribes for them, without themselves being ends of this same whole.

Kant rejected such a view of self-consciousness as early as 1762 and this in part led him to embrace an alternative explanation of the unity of a multiplicity that is characteristic of reason. Kant rejected this view because he came to see through his pre-critical investigations, firstly, that the modal concepts of real possibility/actuality/necessity are inherently *relative* concepts (i.e. they presuppose a condition), and secondly, that the faculty of judgment has the unique feature of being an *intentional* activity of consciousness (i.e. an activity in which the mind consciously and actively relates itself to an object). As a result of these two insights, Kant slowly came to recognize that something can only be necessary *for consciousness* if in fact it is judged to be necessary *by consciousness*, and indeed, since necessity is not an absolute concept, consciousness can only judge something to be necessary relative to a previously given condition of possibility that it explicitly recognizes or holds before itself. From this point on, Kant takes consciousness of necessity *a priori* in regard to any cognition to be proof that it almost self-evidently has nothing to do with objects in themselves.

Following this insight, Kant saw that if the unity of the mind and of its representations is to be something universal and necessary, then it must be a fundamental product of judgment under a condition that is grounded in a universal and necessary, but also *original*, condition of consciousness. Now, the only unity of consciousness of which we are aware is the identical and empty unity of transcendental apperception, a condition that has no inner content, and does not provide any ground for deriving from it the existence and content of a given intuitive manifold. For this reason, the unity of apperception cannot have the character of a common root, since, if it did, then it should be possible to derive from it not just the general unity, but indeed the *specific* unity of the mind as this is embodied in the faculty of judgment. But for this it is in fact required to add the special forms of intuition, space and time; for only in the combination of understanding and intuition, and of their heterogeneous forms in one *complex* of representation, is it possible for knowledge to arise.

Consequently, if there is an objective unity of the mind, then this can only be that of an active synthesis taking place within consciousness that aims at and produces this unity. In other words, the empty unity of apperception may be presupposed as a general condition, but it only becomes the unity of the mind by being carried over, though *a conscious act of synthesis*, into a whole that incorporates all of the sub-functions of mental activity (i.e., other modes of representation) into one. Thus, the specific laws of synthesis derive not from this bare unity, as from a root, but rather from the fact that they describe the only way in which the *given* manifold of mental activities that combine in a judgment *can* be combined into a unity by consciousness itself. This means that the specific form of the laws, the observance of which constitute the objective unity of the mind, derive as much from the *specific* conditions of thought, as from the bare principle of unity that governs the synthesis. The unity of reason, then, is not one that precedes and only later separates (*"getrennt"* Hegel calls it) itself out in into a manifold of mental faculties and capacities. It is rather the projected unity of a specific manifold that it "finds" within itself. *The unity of reason, as Kant envisages it, is a teleological or purposive unity whose goal is the incorporation of the manifold into a functioning whole the a priori form of which is precisely determined by the specific manifold it will serve to unify.*[7] To borrow a line from Charles Taylor, this structure is teleological precisely in the sense that the "order is itself in some way a factor in its own production" (Taylor 1964, p. 5). In this case it is the empty unity of the ego, as supreme condition of self-consciousness, that makes the unity of reason in the object necessary for us, while it is the specific characters of the functions of reason that make this object

---

[7] I hesitate to say, with certain commentators, that its goal is to "preserve" the unity of apperception, since this description only applies to the theoretical version of the problem, and even then only if we leave out the practical significance of theoretical cognition. Here I am rather trying to outline the general form of the unity of reason, which I think is operative in every dimension of Kant's philosophy. In the practical realm, I think it hardly apt to call it a matter of "preserving" the unity of the practical self, since from the perspective of ourselves as worldly beings (a view that has as much reality as that of ourselves as noumenal beings standing over and judging our phenomenal counterparts), the fulfillment of what the law commands is certainly something that must first be *achieved*. To reduce the matter to one of preservation is, in my view, to oversimplify the complex existential situation of the moral self. *Synthesis*, after all, is not a matter of inertia or keeping hold of what is already in hand, but of actively reaching out and combining what is not yet a unity.

necessary in a specific way, i.e. as obeying a distinct set of laws. Thus the possible manner in which the mind may actually become unified into a whole is represented in the mind prior to any unification, i.e., as an *a priori* idea, which subsequently guides the very synthesis whereby the mind actually comes to compose the sort of whole originally sketched out in the idea.

Still, the question remains: Why should this carrying over of a subjective unity into the manifold of mental activities result in something objective and thus unified in itself, rather than just an artfully constructed aggregate of thoughts? After all, the unity of reason must be universal and necessary; not the arbitrary unity of this or that mind, but rather the legislative unity that is prescribed for all minds by virtue of rationality alone. If we reject the common root theory, there still remain two other possible ways in which a manifold can be united into a whole, namely, either technically or architectonically. I will examine these in turn.

Technical unity has the following structural features: a) it is the unity of a manifold that is combined according to an arbitrary form or end; b) because the form is arbitrary, it does not unify the manifold from within, but rather serves to collect the manifold into an aggregate of a general character; c) it is teleological in the sense that the form, as represented before the act of combination, is a factor in the production of the whole that exhibits that form; d) finally, because the form is arrived at independently of the manifold it is to unify, it is not always possible to bring technical unity into a given manifold. For instance, it is impossible to bring the technical unity of an arch into a manifold of dry sand particles, since the properties of the parts simply do not allow themselves to be combined in this way. Likewise, it is impossible on Leibniz's view for God to bring the technical unity of an absolutely perfect world into the material of creation, because the eternal essences allow of being combined only into the best possible. This also reveals e) that even when it *is* possible to bring technical unity into a manifold, it is the properties of the parts, and not the form of the whole that makes such unity really possible.[8]

Architectonic unity, which is the kind Kant always ascribes to reason, manages to combine various features of the unity that would drive from a common root and from technical unity by adopting a *critical* or *transcendental* standpoint on the unity of reason. The first step that Kant takes is to recognize that the unity of reason cannot simply be of *either* of the previous kinds. It cannot be tech-

---

[8] Unless one hits on a natural machine, as Leibniz calls it, or a work of genius. In this hypothetical case, there would be an accidental agreement between the form arbitrarily adopted for a given manifold and the inner form that really makes it possible for the manifold to become a whole of that specific form.

§. 1. The Unity of Reason — 385

nical unity, because then it would not be normative, i.e. necessary, since the rule would bear no essential relation to the possibility of the parts. However, it cannot be derivative of a common root, because then we could not possibly know it *as* normative, since the source of its normativity would lie outside of consciousness entirely. Yet, and this is the second step, Kant also recognizes that the unity of reason has to possess features of *both* these forms of unity. It must be technical, because it must depend on nothing but our own free consciousness. And it must also be traced to a common root as from a necessary prior condition, because otherwise it would be entirely arbitrary, and thus not necessary or legislative.

Kant's solution to this problem lies in the distinction between the transcendental and the metaphysical. From a transcendental point of view, we can outline and catalogue all the principles of any possible act of reason through an analysis of the *essential* and *pure idea* of such an act. The results of this analysis reveal a manifold the elements of which, transcendentally speaking, are entirely contingent for us, but which nevertheless form a whole *teleologically* in relation to the idea of a specific kind of act or product of reason. In other words, this analysis does not in the least reveal why we have precisely these elements and no others, and it does not give us any reason to think that the employment of them together should be absolutely necessary. Nevertheless, knowledge of the elements does allow us to map out and catalogue the possible ways in which they may be employed in combination to bring about the type of act in question. These possible modes of combination are expressed in rules of possible acts of combination according to the form: "If these specific elements are to be employed in combination, then they can only be combined in certain ways or according to certain general *a priori* forms." It is the consciousness of this necessary combination as a condition of possibility that serves to unify these elements into the form of a system.

To this point, there is not a whit of necessity, but merely a transcendental outline of the rules of any possible act of reason that just happens to be based upon certain conditions we discover originally in ourselves. From a transcendental point of view, this hypothetical unity of the mind not only matches but even *transcends* the freedom of a technical unity, since the rules for combining the elements are entirely and originally derived from the goal of performing a specific complex act of reason, which considered in itself is freely presupposed. In other words, unlike the case of technical unity, which is limited by the material which it seeks to unify, the transcendental or architectonic unity of the mind provides the very conditions of the transcendental "matter" which may come before it. What is more, in this very conditioning of the matter, reason is able to represent its own unity as absolutely internal or essential to the matter itself – and to this extent it freely creates its objects. The key point here is that if this synthetic activity is taken up in this absolutely free or self-sufficient manner, then the rules that govern this act are also freely taken up in and through consciousness itself. It is this freedom that is required for the transparency of theoretical consciousness, and for the transparency required for the possibility for the mind to know the essential determinations of its object.

If, however, we change our point of view to the empirical level, or the level on which actual actions of reason take place, then the same rules, which transcendental reflection showed to be freely adopted, take on the aspect of necessity in relation to each and every *particular* act of the mind. Viewed in this manner, these transcendental structures found what Kant would call the "metaphysical" structure of reason. This metaphysical structure is nothing but the same transcendental structure *insofar as* it is viewed as the ground making necessary certain operations of reason in its actual use because without such operations no particular use of reason would be possible *at all*. That is, when we actually set about using reason in a specific way, we are no longer on the transcendental and hypothetical level. We are rather actually taking the deliverances of the previous elements of representation, and combining them with the transcendentally recognized *goal* of performing an activity of a certain general type, or with a specific general kind of unity. Thus, the rules discovered by transcendental reflection, when reformulated *specifically in relation to any actual act of reason* (which means *after* the mind is already committed, as it were, to a certain transcendental and hence universal goal) no longer have the hypothetical form. Rather, the rules of possible combination are at the same time *laws*, i.e. rules with necessity, in relation to all possible *particular* mental acts of this specific type. Indeed, once the transcendental structures are assumed, then these laws follow *identically*, and in this is grounded their specific truth. As for the teleological character of this activity, it should be noted that the object of reason in this case is not necessarily purposive in itself, or objectively, but rather its very objectivity lies in its purposiveness for reason, i.e., in its fulfilling the transcendental goal set out by reason *a priori*. According to context, then, the object will be viewed as purposive in itself, as in teleological judgments, only to the extent that such purposiveness is required in order for the object to be purposive for reason as well. In other cases, as in regard to the first constitution of nature by the understanding, the object is non-purposive because this faculty must be able to completely anticipate the conceptual structure of its object *qua* object. Thus if there were – on the basic level of objectivity as such – an inner form of the object aside from what can be expressed in the categories, then this would be a ground for the falsity, or at least of the incompleteness, of objectivity as such.

Notably, this interpretation shows how the two distinct teleological views that Hegel detected in Kant can in fact both fit together in a single consistent account according to the transcendental and metaphysical standpoints. Firstly, it is clear from the transcendental account how the unity of reason is absolutely purposive and self-limiting, namely insofar as it is a unity in which the character of the whole is determined as much by the character of the parts, as the operations of the parts are determined by their having to be able to be combined into a whole. It is also self-limiting because the laws of synthesis for this combination follow exclusively from the specific character of the parts, insofar as these are to be brought into a whole. Now this very same teleological structure, viewed as the ground of the specific activities of reason, can be seen as the origin of a perpetual striving. This is because the unity of the whole consists only in the very *activity of combining of which we are conscious* in accordance with the laws that make such combination possible. The transcendental and teleological unity of reason is not something that allows of being produced, and then set aside; it is rather essentially the unity of a complex real activity. Put differently, the unity of reason is the unity of a synthesis, and a synthesis does not exist except in act. *The pure idea of reason is the idea of an essentially dynamic and active whole.* To complete the synthesis absolutely would thus be to overcome the original multiplicity that made the synthesis both possible and necessary, which is indeed the very condition of self-consciousness. Now, because consciousness has before it *a priori* both the complete idea of a possible whole, and also the awareness of its synthetic act of bringing the manifold into agreement with this idea, the unity of reason has the basic structure of an end, as Kant often states. The idea, in other words, serves as an archetype or model for all the actual operations of the empirical mind, and against which their perfection can be measured. And yet this idea is a pure or free product of reason with no external measure of its own.

§. 2. Kant's Concept of Philosophy

> Kant discovered [...] the inner character of the system of reason as a law of spirit for the first time. He understands the concept of philosophy in general in accordance with this. Since philosophy looks toward those concepts and representations by which all knowledge of beings is guided and back to which it is deduced, it treats such things in which the totality of what is knowable comes to its comprehensive end which is at the same time a beginning. Such an end is in Greek, *telos*. The knowing explication of this most extreme and highest focus of all the rays of knowledge through knowledge, this *logos* itself, is the *logos* of *telos*, teleology. Thus, Kant defines the essence of philosophy briefly in the expression: philosophy is *teleologia rationis humanae*. (Heidegger 1986, p. 38)

It is sometimes claimed that Kant definitively altered our conception of philosophy, indeed that the advent of critical philosophy marks an indelible break within the tradition. At other times, Kant is depicted as the great restorer and rediscover of philosophy in the true sense of the word, as one who whether by dint of luck, or with the surety of a sleep-walker, found his way back to the original philosophical insights of the Greeks. If we are to be fair to the richness of its consequences, it seems we must view the Kantian philosophy as in some sense *both* the chief exponent of the modern anti-teleological Weltanschauung, and the first philosophy since Aristotle's to revive the idea of intrinsic purposiveness for philosophy.[9]

These contradictions, I suggest, arise not from a want of decisive evidence, but from the copiousness and complexity of Kant's statements on the nature of his philosophy and on its relation to the philosophical tradition.[10] As Eckart Förster has noted, "few philosophers have thought as long and as deeply as Kant about the nature of philosophy" (Förster 1989, p. 285). Yet, unfortunately, the general nature of Kant's philosophical vision is one of the least discussed topics in the secondary literature, and only a few commentators, it seems, are willing to take Kant's statements on the nature of philosophy to be anything more than outmoded window-dressing for his more lasting contributions to epistemology and ethics.

Of course, there are exceptions, although the prevailing view even among the majority of Kant's advocates is that his reflections on philosophy are constantly changing at best, "inchoate" and "clearly inadequate" at worst.[11] Susan Neiman, for instance, has interpreted Kant's entire body of work as a reflection on the nature of the philosophical project. In her view, Kant's concept of philosophy should reflect, and be reflected in, his understanding of the unity of reason, since "no activity seems more characteristic of reason than the practice of philosophy." Her idea seems to be that since Kant understands philosophy to be the self-knowledge of reason, he must also understand the practice of philosophy to be the act of living in accordance with this self-knowledge. Thus Kant's

---

9 As Hegel claims.
10 Kant himself explicitly makes claims to absolute originality and to complete orthodoxy. The ideas of pure reason, we are told, are what Plato really had in mind, while the critical philosophy itself is the true "apology" for Leibniz. The doctrine of the highest good found in the *KpV* is actually a resolution of the debate between the Stoics and Epicureans, Kant often suggests, and even Wolff, Baumgarten, and Mendelssohn were important way stations on the journey to criticism.
11 Förster thinks Kant never reached a settled view. The latter is the view expressed in Neiman 1994, p. 185–186.

§. 2. Kant's Concept of Philosophy — 389

theory of philosophical practice should be the highest and most complete expression of his understanding of the unity of reason.

Although differently motivated, Neiman makes an objection to Kant's theory that is of the same spirit as Hegel's noted at the beginning of this chapter. As she explains, "Kant's work reflects a tension between two wholly diverse conceptions of philosophy and hence of his own procedure, as well as whatever is to succeed it" (Neiman 1994, p. 185). The tension, as she sees it, is between an open-ended regulative conception of "philosophy as an ideal," and a constitutive conception of philosophy as a closed and finished science. Unlike Hegel, however, Neiman finds the view of philosophy as infinite progress to be the more palatable, and worth developing into what she describes as an anthropologically-based vision of philosophy as an ongoing project of human self-discovery. The constitutive view of philosophy, she believes, has no real place in an enterprise which is as open and critical as she believes Kant's to be. As a consequence, it must be abandoned as a mere dogmatic remnant of his misguided attempts to make philosophy scientific and complete. Kant, she states, was unaware of this tension and in his actual writings the two conceptions "are not developed enough to constitute two coherent accounts of the nature of philosophy, let alone one" (Neiman 1994, p. 185). Without discussing many of the details of Kant's theory, presumably because there is not much to discuss, Neiman draws her conclusion: "Reason's justification of itself will be regulative; if philosophy is an idea of reason, nothing else makes sense" (Neiman 1994, p. 196). As a result, the unity of reason too will be a regulative principle.

In the previous section of this chapter, we have refuted the idea that the unity of reason for Kant is always and only regulative. Before we can apply this to Kant's concept of philosophy, however, we must also refute the myth that Kant has no general theory of philosophy at all. The main reason commentators give for this claim is that Kant's comments on philosophy appear to be inconsistent. This is certainly puzzling, since Kant's description of the nature of philosophy – and particularly those features claimed to be inconsistent by commentators – remained essentially unchanged, except for some small details, from the late 1760s through the *Opus postumum*. This alone, of course, is not a sufficient defense, since Kant is routinely accused of cleaving to monumental inconsistencies, not only in the same work, but even in the same sentence. The only acceptable defense, then, is a reconstruction of Kant's concept of philosophy. If it can be shown that this concept is fully consistent with his understanding of the unity of reason, and also that his seemingly inconsistent claims about philosophy can be reconciled when understood as exhibiting such teleological-systematic unity, then this will fulfill the task of this chapter.

§. 2.1. Philosophy "in sensu scholastico" and "in sensu cosmico"

In the *Critique of Pure Reason*, Kant famously defines philosophy in a twofold sense, namely, as a scholastic concept and as a world concept. In the former meaning, philosophy is essentially and entirely concerned with achieving a perfectly systematic comprehension of all knowledge. In the *FM*, Kant explains more fully that "the explanation of metaphysics according to the notion of the schools will be that it is the system of all principles of purely theoretical rational knowledge through concepts; or in brief, that it is the system of pure theoretical philosophy" (AA 20:261). In his lectures on logic, Kant explains that the chief goals of this kind of philosophy are the collection and logical perfection of our cognitions. Kant also characterizes it as a sort of skill, and the scholastic philosopher as an artisan or craftsman of reason (*Log* 09:23–24). Kant explains, however, that even under this concept, philosophy is but a mere idea, i.e. an objective "archetype for the assessment of all attempts to philosophize, which should serve to assess each subjective philosophy" (A838/B866).

The claim that such philosophy is an idea should not be understood necessarily as something negative, although it is usually taken in this way. In one respect, to be sure, this connotes incompleteness or that philosophy *in sensu scholastico* is a work-in-progress. But this is not Kant's real meaning, since the form of such a philosophy is entirely given in the canons of logical analysis and system construction. His point is rather that philosophy even in this sense is and will remain an idea precisely because it is something alive, or is something that consists essentially in an *activity of philosophizing*. Philosophy *qua* science is nothing but the self-consistent activity of reason in its reflection upon objects of whatever kind. That such a kind of thinking is complete does not mean, in the first instance, that it has all been written down somewhere in a book, but rather that the exercise of thought in any one respect, or in regard to any one object, is such that it takes into account and agrees with the whole of reason's purposive activity. By asserting that even philosophy in a scholastic sense is an idea, Kant is stressing that it has the essential role of seeking and fulfilling an essential end, i.e. the scientific perfection of knowledge, and that it does this precisely by providing a model or archetype for the general form of all philosophical activity. Philosophy in this sense is clearly highly valued by Kant, for whom science is the only secure path to wisdom. However, if philosophy is reduced merely to this, and thus if the scholastic form of cognition becomes the sole purpose of our intellectual activities, then it is surely defective, and in a certain sense is not to be entitled either philosophy or wisdom. Such a defect shows itself, Kant believes, through the fact that what reason is most interested in and directed towards, namely the super-sensible, proves to be inaccessible to reason in a merely theoretical employment. This leads reason necessarily to search for another source of metaphysics, and for the satisfaction of its endeavors.

By contrast, according to the world concept, which is that at which reason ultimately aims, philosophy is a doctrine of wisdom, which Kant defines as "the knowledge of the good or of that which is entirely good (in all actual relations) [derived] from the idea of the whole and as a ground of choice," (*Relf* 3643) and as "the (subjective) principle of the unity of all ends according to reason, consequently happiness unified with morality" (*Refl* 3647). In the *Critique of Pure Reason*, Kant defines it more precisely as "the science of the relation of all cognition to the essential ends of human reason (*teleologia rationis humanae*)" (*KrV* A839/B867). Very simply, philosophy as a doctrine of wisdom is nothing but morality insofar as it is extended to include a practical-dogmatic metaphysics, i.e. the rational belief in certain theoretically formulated propositions for the sake of the realization of our duty. "This [moral] law," Kant explains, "as the principle of wisdom leads our reason in its practical use to the final end of a highest wisdom: the greatest happiness combined with virtue as the final end of all things, which however, as far as we can see, makes necessary an eternality of our existence and a moral creator of the world to effect the world-constitution required for this end" (*Refl* 6432). This kind of metaphysics proves itself to be practically constitutive, and indeed to be a complete and closed system of cognitions:

> Metaphysics, on this showing [as practical-dogmatic wisdom], is itself only the Idea of a science, as a system which, after the completion of the critique of pure reason, can and should be constructed, and for which, the building materials and specifications are to hand: a whole which, like pure logic, neither needs nor is capable of any enlargement, and must likewise be constantly occupied and kept in structural repair, if spiders and satyrs, who will never be backward in seeking accommodations here, are not to settle in and make it uninhabitable for reason. (*FM* 20:310)

Again, Kant writes that:

> Philosophy as doctrine of wisdom enjoys this advantage over philosophy as speculative science by virtue of arising from nothing else but pure practical rationality, i.e., morality, so far as it has been derived from the concept of freedom, as a principle super-sensible, indeed, but practically knowable *a priori*. (*FM* 20:301)

Philosophy in this world concept, it must be noted, is yet still merely a doctrine, i.e. a set of teachings to be followed, developed, and practiced, although it is to be sure a doctrine of the highest good and thus of the genuine end of humanity.

Philosophy in its most proper sense, however, is yet more than this set of teachings, even moral ones. It is directed rather at the *attainment* of wisdom, which consists in *living* a life thoroughly determined in accordance with the ideal whole of all ends. It thus requires not only the possession of a doctrine of wisdom, but also that we actually live in accordance with what it teaches. Genuine wisdom in this respect is, as Kant says, an archetype which can never be achieved, not only because it would require us to live perfectly in accord with the moral law (something impossible), but moreover because any *particular* life would by that very fact be unable to equal the *universal* model of perfection. The goal of the philosophical life, in this sense, is thus not to achieve the whole of all ends through oneself, but rather to pursue those particular ends that are possible in accordance with such an idea of a whole of all possible ends. The goal of philosophy in this sense, which is also a duty, is to strive towards becoming a person of wisdom. By contrast with the mere craftsman of reason, which is what the scholar proves ultimately to be, the philosopher in the true sense, as a person possessing wisdom, is the very idea of the "legislator of human reason" (*KrV* B867). It is, in other words, the idea of a being that is perfectly identical with the legislative archetype of reason itself:

> Only philosophy can achieve the highest degree of being a law-giver of human reason. As such it is the doctrine of wisdom and has the rank over all human knowledge. Does it however also already exist according to this idea? As little as a true Christ actually exists, does a philosopher in this sense have an existence. They are both archetypes. An archetype does not remain one if it can be achieved. It should serve purely as a guiding rule. The philosopher is only an idea. Perhaps we will throw a glance to it and can follow it in some parts, but in no way will we entirely achieve it. The philosopher has an insight into the rules of wisdom, the wise person, however, acts according to them. Of this I can only say that he philosophizes who endeavors to establish the highest ends and the destiny of his reason; however, if he has achieved this, then he is already in the temple of wisdom. (*PhilEnz* 29:8)

This is philosophy in the practical sense, and it is that by relation to which all philosophy, and indeed all thinking, first gains its value for Kant.

However, human beings are not only acting beings; we are moreover beings that act *from representations*, and not just any representations, but indeed from general ones. The nature of our actions is thus dependent upon the *nature of the concepts* from which we act. Furthermore, perfection in regard to the cognition of general representations is what Kant calls "science." Thus philosophy, as both a doctrine of wisdom and as wisdom itself, actually presupposes philosophy in the scholastic sense:

> In a word, science (critically sought and methodically directed) is the narrow gate that leads to the doctrine of wisdom, if by this is understood not merely what one ought to do but what ought to serve teachers as a guide to prepare well and clear the path to wisdom which everyone should travel, and to secure others against taking the wrong way; philos-

> ophy must always remain the guardian of this science, and though the public need take no interest in its subtle investigations it has to take an interest in the doctrines which, after being worked up in this way, can first be quite clear to it. (*KpV* 05:163)
>
> For science has an inner true worth only as an organ of wisdom. As such it is also indispensable to wisdom, so that one should well maintain: wisdom without science is a shadow of a perfection to which we will not attain. (*Log* 09:26; my translation)

Philosophy in the scholastic sense can thus prove to be the "custodian" of philosophy, or better, philosophy's guardian of the "narrow gate" towards its own destiny. It is necessary for it to perform this task precisely because our actions always presuppose cognitions as their basis, and because our pure practical faculty is itself essentially rational and reflective, given to dialectic, rationalization and enthusiasm. Thus to determine ourselves to act in a certain way requires that we have a system of concepts for the reflective governance of our actions.

Yet if philosophy as the doctrine of science is able to discharge this function, then it is really more than is contained in the scholastic concept. For it is essential to the perfection of philosophical cognition, particularly in regard to wisdom, for the philosopher to determine the nature, sources and limits of his cognitions. This means that it is a condition of wisdom that the unity of reason be outlined and thereby established, because it is through the idea of this unity that the sum of all ends first becomes systematic or architectonic. As we will see more fully below, this philosophy, which as a doctrine of science is at the same time an essential part of the doctrine of wisdom, and for this reason has a worth beyond any mere scholastic exercise, is precisely what Kant entitles "transcendental philosophy."

§. 2.2. Unity of Reason and the History of Philosophy

We saw in previous chapters, and also in the first part of the present one, that Kant recognizes in the unity of reason the character of a pure faculty that articulates and develops itself from its own internal and absolutely original source, and which has for its only criterion of truth the systematic and purposive harmony of its own dynamic unfolding. In *FM*, Kant draws a direct parallel between this dynamic unfolding and the specifically *historical* progress of philosophy. The initial insight for drawing up this parallel seems to be that, since pure philosophy is really of no empirical use, the only incentive for engaging in it must lie in the dynamics of reason itself, i.e. it must be the case that the kind of cognition peculiar to philosophy provides an original incentive to pure philosophical reflection. "Philosophizing," Kant explains, is a gradual development of human reason, and this cannot have set forth, or even have begun, upon the empirical path, and yet indeed [also] by mere concepts. There must have been a need of reason (theoretical or practical) which obliged it to ascend from its judgments about things to the grounds thereof, up to the first, initially through common reason, e.g., from world-bodies and their motion. But purposes were also encountered: and finally, since it was noticed that rational grounds can be sought concerning all things, a start was made with enumerating the concepts of reason (or those of the understanding) beforehand, and with analyzing thinking in general, without any object. (*FM* 20:340–341)

The beginning of philosophy thus has its roots in the character of this very kind of cognition. So too does the particular historical path which philosophy has followed ever since:

> A history of philosophy is of such a special kind, that nothing can be told therein of what has happened, without knowing beforehand what should have happened, and also what can happen. Whether this has been investigated beforehand or whether it has been reasoned out haphazardly. *For it is the history, not of the opinions which have chanced to arise here or there, but of reason developing itself from concepts.* We do not want to know what has been reasoned out, but what has been reasoned out by reasoning through mere concepts. Philosophy is to be viewed here as a sort of rational genius, from which we demand to know what it should have taught, and whether it has furnished this. (*FM* 20:343; emphasis added)

> Whether a *history* of philosophy might be written mathematically; how dogmatism must have arisen, and from it skepticism, and from both together criticism. But how is it possible to bring history into a system of reason, which requires the contingent to be derived, and partitioned, from a principle? (*FM* 20:342)

In the continuation of the same passage, Kant asks again the same question, but now answers it in the affirmative:

> Whether a schema could be drawn up *a priori* for the history of philosophy, with which, from the extant information, the epochs and opinions of the philosophers so coincide, that it is as though they had had this very schema themselves before their eyes, and had progressed by way of it in knowledge of the subject.
> Yes! if, that is, the idea of a metaphysic inevitably presents itself to human reason, and the latter feels a need to develop it, though this science lies wholly prefigured in the soul, albeit only in embryo. (*FM* 20:343)

Kant clearly has not worked out these ideas in great detail, and yet the basic idea is clear enough. The structure of reason, and so also the unity of reason, is what grounds and makes possible the very notion of philosophical progress. This is because thinking does not belong to philosophy unless it can be shown to occupy a place in the unfolding of reason's dynamic unity. Thus to tell the history of philosophy, we already have to know what philosophy *should* be on the basis of its idea, and to be able to determine from this the systematic unity of the historical events themselves.

Now, we have seen in previous chapters that philosophy consists ultimately of these parts: 1) a theoretical-dogmatic science; 2) a realization that theoretical knowledge of the super-sensible, which was previously thought to be the goal of all philosophy, is impossible; 3) a transcendental or critical investigation of the sources and limits of cognition based upon its pure idea; 4) a transition to a practical-dogmatic metaphysics based on the moral law; 5) and finally, an attempt to live a life of wisdom, which is the true goal and source of value for philosophy as a whole. In the *FM*, Kant goes so far in tracing out the parallel between the history of philosophy and the structure of the system of reason, that he attempts to equate these parts of his own philosophy with the historical stages of philosophy itself, namely theoretical dogmatism, skepticism and criticism, and then to parallel these with the triad of traditional philosophical sciences, ontology, cosmology and theology. All of these parts of philosophy, as Kant articulates them in *FM*, are seen to form a necessary progression towards the final end of the human being. Thus although they each also stand under their own particular idea and thus possess within themselves the unity of reason or, what is the same, the form of a science, the whole series itself stands under a single all-encompassing idea, namely that of the legislator of human reason as the unity of reason in its complete fulfillment and employment. Every part of this series, as well as the series as a whole, forms a complete and closed system sufficient to its essential task, and yet this completion is not a cessation of all activity and of all life, but rather is precisely the perfection of reason in its highest dynamic and purposive employment.

Thus, for the pursuit of wisdom there must exist a constitutive concept of the unity of reason to serve as a guide in our conscious determination of the objects of our reason, so that these may fit into an absolute whole of all ends. This applies as much to the unity of reason itself as to the unity of its historical unfolding. This *a priori* and pure idea of the systematic whole, whose fulfillment would be genuine wisdom, is first established in *transcendental philosophy*. As Kant writes:

> Wisdom is the attribute of the most perfect reason, be it of theoretical or also moral//practical relations. [...] Wisdom is the sum-total of the ends of the most perfect reason. The concept of it represents an absolute whole of such, not as aggregate but as unified into a system. Transcendental philosophy is the All of the ideas of pure (not empirically affected) reason in the system insofar as this constitutes itself into a system of synthetic knowledge *a priori* and makes itself into an object [...]. – It departs from what is formal in this knowledge and proceeds to what is material, namely the possibility of experience that can only be one (there are as little *experiences* as there are *matters*). (*OP* 21:132)

Again,

> Philosophy is the love of the rational being for the highest ends of human reason. World-wisdom is either the theoretical knowledge of this: the knowledge of the *philosopheme*. Since, however, to be wise surpasses human capacities and only God, i.e. the being that fulfills all ends, is wise; world-wisdom is, and is nothing else than, true real love of wisdom. – The highest standpoint of human practical reason is a striving of knowledge towards wisdom (philosophy). The *nosce te ipsum*. – The system of knowledge, insofar as it contains what leads to wisdom, is transcendental philosophy. (*OP* 21:121)

Conclusion

Kant's is a philosophy of the outermost boundary of human reason. As he understands it, this boundary is not a lifeless and stable membrane which separates reason from the transcendent, but rather the dynamic foundation of all our conscious activities. It marks out that towards which reason essentially strives, and against which reason measures the distance it has traversed. What is more, in complete accordance with the stringent requirements Aristotle places on the use of the locution "for the sake of which," the individual acts or judgments of reason belong to the purposive whole of human cognition, in Kant's view, only to the extent that their inner essential form can be shown to only be possible through a relation, essential to self-consciousness, to the form of the whole. For this reason, the boundary is neither entirely immanent, nor entirely transcendent; according to Kant it in fact transcends this very dichotomy, because it is the foundation and essence of human reason. Thus, while from within reason, or from a metaphysical standpoint, the notion of a boundary can be shown to be an internal requirement of any actual employment of reason, the *absolute* justification of any such boundary would require reason to reach beyond itself, thereby cancelling the very conditions that make knowledge possible and meaningful.

I think it is truly remarkable and certainly well worth noting how close this idea of Kant's comes to reproducing an originally Greek insight which was also exploited by Leibniz, namely, that if correctly understood in their relation to being as *activity*, the concepts of goal (*telos*) and boundary (*peras*) are interchangeable and indeed linguistically coincide in the term "end." In other words, the end as idea is the concentrated image of the law of a being's own activity, and indeed to the extent being is act, it is being itself. As such, the end is both the defining boundary or essential limit, and the measure of completeness or perfection. As Arisotle's *Metaphysics* reads,

Moreover, the final cause is an end, and as such it does not exist for the sake of something else but others exist for its sake. Thus, if there is to be such one which is last, the process will not be infinite; but if there is no such, there will be no final cause. But those who introduce an infinite series are unaware of the fact that they are eliminating the nature of the good, although no one would try to do anything if he did not intend to come to a limit. Nor would there be intellect in the world; for, at any rate, he who has an intellect always *acts* for the sake of something, and this is a limit, for the end is a limit. (Aristotle 1970, 994b9–16)

Another way of approaching the teleological character of Kant's notion of boundary is by returning to the first formulation of the problem of synthetic *a priori* judgments, namely, *How is it possible to for self-consciousness to possess absolutely basic laws?* The boundary concepts of human reason are nothing more than the objective correlates of reason's various activities, activities that are made possible by reason's transcendental conditions and laws. Reason, however, as both theoretical and practical, actually performs a manifold of particular actions, which when taken individually are mere contingent *facta* in the history of reason. Nevertheless, in the self-conscious performance of these specific acts, reason necessarily has before it the transcendental structure that stems from its own foundation, which instills it with a sort of *habitude* for knowledge and action. Thus *relative to the performance of these acts*, and because it makes such acts possible in the first place, this transcendental structure is recognized by self-consciousness as normative. Put differently, the self-conscious act of forming our particular cognitions and actions *in full consciousness of these boundary concepts* is a condition of possibility of such cognitions and actions, since it is only in this way that they agree with the conditions of human self-consciousness. But a condition of possibility, when considered relative to that which is actual, and which is made possible by it, is in that very respect *necessary*, which for Kant always means *recognized as necessary by reason itself*.

It is thus precisely as necessary and normative for all particular performances of reason that the concept of the boundary has the look and feel of the transcendent; for it is indeed recognized as transcending and measuring all particular self-conscious rational activities. Nevertheless, when taken absolutely, i.e. not merely relative to reason's own performances, but rather in relation to all that might be possible in itself, the same boundary has no recognizable foundation or external source of its legitimacy. Seen from an external point of view, the very *thought* of the boundary loses all necessity, and thus all objective validity. Indeed, this is a point at which reason alone sustains itself and establishes its own autonomy. It is for this reason that the boundary concepts, although the objects they represent are not immanent, nevertheless have merely an immanent employment, i.e. a function and significance merely relative to reason's own activities.

Finally, the critical philosophy, I believe, is misunderstood if one thinks that through it Kant's goal was to put all our philosophical problems to rest. His intention was rather to eliminate the false problems, while opening up a space within which the genuine problems of philosophy could reveal themselves in their true depth, and impress upon us the sort of force and fascination that is proper to their nature. It just so happens to be that the false problems of philosophy chiefly derive in his view from our desire for unbounded knowledge, while the true problems relate to something much more difficult, but perhaps still possible, namely, the duty to become good human beings. Philosophy, as the pursuit of wisdom, then, is something that cannot be provided with a definitive answer, but is rather like a voice that rings forever in our conscience as a call to self-knowledge, moral cultivation and betterment of our fellow human beings.

Brief Outline of Kant's Conception of Teleology

Kant's philosophy in both the pre-critical and the critical periods is characterized by a double standpoint on objects and their essences, and it is in regard to the relation of these two standpoints that the characteristic teleology of the Kantian world-view is revealed. What Kant calls a "transcendental" standpoint has been adopted when the object is considered in regard to its essence, and particularly in regard to the grounds that constitute this essence and its possibility, while what he calls the "metaphysical" standpoint is adopted when the specifically-determined essence of an object is considered in relation to its own consequences, or when it is viewed as a ground of further possible determinations. Put differently, if the metaphysical can be said to consider the essences of things and their consequences, then the transcendental can be said to consider what is essential to the essences. Therefore, transcendental philosophy is in both the critical and pre-critical periods, as Kant acutely describes it, the "metaphysics of metaphysics."

In the pre-critical period in particular, Kant's investigations lead him to the conclusion that these two standpoints are connected in a uniquely teleological way. Namely, when an object, or in this case a substance, is genuinely considered in regard to its real essence or, what is the same, in regard to its real possibility, this can only be done by cognizing it against the background of the sum-total of all real possibility. Furthermore, since this reality is precisely that found in the dynamic perfection of creation itself, all real possibility must be coextensive with all reality manifest in the world-whole unfolding in both infinite space and infinite time. For these reasons, it can be concluded that the act of real determination through which God creates the individual in regard to its essence, and thus with regard to the totality of its real internal determinations, is *at the same* time an act that determines the individual through the idea or schema comprising the totality of all possible and actual real relations (or grounds) with other members of the world-whole. God's act of creating and thus determining the inner essence of the individual is thus an absolutely teleological act in which the whole of creation is constituted as an absolutely organic totality, the whole through each part, and each part through the whole. It is, transcendentally considered, unconditionally and absolutely the product of a causality acting on the basis of an idea of a real whole or community of substances that is to be brought about through this very act.

If we incorporate into this the previous distinction between the transcendental and the metaphysical standpoints, it can therefore be concluded that the infinite wealth of specific purposive and harmonious relations that are found to be the consequences of the essences of things (i.e., metaphysically considered), is originally founded upon, and a consequence or specification of, the internal teleology of things seen transcendentally, which latter is the ground of their possible real community. And yet, this is no *mere* consequence, because the very same real consequences that appear within the metaphysical perspective, and which really arise for the first time through the interactions of things in community, are *at the same time* contained in the original idea or schema in accordance with which essences are first constituted. Kant discovers, therefore, that the transcendental perspective already itself possesses an essential relation to the metaphysical, just as the internal determinations of all things possesses an essential relation to the whole of creation. The condition of the transparency of teleological activity is therefore perfectly achieved in the interrelation of the two dimensions that become visible when the transcendental and the metaphysical perspectives are adopted.

In the critical period, this same double standpoint is fundamentally reinterpreted. If previously Kant arrived at the concept of a sum-total of reality in order to provide a ground for the complete determination of individuals, and arrived at the idea of God as the self-sufficient ground of this sum-total by means of a *purification* of it, then in the critical period Kant sees *reason itself* as presupposing just such a sum-total as a principle of complete determination, and arrives at the ideal of God (i.e. the ideal of pure reason, not as the sum-total of realities, but as their *ground*) through a purification of the very idea of reason as a pure faculty of principles. The key to this transition and indeed to Kant's transformed employment of the transcendental/metaphysical distinction lies in this conception of the *purification* of reason. In the critical perspective, we can encounter the real only through sensation and can cognize it only as appearance, because of the essential link Kant discovers between self-consciousness and consciousness of the necessity in our representations, or better, in our judgments through which objects are first constituted. This means that transcendental philosophy, understood as a science of the essences of things and of the source of what is necessary in them, no longer concerns things in themselves and absolutely, but rather concerns that which belongs to them essentially and necessarily as objects of human reason. As in the pre-critical period, Kant recognizes that such necessity, if it is to be cognized by reason, must have its source in a genuinely independent and self-sufficient ground into which reason also has complete insight. But what can reason have insight into absolutely prior to any affection from without? The critical answer is that such insight is possible only in regard to reason's own workings, its own pure essence. If the idea of God as the independent being is arrived at in the pre-critical period by means of the purification of all given realities from negations, so the pure idea of reason is arrived at in the critical philosophy through a *purification* of reason from all that is empirical. Critical transcendental philosophy is thus founded in an act of the purification of reason and the analytical unfolding from within itself of its own pure idea. Pure reason as an absolute and self-sufficient unity thus becomes the absolute ground of the possibility of everything that can be reason's own object, firstly in a theoretical and finally in a moral respect.

And here too we find that there arises a transcendental teleology, not of substances in themselves, but rather of all possible objects of reason of whatever kind. Here pure reason as a whole, thus in the combination of its theoretical and practical uses, postulates freely the idea of a being that is a moral ground of all real possibility, so that by acting and determining itself under this idea all objects determined by reason fit within an absolute systematic whole. By means of this, in all its particular acts whereby it determines objects in regard to reality, reason *synthetically* and *essentially* forms the objects as parts under and in view of precisely this absolute whole. This absolute whole is therefore an end, indeed the final end of reason, and it internally structures the essences of all objects of reason transcendentally. This idea, through which an absolute whole is first provided with a principle, is, as we have seen, one also formed with an *internal* relation to the parts themselves. The whole precedes them in idea, as the archetype of their unity, but it is nevertheless the idea of a unity of precisely these and no other parts in their complete determinacy, thus also in their empirical relations. The transcendental unity of reason is thus not only teleological in the respect that it is an archetype that provides an absolutely unified, thus purposive, horizon of objectivity, but also in the sense that it provides the ground for a unity that is brought about and exists essentially in the actual whole (i.e. real community) of these parts in their *own* relations (viewed metaphysically). If viewed in its purity or as regards its essence and inner real possibility, each object of reason therefore contains an essential connection, and indeed a reference to a complete ground of agreement, with absolutely all of its possible relations to other members of the whole of possible experience determined both theoretically and morally. This transcendental unity, the unity of reason, is not imposed upon but is precisely *realized* in and through the whole that is reason's theoretical and practical cognitions. So here, again, the core of Kant's teleological world-view, understood now however as the teleology of human reason, is located precisely in the essential relation he discovers between the transcendental and the metaphysical aspects of reason's activity.

My essential claim has been that in the philosophy of the critical Kant real determination, when properly understood in terms of the grounds that make it possible, is *per se* teleological. This idea, Kant himself came to see, is already contained in Leibniz's claim that the principle of sufficient reason is a teleological principle. This insight was clouded in Kant's predecessors by the issue of the absolute necessity of essences, i.e. the eternal truths. The unconditionally necessary determinations of essences and of mathematical essences in particular are not teleological, they believed, because they are *per se* determinate, and thus allow of no external real ground of determination, and certainly not one that would act by means of representations. For this reason, in Wolff and others the doctrine of the necessity of essences preserves a kind of determinacy that is not teleological. However, Kant's pre-critical understanding of even the necessary properties of space as grounded in the divine being, and thus as not necessary *per se*, but as consequences of God and necessary only in relation those things for which they provide the essences, explodes this distinction once again so that all real determination can be seen as attesting to the real character of its cause, and as such is subject to an internal teleology.

This idea of the radical contingency of essences, and the new understanding of them as "transcendentally" constituted by and for the sake of a real form, is what I then interpret as making possible Kant's critical reinterpretation of theoretical reason in terms of the understanding's determination of perceptions on the basis of and for the sake of the unity of apperception – which alone is possible by making use of the categories as modes of determination – and the fusing together of theoretical and practical reason. For this makes reason in all its determining activities essentially an active and purposive power, i.e. by virtue of this common purposive structure of reason all its functions can be brought under the single purposive function of self-determination. This is discovered to be the inner teleology of reason in its self-determining activity, and it explains why the objects reason presents to itself are always purposive for it.

We have also seen that practical determination by means of the moral law, which forms the core of Kant's critical philosophy, the very linchpin of the unity of reason, is understood by Kant as being teleological *per se*. This is because it is practical determination by means of this law alone that exhibits objectively real purposiveness of the highest kind. My main reasons for this claim were: 1) Determination "of the action for the sake of the law alone" contains Kant's very transcendental definition of purposiveness (*KU* 05:219–220). Morally estimable acts are alone possible through the efficient causality of a unique representation, and the relation of all actions which have this purposive act (intention) as their basis exhibit a complete and universal unity of all possible ends under the idea of the highest good. 2) Natural ends cannot be guaranteed or even regarded as objectively real, because they must be both natural and intentional (i.e. they must both be purposive for theoretical reason, which requires mechanical unity, and for reason, which requires absolute unity). But the moral law, as Kant says, guarantees the objective reality of determination by means of the law – or freedom – and thus for the first time of a real teleological causality. When, in the *KU*, Kant claims that in the human being alone do we find a causality that is genuinely teleological, I take him as meaning precisely this. 3) Kant derives the categorical imperative precisely by deriving the most unlimited form of teleological causality. Namely, he begins with the idea of a will, or something that has causality according to and for the sake of its representations, an intentional cause, and then removes from this idea all specific limitations (particular ends). This removal, which is a construction of the idea of the pure will, should be understood – I have argued – not as a removal of the will from any relation to ends, but rather a removal of the restriction of the will – uncovering its inner reality – to any particular object, which leaves behind the universal form of all willing, unlimited willing, thus unlimited relation to ends, which is the real essence of willing as such. If action for an end is therefore teleological insofar as it relates to some object that is its purpose, then the pure will is absolutely teleological because it relates to and possesses the form of an absolute whole of all possible objects of willing. It is from this universal purposiveness (without a limited purpose) inhering in determination by the pure will that we derive constitutively what our ends should be, and are assured that by this fact they will cohere with the absolute end of pure practical reason.

The kind of universal teleology developed by Kant, I am aware, is not what one usually takes teleology to mean. Yet I have argued that it can properly be called "teleological" because it is arrived at by Kant in an investigation into the inner reality of all particular teleological determination, and that this – generally – is one of the absolutely central insights that both distinguishes the critical philosophy, and makes possible its fundamental claims that the essences of all objects are literally *produced* through a synthesis carried out by the rational mind, and based upon its own *a priori* forms; that because of this, the objects of cognition can be said to "reflect" the inner structure of reason, i.e. they are created after its own image; and that reason performs such an activity in order to fulfill its own needs, and in order to relate to itself as a final end.

Bibliography

I. Translations Consulted

Unless otherwise noted, translations used in this work are from the Cambridge Edition of the Works of Immanuel Kant, edited by Paul Guyer and Allen W. Wood, published by Cambridge University Press. On occasion, I also quote from the following translations of Kant's works.

GMS
Paton, H. J. (Trans.)(1964): New York: Harper & Row.

KpV
Beck, Lewis White (Trans.)(1993): New York: Macmillan Publishing Company.
Pluhar, Werner S. (Trans.)(2002): Indianapolis: Hackett Publishing Company.

KrV
Smith, Norman Kemp (Trans.)(1965): New York: St Martin's Press.

KU
Meredith, James Creed (Trans.)(1952): Oxford: Clarendon Press.
Pluhar, Werner S. (Trans.)(1952): Indianapolis: Hackett Publishing Company.

Prol
Carus, Paul (Trans. 1977): Revised by James W. Ellington. Indianapolis: Hackett.
Lucas, Peter G. (Trans.)(1959): Manchester: University Press.

II. Primary Sources

Aquinas, St. Thomas (1997): *Basic Writings of Saint Thomas Aquinas*. Vol. 1. Pegis, Anton C. (Ed.). Indianapolis: Hackett.
Aristotle (1968). *Physics*. In: Aristotle in Twenty-Three Volumes. Loeb Classical Library. Wickstead, H. P. and F. M. Cornford (Trans.). Vols. 5 and 6. Cambridge: Harvard University Press, 1968.
Aristotle (1970): *Aristotle's Metaphysics*. Apostle, Hipocrates G. (Trans.). Bloomington: Indiana University Press.
Aristotle (1999): *Aristotle's Metaphysics*. Sachs, Joe (Trans.). Santa Fe: Green Lion Press.
Arnauld, Antoine and Pierre Nicole (1996): *Logic or the Art of Thinking*. Jill Vance Buroker (Trans.). Cambridge: Cambridge University Press.
Ayer, Alfred Jules (undated): *Language, Truth and Logic*. New York: Dover Publications.
Ayer, Alfred Jules (2006): *Probability & Evidence*. New York: Columbia University Press.
Bacon, Francis (2000): *The New Organon*. Jardine, Lisa and Michael Silverthorne (Eds.). Cambridge: Cambridge University Press.
Baumgarten, Alexander Gottlieb (1973): *Acroasis Logica in Christianum L. B. De Wolff.* Hildesheim: Georg Olms Verlag.

Baumgarten, Alexander Gottlieb (2004): *Metaphysik.* Meier, Ge. Friedr. (Trans.), with remarks by Joh. Aug. Eberhard. Second edition, 1783. Jena: Dietrich Scheglmann Reprints.
Bergson, Henri (1911): *Creative Evolution.* Mitchell, Arthur (Trans.). New York: Henry Holt.
Brucker, Johann Jakob (1742–1744): *Historia Critica Philosophiae.* 6 Vols. Leipzig.
Crusius, Christian August (1749): *Anleitung über natürliche Begebenheiten ordentlich und vorsichtlich nachzudencken.* Parts I and II. Leipzig: Johann Friedrich Gleditsch.
Crusius, Christian August (1751): *Anweisung vernünftig zu leben.* Second enlarged edition. Leipzig: Johann Friedrich Gleditsch.
Crusius, Christian August (1766): *Ausfürliche Abhandlung von dem rechten Gebrauche und der Einschränkung des sogenannten Satzes vom Zureichenden oder besser Determinirenden Grunde.* Translated from Latin into German by Christian Friedrich Krause. Leipzig: Johann Christian Langenheim.
Crusius, Christian August (1964): *Entwurf der nothwendigen Vernunft-Wahrheiten, wiefern sie den zufälligen entgegen gesetzt werden.* Die philosophische hauptwerke. Vol. 2. Hildesheim: Georg Olms.
Crusius, Christian August (1965): *Weg zur Gewissheit und Zuverlässigkeit der menschlichen Erkenntnis.* Die philosophische hauptwerke. Vol. 3. Hildesheim: Georg Olms.
Chisholm, Roderick M (1946): "The Contrary-To-Fact Conditional." In: *Mind*, p. 289–307.
Copernicus, Nicholas (1995): *On the Revolutions of the Heavenly Spheres.* Wallis, Charles Glenn (Trans.). Amherst: Prometheus Books.
Davidson, Donald (1980): *Essays on Actions and Events.* Oxford: Clarendon Press.
Descartes, René (1985): *The Philosophical Writings of Descartes.* Cottingham, John and Robert Stoothoff and Dugald Murdoch (Trans.). 3 Vols. Cambridge: Cambridge University Press.
Ducasse, C. J (1949): "Explanation, Mechanism, and Teleology." In: *Readings in Philosophical Analysis.* Feigl, Herbert and Wilfrid Sellars (Eds.). New York: Appleton-Century-Crofts, p. 540–544.
Enfield, William (2001): *The History of Philosophy. From the Earliest Periods: Drawn Up From Brucker's Historia Critica Philosophiae.* Vols. 1 and 2. 1837. With an introduction by Knud Haakonssen. No place of publication given: Thoemmes Press.
Epictetus (1807): *The Works of Epictetus.* Carter, Elizabeth (Trans.) Vol. 2. London: Rivington.
Feynman, Richard (1944): *The Character of Physical Law.* New York: Modern Library.
Fichte, Johann Gottlieb (1845/6): *Johann Gottlieb Fichtes sämmtliche Werke.* Ed. Immanuel Hermann Fichte.
Fichte, Johann Gottlieb (1834/5): *Johann Gottlieb Fichtes nachgelassene Werke.* Ed. Immanuel Hermann Fichte.
Fichte, Johann Gottlieb (1982): *Science of Knowledge.* Heath, Peter and John Lachs (Ed. and Trans.). Cambridge: Cambridge University Press.
Fichte, Johann Gottlieb (1987): *The Vocation of Man.* Preuss, Peter (Trans.). Indianapolis: Hackett Publishing Company.
Fichte, Johann Gottlieb (1992): *Foundations of Transcendental Philosophy: (Wissenschaftslehre) nova method (1796/99).* Breazeale, Daniel (Ed. and Trans.). Ithaca: Cornell University Press.
Fichte, Johann Gottlieb (1993): *Fichte's Wissenschaftslehre of 1794: A Commentary on Part 1.* Heath, Peter and John Lachs (Trans.). With a commentary by George J. Seidel. West Lafayette, IN: Purdue University Press.
Fichte, Johann Gottlieb (1994): *Introductions to the "Wissenschaftslehre" (1797–1800).* Breazeale, Daniel (Ed. and Trans.). Indianapolis: Hackett Publishing Company.

Fichte, Johann Gottlieb (2001): "Review of Leonard Creuzer, *Skeptical Reflections on the Freedom of the Will, with Reference to the Latest Theories of the Same, with a Foreword by Professor Schmid.*" In: *The Philosophical Forum.* Daniel Breazeale (Trans.), p. 289–96.

Fichte, Johann Gottlieb (2005a): *The Science of Knowing: J. G. Fichte's 1804 Lectures on the "Wissenschaftslehre."* Wright, Walter E. (Trans.). New York: SUNY.

Fichte, Johann Gottlieb (2005b): *The System of Ethics.* Breazeale, Daniel and Günter Zöller (Eds.) Cambridge: Cambridge University Press.

Frege, Gottlob (1980): *The Foundations of Arithmetic: A Logico-Mathematical Inquiry into the Concept of Number.* Austin, J. L. (Trans.). Evanston: Northwestern University Press.

Goodman, Nelson (1983): *Fact Fiction and Forecast.* Cambridge, Mass.: Harvard University Press.

Gottsched, Johann Christoph (1756): *Erste Gründe der gesammten Weltweisheit.* Sixth and improved edition. Vol. 1. Leipzig: Breitkopf.

Hegel, G. W. F. (1968): *Lectures on the History of Philosophy.* Vol. 3. Haldane, E. S. and Frances H. Simon (Trans.). London: Routledge and Kegan Paul.

Hegel, G. W. F. (1974): *Lectures on the Philosophy of Religion: Together with a Work on the Proofs of the Existence of God.* Vols. I-III. Speirs, E. B. and J. Burdon Sanderson (Trans.). New York: Humanities Press.

Hegel, G. W. F. (1987): *Lectures on the Philosophy of Religion: Vol. 2 Determinate Religion.* Hodgson, Peter C. (Ed.) and R. F. Brown, P. C. Hodgson, and J. M. Stewart (Trans.). Berkeley: University of California Press.

Hegel, G. W. F. (1990): *Wissenschaft der Logik: Die Lehre vom Sein (1832).* Hamburg: Felix Meiner Verlag.

Hegel, G. W. F. (1991): *The Encyclopedia Logic: Part I of the Encyclopedia of Philosophical Sciences with the Zusätze.* Geraets, T. F. and W. A. Suchting and H. S. Harris (Trans.). Indianapolis: Hackett Publishing Company.

Hegel, G. W. F. (1993): *Science of Logic.* Miller, A. V. (Trans.). Atlantic Highlands: Humanities Press International.

Hegel, G. W. F. (1994): *Wissenschaft der Logik: Die Lehre vom Begriff (1816).* Hamburg: Felix Meiner.

Hegel, G. W. F. (1995): *Lectures on the History of Philosophy.* Vol. 3. Haldane, E. and F. Simson (Trans.). Lincoln: University of Nebraska Press.

Heidegger, Martin (1986): *Schelling's Treatise on the Essence of Human Freedom.* Ohio University Press.

Heine, Heinrich (2007): *On the History of Religion and Philosophy in Germany and Other Writings.* Pollack-Milgate, Howard (Trans.) and Terry Pinkard (Ed.). Cambridge: Cambridge University Press.

Hempel, Carl G. (1965): *Aspects of Scientific Explanation and Other Essays in the Philosophy of Science.* New York: The Free Press.

Hempel, Carl G. (1966): *Philosophy of Natural Science.* Englewood Cliffs, New Jersey: Prentice-Hall.

Hoffmann, Adolph Friedrich (1736): *Beweisthümer derjenigen Grund-Wahrheiten aller Relgion und Moralität Welche die in der Wolfischen Philosophie befindlichen Gegensätze haben geleugnet, und über den Haufen geworfen werden wollen.* Frankfurt and Leipzig.

Hoffmann, Adolph Friedrich (2010): *Vernunftlehre.* Ecole, Jean and Robert Theis, Werner Schneiders and Sonia Carbonici-Gavanelli (Eds.). 2 vols. Christian Wolff Gesammelte

Werke Materialien und Dokumente. Volume 99.1 and 99.2. Hildesheim, Zürich, New York: Georg Olms Verlag.
Hume, David (1896): *A Treatise of Human Nature*. Selby-Bigge, L. A. (Ed.). Oxford: Clarendon Press.
Kant, Immanuel (1981). Reflexionen und Textemendationen aus dem Handexemplar der Kritik der praktischen Vernunft. Transcribed by Gerhard Lehmann. In: *Kantstudien*. Vol. 72, p. 132–139.
Kant, Immanuel (1999). *Correspondence*. Zweig, Arnulf (Trans. and Ed.). Cambridge: Cambridge University Press.
Knutzen, Martin (2006): *Philosophischer Beweiss von der Wahrheit der Christlichen Religion*. Fourth edition, 1747. Hildesheim: Georg Olms Verlag.
Lange, Joachim (1736). *Kurtzer Abriss der Wolfianischen Philosophie*. In Hoffman, *Beweisthümer*, Franckfurt and Leipzig: 1736. 1–12.
Leibniz, G. W. (1951): *Selections*. Wiener, Philip P. (Ed.). New York: Charles Scribner's Sons.
Leibniz, G. W. (1969): *Philosophical Papers and Letters*. Loemker, Leroy E. (Trans.). 2nd edition. Dordrecht: Kluwer Academic Publishers.
Leibniz, G. W. (1989): *Philosophical Essays*. Ariew, Roger and Daniel Garber (Trans.). Indianapolis: Hackett Publishing Company.
Leibniz, G. W. (1990): *Theodicy*. Huggard, E. M. (Trans.) and Austin Farrer (Ed.). Chicago: Open Court.
Leibniz, G. W. (1996): *New Essays on Human Understanding*. Remnant, Peter and Jonathan Bennett (Trans. and Ed.). Cambridge: Cambridge University Press.
Maimon, Salomon (2004). *Versuch über die Transzendentalphilosophie*. Hamburg: Felix Meiner Verlag.
Maupertuis, Par M. de (1751): *Essai de Cosmologie*. Published in German the same year as *Versuch einer Cosmologie*. Berlin: C. G. Nicolai.
McDowell, John (1996): *Mind and World*. Cambridge. Mass.: Harvard University.
McDowell, John (1998a): "Having the World in View: Sellars, Kant, and Intentionality." In: *The Journal of Philosophy*, 95, p. 431–450.
McDowell, John (1998b): *Mind, Value, and Reality*. Cambridge, Mass.: Harvard University.
McDowell, John. (2009): *Having the World in View: Essays on Kant, Hegel, and Sellars*. Cambridge, Mass.: Harvard University Press.
Meier, Georg Friedrich (1752): *Auszug aus der Vernunftlehre*.
Meier, Georg Friedrich (1755): *Metaphysik: Erster Theil*. Halle: Johann Justinus Gebauer.
Meier, Georg Friedrich (1756): *Metaphysik: Zweyter Theil*. Halle: Johann Justinus Gebauer.
Meier, Georg Friedrich (1765a): *Metaphysik: Dritter Theil*. Second edition, Halle: Johann Justinus Gebauer.
Meier, Georg Friedrich (1765b): *Metaphysik: Vierter Theil*. Second edition. Halle: Johann Justinus Gebauer.
Mendelssohn, Moses (1931): *Gesammelte Schriften*. Elbogen, I. and J. Guttmann and E. Mittwoch (Eds.). Berlin: Akademie-Verlag.
Mendelssohn, Moses (1979): *Morgenstunden oder Vorlesungen über das Dasein Gottes*. Bourel, Dominique (Ed.). Stuttgart: Phillipp Reclam.
Mendelssohn, Moses (2007): *Phädon, or On the Immortality of the Soul*. Noble, Patricia (Trans.). Berlin: Peter Lang.
Mendelssohn, Moses (1821): *Phädon oder über die Unsterblichkeit der Seele*. Friedländer, David (Ed.). Sixth edition. Berlin: Nicolaischen Buchhandlung.

Mendelssohn Moses (1789): *Phaedon; or, the Death of Socrates*. Cullen, Charles (Trans.). London: J. Cooper.
Mendelssohn, Moses (1997): *Philosophical Writings*. Dahlström, Daniel O. (Trans.). Cambridge: Cambridge University Press.
Mendelssohn, Moses (1989): *Schriften über Religion und Aufklärung*. Thom, Martina (Ed.). Leipzig: Union Verlag Berlin.
Newton, Isaac (1974): *Newton's Philosophy of Nature: Selections from His Writings*. Thayer, H. S. (Ed.). New York: Hafner Press.
Newton, Isaac (2004): *Philosophical Writings*. Janiak, Andrew (Ed.). Cambridge: Cambridge University Press.
Nietsche, Friedrich (1980). *Jenseits von Gut und Böse*. In: Colli, Giorgio and Mazzino Montinari (Eds.) *Sämtliche Werke*. Band 5. Kritische Studienausgabe in 15 Bänden. München and New York.
Peirce, Charles Sanders (1998): *The Essential Peirce: Selected Philosophical Writings Vol. 2 (1839–1913)*. Edited by the Peirce Edition Project. Bloomington and Indianapolis: Indiana University Press.
Plato (1973): *Theaetetus:* McDowell, John (Trans.). Oxford: Clarendon Press.
Plato (1996): *The Collected Dialogues*. Hamilton, Edith and Huntington Cairns (Ed.). Princeton: Princeton University Press.
Pope, Alexander (1964): *The Poems of Alexander Pope, Volume III i: An Essay on Man*. Mack, Maynard (Ed.). New Haven: Yale University Press.
Popper, Karl R. (1983): *Realism and the Aim of Science*. Totowa, New Jersey: Rowman and Littlefield.
Quine, W. V. O. (1977): "Natural kinds." In: Schwartz 1977, p. 155–175.
Reimarus, Hermann Samuel (1772): *Die vornehmsten Wahrheiten der natürlichen Religion*. Fourth edition, Hamburg: Johann Carl Bohn.
Reimarus, Hermann Samuel (1979): *Vernunftlehre*. Munich: Carl Hanser Verlag.
Reinhold, C. L. (1972): *Briefe über die Kantische Philosophie*. 2 vols. Leipzig.
Reinhold, C. L. (2003): *Beiträge zur Berichtigung bisheriger Mißverständnisse der Philosophen: Erster Band, das Fundament der Elementarphilosophie betreffend*. Fabbianelli, Faustino (Ed.). Hamburg: Felix Meiner Verlag.
Rousseau, Jean-Jacques (1979): *Emile or On Education*. Bloom, Alan (Trans.). Place of publication not given: Basic Books.
Rousseau, Jean-Jacques (1987): *The Basic Political Writings*. Cress, Donald A. (Trans.) with an introduction by Peter Gay. Indianapolis: Hackett Publishing Company.
Rousseau, Jean-Jacques (1990): "On Theatrical Imitation: An Essay Drawn from Plato's Dialogues." In: Scott, John T. (Trans.). *The Collected Writings of Rousseau Vol. 7: Essay on the Origin of Languages and Writings Related to Music*. London: University Press of New England.
Schelling, F. W. J. (1967): *Ausgewählte Werke*. 4 vols. Darmstadt: Wissenschaftliche Buchgesellschaft.
Schelling, F. W. J. (1980): *Of the I as Principle of Philosophy, or On the Unconditional in Human Knowledge*. In: Marti, Fritz (Trans.). *The Unconditional In Human Knowledge*. Lewisburg: Bucknell University Press.
Schelling, F. W. J. (1988): *Ideas for a Philosophy of Nature*. Harris, Errol E. and Peter Heath (Trans.). Cambridge: Cambridge University Press.

Schelling, F. W. J. (1997): *System of Transcendental Idealism (1800)*. Heath, Peter (Trans.). Charlottesville: University Press of Virginia.
Schelling, F. W. J. (2000): *System des Transzendentalen Idealismus*. Hamburg: Felix Meiner Verlag.
Schelling, F. W. J. (2004): *First Outline of a System of the Philosophy of Nauture*. Peterson, Keith R. (Trans.). New York: SUNY.
Schlegel, Friedrich (1971): *"Lucinde" and the Fragments*. Firchow, Peter (Trans.). Minneapolis: University of Minnesota Press.
Scotus, Duns (1987): *Philosophical Writings*. Wolter, Allen (Trans.). Indianapolis: Hackett Publishing.
Thomasius, Christian (1968a): *Ausübung der Sittenlehre*. Hildesheim: Georg Olms Verlag.
Thomasius, Christian (1968b): *Ausübung der Vernunftlehre*. Hildesheim: Georg Olms Verlag.
Thomasius, Christian (1968c): *Einleitung zu der Vernunftlehre*. Hildesheim: Georg Olms Verlag.
Thomasius, Christian (1968d): *Einleitung zur Sittenlehre*. Hildesheim: Georg Olms Verlag.
Wolff, Christian (1735): *Philosophia Rationalis sive Logica*. Third corrected edition. Verona.
Wolff, Christian (1741): *Vernünfftige Gedancken von den Absichten der natürlichen Dinge*. Fourth edition. Halle: Rengerischen Buchhandlung.
Wolff, Christian (1747): *Vernünfftige Gedancken von Gott, der Welt und der Seele des Menschen, auch allen Dingen überhaupt*. New enlarged edition. Halle: Rengerischen Buchhandlung.
Wolff, Christian (1749): *Vernünfftige Gedancken von den Kräfften des menschlichen Verstandes und ihrem richtigen Gebrauche wu Erkäntniss der Wahrheit*. New edition. Halle: Rengerischen Buchhandlung.
Wolff, Christian (1752): *Vernünftige Gedancken von der Menschen Thun und Lassen*. New edition. Halle: Rengerischen Buchhandlung.
Wolff, Christian (1963): *Preliminary Discourse on Philosophy in General*. Blackwell, Richard J. (Trans.): Indianapolis: Bobbs-Merrill.
Wolff, Christian (1983): *Der Vernünfftige Gedanken von Gott, der Welt und der Seele des Menschen, auch allen Dingen überhaupt, anderer Teil, bestehend in ausfürlichen Anmerckungen*. Fourth edition, 1740. Reprinted in Gesammelte Werke Materialien und Dokumente. I. Abt. Vol. 3, Hildesheim: Georg Olms Verlag.
Wolff, Christian (2003): *Logic, or Rational Thoughts on the Powers of the Human Understanding; with their Use and Application in the Knowledge and Search of Truth*. Trans. anonymous, 1770. Hildesheim: Georg Olms Verlag.
Wolff, Christian (2005): *Erste Philosophie oder Ontologie: Latin – Deutsch*. Latin and German. Effertz, Dirk (Trans.). Hamburg: Felix Meiner Verlag.
Wüstemann, Justin Elias (1757): *Einleitung in das philosophische Lehrgebäude des Herrn D. Crusius*. Wittenberg: Samuel Gottfried Zimmermann.
Xenophon (2005): *Conversations with Socrates*. Bysshe, Edward (Trans.). New York: Barnes & Noble.

III. Secondary Sources

Adickes, Erich (1895): "Beiträge zur Entwicklungsgeschichte der Kantischen Erkenntnisstheoriel." In: *Kantstudien*. Kiel and Leipzig: Lipsius & Tischer.
Aertsen, Jan A. (1996): *Medieval Philosophy and the Transcendentals: The Case of Thomas Aquinas*. Leiden: E. J. Brill.
Aertsen, Jan A. (2000): "Transcendens – Transcendentalis: The Geneology of a Philosophical Term." In: *L'Élaboration du Vocabulaire Philosophique au Moyen Âge: Actes du Colloque international de Louvain-la-Neuve et Leuven 12–14 septembre 1998*. Hamesse, Jacqueline and Carlos Steel (Eds.). Turnhout, Belgium: Brepols Publishers.
Allison, Henry E. (1973): *The Kant-Eberhard Controversy*. Baltimore: Johns Hopkins University Press.
Allison, Henry E. (1989): "The 'Hidden Circle' in Groundwork III." In: *Proceedings: The Sixth International Kant Congress*. Funke, G. and Th. M. Seebohm (Eds.). Washington, D. C.: University Press of America, p. 149–60.
Allison, Henry E. (1990): *Kant's theory of freedom*. Cambridge: Cambridge University Press.
Allison, Henry E. (1991): "Kant's Antinomy of Teleological Judgment." In: *Southern Journal of Philosophy*. Vol. 30 supplement, p. 25–42.
Allison, Henry E. (1998): "Pleasure and Harmony in Kant's Theory of Taste: A Critique of the Causal Reading." In: Parret 1998, p. 466–83.
Allison, Henry E. (2000): "Where Have all he Categories Gone? Reflections on Longuenesse's Reading of Kant's Transcendental Deduction." In: *Inquiry*. Vol. 43, p. 67–80.
Allison, Henry E. (2001): *Kant's Theory of Taste: A Reading of the "Critique of Aesthetic Judgment."* Cambridge: Cambridge University Press.
Allison, Henry E. (2004): *Kant's Transcendental Idealism: An Interpretation and Defense*. Revised and enlarged edition. New Haven, Conn.: Yale University Press.
Ameriks, Karl (2000): *Kant's Theory of Mind: An Analysis of the Paralogisms of Pure Reason*. Second edition. Oxford: Oxford University Press.
Ameriks, Karl (2001): "Kant's Notion of Systematic Philosophy: Changes in the Second *Critique* and After," In: Fulda 2001, p. 73–91.
Andersen, Svend (1983): *Ideal und Singularität*. In: *Kantstudien*. Ergänzungshefte 116. Berlin: Walter de Gruyter.
Anderson, Abraham (1998): "On the Practical Foundation of Kant's Response to Epistemic Skepticism." In: *Kantstudien*. Vol. 89, p. 145–166.
Anton, John Peter (1957): *Aristotle's Theory of Contrariety*. New York: Humanities Press.
Aquila, Richard E. (1979): "A New Look at Kant's Aesthetic Judgment." In: *Kantstudien*. Vol. 70, p. 17–34.
Aquila, Richard E. (1986): "Comments on Manfred Baum's 'The B-Deduction and the Refutation of Idealism.'" In: *The Southern Journal of Philosophy*. Vol. 25, p. 109–114.
Aquila, Richard E. (1991): "Unity of Organism, Unity of Thought, and the Unity of the *Critique of Judgment*." In: *Southern Journal of Philosophy*. Vol. 30 supplement, p. 139–55.
Aquinas, St. Thomas (1997): *Basic Writings of Saint Thomas Aquinas*. Vol. 1. Pegis, Anton C. (Ed.). Indianapolis: Hackett Publishing Company.
Auxter, Thomas (1982): *Kant's Moral Teleology*. Macon: Mercer University Press.
Barnard, F. M. (1971): "The 'Practical Philosophy' of Christian Thomasius." In: *Journal of the History of Ideas*. Vol. 32, p. 221–246.

Baum, Manfred (1979): "Transcendental Proofs in the *Critique of Pure Reason*." In: Bieri, Peter, Rolf-P. Hostrmann and Loranz Krüger (Eds.). *Transcendental Arguments and Science*. Dordrecht: Springer, p. 3–26.
Baum, Manfred (1986): "The B-Deduction and the Refutation of Idealism." In: *Southern Journal of Philosophy*. Vol. 25, p. 89–107.
Baum, Manfred (1989): "Der Aufbau der Deduction der Kategorien." In: Funke, G. and Th. M. Seebohm (Eds.). *Proceedings: Sixth International Kant Congress*. Washington, D. C.: University Press of America, p. 143–156.
Baum, Manfred (1989): "Kant on Cosmological Apperception." In: *International Philosophical Quarterly*. Vol. 29, p. 281–9.
Baum, Manfred (1995): "Über die Kategoriendeduction in der 1. Auflage der *Kritik der reinen Vernunft*." In: Robinson 1995, p. 467–82.
Baum, Manfred (2001): "Systemform und Selbsterkenntnis der Vernunft bei Kant." In: Fulda 2001, p. 25–40.
Beck, Lewis White (1963): *A Commentary on Kant's "Critique of Practical Reason."* Chicago: University of Chicago Press.
Beck, Lewis White (1967): "Kant's Theory of Definition." In: Gram 1967, p. 215–27.
Beck, Lewis White (1978a): "Analytic and Synthetic Judgments before Kant." In: *Essays on Kant and Hume*. New Haven: Yale University Press, p. 80–100.
Beck, Lewis White (1978b): "Lovejoy as a Critic of Kant." In: *Essays on Kant and Hume*. New Haven: Yale University Press, p. 61–79.
Beck, Lewis White (1987): "Five Concepts of Freedom in Kant." In: Szrednicki, Jan T. J. (Ed.). *Stephan Körner – Philosophical Analysis and Reconstruction*. ed. Jan T. J. Dordrecht: Martinus Nijhoff Publishers, p. 35–51.
Beck, Lewis White (1996): *Early German Philosophy: Kant and His Predecessors*. Bristol: Thoemmes Press.
Beckner, Morton (2006): "Teleology." In: Borchert, Donald M. (Ed.). *Encyclopedia of Philosophy*. 2nd edition. New York: Thompson Gale, p. 384–8.
Beiser, Frederick C. (1992): "Kant's intellectual development: 1746–1781." In: Guyer 1992, p. 26–61.
Beiser, Frederick C. (2006): "Moral Faith and the Highest Good." In: Guyer, Paul (Ed.). *The Cambridge Companion to Kant and Modern Philosophy*. Cambridge: Cambridge University Press, p. 588–629.
Benden, Magdalene (1972): *Christian August Crusius: Wille und Verstand als Prinzipien des Handelns*. Abhandlungen zur Philosophie, Psychologie und Pädagogik. Vol. 73. Bonn: Bouvier Verlag.
Bennett, Jonathan (1976): *Linguistic Behaviour*. Cambridge: Cambridge University Press.
Bennett, Jonathan (1991):"Folk-psychological explanations." In: Greenwood, John D. (Ed.). *The future of folk psychology: intentionality and cognitive science*. Cambridge: Cambridge University Press.
Bennett, Jonathan (2005): "Leibniz's Two Realms." In: Rutherford, Donald and J. A. Cover (Eds.). *Leibniz: Nature and Freedom*. Oxford: Oxford University Press, p. 135–155.
Beversluis, John (1974): "Kant on Moral Striving." In: *Kantstudien*. Vol. 65, p. 67–77.
Bittner, Rüdiger and Konrad Cramer, (Eds.) (1975): *Materialien zu Kants 'Kritik der praktischen Vernunft.'* Suhrkamp: Frankfurt am Main.
Blumenberg, Hans (1983): "Self-Preservation and Inertia: On the Constitution of Modern Rationality." In: Christensen 1983, p. 209–56.

Blumenberg, Hans (1987): *The Genesis of the Copernican World*. Wallace, Robert M. (Trans.). Cambridge, Mass.: M. I. T. Press.
Bowman, Curtis (2003): "A Deduction of Kant's Concept of the Highest Good." In: Journal of Philosophical Studies. Vol. 28, p. 45–63.
Brandt, Reinhard (1995): *The Table of Judgments: Critique of Pure Reason A67–76;B92–101*. Watkins, Eric (Trans.). North American Kant Society Studies in Philosophy. Vol. 4. Atascadero, California: Ridgeview.
Brandt, Reinhard (1998): "Zur Logik des ästhetischen Urteils." In: Parret 1998, p. 229–45.
Brandt, Reinhard (2003): "The Guiding Idea of Kant's Anthropology and the Vocation of the Human Being." In: Jacobs 2003, p. 85–104.
Breazeale, Daniel and Tom Rockmore (Eds) (2001). *New Essays in Fichte's "Foundation of the Entire Doctrine of Scientific Knowledge."* Amherst, NY: Humanity Books.
Brecht, Martin (1993): "August Hermann Francke und der Hallische Pietismus." In: Brecht, Martin (Ed.). *Gescheidnis des Pietismus*. Vol. 1. Göttingen: Vandenhoek & Ruprecht, p. 439–539.
Bronfenbrenner, Martha Ornstein (1975): *The Role of Scientific Societies in the Seventeenth Century*. New York: Arno Press.
Carboncini, Sonia (1989): "Die thomasianisch-pietistische Tradition und ihre Fortsetzung durch Christian August Crusius." In: *Christian Thomasius, 1655–1728: Interpretationen zu Werk und Wirkung*. Schneiders, W. (Ed.). Hamburg: Meiner Verlag, p. 287–304.
Carboncini, Sonia (1991): *Transzendentale Wahrheit und Traum: Christian Wolffs Antwort auf die Herausforderung durch den Cartesianischen Zweifel*. In: Forschungen und Materialien zur deutschen Aufklärung. Abteilung II: Monographien. Vol. 5. Stuttgart-Bad Cannstatt: frommann-holzboog.
Carriero, John (2009): *Between Two Worlds: A Reading of Descartes's "Meditations."* Princeton: Princeton University Press.
Cassirer, Ernst (1967): "Kant and the Problem of Metaphysics." In: Gram 1967, p. 131–57.
Cassirer, Ernst (1970): *Rousseau Kant Goethe: Two Essays*. Gutmann, James and Paul Oskar Kristeller and John Herman Randall, Jr., (Trans.). Princeton: Princeton University Press.
Cassirer, Ernst (1981): *Kant's Life and Thought*. Haden, James (Trans.). New Haven: Yale University Press.
Cassirer, Ernst (1985): *The Philosophy of Symbolic Forms, Volume 3: The Phenomenology of Knowledge*. Manheim, Ralph (Trans.). New Haven: Yale University Press.
Cassirer, H. W. (1968): *Kant's First Critique: An Appraisal of the Permanent Significance of Kant's Critique of Pure Reason*. London: George Allen & Unwin.
Caswell, M. (2006): "Kant's Conception of the Highest Good, the *Gesinnung*, and the Theory of Radical Evil." In: *Kant Studien*. Vol. 97, p. 184–209.
Christensen, Darrel E, and Manfred Riedel, Robert Spaemann, Reiner Wiehl and Wolfgang Wieland (Eds.) (1983): *Contemporary German Philosophy: Volume 3, 1983*. London: Pennsylvania State University Press.
Ciafardone, Raffaele (1982): "Über das Primat der praktischen Vernunft vor der theoretischen bei Thomasius und Crusius mit Beziehung auf Kant." In: *Studia Leibnitiana*. Vol. 14, p. 127–135.
Collingwood, R. G: (1960): *The Idea of Nature*. New York: Oxford University Press.
Collins, James (1959): *God in Modern Philosophy*. Chicago: Henry Regnery Company.
Collins, James (1977): "Functions of Kant's Philosophy of Religion." In: *The Monist*. Vol. 60, p. 157–80.

Cornford, F. M. (1980): *From Religion to Philosophy: A Study in the Origins of Western Speculation*. Sussex: Harvester Press.
Couturat, Louis (1994): "On Leibniz's Metaphysics." In Woolhouse 1994, vol. 1, p. 1–19.
Craig, Edward (1998): *Routledge Encyclopedia of Philosophy*. London: Routledge.
Curley, E. M. (1972): "The Roots of Contingency." In: Frankfurt, Harry G. (Ed.). *Leibniz: A Collection of Critical Essays*. New York: Anchor Books.
Curley, E. M. (1988): *Behind the Geometrical Method: A Reading of Spinoza's "Ethics."* Princeton: Princeton University Press.
Deleuze, Gilles (1984): *Kant's Critical Philosophy: The Doctrine of the Faculties*. Tomlinson, Hugh and Barbara Habberjam (Trans.). Minneapolis: University of Minnesota Press.
Denis, Lara (2005): "Autonomy and the Highest Good." In: *Kantian Review*. Vol. 10, p. 33–59.
Des Chene, Dennis (1996): *Physiologia: Natural Philosophy in Late Aristotelian and Cartesian Thought*. Ithaca, New York: Cornell University Press.
Despland, Michel (1973): *Kant on History and Religion*. Montreal: McGill-Queen's University Press.
deVries, Willem A. (1991): "The Dialectic of Teleology." In: *Philosophical Topics*. Vol. 19, p. 51–70.
Dörflinger, Bernd (1991): "Teleology and the Problem of Transition." In: *Southern Journal of Philosophy*. Vol. 30, supplement, p. 65–71.
Dörflinger, Bernd (1995): "The Underlying Teleology of the First Critique." In: Robinson 1995, p. 813–26.
Dörflinger, Bernd (2000): *Das Leben theoretischer Vernunft*. Berlin: Walter de Gruyter.
Dorter, Kenneth (1982): *Plato's Phaedo: An Interpretation*. Toronto: University of Toronto.
Doyle, John P (1997): "Between Transcendental and Transcendental: The Missing Link?." In: *The Review of Metaphysics*. Vol. 50, p. 783–815.
Düsing, Klaus (1968): *Die Teleologie in Kants Weltbegriff*. Kantstudien Ergänzungshefte. Vol. 96. Bonn: H. Bouvier Verlag.
Düsing, Klaus (1971): "Das Problem des Höchsten Gutes in Kants Praktischer Philosophie." In: *Kantstudien*. Vol. 62, p. 5–42.
Düsing, Klaus (1990): "Beauty as the Transition from Nature to Freedom in Kant's Critique of Judgment." In: *Nous*. Dahlstrom, Daniel O. (Trans.) Vol. 24, p. 79–92.
Edwards, Jeffrey (2000): *Substance, Force, and the Possibility of Knowledge*. Berkeley: University of California Press.
Engstrom, Stephen (1992): "The concept of the highest good in Kant's moral theory." In: *Philosophy and Phenomenological Research*. Vol. 52, p. 747–80.
Engstrom, Stephen (2002a): "Introduction." In: *Critique of Practical Reason*. Kant, Immanuel. Pluhar, Werner S. (Trans.). Indianapolis: Hackett Publishing Company.
Engstrom, Stephen (2002b): "The Inner Freedom of Virtue." In: Timmons, Mark (Ed.) *Kant's 'Metaphysics of Morals': Interpretive Essays*. Oxford: Oxford University Press, p. 289–315.
Erdmann, Benno (1876): *Martin Knutzen und seine Zeit*. Leipzig: Verlag von Leopold Voss.
Erdmann, Benno (1888): "Kant und Hume um 1762." In: *Archiv für Geschichte der Philosophie*. Vol. 1, p. 62–77 & 216–230.
Fischer, Kuno (1867): *Geschichte der neuern Philosophie: Zweiter Band, Leibniz und seine Schule*. Second edition. Heidelberg: Friedrich Bassermann.

Fisher, Mark and Eric Watkins (1998): "Kant on the Material Ground of Possibility: From *The Only Possible Argument* to the *Critique of Pure Reason*." In: *The Review of Metaphysics.* Vol. 52, p. 369–395.

Förster, Eckart (1989): "Kant's Notion of Philosophy." In: *The Monist.* Vol. 72, p. 285–304.

Förster, Eckart (Ed.) (1989): *Kant's Transcendental Deductions: The Three Critiques and the Opus postumum*. Stanford: Stanford University Press.

Freudiger, Jürg (1996): "Kants Schlussstein: Wie die Teleologie die Einheit der Vernunft stiftet."In: *Kantstudien.* Vol. 87, p. 423–435.

Frierson, Patrick (2003): *Freedom and Anthropology in Kant's Moral Philosophy*. Cambridge: Cambridge University Press.

Fry, Iris (1989): "Kant's Principle of The Formal Finality of Nature and Its Role in Experience." In: *International Philosophical Quarterly.* Vol. 29, p. 67–76.

Fugate, Courtney (2009): "Life and Kant's Critique of Aesthetic Judgment" In: Rhoden, Valerio, Ricardo R. Terra and Guido A. de Almeida (Eds). *Recht und Frieden in der Philosophie Kants*. Akten des X. Internationalen Kant-Kongresses. Berlin and Boston: Walter de Gruyter. Vol. 4, p. 609–621.

Fugate, Courtney (2012): "Did Plato Nearly Discover Synthetic Judgments a priori?" In: *Skepsis: A Journal for Philosophy and Interdisciplinary Research.* Vol. 22, p. 44–50.

Fugate, Courtney (2013): "Teleology, Freedom and the Will in Kant's Moral Philosophy." In: Bacin, Stefano, Alfredo Ferrarin, Claudio La Rocca, and Margit Ruffing (Eds.). *Kant und die Philosophie in weltbürgerlicher Absicht*. Akten des XI. Kant-Kongresses. Berlin and Boston: Walter de Gruyter. Vol. 3, p. 207–218.

Fugate, Courtney (2014): "The Highest Good and Kant's Proof(s) of God's Existence." In: *History of Philosophy Quarterly* (forthcoming).

Fulda, H. F. and J. Stolzenberg (Eds) (2001): *Architecktonik und System der Philosophie Kants*. Hamburg: Felix Meiner Verlag.

Genova, Anthony C. (1974): "Kant's Epigenesis of Pure Reason." In: *Kantstudien.* Vol. 65, p. 259–73.

Genova, Anthony C. (1982): "Kant's Complex Problem of Reflective Judgment." In: *Review of Metaphysics.* Vol. 23, p. 452–480.

Gill, Mary Louise (1989): *Aristotle on Substance: The Paradox of Unity*. Princeton: Princeton University Press.

Gram, Moltke S. (Ed.) (1967): *Kant: Disputed Questions*. Chicago: Quadrangle Books.

Grier, Michelle (2001): *Kant's Doctrine of Transcendental Illusion*. Cambridge: Cambridge University Press.

Gurr, John Edwin, S. J. (1959): *The Principle of Sufficient Reason in Some Scholastic Systems: 1750–1900*. Milwaukee: Marquette University Press.

Guyer, Paul (1991): "Mendelssohn and Kant: One Source of the Critical Philosophy." In: *Philosophical Topics.* Vol. 19, p. 119–152.

Guyer, Paul (1997): "The Unity of Reason: Rereading Kant." In: *The Philosophical Review.* Vol. 106, p. 291–295.

Guyer, Paul (1998): "The Unity of Reason: Pure Reason as Practical Reason in Kant's Early Conception of the Transcendental Dialectic." In: *The Monist.* Vol. 72, p. 139–167.

Guyer, Paul (2000): *Kant on Freedom, Law, and Happiness*. Cambridge: Cambridge University Press.

Guyer, Paul (2001): "From Nature to Morality: Kant's New Argument in the 'Critique of Teleological Judgment.'" In: Fulda 2001, p. 375–404.

Guyer, Paul (2003): "Kant's Principles of Reflecting Judgment." In: Guyer, Paul (Ed.). *Kant's Critique of the Power of Judgment: Critical Essays*. Oxford: Rowman & Littlefield, p. 1–61.
Guyer, Paul (2007): "Perfection, Autonomy, and Heautonomy. The Path of Reason from Wolff to Kant." In: Stolzenberg, Jürgen and Oliver-Pierre Rudolph (Eds.): *Christian Wolff und die europäische Aufklärung*. Akten des 1. Internationalen Christian – Wolff – Kongresses, Halle (Saale), 4.–8. April 2004. Teil I. Christian Wolff Gesammelte Werke Materialien und Dokumente, II.1. Hildesheim, Zürich, New York: Georg Olms Verlag, p. 299–322.
Guyer, Paul (Ed.) (1992): *The Cambridge Companion to Kant*. Cambridge: Cambridge University Press.
Halper, Edward C. (1989): *One and Many in Aristotle's Metaphysics: The Central Books*. Columbus: Ohio State University Press.
Hanna, Robert (2006): *Kant, Science and Human Nature*. Oxford: Oxford University Press.
Heidegger, Martin (1990): *Kant and the Problem of Metaphysics*. Taft, Richard (Trans.). Bloomington: Indiana University Press.
Heidegger, Martin (1998): "Kant's Thesis about Being." In: McNeill, William (Ed.). *Pathmarks*. Cambridge: Cambridge University Press, p. 337–63.
Heidegger, Martin (2002): *The Essence of Human Freedom: an introduction to philosophy*. Sadler, Ted (Trans.). London: Continuum.
Heidegger, Martin (2008): *Basic Concepts of Ancient Philosophy*. Rojcewicz, Richard (Trans.). Bloomington: Indiana University Press.
Heimsoeth, Heinz (1940/41a): "Kants Philosophie des Organischen in den letzten Systementwürfen." In: *Blätter für Deutsche Philosophie*. Vol. 14, p. 81–108.
Heimsoeth, Heinz (1940/41b): "Kants philosophische Entwicklung. Ein Beitrag zum Thema 'Metaphysik' und 'Kritik' im Kantischen Lebenswerk." In: *Blätter für Deutsche Philosophie*. Vol. 14, p. 148–166.
Heimsoeth, Heinz (1956): *Studien zur Philosophie Immanuel Kants: Metaphysicshe Ursprünge und Ontologische Grundlagen*. Kantstudien Ergänzungshefte 71. Köln: Kölner Universitäts-Verlag.
Heimsoeth, Heinz (1966): *Transzendental Dialektik: Ein Kommentar zu Kants Kritik der reinen Vernunft; Erster Teil*. Berlin: Walter de Gruyter.
Heimsoeth, Heinz (1967): "Metaphysical Motives in the Development of Critical Idealism." In: Gram 1967, p. 158–199.
Heimsoeth, Heinz (1967): *Transzendental Dialektik: Ein Kommentar zu Kants Kritik der reinen Vernunft; Zweiter Teil*. Berlin: Walter de Gruyter, 1967.
Heizelmann, J. H. (1913): "Pope in Germany in the Eighteenth Century." In: *Modern Philosophy*. Vol. 10.3, p. 317–64.
Henrich, Dieter (1944/45): "Das Prinzip der Kantischen Ethik." In: *Philosophische Rundschau*. Vol. 2, p. 20–38.
Henrich, Dieter (1953/54): "Zur Theoretischen Philosophie Kants." In: *Philosophische Rundschau*. Vol. 1, p. 124–49.
Henrich, Dieter (1960): *Der Ontologische Gottesbeweis: Sein Problem und seine Geschichte in der Neuzeit*. Tübingen: J. C. B. Mohr.
Henrich, Dieter (1966): "Über Kants Entwicklungsgeschichte," *Philosophische Rundschau*. Vol. 13, p. 252–63.

Henrich, Dieter (1966): "Zu Kants Begriff der Philosophie: Eine Edition und eine Fragstellung." In: *Kritik und Metaphysik Studien: Heinz Heimsoeth zum achtzigsten Geburtstag*. Berlin: Walter de Gruyter, p. 40–59.
Henrich, Dieter (1967): "Kants Denken: Über den Ursprung der Unterscheidung analytischer und synthetischer Urteile." In: *Studien zu Kants Philosophisher Entwicklung*. Hildesheim: Georg Olms Verlagsbuchhandlung, p. 9–38.
Henrich, Dieter (1974): "The Basic Structure of Modern Philosophy." In: *Cultural Hermeneutics*. Vol. 2/1, p. 1–18.
Henrich, Dieter (1982): "The Proof-Structure of Kant's Transcendental Deduction." In: Walker, Ralph C. S. (Ed.). *Kant on Pure Reason*. London: Oxford University Press.
Henrich, Dieter (1989a): "Kant's Notion of a Deduction and the Methodological Background to the First *Critique*." In: Förster 1989, p. 29–46.
Henrich, Dieter (1989b): "The Identity of the Subject in the Transcendental Deduction." In: Schaper, Eva and Wilhelm Vossenkuhl (Eds.) and P. Gorner (Trans.). *Reading Kant*. ed. Oxford: Basil Blackwell.
Henrich, Dieter (1994): *The Unity of Reason*. Velkley, Richard L. (Ed.) and Jeffery Edwards, Louis Hunt, Manfred Kuehn and Guenter Zoeller (Trans.). Cambridge: Harvard University Press.
Henrich, Dieter (2003): *Between Kant and Hegel*. Pacini, David S. (Ed.). Cambridge, Mass.: Harvard University Press.
Herman, Barbara (1993): "Leaving Deontology Behind." In: *The Practice of Moral Judgment*. London: Harvard University Press, p. 209–240.
Hinske, Norbert (1968): "Die Historischen Vorlagen der Kantischen Transzendentalphilosophie." In: *Archiv für Begriffsgeschichte*. Vol. 12, p. 86–113.
Hinske, Norbert (1970): "Verschiedenheit und Einheit der Transzendentalen Philosophien." In: *Archiv für Begriffsgeschichte*. Vol. 14, p. 41–68.
Hinske, Norbert (1970): *Kants Weg zur Transzendentalphilosophie*. Stuttgart: W. Kohlhammer Verlag.
Höffe, Otfried (2006): *Kant's Cosmopolitan Theory of Law and Peace*. Newton, Alexandra (Trans.). Cambridge: Cambridge University Press.
Hund, William (1983): "The Sublime and God in Kant's 'Critique of Judgment.'" In: *The New Scholasticism*. Vol. 57, p. 42–70.
Hunter, Ian (2000): "Christian Thomasius and the Desacralization of Philosophy." In: *Journal of the History of Ideas*. Vol. 61, p. 595–616.
Hunter, Ian (2001): *Rival Enlightenments: Civil and Metaphysical Philosophy in Early Modern Germany*. Cambridge: Cambridge University Press.
Hurka, Thomas (2006): "Teleological Ethics." In: Borchert, Donald M. (Ed.). *Encyclopedia of Philosophy*. 2nd edition. New York: Thompson Gale, p. 382–4.
Irrlitz, Gerd (2002): *Kant Handbuch: Leben und Werk*. Stuttgart and Weimar: J. B. Metzler.
Irwin, T. H. (1992): "Who discovered the Will?." In: *Philosophical Perspectives*. Vol. 6, p. 453–473.
Jacobs, Brian and Patrick Kain (Eds.) (2003): *Essays on Kant's Anthropology*. Cambridge, Uk: Cambridge University Press.
Jaeger, Werner (1967): *The Theology of the Early Greek Philosophers*. Robinson, Edward S. (Trans.) London: Oxford University Press.

Kahn, Chalres H. (1985): "The Place of the Prime Mover in Aristotle's Teleology." In: Gotthelf, Allan (Ed.). *Aristotle on Nature and Living Things: Philosophical and Historical Studies.* Bristol: Bristol Classical Press.

Kim, Jaegwon and Ernst Sosa and Gary S. Rosenktrantz (Eds.) (2009): *A Companion to Metaphysics.* Wiley-Blackwell.

Kleingeld, Pauline (1995): "What Do the Virtuous Hope For? Re-reading Kant's Doctrine of the Highest Good." In: Robinson 1995, p. 91–112.

Kleingeld, Pauline (1998): "Kant on the Unity of Theoretical and Practical Reason." In: *The Review of Metaphysics.* Vol. 52, p. 311–39.

Kleingeld, Pauline (1998): "The Conative Character of Reason in Kant's Philosophy." In: *Journal of the History of Philosophy.* Vol. 36, p. 77–97.

Kleingeld, Pauline (1999): "Kant, History, and the Idea of Moral Development." In: *History of Philosophy Quarterly.* Vol. 16, p. 59–80.

Kleingeld, Pauline (2001): "Nature or Providence? On the Theoretical and Moral Importance of Kant's Philosophy of History." In: *American Catholic Philosophical Quarterly.* Vol. 75, p. 201–20.

Klemme, Heiner F. (2008): "Moralisches Sollen, Autonomie und Achtung. Kants Konzeption der 'libertas indifferentiae' zwischen Wolff und Crusius." In: *Proceedings of the 10th International Kant Congress, Sao Paulo, 2005.* Berlin: Walter de Gruyter, p. 341–353.

Klemme, Heiner F. and Manfred Kuehn (Eds.) (1999): *Immanuel Kant.* 2 vols. The International Library of Critical Essays in the History of Philosophy. Aldershot: Ashgate.

Knittermeyer, Hinrich (1920): *Der Terminus Transcendental in seiner historischen Entwickelung bis zu Kant.* Marburg: Buchdruckerei von Joh. Hamel.

Knittermeyer, Hinrich (1953/54): "Von der klassischen zur kritischen Transzendentalphilosophie." In: *Kantstudien.* Vol. 45, 113–131.

Konhardt, Klaus (1979): *Die Einheit der Vernunft: Zum Verhältnis von theoretischer und praktischer Vernunft in der Philosophie Immanuel Kants.* Regensberg: Forum Academicum.

König, Peter (1994): *Autonomie und Autokratie: Über Kants Metaphysik der Sitten.* Berlin: Walter de Gruyter.

König, Peter (2001): "Die Selbsterkenntnis der Vernunft und das wahre System der Philosophie bei Kant." In: Fulda 2001, p. 41–52.

Korsgaard, Christine M. (1996): "Morality as Freedom." In: Korsgaard, Chrisine M. *Creating the Kingdom of Ends.* Cambridge: Cambridge University Press, p. 159–187.

Korsgaard, Christine M., et al. (1997): *The Sources of Normativity.* O'Neill, Onora (Ed.). Cambridge: Cambridge University Press.

Kraft, Michael (1981): "Thinking the Physico-Teleological Proof." In: *International Journal for Philosophy of Religion.* Vol. 12, p. 65–74.

Kraft, Michael (1982): "Kant's Theory of Teleology." In: *International Philosophical Quarterly.* Vol. 22, p. 41–50.

Kroner, Richard (1956): *Kant's Weltanschauung.* Smith, John E. (Trans.). University of Chicago Press.

Kuehn, Manfred (1983): "Dating Kant's 'Vorlesungen über Philosophische Enzyklopädie.'" In: *Kantstudien.* Vol. 74, p. 302–13.

Kuehn, Manfred (1985): "Kant's Transcendental Deduction of God's Existence as a Postulate of Pure Practical Reason." In: *Kantstudien.* Vol. 76, p. 152–69.

Kuehn, Manfred (1989): "Hume and Tetens." In: *Hume Studies.* Vol. 15, p. 365–75.

Kuehn, Manfred (1995): "The Moral Dimension of Kant's Inaugural Dissertation: A New Perspective on the 'Great Light of 1769'?" In: Robinson 1995, p. 373–92.
Kuehn, Manfred (2003): *Scottish Common Sense in Germany, 1786–1800: A Contribution to the History of Critical Philosophy.* Montreal: McGill-Queen's University Press.
Langthaler, Rudolf (1995): "Zu Kants Idee der 'Practischen Teleologie.'" In: Robinson 1995, p. 827–44.
Leisegang, Hans (1915): "Über die Bedeutung des scholastischen Satzes: 'Quodlibet ens est unum, verum, bonum seu perfectum,' und seine Bedeutung in Kants *Kritik der reinen Vernunft.*" In: *Kantstudien.* Vol. 20, p. 403–21.
Leisegang, Hans (1951): *Denkformen.* Berlin: Walter de Gruyter.
Longuenesse, Béatrice (1995): "The Transcendental Ideal, and the Unity of the Critical System." In: Robinson 1995, p. 521–38.
Longuenesse, Béatrice (1998): *Kant and the Capacity to Judge.* Wolfe, Charles T. (Trans.). Princeton: Princeton University Press.
Longuenesse, Béatrice (2000a): "Kant's Categories and the Capacity to Judge: Responses to Henry Allison and Sally Sedgwick." In: *Inquiry*, p. 91–110.
Longuenesse, Béatrice (2000b): "Point of View of Man or Knowledge of God: Kant and Hegel on Concept, Judgment and Reason." In: Sedgwick, Sally (Ed.). *The Reception of Kant's Critical Philosophy: Fichte, Schelling, and Hegel.* Cambridge, UK: Cambridge University Press.
Longuenesse, Béatrice (2001): "Logical Functions and the World-Whole." In: Fulda 2001, p. 171–192.
Loux, Michael J. (2006): *Metaphysics: A Contemporary Introduction.* London: Routledge.
Lovejoy, Arthur O. (1976): *The Great Chain of Being: A Study of the History of an Idea.* Cambridge: Harvard University Press.
MacIntyre, Alasdair (1966): *A Short History of Ethics.* New York: MacMillan Company.
MacIntyre, Alasdair. (1981): *After Virtue: a study in moral theory.* London: Gerald Duckworth.
MacBeath, A. Murray (1973): "Kant on Moral Feeling." In: *Kantstudien.* Vol. 64, p. 283–314.
Makkreel, Rudolf A. (1990): *Imagination and Interpretation in Kant.* Chicago: University of Chicago Press.
Makkreel, Rudolf A. (1991): "Regulative and Reflective uses of Purposiveness in Kant." In: *Southern Journal of Philosophy.* Vol. 30 supplement, p. 49–63.
Mariña, Jacqueline (2001): "The Religious Significance of Kant's Ethics." In: *American Catholic Philosophical Quarterly.* Vol. 75, p. 179–200.
Martin, Conor (1980): "Emotion in Kant's Moral Philosophy." In: *Philosophical Studies (Ireland).* Vol. 27, p. 16–27.
Martin, Gottfried (1964): *Leibniz: Logic and Metaphysics.* Northcott, J. K. and P. G. Lucas (Trans.). Manchester: Manchester University Press, 1964.
Martin, Gottfried (1974): *Kant's Metaphysics and Theory of Science.* Lucas, P. G. (Trans.). Westport, Conn.: Greenwood Press, 1974.
McFarland, J. D. (1970): *Kant's Concept of Teleology.* Edinburgh: University of Edinburgh Press.
McLaughlin, Peter (1989):*Kants Kritik der teleologischen Urteilskraft.* Bonn: Bouvier Verlag.
Meerbote, Ralf (1972): "Kant's Use of the Notions 'Objective Reality' and 'Objective Validity.'" In: *Kantstudien.* Vol. 63, p. 51–8.
Meerbote, Ralf (1986): "Deleuze on the Systematic Unity of the Critical Philosophy." In: *Kantstudien.* Vol. 77, p. 347–54.

Meerbote, Ralf (1995): "Function and Purpose in Kant's Theory of Knowledge." In: Robinson 1995, p. 845–61.
Mercer, Christina (2001): *Leibniz's Metaphysics: Its Origins and Development*. Cambridge: Cambridge University Press.
Mirus, Christopher (2004a). "Aristotle's Agathon." In: *The Review of Metaphysics*. Vol. 57, p. 515–536.
Mirus, Christopher (2004b). "The Metaphysical Roots of Aristotle's Teleology." In: *The Review of Metaphysics*. Vol. 57, p. 699–724.
Mirus, Christopher (2012). "Order and the Determinate: The Good as a Metaphysical Concept in Aristotle." In: *The Review of Metaphysics*. Vol. 65, p. 499–523.
Möhle, Hannes (1996): "Wille und Moral. Zur Voraussetzung der Ethik des Johannes Duns Scotus und Ihrer Bedeutung für die Ethik Immanuel Kants." In: Honnefelder, Ludiger and Mechtild Dreyer and Rega Wood (Eds.). *John Duns Scotus: Metaphysics and Ethics*. Leiden: E.J. Brill, p. 573–94.
Moors, Martin (1989): "Die Bestimmungsgestalt von Kant's Gottesidee und das Gemeinschaftsprinzip." In: Funke, G. and Th. M. Seebohm (Eds.). *Proceedings: Sixth International Kant Congress*. Washington, D. C.: University Press of America.
Moors, Martin (1998): "Über (Selbst-)Affection, (Un)Form und (Un)Lust: Ideen zu einer Kanonik der ästhetischen Urteilskraft." In: Parret 1998, p. 484–97.
Moors, Martin (2004): "Kant on Religion in the Role of Moral Schematism." In: Desmond, William and Ernst-Otto Onnasch and Paul Cruysberghs. *Philosophy and Religion in German Idealism*. Dordrecht: Kluwer, p. 21–33.
Munzel, G. Felicitas (1999): *Kant's Conception of Moral Character*. Chicago: University of Chicago Press.
Neander, Karen (2006): "Teleology [Addendum]." In: Borchert, Donald M. (Ed.). *Encyclopedia of Philosophy*. 2nd edition. New York: Thompson Gale, p. 388–390.
Neiman, Susan (1994): *The Unity of Reason: Rereading Kant*. Oxford: Oxford University Press.
Neiman, Susan (1995): "Understanding the Unconditioned." In: Robinson 1995, p. 505–20.
Owens, Joseph (1963): *The Doctrine of Being in the Aristotelian 'Metaphysics': A Study in the Greek Background of Mediaeval Thought*. Fourth revised edition. Toronto: Pontifical Institute of Mediaeval Studies.
Parret, Herman (Ed.) (1998): *Kants Ästhetik, Kant's aesthetics, L esthétique de Kant*. Berlin: Walter de Gruyter.
Paton, H. J. (1967a): "Is the Transcendental Deduction a Patchwork?" In: Gram 1967, p. 62–91.
Paton, H. J. (1967b): "The Key to Kant's Deduction of the Categories." In: Gram 1967, p. 247–68.
Paton, H. J. (1970): *The Categorical Imperative: A study in Kant's moral philosophy*. London: Hutchinson of London.
Paulsen, Friedrich (1963): *Immanuel Kant: His Life and Doctrine*. Creighton, J. E. and Albert Lefevre (Trans.). New York: Fredrick Ungar Publishing Co.
Phemister, Pauline (2006): *The Rationalists: Descartes, Spinoza and Leibniz*. Cambridge: Polity.
Pichler, Hans (1910): *Über Christian Wolffs Ontologie*. Leipzig: Verlag der Dürr'schen Buchhandlung.
Picht, Georg (1985): *Kants Religionsphilosophie: Vorlesungen u. Schr.* Eisenbart, Constanze and Enno Rudolph (Trans.). Stuttgart: Klett-Cotta.

Pippin, Robert B. (1987): "Kant on the Spontaneity of Mind." In: *Canadian Journal of Philosophy*. Vol. 17, p. 449–76.
Polonoff, Irving I. (1973): *Force, Cosmos, Monads and Other Themes of Kant's Early Thougt* (sic). Kantstudien Ergänzungshefte 107. Bonn: H. Bouvier Verlag.
Prauss, Gerold (1971): *Erscheinung Bei Kant: Ein Problem der "Kritik der reinen Vernunft."* Berlin: Walter de Gruyter.
Prauss, Gerold (1974): *Kant und das Problem der Dinge an sich*. Bonn: Bouvier.
Prauss, Gerold (1981): "Kants Problem der Einheit theoretischer und praktischer Vernunft," *Kantstudien*. Vol. 72, p. 286–303.
Prauss, Gerold (1983): *Kant über Freiheit as Autonomie*. Frankfurt am Main: Vittorio Klostermann.
Raymaekers, Bart (1998): "The Importance of Freedom in the Architectonic of the *Critique of Judgment*." In: Parret 1998, p. 84–92.
Reich, Klaus (1939a): "Kant and Greek Ethics (I.)." In: *Mind*. Vol. 48, p. 338–54.
Reich, Klaus (1939b): "Kant and Greek Ethics (II.)."In: *Mind*. Vol. 48, p. 446–63.
Reich, Klaus (1992): *The Completeness of Kant's Table of Judgments*. Kneller, J. and M. Losonsky (Trans.). Stanford: Stanford University Press.
Reich, Klaus (2001a): "Die Tugend in der Idee (1964)." In: Reich 2001b, p. 306–313.
Reich, Klaus (2001b) *Gesammelte Schriften*. Manfred Baum, Udo Rameil, Klaus Reisinger and Gertrud Scholz (Eds.). Hamburg: Felix Meiner.
Reich, Klaus (2001c): "Kants 'Einzig möglicher Beweisgrund zu einer Demonstration des Daseins Gottes' (1937)." In Reich 2001b, p. 166–199.
Reich, Klaus (2001d): "Rousseau und Kant." In: Reich 2001b, p. 147–165.
Reich, Klaus (2001e): "Vorwort und Einleitung in 'Immanuel Kant: De Mundi Sensibilis atque Intelligibilis Forma et Principi' (1958)." In: Reich 2001b, p. 263–271.
Reich, Klaus (2001f): "Vorwort und Einleitung in 'Immanuel Kant: Träume eines Geistessehers. Der Unterschied der Gegenden im Raume' (1975)." In: Reich 2001b, p. 348–359.
Rescher, Nicholas (1952): "Contingence in the Philosophy of Leibniz." In: *The Philosophical Review*. Vol. 61, p. 26–39.
Robinson, Hoke (Ed.) (1995): *Proceedings of the Eighth International Kant Congress: Memphis, 1995*. Milwaukee: Marquette University Press.
Rogers, Robert W. (1948): "Critiques of the *Essay on Man* in France and Germany 1736–1755." In: *English Literary History*. Vol. 15, p. 176–193.
Rosales, Alberto (1989): "Zur teleologischen Grundlage der transzendentalen Deduktion der Kategorien." In: *Kant Studien*. Vol. 80, p. 377–404.
Rosenberg, Jay (2005): *Accessing Kant*. Oxford: Clarendon Press.
Ross, David (1953): *Plato's Theory of Ideas*. Oxford: Clarendon Press.
Rossi, Philip (2001): "Autonomy: Toward the Social Self-Governance of Reason," *American Catholic Philosophical Quarterly*. Vol. 75, p. 171–178.
Rutherford, Donald (1995): *Leibniz and the Rational Order of Nature*. Cambridge: Cambridge University Press.
Rutherford, Donald (2004): "Idealism Declined." In: Lodge, Paul (Ed.). *Leibniz and His Correspondents*. Oxford: Cambridge University Press, p. 214–237.
Schilpp, Paul A. (1970): *Kant's Pre-Critical Ethics*. 2nd ed. Evanston: Northwestern University Press.

Schmucker, Josef (1961): *Die Ursprünge der Ethik Kants*. Meisenheim am Glan: Verlag Anton Hain KG.
Schmucker, Josef (1963): "Die Gottesbeweise beim vorkritischen Kant." In: *Kantstudien*. Vol. 54, p. 445–463.
Schmucker, Josef (1966): "Die Originalität des ontotheologischen Arguments Kants gegenüber verwandten Gedankengängen bei Leibniz und in der Schulphilosophie der Zeit." In: *Kritik und Metaphysik Studien: Heinz Heimsoeth zum achtzigsten Geburtstag*. Berlin: Walter de Gruyter, p. 120–33.
Schmucker, Josef (1967): "Die Frühgestalt des Kantischen Ontologischen Arguments in der 'Nova Dilucidatio' und ihr Verhältnis zum 'Einzig Möglichen Beweisgrund' von 1762." In: *Studien zu Kants Philosophischer Entwicklung*. Hildesheim: Georg Olms.
Schmucker, Josef (1972): "On the Development of Kant's Transcendental Theology." In: Beck, L. W. (Ed.). *Proceedings of the Third International Kant Congress*. Dordrecht: D. Reidel Publishing Company, p. 495–500.
Schmucker, Josef (1980): *Die Ontotheology des vorkritischen Kant*. Kantstudien Ergäzungshefte 112. Berlin: Walter de Gruyter.
Schmucker, Josef (1983): *Kants vorkritische Kritik der Gottesbeweise*. Wiesbaden: Franz Steiner Verlag.
Schneeberger, Guido (1952): *Kants Konzeption der Modalbegriffe. Philosophische Forschungen Neue Folge*. Vol. 1. Jaspers, Karl (Ed.). Basel: Verlag für Recht und Gesellschaft Ag.
Schneewind, J. B. (1998): "Kant and Stoic Ethics." In: *Aristotle, Kant, and the Stoics: Rethinking Happiness and Duty*. Engstrom, Stephen and Jennifer Whiting (Eds.). Cambridge: Cambridge University Press, p. 285–301.
Schönfeld, Martin (2000): *The Philosophy of the Young Kant: The Precritical Project*. Oxford: Oxford University Press.
Schrader, George (1953): "The Status of Teleological Judgment in the Critical Philosophy." In: *Kantstudien*. Vol. 45, p. 204–235.
Schwartz, Stephen P. (Ed.) (1977): *Naming, Necessity, and Natural Kinds*. Ithaca, New York: Cornell University Press.
Senderowicz, Yaron M. (2004): "Figurative Synthesis and Synthetic a priori Knowledge," *Review of Metaphysics*. Vol. 57, p. 755–785.
Sensen, Oliver (2011): *Kant on Human Dignity*. Kantstudien Ergänzungshefte 166. Berlin and Boston: De Gruyter.
Shell, Susan Meld (2003): "Kant's 'True Economy of Human Nature': Rousseau, Count Verri, and the Problem of Happiness." In: Jacobs 2003, p. 194–229.
Sidgwick, Henry (1888): "The Kantian Conception of Free Will." In: *Mind*. Vol. 13, p. 405–412.
Silber, John R. (1959a): "Kant's Conception of the Highest Good as Immanent and Transcendent." In: *Philosophical Review*. Vol. 68, p. 469–92.
Silber, John R. (1959b): "The Metaphysical Importance of the Highest Good as the Canon of Pure Reason in Kant's Philosophy." In: *Texas Studies in Literature in Language*. Vol. 1, p. 234–44.
Silber, John R. (1959/60): "The Copernican Revolution in Ethics: The Good Reexamined." In: *Kantstudien*. Vol. 51, p. 85–101.
Silber, John R. (1960): "The Ethical Significance of Kant's Religion." In: Kant, Immanuel. *Religion within the Limits of Reason Alone*. Greene, Theodore M. and Hoyt H. Hudson (Trans.). New York: Harper, p. lxxix-cxxxiv.

Silber, John R. (1963): "The Importance of the Highest Good in Kant's Ethics." In: *Ethics*. Vol. 73, p. 179–97.
Silber, John R. (1974): "Procedural Formalism in Kant's Ethics." In: *Review of Metaphysics*. Vol. 28, p. 197–236.
Silber, John R. (1982): "The Moral Good and the Natural Good in Kant's Ethics." In: *Review of Metaphysics*. Vol. 36, p. 397–438.
Simon, Josef (1983): "Teleological Reflection and Causal Determination." In: Christensen 1983, p. 121–40.
Smith, Norman Kemp (1984): *A Commentary to Kant's 'Critique of Pure Reason.'* Second edition, 1923. London: McMillan Press.
Sparn, Walter (1993): "Philosphie." In: Brecht, Martin (Ed.). *Gescheidnis der Pietismus*. Vol. 4. Göttingen: Vandenhoek & Ruprecht, p. 227–263.
Stark, Werner (2003): "Historical Notes and Interpretive Questions about Kant's Lectures on Anthropology." In: Jacobs 2003, p. 15–37.
Stoeffler, F. Earnest (1971): *The Rise of Evangelical Pietism*. Studies in the History of Relgions. Supplements to Numen, 9. Leiden: Brill.
Stoeffler, F. Earnest (1973): *German Pietism During the Eighteenth Century*. Studies in the History of Religions. Supplements to Numen, 24. Leiden: Brill.
Strawson, P. F. (1966): *The Bounds of Sense: An Essay on Kant's 'Critique of Pure Reason'*. London: Methuen.
Taylor, A. E. (1929): *Plato: The Man and His Work*. London: Methuen.
Taylor, C. C. W. (1969): "Forms as cause in the *Phaedo*." In: *Mind*. Vol. 78, p. 45–59.
Taylor, Charles (1979): *The Explanation of Behaviour*. New York: Humanities Press.
Timmermann, Jens (2007): *Kant's "Groundwork of the Metaphysics of Morals."* Cambridge: Cambridge University Press.
Tonelli, G. (1957/58): "Von den Verschiedenen Bedeutungen des Wortes Zweckmässigkeit in der Kritik der Urteilskraft." In: *Kantstudien*. Vol. 49, p. 154–166.
Tonelli, G. (1976): "Analysis and Synthesis in XXVIII th Century Philosophy prior to Kant." In: *Archiv für Begriffsgeschichte*. Vol. 20, p. 176–213.
Tonelli, G. (1994): *Kant's 'Critique of pure reason' within the tradition of modern logic: A commentary on its History*. Chandler, David H. (Ed.). Zürich: Georg Olms.
Tuschling, Burkhard (1991): "The System of Transcendental Idealism: Questions Raised and Left Open in the *Kritik Der Urteilskraft*." In: *Southern Journal of Philosophy*. Vol. 30 supplement, p. 109–27.
Vaihinger, Hans (1967): "The Transcendental Deduction of the Categories in the First Edition of the Critique of Pure Reason." In: Gram, p. 23–61.
Velkley, Richard (1989): *Freedom and the End of Reason: On the Moral Foundation of Kant's Critical Philosophy*. Chicago and London: University of Chicago Press.
Velkley, Richard (2001): "Metaphysics, Freedom and History: Kant and the End of Reason." *American Catholic Philosophical Quarterly*. Vol. 75, p. 153–170.
Vlastos, Gregory (Ed.) (1971): *Plato: A Collection of Critical Essays*. 2 vol. New York: Anchor Books.
Vleesschower, Herman-J. de (1962): *The Development of Kantian Thought*. Duncan, A. R. (Trans.). London: Thomas Nelson and Sons Ltd.
Wagner, Hans. (1983): "Morality and Religion in Kant." In: Christensen 1983, p. 75–88.

Walford, David (1999): "The Aims and Method of Kant's 1768 *Gegenden im Raume* in the light of Euler's 1748 *Réflexionx sur L'Espace*." In: *British Journal for the History of Philosophy*. Vol. 7, p. 305–332.
Ward, Keith (1972). *The Development of Kant's View of Ethics*. New York: Humanities Press.
Watkins, Eric (1995): "Kant's Theory of Physical Influx," *Archiv für Geschichte der Philosophie*. Vol. 77 , p. 285–324.
Watkins, Eric (1995): "The Development of Physical Influx in Early Eighteenth-Century Germany: Gottsched, Knutzen, and Crusius." In: *The Review of Metaphysics*. Vol. 49, p. 295–339.
Watkins, Eric (2005): *Kant and the Metaphysics of Causality*. Cambridge: Cambridge University Press.
Webb, Clement C. J. (1970): *Kant's Philosophy of Religion*. Oxford: Clarendon Press, 1926. New York: Kraus Reprint Co.
Weber, Emil. (1907): *Die Philosophische Scholastik des deutschen Protestantismus im Zeitalter der Orthodoxie*. Leipzig: Quelle & Meyer.
Werkmeister, W. H. (1980): *Kant: The Architectonic and Development of His Philosophy*. London: Open Court Publishing Company.
Willaschek, Marcus (2010): "The primacy of the practical and the idea of a practical postulate." In: Reath, Andrews and Jens Timmermann (Eds.). *Kant's "Critique of Practical Reason": A Critical Guide*. Cambridge: Cambridge University Press.
Wolter, Allan Bernard (1946): *The Transcendentals and their Function in the Metaphysics of Duns Scotus*. Washington, D. C.: The Catholic University of America Press.
Wood, Allen W. (1970): *Kant's Moral Religion*. Ithaca: Cornell University Press.
Wood, Allen W. (1978): *Kant's Rational Theology*. Ithaca: Cornell University Press.
Wood, Allen W. (1984): "Kant's Compatibilism." In: Wood, Allen W. (Ed.). *Self and Nature in Kant's Philosophy*. Ithaca and London: Cornell University Press, p. 76–83.
Wood, Allen W. (1995): "Humanity as End in Itself." In: Robinson 1995, p. 301–19.
Wood, Allen W. (1999): *Kant's Ethical Thought*. Cambridge: Cambridge University Press.
Wood, Allen W. (2003): "Kant and the Problem of Human Nature." In: Jacobs 2003, p. 38–59.
Woodfield, Andrew (1998): "Teleology." In: Craig, Edward. *Routledge Encyclopedia of Philosophy*. New York: Routledge.
Woolhouse, R. S. (Ed.) (1994): *Gottfried Wilhelm Leibniz: Critical Assessments*. Vols. 1–3. London: Routledge.
Wundt, Max (1953): *Untersuchungen zur Metaphysik des Aristoteles*. Stuttgart: W. Kohlhammer Verlag.
Wundt, Max (1964): *Die deutsche Schulphilosophie im Zeitalter der Aufklärung*. Hildesheim: Georg Olms Verlagsbuchhandlung.
Wundt, Max (1969): *Geschichte der Griechischen Ethik: Band 2. Der Hellenismus*. Aalen: Scientia Verlag.
Wundt, Max (1984): *Kant als Metaphysiker*. Hildesheim: Georg Olms Verlag.
Wundt, Max (1992): *Die deutsche Schulmetaphysik des 17. Jahrhunderts*. Hildesheim: Georg Olms Verlag.
Zammito, John H. (1992): *The Genesis of Kant's "Critique of Judgment."* Chicago: University of Chicago Press.
Zöller, Günter (1989): "Making Sense Out of Inner Sense: The Kantian Doctrine as Illuminated by the Leningrad *Reflexion*." In: *International Philosophical Quarterly*. Vol. 29, p. 263–79.

Zöller, Günter (1998): "From Innate to A Priori: Kant's Radical Transformation of a Cartesian-Leibnizian Legacy." In: *The Monist*. Vol. 72, p. 222–235.
Zöller, Günter (2001): "'Die Seele des Systems': Systembegriff und Begriffssystem in Kants Transzendentalphilosophie." In: Fulda 2001, p. 53–72.
Zuckert, Rachel (2002): "A New Look at Kant's Theory of Pleasure." In: *The Journal of Aesthetics and Art Criticism*. Vol. 60, p. 239–52.

Register

abstraction 55, 122, 126, 137, 141, 153, 155, 158, 225, 231
absurdum practicum 294, 300 f., 304, 328 f.
– as a dilemma 301–302, 328
affinity 29, 52, 54, 150, 365
analogy 15 f., 21, 51 f., 73–75, 78, 128 f., 160, 175, 184, 205, 212, 230–233, 237, 273, 313, 339, 344, 347, 358, 374, 377, 379
analysis 53, 122, 132, 135 f., 142 f., 149–151, 153 f., 161, 178, 186, 191, 225, 366, 369–373, 385, 390
– principles of 153
Anaxagoras 24 f., 264, 268
anthropology, pragmatic 318
appearance 8, 10 f., 153, 155, 157, 161–165, 169–173, 175 f., 196–199, 228, 236, 250 f., 255, 275 f, 283 f., 335, 372, 379, 400
apperception 5, 97, 101, 114, 152, 164, 170, 185–196, 199 f., 236, 239, 255 f., 285, 376, 382 f., 401
– synthetic unity of 185 f., 190–191, 197
– transcendental unity of 5, 101, 164
Aquinas, Thomas 75–78
Aristotle (Aristotelian) 12, 24, 44, 55, 62 f., 66, 75, 95, 101, 104, 122, 125, 134, 144, 248, 249, 266, 348, 388, 396 f.
Arnauld, Anoine 123
Autonomie und Autokratie 55
autonomy 14, 17, 23, 45, 55, 199, 211, 239, 258, 282 f., 288 f., 292–297, 320, 335, 340, 351, 364, 366, 372, 376, 381, 397

Bacon, Francis 87
Baumgarten, Alexander 113, 116 f., 125, 127, 142, 350, 388
BDG (Only Possible Argument) 28 f., 80, 171, 187, 220 f., 227, 232, 235 f.
beauty 65, 76, 80, 95, 103, 337, 344–346, 353, 356, 359
Beck, Lewis White 47, 130, 294, 296–301, 304, 310

belief 293–296, 299–304, 310, 315, 318–319, 326–330, 334, 391
Bennett, Jonathan 60–62, 64–68, 81, 102
Bergson, Henri 57, 59
Berkeley, George 72
Beyond Good and Evil 115
Blumenberg, Hans 15
boundary 3, 143, 197, 213, 284, 396 f.
Brandt, Reinhard 51
Brucker, Johann Jakob 25

Canon of Pure Reason 13
categories 6, 51 f., 66, 82, 97, 116, 123, 125, 127, 142, 153–155, 157 f., 161–166, 177 f., 181, 183–186, 191–194, 196–200, 206 f., 212 f., 217, 225 f., 228–232, 246, 261 f., 378 f., 386, 401
causality 8, 11 f., 24, 30, 38, 52, 57, 60, 62, 67, 71 f., 79, 87, 92, 94, 104–107, 117, 132, 158 f., 209, 211 f., 222, 231 f., 239, 246, 248, 252, 254–259, 261–267, 269–273, 275–277, 279–281, 290 f., 313, 324, 337, 339 f., 347 f., 350 f., 354, 372 f., 375, 399, 402
– final 5, 24, 57, 67, 86, 93–94, 107, 200, 397
character, moral 64, 250, 264, 275, 258, 294, 306, 310, 330
Chisholm, Roderick 84
Collingwood, Robin George 42
concepts 6, 15, 18 f., 45, 47, 85, 97–98, 116, 123, 125 f., 129–130, 134–136, 140, 144–146, 153–157, 161 f., 165, 168, 176–183, 186, 191–192, 205 f., 207, 210, 214 f., 218, 223–226, 263 f., 340, 349, 362, 379, 390, 394
boundary 284, 397
of space and time 193 f.
constitutive 9, 12, 50, 86, 203–205, 211, 223, 229 f., 233 f., 249 f., 256, 275, 277, 279 f., 339, 346 f., 352 f., 355, 361 f., 366, 368, 374–380, 389, 391, 395
content, non-conceptual 116, 143, 146

Copernicus, Nicholas 15f., 91
counterfactual conditionals 84
Couturat, Louis 64–68
Critique of Teleological Judgment 8, 42
Crusius, Christian August 27, 32f., 76, 78, 80, 111, 116, 119, 130–138, 140–143, 145, 147f., 152, 254, 348–352

Darstellung der Wissenschaftsehre 35
Das Leben theoretischer Vernunft 51
Davidson, Donald 102
deduction 6, 51f., 114, 143f., 148, 151, 154, 161–163, 175, 177f., 180–185, 191f., 196f., 199, 206, 225f., 258, 264, 274, 355, 360, 371, 376
– metaphysical 6, 52, 178–181, 192
– objective 162
– transcendental 51, 114, 143, 181–200, 226, 360, 376
deontology 43, 249
De Revolutionibus 91
Descartes, René (Cartesian) 33–34, 38–39, 40, 47, 88, 94, 117, 120, 142, 179
determination (determinations) 6–8, 17, 22, 27, 30–33, 46, 57, 79, 105, 118, 124, 126, 128, 132, 135, 146, 161, 164, 166–170, 172f., 193–196, 198, 200, 206, 208–210, 216f., 219–223, 225f., 230–232, 234, 240, 245f., 248, 253, 255–263, 265, 269, 271, 273–276, 280, 285f., 288, 318, 320f., 327–330, 336f., 339f., 342–344, 347, 351, 355, 358, 367, 374, 386, 395, 398f., 401f.
– real 30–33, 200, 216, 222–223, 399–401
DfS 153
disposition 3, 82–86, 88, 103, 202, 213, 244, 280, 293f., 298, 302, 305, 310, 312, 314, 317, 320–322, 324–326, 328–330, 334f., 340, 344, 358
– moral 293, 294, 310, 314, 320, 324–330, 335, 344
dogmatism 37, 40, 394f.
Dörflinger, Bernd 42f., 51–53, 144, 148, 360
dreams (somnium objective sumptum) 128f., 380

Düsing, Klaus 360
duty 43, 78, 257, 259f., 272, 274, 291, 297–299, 304, 307–315, 324, 326f., 330, 333, 337, 340, 344, 352, 360, 391f., 398
– as divine command, see *religion*
– of virtue 310, 326, 327

end (ends) 3–14, 16, 18, 21–25, 29–33, 35, 37, 39–41, 43f., 48f., 54, 57f., 60, 63, 67, 69, 75–77, 82, 90, 92, 97, 103–107, 123, 135, 144, 154, 167, 171–173, 198f., 205, 210–212, 234, 237, 244f., 249f., 252f., 263–275, 283, 290–294, 296, 298–301, 304–310, 316, 318–321, 323f., 327–330, 332, 334–336, 347, 353, 355, 357f., 360–362, 364–366, 368, 370–375, 381f., 384, 387, 390–393, 395–397, 400, 402f.
– final 3, 18, 23, 25, 32f., 234, 253, 273, 290, 293, 304, 324, 328f., 335, 336, 360, 375, 395, 400, 403
– natural 8, 106f., 210f., 237, 266, 269f., 290, 319, 347, 358, 371f., 374, 402
– of reason 3, 23, 24, 39, 400
– pure doctrine of 5, 9, 269
Enlightenment 26, 39, 118
entelechie 96
Essay on Cosmology 88
Essay on Man 27
essence 7, 13f., 27–31, 50, 54, 80, 83–86, 89, 104, 120f., 124, 126, 134, 137, 150, 152, 161, 163, 166, 171f., 174, 208f., 222, 227, 236, 267–269, 281, 336, 382, 384, 387, 398–402
– of freedom 13, 279, 291, 376
– of judgment 115
– of understanding 135, 142
– of willing 271, 281. 402
experience 5–8, 11f., 18, 21, 35, 40, 44, 52, 54f., 68, 82–84, 92, 97f., 111–129, 131f., 135–138, 140–163, 165–167, 175, 177, 179f., 185, 189, 194, 196–201, 204, 206f., 209–211, 213f., 218, 223–229, 232–234, 237, 239, 243, 252, 261, 264, 267–269, 279–281, 286, 289, 337,

344, 349, 354, 358, 362, 372, 374 f., 377–379, 395, 401
– judgment of 113–116, 123–127, 137, 156
– possibility of 8, 111, 113, 115–117, 119, 127–130, 138 f., 141 f., 165, 177, 185, 194, 198, 379, 385
– pure vs. mixed 137–140
experiment 15, 34, 95, 124, 138, 151, 160
explanation
– deductive-nomological 82–83, 85, 86. 98
– scientific 59, 83, 86, 97, 99, 100
– teleological 59, 60, 81–104, 381

faculty, of judging 7, 51, 115, 125, 152, 155, 182, 208, 213, 233, 359, 382, 383
faith, see *belief*
fatalism, Christian 39
feeling 39, 277, 313 f., 318, 333, 340 f., 344–346, 351, 353–355, 357 f.
– difference between moral and empirical 341
Feynman, Richard 98
Fichte, Johann Gottlieb 4, 33–41, 179, 248, 289
fitness 6, 16, 29–31, 104, 147 f., 154, 156, 160, 171, 365
FM (*What Progress has Metaphysics Made since the Time of Leibniz and Wolff?*) 24, 113, 148, 202, 231, 327, 332–335, 360, 390 f., 393–395
Förster, Eckart 388
freedom 4 f., 10, 12–14, 22, 26 f., 31 f., 35–38, 40–45, 47 f., 50, 55, 62 f., 92, 182, 199, 220, 228, 241, 244, 248, 250–252, 254–265, 267, 269, 271 f., 276 f., 279–285, 287–293, 295 f., 311 f., 326 f., 331, 337–339, 342–346, 350 f., 353, 355–358, 372–376, 385 f., 391, 402
– absolute 36, 199, 276
– as idea 254, 256, 258–260, 276, 373
– as self-constraint or self-mastery 254, 259, 260, 276, 290
– human 27, 31, 50, 252, 276
– of responsibility 254 f., 288, 290
– transcendental 250, 251, 257, 285, 331
Frege, Gottlob 81

Freudiger, Jürg 56
Frierson, Patrick 250, 318

Galileo 42, 91
Garve, Christian 19 f., 322
German Idealism 33, 40, 116, 287
GMS (*Groundwork*) 9 f., 49, 245, 248, 251 f., 256–258, 261, 264, 271, 276–279, 281–283, 286, 288, 298, 308, 314 f.
God 3, 14, 24–33, 39, 41, 54, 63, 65–67, 72, 74–79, 88–93, 100, 112, 151 f., 167, 169, 175, 179 f., 187, 189, 203–205, 208 f., 215 f., 221, 223 f., 229–238, 246, 251, 272 f., 287–289, 292–298, 300–305, 309 f., 315, 318–320, 322–336, 351, 371, 377, 384, 396, 399–401
– symbolic function of 295, 324
– synthetic function of 295, 324, 325, 326
God's existence, teleological argument for, see *inference, teleological, for God's existence*
good 13, 28, 31, 39, 43 f., 46 f., 55 f., 63, 65–67, 71, 77, 113, 125 f., 203, 246, 249, 253, 256 f., 262, 265, 270, 272 f., 285, 292–309, 316–330, 332–335, 337, 340, 343, 351, 355, 360, 364, 375, 388, 391, 397 f., 402
– highest (summum bonum, bonum consummatum) 13, 246, 249, 265, 273, 292–309, 318–335, 360, 364, 375, 388, 391, 402
Goodman, Nelson 84, 99
Grundlage der gesamten Wissenschaftslehre 35
Guyer, Paul 49, 56, 276, 360

happiness 48, 244, 272, 294 f., 297–299, 303–310, 315–319, 321–330, 332 f., 391
harmony 14–16, 19, 22–24, 27–30, 32, 53, 80, 91, 93, 151 f., 172, 174–176, 182, 184, 196, 200–202, 222, 231 f., 237 f., 248, 268, 270, 297, 315, 317, 324, 326 f., 355–358, 370, 382, 393
– of sensibility with understanding 174, 176, 196, 200
– pre-established 175

health 16, 316, 337, 342f.
Hegel, Georg Wilhelm Friedrich 4, 40, 46, 61, 296, 322, 360f., 383, 386, 388f.
Heidegger, Martin 387
Heimsoeth, Heinz 25, 125
Hempel, Carl 102
Henrich, Dieter 46, 51, 131, 181f., 252, 360
Herder, Johann Gottfried von 113, 117
Hermotimus of Clazomenae 24
heteronomy 260, 293, 297, 320, 351
Historia Critica Philosophiae (*Critical History*) 25
Hobbes, Thomas 248
Höffe, Odfried 55
Hoffmann, Adolph 32, 116, 119, 130–143, 145, 147
hope 48, 58, 69, 94, 289, 305, 323f., 330, 332, 337
Hume, David 43, 45, 59, 71, 73f., 78f., 113, 117, 120f., 130, 151

idea 6–8, 13, 15–16, 23, 25, 28, 35, 41, 51, 54–55, 78, 106, 112, 149–152, 154, 168–170, 175, 178, 180, 181, 198–208, 210–217, 219–224, 226–238, 240, 248, 251–253, 260–262, 264–270, 275–277, 279–281, 292, 324f., 327, 329, 353, 355, 357f., 360–378, 384f., 387, 396
– transcendental derivation of 213–215
illusion, transcendental 38, 146, 173, 201–204, 213, 277, 378, 380
imperative, categorical 49f.,249, 253, 258, 260, 265, 283, 286, 295, 299, 337, 402
incentive 201, 257, 277f., 286, 288f., 295, 312–322, 325–330, 333, 335f., 339, 342, 355, 393
inclinations 4, 44, 258, 260, 280, 307, 309, 311, 313, 316, 331, 333, 335, 341f., 352
induction, see *inference, inductive*
inference 29, 38, 59–61, 68, 70–75, 78, 80f., 88, 92, 103f., 114, 120, 122, 124, 148, 188, 204, 236f., 275
– for God's existence 28, 64, 75, 78
– inductive 59, 72f., 80, 81, 90, 92f., 121
– teleological 59, 68–75, 80, 81, 88, 92, 103, 236, 275

intellect, intuitive 272
intention (intentional activity) 18, 26, 49, 55, 58, 67, 69, 72f., 91f., 96, 148, 156, 197f., 206, 212f., 236, 277, 299, 303, 306, 312, 315, 327f., 338, 342, 381, 398, 402
intuition (intuitions) 6, 18, 35, 42, 45, 57, 97, 112, 146, 148, 150f., 155f., 160f., 163, 165f., 168, 170, 172–174, 176–178, 180, 185–196, 199f., 206, 208, 214f., 219, 224, 228, 230, 235, 239, 245, 255f., 261, 268, 272, 274, 295f., 358, 367f., 372, 379, 383
– formal 192–194, 228
„I think" 34, 37, 188, 239

judgment 6–8, 17, 42, 51, 112–116, 119–127, 130–133, 136–139, 142–146, 149–153, 155–160, 162f., 169f., 174, 176–178, 180–183, 185f., 191f., 197f., 200, 203, 206f., 210, 213, 217f., 225f., 228, 230, 233, 235f., 240, 246, 262, 270, 304, 325, 327, 337, 344–347, 353f., 356–359, 368, 375f., 382f., 386, 394, 397, 400
– aesthetic 42, 337, 344, 345–347, 353, 356–359
– definition of 114
– fundamental 119, 121, 127, 142, 155
– intuitive 124, 151, 156, 162, 176f., 240
– logical functions of 178, 192, 197
– of perception 116,129, 155, 158
– provisional 156–159, 225

Kant and the Capacity to Judge 152
Kleingeld, Pauline 51f., 56, 360
Konhardt, Klaus 56, 360
König, Peter 54f., 258
Korsgaard, Christine 252, 260
KpV (*Critique of Practical Reason*) 13, 21, 114f., 181, 213, 243–245, 252, 255–258, 261f., 264f., 267, 271, 276–278, 285–288, 292f., 295f., 298, 304–313, 315–324, 327, 329, 331f., 337, 352–355, 364, 368f., 372f., 375, 388, 393
KrV (*Critique of Pure Reason*) 3, 5–7, 10f., 13–16, 18, 20f., 24, 34, 36, 42, 52, 80,

95, 97, 113–115, 117, 125, 128f., 136, 145, 148, 152f., 155, 157f., 160, 175, 177f., 180, 182, 185–188, 190–193, 197–199, 201–203, 206f., 211, 213–215, 217–220, 222–224, 227f., 230–234, 236–238, 243, 246, 248, 251, 258, 264, 292, 304, 327, 337, 354, 362–367, 370–372, 377–379, 382, 391f.

Lambert, Johann Heinrich   153
law   3, 7, 9, 12–14, 26–29, 31, 33, 35f., 38f., 43–47, 49f., 53–55, 57–67, 70–75, 77, 79–99, 101–104, 113, 116, 118, 128, 133f., 137, 139, 141f., 150, 154, 156, 158–160, 166f., 171, 180, 182f., 189, 197–199, 201, 203, 205f., 209–211, 213f., 223, 225–227, 229, 234, 236–239, 243–245, 248f., 251, 253f., 256–267, 269, 271, 273, 277, 279–293, 296–335, 337, 340–346, 349, 351f., 355f., 358, 360, 363f., 372f., 375f., 379f., 383f., 386f., 391f., 395–397, 402
– empirical   158, 166, 198, 211, 225, 236, 315
– of nature   13, 14, 29, 31, 53, 65, 74, 85, 87–96, 101, 209, 236, 315
– Snell's   26, 65, 67, 93
– teleological   58, 61, 63, 102
– universal mechanical   9, 26, 28, 45, 58, 60, 63–65, 74, 79–81, 90, 93, 94, 98, 102, 103, 211, 209
Leibniz, Gottfried Wilhelm   25–29, 31f., 38f., 49, 58, 64–67, 88f., 93, 95f., 113, 116–118, 121f., 124, 200, 244, 253, 316, 348f., 352, 381, 384, 388, 396, 401
life   10f., 26, 37, 44f., 49, 51–53, 68, 77, 98, 116, 199, 250, 289, 294, 305, 316, 327, 332, 334, 337–339, 342–358, 367, 392, 395
– constitutive moral idea of   347–348
– feeling of   337, 343–346, 351–356
– spiritual   346, 353, 355, 356
Linguistic Behavior   64
Locke, John   120f., 130
logic   34, 55, 112f., 116f., 119f., 124–126, 133, 137, 142, 154, 156, 158, 180, 294, 369, 377, 390f.

Longuenesse, Béatrice   51, 146, 152f.
Lovejoy, Arthur O.   117, 125, 128

MacIntyre, Alasdair   43f., 55
Maimon, Solomon   115
Makkreel, Rudolf   345f.
Malebranche, Nicolas   89
MAN (*Metaphysical Foundations of Natural Science*)   114, 349, 354
Martin, Gottfried   42
mathematics   29, 91f., 131, 193, 337
Maupertuis, Pierre-Louis Moreau de   26, 30, 58f., 64, 88–96, 100f., 104
maxim   182, 203, 205, 207, 211, 213, 215, 222, 227f., 233–239, 243–245, 257f., 262, 274, 282, 285–287, 292f., 295, 305–309, 311–313, 315–320, 322f., 327f., 331, 363, 375–378
– of reason   205, 228, 237, 239
McDowell, John   44–47, 55, 146, 212
mechanism   7f., 26, 45, 48, 57, 59–62, 64f., 70, 74, 79f., 85f., 92, 103f., 253, 266, 337, 351f., 356, 371
Meier, Georg Friedrich   116, 127, 217
Mendelssohn, Moses   25, 221, 348, 388
Metaphysica   116f.
metaphysics (metaphysical knowledge)   3f., 14, 18f., 21, 23f., 26, 34, 46f., 62, 68, 99–101, 113, 125, 133f., 136, 138, 141–143, 149, 151, 208, 249, 253, 278, 281, 290, 293, 298, 301, 331, 333f., 338, 350, 360, 390f., 395f., 398
– practical-dogmatic   14, 293, 334, 391, 395
– traditional   23, 68, 100, 101, 113, 138, 142, 149
method (methodology)   7, 15f., 32, 34, 36, 42, 81, 90, 93, 95, 98, 113, 118, 122, 126, 131, 133–137, 142, 154, 181, 193, 205, 234, 236–238, 243, 311, 338, 355, 368–371, 373
Mind and World   44, 46
modality   293
monads   65, 67
motivation, moral   3, 12, 56, 101, 143, 147f., 252–254, 257, 259, 305f., 308, 319–322, 324
MSI   153, 161, 167, 175, 213

MS (*Metaphysics of Morals*) 182, 255–257, 259 f., 266, 271, 274, 284, 288, 290, 295, 304, 307, 311–314, 318, 325 f., 330, 332 f., 335, 338, 340–342, 353, 360

– Naure, second 44, 45, 212
Neiman, Susan 376, 388 f.
Newton, Isaac 42, 58, 74–78, 89, 94
Nietzsche, Friedrich 115
NTH (*Universal Natural History and Theory of the Heavens*) 28 f., 80, 202 f.

obligation 281, 283, 288, 291, 295 f., 310–313, 315, 325–327, 340
– wide 310, 313, 315, 327
omnitudo realitatis 204, 217, 232, 253
ontology 118 f., 125–127, 133, 141 f., 199, 208, 252, 395
– artificial vs. natural 126
OP (*Opus postumum*) 295, 347, 365, 395 f.
Optics 87, 89
optimism 27
organism (organic) 7, 14, 17, 36, 51–54, 62, 70, 87, 104, 106 f., 182, 199, 211 f., 264, 347, 351, 355 f., 358 f., 365
ought 62, 65, 125, 257, 271, 273, 281, 283 f., 286–289, 297, 306, 331 f., 334, 350, 368, 392

Paton, H. J. 48
pattern 28, 49, 53, 59 f., 62, 64, 68–75, 77 f., 81, 85, 103, 159, 178, 358
perception 6, 67, 88, 101, 111, 114, 116, 119 f., 122–125, 127–129, 132 f., 138–142, 144 f., 154 f., 158, 164, 170, 184, 190, 194, 197 f., 205–207, 210, 226, 239, 351, 353, 362, 379
perfection 6, 12–14, 26–29, 31–33, 39, 47–49, 53 f., 63, 65–67, 76, 88, 90–92, 94 f., 106, 150, 152, 167, 171, 181, 195, 213, 227 f., 231, 235 f., 252 f., 257, 271, 311, 315–317, 353, 356, 368, 370, 375, 387, 390, 392 f., 395 f., 398
– formal 53, 167–175, 195, 356
Phaedo 25, 264
philosophy 3–5, 9, 12–16, 20 f., 24–27, 30, 33 f., 36–38, 40–43, 46–52, 55–58, 60, 62, 65, 68, 78, 81, 97, 104, 111, 113–119, 129, 131, 133, 148 f., 167, 175, 177, 200–202, 213, 218, 222, 236, 238 f., 243, 245, 248, 250 f., 262 f., 273, 278, 288, 292–295, 311, 317, 330 f., 336–338, 345, 348, 360 f., 363, 368, 373, 376, 379, 381, 383, 387–396, 398, 400–402
– history of 393–396
– in sensu cosmico vs. in sensu scholastico 390 f.
– pre-critical 26 f., 30, 53 f., 58 f., 64, 79, 94, 104, 112, 116, 131, 146–148, 151–153, 167, 169–172, 174 f., 178–180, 182, 187, 189, 202, 204, 208, 213, 216, 218, 220, 232 f., 235–238, 253, 268, 273, 338, 348, 365, 371, 378, 382, 398, 400 f.
– pre-Kantian 25, 33 f., 38–40, 58, 117
– transcendental 5, 13, 15, 16, 42, 111, 113, 114, 129, 149, 200, 201, 239, 373, 393–398, 400
physico-theology 236 f.
Pichler, Hans 117, 128 f.
Pierce, Charles Sanders 57
plasticity 58, 62, 103
Plato 25, 101, 148, 152, 172, 248, 267 f., 348, 388
PND (*New Elucidation*) 28, 80, 202
Pope, Alexander 27, 89, 203
postulation 14 f., 223, 294–296, 298, 315, 318 f., 323, 327 f., 332, 334 f., 339, 355, 362, 374
principle
– material 133–140, 142, 214–216, 348
– of complete determination 38, 168, 218, 220–222, 274, 399
– of contradiction 30, 118, 130–136, 203, 216
– of least action 26, 58, 88, 90 f., 93
– of sufficient reason 38, 128–130, 132, 200, 254, 401
Principles of Philosophy 88, 119
Prol (*Prolegomena to Any Future Metaphysics*) 3, 17, 34, 114, 129
proportionality, of happiness to virtue 304–305
purpose (purposes), see *end*

purposiveness 6, 13–15, 21, 51, 53 f., 57, 60, 67, 74, 77, 87, 92, 101, 107, 148, 152, 160, 171–175, 197, 205, 209, 211 f., 227, 237, 264–270, 272, 275, 281, 284, 334, 356 f., 374, 386, 388, 402

Quine, Willard van Orman 84, 88, 98 f.

reality 3, 5, 8–13, 23, 47, 55, 60, 65 f., 79, 84 f., 92, 94, 98 f., 101, 113, 116, 132–138, 140–142, 157, 167 f., 171, 176, 179, 184, 199, 203, 214–224, 232, 246, 249–253, 260, 266, 269, 271, 273, 275, 277, 279 f., 287, 291 f., 324, 331, 334, 336, 339, 355 f., 368, 372 f., 375, 379, 383, 398–400, 402
– objective 5, 8, 13, 46, 113, 116, 132, 134–138, 140, 141, 179, 199, 223, 253, 266, 269, 273, 277, 292, 334, 339, 368, 372, 379, 402
– practical objective 253, 277
reason
– conditioned-practical 244–246, 264, 285, 287, 315–319, 335
– critique of pure 16, 18–20, 23, 96, 111, 113, 115, 117, 246, 390 f.
– fact of 46 f., 55, 286, 331
– hypothetical use of 160
– practical, pure 4 f., 9–12, 14, 22 f., 49, 101, 213, 245 f., 258, 261, 264, 266, 269, 273–275, 280, 284–286, 292, 304, 307, 318 f., 324, 326, 329 f., 333–335, 355, 362, 368, 373–375, 380, 391, 393, 402
– unity of 12, 20 f., 30, 54, 56, 227–228, 230, 239, 240, 251, 294, 335, 360 f.
receptivity 45 f., 155, 200, 223, 369
reflection 8, 16, 19, 21, 24, 34, 38, 40–42, 45, 71, 80, 82, 89, 91, 93, 95, 97, 99, 132, 141, 153, 157 f., 161, 173, 183, 189 f., 201 f., 204, 225, 228 f., 234 f., 238, 243, 262 f., 268, 270, 284 f., 315, 330, 351, 358, 366, 378, 382, 386, 388, 390, 393
regulative 7 f., 112, 204, 211, 221, 224, 228–231, 234–236, 238, 243, 249, 251, 280, 292, 336, 347, 358, 361–363, 368, 374–380, 389
Reinhold, Karl Leonhard 115

religion 79, 219, 233, 249, 272, 278, 296, 300, 304, 323 f., 327, 330, 343
RGV (Religion within the Boundaries of Mere Reason) 107, 249, 259, 295, 331 f., 343
Rosales, Alberto 51, 144
Rosenberg, Jay 51, 144
Rousseau, Jean-Jacques 292

Schelling, Friedrich Wilhelm Joseph von 4, 40, 372
schema (schemata) 28, 96, 200, 205, 208–210, 212, 230, 365, 367, 372, 394, 399
Schneewind, Jerome 43
science 15–20, 28, 34–36, 42 f., 45, 47, 60, 73, 79, 83, 90, 93 f., 96, 99, 104, 114, 118 f., 125 f., 131, 138, 143, 153, 175, 178, 198, 202, 249, 267, 292, 319, 337 f., 347, 354, 360, 365 f., 369–371, 373, 389–395, 400
self-consciousness 12, 33–35, 38, 41, 111, 133 f., 145 f., 164 f., 190, 195, 198, 200, 202 f., 207, 230, 234, 243, 246, 252, 254, 262, 276–278, 281–286, 289, 291, 331, 333, 335, 354, 366, 373, 376 f., 381–383, 387, 396 f., 400
self-sufficiency 23 f., 37, 53 f., 63, 178, 273, 351
Sellars, Wilfrid 51
Sidgwick, Henry 254, 256
Simon, Josef 51, 77
Smith, Norman Kemp 44, 115, 255, 367
Socrates 25, 253 f., 264
space and time 6, 105, 143, 145, 161–171, 175–177, 185, 190, 192–197, 199 f., 223, 228 f., 236, 239, 274, 378, 383
– purposive structure of, see perfection, formal
– singularity of 166, 185, 192–194
Spinoza 98, 248, 328
spontaneity 17, 21, 23, 45 f., 57, 179, 187–189, 200, 223, 252, 256, 264, 295, 337–339, 342, 350 f., 355 f., 358, 362, 372
Stoicism 44, 310
strength, moral 59, 76, 78, 80 f., 211, 260, 288, 293 f., 310–315, 318, 325 f., 330, 333, 337, 339, 341–343, 352 f., 355, 357, 360, 365

striving, moral   5, 9–12, 39, 48, 58, 62f.,
  95, 103, 244, 249f., 252, 254, 276,
  293f., 302, 310, 312, 314, 322, 360, 387,
  396
subreption   143, 201, 233f.
symbol (symbolic), see *analogy*
synthesis, principles of 153   6, 22, 52, 93,
  97, 114, 129, 131, 135, 147, 153f., 164f.,
  177, 184–196, 200, 215, 218, 239f., 256,
  283f., 287, 296, 319, 366, 383f., 387,
  403
System of Ethics   37, 40

Taylor, Charles   60f., 81, 102, 157, 383
teleology   3–9, 12–15, 17, 20f., 25–27,
  29–33, 37–44, 46–58, 60–68, 80f.,
  83, 85–88, 91, 93, 95–101, 103f.,
  106f., 109, 111f., 117, 147f., 167, 171,
  173, 175, 182, 185, 196, 199–202, 204f.,
  209f., 222f., 232, 237f., 241, 246, 248–
  254, 264, 267, 269, 272, 334–336, 339,
  356, 358, 360f., 374, 387, 398–402
– moral   12, 13, 14, 47, 49, 267, 269, 272,
  334, 335, 374
– transcendental   7, 14, 29, 37, 104, 111, 112,
  117, 167, 185, 200, 205, 209, 232, 237, 238,
  324, 374, 400
TG   348f.
Thales   74
The Categorical Imperative   48–50, 249,
  253, 258, 260, 265, 286, 295, 402
The Explanation of Behavior   61
Theodicy   27, 31
theology   13f., 43, 79, 94, 223, 235, 243,
  395
– transcendental   13, 14, 223, 243
thing in itself   169, 232, 283
Thomasius, Christian (Thomasian)   26, 118,
  142
TP   273, 309, 313, 315, 317, 319, 329
transcendental turn   41f., 46
transparency   105f., 188, 257, 265, 386, 399
truth   15, 18, 25f., 30–32, 34, 41, 43, 47,
  52f., 81, 83–86, 93, 98, 102, 118–122,
  125f., 128f., 133, 139, 142, 151f., 155–
  163, 174, 176, 187, 191, 201, 207, 214,
  225–228, 248, 250, 293, 354, 360, 369,
  380, 386, 393, 401
– empirical criterion of   225
– transcendental   128

UD (*Prize Essay*)   131, 136
ÜE   175, 184
ÜGTP   4–10, 13, 15, 21, 269, 283
unity
– absolute   5, 12, 21, 22, 24, 54, 154, 179,
  187, 198, 215, 232, 364, 365, 368, 402
– architectonic   384f.
– collective   107, 206–208, 210, 216, 358
– distributive   206f., 210, 216
of the will   264, 291
– organic   16, 18, 35–37, 51, 53, 106f., 222,
  338, 346–348, 354, 365, 399
– technical   263, 281, 299, 329, 384f.
– teleological   6, 21, 24, 54, 58, 79, 80, 104,
  152, 167, 173, 175, 197–199, 207, 240, 264,
  272, 273, 291, 360f., 381
unity condition, Bennett's   61, 64, 104
unmoved mover   62f., 348

value   24, 33, 43f., 48–50, 69, 99, 155,
  250, 292, 327, 392, 395
VAVT (*On a Recently Prominent Tone*)   148
Velkley, Richard   42, 360f.
*Vernünfftige Gedanken von den Absichten
  der natürlichen Dinge* (*German Teleology*)   26, 31
Versuch vom Wesen des Geistes   26
virtue   14, 30, 37, 41, 44, 54, 63, 67, 78,
  104, 106f., 123, 132f., 137, 155f., 165,
  170, 174, 198, 222, 248, 253, 255–257,
  260, 273, 279, 292, 294f., 297–299,
  305, 307, 309–313, 315–318, 321–327,
  330, 332–335, 340–344, 355f., 358,
  365, 374f., 381, 384, 391, 401
Vocation of Man   27, 37, 40

Ward, Keith   48, 60
whole
– absolute   23, 163, 166, 178, 179, 185, 200,
  210, 253, 365, 395, 400, 402
– purposive   51, 112, 151, 361, 362, 396

will
- divine   23, 26, 29, 31f., 37, 79, 90, 174f., 208–210, 222, 243, 268, 270f., 273, 275, 295, 304, 324, 330, 366, 373, 381, 401
- empirical   12, 254, 255, 264, 275, 276, 279–286
- holy   63, 276
- noumenal   250, 254, 264
- phenomenal   254, 275–276, 280
- pure   47, 55, 245, 246, 253, 257, 259, 261, 264, 266–276, 280, 281, 283–288, 318–321, 402

wisdom   3, 13, 22–24, 66, 89f., 92, 237, 272, 292f., 320, 360, 364, 390–393, 395f., 398
Wolff, Christian   25–27, 29, 31, 47, 111, 113, 116–133, 136f., 139–143, 145, 147f., 151, 155, 244, 253, 315–317, 350, 352, 381, 388, 401
Wood, Allen   10f., 49f., 250, 252, 294, 296f., 300–306, 308, 310, 328
Wright, Larry   62
Wundt, Max   25, 113

Zammito, John   345f.

www.ingramcontent.com/pod-product-compliance
Lightning Source LLC
Chambersburg PA
CBHW050848160426
43194CB00011B/2068